AF841579

THE VATICAN IN THE FAMILY OF NATIONS

Based on a collection of statements delivered between 2003 and 2015, *The Vatican in the Family of Nations* provides a new understanding of the social doctrine and actions of the Catholic Church in international law and relations. These statements address contemporary issues that stir deep emotional responses, from disarmament, migrations, trade and intellectual property to discrimination and freedom of conscience. This volume disputes irrational fears of newcomers, offers reasonable adaptations to allow for peaceful coexistence and insists on investigating the root causes of today's conflicts and displacements. As an independent voice, the Holy See offers these reflections with the view of prioritizing the common good before confessional interests, even when their aims and ends converge. In this sense, this book is a unique collection in international literature on the intersection of theology, human rights and social issues, which opens courageous new paths for the future.

Archbishop Silvano M. Tomasi, C.S., Apostolic Nuncio, is a Member and Delegated Secretary of the Dicastery for Promoting Integral Human Development. He became a priest in New York in 1965 and holds a PhD in Sociology from Fordham University. A member of the Congregation of the Missionaries of St Charles-Scalabrinians, he served as Provincial Superior of their New York Province. He has worked and written in the area of migration. He has served as founding Director of the Center for Migration Studies of New York, as Director of Pastoral Care of Migrants and Refugees at the USCCB in Washington, as Secretary of the Pontifical Council for Migrants and Itinerants in Rome, as Nuncio in Ethiopia, Eritrea and Djibouti, and Observer to the African Union. He was the Permanent Observer of the Holy See to the United Nations Office and other International Organizations in Geneva from 2003 to 2016.

THE VATICAN IN THE FAMILY OF NATIONS

Diplomatic Actions of the Holy See at the UN and Other International Organizations in Geneva

SILVANO M. TOMASI

Holy See Mission to the UN and other International Organizations

ASSISTED BY

Antoine Abi Ghanem

Holy See Mission to the UN

Vincenzo Buonomo

Pontificia Università Lateranense

Richard Gyhra

Holy See Mission to the UN

Carlo Maria Marenghi

Holy See Mission to the UN

Stefano Saldi

Holy See Mission to the UN

Robert J. Vitillo

Holy See Mission to the UN

CAMBRIDGE
UNIVERSITY PRESS

CAMBRIDGE
UNIVERSITY PRESS

University Printing House, Cambridge CB2 8BS, United Kingdom

One Liberty Plaza, 20th Floor, New York, NY 10006, USA

477 Williamstown Road, Port Melbourne, VIC 3207, Australia

4843/24, 2nd Floor, Ansari Road, Daryaganj, Delhi - 110002, India

79 Anson Road, #06-04/06, Singapore 079906

Cambridge University Press is part of the University of Cambridge.

It furthers the University's mission by disseminating knowledge in the pursuit of education, learning and research at the highest international levels of excellence.

www.cambridge.org
Information on this title: www.cambridge.org/9781107179301
DOI: 10.1017/9781316681701

© Silvano Maria Tomasi 2017

This publication is in copyright. Subject to statutory exception and to the provisions of relevant collective licensing agreements, no reproduction of any part may take place without the written permission of Cambridge University Press.

First published 2017

Printed in the United Kingdom by Clays, St Ives plc

A catalogue record for this publication is available from the British Library

Library of Congress Cataloging-in-Publication data
Names: Tomasi, Silvano M., author.
Title: The Vatican in the family of nations : diplomatic actions of the Holy See at the UN and other international organizations in Geneva / Silvano M. Tomasi, Holy See to the UN and other International Organizations ; assisted by Antoine Abi Ghanem, Attachbe for Disarmament and Security Affairs at the Holy See Mission; Vincenzo Buonomo, Pontificia Universita Lateranese; Richard Gyhra, Holy See Mission to the UN; Carlo Maria Marenghi, Holy See Mission to the UN; Stefano Saldi; Holy See Mission to the UN; Robert J. Vitillo, Holy See Mission to the UN.
Description: New York : Cambridge University Press, 2017. |
Includes bibliographical references and index.
Identifiers: LCCN 2017003103 | ISBN 9781107179301 (hardback)
Subjects: LCSH: Catholic Church – Foreign relations. | Christianity and international relations – Catholic Church. | Church and social problems – Catholic Church. | BISAC: LAW / International.
Classification: LCC KBU4076.T66 2017 | DDC 327.456/34 – dc23
LC record available at https://lccn.loc.gov/2017003103

ISBN 978-1-107-17930-1 Hardback

Cambridge University Press has no responsibility for the persistence or accuracy of URLs for external or third-party internet websites referred to in this publication, and does not guarantee that any content on such websites is, or will remain, accurate or appropriate.

CONTENTS

CONTRIBUTORS

Revd Antoine Abi Ghanem is the Attaché for Disarmament and Security Affairs at the Permanent Mission of the Holy See to the United Nations and other International Organizations in Geneva. From 1992 to 1998 he served as Secretary General of the Lebanese Maronite Order and since 2000 he has been working for the Permanent Mission of the Holy See. He holds a Licentiate in Theology from the Pontifical Faculty of Theology of the Holy Spirit University of Kaslik (USEK) and a Diploma of advanced studies in Philosophy from the Paris-Sorbonne University.

Vincenzo Buonomo is Professor of International Law and Organization at the Institute of Law, Pontifical Lateran University, where he also teaches international law of human rights. Former Dean, and current Coordinator of the PhD Programmes of the School of Law, he has written extensively in the fields of international law, diplomatic law and institutional international governance, with a particular focus on the evolving promotion and protection of human rights. He serves as Legal Adviser in the Delegation of the Holy See to conferences and meetings of the United Nations, FAO, IFAD, OSCE and Council of Europe. He participates at the UN World Conference on Human Rights, UN Diplomatic Conference on the Establishment of the International Criminal Court and FAO Word Summits on Food and Food Security. Dr Buonomo is Counsellor of the Vatican City State.

Msgr Richard Gyhra was First Secretary at the Permanent Mission of the Holy See in Geneva from 2013 to 2016. He was ordained a priest in 1999 for the Diocese of Lincoln, Nebraska (USA). After completing his studies at the Pontifical Ecclesiastical Academy and obtaining a Doctorate in Sacred Theology, he entered the diplomatic service of the Holy See in 2010.

Carlo M. Marenghi is the legal advisor on intellectual property and trade matters of the Holy See Permanent Mission to the United Nations and specialized agencies in Geneva. He received his PhD in International Law summa cum laude from the Pontifical Lateran University in the Vatican City. Dr Marenghi has written extensively and published on health, trade, intellectual property and labour and human rights, including from the perspective of the social doctrine of the Catholic Church. Since 2015, Dr Marenghi is also an international lecturer at Webster University in Geneva.

Stefano Saldi is the Attaché for Disarmament, Migrants and Refugees issues of the Permanent Mission of the Holy See to the United Nations and other

International Organizations in Geneva. He completed his graduate studies in European and international politics from the Catholic University of the Sacred Heart in Milan, during which he spent a research year abroad at Creighton University. After a brief experience at the Italian Chamber of Commerce in Vancouver, Canada, he joined the Permanent Mission of the Holy See to the United Nations and other International Organizations in Geneva in January 2014. In 2016 he was awarded the United Nations Fellowship on Disarmament.

Msgr Robert J. Vitillo completed graduate studies in theology, clinical social work and management. He is a Catholic priest of the Diocese of Paterson, New Jersey (USA). He served in Catholic Church-related charitable agencies at local, national and global levels. Between 2005 and 2016, he coordinated the Caritas Internationalis Delegation to the UN in Geneva. He currently serves as the Secretary General of the International Catholic Migration Commission and as the Attaché for Health at the Permanent Mission of the Holy See to the UN in Geneva.

PREFACE

The Holy See's Diplomatic Mission in Today's World

CARDINAL PIETRO PAROLIN*

The Catholic Church, consistent with her 'catholicity', has constantly engaged cultures and societies to share the message of Jesus of Nazareth. History demonstrates how deeply, from the very beginning, the Church cared for vulnerable and marginalized groups of society. She has adapted her action according to the evolving needs of society by promoting science, agriculture and trade, through the establishment of the first universities, and by advocating peaceful relations among peoples. The Holy See, in particular, has often taken the initiative, as a voice of mediation and moral reference, to call for a peaceful solution of differences and the promotion of the dignity of every man and woman as created in the image of God.

Today, in our interconnected world, the Holy See continues to exercise its diplomatic activity in accordance with international law and established practice. It is, however, distinct from other States in that it does not have any particular commercial, military or political aims to defend or pursue. Rather, her diplomatic activity serves the universal mission of the Holy Father, which is essentially a spiritual mission, at the service of the Gospel and the common good of the human family:

> This is the only strength that makes her universal and credible to people and the world; this is the heart of her truth, that does not erect walls of division, but makes herself a bridge that builds communion and calls for the unity of the human race. This is her secret power that feeds her tenacious hope, invincible notwithstanding temporary defeats.[1]

In this sense, it is often said that the Holy See exercises 'soft-power' diplomacy, namely a diplomacy which does not depend on military, political or economic strength but on the ability to persuade. The Holy See, one could say, acts as a voice of conscience, at the service of the common good, by drawing attention to the anthropological, ethical and religious aspects of the various questions affecting the lives of peoples, nations and the international community as a whole.

* His Eminence Cardinal Pietro Parolin is the Secretary of State of the Holy See.

[1] Pope Francis, 'To the Future Diplomats of the Holy See'. *L'Osservatore Romano*, 26 June 2015, p. 8.

At the heart of this mission is a clear idea of the human person, who possesses an innate dignity that must always be respected, ultimately because he or she is created in the image and likeness of God, and endowed with reason, will and freedom. This vision of the human person is fundamental to the Church's social teaching, which has continued to develop over the centuries, particularly over the past two hundred years, as it addresses concerns regarding the organization of society and other challenges affecting the human person's social dimension, such as relations with the family, economics, culture, politics, justice, human rights, peace and the environment. 'The development of the Church's social teaching' represents a synthesis between faith and reason 'with regard to social issues; this teaching is called to be enriched by taking up new challenges'.[2] The diplomatic activity of the Holy See continually refers to this teaching, which, to a large extent, is based upon the natural moral law and is therefore not dependent on one's particular religious beliefs. This teaching provides a basis for peaceful social coexistence, since it can lead to a universal consensus expressive of the common nature of all persons.

The diplomatic activity of the Holy See, the product of an ancient and proven practice whose essential role is spiritual, as Pope Paul VI observed in speaking to the Diplomatic Corps accredited to the Holy See, responds to the present developments in the international arena and to the demands and crises witnessed in the contemporary world. Key aspects of this mission are the promotion of the unity of the human family, fostering dialogue among nations and inspiring cooperation among peoples with a view to the common good and peaceful coexistence. Pope John Paul II, speaking to the Apostolic Nuncios in Africa, recommended them to 'continue with every effort to be witnesses of communion, by supporting the overcoming of tensions and misunderstandings, the victory over the temptation of particularism and the reinforcement of the sense of belonging to the one and undivided People of God'.[3]

There is a strict correlation between the diplomatic activity of the Holy See and the apostolic mission of the Church, namely, the proclamation of the Good News of Jesus. The mission of the Church may be

[2] Cf. Pope Francis' Encyclical Letter, *Laudato Si'*, § 63.

[3] Pope John Paul II, Address to Apostolic Nuncios in Africa, 25 September 2004: 'Continuate con ogni impegno ad essere *testimoni di comunione*, favorendo il superamento delle tensioni e delle incomprensioni, la vittoria sulla tentazione del particolarismo, il rafforzamento del senso di appartenenza all'unico ed indiviso Popolo di Dio.'

expressed in the mandate of Christ: 'Go, teach and baptize' (Mt 28:18–20). It indicates the necessity of proclaiming salvation in Jesus Christ in such a way that the proclamation reaches everyone. This proclamation has used different methods in the course of history, adapting itself to different circumstances related to the presence of the faith community in society. Saint Paul reasoned from the sources of the Old Testament, from the philosophy of his day and from cultural experience as seen in his well-known speech in Athens. Charlemagne imposed the faith even with the sword on some German tribes. Matteo Ricci adopted the local culture in China as far as possible, becoming a Chinese sage in the process. In colonial times, in Africa and Latin and North America, politics and economic interests often were not separate from religious goals.

Today, societies tend to function in a democratic style and globalization has introduced a pluralization within them – virtual or real – as a result of which totally closed societies are a rare case. Instead, a plurality of religions, cultures and life-styles coexist in the same society, especially in those that are more technologically advanced. Globalization is also spreading a culture that is new in the sense that it is no longer linked to the history of a people, to a geographic region or even to a specific religious tradition. It seems rather a culture derived from the evolution of the underlying philosophy of individualism of the American and French Revolutions. In this evolution, the ideas of the person and of the individual have come apart. On one side, the Christian concept of the person with its relations to others and consequent responsibilities; on the other side, the self-accountable individual, who justifies his or her choices on the basis of internal assurance (expressed with statements like: 'I feel good', 'it's my choice', 'one choice is as good as another', etc.). This type of individual becomes a world closed in on himself, protecting his satisfaction. The notion of an objective norm disappears. Even religion becomes totally subjective. Thus, before the tendency of society to relegate religion to the private sphere, the individualistic culture had already effectively done so. Today, public culture is both pluralistic and individualistic. Pluralism (a sociological fact) and relativism (a philosophical consideration) make up the social context of the present obligation to announce the Christian message. On the other hand, the religious factor has become the centre of a lively discussion concerning its return to public life and politics. The global return of religion is a puzzling phenomenon and there are various interpretations and theories to explain it. But the fact of this resurgence is generally accepted and international politics needs to take it into account.

Confronted with such a situation, the diplomatic role of the Holy See takes on a socio-political engagement in order to change the unjust structures of society, the structures of sin. It highlights the international dimension of problems on both technical and religious levels; it gives visibility to the action of the Church within public structures; it develops expertise in order to dialogue with other actors in a pluralistic context. In this way, the message of the Gospel becomes the leaven of society.

The multilateral dimension of international relations, with its ever-increasing complexity of methods and regulations, is part of the global dimension that characterizes our present age. For the diplomacy of the Holy See, the challenge is twofold. On the one hand, it considers itself obliged to be well formed and well prepared, acknowledging that one cannot function in the framework of intergovernmental institutions without the necessary expertise, technical capacity and true professionalism. On the other hand, as an ecclesial reality, the Holy See must evaluate whether the 'if and how' of what emerges corresponds effectively to the good of the human family and whether it is not limited by particular interests which could easily compromise peace initiatives. Such a 'road map' is necessarily connected with prevention, not only as far as conflicts and wars are concerned, but also for the protection of human dignity and human rights. Poverty, underdevelopment, natural disasters, the economic crisis and other situations are among the priorities of the Holy See, which uses its internationally recognized diplomatic status to engage with them.

In fact, the Holy See enjoys full international subjectivity as well as absolute independence, as recognized by the Lateran Treaty of 1929 which legally settled the dispute commonly known as the 'Roman Question' and, inter alia, created the Vatican City State under the full sovereignty of the Pope.[4] The international activity of the Holy See is manifested objectively in various ways: the right to active and passive delegation, the exercise of *ius contrahendi* in stipulating treaties and participation in international organizations, as well as mediation initiatives and the use of her good offices to facilitate dialogue in situations of conflict, without seeking any advantage for itself but only the good of the entire human family.[5] Bilateral and multilateral diplomacy

[4] Cf. Vincenzo Buonomo, 'Vatican', in Gerhard Robbers (ed.), *Encyclopedia of World Constitutions*, New York: Facts on File, 2007.

[5] *Compendium of the Social Doctrine of the Church*, Vatican: Libreria Editrice Vaticana, 2004, § 444.

is therefore part of the Church's mission in the international arena and it has taken on a truly 'catholic' dimension. The Holy See presently has full diplomatic relations with 182 states and with the European Union and the Sovereign Military Order of Malta.[6] It recently signed its first treaty with the State of Palestine in June 2015, thus calling for courageous decisions to end the Israeli–Palestinian conflict and hoping that 'the much desired two-State solution may become a reality as soon as possible'.[7] The Holy See is present in the United Nations with Permanent Observer status, and is a member of seven UN organizations or agencies, an observer in eight others and a member or observer in five regional organizations.[8]

Today's international organizations have a direct influence on the formation of international public culture. The presence of the message of the Gospel has to be articulated in ways that can reach people of today. That is why the Popes and the Second Vatican Council[9] have established an ongoing dialogue with the contemporary world, a dialogue that is founded on the common ground of the human person. Although we live in a context of pluralism, we share a common humanity. Hence, Pope John Paul II summed up this approach by saying: 'Man is the way of the Church.' He added: 'The universal vocation of the Church must be to the eyes of everyone a proof of its disinterestedness and impartiality. It is

[6] http://press.vatican.va/content/salastampa/en/bollettino/pubblico/2017/01/09/170109b.html.

[7] Address of His Excellency Archbishop Paul Richard Gallagher, Secretary for Relations with States of the Holy See on the occasion of the Signing Ceremony of the Comprehensive Agreement between the Holy See and the State of Palestine, 26 June 2015.

[8] For an exhaustive list of the international organizations in which the Holy See has full member or observer status, please refer to the Appendix.

[9] Second Vatican Ecumenical Council, Pastoral Constitution on the Church in the Modern World, *Gaudium et Spes*, § 42: 'since in virtue of her mission and nature she is bound to no particular form of human culture, nor to any political, economic or social system, the Church by her very universality can be a very close bond between diverse human communities and nations … With great respect, therefore, this council regards all the true, good and just elements inherent in the very wide variety of institutions which the human race has established for itself and constantly continues to establish. The council affirms, moreover, that the Church is willing to assist and promote all these institutions to the extent that such a service depends on her and can be associated with her mission. She has no fiercer desire than that in pursuit of the welfare of all she may be able to develop herself freely under any kind of government which grants recognition to the basic rights of person and family, to the demands of the common good and to the free exercise of her own mission', www.vatican.va/archive/hist_councils/ii_vatican_council/documents/vat-ii_const_19651207_gaudium-et-spes_en.html.

man, as man, that concerns it, and all the more so in that it sees in him the image of the Creator, the brother of Christ.'[10]

Thus, the increasing involvement of the Holy See in multilateral diplomacy is the result of the conviction that the human person has to be protected and served. This is a basic expression of the unconditional love of neighbour on a universal scale.[11] The recent Papal visits to the United Nations and the International Labour Organization adopted the language of human rights. Without hiding or underplaying the specific Catholic identity and the centrality of Christ, the proposal has been one of joining forces in making society an environment worthy of every human person everywhere and inclusive of all peripheries. In this context of dignity and freedom, the option of faith can truly be a genuine response.

The aspirations and the claims of the masses of people in developing countries are, in fact, formulated more explicitly in the language of human rights because the awareness of the dignity of every human person has become a common acquisition. Political movements justify their actions by appealing to the rights flowing from our common human dignity. Providing a just answer to these expectations is a way to guarantee peace and development.

All pronouncements of the Holy See aim at the salvation of the person and of society and keep alive the conviction that change is possible and that solutions are possible to the outstanding problems of our time. Therefore, the active participation of the Holy See in international affairs is an essential part of the Church's mission and a contribution to finding appropriate answers. There are differences, even fundamental ones, in the way the Holy See proposes solutions and the way other States do, and in the motivations used, but there are also convergences. For example, the social doctrine of the Church and the fundamental human rights found in UN charters and instruments share many points in common. Indeed, there is a different anthropological perspective for the Holy See which balances the prevalence of pragmatic, economic approaches marked in the UN system, but the objective is the same: respect for the human person and the search for the common good. There is also convergence

[10] Pope John Paul II, Address to the Diplomatic Corps, 15 January 1983: 'La vocation universelle de l'Église devrait être aux yeux de tous une garantie de son désintéressement et de son impartialité. C'est l'homme, en tant qu'homme, qui l'intéresse, d'autant plus qu'elle voit en lui l'image du créateur, le frère du Christ.'

[11] 'I was hungry and you fed me, thirsty and you gave me a drink; I was a stranger and you received me in your homes' (Mt 25:35). The solidarity demanded by this parable of the final judgement is simply a response to need without strings attached.

in the recognition that international institutions should be restructured to allow everyone to participate and that real reform should overcome vested interests.

The specific agenda of the Holy See for multilateral diplomacy in many ways reflects the concerns of the international community. It gives its own reading of current reality in the light of experience obtained on the ground, and a non-partisan approach of the social doctrine developed so far of acceptance of 'natural law' and the human rights derived from it. From this perspective, the Holy See dialogues especially with the sectors of the UN system that concern religious freedom, the right to development and the right to life, women, the protection of uprooted people, emergency responses to humanitarian crises, disarmament and the promotion of peace, the right to health, the role of labour and the rights of workers, and the environment, climate change, intellectual property and information technologies, among others.

The overarching mission of the Holy See, which remains unchanged, encourages dialogue with our contemporary culture and proposes integral human development. This strategy serves the pursuit of peaceful coexistence, a constructive international collaboration and the affirmation and even rejuvenation of our Catholic identity. While affirming, among others, the truth about creation, the human person, the human family as one with a common destiny, the diplomacy of the Holy See remains a moral voice and an appeal to conscience that sustain the common good.

Working to renew the moral dimension within international relations is one of the contributions that Papal diplomacy offers. The Holy See, however, is not satisfied with the mere observation of events or the evaluation of their implications, nor can it remain only a critical voice. In fact, it is called to act so as to facilitate coexistence and cohabitation among the various nations in order to promote a genuine fraternity among peoples, in which the term 'fraternity' is synonymous with effective collaboration, with genuine cooperation – that is unanimous and orderly – and of a solidarity structured in favour of both the common good and the good of the individual.[12]

The Holy See, in substance, acts in the international scene not to guarantee general security – which nowadays is made harder than ever due

[12] Cardinal Secretary of State Pietro Parolin, Lectio Magistralis: 'L'attività diplomatica della Santa Sede a servizio della Pace', 'Dies Academicus', Pontificia Università Gregoriana, 11 March 2015.

to constant instability – but to endorse the idea of peace as a result of just relationships, the observance of international norms and the protection of fundamental human rights, beginning with the most vulnerable. That peace, as Pope Paul VI once said, quoting the Pastoral Constitution *Gaudium et Spes*, does not stem simply from 'the absence of war; nor can it be reduced solely to the maintenance of a balance of power between enemies'.[13] Nations, as architects of their own development, can relate to each other through mutually shared objectives and practices and thus create a well-founded sense of the common good. Even more so, they can give life to the Institutions at the heart of the international community which are capable of fulfilling a role without compromising the identity, dignity and the responsible freedom of each State. The service of these Institutions includes accepting the needs of various peoples and discovering the capacities of others. Such an approach counters the 'globalization of indifference' and pure utilitarian egoism so as to do something good for others through international bodies.[14]

The present volume clearly emphasizes the active presence of the Holy See at the United Nations and other International Organizations in Geneva. This collection of the numerous speeches pronounced illustrates the vast array of issues addressed by the Permanent Mission of the Holy See in Geneva and represents a continued development of the social doctrine of the Catholic Church as new responses are given to the innovations and challenges introduced by technology and the changing geopolitical landscape. As such, this volume provides not only a useful tool for research on contemporary issues but also documents the years of active and fruitful engagement of the Holy See Mission in the multilateral context of Geneva.

[13] *Gaudium et Spes*, § 78.

[14] Preface by Pope Francis, in Tarcisio Bertone, *La diplomazia pontificia in un mondo globalizzato*, ed. Vincenzo Buonomo, Vatican City: Libreria Editrice Vaticana, 2013.

METHODOLOGICAL NOTE

This volume is the first comprehensive collection of the Holy See's[1] diplomatic actions and statements at the United Nations and other International Organizations in Geneva from 2003 to 2015.

International Geneva is assuming an increasingly significant role as the seat of the humanitarian, human rights, disarmament and trade concerns of the countries of the world. In addition, new political negotiations have moved to this city where much of the preparatory work and drafting processes of the United Nations are carried out. Thus, the local saying goes, 'the dishes are prepared and cooked in Geneva and eaten in New York'.

Through a combined approach of the analysis of contemporary problems that are at the cutting edge of society and of the response to these new developments, the activity of the Holy See opens the way for the advancement of an ethical perspective necessary to move forward in a constructive way. This volume, therefore, aims at contributing an understanding of crucial new developments in the field of human rights, economy, finance, intellectual property, disarmament, health and migration from a perspective rooted in the Greco-Roman and Christian anthropological and intellectual traditions. At the same time, the volume serves as a testimony to and as evidence of how the centuries-old social doctrine of the Catholic Church has evolved and is able to respond to new challenges from its inner strength. Some of the suggestions emerging in the various parts of the volume could also serve as an inspiration for future policies and concerted action by the international community.

This volume is more than a valuable collection of the statements delivered by the Permanent Observer of the Holy See at the United Nations and other International Organizations in Geneva on the main contemporary issues which demand consideration and concern from the international community. This work fulfils a twofold aim. On the one hand, this compilation underscores the Holy See's support for multilateral diplomacy and its encouragement for all efforts aimed at improving the United Nations structure towards greater effectiveness and credibility. On the other hand, it witnesses to the diplomatic activity of the Vatican in the international arena.

[1] On the nature of the constitutional history of the Holy See, see Buonomo, 'Vatican', in Robbers, *Encyclopedia of World Constitutions*, p. 1007.

The time period covered (2003–15) represents the years during which I served as Apostolic Nuncio to the UN – the longest tenure of a Permanent Observer of the Holy See to the United Nations in Geneva. Thus, this volume offers the possibility of documenting the Holy See's position on a very wide spectrum of issues at different historical times. As all the Statements have been officially approved by the Secretariat of State of the Holy See, they reflect the formal position of the Holy See regarding key and evolving issues affecting the international community and posing new ethical challenges.

A detailed Preface by His Eminence Cardinal Pietro Parolin, Secretary of State of the Holy See, provides a framework for the book and gives an extensive overview of today's diplomacy of the Holy See. The participation of the Holy See in UN activities was initiated in 1964 under Pope Paul VI. It was further clarified by the 2004 United Nations General Assembly Resolution 58/314 that acknowledged that 'the Holy See, in its capacity as an Observer State, shall be accorded the rights and privileges of participation in the sessions and work of the General Assembly and the international conferences convened under the auspices of the Assembly or other organs of the United Nations, as well as in United Nations conferences'.[2] The Resolution is linked to an interpretative Note of the Secretary General.[3] This Note explains the observer status of the Holy See at the United Nations as *de facto* equal to that of the Member States except for the right to vote and to put forward candidates in the General Assembly. Quite symbolically, in October 2015, the flag of the Holy See was raised among the other flags at the United Nations in Geneva.

The multilateral diplomacy of the Holy See in Geneva is engaged in the United Nations and in numerous international organizations that deal with a broad range of concerns. In the span of time considered in this volume (2003–15), the Holy See delivered 242 major Statements. As the Permanent Observer of the Holy See to the United Nations and other International Organizations in Geneva I delivered the majority of them, unless otherwise indicated. For convenience, the statements included in this volume are grouped into six different chapters. Each is contextualized by an introduction that sets the relevant political and historical background and highlights the official position of the Holy See. These introductions present the main contributions of the Holy See at the

[2] Cf. United Nations General Assembly, Doc. A/58/314.

[3] Cf. United Nations, Note by the Secretary General to the General Assembly Resolution 58/871.

multilateral level and serve to ensure the cohesive structure and unity of the volume as a whole. The leitmotif of the Holy See interventions remains the same throughout the volume: the centrality of the human person as the protagonist of development, which is the foundation of the presence of the Holy See in multilateral fora.

Additionally, within each chapter, the Statements have been divided into sections, further narrowing down their scope to provide researchers with a convenient, organized and research-friendly analysis.

Chapter I, 'The Human Person at the Center of Fundamental Rights and Protagonist of Development', covers the Statements delivered at the United Nations Commission on Human Rights and the United Nations Human Rights Council. The interventions illustrate how the Holy See's engagement and commitment develop in a two-pronged approach: first, in the proclamation of the Christian foundations of human rights with their universality and indivisibility, and, second, in the denunciation of any violations of basic human rights. These discourses consistently reflect and cover a wide variety of issues affecting the life of the family of nations.

Chapter II, 'Freedom as the Foundation of Human Relations and Social Coexistence', instead, is mostly dedicated to freedom of religion, which has always been a subject of great consideration. This is seen in its regulation by domestic or international legal systems as well as in the mixed interest within the institutions of the international community. The public dimension of religion – a practical reality formed by worship, teaching, training, institutional framework, organization and relationships – paves the way to the complexity surrounding the inherent rights of the human person. *Protection* and *limitations* are the two key elements surrounding any debate on religious freedom that is a fundamental right because of its direct connection to the human person. In fact, it also serves a strategic role in evaluating and ensuring the proper attention and guarantee acknowledged by the public authorities regarding such dignity. The interventions of the Holy See repeatedly recall the description and delimitation of the content of the right to religious freedom. This is not to deprive the right of some of its components or to restrict its scope, but as a guarantee for its full protection and implementation, thereby preventing an erroneous – or at least partial – interpretation which can lead to other kinds of limitations.

Chapter III, 'The Economy as a Means, Not an End', covers the activity of the Holy See at the World Trade Organization, the World Intellectual Property Organization and the International Labour Organization.

At present, the international community continues to call for changes in the way the global economy is ordered and managed. The profound political, economic and institutional crises open a new challenge for the social doctrine of the Church: renewing the semantics of the economy and finance. This does not only mean that it has the duty to identify an intrinsic and autonomous ethics but that it should frame it in the context of other human activities. Economics and finance are not abstract concepts separated from the actors that are engaged in them in social, political, national and supranational contexts. The development of the social doctrine of the Church, especially since the innovative teaching found in *Rerum Novarum*, the Encyclical Letter 'On Capital and Labour' (1891) of Pope Leo XIII, implemented and revealed in the statements delivered by the Holy See, is a clear example of how the Holy See addresses new moral issues that affect the economy and social justice.

As States continue to increase their military capabilities to meet new and asymmetrical challenges in an increasingly dangerous world, Chapter IV, 'The Quest for Peace', serves as a starting point and an invitation to deepen the knowledge of the activity of the Holy See in the area of disarmament and to promote commitment to serve the noble cause of peace through disarmament. In this context, the Holy See, inspired by its teaching on the unity of the human family and on justice and peace, desires to make its contribution to initiatives like disarmament which promote security, mutual trust and peaceful co-operation in relations among peoples. It considers it a moral obligation to join the international community as an active player in the creation and shaping of appropriate mechanisms and negotiated treaties that limit and regulate the use of arms, and to allocate funds for social needs.

The interventions of the Holy See contained in Chapter V, 'Solidarity with all Humanity', reveal once again her active participation at the multilateral level. Be it at the World Health Organization, at the International Conferences of the Red Cross or at the Human Rights Council of the United Nations, the Holy See has always decried the disparity among nations and the many situations of inequality, poverty and injustice, which 'are signs not only of a profound lack of fraternity, but also of the absence of a culture of solidarity'. In the course of its diplomatic activities, the Holy See focuses much of its concern on the plight of the poorest and most vulnerable members of society, those who are often marginalized from access to social protection, care and enjoyment of rights and dignity. Thus, the principle of solidarity inspires the engagement of the Holy See within multilateral organizations.

Chapter VI, 'People on the Move: The Challenge of the Twenty-first Century', mostly contains the statements delivered to the UNHCR (the United Nations Refugee Agency) and the International Organization for Migration. People on the move constitute an age-old experience and are important players in the unfolding of history. Ours has been called the 'age of migration'. With some 250 million people living and working in a country different from the one in which they were born, and with more than 700 million internal migrants, one person in every seven in the world is a migrant. Globalization is both a cause and a result of human mobility extending in many directions: South to North, South to South, and North to South. Projections for the future provide evidence that the phenomenon of human mobility will remain a critical social concern. The interventions delivered by the Holy See in this regard aim at supporting the process of a greater humanization of the global movement of people, at addressing the root causes of economic imbalances and violence and the need of a new governance of human mobility in all its forms. They highlight the evidence that in the medium and long term migration benefits the countries of origin and of arrival, and the migrants themselves.

Finally, an extensive conclusion to the volume, 'A Beacon of Inspiration for the Family of Nations', by António Manuel de Oliveira Guterres, current Secretary General of the United Nations and a long-standing United Nations High Commissioner for Refugees as well as former Prime Minister of Portugal, contributes to enriching the volume from a different perspective. The quest for peace, the respect for human rights and the dignity of the human person and the promotion of justice and social progress are the same founding principles that the leaders of the world agreed to abide by in 1945. However, more than seventy years after this solemn declaration, its realization remains unfulfilled. Through its statements, the Holy See prompts the international community and its institutions to take a 'risk of solidarity', renewing the moral dimension within international relations so that the human family may live peacefully and develop justly together.

ABBREVIATIONS

ACP	African, Caribbean and Pacific Group
AD	Anti-dumping measures
AFTA	ASEAN Free Trade Area
APEC	Asia-Pacific Economic Cooperation
APLC	Anti-Personnel Landmines Convention
ASEAN	Association of Southeast Asian Nations
BRIC	Brazil, Russia, India, China
BWC	Biological Weapons Convention
CBD	Convention on Biological Diversity
CCM	Convention on Cluster Munitions
CCW	Convention on Certain Conventional Weapons
CDIP	Committee on Development and Intellectual Property
CEDAW	Convention on the Elimination of All Forms of Discrimination against Women
CMW	International Convention on the Protection of the Rights of All Migrant Workers and Members of Their Families
COP 21	Conference of the Parties 21
CRC	Convention on the Rights of the Child
CTBT	Comprehensive Nuclear-Test-Ban Treaty
DDA	Doha Development Agenda
DSB	Dispute Settlement Body
DSU	Dispute Settlement Understanding
ECOSOC	UN Economic and Social Council
EFTA	European Free Trade Association
ERW	Explosive Remnants of War
EU	European Union
ExCom	Executive Committee (UNHCR)
FAO	Food and Agriculture Organization
GATS	General Agreement on Trade in Services
GATT	General Agreement on Tariffs and Trade
GDP	gross domestic product
GFMD	Global Forum on Migration and Development
GR	Genetic Resources
GRI	Global Reporting Initiative
GRTKF	Genetic Resources, Traditional Knowledge and Folklore
GSP	Generalized System of Preferences
HIPCs	Heavily Indebted Poor Countries

ICARA I	1981 International Conference on Assistance to Refugees in Africa
ICARA II	1984 International Conference on Assistance to Refugees in Africa
ICCPR	International Covenant on Civil and Political Rights
ICERD	International Convention on the Elimination of All Forms of Racial Discrimination
ICESCR	International Covenant on Economic, Social and Cultural Rights
ICMC	International Catholic Migration Commission
ICRC	International Committee of the Red Cross
IDM	International Dialogue on Migration
IDPs	Internally Displaced Persons
IED	Improvised Explosive Device
IGC	Intergovernmental Committee on Intellectual Property and Genetic Resources, Traditional Knowledge and Folklore
IHL	international humanitarian law
ILO	International Labour Organization
IMF	International Monetary Fund
IOM	International Organization for Migration
IPRs	intellectual property rights
ITC	International Trade Centre
ITO	International Trade Organization
LAWS	lethal autonomous weapon systems
LDCs	least developed countries
MDGs	Millennium Development Goals
MEA	Multilateral Environmental Agreement
MFN	most favoured nation
MOTAPM	mines other than antipersonnel mines
MTN	multilateral trade negotiations
MVT	Marrakesh Treaty to Facilitate Access to Published Works for Persons Who Are Blind, Visually Impaired, or Otherwise Print Disabled
NAFTA	North American Free Trade Agreement
NEW START	New Strategic Arms Reduction Treaty
NPT	Non-Proliferation Treaty
OECD	Organisation for Economic Co-operation and Development
OHCHR	Office of the United Nations High Commissioner for Human Rights
OSCE	Organization for Security and Cooperation in Europe

PCT	Patent Cooperation Treaty
RTD	Right to Development
SDT	special and differential treatment
SCCR	Standing Committee on Copyright and Related Rights
SCP	Standing Committee on Patents
SDGs	Sustainable Development Goals
SELA	Latin American Economic System [Sistema Económico Latinoamericano y del Caribe]
SPS	sanitary and phytosanitary measures
SRBHR	Special Rapporteur on Business and Human Rights
START	Strategic Arms Reduction Treaty
TBT	technical barriers to trade
TCEs	Traditional Cultural Expressions
TK	Traditional Knowledge
TNC	Trade Negotiations Committee
TPP	Trans-Pacific Partnership
TPRB	Trade Policy Review Body
TPRM	Trade Policy Review Mechanism
TRIMs	trade-related investment measures
TRIPS	trade-related aspects of intellectual property rights
UDHR	Universal Declaration of Human Rights
UN	United Nations
UNCTAD	United Nations Conference on Trade and Development
UNDP	United Nations Development Program
UNDSS	United Nations Department of Safety and Security
UNEP	United Nations Environment Program
UNFCCC	United Nations Framework Convention on Climate Change
UNHCR	United Nations High Commissioner for Refugees
UNIDIR	United Nations Institute for Disarmament Research
UNODC	United Nations Office of Drugs and Crime
UPOV	International Union for the Protection of New Varieties of Plants
UR	Uruguay Round
VIPs	Visually Impaired and otherwise Print Disabled
WFP	World Food Program
WHA	World Health Assembly
WHO	World Health Organization
WIPO	World Intellectual Property Organization
WTO	World Trade Organization

I

The Human Person at the Center of Fundamental Rights and Protagonist of Development

Introduction

After the crimes and horrors of the Second World War, the Universal Declaration of Human Rights (UDHR), adopted by the UN in 1948, set the protection, promotion and respect of the human person as the central concern of the international community. This concern had inspired the drafters of the UN Charter when they proclaimed:

> We the peoples of the United Nations determined to save succeeding generations from the scourge of war, which twice in our lifetime has brought untold sorrow to mankind, and to reaffirm faith in fundamental human rights, in the dignity and worth of the human person, in the equal rights of men and women and of nations large and small ... and to promote social progress and better standards of life in larger freedom, and for these ends to practice tolerance and live together in peace with one another as good neighbors ... for the promotion of the economic and social advancement of all peoples ... have resolved to combine our efforts to accomplish these aims.[1]

The UDHR affirms that the 'recognition of the inherent dignity and of the equal and inalienable rights of all members of the human family is the foundation of freedom, justice and peace in the world.'[2]

The centrality of the human person recognized by the international community found its roots in the long journey of humankind from Greek philosophy, Roman jurisprudence and Christian inspiration. Pope John Paul II hailed the Declaration as 'a true milestone on the path of humanity's moral progress',[3] adding that 'all the subsequent international documents on human rights declare this truth anew.'[4] It recognizes and affirms that human rights stem from the inherent dignity and worth of the human person and that these rights apply to every stage of life and to every political, social, economic and cultural situation. In his address to the General Assembly, Pope Benedict XVI also praised the UDHR as 'the outcome of a convergence of different religious and cultural traditions, all of them motivated by the common desire to place the human person at the heart of institutions, laws and the workings of society, and

[1] Charter of the United Nations, Preamble, www.un.org/en/documents/charter/preamble.shtml.

[2] Universal Declaration of Human Rights, Preamble, www.un.org/en/documents/udhr/.

[3] Pope John Paul II's Message for the 1999 World Day of Peace, http://w2.vatican.va/content/john-paul-ii/en/messages/peace/documents/hf_jp-ii_mes_14121998_xxxii-world-day-for-peace.html.

[4] Ibid.

to consider the human person essential for the world of culture, religion and science'.[5] Thus, the universality of human rights finds its justification in the fact of the universality of man's common nature.

Human rights constitute the ethical substratum of international relations.[6] Therefore, the advancement of their universality and indivisibility, essential for the construction of a peaceful society and for the overall development of individuals, peoples and nations, remains at the heart of the position of the Holy See in the international arena.

The language of the original UN human rights discourse and that of the Holy See converge to a very significant degree. However, one may observe a recent trend wherein increasing efforts have been made to change the content and meaning of the human rights language in various UN Conventions and Declarations. There is a tendency to reinterpret them according to a 'post-modern' conception of the human person. From this perspective, the individual is considered an end in him/herself. Such a myopic understanding of the person and of human rights that focuses solely on the fulfilment of individual desires, suffocates the aspiration towards the other, thus encouraging a selfishness that often leads to emptiness and death. However, the promotion of the dignity of the human person and of a just international order based on the respect for natural law and non-negotiable ethical principles explains the constant support given by the Holy See to the original ideas of the UN Charter and the UDHR. The position of the Holy See consistently points out the four pillars on which social order should rest, which were formulated by Pope John XXIII: 'nations are the subjects of reciprocal rights and duties. Their relationships, therefore, must likewise be harmonized in accordance with the dictates of truth, justice, willing cooperation, and freedom. The same natural law that governs the life and conduct of individuals must also regulate the relations of political communities with one another.'[7]

Generally, the diplomatic activity and representation of the Holy See in the field of human rights includes informal consultations relating to Resolutions of the UN Human Rights Council (HRC), official interventions, as well as the hosting of round tables, conferences and side

[5] http://w2.vatican.va/content/benedict-xvi/en/speeches/2008/april/documents/hf_ben-xvi_spe_20080418_un-visit.html.

[6] Ibid.

[7] Pope John XXIII, *Pacem in Terris*, Encyclical Letter on Establishing Universal Peace in Truth, Justice, Charity, and Liberty, Vatican City, 11 April 1963, para. 80, http://w2.vatican.va/content/john-xxiii/en/encyclicals/documents/hf_j-xxiii_enc_11041963_pacem.html.

events.[8] These activities aim at developing a global culture that meets the needs of all people, rich and poor, through an advocacy based on a justice-oriented Christian anthropology. As stated by Pope Francis: 'our duty is to continue to insist, in the present international context, that the human person and human dignity are not simply catchwords, but pillars for creating shared rules and structures capable of passing beyond purely pragmatic or technical approaches in order to eliminate divisions and to bridge existing differences.'[9] This diplomacy of universal values is prompted by the conviction that the human person is open to transcendence. Pope John Paul II eloquently recalled this importance: 'Every person, created in the *imago Dei*, i.e. the image and likeness of God, and therefore radically oriented towards the Creator, is constantly in relationship with those possessed of the same dignity. Promoting and defending the good of the individual is thus to serve the common good, which is where rights and duties converge and reinforce one another.'[10] The same Pontiff cautions that: 'The history of our time has shown in a tragic way the danger which results from forgetting the truth about the human person … it must be said again that no affront to human dignity can be ignored, whatever its source, whatever actual form it takes and wherever it occurs.'[11]

The attention given to the rights of every human person is clearly manifest in the interventions delivered by the Holy See to the former Commission on Human Rights and then to the Human Rights Council. These discourses consistently reflect the universality and indivisibility of human rights[12] and cover a wide variety of issues affecting the life of the family of nations. The United Nations Commission on Human Rights was established in 1946 'to weave the international legal fabric that protects the fundamental rights and freedoms and to set standards to govern the conduct of States.[13] Over the course of its existence, however, the

[8] For instance, the Holy See has organized official side-events at the United Nations on the following topics: migration, freedom of religion, protection of Christians in the Middle East, etc.

[9] http://w2.vatican.va/content/francesco/en/speeches/2013/june/documents/papa-francesco_20130620_38-sessione-fao.html.

[10] http://w2.vatican.va/content/john-paul-ii/en/messages/peace/documents/hf_jp-ii_mes_14121998_xxxii-world-day-for-peace.html.

[11] Ibid.

[12] Cf. 'The Respect of All Human Rights is the Source of Peace' (2007); 'Human Dignity is the Pillar of Human Rights' (2008); 'A Reaffirmation of the Supreme Value of Human Dignity' (2008).

[13] www2.ohchr.org/english/bodies/chr/.

Commission came under intense criticism for its politicized membership that included countries with horrendous human rights records. It was also considered ineffective and unable to address urgent human rights crises, and reproached for its selective and politicized decision-making.[14] These criticisms culminated in a UN reform process on 15 March 2006 when the General Assembly adopted Resolution A/RES/60/251[15] establishing the Human Rights Council (HRC): a new, stronger institution to replace the Commission on Human Rights, where human rights would be treated as the UN's 'third pillar' along with security and development. The HRC is an intergovernmental body within the United Nations consisting of forty-seven Member States elected by the General Assembly. Regular sessions of the Council are convoked three times a year (March, June and September). Upon the request of one-third of the Member States, the Council may also hold a Special Session to address urgent human rights violations and emergencies at any time. A significant innovation of the HRC is the Universal Periodic Review (UPR) that systemically examines every four years how States implement human rights. The HRC is the organ of the UN responsible for the promotion and protection of human rights around the globe and for addressing situations of human rights violations and making recommendations on them.[16]

The interventions of the Holy See in the promotion and defence of the primacy of the human person, including the right to life, represent the most substantial section of this chapter. The right to life is the condition for the exercise of all other rights and requires a commitment to uphold life from conception to natural death. Recent evolutions and trends in public culture, particularly in some Western countries, accompanied by breakthroughs in the field of genetic engineering, pose a significant challenge. In response, the Holy See coherently upheld that 'the right to life must be promoted and safeguarded with appropriate legal and political guarantees, for no offence against the right to life, against the dignity of any single person, is ever unimportant.'[17] This also includes the need to

[14] Julie A. Mertus, *The United Nations and Human Rights: A Guide for a New Era*, 2nd edn, London: Routledge, 2009.

[15] www2.ohchr.org/english/bodies/hrcouncil/docs/A.RES.60.251_En.pdf.

[16] www.ohchr.org/EN/HRBodies/HRC/Pages/AboutCouncil.aspx. The Council is made up of 47 United Nations Member States which are elected by the United Nations General Assembly.

[17] http://w2.vatican.va/content/john-paul-ii/en/messages/peace/documents/hf_jp-ii_mes_14121998_xxxii-world-day-for-peace.html.

ensure adequate care for the sick and the elderly[18] and to support the role of the family as the fundamental cell of society. The right to life includes 'the right of the child to develop in the mother's womb from the moment of conception; the right to *live in* a united family and in a moral environment conducive to the growth of the child's personality'.[19] This principle is also recalled in the preamble of the UN Convention on the Rights of the Child, 'The child by reason of his physical and mental immaturity, needs special safeguards and care, including appropriate legal protection, before as well as after birth.'[20]

The protection of children has become an even greater concern for the Holy See. The scourge of child abuse and any form of sexual violence against children and young people[21] have been repeatedly and unambiguously condemned. For example, Pope Benedict XVI declared that 'sexual abuse of minors is always a heinous crime', and it is also a 'grave sin that offends God and human dignity'.[22]

The interventions contained in this chapter illustrate how the Holy See's engagement and commitment develop in a two-pronged direction: first, in the proclamation of the Christian foundations of human rights with their universality and indivisibility, and, second, in the denunciation of any violations of basic human rights. This approach is what brought the Holy See to ratify the following UN Conventions: International Convention on the Elimination of All Forms of Racial Discrimination (1969); Convention against Torture and Other Cruel, Inhuman or Degrading Treatment or Punishment (1987); Convention on the Rights of the Child (1990) and to submit periodic reports.

Experience shows that between the noble ideals proclaimed and legislated and their practical implementation, there remains a wide gap. It becomes a duty for the Holy See to be the voice of conscience, sustaining and promoting those rights that are all too often violated. In addition to the right to life, it defends the right to access to safe drinking water and basic sanitation, the right to adequate housing,[23] the right to education

18 Cf. 'The Right to Health of Older Persons' (2011).

19 Pope John Paul II, Encyclical Letter, *Centesimus Annus*, § 47, https://w2.vatican.va/content/john-paul-ii/en/encyclicals/documents/hf_jp-ii_enc_01051991_centesimus-annus.html.

20 www.ohchr.org/en/professionalinterest/pages/crc.aspx. In this regard, see 'Maternal Mortality and the Human Rights of Women' (2008) and 'Preserving Life for Both Mother and Child' (2010).

21 Cf. 'The Social Wound of Forced Conscription of Children' (2013).

22 Cf. 'We Must Combat Sexual Violence against Children' (2010), 'The Scourge of Sexual Abuse against Minors' (2012).

23 Cf. 'A House is Much More than Just a Roof' (2012).

and the right to food. On the last, especially in the wake of the surge in global food prices following the economic and financial crisis that threatened the stability of many developing countries, several statements have been delivered at the Human Rights Council.[24] Likewise, it has repeatedly asserted the need to eradicate hunger worldwide, which can be seen as a 'slow death' depriving children of their natural developmental opportunities. A clear direction is given by Pope Francis as he calls 'to bring down the barriers of individualism, of being shut-in on ourselves, of the slavery of profit at all cost'[25] and to overcome the throw-away culture.[26]

Finally, a major objective for the Holy See remains the need significantly to advance the right to development and the right to international solidarity. In her interventions in the UN fora, the Holy See stresses: the unity of origin and a shared destiny of the human family; the equal dignity of every person; integral human development, namely, the intimate and indissoluble link between the development of societies at large and the development of the human person in both the physical and spiritual aspects; and the need for solidarity and subsidiarity in the search of a healthy and sustainable development.[27] Solidarity is not simply an option but a duty.[28] UN data revealed that, in 2014, over 2.2 billion people (over 15 per cent of the world's population) are still estimated to be either near, or living in, poverty with overlapping deprivations in health, education and living standards.[29] Because of such tragic and unjust situations, the Holy See has insisted on the need to recognize legally the principle of solidarity[30] in addressing these widespread inequalities, which Pope Francis defines as 'the root of social evil'.[31]

In a globalized culture, the human person seems increasingly subjugated and exploited by ideological and economic systems. Hence, it becomes even more compelling for the Holy See to reaffirm that human dignity must remain the source of all human rights. At a time when the media highlight the most tragic conflicts around the world, the economic

[24] Cf. 'How Can We Feed the 854 Million? The Cost of Hunger Worldwide' (2008); 'Ensure that Food Flows to Those in Need' (2011).

[25] www.vatican.va/holy_father/francesco/messages/food/documents/papa-francesco_20131016_messaggio-giornata-alimentazione_en.html.

[26] Cf. 'The Right to Food Requires Social Solidarity among All Peoples' (2014).

[27] *Compendium of the Social Doctrine of the Church*, § 446.

[28] Cf. 'Implementing the Right to Development for Justice and Peace' (2014); 'A Duty of Collaboration across Political and Geographical Lines' (2005).

[29] UN Special Rapporteur on the Eradication of Extreme Poverty, 17 Oct. 2014, www.ohchr.org/SP/NewsEvents/Pages/DisplayNews.aspx?NewsID=15175&LangID=E.

[30] Cf. 'A Globalization of Solidarity' (2014).

[31] Tweet by Pope Francis @pontifex, 28 April 2014.

and financial crisis and the clash of civilizations and cultures, the Holy See advocates a 'civilization of love', the fruit of the universal values of peace, solidarity, justice and freedom. The diplomatic activity and advocacy of the Holy See in the field of human rights accompanies all peoples, especially the most suffering and vulnerable. It provides a ray of hope that transforms the pains of recent history into a renewed sense of human dignity.

List of Statements

1 Right to Life

- MATERNAL MORTALITY AND THE HUMAN RIGHTS OF WOMEN, 8th Session of the Human Rights Council – Item 3: *Maternal Mortality and the Human Rights of Women* (5 June 2008)
- PRESERVING LIFE FOR BOTH MOTHER AND CHILD, 14th Session of the Human Rights Council: *Maternal Mortality Panel* (14 June 2010)
- PRACTICES IN ADOPTING A HUMAN RIGHTS-BASED APPROACH TO ELIMINATE PREVENTABLE MATERNAL MORTALITY AND HUMAN RIGHTS, 18th Session of the Human Rights Council – Item 3 (15 September 2011)
- EARLY MARRIAGES, ADOLESCENT AND YOUNG PREGNANCIES, 130th Session of the Executive Board, World Health Organization, re: Agenda Item 6.4, 16 (1 December 2011)
- PLACING PRIORITY ON REDUCING INFANT AND MATERNAL MORTALITY RATES, 21st Session of the Human Rights Council – Item 8: *Vienna Declaration and Programme of Action* (24 September 2012)
- RECOMMENDATIONS OF THE COMMISSION ON LIFE-SAVING COMMODITIES FOR WOMEN AND CHILDREN, 132nd World Health Organization Executive Board, re: EB 132/ Conf. Paper/1 – Draft Resolution on Implementation of the recommendations of the Commission on Life-Saving Commodities for Women and Children (23 January 2013)
- THE INADMISSIBILITY OF THE DEATH PENALTY, Statement delivered to the 28th Session of the Human Rights Council – Item 1: *The Question of the Death Penalty* (4 March 2015)

2 Rights of the Child

- TO RESPECT THE CHILDREN IS TO RESPECT ALL HUMANITY, 4th Session of the Human Rights Council (23 March 2007)

- WE MUST COMBAT SEXUAL VIOLENCE AGAINST CHILDREN, 13th Session of the Human Rights Council: *Annual Full-Day Meeting on the Rights of the Child* (10 March 2010)
- GUIDELINES ON THE OPTIONAL PROTOCOL TO THE CONVENTION ON THE RIGHTS OF THE CHILD TO PROVIDE A COMMUNICATION PROCEDURE (OPC), 17th Session of the Human Rights Council – Item 5, Geneva (6 June 2011)
- THE SCOURGE OF SEXUAL ABUSE AGAINST MINORS, 19th Session of the Human Rights Council – Item 3: *Violence against Children* (8 March 2012)
- CHILD'S RIGHT TO HEALTH, 22nd Session of the Human Rights Council, *Annual Full-Day Meeting on the Rights of the Child* (7 March 2013)
- THE SOCIAL WOUND OF FORCED CONSCRIPTION OF CHILDREN, 24nd Session of the Human Rights Council – Item 3: *Children and Armed Conflict* (10 September 2013)
- PRESENTATION OF THE PERIODIC REPORT OF THE HOLY SEE TO THE COMMITTEE ON THE CONVENTION OF THE RIGHTS OF THE CHILD AND THE OPTIONAL PROTOCOLS, *Committee on the Convention of the Rights of the Child and the Optional Protocols* (16 January 2014)
- IMPLICATIONS OF FAMILY BREAKDOWNS ON THE VIOLENCE AGAINST CHILDREN, 25th Session of the Human Rights Council – Item 3: *Reports of the Special Rapporteurs on Sale of Children, Child Prostitution and Child Pornography; Violence against Children; and Children in Armed Conflict* (13 March 2014)
- SYRIAN CHILDREN IN LIMBO: LIFE WITHOUT A LEGAL IDENTITY AND POOR EDUCATION, 28th Session of the Human Rights Council – Item 4: *Report of the Independent International Commission of Inquiry on the Syrian Arab Republic* (17 March 2015)

3 Human Dignity and the Right to Basic Needs

- THE RESPECT OF ALL HUMAN RIGHTS IS THE SOURCE OF PEACE, 6th Session of the Human Rights Council on the beginning of the Year of Commemoration of the 60th Anniversary of the Universal Declaration of Human Rights (10 December 2007)
- HUMAN DIGNITY IS THE PILLAR OF HUMAN RIGHTS, 7th Session of the Human Rights Council (5 March 2008)
- HOW CAN WE FEED THE 854 MILLION? THE COST OF HUNGER WORLDWIDE, 7th Special Session of the Human Rights Council on

the negative impact of the worsening of the world food crisis (22 May 2008)

- SEEK JUSTICE FROM VIOLATIONS: THE OPTIONAL PROTOCOL TO THE INTERNATIONAL COVENANT ON ECONOMIC, SOCIAL AND CULTURAL RIGHTS (ICESCR), 8th Session of the Human Rights Council on the Report of the Chairperson of the Working Group on an Optional Protocol to the ICESCR (4 June 2008)
- A REAFFIRMATION OF THE SUPREME VALUE OF HUMAN DIGNITY: 60TH ANNIVERSARY OF THE UNIVERSAL DECLARATION OF HUMAN RIGHTS, Human Rights Council Commemorative Session on the occasion of the 60th anniversary of the Universal Declaration of Human Rights (12 December 2008)
- THE RIGHT TO SAFE DRINKING WATER AND BASIC SANITATION, 15th Session of the Human Rights Council: *Interactive Dialogue on Human Rights* (16 September 2010)
- RIGHT TO FOOD: ENSURE THAT FOOD FLOWS TO THOSE IN NEED, 16th Session of the Human Rights Council (8 March 2011)
- THE ROLE OF RELIGIOUS ORGANIZATIONS IN UNIVERSAL EDUCATION, 2011 High-Level Segment of the Economic and Social Council (6 July 2011)
- A HOUSE IS MUCH MORE THAN JUST A ROOF: THE RIGHT TO ADEQUATE HOUSING, 19th Session of the Human Rights Council – Item 3: *Adequate Housing* (23 March 2012)
- EDUCATION IS A VITAL CONDITION FOR PROGRESS, 20th Session of the Human Rights Council: *Presentation of the Report of the Special Rapporteur on the Right to Education* (27 June 2012)
- THE RIGHT TO FOOD REQUIRES SOCIAL SOLIDARITY AMONG ALL PEOPLES, 25th Session of the Human Rights Council – Item 3: *Report of the Special Rapporteur on the Right to Food* (10 March 2014)

4 Right to Development

- SUBSIDIARITY AND SOCIAL INCLUSION FOR DEVELOPMENT, 60th Session of the Human Rights Commission – Item 7: *The Right to Development* (24 March 2004)
- A DUTY OF COLLABORATION ACROSS POLITICAL AND GEOGRAPHICAL LINES, 61st Session of the Commission on Human Rights (22 March 2005)
- IMPLEMENTING THE RIGHT TO DEVELOPMENT FOR JUSTICE AND PEACE, Right to Development anniversary: '*Sustainable Development*

with Dignity and Justice for All – Realizing the Right to Development for Present and Future Generations' (2 December 2014)

5 Right to International Solidarity

- GLOBAL INTERDEPENDENCE SHOULD BE ANIMATED BY A 'GLOBALIZATION' OF SOLIDARITY, 26th Session of the Human Rights Council – Item 3: *Interactive Dialogue with the Independent Expert on Human Rights and International Solidarity* (13 June 2014)

6 Rights of the Family

- THE FAMILY MUST REMAIN THE FUNDAMENTAL CELL OF SOCIETY, 26th Session of the Human Rights Council, Item 8 – General Debate, Geneva (24 June 2014)

7 Right to a Safe and Healthy Environment

- THE DEGRADATION OF NATURE, A MIRROR OF OUR CULTURE, High-Level Segment of the 24th Meeting of the States Parties to the Montreal Protocol on Substances that Deplete the Ozone Layer (15 November 2012)
- THE ADVERSE IMPLICATIONS OF CLIMATE CHANGE ON POVERTY AND DEVELOPMENT, 28th Session of the Human Rights Council – Item 1: *Full-Day Discussion on Human Rights and Climate Change* (6 March 2015)
- OUR COMMON RESPONSIBILITY TOWARDS CREATION, 28th Session of the Human Rights Council – Item 3: *Human Rights Obligations Relating to the Enjoyment of a Safe, Clean, Healthy and Sustainable Environment* (9 March 2015)

1 RIGHT TO LIFE

MATERNAL MORTALITY AND THE HUMAN RIGHTS OF WOMEN*

Mr President, distinguished Members of the Panel,

As has been stated by the Members of the Panel, the percentage of deaths of women from pregnancy-related causes is unacceptably high. As the Secretary General Ban Ki Moon explained during his Address concerning the Food crisis, the reduction of maternal mortality as described in the Millennium Development Goals is the only goal on which no real progress has been made.

The Catholic Church, through its many hospitals and maternal clinics, in cities but also in difficult-to-reach places, has been a pioneer, and in many cases still is, in assisting pregnant women and mothers medically, psychologically and socially, before, during and after birth of their child.

As the Panel has explained so well, maternal mortality is an urgent Human Rights issue which touches not only upon the rights of women but also upon the right to life. Within this context, abortion is at times presented as an alternative. In reality, however, it increases the distress of the mother-to-be, already anxiety stricken, placing her in front of a false and impossible dilemma to choose between her life and the life of her child, while the majority of complications during pregnancy and labour are caused because of lack of medical skills, lack of hygiene and lack of antibiotics. It goes without saying that in the case of abortion the right to life of the unborn baby is violated. Human Rights are universal and indivisible: one cannot seek to safeguard one right by sacrificing the most basic of all rights, the right to life of a defenseless human being. Abortion is no alternative.

I would like to recall the Council's attention to the fact that abortion is not mentioned in any binding international document and that no country is under the obligation to legalize abortion. On the contrary, the Convention on the Rights of the Child states in its preamble: 'The child by reason of his physical and mental immaturity needs special safeguards and care, including appropriate legal protection, before as well as after birth.'

Thank you, Mr President.

* Statement delivered at the 8th Session of the Human Rights Council – Item 3: *Maternal Mortality and the Human Rights of Women*, 5 June 2008.

PRESERVING LIFE FOR BOTH MOTHER AND CHILD*

Mr President,

Based on the significant commitment and experience of the Catholic Church in assisting mothers and newborn babies, since the earliest of times, especially through its hospitals and maternity and pediatric clinics, my Delegation wishes to express its urgent concerns about the shocking number of maternal deaths that continue to occur – estimated by reliable indicators at 350,000 a year – most especially among the poorest and most marginalized and disenfranchised populations.[1]

The Holy See's approach to Maternal Mortality is holistic, since it gives priority to the rights of mothers and children, both those already born and those awaiting birth in the womb of the mother. Not surprisingly, a strong correlation is revealed between statistics related to Maternal Mortality and those related to Neonatal Death, indicating that many measures aimed at combating Maternal Mortality, in fact, also contribute to a further reduction of Child Mortality. Moreover, we should not forget that 3 million babies die annually during their first week of life, another 3 million are stillborn, 2.3 million children die each year during their first year of life.

Mr President,

Improvements to reduce Maternal Mortality have been made possible due to higher per capita income, higher education rates for women and increasing availability of basic medical care, including 'skilled birth attendants'. A recent study on Maternal Mortality has suggested that Maternal Mortality in Africa could be significantly reduced if HIV-positive mothers were given access to antiretroviral medications. The availability of emergency obstetric care, including the provision of universal pre- and post-natal care, and adequate transport to medical facilities (when necessary), skilled birth attendants, a clean blood supply and a clean water supply, appropriate antibiotics and the introduction of a minimum age of 18 years for marriage, are all measures that could benefit both

* Statement delivered at the 14th Session of the Human Rights Council: *Maternal Mortality Panel*, 14 June 2010.

1 According to a study published in the medical journal, the *Lancet*, vol. 375, no. 9726 (8 May 2010): 1609–23, there are approximately 350,000 maternal deaths *per annum* worldwide; WHO and UNICEF estimate 500,000 such deaths each year (the difference is attributed to different approaches to statistical modelling).

mothers and their children. Most importantly, if the international community wishes to effectively reduce the tragic rates of Maternal Mortality, respect for and promotion of the right to health and of access to medications must not only be spoken about, but also be put into action, by States as well as by non-governmental organizations and by civil society.

Mr President,

Policies aimed at combating Maternal Mortality and Child Mortality need to strike a delicate balance between the rights of mother and those of the child, both of whom are rights bearers, the first of which is the right to life. The maternity clinics and hospitals promoted by the Catholic Church do exactly that: they save the lives both of mothers and of child, born and yet-to-be-born.

Thank you, Mr President.

PRACTICES IN ADOPTING A HUMAN RIGHTS-BASED APPROACH TO ELIMINATE PREVENTABLE MATERNAL MORTALITY AND HUMAN RIGHTS*

Madam President,

The Delegation of the Holy See has reviewed with careful attention the Report on 'Practices in adopting a human rights-based approach to eliminate preventable maternal mortality and human rights',[1] the 2010 Resolution 15/17 of the Human Rights Council on 'Preventable maternal mortality and morbidity and human rights: follow-up to Council resolution 11/8' as well as Resolution 11/8.[2] The latter resolution expressed 'grave concern at the unacceptably high global rate of preventable maternal mortality and morbidity', recognized this phenomenon as a 'health, development and human rights challenge', and encouraged States and other relevant stakeholders, including national human rights institutions and non-governmental organizations, to give 'increased attention and resources to preventable maternal mortality and morbidity' in the context of the engagement to protect human rights.

Despite such strongly articulated commitments, however, the international community must recognize, with deep regret, that it has made insufficient progress in preventing some 350,000 deaths that occur annually during pregnancy and childbirth. Thus my Delegation believes it necessary to affirm, once again, that 'every woman is equal in dignity to man, and a full member of the human family, within which she has a distinctive place and vocation that is complementary to but in no way less valuable than man's'.[3]

My Delegation is pleased to note three of the 'common features of good and effective practices to reduce maternal mortality and morbidity' to which attention was called by the report being discussed today:

* Statement delivered at the 18th Session of the Human Rights Council – Item 3: 15 September 2011.

1 UN Doc. A/HRC/18/27, 8 July 2011.

2 Human Rights Council, 15th Session, Resolution 15/17. Preventable maternal mortality and morbidity and human rights: follow-up to resolution 11/8, 7 October 2010; 11th Session, Resolution 11/8, June 2009.

3 Letter of Pope John Paul II to the Secretary General of the International Conference on Population and Development, from the Vatican, 18 March 1994, para. 8,http://vatican.va/holy_father/john_paul_ii/letters/1999/documents/hf_jp_ii_let_19031994_populations-develop_en.html.

(1) Broad social and legal changes to enhance women's status by promoting equality between men and women, elimination of early age marriage and the consequent promotion of delay in onset of sexual activities, improvement of social, economic, health and nutritional status of women and girls, and elimination of such harmful practices as female genital mutilation and domestic violence; (2) Strengthening health systems and primary health care to improve access to, and use of, skilled birth attendants and emergency obstetric care for complications; and (3) Improving monitoring and evaluation of State obligations to ensure the accountability of all actors and to implement policies.

The Catholic Church maintains an extensive network of health services in all parts of the world and, in particular, offers outreach to poor and rural communities that often are excluded from access to government-sponsored services. Some Catholic organizations have developed specialized services for fistula repair, provide holistic treatment and societal re-integration of the victims of domestic violence, and promote integral development and education of women and girls. Moreover, Catholic organizations are active in advocacy, on global, regional, national, and local levels, for policies and practices that protect the rights of women and girls. Thus my Delegation wishes to assure you, Madam President, of its strong support for the above-mentioned elements of good practice.

With regard to two other elements proposed by the report as so-called 'features of good practice' to reduce maternal morbidity and mortality – that is 'increasing access to contraception and family planning' and addressing so-called 'unsafe abortion for women', the Holy See wishes to express its strong disagreement. My Delegation believes that 'particular attention should be given to securing for husband and wife the liberty to decide responsibly, free from all social or legal coercion, the number of children they will have and the spacing of their births. It should not be the intent of governments or other agencies to decide for couples but, rather, to create the social conditions which will enable them to make appropriate decisions in the light of their responsibilities to God, to themselves, and to the society of which they are part, and to the objective moral order.'[4] We believe, moreover, that 'abortion, which destroys existing human life ... is never an acceptable method of family planning, as was recognized by consensus at the Mexico City United Nations International Conference on Population (1984).' Thus we find it totally unacceptable for so-called 'safe abortion' to be promoted by the Report being

[4] Ibid., para. 3.

discussed during the current Session of the Human Rights Council or, perhaps even more significantly, by the United Nations Global Strategy for Women's and Children Health, launched by the UN Secretary General in September 2010.

Madam President,

The above-cited concerns are substantiated by evidence-based data. The World Health Organization (WHO) has demonstrated that women in Africa die primarily from five major causes: hypertensive diseases, obstructed labour, haemorrhage, sepsis and infection, and HIV-related diseases.[5] The interventions known to address such medical crises include training and employment of skilled birth attendants, provision of antibiotics and uterotonic medications, and improvement of blood banking. My Delegation finds totally unacceptable any attempts to divert much-needed financial resources from these effective and life-saving interventions to increased programs of contraception and abortion, which aim at limiting procreation of new life or at destroying the life of a child.

In conclusion, the Holy See Delegation expresses the firm hope that the international community will succeed in reducing maternal morbidity and mortality by promoting effective interventions that are based on deep and abiding values as well as on scientific and medical knowledge and that are respectful of the sacredness of life from conception to natural death, for '[t]he presence of a mother within the family is so important for the stability and growth of this fundamental cell of society, that it should be recognized, commended and supported in every possible way.'[6]

[5] Khalid S. Khan et al., 'WHO Analysis of Causes of Maternal Deaths: A Systematic Review', *Lancet*, vol. 367, no. 9516 (1 April 2006): 1066–74.

[6] Pope Benedict XVI, Address at Meeting with Catholic Movements for the Promotion of Women, Parish of St Anthony, in Luanda, Angola, 22 March 2009,www.vatican.va/holy_father/benedict_xvi/speeches/2009/march/documents/hf_ben-xvi_spe_20090322_promozione-donna_en.html.

EARLY MARRIAGES, ADOLESCENT AND YOUNG PREGNANCIES*

Mr Chairman,

Thank you for the opportunity to speak on this important topic. The Holy See Delegation understands the serious risks incurred by young women and men when they are influenced or, worse yet, forced to contract marriage before they have developed the physical and affective maturity to make and keep a permanent and mutually faithful commitment as husband and wife.

The report prepared by the Secretariat already points out the necessity to influence family and community norms related to delay of marriage among young people, to the retention of girls in school, especially at primary and secondary levels, and to the encouragement of men and boys to call into question prevailing norms and stereotypes that can be harmful to women, girls, families, and communities.

Our Delegation wishes to register its serious concern, however, with regard to the recommendations in the Secretariat report that promote access to so-called 'emergency contraceptives' and to so-called 'safe abortion care'. Re-affirming that human life begins at the moment of conception and that life must be defended and protected, the Holy See can never condone abortion or policies that favour abortion.[1]

Mr Chairman, our Delegation 'does not consider abortion or abortion services to be a dimension of reproductive health or reproductive health services ... [nor does it] endorse any form of legislation which gives legal recognition to abortion',[2] which is the very antithesis of human rights.

* Statement delivered at the 130th Session of the Executive Board, World Health Organization, re: Agenda Item 6.4, 1 December 2011.

1 Cf. Statement of the Holy See at the Concluding Session of the 21st Special Session of the General Assembly for the Overall Review and Appraisal of the Implementation of the Programme of Action of the International Conference on Population and Development New York, 2 July 1999.

2 Cf. Reservations and Statement of Interpretation by the Holy See Delegation during concluding session of the Fourth World Conference on Women, Beijing, 15 September 1995, www.its.caltech.edu/~nmcenter/women-cp/beijing3.html.

PLACING PRIORITY ON REDUCING INFANT AND MATERNAL MORTALITY RATES*

Madam President,

The 1993 Vienna Declaration and Programme of Action reminded States that 'particular priority should be placed on reducing infant and maternal mortality rates.'[1] The Delegation of the Holy See notes some signs of hope in reports by the World Health Organization that deaths due to maternal conditions[2] have decreased significantly between 1990 and 2010.[3] However, the situation cited in the current report by the High Commissioner for Human Rights,[4] namely, that 287,000 women died due to maternal conditions and between 10 and 15 million mothers suffered debilitating conditions during 2010, is truly tragic.

We wish to point out further concerns arising from the above-cited Report and influencing the Resolution of the Human Rights Council presently introduced on this issue during this 21st Session. First of all, the Report uses ambiguous terms and dubious arguments in maintaining that 'maternal mortality and morbidity is a product of discrimination against women, and denial of their human rights, including sexual and reproductive health rights.'[5] According to the World Health Organization, the following are included as major causes of maternal mortality and morbidity: severe bleeding (mostly bleeding after childbirth), infections (usually after childbirth), high blood pressure during

* Statement delivered at the 21st Session of the Human Rights Council – Item 8: *Vienna Declaration and Programme of Action*, 24 September 2012.

1 Vienna Declaration and Programme of Action, 25 June 1993, Article 47.

2 Deaths due to maternal conditions = deaths of women during pregnancy, childbirth, or in the 42 days after delivery. A maternal death is defined as 'the death of a women while pregnant or within 42 days of termination of pregnancy, irrespective of the duration and site of the pregnancy, from any cause related to or aggravated by the pregnancy or its management but not from accidental or incidental causes' (Source: *Trends in Maternal Mortality: 1990–2008: Estimates Developed by WHO, UNICEF, UNFPA and the World Bank*, Geneva: World Health Organization, 2010).

3 World Health Organization et al., *Trends in Maternal Mortality: 1990–2010*, Geneva: World Health Organization, 2012.

4 'Technical Guidance on the Application of a Human Rights Based Approach to Implementation of Policies and Programmes to Reduce Maternal Morbidity and Mortality: Report of the Office of the United Nations High Commissioner for Human Rights', UN Doc. A/HRC/21/22.

5 Ibid., para. 14, under general principles section.

pregnancy (pre-eclampsia and eclampsia).[6] By ignoring these important health conditions, the Report gives a biased view of causality in this health emergency for mothers and children. Additional evidence-based determinants of maternal morbidity and mortality have been identified as weaknesses in health infrastructure, including absence of a skilled birth attendant during the birth process, unsanitary medical environment, lack or insufficiency of emergency medical and surgical facilities and supplies, including antibiotics and surgical gloves. Consequently, a lot of maternal deaths are preventable with basic health care, adequate nutrition and competent obstetric care throughout pregnancy, delivery and postpartum.

With regard to ensuring 'universal access … in the national plan – as essential for improving maternal health', the Report points to 'management of unintended pregnancies, including access to safe abortion services, wherever legal' as a major component in assuring maternal health and includes abortifacients, such as misoprostol and mifepristone, as essential medicines to be included in the facilitation of universal access. Thus the Report seems to give abortion, the main aim of which is to terminate the life of a child, precedence over such urgent interventions aimed at saving the lives of both mothers and children as 'appropriate antenatal care; detection of domestic violence; management of pre-labour rupture of membranes and pre-term labour; induction of labour for prolonged pregnancy; prevention and management of post-partum hemorrhage; caesarean sections; and appropriate post-partum care'.

My Delegation wishes to register additional serious concerns with regard to the recommendations in the High Commissioner's Report that promote access to so-called 'emergency contraceptives' and to so-called 'safe abortion care'. Re-affirming that human life begins at the moment of conception and that life must be defended and protected, the Holy See can never condone abortion or policies that favour abortion.[7]

Moreover, the Holy See 'does not consider abortion or abortion services to be a dimension of reproductive health or reproductive health

[6] www.who.int/mediacentre/factsheets/fs348/en/index.html.

[7] Cf. Statement of the Holy See at the Concluding Session of the 21st Special Session of the General Assembly for the Overall Review and Appraisal of the Implementation of the Programme of Action of the International Conference on Population and Development New York, 2 July 1999.

services … [nor does it] endorse any form of legislation which gives legal recognition to abortion',[8] which is the very antithesis of human rights.

With regard to the frequent references in the Report to the expression 'sexual and reproductive health and rights', the Holy See points out that such a totally unbalanced attention to sexual and reproductive health fails to address the complex and underlying causes responsible for maternal mortality and morbidity[9] in an integrated and complete manner and in a way that respects the full dignity of all members of the family.

In similar regard, my Delegation wishes to express concern about the claim advanced in this Report that 'if abortion laws are overly restrictive, responses by providers, police and other actors can discourage care-seeking behavior', thus implying that the lack of so-called 'legal' abortion is a cause of maternal mortality. This statement is unfounded and lacked citation of any evidence to demonstrate its validity. In fact, in a 2010 Report by the World Health Organization, contrary evidence can be found, namely that, during 2008, three countries that permitted 'legal' abortion, i.e., Guyana, Ethiopia and Nepal, had significantly higher numbers of maternal deaths per 100,000 births, than three countries, from their respective regions, that did not allow abortion, i.e., Chile, Mauritius and Sri Lanka.[10]

A final concern from my Delegation relates to the recommendation in the Report that national plans 'should address improved access for adolescents to comprehensive sexuality education, sexual and reproductive health information and care, including family planning'. This recommendation fails to recognize the role of parents. The Universal Declaration of Human Rights recognizes that 'Parents have a prior right to choose the kind of education that shall be given to their children' (Art. 26.3). Thus my Delegation maintains that 'parents must be always free to transmit to their children responsibly and without constraints, their heritage of faith, values, and culture,'[11] as well as the need for all rights to be accompanied by concomitant responsibilities. Moreover, the Holy

8 Cf. Reservations and Statement of Interpretation by the Holy See Delegation during concluding session of the Fourth World Conference on Women, Beijing, 15 September 1995, www.its.caltech.edu/~nmcenter/women-cp/beijing3.html.

9 Cf. Final Statement of the Holy See Delegation to the 4th World Conference on Women, Beijing, 15 September 1995, as recorded in Report of the 4th World Conference on Women, Beijing, 1995, www.un.org/womenwatch/daw/beijing/pdf/Beijing%20full%20report%20E.pdf.

10 World Health Organization et al., *Trends in Maternal Mortality: 1990–2008*, Geneva: World Health Organization, 2010, p. 33.

11 Pope Benedict XVI's Message for the 2011 World Day of Peace.

See wishes to point out the role of parents in educating their children in authentic human love as self-giving in communion and friendship with God and others through the exercise of authentic freedom and respect for one's own body and those of others. Lastly, it is essential the involvement of parents in witnessing and teaching to their children that the self-giving in married love of a man and a woman expresses itself through the body, the complementarity and totality of self-giving, and that such sexual giving belongs to this married love, and to this love alone any national plan or recommendation advanced by the High Commissioner or by this Human Rights Council cannot and should not ignore or bypass parents' rights.

Thank you, Madam President.

RECOMMENDATIONS OF THE COMMISSION ON LIFE-SAVING COMMODITIES FOR WOMEN AND CHILDREN*

The Holy See wishes to note that Catholic Church-affiliated medical care as well as that associated with other major faith traditions contributes greatly toward reduction in morbidity and mortality for significant numbers of mothers, newborns, and children throughout the world, but most especially in developing countries and among the poorest and most marginalized sectors of society. These organizations agree strongly with the need to achieve further reductions in the loss of life and prevention of illness through increased access to affordable interventions that are respectful of the life and dignity of all mothers and children at all stages of life, from conception to natural death.

It is specifically in this regard that the Holy See wishes to raise grave concern with the consideration being given by the Executive Board to affirm and promote so-called 'Emergency Contraception', which was included as one of the strategies recommended by the Commission on Life-Saving Commodities for Women and Children. It is well known that, when conception already has occurred, the substances used in 'emergency contraception' produce an abortifacient effect. For my Delegation, it is totally unacceptable to refer to a medical product that constitutes a direct attack on the life of the child *in utero* as a 'life-saving commodity' and, much worse, to encourage increasing use of such substances in all parts of the world.

As it has done on many previous occasions, the Holy See reiterates that it does not consider abortion or abortion services to be a dimension of reproductive health or reproductive health services.

It urges the international public health community to focus its attention, energy, expertise and finances on procedures and commodities that defend and preserve life at all stages, including life *in utero*, such as those listed as 'Maternal, Newborn, and Child Health Commodities' and proposed as recommendations in the above-cited Commission Report.

* Statement delivered at the 132nd WHO Executive Board, re: EB 132/ Conf. Paper/1 – Draft Resolution on Implementation of the Recommendations of the Commission on Life-Saving Commodities for Women and Children, 23 January 2013.

THE INADMISSIBILITY OF THE DEATH PENALTY*

Mr Chairman,

The Delegation of the Holy See is pleased to take part in this first biennial high-level panel discussion on the question of the death penalty and joins an increasing number of States in supporting the fifth United Nations General Assembly resolution calling for a global moratorium on the use of the death penalty. Public opinion and support of the various provisions aimed at abolishing the death penalty, or suspending its application, is growing. This provides a strong momentum which this Delegation hopes will encourage States still applying the death penalty to move in the direction of its abolition.

The position of the Holy See on this issue has been more clearly articulated in the past decades. In fact, twenty years ago, the issue was framed within the proper ethical context of defending the inviolable dignity of the human person and the role of the legitimate authority to defend in a just manner the common good of society.[1] Considering the practical circumstances found in most States, as a result of steady improvements in the organization of the penal system, it appears evident nowadays that means other than the death penalty 'are sufficient to defend human lives against an aggressor and to protect public order and the safety of persons'.[2] For that reason, 'public authority must limit itself to such means, because they better correspond to the concrete conditions of the common good and are more in conformity to the dignity of the human person.'[3]

Political and legislative initiatives being promoted in a growing number of countries to eliminate the death penalty and to continue the substantive progress made in conforming penal law both to the human dignity of prisoners and the effective maintenance of public order are moving in the right direction.[4]

Pope Francis has further emphasized that the legislative and judicial practice of the State authority must always be guided by the 'primacy of human life and the dignity of the human person'. He noted as well 'the possibility of judicial error and the use made by totalitarian and dictatorial

* Statement delivered to the 28th Session of the Human Rights Council – Item 1: *The Question of the Death Penalty*, 4 March 2015.

1 Pope John Paul II, *Evangelium Vitae*, 25 March 1995, § 56. 2 Ibid.

3 Ibid. 4 Cf. Pope Benedict XVI, General Audience, 30 November 2011.

regimes … as a means of suppressing political dissidence or of persecuting religious and cultural minorities'.[5]

Thus, respect for the dignity of every human person and the common good are the two pillars on which the position of the Holy See has developed. These principles converge with a similar development in international human rights law and jurisprudence. Moreover, we should take into account that no clear positive effect of deterrence results from the application of the death penalty and that the irreversibility of this punishment does not allow for eventual corrections in the case of wrongful convictions.

Mr Chairman,

My Delegation contends that bloodless means of defending the common good and upholding justice are possible, and calls on States to adapt their penal system to demonstrate their adhesion to a more humane form of punishment. As for those countries that claim it is not yet feasible to relinquish this practice, my Delegation encourages them to strive to become capable of doing so.

In conclusion, Mr Chairman, the Holy See Delegation fully supports the efforts to abolish the use of the death penalty. In order to arrive at this desired goal, these steps need to be taken: (1) to sustain the social reforms that would enable society to implement the abolition of the death penalty; (2) to improve prison conditions, to ensure respect for the human dignity of the people deprived of their freedom.[6]

Thank you, Mr Chairman.

[5] Pope Francis, Address to the Delegates of the International Association of Penal Law, 23 October 2015, nos. I and II.b.

[6] Cf. Ibid.

2 RIGHTS OF THE CHILD

TO RESPECT THE CHILDREN IS TO RESPECT ALL HUMANITY*

Mr President,

The Delegation of the Holy See very much welcomes the attention given to child protection and to children's rights in recent studies and debates. In fact the child should not only be placed high on the political agenda but right at the center of concern: the future of society depends on children and on how they are prepared for it, and their vulnerability calls for special protection. A child is neither an instrument nor an object. The United Nations Convention on the Rights of the Child attributes to the child the fundamental rights of a person; it recognizes the child to have the same equality and dignity as any adult person. In its preamble, it affirms that because of its immaturity the child 'needs special safeguards and care, including appropriate legal protection before as well as after birth'. Respect of children is respect of humanity.

In many cases, due to lack of will and of resources, good legal provisions and public policies are not implemented, with grave consequences for children. They often become the first victims of famines and wars. They are crippled by unexploded munitions, deprived of schooling, lack sufficient food, are obliged to sleep and survive on sidewalks in urban centers, sick with AIDS, malaria and tuberculosis (TB), without the possibility of medicaments, sold to traffickers, recruited into irregular armies, uprooted by forced displacements, compelled into long hours of debilitating work. These millions of young victims are a vivid symbol of existing inequalities and failing systems. Unfortunately, these are not the only contradictions affecting children in our globalized world. To many children, the right to life is denied; prenatal selection eliminates both babies suspected to be with disabilities and female children simply because of their sex and thus deny the equal and intrinsic value of disabled persons and of girls for their families and for society. In a variety of ways violence against children goes on, a humiliating violation of their rights as human beings.

If respect of the human rights of children measures the health of a society, then the legal recognition of these rights is urgent. The first

* Statement delivered at the 4th Session of the Human Rights Council, 23 March 2007.

right of children is that of being born and educated in a welcoming and secure family environment where their physical, psychological and spiritual growth is guaranteed, their potential is developed and where the awareness of personal dignity becomes the base for relating to others and for confronting the future. The target of eliminating violence against children and of providing a constructive and healthy context for their development demands that the State and society concretely support and enable the family to carry out its task. A vital way, in fact, to counteract the vulnerability of children is to strengthen the families in which they are meant to grow, to thrive, and to be formed as responsible and productive citizens in their local communities and in the wider society. Governments must assume their rightful role to protect and promote family life because the family has obvious vital and organic links with society. The creation of conditions leading to peace and economic progress, a continued responsibility of the national and the international communities, will open the way to reducing and eventually eliminating those situations that hurt children in a disproportionate way. My Delegation certainly agrees that all forms of violence against children are unjustifiable, preventable and must be stopped.

A coherent effort to eliminate violence against children will therefore reject the exaltation of violence in the public culture of society. Education becomes a critical instrument to instil not just tolerance for coexistence in today's societies experiencing everywhere a greater pluralism, but appreciation and respect of others, openness to dialogue in a concerted search for the common good, and even to love as a more constructive bond for the orderly functioning of society. It would turn into a new form of violence against children if the State were to impose a specific model of moral conscience on children without taking into consideration the moral and religious convictions of parents. Civil society has a major role to play in supporting the family and counteracting all forms of violence against children. On her part, the Catholic Church's over 300,000 social, caring and educational institutions work daily to ensure both a peace-oriented and creative education for children, and the development of their talents, and to provide the reintegration of abused and neglected children into their families, if possible, and into society.

Mr President,

Children are both weakness and hope. To pursue the defense of their rights and the elimination of all forms of violence against them remains an institutional challenge for the international community. Success will be reached if priority is given to the natural role of the family and to the public culture that recognizes that children too are full human persons.

Thank you, Mr President.

WE MUST COMBAT SEXUAL VIOLENCE AGAINST CHILDREN*

Mr President,

'Sexual abuse of minors is always a heinous crime.' To this unambiguous condemnation of sexual violence against children and young people, the Holy Father Pope Benedict XVI has added the religious dimension, pointing out that it is also a 'grave sin' that offends God and human dignity. The child's physical and psychological integrity is violated with destructive consequences. Studies have shown that abused children react in different ways to sexual violence and have a higher likelihood of teen pregnancy, homelessness, risk of drug and alcohol dependence. In a word, the evil committed against these little ones often stigmatizes them for their entire life.

As you are aware, in the last years, Catholic clergy, religious and lay workers in a number of countries have been accused, and several have been convicted, of child abuse. There is no excuse for this behavior, which is a grave betrayal of trust. In some cases, heavy fines had to be paid while in other cases the culprits were given custodial sentences. Protection from sexual aggression remains high on the agenda of all church institutions as they struggle to come to terms with this serious problem. Likewise, concrete measures to ensure transparency and assistance to the victims and their families are the way to alleviate the pain, grief and bewilderment caused by the abuse that has occurred.

The Catholic community continues its efforts to deal decisively with this problem. Thus, those who are found guilty of these crimes are immediately suspended from exercising their office and are dealt with according to the norms of civil and canon laws. Other legal measures have been taken in order to ensure that children and young people cared for in schools and institutions are safe. Many of the measures taken, legal or administrative, deal with recognition and punishment of abuse. Prevention is the best medicine, and this begins with education and promoting a culture of respect of the human rights and human dignity of every child, and especially through the implementation of efficient methods for the recruitment of school personnel.

Could the panel share some best practices that can help children to recognize and report the improper behavior of educators and caregivers?

* Statement delivered at the 13th Session of the Human Rights Council: Annual Full-Day Meeting on the Rights of the Child, 10 March 2010.

GUIDELINES ON THE OPTIONAL PROTOCOL TO THE CONVENTION ON THE RIGHTS OF THE CHILD TO PROVIDE A COMMUNICATION PROCEDURE (OPC)*

Mr President,

At the outset, my Delegation would like to congratulate all the stakeholders that engaged in the preparation of the draft Optional Protocol to the Convention on the Rights of the Child to provide a communication procedure (OPC), which will become a significant instrument of the human rights system.

Beyond the legal aspect, the Optional Protocol to the CRC provides a word of hope and encouragement to those children and young people whose innocence and human dignity have been wounded by the cruelty that can be present in the world of adults. If all States, UN agencies, civil society and faith-based institutions work together in a more effective partnership, they will be able to ensure love, care and assistance to those affected by violence and abuse. Moreover, they will foster a world where these children can pursue their dreams and aspirations of a future free of violence.

'The best interests of the child shall be a primary consideration'[1] and the precondition to realize the future thus envisioned. In fact, we are 'convinced that the family, as the fundamental group of society and the natural environment for the growth and well-being of all its members, and particularly children, should be afforded the necessary protection and assistance so that it can fully assume its responsibilities within the community.'[2] In line with the CRC that recognizes the family as essential, the Holy See believes that the best interests of the child are primarily served in the context of the traditional family.

* Statement delivered at the 17th Session of the Human Rights Council – Item 5, Geneva: 6 June 2011.

1 United Nations General Assembly, Art. 3.1 of the Convention on the Rights of the Child, 1989, p. 1.

2 United Nations General Assembly, Preamble to the Convention on the Rights of the Child, 1989, p. 1.

Mr President,

More than fifty years ago, in the Declaration of the Rights of the Child, the General Assembly proclaimed that 'The child shall enjoy special protection, and shall be given opportunities and facilities, by law and by other means, to enable him to develop physically, mentally, morally, spiritually and socially in a healthy and normal manner and in conditions of freedom and dignity.'[3] This continues to be of great importance now, as it was then, and points to the responsibility of the entire international community to pursue its essential work of promoting the dignity and well-being of all children and adolescents everywhere. In 2009, Pope Benedict XVI made an appeal to the international community to increase its effort to offer an adequate response to the tragic problems experienced by far too many children: 'May a generous commitment on everyone's part not to be lacking so that the rights of children may be recognized and their dignity given ever greater respect.'

Mr President, the Holy See looks at this new Optional Protocol to the Convention of the Rights of the Child to provide a communication procedure as an opportune contribution to strengthening the human rights system. May it also bring us closer to our ultimate goal: the unconditional preservation and respect of the dignity of every single person, woman or man, adult or child.

Thank you, Mr President.

[3] United Nations General Assembly, Declaration of the Rights of the Child, 1959, p. 1.

THE SCOURGE OF SEXUAL ABUSE AGAINST MINORS*

Madam President,

The Delegation of the Holy See wishes to express its deep concern, as already has been shared by other Delegations, regarding the plight of innocent children whose physical, emotional, and spiritual well-being have been seriously wounded as a result of violence to which they have been subjected. As the United Nations Secretary General Mr Ban Ki-moon noted during his address at a special event to encourage ratification of Optional Protocols to the Convention on the Rights of the Child, 'Childhood is a time of innocence and learning, a time for building character and finding a safe route to adulthood. But the sad truth is that too many children in today's world suffer appalling abuse.'[1]

While the Special Representative of the Secretary General on Violence against Children reported on positive developments in several regions of the world, she also details many persistent challenges to be confronted in order to assure the safety and well-being of children in all sectors and circumstances of social life and welfare. Some 300,000 children are involved in more than 30 conflicts worldwide, and they are used as combatants, messengers, porters, cooks, suicide-bombers and are even forced to have sexual relations. Most of them are brutally recruited. Some 115 million of the world's 215 million child laborers are caught in hazardous work. Most regrettably, studies have demonstrated that violence against children can take place in many settings: at home, in school or other educational settings, in institutions or other residential care settings for children whose parents cannot provide adequate and appropriate care, in the workplace and in prisons or other types of detention centers. Added to these traditional risks of abuse are the new technologies that, as demonstrated by evidence-based research, often bombard children with damaging and frightening images and information or naively participate in fora that are manipulated by persons interested in preying on such children for selfish and harmful motives.[2] Sexual violence against children is

* Statement delivered at the 19th Session of the Human Rights Council – Item 3: *Violence against Children*, 8 March 2012.

[1] Remarks of UN Secretary General, 27 May 2010, www.ohchr.org/EN/NewsEvents/Pages/Newpushtoprotectchildren.aspx.

[2] Cf. Lost in Cyber World, a project explaining the dangers harboured by the Internet – Information for parents and educators, IN VIA Project, Social Network of the Archdiocese of Berlin, September 2011.

particularly disturbing and requires heightened attention, not only from State governments and law enforcement agencies, but also from each and every component of society, since all members of the human family must share in the responsibility to protect our children, by helping them enjoy their God-given human dignity, and accompanying them as they mature in a caring and wholesome manner.

Madam President, this Delegation is acutely aware of the very regrettable actions perpetrated by some religious ministers who have betrayed the very values which they preach on behalf of their respective faith traditions, by committing aberrant acts of sexual abuse against children. My Delegation wishes to inform that the Catholic Church continues to develop and adopt decisive measures aimed at carefully monitoring the actions taken by church-related structures to help to prevent future occurrences of sexual abuse against children within religious settings. Indeed, the Church has stated on numerous occasions that, without prejudice to the sacramental internal forum, the prescriptions of civil law regarding the reporting of such crimes to the designated authority should always be followed.[3] During a recent high-level meeting on this topic, held in Rome, a new Internet-based 'Center for Child Protection' was launched with the aim of assisting Catholic Church-related institutions in educating clergy and other church-related personnel in the prevention of child abuse.[4]

In a recent address to bishops from the United States of America, Pope Benedict XVI 'acknowledge[d] personally the suffering inflicted on the victims [of sexual abuse] and the honest efforts made both to ensure the safety of our children and to deal appropriately and transparently with allegations as they arise'. The Holy Father further expressed the 'hope that the Church's conscientious efforts to confront this reality will help the broader community to recognize the causes, true extent and devastating consequences of sexual abuse, and to respond effectively to this scourge which affects every level of society', and noted that, 'just as the Church is rightly held to exacting standards in this regard, all other institutions, without exception, should be held to the same standards.'[5]

[3] Cf. Circular letter to assist Episcopal Conferences in developing guidelines for dealing with cases of sexual abuse of minors perpetrated by clerics (3 May 2011), www.vatican.va/roman_curia/congregations/cfaith/documents/rc_con_cfaith_doc_20110503_abuso-minori_en.html.

[4] Cf. http://elearning-childprotection.com/.

[5] Address of Pope Benedict XVI to the Bishops of the United States of America on their 'Ad Limina' Visit, Vatican City, 26 November 2011, www.vatican.va/holy_

Madam President, this Council, and society as a whole, should not deceive itself into thinking that sexual abuse against minors is restricted to some institutions. It has insidiously infiltrated all elements of society and most often occurs within the family, the local neighborhood, and the child's immediate social circle. It must honestly be acknowledged and effectively prevented in order to safeguard the safety and the physical and emotional health of children who, in turn, constitute the future of society.

father/benedict_xvi/speeches/2011/november/documents/hf_ben-xvi_spe_20111126_bishops-usa_en.html.

CHILD'S RIGHT TO HEALTH*

Mr President,

My Delegation welcomes the focus on the Child's Right to Health during this Annual Discussion. Allow me to call special attention to the situation of children living with HIV or with HIV/TB co-infection – a topic that could have received more extensive consideration in the Report of the High Commissioner in preparation for this important discussion.

Despite evidence that treatment is very successful in children living with HIV, even in resource-limited settings, there remain significant obstacles to expanding access for children living with HIV to such life-saving and life-enhancing treatment. In fact, only 28 per cent of children living in low- and middle-income countries in need of highly active antiretroviral treatment, or HAART, are currently able to benefit from such medications, compared with 50 per cent of adults living with HIV who have access to ART.[1] As a result, 30 children under 15 years of age living with HIV die every hour.[2] For children living with both HIV and TB, the situation is even worse; despite the fact that TB remains the main cause of death among children with AIDS, pediatric drug formulations are not available to treat HIV/TB co-infection in children.

One major barrier to treating children with HIV is the difficulty of detecting the infection in babies younger than 18 months. In high-income countries, children can be diagnosed accurately within 48 hours of birth. However, the specialized and sophisticated tests that permit such diagnosis among infants are not commonly available in low-income countries because they require expensive laboratory equipment and trained staff. Moreover, the scale-up of testing programs for children requires investment in training and technical assistance for health care providers, improvement of laboratory capacity and facilities, and referral networks and community mobilization.

We know, of course, that 90 per cent of HIV infection among children is transmitted from a mother who is living with the virus to her child while still in the womb, during the birth process, or during breastfeeding.

* Statement delivered at the 22nd Session of the Human Rights Council, *Annual Full-Day Meeting on the Rights of the Child*, 7 March 2013.

[1] UNAIDS, Report on the Global AIDS Epidemic, December 2012.

[2] UNAIDS Report, 'Together We Will End AIDS', July 2012.

Even though interventions are available to prevent the transmission of HIV from mother to child, approximately 330,000 children were newly infected with HIV during 2011,[3] mainly through mother-to-child transmission. If access to special programs to prevent mother-to-child transmission through early diagnosis of the mothers and through provision of antiretroviral treatment to such mothers immediately upon diagnosis were increased, the number of children newly infected with HIV would soon decrease. Moreover, the immediate initiation of HAART among children born to HIV-positive mothers would delay the onset of HIV-related illnesses among such children.

Without adequate care and treatment, up to one-third of all children born with HIV die before their first birthday, and half of them will die before they are two years old. Yet children treated with HAART must take three or more different antiretroviral drugs several times a day in order to avoid developing resistance to a single drug, and therefore to prevent the further progression of HIV disease. These medicines must be formulated differently than those for adults, and in a way that takes into consideration the climatic conditions in the areas in which they will be distributed and used. It also should be noted that, in many low-income settings, clean drinking water, adequate nutrition, and a continuous supply of electricity are not always available and can therefore further jeopardize the quality of treatment that a child can access. Indeed, an insufficient variety of formulations of antiretroviral medicines are available for specific use among children, 'largely because the HIV medicine market for children was judged too small to warrant investments in such research'.[4]

Mr President, the above-mentioned barriers thwart the ability of the child to enjoy and exercise his or her right to the highest attainable standard of physical and mental health, recognized, inter alia, in the Convention on the Rights to the Child. My Delegation speaks here not merely in an abstract or legalistic manner but on the basis of information and lived experience reported by Catholic Church-related organizations engaged in promoting and protecting the child's right to health in every part of the world. A recent study conducted by the Catholic HIV/AIDS Network, an informal network of Catholic Church-related organizations engaged in providing financial and technical assistance support to HIV programs in developing countries reports significant engagement by such programs

[3] Ibid.

[4] 'Paediatric HIV: From a Human Rights Lens', Caritas Internationalis HAART for Children Newsletter, Issue 2, June 2012, Interview with Professor Daniel Tarantola.

in efforts to eliminate mother-to-child transmission of the virus, to promote comprehensive and early diagnosis and treatment of those children who have been infected, and to confront the social stigma and ignorance that often obstructs the effective and efficient implementation of such programs. This report was discussed in a parallel event, held on 6 March 2013, in conjunction with the 22nd Session of this Council.

In an appeal on World AIDS Day 2012, Pope Benedict XVI noted with much urgency: 'HIV/AIDS particularly affects the poorest regions of the world, where there is very limited access to effective medicines. My thoughts turn in particular to the large number of children who contract the virus from their mothers each year, despite the treatments which exist to prevent its transmission. I encourage the many initiatives that, within the scope of the ecclesial mission, have been taken in order to eradicate this scourge.'[5]

Mr President, my Delegation sincerely hopes that this Council itself will appeal to the Member States of the United Nations to invest funds and collaborate closely with pharmaceutical companies and research institutes in order to preserve and advance the life and dignity of children living with HIV or with HIV/TB co-infection by providing them with available, affordable and accessible diagnostic tools and medications and thereby assuring their full enjoyment of the right to health.

[5] www.vatican.va/holy_father/benedict_xvi/audiences/2012/documents/hf_ben-xvi_aud_20121128_en.html.

THE SOCIAL WOUND OF FORCED CONSCRIPTION OF CHILDREN*

Mr President,

The scourge of recruiting child soldiers today continues in several countries, with an estimated 250,000 children fighting all over the world, a substantive percentage of whom are girls. Most are recruited by force and some lured by false promises of an escape from extreme poverty and the assurance of a daily meal. They find themselves sexually exploited, forced to kill, deprived of basic human rights and robbed of a normal future. Child soldiers remain a challenge for the international community, still struggling to protect these children from the impact of violence. As the Special Rapporteur indicates, it is urgent to stop recruitment by both governmental and non-governmental groups so that these children may be able to overcome the difficulties of their environment and have access to education and a normal family life.

The Holy See is very much aware of these facts and emphasizes the importance and essential social value of a healthy childhood since, in fact, '[n]o country on earth, no political system can think of its own future otherwise than through the image of these new generations.'[1] Recruiters thwart the development of these children and rob them of the right to learn peace as a way for productive coexistence in society and the right to enjoy the family as the natural school for peace and healthy growth.

International law provides special protection for children, but the gap between legislation and implementation remains very wide. Thus we see that these children are abused and maimed; even when they are lucky enough to survive, a psychology of hate is inculcated in their hearts. Respect for the Convention on the Rights of the Child and its Optional Protocol on the Involvement of Children in Armed Conflict (2000) can go a long way to remedy these evils, and ratification of this Optional Protocol should become a priority for those States that have not already taken such action.

The civil and religious organizations that work for the full implementation of these instruments deserve commendation and support. In

* Statement delivered at the 24nd Session of the Human Rights Council – Item 3: *Children and Armed Conflict*, 10 September 2013.

1 Pope John Paul II, Address to the General Assembly of the United Nations (2 October 1979).

fact, they show, through their action, the recognition of the equal dignity of children as human persons created in the image of God.

On such foundation, it is possible to devise new and creative ways to prevent forced or voluntary recruitment of children into armed forces and to develop new programs for their de-mobilization and rehabilitation. A critical component of such programming would be the establishment of transitional centers where children could be prepared for re-integration into family life and mainstream society. On its part, the Catholic Church, like other religious and voluntary organizations, is engaged in the provision of specialized support to the survivors of such violence, including shelter, food, clothing, education, as well as counselling and other trauma-healing services, spiritual accompaniment, and reconciliation with families.

The link between extreme poverty and social deprivation facilitates conflicts and the forced conscription of children into armed groups. Thus the building of a protective environment for children requires economic and social development and, above all, access to education and the formation of public opinion that values children and is committed to their future. Some practical steps to achieve these goals should include: monitoring the quantitative phenomenon of child recruitment, scrutinizing the degree of respect for international and humanitarian law, raising the minimum age for recruitment by States to eighteen years, providing children with the knowledge, skills and technical capacities for eventual employment, and strengthening the bonds of family life.

Mr President,

Society should not allow the talents and energies of children and young people to be dispersed in pursuit of destructive goals but rather assist that they be focused on the common good and on constructing a culture of peace, dialogue and solidarity. Indispensable to achieve the elimination of the social wound of child soldiers is the work and achievement of peace. In such a pursuit, 'religions can and must offer precious resources to build a peaceful humanity, because they speak of peace to the human heart.'[2]

[2] Pope Benedict XVI, Pastoral Visit to Naples, and Address to Heads of Delegations Taking Part in the International Encounter for Peace, 2007.

PRESENTATION OF THE PERIODIC REPORT OF THE HOLY SEE TO THE COMMITTEE ON THE CONVENTION OF THE RIGHTS OF THE CHILD AND THE OPTIONAL PROTOCOLS*

The protection of children remains a major concern for contemporary society and for the Holy See. Already the UN report on Violence against Children, issued in 2006, cited shocking WHO estimates that 150 million girls and 73 million boys under 18 'experienced forced sexual intercourse and other forms of sexual violence involving physical contact'.[1] Even if they contain a significant margin of error, these estimates should never be ignored nor overshadowed by other priorities or interests on the part of the international community. Moreover, this estimate does not include projections on the number of victims of child labour and child trafficking, whether for sexual exploitation, forced work, sale of organs and other shameful reasons. Although little is known about its magnitude, the International Labour Organization, in 2002, estimated that there were 1.2 million children being trafficked each year.[2]

Abusers are found among members of the world's most respected professions, most regrettably, including members of the clergy and other church personnel.[3] This fact is particularly serious since these persons have great trust placed in them and they are called to levels of service

* Presentation of the Periodic Report of the Holy See at the Committee on the Convention of the Rights of the Child and the Optional Protocols, Committee on the Convention of the Rights of the Child and the Optional Protocols, 16 January 2014.

1 www.unicef.org/violencestudy/I.%20World%20Report%20on%20Violence%20against%20Children.pdf.

2 International Labour Organization, *Every Child Counts: New Global Estimates on Child Labour*, Geneva: International Labour Office, 2002. Difficult as it is to collect reliable statistics in this area, they could at least indicate the vastness of the problem. For example, global statistics provided by ARC of Hope for Children present the following picture in 2013:

- 40 million children subjected to abuse each year;
- suicide is the third leading cause of death among adolescents worldwide;
- 30% of severely disabled children in special homes in the Ukraine die before 18 years of age;
- approximately 20% of women and 5% to 10% of men report being sexually abused as children, while 25% to 50% of all children report being physically abused;
- 3 million young girls are subjected to genital mutilation every year.

3 John Jay College Research Team, 'The Causes and Context of Sexual Abuse of Minors by Catholic Priests in the United States, 1950–2010', Washington, DC: United States Conference of Catholic Bishops, 2011.

that are to promote and protect all elements of the human person, including physical, emotional and spiritual health. This relationship of trust is critical and demands a higher sense of responsibility and respect for the persons served.

Confronted with this reality, the Catholic Church at large, as well as other religious structures in other faith traditions, has undergone a serious examination of conscience. The Catholic Church has delineated carefully policies and procedures designed to eliminate such abuse; to investigate, report and collaborate with respective legal authorities on even any suspicion of such cases; and to listen carefully and to address the impact such situations have on survivors of abuse and on their families. While the vast majority of church personnel and institutions have provided, and continue to provide, a wide variety of services to children by educating and by supporting their families, to protect them, and to respond to their physical, emotional, and spiritual needs, a small percentage of these persons has committed abuses and has rightly been adjudicated and punished by the competent authorities in their respective countries. Although fines have been imposed and paid, it must be recognized that no amount of payment can ever compensate for broken trust and defiled dignity.

The response of the Catholic Church has been articulated at two levels. The local Churches, in line with the legal authorities in their respective countries, have developed, enacted and monitored compliance with internal guidelines that aim at preventing and eliminating any additional abuse and dealing promptly and in accordance with local law if it does occur. For example, the Catholic Church in the United States enacted a Charter for the Protection of Children and Young People and a series of related measures.[4] Other practical initiatives have been

[4] The revised Charter for the Protection of Children and Young People was a footnote text developed by the Ad Hoc Committee for Sexual Abuse of the United States Conference of Catholic Bishops (USCCB). It was approved by the full body of US Catholic bishops at its June 2005 General Meeting, and this second revision was approved at the June 2011 General Meeting. The revised 'Essential Norms for Diocesan/Eparchial Policies Dealing with Allegations of Sexual Abuse of Minors by Priests or Deacons' was developed by the Ad Hoc Committee on Sexual Abuse of the USCCB and by the Vatican–US Bishops' Mixed Commission on Sex Abuse Norms. They were approved by the full body of bishops at its June 2005 General Meeting, received the subsequent *recognitio* of the Holy See on 1 January 2006, and were promulgated 5 May 2006. The revised *Statement of Episcopal Commitment* was developed by the Ad Hoc Committee on Bishops' Life and Ministry of the USCCB. It was approved by the full body of US Catholic bishops at its November 2005

undertaken – for example, the production of e-courses by the Pontifical Gregorian University together with the University of Munich and the identification of good practices by the Bureau International Catholique de l'Enfance, and these have a transnational accessibility.

At the level of the Holy See, the response has been in accord with its direct responsibility over the territory of Vatican City State. In this regard, special legislation has been enacted and covers the State and its population.[5] At the same time, the Holy See has formulated guidelines that will enable local Churches to develop effective measures within their jurisdiction and in conformity with canonical legislation pertaining to the internal discipline of the Catholic community.

The result of the combined action taken by local Churches and by the Holy See presents a framework that, when properly applied, will eliminate occurrence of child sexual abuse by clergy and other church personnel. In fact, other States and institutions might wish to consider these policies and practices as they fortify their own efforts to eliminate the tragic and destructive situation of child sexual abuse.

The Holy See's Report provides answers with the firm intention to specifically address the questions from the Committee and to list the various measures already enacted in response to them.

While much attention has been given to the lamentable impact of child abuse, in whatever form, we should acknowledge, as well, the urgent need to awaken, in a more determined way, the more extensive responsibilities entailed in the overall care and formation of children as they grow to be contributing, productive and valuable members of society. At the present time, as before the development and entry into effect of the Convention on the Rights of the Child and of its Additional Protocols, both the local Catholic Churches and the Holy See, according to their respective areas

General Meeting and then again in 2011. This revised edition, containing all three documents, is authorized for publication by the undersigned.

5 The competent Judicial Authorities of Vatican City State shall now also exercise penal jurisdiction over these crimes and according to the laws transformed in Vatican City State Law No. VIII, of 11 July 2013, containing Supplementary Norms on Criminal Law Matters; in Vatican City State Law No. IX, of 11 July 2013, containing Amendments to the Criminal Code and the Criminal Procedure Code, when such crimes are (a) committed by persons deemed 'public officials' (e.g. persons working within the Roman Curia and related institutions as well as diplomatic personnel in missions around the world); (b) committed by the same in the exercise of their functions; and (c) if the perpetrator is physically present in the territory of Vatican City State and has not been extradited. See in particular, Vatican City State Law No. VIII of 11 July 2013, containing Supplementary Norms on Criminal Law Matters and Vatican City State Law No. IX of 11 July 2013, containing Amendments to the Criminal Code and the Criminal Procedure Code.

of responsibility, have been engaged in assuring a broad range and scale of vital social, health and educational services, thereby accompanying families to form and protect children. One need only think, for example, of the network of Catholic schools, from elementary to secondary to higher education levels, sponsored by Catholic religious orders, and dioceses, and local parishes, that provide vital formal and informal education to more than 50 million children worldwide, and often delivered in rural areas and among marginalized population whom even governments are unable to reach.[6]

There is no excuse for child abuse and even one case is a case too much. Child abuse can never be justified, whether committed in the home, in schools, in community and sports programs, in religious organizations and structures. Pope John Paul II stated that the sexual abuse of young people is 'by every standard wrong and rightly considered a crime by society; it is also an appalling sin in the eyes of God.'[7] For this reason, the Holy See, and local Church structures in all parts of the world, are committed to holding inviolable the dignity and entire person of every child – body, mind, and spirit. Thus they unconditionally prioritize the protection of all children, and will steadfastly continue their efforts to eliminate all forms of child abuse and to effectively pursue the adjudication of any such occurrence.

Clearly this is the policy of the recent Popes. Three years ago, Pope Benedict XVI clearly asked forgiveness for the crimes of sexual abuse committed by the clergy and committed the Catholic Church to work toward the elimination of this evil activity: 'We … insistently beg forgiveness from God and from the persons involved [in sexual abuse], while promising to do everything possible to ensure that such abuse will never occur again; and that in admitting men to priestly ministry and in their formation we will do everything we can to weigh the authenticity of their vocation and make every effort to accompany priests along their journey, so that the Lord will protect them and watch over them in troubled situations and amid life's dangers.'[8]

6 As of 2011, the Church operates the world's largest non-governmental school system. Roy Gardner, Denis Lawton and Jo Cairns, *Faith Schools: Consensus or Conflict?*, London: Routledge, 2005, p. 148.

7 Pope John Paul II, Address to the Cardinals of the United States and Conference Officers, 23 April 2002.

8 Pope Benedict XVI, Homily on the Feast of the Sacred Heart of Jesus, St Peter's Square, Vatican City, 11 June 2010, www.vatican.va/holy_father/benedict_xvi/homilies/2010/documents/hf_ben-xvi_hom_20100611_concl-anno-sac_en.html.

Pope Francis clearly stated his intentions to follow the careful attention given by his predecessors to this serious problem by sharing his own deep concern with the Bishops of the Netherlands and offering them some strong counsel: 'In particular, I want to express my compassion and assure my prayers to all victims of sexual abuse and their families; I ask you to continue to support them along their painful path of healing, undertaken with courage.'[9] He undertook new action and has created a Commission for the Protection of Minors, with the aim of proposing new initiatives for the development of safe environment programs for children and improving efforts for the pastoral care for victims of abuse around the world.[10]

In conclusion,

The variety of measures undertaken and the new mentality created should open a better future for all children: healing past wounds and assuring their protection for the future.

[9] Pope Francis, Address to the Episcopal Conference of the Netherlands, Vatican City, 2 December 2013, www.vatican.va/holy_father/francesco/speeches/2013/december/documents/papa-francesco_20131202_presuli-paesi-bassi_fr.html.

[10] Briefing on the Meeting of the Council of Cardinals, 5 December 2013. At the briefing on 5 December, at 1 p.m., alongside the Director of the Holy See Press Office, there participated Cardinal Sean Patrick O'Malley, archbishop of Boston, member of the Council of Cardinals, who gave the following Declaration:

Continuing decisively along the lines undertaken by Pope Benedict XVI, and accepting a proposal presented by the Council of Cardinals, the Holy Father has decided to establish a specific *Commission for the Protection of Minors*, with the aim of advising Pope Francis on the Holy See's commitment to the protection of children and in pastoral care for victims of abuse. Specifically, the Commission will:

(1) Study present programmes in place for the protection of children.
(2) Formulate suggestions for new initiatives on the part of the Curia, in collaboration with bishops, Episcopal conferences, religious superiors and conferences of religious superiors.
(3) Indicate the names of persons suited to the systematic implementation of these new initiatives, including lay persons, religious and priests with responsibilities for the safety of children, in relations with the victims, in mental health, in the application of the law, etc.

The composition and competences of the Commission will be indicated shortly, with more details from the Holy Father in an appropriate document.

Cardinal O'Malley then quoted some of the lines of action proposed by the Commission under constitution.

IMPLICATIONS OF FAMILY BREAKDOWNS ON THE VIOLENCE AGAINST CHILDREN*

Mr President,

The reports of the Special Rapporteurs dealing with various forms of violence and exploitation directed against children form a tragic litany of willful harm to the dignity, wellbeing and future development of the world's most innocent and vulnerable citizens. My Delegation is left with particularly serious concerns having read in one report after another that the international community possesses little understanding of the dimensions of such problems as the sale of children, child prostitution, child pornography and the horrendous violence against those affected by albinism. In the present day and age, we surely need to develop the political will, analytical capacity and firm commitment to take effective action, at the individual, community, national, regional and global levels, to address, adjudicate and eliminate these crimes.

In a recent address to the new Ambassadors accredited to the Holy See on the occasion of the presentation of their credentials, Pope Francis encouraged more a focused and intense attention by governments to the 'scourge' of human trafficking, which he labeled a 'crime against humanity', 'a true form of slavery, unfortunately more and more widespread, which concerns every country, even the most developed'. He made a further appeal: 'People of good will, whether or not they profess religious beliefs, must not allow these women, men and children to be treated as objects, to be deceived, raped, often sold and resold for various purposes, and in the end either killed or left devastated in mind and body, only to be finally thrown away or abandoned.'[1]

The Special Rapporteurs pointed to similar patterns of vulnerability that constitute the root causes of abuse perpetrated against children. Such conditions include abject poverty, economic and social crises, civil and political conflicts and the widespread violence resulting from such disorders. My Delegation noted with particular interest that family breakdown was acknowledged as a serious contributing factor to the violence

* Statement delivered at the 25th Session of the Human Rights Council – Item 3: *Reports of the Special Rapporteurs on Sale of Children, Child Prostitution and Child Pornography; Violence against Children; and Children in Armed Conflict*, 13 March 2014.

[1] www.vatican.va/holy_father/francesco/speeches/2013/december/documents/papa-francesco_20131212_credenziali-nuovi-ambasciatori_en.html.

against children. For many years, the Holy See has made efforts to alert the international community to the alarming fact that the number of broken and troubled families is 'on the rise, not simply because of the weakening sense of belonging so typical of today's world, but also because of the adverse conditions in which many families are forced to live, even to the point where they lack basic means of subsistence'.[2] For this reason, the international community must acknowledge the need to enact suitable policies aimed at supporting, assisting and strengthening the family. The promotion of strong family values and provision of social and economic help to families in particular need will, at the same time, prove effective in reducing domestic violence and sexual abuse, which regrettably is the most frequently occurring cause of harm to women and children.

Mr President, with regard to the situation of children in armed conflict, my Delegation insists that 'full respect for humanitarian law remains essential. It is unacceptable that unarmed civilians, especially children, become targets.'[3] Together with all people of good will, we are deeply grieved by the fact that the youngest members of society so often are robbed of their childhood and forced to become soldiers, or are kidnapped, wounded and killed in armed conflicts.

Thank you, Mr President.

[2] www.vatican.va/holy_father/francesco/speeches/2014/january/documents/papa-francesco_20140113_corpo-diplomatico_en.html.

[3] Ibid.

SYRIAN CHILDREN IN LIMBO: LIFE WITHOUT A LEGAL IDENTITY AND POOR EDUCATION*

Mr President,

Conflicts forced a staggering 5.5 million people to flee their homes in the first six months of 2014. This represents a major addition to the record of 51.2 million worldwide who already were forcibly displaced by the end of 2013.[1] The Independent International Commission of Inquiry on the Syrian Arab Republic recently informed that, since the start of the crisis, 'more than 10 million Syrians have fled their homes. This amounts to almost half of the country's population, now deprived of their basic rights to shelter and adequate housing, security and human dignity. Many are victims of human rights violations and abuses and are in urgent need of protective measures and support.' To compound this tragedy, more than 3 million people, most of them women and children, have fled the Syrian Arab Republic and are refugees in neighboring countries.[2] Violence continues to produce victims in the Middle East in particular, but elsewhere as well, where hatred and intolerance are the criteria for inter-group relations. The human rights of these forcibly displaced people are systematically violated with impunity. A variety of sources have provided evidence on how children suffer the brutal consequences of a persistent status of war in their country. Children are recruited, trained and used in active combat roles, at times even as human shields in military attacks. The so-called Islamic State (ISIL) group has worsened the situation by training and using children as suicide bombers; killing children who belong to different religious and ethnic communities; selling children as slaves in markets; executing large numbers of boys; and committing other atrocities.[3] In camps throughout the Middle East, children constitute approximately half of the refugee population and they are the most vulnerable demographic group in times of conflict and

* Statement delivered at the 28th Session of the Human Rights Council – Item 4: *Report of the Independent International Commission of Inquiry on the Syrian Arab Republic*, 17 March 2015.

[1] UNHCR, Mid-Year Trends 2014, p. 3.

[2] *Report of the Independent International Commission of Inquiry on the Syrian Arab Republic*, Human Rights Council (27th Session), 5 February 2015.

[3] UN Committee on the Rights of the Child, Concluding Observations on the Combined Second to Fourth Periodic Reports on Iraq, p. 5, point 23(a), 4 February 2015.

displacement. Their life in exile is full of uncertainty and daily struggles. 'Many are separated from their families, have difficulties accessing basic services, and live in increasing poverty. Only one in two Syrian refugee children in the neighboring countries is receiving education.'[4] Beyond the specific conditions faced by internally displaced children and those in the refugee camps of the region and beyond the enormous tragedies affecting them, it seems important to envision their future, by focusing on three particular areas of concern.

First, the world must deal with the situation of millions of stateless children, who as such according to the law were never born. The United Nations estimates that approximately 30,000 of these children can be found in Lebanon alone. Moreover, due to the Middle Eastern conflicts and massive uprooting of families, several thousand unregistered children are scattered in camps and other asylum countries.[5] These are 'phantom kids' whose parents have escaped from Syria but whose name and date of birth were never registered at any office. In fact, UNICEF reports that 3,500 children 'officially' do not have a family or an identity. This occurs because all personal documents have been destroyed under the rubble of war or, at times, simply because their parents did not have the time or the money to certify their birth. Stateless children cross international borders alone and find themselves completely abandoned. The number of stateless persons in the world reaches 10 million. While all face grave difficulties, those fleeing Syria face challenges that are even more dramatic: a child below eleven years of age and without documents has no access even to the most basic services. These children obviously cannot go to school and they are likely to be adopted illegally, recruited in an armed group, abused, exploited or forced into prostitution. Every child has the right to be registered at birth and thus to be recognized as a person before the law. The implementation of this right opens the way for access to the enjoyment of other rights and benefits that affect the future of these children. Simplifying mechanisms and requirements for registration, waiving fees, advocating for refugee inclusive registration legislation, represent steps to solve the plight of stateless children.

Second, another key component that shapes the future of uprooted children is education. Both in Syria and in refugee camps in the region,

[4] A. Guterres' speech at the opening session of the 'Investing in the Future' conference in Sharjah, 15 October 2014.

[5] UNICEF, Monthly Humanitarian Situation Report, Syria Crisis, 14 October–12 November 2014.

provision of education has become extremely problematic. Some 5,000 schools have been destroyed in Syria,[6] where more than one million and a half students no longer receive an education and where attacks against school buildings continue. The extremists from ISIL already have closed a great number of schools in the zones under their control. The dangerous condition of the country does not permit children to attend school nor to have access to a proper education. The international community as a whole seems to have misjudged the extent of the Syrian crisis. It was thought by many that the Syrian refugee flow was temporary and such refugees would leave their countries of asylum in a matter of months. Now, after four years of conflict, it appears likely that these refugees will remain and the locals have to learn to live side by side with them. As a result of the conflict, children are behind in their education and are missing the enjoyment of their childhood. In the camps, there are only 40 teachers for more than 1,000 students aged 6 to 17. Most of the teachers are volunteers, and often refugees themselves. Classes focus on drawing and music to help ease the trauma; writing and mathematics are taught when books are available. In Turkey, children face additional problems because of the language barrier. These refugees speak Arabic or Kurdish, so they cannot attend public schools where only Turkish is spoken. For different reasons, whether in their home countries or in the refugee camps, children find an inadequate education system that jeopardizes their future. Everywhere there is an urgent need for an education system that could absorb these children and bring some normalcy to their lives.

Third, another disruptive consequence of the continuing violence that torments the Middle East is the separation of family members, which forces many minors to fend for themselves. The root of the destabilization of society is the generalized violence that leads to the breaking down of the family, society's basic social unit. To prevent the further exploitation of children and to protect them properly, an additional effort should be made to facilitate the reunification of minors with their respective families.

[6] *Report of the Independent International Commission of Inquiry on the Syrian Arab Republic*, Human Rights Council (27th session), 5 February 2015.

Mr President,

The right to a legal identity, to an adequate education and to a family are key elements and specific requirements in a comprehensive system of protection for children. Such measures require the close collaboration of all stakeholders. Access to quality education and psycho-social care, together with other basic services, is extremely important. However, children cannot benefit from such services unless they are registered at birth and their families and communities are supported to protect them better. If the violence does not stop and the normal pace of education and development is not resumed, these children are at risk of becoming a lost generation.

Peace in Syria and the Middle East is the priority for healthy growth of all children. With conviction, during his pilgrimage to the Holy Land, Pope Francis stated: 'May the violence cease and may humanitarian law be respected, thus ensuring much needed assistance to those who are suffering! May all parties abandon the attempt to resolve issues by the use of arms and return to negotiations. A solution will only be found through dialogue and restraint, through compassion for those who suffer, through the search for a political solution and through a sense of fraternal responsibility.'[7]

Thank you, Mr President.

[7] Address of Pope Francis to the Meeting with Refugees and Disabled Young People, Latin Church, Bethany beyond the Jordan, 24 May 2014.

3 HUMAN DIGNITY AND THE RIGHT TO BASIC NEEDS

THE RESPECT OF ALL HUMAN RIGHTS IS THE SOURCE OF PEACE*

Mr President,

First of all, the Delegation of the Holy See congratulates you and the High Commissioner for Human Rights and her Office on the important initiative to organize appropriate celebrations to mark the 60th anniversary of the Universal Declaration of Human Rights (UDHR).

On December 10th 1948, at the Palais de Chaillot in Paris, the United Nations General Assembly took an historical decision and adopted the UDHR. The Universal Declaration remains the single most important reference point for cross-cultural discussion of human freedom and dignity in the world and represents the customary law base for any discussion about Human Rights.

The rights presented in the UDHR are not conferred by States or other institutions but they are acknowledged as inherent to every person, independent of, and in many ways the result of, all ethical, social, cultural and religious traditions. Human dignity goes beyond any difference and it unites all humans in one family; as such, it requires all political and social institutions to promote the integral development of any person, as an individual and in his or her relation with the community.

Human dignity concerns democracy and sovereignty, but goes at the same time beyond them. It calls upon all actors, both governmental and non-governmental, both faith and other communities, State and non-State actors to work for freedom, equality, social justice for all human beings, while respecting the world's cultural and religious mosaic. The very fact that we share a common human dignity provides the indispensable base that sustains the inter-relatedness and indivisibility of human rights, social, civil and political, cultural and economic.

The integral development of the person finds its full and complete realization in community life, which, in turn, finds the root of its existence in the fundamental rights and the dignity with which each person is

* Statement delivered at the 6th Session of the Human Rights Council on the beginning of the Year of Commemoration of the 60th Anniversary of the Universal Declaration of Human Rights, 10 December 2007.

endowed. The rights, recognized in the UDHR, are not subject to historical ups and downs or convenient interpretations, but find their balance and reference in the centrality of human dignity.

In this context, the important debate on the relation between freedom of speech and expression, on the one hand, and respect for religion and religious symbols, on the other, finds a solution in human dignity. I can only increase my own dignity, that is to enjoy human rights to the full, when I respect the dignity of others. Freedom of religion for all, and education to implement such freedom, become the main road for respect of all beliefs and convictions.

In fact, human dignity is the basis for the implementation of all human rights and, at the same time, the point of reference to identify national interests, thus avoiding the 'double danger' of extreme individualism and of collectivism. It is also normative in the adoption of measures in any field where the human person expresses himself, in work and economy, science and security, health and similar areas.

The Universal Declaration recognizes that the respect of all human rights is the source of peace. The concept of peace, as expressed in Article 28, affirms that 'Everyone is entitled to a social and international order in which the rights and freedoms set forth in this Declaration can be fully realized.' Peace is not only conceived as an absence of violence but includes also cooperation and solidarity, at the local and international levels, as a necessary way in order to promote and to defend the common good of all people.

Sixty years after the Declaration many members of the human family are still far from the enjoyment of their rights and basic needs. Human security is still not ensured. The occasion of the 60th Anniversary of the Declaration, launched today, can show that every person, as an individual or as a member of a community, has the right and the responsibility to defend and implement all human rights. An African aphorism puts it like this: 'To be human is to affirm one's humanity by recognizing the humanity of others, and on that basis to establish humane relations with any person.'

Thank you, Mr President.

HUMAN DIGNITY IS THE PILLAR OF HUMAN RIGHTS*

Mr President,

The current debates at the Human Rights Council (HRC) provide a useful supplement of reflection that leads us to the heart of the world's expectations: a recognition of fundamental rights and their implementation. But underneath the statement of high ideals, different perceptions and convictions risk building barriers and stifle concrete respect for people. Perhaps history can help us out of the impasse. Walls and fences built to keep peoples apart have not blocked their movement in the long run nor prevented the flow of ideas and exchanges. At this moment in time dialogue appears more urgent than ever both to sustain mutual knowledge and to prevent dangerous misunderstandings. Now that the HRC has successfully completed its organizational structure and developed its operational mechanisms, the Delegation of the Holy See believes that an even more critical task is left to accomplish: the building of a larger sense of trust and a more precise understanding of the different points of departure and of the different visions that persist in the interpretation and daily implementations of human rights.

The core rules of human rights are often coloured by the historical experience and cultural traditions of the States and regions where they must be applied. In particular, it seems that at the root of various conflicting positions is the focus of attention placed on the relationship between persons and collectivities. Thus, it becomes important to clarify and identify where the source and foundation of human rights are found. In reality the very expression 'human rights' offers the key for an appropriate understanding because it deals exactly with what is 'human', that is the common link among every person and the foundation of human rights.

The great progress achieved in articulating human rights and in improving their application is due in large part to the wisdom of the framers of the Universal Declaration of Human Rights where the universal value of the inherent dignity and worth of the human person was deliberately agreed upon as the cornerstone of all rights. Avoiding a purely collectivist or individualistic approach to human rights, this historical document sets out rights as well as duties and thus it establishes a range of connections between the individual, community and society.

* Statement delivered at the 7th Session of the Human Rights Council, 5 March 2008.

In this way, rights attributed to groups or collective entities are rooted in the dignity inherent equally in each of their individual members. This approach cannot be turned upside down by deriving fundamental rights of persons from the community to which they belong as if it were the subject of basic rights. If the latter were the case, the whole architecture of human rights would crumble. But human rights are universal, interdependent and indivisible: civil, political, economic, social and cultural, and all require effective implementation through an engagement at various levels of social life, of the village, the city, the nation and the international community through its institutions. An integral implementation of all human rights expresses the concrete position of the person in society. A new understanding of the tension between individual persons and community becomes possible by balancing the attention to the rights of the individual within a social dimension. In this context, it remains a concerted responsibility to eliminate those destructive structures that see war, the arms race and unlimited military spending, unbridled profit and unfair trade as acceptable options since they undermine the universal protection of human rights. An essential expression of human dignity is the right to freedom of religion, and here as well the tension between individual persons and community takes on significant dimensions that demand new reflection stemming from the solid base of the UDHR and the two Covenants of 1966.

A person's fundamental right to believe and to practice a specific religion, in the ways proper to it, provided these will not discriminate or condone, for example, torture, genocide or slavery, is the juridical foundation of the organized form of that belief, of its functioning in freedom and of its preserving and defending its own specific identity. It is a bottom-up approach. With his fundamental rights, starting with that of religious freedom, the individual person contributes to defend the identity and the freedom of the organized form of his religion and develops harmoniously in relation to others. Identities, however, cannot be used as a means to justify violations of human rights that are a common heritage of the entire human family and of every culture. Then, respect of the human person from conception to natural death is the only measure to judge any policy, be it the fight against terrorism or the fight against hunger and underdevelopment. Dialogue and interaction become possible when our common human dignity is the guiding value. On its part, the State does not have the power to create human rights by enacting a law, but it has only the capacity to recognize and discipline their existence and ensure their protection, specifically in case of discrimination. Persons then can exercise their human rights individually and in community: it is a continuum for the common good.

Mr President,

As the UN Special Rapporteur on Freedom of Religion or Belief has reminded the Council, present instruments protect religious freedom in its manifold manifestations and forbid any advocacy of national, racial and religious hatred that leads to discrimination or violence. The implementation in every country of existing human rights protection instruments, especially the UDHR and the related Covenants, is the best way to ensure respect of all beliefs and of a peaceful coexistence within pluralistic and interactive contemporary societies. Unfortunately, victims of religious intolerance are particularly numerous where the international law of human rights is not incorporated into national legislations that risk in this way allowing impunity of violators of fundamental human rights. The way ahead includes a renewed engagement in appropriating through education the juridical instruments developed by international law. But it is not enough to communicate a series of documents. It is important to change attitudes, a long-range process that transforms the person and ensures an effective support for dignity and freedoms such as freedom of religion and expression and freedom from want and fear.

In conclusion, Mr President, allow me to recall the well-known aspiration of Pope John XXIII, a still valid and timely message expressed in *Pacem in Terris*, 'that the United Nations Organization may be able progressively to adapt its structure and methods of operation to the magnitude and nobility of its tasks. May the day be not long delayed when every human being can find in this organization an effective safeguard of his personal rights; those rights, that is, which derive directly from his dignity as a human person, and which are therefore universal, inviolable and inalienable. This is all the more desirable in that men today are taking an ever more active part in the public life of their own nations, and in doing so they are showing an increased interest in the affairs of all peoples. They are becoming more and more conscious of being living members of the universal family of mankind' (§ 145). The HRC, as the other organs of the United Nations, are called to realize this wish in our time. The human family and the peoples of the United Nations cannot wait another 60 years.

Thank you, Mr President.

HOW CAN WE FEED THE 854 MILLION? THE COST OF HUNGER WORLDWIDE*

Mr President,

The Delegation of the Holy See fully supports the priority attention accorded to the current food crisis by means of this special session of the Human Rights Council. The primary tasks before the global community are to develop a coherent response within the context of the multiple initiatives underway and to 'mainstream' this crisis within the framework of human rights. We are faced with the overwhelming challenge to adequately feed the world's population at a time when there has been a surge in global food prices that threatens the stability of many developing countries. This calls for urgent concerted international action. This crisis shines a 'red light' of alarm on the negative consequences affecting the long-neglected agriculture sector when more than half of the world's population struggle to make their livelihood through such work. It calls attention to the dysfunction of the global trade system when four million people annually join the ranks of the 854 million plagued by chronic hunger. Hopefully, this session will open the eyes of public opinion on the worldwide cost of hunger, which so often results in lack of health and education, conflicts, uncontrolled migrations, degradation of the environment, epidemics, and even terrorism.

The international community long has recognized a right to food in the Universal Declaration of Human Rights of 1948 (Art. 25) and in the International Covenant on economic, social and cultural rights of 1966 (Art. 25), just to mention some juridical instruments that proclaim the fundamental right to freedom from hunger and malnutrition. Conferences and Declarations of intergovernmental agencies rightfully have concluded that hunger is not due to lack of food but rather is caused by the lack of access, both physical and financial, to agricultural resources. The first Millennium Development Goal aims to reduce by one-half the number of the people living in extreme poverty and hunger by the year 2015. Society must confront the hard fact that stated goals very often are not matched by consistent policies. As a result, many millions of men, women and children face hunger every day. Higher prices may cause some inconvenience to families in developed countries since they find

* Statement delivered at the 7th Special Session of the Human Rights Council on the negative impact of the worsening of the world food crisis, 22 May 2008.

it necessary to spend 20 per cent of their income on food. However, such prices are life threatening for the one billion people living in poor countries since they are forced to spend nearly all their daily income of US$1 per day in search of food. The grave task before us is to design and implement effective policies, strategies, and actions that will result in food sufficiency for all.

The problem of adequate food production is more than a temporary emergency. It is structural in nature and should be addressed in the context of economic growth that is just and sustainable. It requires measures dealing not only with agriculture and rural development but also with health, education, good governance, the rule of law, and respect for human rights. The impact of international trade on the right to food and the liberalization of trade in agricultural products tend to favour multinational enterprises and therefore to harm production by the small local farms, which represent the base of the food security in developing countries. A renewed commitment to agriculture, especially in Africa, appears necessary. To this end, investments in agriculture and rural development are important. Moreover, the duty of solidarity toward the most vulnerable members of society must be recognized. When seen through this ethical perspective, hoarding and price speculation are unacceptable and individual property rights, including those of women, must be recognized. The priority in food production should be to benefit people. Unfair subsidies in agriculture need to be eliminated. To remedy the limitations faced by small farms, cooperative structures can be organized. The utilization of land for food production and for the production for other resources eventually has to be balanced, not by the market, but by mechanisms that respond to the common good.

Mr President,

In this complex and urgent debate on the right to food, a new mentality is required. It should place the human person at the center and not focus simply on economic profit. Due to lack of food, too many poor die each day, while immense resources are allocated for arms. The international community must be galvanized into action. The right to food regards the future of the human family as well as peace in the global community.

SEEK JUSTICE FROM VIOLATIONS: THE OPTIONAL PROTOCOL TO THE INTERNATIONAL COVENANT ON ECONOMIC, SOCIAL AND CULTURAL RIGHTS (ICESCR)*

Mr President,

The Delegation of the Holy See associates itself with previous speakers to thank the Chairperson of the Open-ended Working Group on an Optional Protocol to the International Covenant on Economic, Social and Cultural Rights (ICESCR), Catarina de Albuquerque for her efforts and firmness to carry out her work.

In the fight against poverty, especially extreme poverty, the international community has set for itself specific objectives like the Millennium Development Goals, which are an important road leading to a more universal development. The various 'instruments of the United Nations and its specialized agencies concerning the *integral development* of the human being, economic and social progress and development of all peoples' (Declaration on the Right to Development, Res. 41/128 of 4 December of 1986, Preamble, 5) sustain, in fact, a culture of justice and global solidarity.

The ICESCR serves as a major framework for the achievement of these goals. The steps that have been taken to increase its effectiveness through new mechanisms are a sign of the continued determination to look at the implementation of all human rights in a balanced way. The universal value of human dignity requires the promotion and protection of all human rights without distinction of any kind. The new Optional Protocol of the ICESCR, therefore, represents a positive step towards a fair social and international order.

Historically, economic, social and cultural rights were considered too vague to be justiciable and a base for an individual complaint procedure. In a way they were looked at as second-rate human rights. Now the text presented at the 8th Session of the Human Rights Council is a good compromise. The new Optional Protocol, through an Inquiry and Communication system, gives the possibility to individuals and groups to seek justice from violations, and it reinforces existing mechanisms for an effective monitoring of the activity of States.

* Statement delivered at the 8th Session of the Human Rights Council on the Report of the Chairperson of the Working Group on an Optional Protocol to the ICESCR, 4 June 2008.

The experience of other Treaty bodies shows that these procedures can help to clarify and implement the normative content of a particular provision; to lead monitoring systems to a more focused and disciplined legal approach; to concentrate on a concrete violation of human rights, keeping in mind that coherence is needed to avoid their fragmentation.

While different approaches to human rights can emerge, in the light of the 'inherent dignity and of the equal and inalienable rights of all members of the human family' (UDHR, Preamble, 1) it would be possible to arrive at a fair agreement. In this way, differences should open the way to a more dynamic recognition, promotion and protection of human rights and not stifle their universal implementation. In this connection, there is a need to adopt a comprehensive and holistic approach under which all human rights would be covered and reservations should not be permitted.

Mr President,

The new Protocol will fill a gap in the international human rights system. However, our work is not finished until every person will enjoy the right 'to a standard of living adequate for the health and well-being of himself and of his family' (UDHR, Article 25).

Thank you, Mr President.

A REAFFIRMATION OF THE SUPREME VALUE OF HUMAN DIGNITY: 60TH ANNIVERSARY OF THE UNIVERSAL DECLARATION OF HUMAN RIGHTS*

Mr President,

The Universal Declaration of Human Rights (1948) is a memorable moment in the history of human coexistence and a great expression of a universal juridical civilization founded on human dignity and oriented toward peace. The Delegation of the Holy See fully supports the decision of the Human Rights Council to specially observe the 60th anniversary of this Declaration. After the horrors of the Second World War, the Declaration solemnly reaffirmed the supreme value of the human dignity of every person and people, without any distinction based on sex, social condition, ethnicity, culture, or political, religious or philosophical convictions. With this document, human dignity finally is recognized as the essential value on which rests an international order that is truly peaceful and sustainable. The UDHR proclaims: 'All human beings are born free and equal in dignity and rights. They are endowed with reason and conscience and should act towards one another in a spirit of brotherhood' (Art. 1). The Holy See celebrates the 60th Anniversary of the UDHR, first, by recalling the great sense of unity, solidarity and responsibility that led the United Nations to proclaim universal human rights as a response to all persons and peoples weighed down by the violation of their dignity, a task that even today challenges us. Then, it has promoted events, educational programs, assistance initiatives worldwide, in particular for children, women and vulnerable groups, so that God, as His Holiness Pope Benedict XVI said on 10 December 2008, 'may allow us to build a world where every human being will feel accepted in his/her full dignity, and where relations among persons and among peoples are based on respect, dialogue and solidarity'. Thirdly, it has highlighted once more the fact that human rights are at risk if not rooted on the ethical foundation of our common humanity as created by God who has given everyone the gifts of intelligence and freedom.

Human rights have an indispensable social role. They remain 'the most effective strategy for eliminating inequalities between countries and

* Statement delivered at the Human Rights Council Commemorative session on the occasion of the 60th anniversary of the Universal Declaration of Human Rights, 12 December 2008.

social groups, and for increasing security'.[1] For the protection of individuals and society, the Holy See incessantly has reaffirmed the centrality of human rights and the role of the United Nations Organization in upholding this common patrimony of the human family. Human freedom and creativity have given rise to different models of political and economic organization in the context of different cultures and historical experiences. 'But it is one thing to affirm a legitimate pluralism of "forms of freedom", and another to deny any universality or intelligibility to the nature of man or to the human experience.'[2] A healthy realism, therefore, is the foundation of human rights, that is, the acknowledgement of what is real and inscribed in the human person and in creation. When a breach is caused between what is claimed and what is real through the search of so-called 'new' human rights, a risk emerges of reinterpreting the accepted human rights vocabulary to promote *mere desires* and measures that, in turn, become a source of discrimination and injustice and the fruit of self-serving ideologies. By speaking of the right to life, of respect for the family, of marriage as the union between a man and a woman, of freedom of religion and conscience, of the limits of the authority of the State before fundamental values and rights, nothing new or revolutionary is said, and both the letter and the spirit of the Declaration are upheld, and coherence with the nature of things and the common good of society is preserved.

This anniversary of the Declaration leads us also to reflect on its implementation. In a world of too many hungry people, too many violent conflicts, too many persons persecuted for their beliefs, there remains a long road to walk and the duty to eliminate every discrimination so that all persons can enjoy their inherent equal dignity. In pursuing this goal, there are reasons for hope in the developments that have been generated by the UDHR. The family, 'the natural and fundamental group unit of society' (Art. 16(3)), can be the first 'agency' of protection and promotion of human dignity and fundamental rights. This is in line with the UDHR as well as with the Holy See's Charter of the Rights of the Family, whose 25th anniversary is celebrated this year.[3] The United Nations Organization and its specialized Agencies, this Council in particular, are

1 www.vatican.va/holy_father/benedict_xvi/speeches/2008/april/documents/hf_ben-xvi_spe_20080418_un-visit_en.html.

2 www.vatican.va/holy_father/john_paul_ii/speeches/1995/october/documents/hf_jp-ii_spe_05101995_address-to-uno_en.html.

3 www.vatican.va/roman_curia/pontifical_councils/family/documents/rc_pc_family_doc_19831022_family-rights_en.html.

called to faithfully translate the principles of the UDHR into action by supporting States in the adoption of effective policies truly focused on the rights and sense of responsibility of everyone. International pacts and regional agreements derived from the UDHR coalesce into a body of international law that serve as necessary reference.

In conclusion, Mr President, every human being 'is entitled to a social and international order in which the rights and freedoms' set forth in the UDHR can be fully realized (Art. 28). Every human being has the right to an integral development and 'the sacred right' to live in peace.[4] On such premises, human rights are not just entitlement to privileges. They are rather the expression and the fruit of what is noblest in the human spirit: dignity, aspiration to freedom and justice, search for what is good, and the practice of solidarity. In the light of the tragic experiences of the past and of today, the human family can unite around these values and essential principles, as a duty toward the weakest and needier and toward future generations.

Thank you, Mr President.

[4] United Nations General Assembly, Declaration on the Right of People to Peace, Resolution 39/11, 12 November 1984, p. 1.

THE RIGHT TO SAFE DRINKING WATER AND BASIC SANITATION*

Mr President,

Please allow me to begin by thanking the Independent Expert for her Report on the issue of human rights obligations related to access to, and delivery of, safe drinking water and sanitation services and the responsibility of the participation of non-State service providers in this context.

The availability of fresh water has now become correlated more obviously to human rights like the right to life and health. While in the Millennium Development Goals (MDGs) the international community has set itself the goal of halving by 2015 the number of people globally without sustainable access to safe drinking water and basic sanitation, nearly 900 million people today continue to rely on unimproved water sources for their drinking, cooking and other basic needs. Today, approximately 2.5 billion people around the world – approximately half the developing world – are unserved by improved sanitation conditions. As a result, nearly 1.8 million children under the age of 5 die annually from diarrhoeal diseases (such as cholera, typhoid and dysentery) attributable to a lack of safe drinking water and basic sanitation options. Many other human illnesses can be traced back directly to the inadequate supply of fresh water for drinking and basic hygiene.[1]

Many obstacles impede progress toward achieving the proposed goals, not least the inability of administrators to ensure a fair distribution of water resources in the peripheral areas and slums of large urban centers because of lack of funding or technical capacity. Poor people often suffer, not so much from a scarcity of water itself, but rather from the economic inability to access it.[2] According to current and prevalent thinking, water primarily is regarded as a commodity, and its price should be based on the principle of profit. This concept is based on the theory that the cost of everything usable must be covered by the consumer. Thus, in line with such thinking, even the poorest people should 'pay' for access to

* Statement delivered at the 15th Session of the Human Rights Council: Interactive Dialogue on Human Rights, 16 September 2010.

1 United Nations Environment Programme, 'The Greening of Water Law: Managing Freshwater Resources for People and the Environment', New York, 2010.

2 As noted in the 2006 report of the United Nations Development Program (UNDP), entitled Beyond Scarcity: Power, Poverty and the Global Water Crisis.

the fifty liters of drinking water considered by the World Health Organization for minimal daily subsistence. But it is impossible today to talk about 'common good', or about respect for fundamental human rights, without taking into account the right to live in a healthy environment. Water is a social, economic and environmental asset whose management must be based on social responsibility, a mentality of ecological behavior and of solidarity within countries and globally. The dignity and well-being of the human person must be the central point of convergence of all issues related to development, environment, and water. It follows that access to water should be available to everyone now and in the future since without it people cannot be actors of their own development. In particular, everyone, including the poor, should be engaged in decisions and policymaking related to water management.

The fight against poverty and hunger requires more and more targeted interventions and solidarity in order to guarantee universal access to water for personal survival, health, and for the development of agriculture and the production of food. Thus the Catholic Church teaches that 'by its very nature water cannot be treated as just another commodity among many, and it must be used rationally and in solidarity with others. The distribution of water is traditionally among the responsibilities that fall to public agencies, since water is considered a public good. If water distribution is entrusted to the private sector it should still be considered a public good ... Without water, life is threatened. Therefore, the right to safe drinking water is a universal and inalienable right.'[3]

Mr President, once again we state our appreciation for the Report presented to the Council. In conclusion, my Delegation would like to underscore the State's and the private sector's synergy and responsibility in sub-contracting water and sanitation services and in adopting targeted measures to reach the most marginalized; in developing research facilities for an efficient use of water in urban conglomerates and in agriculture; in controlling the use of chemical fertilizers for their impact on rivers and underground water-bearing strata and the consequent dangers on health; in highlighting the cost-efficient ways that the management and provision of water resources, water services and sanitation contribute in addressing the Millennium Development Goals.

Thank you, Mr President.

[3] *Compendium of the Social Doctrine of the Church*, § 485, www.vatican.va/roman_curia/pontifical_councils/justpeace/documents/rc_pc_justpeace_doc_20060526_compendio-dott-soc_en.htm.

RIGHT TO FOOD: ENSURE THAT FOOD FLOWS TO THOSE IN NEED*

Mr President,

The right to food is a basic right because it is intrinsically linked to the right to life. Almost a billion people, however, do not enjoy this right. The challenge for the world's community is 'to tackle one of the gravest challenges of our time: freeing millions of human beings from hunger, whose lives are in danger due to a lack of daily bread.'[1] Two conditions are involved: there must be safe food available in sufficient quantity; each person should have access to food. Special attention should be directed to the 2.5 billion people dependent on agriculture for their daily sustenance. Among this population are found most of the people who suffer from malnutrition and hunger. Solutions exist to improve the situation, but they demand vigorous action by the governments and peoples of the countries concerned. The international community is also expected to act. My Delegation would like to indicate some conditions it thinks necessary for the enjoyment of the human right to food and the development of policies of food security as a prerequisite for self-sufficiency.

First, it is necessary to recognize and strengthen the central role of agriculture in economic activity; thus, to reduce malnutrition in rural areas, production per person must increase in order to enhance local, regional or national food independence. Investments to improve productivity are required in the areas of seeds, training, sharing of tools for cultivation and of the means for marketing. Structural changes are also demanded according to the specificity of individual states. For example, we must ensure security of land tenure for farmers, especially for those with small landholdings. The customary right of land ownership may be reconsidered. A clear property right gives the farmer the opportunity to pledge his land in exchange for seasonal credit to purchase necessary inputs. In addition, the aim of land tenure has now become increasingly important in the face of the expansion of the phenomenon of land grabs. In Sub-Saharan Africa, 80 per cent of the land is occupied by the poor

* Statement delivered at the16th Session of the Human Rights Council, 8 March 2011.

[1] Pope Benedict XVI, Message to Mr Jacques Diouf, Director General of FAO, on the occasion of World Food Day 2007.

who have no land titles. In addition, membership in cooperatives and access to information services would strengthen productivity.

We must ensure that food flows to those who need it. The current food crises have shown that some regions are facing serious shortfalls, and in areas that traditionally produce food the stocks are now exhausted or limited. These circumstances entail strong restrictions to food aid in emergency situations. The smooth flow of food products involves several conditions: local markets should be efficient, transparent and open; information must flow efficiently; investment in roads, transport and storage of crops is indispensable. Barriers to exports that have been decided by sovereign states must be limited. These barriers temporarily exacerbate deficits in importing countries and strongly raise prices; finally, food aid that plays a vital role in cases of disasters must not disrupt local agricultural production. For example, the distribution of large amounts of food either free or cheap can ruin the farmers of the region who can no longer sell their products. In so doing, we jeopardize the future of local agriculture.

Adequate measures, therefore, should be taken to protect farmers against price volatility which has a strong impact on food security for several reasons: high prices make food unaffordable for the poor and low prices give farmers the incorrect information on needed seedlings after harvest for the following year. To prevent price volatility or at least weaken its impact, local food crops need to be protected against sudden disruptions in international prices. The customs duty at the entrance of an importing country (or the cyclical adjustment of special and differential treatment) must take into account both the needs of poor consumers and secondly the price to be paid to small farmers so they may afford a dignified standard of living and promote production. Speculation should be limited to the actors necessary for the proper functioning of the future markets. Governments should refrain from introducing measures that increase volatility, and are called to reconsider that food cannot be like any commodity, a matter of speculation or an instrument of political pressure. The establishment of regional stockpiles of raw food (cereals, oil, sugar) can have a twofold benefit: these stocks can be sold at an affordable price in case of shock and they can play a moderating role against the volatility of local prices.

The availability of food is not a sufficient factor to ensure food for everyone. People must have sufficient income to purchase food or food should have an affordable price for the poor. This raises the question of a comprehensive safety net that may consist in making available food products at subsidized prices for the poorest people at a regional level. The level of subsidy would vary according to the market price so that the cost of subsidized food can remain stable. It is illusory to believe there is a 'good price' for wheat or corn. The price that a poor consumer may be able to pay may not correspond with what a small African farmer needs to live. We must construct mechanisms that bridge the gap between these two prices and for the poorest countries solidarity requires that they be internationally funded.

A recent development in the world search for food security regards the purchase or rent of large extensions of arable land on the part of foreign organizations in countries other than their own. It seems a reasonable precondition to require that the people who are in the area should be respected, included in the project, and that the level of food security in the region should be increased. This said, investment in the relief of hunger and agriculture is essential to eradicate hunger and malnutrition.

In conclusion, Mr President, food insecurity is not inevitable, given the vast agricultural and pastoral areas to be exploited still. With a concerted and determined action sustained by the ethical conviction that the human family is one and must move forward in solidarity, urban and rural populations together, the right to food can be implemented for every person.

THE ROLE OF RELIGIOUS ORGANIZATIONS IN UNIVERSAL EDUCATION*

Mr President,

The theme of this Annual Ministerial Review, 'Implementing the internationally agreed goals and commitments in regard to education', is of urgent importance to the overall achievement of integral human development well into the future of the human family. Education is, first of all, a fundamental right of the human person and the validity of all development policies is measured by their respect of the human right to education. In fact, education plays a fundamental role in achieving sustained and equitable economic growth, poverty eradication and sustainable development and reducing inequity and inequality. It is indispensable to protect and affirm the transcendent dignity of every man and woman.

The international community has made significant progress in reducing the number of children without access to primary education. However, as of 2008, some 67.5 million children remained out of school, and according to the 2011 Global Monitoring Report, if the current trajectory is maintained, the international community will not be able to attain the goal of universal primary education by 2015. Among the least developed countries, three countries report enrolment rates below 50 per cent, and only 17 countries report rates above 80 per cent.

This year marks the 25th Anniversary of the Declaration of the Right to Development. On this occasion, we should recall that a more just social context, including deeper commitment to efforts at the eradication of poverty, will positively influence access to education, most especially for children living in low-income, rural, and marginalized circumstances. However, the quality of life depends not only on the overcoming of economic poverty, but on the cultural level, the quality of human relations, and the quality of inter-personal relationships among people, goals that could be achieved only through education.

Also to be noted is that some 28 million children not attending school live in countries affected by conflict. In addition, many people live in environments affected by political violence, organised crime, exceptionally high murder rates or low-intensity conflicts. Such forms of so-called 'lesser violence' can cause as much, if not more, destruction than more formal wars and civil conflicts. People in such situations are

* Statement delivered at the 2011 High-Level Segment of the Economic and Social Council, 6 July 2011.

more than twice as likely as people in other developing societies to be malnourished, three times as likely to be deprived of primary school attendance, and almost twice as likely to die in infancy. Thus, a deeper commitment by the international community to peace, reconciliation and solidarity can exert a positive influence on the enjoyment of the right to universal education.

Fundamental human rights are inter-related and require respect of one for the other. In particular, the right to education cannot be isolated from the promotion and implementation of greater justice and equity within and among societies. As the UN Economic and Social Council (ECOSOC) Committee has stated, the right to education 'is the epitome of the indivisibility and interdependence of all other human rights'.[1] In accord with the UN Covenant on Economic, Social, and Cultural Rights, primary education must be obligatory and freely accessible to all (Art. 13(2–4)).

The State has an essential responsibility to assure the provision of educational services. At the same time, the right to educate is a fundamental responsibility of parents, churches and local communities. Thus public institutions, especially at the local level, organizations of civil society and also the private sector, could offer their unique and respective contributions to the attainment of universal access to education. In this context, civil society should also be able to provide alternative services, implement innovative actions, and even exercise a critical function that can mobilize social forces to assist the State in carrying out its overall educational responsibilities by respecting the principle of subsidiarity. Moreover, the critical role played by civil society educational programs should be recognized and encouraged. In fact, the educational system functions correctly when it includes the participation, in planning and implementation of educational policies, of parents, family and religious organizations, other civil society organizations and also the private sector.

For centuries, religious groups have supported basic education and, in fact, were the first institutions to provide basic education to the poorest populations. We may look, for example, at the experience and the direct contribution of the Catholic Church in the area of education. There are some 200,000 Catholic primary and secondary schools located in every continent of the world with some 58 million students and 3.5 million teachers. They are characterized by an open and comprehensive approach without distinctions of race, sex or social condition. The human person always remains at the center of the educational endeavor, since education

[1] United Nations Committee on Economic, Social, and Cultural Rights, 1999, para. 2.

is genuine when it humanizes and personalizes so that, in turn, the person may humanize the world, shape culture, transform society, and construct history. In close contact with the students' families, whose freedom to decide the education of their children is a natural right, Catholic schools accompany students toward maturity and the ability to make free, reasoned, and value-based decisions. While safeguarding their identity, these schools welcome students from every ethnic and religious background and socio-economic class.

In our global world, the key role of education becomes even more essential to enable the peaceful coexistence and mutual appreciation among all sectors of society. The simple transmission of technical information is inadequate. The goal of education has to extend to the formation of the person the transmission of values, such as a sense of individual and social responsibility, a work ethic, a sense of solidarity with the entire human family.

In this educational process, the State should respect the choices that parents make for their children and avoid attempts at ideological indoctrination. The Covenant on Economic, Social, and Cultural Rights says that 'The States Parties to the present Covenant undertake to have respect for the liberty of parents and ... to choose for their children schools, other than those established by the public authorities ... and to ensure the religious and moral education of their children in conformity with their own convictions.'[2] And this includes the right to make moral judgments on moral issues. Religious organizations are uniquely positioned to promote equitable outcomes for the most vulnerable children and families. Moreover, such educational institutions often reach those communities, for example, in rural and remote areas, that remain uncovered by governmental policies. The continuing engagement of religious organizations in advocating for and implementing the right of every person to basic and good-quality education enhances the achievement of the authentic education-related objectives of the Millennium Development Goals. For the best educational results, a close cooperation between parents and schools must be fostered.

[2] International Covenant on Economic, Social and Cultural Rights, adopted 16 December 1966 and entry into force 3 January 1976, Art. 13(3).

Mr President,

As proposed in the Outcome Document, my Delegation believes that the whole educational effort should be socially contextualized within a spirit of justice and through practical measures that make education better suited for the twenty-first century. In order to accomplish this, for example, the State and civil society must assure high-quality formation of teachers so that they recognize their role as a special mission and so that their service is recognized accordingly. To reach the desired goal of universal access to education, all elements of society must participate. Civil society, especially religious organizations and parents' associations, stands ready to offer its contribution, but public financial resources must be made available in order to assure fairness for its strong engagement in educational processes in line with parents' choices. With regard to children and young people who already have been excluded from the educational system, society can and must ensure a 'second chance'; once again, religious organizations are well placed to offer sensitive outreach through programs for drop-outs, children with special needs, and other vulnerable children. This extra effort renders future benefits to society in terms of productivity of beneficiaries from such special programs that pay off in prevention of crime, disordered behavior, and high unemployment rates. Information and communication technology, kept at low cost, can open a new chapter in training possibilities, mobile education as well as in education management.

Policymakers tend to see education as mainly a key to economic survival. Learning skills such as good literacy and numeracy combined with habits of the mind such as creativity makes education functional to the economy. But the horizon needs widening. As Pope Benedict XVI observes: 'the person grows to the extent she experiences what is good and learns to distinguish it from what is evil, beyond the calculation that considers only the consequences of a single action or that uses as a criterion of judgement the possibility to doing it.' The educational responsibility of all who have at heart the city of man and the welfare of future generations requires both a continued engagement for a free and accessible primary education as well as for its quality. Secondary and higher education should also be made available and accessible. Education, in fact, is not only 'directed to the full development of the human personality and the sense of its dignity', but it is also a means for the participation of the individual in a free society and an instrument that promotes mutual understanding and 'friendship among all nations and all racial, ethnic or religious groups'.[3] No less fundamental an aim of education is the transmission and development of common cultural and moral values in whose reference the individual and society find their identity and worth.

Mr President,

Meeting the international goal of education that boys and girls everywhere be able to complete a full course of primary schooling is therefore an ineludible requirement. The imposition of economic conditionalities that hurt this objective would be miscalculated solidarity. Openness to partnerships from civil society and the private sector can effectively contribute to the common objective when fairness in the sharing of resources is taken into account. In conclusion, it is the same concern that moves all stakeholders to action in our rapidly changing and interconnected world, to make children and young people the best hope for the future.

[3] Ibid., Art. 3(1).

A HOUSE IS MUCH MORE THAN JUST A ROOF: THE RIGHT TO ADEQUATE HOUSING*

Mr President,

Let me begin by thanking Ms Raquel Rolnik, Special Rapporteur on Adequate Housing as a component of the right to an adequate standard of living and the right of non-discrimination in this thereon,[1] for her report to the Council focused on women's right to adequate housing.

The Report rightly points out the progress and legal developments carried out in various countries and aimed at facilitating the full realization of this right by women. In turn, the Report shows concern about the still existing loopholes and socio-cultural situations that in some regions continue to hinder the women's full enjoyment of the right to adequate housing, to their status as mother, wife, widow, orphan or to their equal treatment with men in the distribution of family possessions, of land and property in general.

Therefore, the legal protection of a woman's right to adequate housing is of interest to us all and now it requires specific measures because in many places for various reasons women are heads of household and have the sole responsibility for the education, upbringing and support of their children. This situation is most dramatic when the lack of adequate housing comes together with factors such as poverty and unemployment which in turn force many women to migrate and leave their children not only without a home but also under the care of others.

To promote women's right to adequate housing is also a way to combat discrimination against women[2] and domestic violence. In most cases women and children are the most affected by these scourges. In many contexts, both the woman and her child are forced to endure inhumane treatment mainly due to the lack of a place to live and be protected.

* Statement delivered at the 19th Session of the Human Rights Council – Item 3: *Adequate Housing*, 23 March 2012.

[1] UN Doc. A/HRC/53.

[2] Cf. Convention on the Elimination of All Forms of Discrimination against Women (Art. 14, 2 h).

Mr President,

The Holy See is convinced 'that a house is much more than just a roof, but the place where a person realizes and lives her own life, but also where she builds in some way her deepest identity and her relations with others'.[3] It has therefore kept the subject of housing constant among its concerns. My Delegation, therefore, reaffirms the general principle of the right to housing for all as a fundamental human right[4] and, in this regard, it calls for greater protection and legal guarantees for women at the moment of pregnancy and maternity so they may enjoy the full right to adequate housing. This prerequisite reflects the fact that in these circumstances both the mother and the newborn child are exposed to increased vulnerability and thus necessitate particular assistance.[5]

Similarly, this Delegation agrees that priority should be given to women with children and to families where the father is away for work when the State develops programs of construction, distribution and allocation of housing. It recommends as well that in the process of building these houses the State should provide basic social services like health, education, drinking water and a healthy environment so as to allow women and their children to develop a normal life.[6] The Holy See also recommends ensuring, particularly in the 'Forced Evictions' cases, that relocations be put in practice taking into account the mandatory value of families' unity. More, we recommend ensuring a new arrangement that will guarantee adequate housing conditions especially for women with children, granting accessibility and proximity of schools and child care services.

Finally, my Delegation also urges all those responsible for, and involved in the search for, a solution to the housing problem in general and for adequate housing for women in particular 'to make their contribution in order to have adequate policies to deal with the more

3 Cf. Pope John Paul II, Letter to Hon. Cardinal Roger Etchegaray, President of the Pontifical Commission 'Justice and Peace', 8 December 1987.

4 Cf. Universal Declaration of Human Rights (Art. 25(1)), International Covenant on Economic, Social and Cultural Rights (Art. 11(1)), Convention on the Elimination of All Forms of Racial Discrimination (Art. 5, and (iii)), I United Nations Conference on Human Settlements (Habitat I), Vancouver, 1976; II United Nations Conference on Human Settlements (Habitat II), Istanbul, 1996.

5 Cf. Universal Declaration of Human Rights (Art. 25(2)).

6 Cf. Convention on the Rights of the Child (Art. 27(1 and 3)).

urgent situations and to remove the obstacles that impede finding the specific economic, legal and social rules capable to promote more favourably the resolution of these problems'.[7]

Thank you, Mr President.

[7] Cf. Pope John Paul II, Letter to Hon. Cardinal Roger Etchegaray, President of the Pontifical Commission 'Justice and Peace', 8 December 1987.

EDUCATION IS A VITAL CONDITION FOR PROGRESS*

Madam President,

The Delegation of the Holy See supports what the Report of the Special Rapporteur on the Right to Education states, that 'it is essential to promote the right to education as entitlement in terms of universal access to basic education, and as empowerment in terms of acquisition of knowledge, skills and competencies and their quality.'

The Special Rapporteur notes that millions of children are not attending primary school in low-income countries and countless children go through five years of education without learning basic reading, writing and math skills. Education, however, is required to promote a culture of peace, mutual respect and international solidarity. It should be provided to children of both sexes and without any discrimination based on their religion, national or ethnic origin, race, color, wealth or disability. As the Report underlines, it implies a cooperative approach for its success: adequate infrastructure and facilities and a school environment in which teachers, parents and communities are all active participants in school life.

On the other hand, the inalienable right of parents to choose the kind of education that shall be given to their children remains an irreplaceable priority, as the Universal Declaration of Human Rights states.[1] This right is connected with the transmission of human life and the unique loving relationship between parents and children.

Education is comprehensive and concerned with 'the integral formation of the person, including the moral and spiritual dimension, focused upon man's final end and the good of the society to which he belongs. Therefore, in order to educate in truth, it is necessary first and foremost to know who the human person is, to know human nature.'[2] The Report of the Special Rapporteur on the right to education rightly refers to various international instruments that affirm that education should be aimed at the full development of the human personality and the sense of its dignity. For example, for Article 13 of the International

* Statement delivered at the 20th Session of the Human Rights Council – Presentation of the Report of the Special Rapporteur on the Right to Education, 27 June 2012.

1 'Parents have a prior right to choose the kind of education that shall be given to their children', Art. 26.

2 Pope Benedict XVI's Message for the 2012 World Day of Peace, 'Educating young people in justice and peace'.

Covenant on Economic, Social and Cultural Rights education should 'enable all persons to participate effectively in a free society, promote understanding, tolerance and friendship among all nations and all racial, ethnic or religious groups ... ' In this perspective, it is easy to understand that, by exercising its mission to educate, the family contributes to the common good and constitutes the first school of social virtue, which all societies need.

In its social function, education is an indispensable condition for progress and the improvement of the quality of life. It develops personal talents and places them at the service of society, a process that leads to innovation and moves forward the economy whose real propelling force are prepared and responsible persons aware that the goal to be achieved is the common good. The implementation of the right to education remains a real challenge; if carried out in all countries, however, it will bear fruit for both individuals and society.

Thank you, Madam President.

THE RIGHT TO FOOD REQUIRES SOCIAL SOLIDARITY AMONG ALL PEOPLES*

Mr President, my Delegation welcomes the opportunity to address this Council on the urgent need for governments and the global society better to respect, protect, facilitate, and fulfill the human right to food. We are deeply grateful to the outgoing Special Rapporteur for his significant efforts in this regard and express the sincere hope that additional progress will be made in order to ensure that the right to food is not 'reduced to a right not to starve' and will truly be acknowledged as 'an inclusive right to an adequate diet and all the nutritional elements' needed 'to live a healthy and active life, and the means to access them'.[1]

The international community has indeed made progress in addressing food security. On the occasion of World Food Day 2013,[2] the UN Food and Agriculture Organization reported that, since the end of the Second World War, the availability of food per person has increased by more than 40 per cent. It further advised, however, that hunger still afflicts more than 840 million people but is much less evident since it persists mainly among those living in developing countries. This type of hunger manifests itself as a 'slow death' caused by under-nutrition, depriving children of opportunities and the achievement of such developmental milestones as growth within normal standards, neuromotory development, and school performance, all of which are taken for granted by well-nourished people who live in high-income countries … 'this is a real scandal.'[3]

Mr President, in his Message for the most recent World Food Day, Pope Francis strongly asserted that 'hunger and malnutrition can never be considered a normal event to which one must become accustomed, as if it were part of the system.'[4] In order to break this vicious cycle, we need to take structural measures such as the enactment of framework laws at the national level and the development of just food policies. We also need

* Statement delivered at the 25th Session of the Human Rights Council – Item 3: *Report of the Special Rapporteur on the Right to Food*, 10 March 2014.

1 www.ohchr.org/Documents/HRBodies/.../A-HRC-19-59_en.pdf.

2 Mr José Graziano Da Silva, Director General, FAO, 'La sicurezza alimentare è la sfida del futuro', *L'Osservatore Romano*, 19 September 2013.

3 www.vatican.va/holy_father/francesco/messages/peace/documents/papa-francesco_20131208_messaggio-xlvii-giornata-mondiale-pace-2014_en.html.

4 www.vatican.va/holy_father/francesco/messages/food/documents/papa-francesco_20131016_messaggio-giornata-alimentazione_en.html.

well-developed processes, including implementation and monitoring of policies as well as adequate resource allocations. Finally, we must carefully analyze outcomes and impact based on statistics related to hunger and under-nutrition and on indicators related to the availability of food, sufficient revenue and affordable prices to buy proper nourishment for families and the more vulnerable members of society.

In a certain sense, Mr President, Pope Francis has outlined a 'road map' aimed at further advancing the full implementation of the right to food. 'Something has to change, in ourselves, in our mentality, in our society', he urged, proposing that 'an important step is to bring down, with determination, the barriers of individualism, of being shut-in on ourselves, of the slavery of profit at all cost.'[5] My Delegation, therefore, suggests that the achievement of the right to food requires social solidarity among all peoples, in addition to the legal and policy-related safeguards already established by this Council.

At the national level, this requires adequate public and private investment to enable small-scale farmers to increase productivity, to attain adequate revenue surplus to improve the conditions under which they farm and to be able count on long-term prospects of sufficient income to support their families. Special attention will be needed to facilitate the empowerment and participation of rural women to enhance agriculture and rural development. With regard to the private sector, we must strive for more equitable distribution of resources, one that does not disadvantage small, local food producers. In the provision of humanitarian assistance, access to food and resources by affected populations needs to be assured both within and across borders. Development assistance should include agricultural components so that the right to produce and market food can be assured without discrimination.

Solidarity at the international level is equally important in efforts to guarantee the right to food. The agreement reached in Bali, during the ninth Ministerial Conference of the World Trade Organization 'on public stockholding for food security purposes' is on the same line and is a clear example of how multilateralism can regain its central role in addressing new problems, tackling new opportunities, and, most importantly, promoting freer and more equitable trade, not as an end in itself, but as one of the many approaches to ending poverty for all. The implementation of this interim agreement would provide a more secure, stable and equitable access to food for countries that need it.

[5] Ibid.

During the current International Year of Family Farming, Mr President, my Delegation would urge this Council to include, as a special component of its efforts to advance and preserve the human right to food, 'education in solidarity and in a way of life that overcomes the "throw away culture" and really puts every person and his/her dignity at the center, as is characteristic of the family.'[6]

Thank you, Mr President.

[6] Ibid.

4 RIGHT TO DEVELOPMENT

SUBSIDIARITY AND SOCIAL INCLUSION FOR DEVELOPMENT*

Mr Chairman,

The pace of change has accelerated in a very tangible and visible way in recent years. Technology advances and the interconnectedness that economic processes and information have brought about demand difficult adjustments for the world of work and for political systems. New and serious venues are needed to assess the impact of globalization especially on the poorer and more vulnerable members of societies. The Delegation of the Holy See views the current discussion on the Right to Development as an especially important and timely dialogue within the United Nations at this time when the gap between incomes in the richest and poorest countries seems widening. Globalization has allowed the emergence of a true planetary conscience more sensitive to injustice, to poverty, to discrimination, to degradation of the environment, and with greater expectations that a convergence of efforts will remedy these shortcomings. A positive result of the many debates on development has highlighted the fact that a synergy is required between economic growth, that adds to the material well-being of society and of individuals, and the growth of the whole person and her/his human rights.

The Right to Development connects and animates the promotion and protection of the two interdependent Covenants of human rights that serve as lungs providing oxygen for the flourishing of civil society. Civil and political rights and economic, social and cultural rights are mutually reinforcing and development is the fruit of their implementation. The Declaration on the Right to Development adopted by the General Assembly in 1986 is unique among other international human rights standards in that it identifies the individual person as the focus and beneficiary of the right, with the State as the primary duty bearer. At the same time, it makes an explicit connection between this right and the obligation for international cooperation to assist individual States in their duties as the primary promoter and protector of the individual's right to development. If globalization makes the single State less autonomous it imposes greater

* Statement delivered at the 60th Session of the Human Rights Commission – Item 7: *The Right to Development*, 24 March 2004.

responsibility on the international community to help it in securing the right to development. In this global partnership, resources allocation plays a crucial role and their priority should be directed to enhance the creativity of individuals, women and men, so that they remain the real protagonists of any development. Unfortunately, writes Pope John Paul II, 'many people, perhaps the majority today, do not have the means which would enable them to take their place in an effective and humanly dignified way within a productive system in which work is truly essential. They have no possibility of acquiring the basic knowledge which would enable them to express their creativity and develop their potential' (Encyclical Letter, *Centesimus Annus*, § 33) The indispensable convergence of human rights and economic policies becomes self-evident.

The interdependence of rights and responsibilities among the individual, family, State and international community is a frequent theme in the social teaching of the Holy See and this interdependence is quickly becoming part of most discussions about the impact of globalization. However, we believe that States have the primary responsibility to promote, protect and implement the Right to Development. The complementarity of different stakeholders proves effective and productive when subsidiarity is respected and the same goal is pursued of social inclusion and development of personal capabilities. Thus, in dealing with the international system of governance, States, including the poorest, should be permitted rightful access to the decision-making procedures of organizations and institutions which affect their future.

It is to be expected that, with its wide and novel scope, discussion about the Right to Development will be a difficult challenge to the United Nations community. However, the last Working Group has offered a hopeful indication that future RTD discussions can be more concrete by involving States, the UN Agencies, the International Financial, Trade, and Development Institutions, and representatives of civil society.

Mr Chairman, future discussions about RTD within the proposed Task Force and within the Working Group could provide valuable opportunities for us to learn from the experience of various segments of society while working through a convergence of opinions that could lead to a more effective promotion of civil, cultural, economic, political and social rights that protect each person's and each country's right to development, that is one framework of integral development.

A DUTY OF COLLABORATION ACROSS POLITICAL AND GEOGRAPHICAL LINES*

Mr Chairperson,

The Delegation of the Holy See extends to you, to the High Commissioner, and the Bureau, its congratulations and all best wishes of success for the work of this 61st Session of the Commission on Human Rights.

Mr Chairperson,

All poverty indicators give evidence of a disturbing gap between developed and developing countries. The equal right of people to take their seat at the table of the common banquet is not recognized.[1] Health conditions are worsening in some regions not least because of the pandemics of HIV/AIDS, malaria and TB. Illiteracy persists and access to food and drinking water is denied to too many people. Almost 20 years since the Declaration on the Right to Development in 1986, large segments of the human populations are still cut off from a right that is so clearly proclaimed in this important document: 'The right to development is an inalienable human right by virtue of which every human person and all peoples are entitled to participate in, contribute to, and enjoy economic, social, cultural and political development, in which all human rights and fundamental freedoms can be fully realized' (Art. 1(1)).

The commendable work carried out by the Working Group and the High-Level Task Force on the Implementation of the Right to Development highlights the importance of a comprehensive approach of all sectors of civil society, of states and of the international community, if the operationalization of the right to development is to make progress. Specific and concrete measures translate widely agreed principles of solidarity into a better life for the poor of the world. A renewed mobilization of efforts is called for since the achievement of the Millennium Goals appears at this point a very elusive target for the least developed countries and important occasions are ahead for the international community when the impact of trade and of official development assistance on development will be carefully dealt with. In fact, governments should

* Statement delivered at the 61st Session of the Commission on Human Rights, 22 March 2005.

1 Pope John Paul II, Encyclical Letter, *Sollicitudo Rei Socialis* (1987), § 33.

feel encouraged in proposing concrete measures for the right to development by the extraordinary generosity shown by the people of the world in responding to the recent tsunami tragedy.

Experience shows that the implementation of the right to development is successful if centered on the human person and on human communities, as the Declaration on the Right to Development states, and these should be the active participants and beneficiaries of this right. The network of educational and health care institutions and the relief agencies, for instance, conducted by faith-based organizations mainly for the poorest people of the world, prove to be motors of change and empowerment rightly because they focus directly on the human person and on an understanding of sustainable development that keeps a balanced relationship between the needs of individual persons and the communities they belong to and between people and the environment. An inclusive approach therefore will take into account together with 'sound economic policies that foster growth with equity' the priority of the human person and of human dignity and aspirations.

To the right to development corresponds a duty of collaboration across political and geographical lines. The dynamics of this process involve rich and poor countries in taking steps in two major areas that condition the implementation of the right to development: human rights and trade. In particular, current negotiations regarding the opening of the markets of developed countries to the agricultural products of the South and the lowering of entry taxes for these products will make the international trade system responsive to the social impact of its agreements. On the other hand, good governance, for example, will impact the whole quality of life. This Delegation also supports the renewed calls to cancel the external debt of highly indebted poor countries and others as well and to comply with the agreed commitment to provide 0.7 per cent of GNP for Official Development Assistance.

But development is not a homogenizing process that flattens local cultures and values and takes away the creative responsibility of national and local communities. The respect and the positive appreciation of these communities add to the richness of the process, strengthen it and favour positive results. In the past, for not listening to local communities, some development projects ended up as cathedrals in the desert. A great service that international cooperation can contribute is of course assistance in capacity building, especially through education equally of young women and men, that allows the blooming of local talent and consequent self-reliance.

As the debate and the refinement of proposals continue in this critical area of development as a right for everyone, the incorporation of this right in the decisions of the financial institutions, in financial and trade exchanges, will support a global partnership for development that will give new impetus to its implementation. The road ahead is long and not without obstacles. A patient work of negotiations, a holistic approach, can open the way to success. The Delegation of the Holy See has been a constant advocate of development, supports the inclusion of social development policies in the future agenda of the Working Group as well as the comprehensive concept of development agreed at the 1995 Copenhagen Declaration on Social Development, one that is political, economic, cultural, ethical and spiritual.

IMPLEMENTING THE RIGHT TO DEVELOPMENT FOR JUSTICE AND PEACE*

Mr High Commissioner,

Excellencies and Distinguished Delegates,

Ladies and Gentlemen,

I am grateful to the Office of the United Nations High Commissioner for Human Rights for organizing this initiative to commemorate the anniversary of the UN Declaration on the Right to Development. I am also honored to have this occasion to present a brief reflection on the implementation process of this right. At stake are the pursuit of a more equitable world and of a peaceful coexistence for an increasingly pluralistic world. This occasion affords us the opportunity to consider the Declaration on the Right to Development, the principles on which it stands, and to take stock on the progress the international community has made in this very important area of concern.

Thirty years ago a formal declaration on the Right to Development was prompted by social and political circumstances demanding a coordinated response to existing inequalities. Today, the global human family is still confronted with serious crises and challenges. UN data tell us that over 2.2 billion people – more than 15 per cent of the world's population – are estimated to be either near or living in 'multidimensional' poverty with overlapping deprivations in health, education and living standards.[1] The economic and social gap between the 'haves' and 'have-nots' is widening. State and non-State actors are engaged in numerous serious and violent conflicts. They cause hundreds of thousands of victims. Pope Francis caught the public imagination when he defined the current situation a 'World War Three … in pieces'.[2] These injustices and wars inhibit effective progress toward the implementation of the right to development. One might go so far as to deduce

* Statement delivered at the Right to Development anniversary: '*Sustainable Development with Dignity and Justice for All – Realizing the Right to Development for Present and Future Generations*', 2 December 2014.

1 UN Special Rapporteur on the Eradication of Extreme Poverty, 17 October 2014, www.ohchr.org/SP/NewsEvents/Pages/DisplayNews.aspx?NewsID=15175&LangID=E.

2 Pope Francis, Homily in Redipuglia, Italy, 13 September 2014.

that, in some cases, a combination of national interests, arms trade, greed and power ambition block the political will of many States from seriously pursuing the path of justice and peace as prescribed by the founding documents of the UN. These elements provide evidence that the ideals of equality and solidarity that inspired the Universal Declaration of Human Rights and the treaties derived from this Declaration have lost their credibility for some people and that the culture supporting them has changed. Perhaps this reflection on how to universalize the implementation of the Declaration on the Right to Development can help us look at the fundamental principles that underlie this very right.

The social doctrine of the Catholic Church presents a few very fundamental notions, many explicitly articulated in the UN Declaration itself, as necessary for the proper approach and for the promotion of the right to development. These basic concepts are: (1) the unity of origin and a shared destiny of the human family; (2) the equal dignity of every person and of every community; (3) the universal destination of the goods of the earth; (4) human development must be integral embracing the whole person; (5) the human person must be at the center of every social activity; (6) solidarity and subsidiarity are necessary for a healthy development.[3] These principles are mutually intertwined, interdependent and essential for a right to development that can lead society out of its deep crises. Of these, I would like to highlight two in particular: equality of persons based on human dignity and the centrality of the human person and solidarity.

We can see a very strong, and necessary, I might add, convergence of the social doctrine of the Church and the Declaration on the Right to Development in the importance given to the dignity of the human person. For any realistic development of society, the most basic and simple starting point is the realization that every human person is created free and with an equal and inviolable dignity. Yet, it is precisely this basic point that is most often obfuscated or, in some cases, completely ignored, and this leads to all sorts of injustices and abuses of human rights. As Pope Francis remarked to the European Parliament, 'Promoting the dignity of the person means recognizing that he or she possesses inalienable rights which no one may take away arbitrarily, much less for the sake of

[3] Cf. *Compendium of the Social Doctrine of the Church*, § 446.

economic interests.'[4] When the equal dignity of the human person is not respected, whether collectively as in the case of States and institutions, or individually, other more 'pragmatic' or 'utilitarian' categories become the criteria by which society operates. In such a fundamental shift of mentality emerge categories of 'values' that place the human person at the service of some other 'material gain or value'. The person becomes functional to consumerism or political power. In these cases, the dignity of others is considered worth being 'sacrificed' for some greater material good.

In this perspective, perhaps all too prevalent in many cultures, a major factor becomes evident: the *de facto* categorization of persons into 'classes' or 'groups' as means more or less useful to economic or political 'progress'. This dangerous approach is very much in need of our reflection and discussion; its negative effects, including the fact that it does not embrace the 'notion of development in its "entirety"', are to be acknowledged. Pope Francis in his social Apostolic Exhortation, *Evangelii Gaudium*, observes: 'Inequality is the root of social ills. The dignity of each human person and the pursuit of the common good are concerns which ought to shape all economic policies. At times, however, they seem to be a mere addendum imported from without in order to fill out a political discourse lacking in perspectives or plans for true and integral development.'[5] The task then before the international community and all individual stakeholders is striving to reclaim the centrality of the human person and the common good as essential for integral human development. In this way, the seemingly insurmountable and lopsided perspective that gives preference to merely economic and political gains can be overcome. But two conditions are required. The first, the ideology of extreme individualism that has become pervasive should be reconsidered as it contradicts or ignores the rights of others; the second, a renewed effort to place again the human person as the end to which all political and economic decisions must be aimed.

A natural consequence of the respect for the centrality of the human person and the pursuit of the common good of the human family is an effective exercise of solidarity. Solidarity is more than a mere sentiment

[4] Pope Francis, Speech to European Parliament, 25 November 2014.

[5] Pope Francis, Apostolic Exhortation, *Evangelii Gaudium*: The Joy of the Gospel (Washington, DC: United States Catholic Conference, 2013), §§ 202–3.

of compassion for the victims of injustice and for the underprivileged. Rather, in its proper sense and implementation, solidarity is an obligation of all persons and of all nations to co-operate with one another in our globalized world and to work collectively towards 'eliminating obstacles to development'.[6] Perhaps the term 'solidarity' in its often misused colloquial sense has been misunderstood. More than a mere expression of 'random acts of kindness', solidarity 'presumes the creation of a new mindset which thinks in terms of community and the priority of the life of all over the appropriation of goods by a few'.[7] As such, solidarity leads beyond the radical individualism and materialism, found in so many cultural contexts, and toward the consideration of the plight of others, toward a change of worldview, in particular, with regard to the distribution of goods and resources which should not be at the service of a few privileged, but of all.

'Solidarity is a spontaneous reaction by those who recognize that the social function of property and the universal destination of goods are realities which come before private property. The private ownership of goods is justified by the need to protect and increase them, so that they can better serve the common good; for this reason, solidarity must be lived as the decision to restore to the poor what belongs to them. These convictions and habits of solidarity, when they are put into practice, open the way to other structural transformations and make them possible. Changing structures without generating new convictions and attitudes will only ensure that those same structures will become, sooner or later, corrupt, oppressive and ineffectual.'[8]

The transformative vision necessary to make the right to development effective comes from the values that sustain it. In this effort to address root cause, systemic issues and structural changes there is a convergence between the Declaration on the right to development and the social doctrine of the Church. In particular, the Declaration affirms the right to development as a human right (Art. 1); the human person as the central subject of development (Art. 2(1)); all human beings have a responsibility for development (Art. 2(2)); States have the duty to co-operate with each other in ensuring development (Art. 3). The equal dignity of every person, the centrality of the person, and solidarity, are essential components that we must preserve and implement in all of the

[6] UN Declaration on the Right to Development, Art. 3.3.
[7] Pope Francis, *Evangelii Gaudium*, § 188. [8] Ibid., § 189.

economic and political decisions on the international and local levels. Indeed, these two principles undergird the right to development and certainly apply to every sector of life. If I may, I would like briefly to underscore two areas in particular in which there is urgent need of such attention: trade and migration.

The crisis witnessed in the Doha development agenda in the WTO negotiations admits to the necessity of finding ways of collaboration, placing the centrality of the human person in the prime place, rather than subservient to markets and economic advantage. The multilateral trade negotiations should return to their central role in addressing new problems, capitalizing on new opportunities, and, most importantly, in promoting a freer and more equitable trade, not as an end to itself, but as one of many tools to end poverty for all. The agreement just reached in the WTO moves in the positive direction and hopefully will accelerate the conclusion of the Doha Development Agenda.

The Global Forum on Migration and Development (GFMD) has documented how a justly managed migration can become a resource for the benefit and development of countries of origin, arrival and for the migrants themselves. This goal is achieved when a global governance that prioritizes the person of the migrants and their human rights and is open to a fair acceptance of newcomers as partners in development shows their contribution without prejudice and realistically acknowledges their positive presence. The multilateral fora, even if imperfect, are the only place where all States have an equal voice that can ease the search for the common good of all.

In conclusion, my hope is that the emphasis placed on the Declaration on the Right to Development will serve as a catalyst to the proper implementation of its clear principles for the progress of the common good and the improvement of all sectors of life for people. Multilateral action can become effective and overcome current tragedies and protracted situations of misery. I wish to close with the words, once again, of Pope Francis: 'In the case of global political and economic organization, much more needs to be achieved, since an important part of humanity does not share in the benefits of progress and is in fact relegated to the status of second-class citizens. Future Sustainable Development Goals must therefore be formulated and carried out with generosity and courage, so that they can have a real impact on the structural causes of poverty and hunger, attain more substantial results in protecting the environment, ensure dignified and productive labor for all, and provide appropriate protection for the family, which is an essential element in sustainable human and social development. Specifically, this involves challenging all forms of injustice and resisting the "economy of exclusion", the "throwaway culture" and the "culture of death" which nowadays sadly risk becoming passively accepted.'[9]

[9] Pope Francis, Address to the Secretary General of the United Nations and other Directors of Various International Organizations, 5 May 2014.

5 RIGHT TO INTERNATIONAL SOLIDARITY

GLOBAL INTERDEPENDENCE SHOULD BE ANIMATED BY A 'GLOBALIZATION' OF SOLIDARITY*

Mr President,

As States and civil society continue intensive efforts to plan strategically the future development of our planet and its peoples, we continue to be burdened, at this moment of history, with a long-term financial crisis. It has deeply affected not only those high-income economies where it was initiated, but also those struggling economies that depend so much on global opportunities in order to emerge from centuries-long oppression by abject poverty or by the remnants of colonialism, or by more recent unjust trade policies.

Moreover, in view of the escalating conflicts between and within various States, the human family often appears incapable of safeguarding peace and harmony in our troubled world. Nor can we ignore the destructive effects wrought by climate change both on the natural patrimony of this earth and on all women and men who have been made the stewards of creation.

Among the diverse causes of human suffering we must also consider the role of personal greed, which leads to the literal 'enslavement' of millions of women, children, and men in clear situations of abuse and total disregard for the human person. Similarly, we must also consider the situation of people in low-paid employment who work under extremely negative conditions from which they see no way of escape. In the face of these seemingly insurmountable challenges, we must recognize the constant refrain: the poor and marginalized citizens of our world suffer the most negative effects and find it increasingly more difficult to extract themselves from their daily suffering.

Such tragic and unjust situations led Pope Francis to exclaim recently: 'inequality is the root of social evil'[1] and to insist that 'money must serve, not rule!'[2] Indeed, the inequalities in our present-day

* Statement delivered at the 26th Session of the Human Rights Council – Item 3: *Interactive Dialogue with the Independent Expert on Human Rights and International Solidarity*, 13 June 2014.

[1] Tweet by Pope Francis @pontifex, 28 April 2014.

[2] Pope Francis, *Evangelii Gaudium*, § 58.

society cause the gap between the rich and the poor to fester and to produce deep fissures in relations among people on local, national, regional, and global levels.

Mr President,

Relying on the well-articulated Social Teaching of the Catholic Church, my Delegation proposes the principle and practice of solidarity as the only effective means to exit from the vicious cycle of poverty, of profiting at the expense of others, and of conflicts in this world. Solidarity is not a mere feeling of vague compassion, but rather, as Pope Paul II stated, 'it is a firm and persevering determination to commit oneself to the common good; this is to say, to the good of all and of each individual, because we are all really responsible for all.'[3] The Independent Expert on the Human Rights and to International Solidarity, in turn, focuses on the implementation of this principle in relations between States by observing that it 'is a vital component of the duty of States to provide and seek international cooperation and assistance in the implementation of their human rights obligations.'[4]

Recent history has already confirmed the fact that global interdependence in our time is evident in such areas as public health, economy and the environment. However, such interdependence must be animated and driven by a spirit of solidarity. Understood and applied in this manner, solidarity can prevent, or at least, mitigate the impact of the global challenges, which are only too well known by all sectors of today's society. Mere international cooperation, for example, can be perceived as a form of political 'palliative care', never tackling the root causes of the imbalances between developed and developing countries, nor removing the structural obstacles that generate poverty worldwide. On the other hand, full implementation of the principle of solidarity can shift the focus from cooperation based on a logic of profit extracted from one country by another to one based on mutual help in a spirit of brotherhood exercised without any conditionality.

On the micro level, the recognition of the principle of solidarity can help to elicit the support of individuals and communities in first resisting, and then resolving, such seemingly intractable problems as human

[3] Pope John Paul II, Encyclical Letter, *Sollicitudo Rei Socialis* (1987), § 38.

[4] Report of the Independent Expert on human rights and international solidarity, UN Doc. A/HRC/26/34, available at www.ohchr.org/EN/HRBodies/HRC/RegularSessions/Session26/Pages/ListReports.aspx.

trafficking. Thus, the UN Office on Drugs and Crime launched a public awareness campaign asking people to self-reflect on this social scourge and to avoid any economic involvement in businesses that are based on such illegal activities. The Independent Expert makes reference to 'preventive solidarity'[5] as an appropriate and needed response to climate-related disasters. How many of us respond immediately, with donations of money or material goods, when such disasters strike and we see the evidence of massive destruction of homes, community infrastructure and human life? But, would it not be much better if we demonstrated solidarity by joining skill, expertise, experience, and resources to strengthen efforts at disaster preparedness and building of sturdy structures to withstand the forces of nature? In a similar way, how many more tragedies of migrants, and of would-be migrants, do we need to experience before we finally prompt a new comprehensive approach that favours prevention rather than a so-called 'cure'?

Indeed, in the global arena, '[o]ne also senses the urgent need to find innovative ways of implementing the principle of the responsibility to protect and of giving poorer nations an effective voice in shared decision-making. This seems necessary in order to arrive at a political, juridical and economic order which can increase and give direction to international cooperation for the development of all peoples in solidarity.'[6]

Mr President,

Solidarity comes from an absolutely binding ethic; it is not simply an option, but rather a duty. It becomes, therefore, urgent to continue the effort and arrive at a full recognition and legal application of the principle of solidarity. In order to fully implement this principle, all members of the human family are called 'to change the … attitudes which define each individual's relationship with self, with neighbor, with even the remotest human communities, and with nature itself; and all of this in view of higher values such as the common good or … the development of the whole person and of all peoples.'[7]

[5] Ibid. [6] Pope Benedict XVI, *Caritas in Veritate* (2009), § 67.
[7] Pope John Paul II, Encyclical Letter, *Sollicitudo Rei Socialis* (1987), § 38.

6 RIGHTS OF THE FAMILY

THE FAMILY MUST REMAIN THE FUNDAMENTAL CELL OF SOCIETY*

Mr President,

My Delegation supports the importance given by the United Nations to the twentieth anniversary observance of the International Year of the Family. This significant event was recently highlighted in a special way, on 15 May 2014, during the International Day of Families, under the theme: 'Families Matter for the Achievement of Development Goals'. Surely, the choice of this theme had a strong relationship to Resolution 2012/10, adopted by ECOSOC, that stressed the need 'for undertaking concerted actions to strengthen family-centered policies and programs as part of an integrated, comprehensive approach to development' and that invited States, civil society organizations and academic institutions 'to continue providing information on their activities in support of the objectives of and preparations for the twentieth anniversary.'

This Council is well aware, Mr President, of the strong debates held in this very chamber about the nature and definition of the family. Such discussions often lead States to conclude that the family is more of a problem than a resource to society. Even the United Nations materials prepared for the observance of this Anniversary Year stated: 'Owing to rapid socio-economic and demographic transformations, families find it more and more difficult to fulfill their numerous responsibilities.'[1] My Delegation believes that despite past or even current challenges, the family, in fact, is the fundamental unit of human society. It continually exhibits a vigor much greater than that of the many forces that have tried to eliminate it as a relic of the past, or an obstacle to the emancipation of the individual, or to the creation of a freer, egalitarian and happy society.

The family and society, which are mutually linked by vital and organic bonds, have complementary functions in the defense and advancement of the good of every person and of humanity.[2] The dignity and rights of the individual are not diminished by the attention

* Statement delivered at the 26th Session of the Human Rights Council – Item 8: General Debate, Geneva, 24 June 2014.

1 http://undesadspd.org/Family/InternationalObservances/TwentiethAnniversaryofIYF2014.aspx.

2 Pontifical Council for the Family, 'Charter on the Rights of the Family,' 1983, file:///Users/BobNewMBP/Documents/Pontifical%20Council%20for%20the%20Family/

given to the family. On the contrary, most people find unique protection, nurture, and dynamic energy from their membership in a strong and healthy family founded upon marriage between a man and a woman. Moreover, ample evidence has demonstrated that the best interest of the child is assured in a harmonious family environment in which the education and formation of children develop within the context of lived experience with both male and female parental role models.

The family is the fundamental cell of society where the generations meet, love, educate, and support each other, and pass on the gift of life, 'where we learn to live with others despite our differences and to belong to one another.'[3] This understanding of the family has been embraced throughout history by all cultures. Thus, with good reason, the Universal Declaration of Human Rights recognized unique, profound, and uncompromising rights and duties for the family founded on marriage between a man and a woman, by declaring as follows: '(1) Men and women of full age, without any limitation due to race, nationality or religion, have the right to marry and to found a family. They are entitled to equal rights as to marriage, during marriage and at its dissolution. (2) Marriage shall be entered into only with the free and full consent of the intending spouses. (3) The family is the natural and fundamental group unit of society and is entitled to protection by society and the State.'

Mr President, during this historic anniversary observance, the Holy See Delegation firmly maintains that the family is a whole and integral unit, which should not be divided or marginalized. The family and marriage need to be defended and promoted not only by the State but also by the whole of society. Both require the decisive commitment of every person because it is starting from the family and marriage that a complete answer can be given to the *challenges* of the present and the *risks* of the future.[4] The way forward is indicated in the fundamental human rights and related conventions that ensure the universality of these rights and whose binding value need to be preserved and promoted by the international community.

Charter%20of%20the%20Rights%20of%20the%20Family,%2022%20October%201983%C2%A0.webarchive.

[3] Pope Francis, *Evangelii Gaudium*, § 66, http://w2.vatican.va/content/francesco/en/apost_exhortations/documents/papa-francesco_esortazione-ap_20131124_evangelii-gaudium.html.

[4] Pontifical Council for the Family, 'The Family and Human Rights', 2000, www.vatican.va/roman_curia/pontifical_councils/family/documents/rc_pc_family_doc_20001115_family-human-rights_en.html.

7 RIGHT TO A SAFE AND HEALTHY ENVIRONMENT

THE DEGRADATION OF NATURE, A MIRROR OF OUR CULTURE*

Mr President,

The 25th anniversary of the Montreal Protocol is a good occasion to pause and look back at the positive developments it brought about. Equally important remains the need to reflect on the future of this Protocol.

The ozone layer is a tiny and fragile but very essential part of creation. The human family depends on creation to sustain its life. The progress that the international community has achieved thanks to this Protocol in recovering the ozone layer promises more advances for the future so the ozone layer soon can again be our strong protecting shield.

Besides, this Protocol helps also in the protection of climate in general as the phase-out of ozone-depleting substances under this body has resulted in a significant reduction of greenhouse gas emissions.

While some important issues remain unresolved, a sense of responsibility for the next generations should prompt continued efforts. How can we manage to arrive at a clear and firm political will necessary to reach agreement on further measures that would efficiently address the urgent need for enhanced protection of creation as a whole?

Part of the answer is a strong cooperation between the Montreal Protocol and other multilateral environmental agreements and this can set new standards of successful cooperation between different Protocols. In such a process it is vital to take into account the concerns of the poorer and more vulnerable countries and to assist them to meet the challenges they face. The principle of common but differentiated responsibility leads in this direction and encourages common action. It is also required to ensure continued integrity on the part of the assessment panels responsible for providing independent and unbiased technical advice and recommendations to the Parties to the Protocol so they may take correct decisions.

* Statement delivered at the High-Level Segment of the 24th Meeting of the States Parties to the Montreal Protocol on Substances that Deplete the Ozone Layer, 15 November 2012.

Mr President,

The human family is currently experiencing several crises, economic, nutritional, environmental, and social – all deeply interlinked. They oblige us to redesign our way, to establish new guidelines and to find new forms of engagement through discernment and creative thinking.

The topics discussed under environmental treaties in the past days are very closely linked with human rights issues. Increased ultraviolet radiation as a consequence of a depleted ozone layer can result in an increase in eye cataracts, and yet access to medical treatment is not easy for poor people in developing countries where blindness causes not only social problems but also high costs. Another example is forced migration due to the rising sea level.

The latter issue is linked with greenhouse gases, not necessarily with ozone-depleting substances. Seen, however, in a holistic approach, it would be wise to use synergies by combining different instruments provided by all relevant Protocols thus contributing a more efficient approach to the pertinent issues.

Protection of creation in all its aspects is a duty of solidarity toward future generations and technical advances should be placed at the service of this basic value.

In this context, the Montreal Protocol is a good example. Civil society, local authorities and industry have joined together in the past 25 years with an impressive series of initiatives to phase out production and consumption of certain substances that deplete the ozone layer and this has been possible only due to the adoption of alternatives developed and introduced on a large scale, a clear example of successful synergies.

Technical solutions are necessary, but not sufficient. From the beginning, the Montreal Protocol laid focus on information, education, and the formation of a sense of responsibility in children and adults towards environmentally sound patterns of development and the stewardship of creation. This course is to be followed also in the years to come.

Mr President,

The Holy See is making significant efforts in environmental protection. It gives particular attention to promoting an education in environmental responsibility in a way that also seeks to safeguard the moral conditions for an authentic human ecology. Worldwide, many Catholic educational institutions are engaged in promoting such a model of education. Moreover, Episcopal Conferences, Dioceses, parishes and faith-based

NGOs have been devoted to advocacy and management of ecological programs for a number of years.

These efforts are targeting our life-styles, as the current dominant models of consumption and production are often unsustainable from the point of view of social, environmental, economic and moral analysis. We must practice a lifestyle through which we can safeguard creation – soil, water and air – as a gift entrusted to everyone and the base and prerequisite for our life. Above all we must prevent mankind from destroying itself. The degradation of nature is like a mirror of the culture: when the human ecology is respected within society, the environmental ecology will benefit. The way humanity treats the environment influences the way it treats itself.

In his recent Encyclical *Caritas in Veritate*, and in his Message for the 2010 World Day of Peace, Pope Benedict XVI addressed to all those involved in the environmental sector an inescapable question: how can we hope that future generations respect the natural environment when our educational and social systems as well as our laws do not help them to respect themselves?

Mr President,

The environment – notably ozone layer protection and related actions – entails a shared responsibility toward the entire human family, especially the poor and the future generations. There is an inseparable link between the protection of creation, education and an ethical approach to the economy and development. The Holy See hopes that a holistic approach will be shared by everyone and lead to the integral development of all persons, countries and creation itself.

Thank you, Mr President.

THE ADVERSE IMPLICATIONS OF CLIMATE CHANGE ON POVERTY AND DEVELOPMENT*

Mr President,

The Holy See is encouraged by the growing efforts to address global climate change initiated by a variety of stakeholders.

There is increased evidence that the poorest people in the more vulnerable countries will bear most of the burden of adapting to climate change consequences which they had almost no role in creating.[1] As we look toward the 2015 United Nations Climate Change Conference in Paris, we are offered a significant opportunity to make two ethical decisions. First, the nations of the world need to commit themselves to curbing carbon emissions at a minimum level to avoid dangerous anthropogenic interference with the climate system; and secondly, the nations of the world must sufficiently fund adaptation measures needed by vulnerable nations and peoples to withstand the impacts of climate change. Our concern for the common good of the planet, and for humanity, urges us to recognize our sense of interdependence with both nature and one another. No one is exempt from either the impacts of climate change or our moral responsibility to act in solidarity with one another to address this global concern.

We believe that such decisions will demonstrate humankind's commitment to showing respect for the environment, for those who suffer the most, and for the sake of present and future generations. While science continues to research the full implications of climate change, the virtue of prudence calls us to take the responsibility to act to reduce the potential damages, particularly for those individuals who live in poverty, for those who live in very vulnerable climate impact areas, and for future generations. As Pope Francis underlined, 'The effective struggle against global warming will only be possible with a responsible collective answer, that goes beyond particular interests and behavior and is developed free

* Statement delivered at the 28th Session of the Human Rights Council – Item 1: *Full-Day Discussion on Human Rights and Climate Change*, 6 March 2015.

1 As pointed out by the United Nations Development Programme (UNDP), 'In the Netherlands, people are investing in homes that can float on water. The Swiss Alpine ski industry is investing in artificial snow-making machines', but '[i]n the Horn of Africa, "adaptation" means that women and young girls walk further to collect water.' In the Ganges and Mekong Deltas, 'people are erecting bamboo flood shelters on stilts' and 'planting mangroves to protect themselves against storm surges'.

of political and economic pressures ... On climate change, there is a clear, definitive and ineluctable ethical imperative to act ... The establishment of an international climate change treaty is a grave ethical and moral responsibility.'[2]

Mr President,

Solidarity with the most vulnerable nations and peoples that are experiencing the impact of climate change in a more prominent and immediate way impels us to contribute to improving their situation and defending their right to development. Poverty and climate change are now intimately linked. Strategies to address the first need to take into account the latter and vice versa.

In fact, poor people living in developing countries are particularly vulnerable given their disproportionate dependency on climate-sensitive resources for their food and livelihoods.[3] The Special Rapporteur on the Right to Food has documented how extreme climate events are increasingly threatening livelihoods and food security. Indeed, an estimated 600 million people will face malnutrition due to climate change, with increasing malnutrition rates in South Asia and sub-Saharan Africa in particular.[4]

Moreover, the proliferation of floods and storms and the rising of the sea level are showing some of the effects that climate change will have also on the human right to adequate housing. The erosion of livelihoods, partly caused by climate change, is a main 'push' factor for increasing rural to urban migration. Many will move to urban slums and informal settlements where they will be forced to build shelters in hazardous areas.[5] Already today, an estimated one billion people live in urban slums, on fragile hillsides or flood-prone river banks, which are acutely vulnerable to extreme climate events.

As we continue to search for viable solutions, we know that the path to a more just and sustainable future is complex and often uncertain. In

[2] Message of Pope Francis to the President of COP 20 under the United Nations Framework Convention on Climate Change (UNFCCC).

[3] IPCC AR4 WG II, p. 359. United Nations Millennium Project 2005, Halving Hunger: It Can Be Done, Task Force on Hunger, p. 66. Furthermore, according to the Human Rights Council Special Rapporteur on the right to food, 'half of the world's hungry people ... depend for their survival on lands which are inherently poor and which may be becoming less fertile and less productive as a result of the impacts of repeated droughts, climate change and unsustainable land use' (UN Doc. A/HRC/7/5, para. 51).

[4] www.ifpri.org/. [5] UN Doc. A/63/275, paras. 31–38.

our collective work to address global climate change, the Holy See is committed to working with all people of good will and it pledges its support for efforts that advance the common good, respect for human dignity and a special care for the most vulnerable.

The Holy See hopes as well that the pledged contributions to the Green Climate Fund will continue to increase so as to enable the most vulnerable nations to mitigate, and adapt to, the effect of climate change more effectively. Finally, the continuing and deepening collaboration and engagement of civil society and the private sector is a welcome sign. All of these measures should improve the chances for meaningful and constructive steps to address climate change at the forthcoming Paris Conference. The expected new agreement should embody binding measures of responsibility and solidarity for an effective action by the international community to address together the threats resulting from climate change. Climate change is, in fact, an issue of justice for everyone. The new instrument should rest on that justice, which must guide our deliberations in the weeks to come. Both developed and developing countries have a responsibility to protect: they constitute the one human family of this earth with an equal mandate to manage and protect creation in a responsible manner to ensure that also our future generations find a world that allows them to flourish.

OUR COMMON RESPONSIBILITY TOWARDS CREATION*

Mr President,

As the Holy See stated during the UN Climate Summit, the enjoyment of a sustainable environment is an issue of justice, respect and equity. Environmental degradation can and does adversely affect the 'enjoyment of a broad range of human rights'.[1] The Human Rights Council itself has stated, 'environmental damage can have negative implications, both direct and indirect, for the effective enjoyment of human rights.'[2] These situations must be approached from the perspective of the principle of common and distributive justice. Contributive justice in the sense that all shall contribute according to their financial and technological possibilities; distributive justice, in order to provide to each country the know-how as well as the possibility to develop, to produce goods and to deliver services. Reparative justice implies that those who have benefited more from the use of natural resources, and having thus damaged the environment more, have a special duty to work for its restoration and care.

Human rights obligations and commitments have the potential to inform and strengthen international, regional and national policymaking in the area of environmental protection and urge States 'to take human rights into consideration when developing their environmental policies' (Resolution 16/11). This Council, as well as the parties to the United Nations Framework Convention on Climate Change, has stated that States should, in all climate change-related actions, fully respect human rights.[3] The human rights obligations relating to the environment also include substantive obligations to adopt legal and institutional frameworks that protect against environmental damage that would interfere with the enjoyment of human rights, including harm caused by private actors. As my Delegation has already stated in the intervention on Transnational Corporations, we reiterate our call to protect human rights from environmental harm. States have to strike a balance between environmental protection and other legitimate societal interests. But the balance should be reasonable and not result in unjustified and foreseeable infringements of human rights.

* Statement delivered at the 28th Session of the Human Rights Council – Item 3: *Human Rights Obligations Relating to the Enjoyment of a Safe, Clean, Healthy and Sustainable Environment*, 9 March 2015.

[1] Cf. UN Doc. A/HRC/22/43, para. 34. [2] Cf. Resolution 16/11.

[3] Resolution 18/22; and FCCC/CP/2010/7/Add.1, decision 1/CP.16.

In this regard, the Holy See would like to express its appreciation for the good practice of preparing 'sustainability reports', which describe the economic, environmental and social impacts caused by companies' everyday activities. The comprehensive guidelines prepared by the Global Reporting Initiative provide a framework for measuring and reporting sustainability-related impact and performance, inclusive of indicators relating to the protection of human rights and the environment.[4]

It is a matter of justice to help poor and vulnerable people who suffer from causes largely not of their making and beyond their control. One concrete step would be to make available to them the best in adaptation and mitigation technology. Now, all eyes are focused on the Twenty-first Conference of Parties to the UNFCCC and the Eleventh Meeting of the Parties to the Kyoto Protocol, which will take place in Paris in December 2015. There, the poor and the rich will be winners if we could reach an agreement on a post-2020 international regime, in which all the nations of the world, including the biggest emitters of greenhouse gases, bind themselves to a universal agreement on climate.

In conclusion, Mr President,

As Pope Francis stated in different circumstances: 'Even if "nature is at our disposition" all too often we do not "respect it or consider it a gracious gift which we must care for and set at the service of our brothers and sisters, including future generations". Here too what is crucial is responsibility on the part of all in pursuing, in a spirit of fraternity, policies respectful of this earth which is our common home.' The responsibility to protect the environment, whether as a developed or a developing country, rests on the shoulders of us all. Taking into consideration the good practices highlighted by the Special Rapporteur, we should not avoid the urgent work that remains to be done for ensuring that future generations might find a world that will allow them to lead prosperous lives.

[4] Report of the Independent Expert on the Issue of Human Rights Obligations Relating to the Enjoyment of a Safe, Clean, Healthy and Sustainable Environment, UN Doc. A/HRC/28/61, para. 81.

EXPLANATORY NOTES

Commission on Life-Saving Commodities for Women and Children

In 2012, the UN Commission on Life-Saving Commodities for Women's and Children's Health called on the global community to increase access to and appropriate use of thirteen life-saving commodities addressing the leading preventable causes of death during pregnancy, childbirth and childhood by 2015. Among its strategy, it also promoted reproductive health commodities, so-called 'Emergency Contraception' (www.unfpa.org/publications/un-commission-life-saving-commodities-women-and-children).

Committee on the Rights of the Child

The Committee on the Rights of the Child is the body of 18 Independent experts that monitors the implementation of the Convention on the Rights of the Child by its States Parties.

COP 21 – Conference of the Parties 21

The 2015 United Nations Climate Change Conference in Paris, also referred to as COP 21, was held in Paris, France, from November 30 to December 12, 2015. It was the 21st yearly session of the Conference of the Parties to the United Nations Framework Convention on Climate Change (UNFCCC) adopted in Rio in 1992 and the 11th Session of the Meeting of the Parties to the 1997 Kyoto Protocol (www.cop21paris.org/).

Copenhagen Declaration on Social Development (1995)

At the World Summit for Social Development, held in March 1995 in Copenhagen, governments reached a new consensus on the need to put people at the center of development. It pledged to make the conquest of poverty, the goal of full employment and the fostering of social integration overriding objectives of development (www.un-documents.net/cope-dec.htm).

CRC – Convention on the Rights of the Child

The Convention on the Rights of the Child was adopted by the General Assembly Resolution 44/25 of 20 November 1989 and entered into force on 2 September 1990. Two Optional Protocols to the Convention, on involvement of children in armed conflict and on sale of children, child prostitution and child pornography were adopted in 2000 by the United Nations General Assembly, while a third Optional Protocol on a communications procedure, which allows individual children to submit complaints regarding specific violations of their rights under the Convention and its first two Optional Protocols, was adopted in 2011 (www.ohchr.org/EN/ProfessionalInterest/Pages/CRC.aspx).

Declaration on the Right to Development

The Declaration on the Right to Development contains 10 articles and was adopted by the General Assembly by Resolution 41/128 of 4 December 1986. Article 1 of the Declaration proclaims that the right to development is an inalienable human right, while Article 2 identifies the human person as the central subject of development (www.un.org/documents/ga/res/41/a41r128.htm).

ECOSOC – UN Economic and Social Council

The Economic and Social Council is one of the six principal organs of the United Nations System established by the UN Charter in 1945. It consists of 54 Members of the United Nations elected by the General Assembly. ECOSOC coordinates economic, social and related work of the 14 United Nations specialized agencies, functional commissions and five regional commissions. It serves as the central forum for discussing international economic and social issues, and for formulating policy recommendations addressed to Member States and the United Nations system. It is also responsible for the follow-up to major UN Conferences and Summits (www.un.org/en/ecosoc/).

GFMD – Global Forum on Migration and Development

The Global Forum on Migration and Development (GFMD) was created during the United Nations General Assembly 14–15 September 2006 High-Level Dialogue on International Migration and Development to address the linkages between migration and development in practical and action-oriented ways. It is an informal, non-binding, voluntary and government-led process that marks the culmination of more than a decade of international dialogue on the growing importance of the linkages between migration and development (www.gfmd.org/).

GRI – Global Reporting Initiative

The GRI is an international independent organization that helps businesses, governments and other organizations understand and communicate the impact of business on critical sustainability issues such as climate change, human rights, corruption and many others (https://www.globalreporting.org/Pages/default.aspx).

High Commissioner for Human Rights

The High Commissioner for Human Rights is the principal human rights official of the United Nations. He heads the OHCHR and supervises the Human Rights Council at the United Nations Office in Geneva (www.ohchr.org/EN/AboutUs/Pages/HighCommissioner.aspx).

Holy See's Charter of the Rights of the Family

The Charter of the Rights of the Family was 'presented by the Holy See to all persons, institutions and authorities concerned with the mission of the family in today's world' on 22 October 1983. The document is composed of a preamble followed by 12 Articles and contains the formulation of those inalienable rights that are inherent to that natural and universal society that is the family composed of husband, wife and children, that States have the duty to defend (www.vatican.va/roman_curia/pontifical_councils/family/documents/rc_pc_family_doc_19831022_family-rights_en.html).

ICCPR – International Covenant on Civil and Political Rights

The ICCPR was adopted in 1966 by General Assembly Resolution 2200A. The Covenant elaborates further the civil and political rights and freedoms listed in the Universal Declaration of Human Rights (www.ohchr.org/en/professionalinterest/pages/ccpr.aspx).

ICESCR – International Covenant on Economic, Social and Cultural Rights

The ICESCR was adopted in 1966 by General Assembly Resolution 2200A. Together with the Universal Declaration of Human Rights and the ICCPR make up the International Bill of Human Rights. (www.ohchr.org/EN/ProfessionalInterest/Pages/CESCR.aspx).

International Year of the Family

Established by the United Nations General Assembly in 1994 to raise awareness of the importance of the family, to promote knowledge of socio-economic and demographic trends affecting families and to stimulate efforts to respond to challenges faced by families.

Mexico City United Nations International Conference on Population and Development

The Fifth International Conference on Population and Development was held in Mexico City in 1994 under the auspices of the United Nations. As a result, a new Program of Action was adopted as a guide for national and international action in the area of population and development for the next 20 years (www.un.org/en/development/devagenda/population.shtml).

Millennium Development Goals (MDGs)

The Millennium Development Goals were adopted at the UN Millennium Summit in New York in September 2000. The MDGs are eight time-bound international targets – that were committed to being achieved by 2015 – for addressing extreme poverty in its many dimensions such as income poverty, hunger, disease, lack of adequate shelter, and exclusion, while promoting gender equality, education, and environmental sustainability (www.unmillenniumproject.org/goals/).

Montreal Protocol

The Montreal Protocol on Substances that Deplete the Ozone Layer was adopted by the Conference of Plenipotentiaries on the Protocol on Chlorofluorocarbons to the Vienna Convention for the Protection of the Ozone Layer, held in Montreal in 1987. It was designed to reduce the production and consumption of ozone depleting substances in order to reduce their abundance in the atmosphere, and thereby protect the earth's fragile ozone layer (https://treaties.un.org/pages/ViewDetails.aspx?src=TREATY&mtdsg_no=XXVII-2-a&chapter=27&lang=en).

OHCHR – Office of the United Nations High Commissioner for Human Rights

The OHCHR works to promote and protect the human rights that are guaranteed under international law and stipulated in the Universal Declaration of Human Rights of 1948. The Office was established by the United Nations General Assembly on 20 December 1993 in the wake of the Vienna Declaration and Programme of Action (www.ohchr.org/EN/Pages/Home.aspx).

Special Procedures of the Human Rights Council: Independent Expert/Special Rapporteur

The special procedures of the Human Rights Council are independent human rights experts with mandates to monitor, advise and publicly report on human rights situations in specific countries or territories (country mandates), or on major phenomena of human rights violations worldwide (thematic mandates). Special procedures are either an individual ('Special Rapporteur' or 'Independent Expert') or a working group composed of five members, one from each of the five United Nations regional groupings: Africa, Asia, Latin America and the Caribbean, Eastern Europe and the Western group. They are appointed by the Human Rights Council and serve in their personal capacities to a maximum of six years. Special Procedures report annually to the Human Rights Council and the majority of the mandates also report to the General Assembly (www.ohchr.org/EN/HRBodies/SP/Pages/Introduction.aspx).

Sustainable Development Goals (SDGs)

The Sustainable Development Goals are a universal set of goals, targets and indicators that UN Member States will be expected to use to frame their agendas and political policies over the next 15 years. They were adopted at the United Nations Sustainable Development Summit in September 2015 in New York, where world leaders adopted the 2030 Agenda for Sustainable Development. This Agenda includes a set of 17 SDGs to end poverty, fight inequality and injustice, and address climate change by 2030. The Sustainable Development Goals build on the Millennium Development Goals. While the MDGs, in theory, applied to all countries, in reality they were considered targets for poor countries to achieve, with financial assistance from wealthy States. Conversely, every country will be expected to work towards achieving the SDGs (https://sustainabledevelopment.un.org/sdgs).

Task Force on the Implementation of the Right to Development

The high-level task force on the implementation of the right to development was established by the Commission on Human Rights, in its resolution 2004/7, and the Economic and Social Council, by its decision 2004/249, at the recommendation and within the framework of the intergovernmental Working Group on the Right to Development, in order to assist it in fulfilling its mandate (www.ohchr.org/EN/Issues/Development/Pages/HighLevelTaskForce.aspx).

UDHR – Universal Declaration of Human Rights

The Universal Declaration of Human Rights is a milestone document in the history of human rights. Drafted by Representatives with different legal and cultural backgrounds from all regions of the world, the Declaration was proclaimed by the United Nations General Assembly in Paris on 10 December 1948, General Assembly Resolution 217A as a common standard of achievements for all peoples and all nations. It set out, for the first time, fundamental human rights to be universally protected (www.un.org/en/universal-declaration-human-rights/).

UNFCCC and Kyoto Protocol

The United Nations Framework Convention on Climate Change is an international environmental treaty that was opened for signature at the Earth Summit held in Rio de Janeiro in 1992 and came into force in 1994. The ultimate objective of the Convention is 'to stabilize greenhouse gas (GHG) concentrations in the atmosphere at a level that will prevent dangerous human interference with the climate system' (http://newsroom.unfccc.int/). The Convention was complemented by the 1997, legally binding, Kyoto Protocol. Recognizing that developed countries are principally responsible for the current high levels of GHG emissions in the atmosphere as a result of more than 150 years of industrial activity, the

Protocol places a heavier burden on developed nations under the principle of 'common but differentiated responsibilities' (http://unfccc.int/kyoto_protocol/items/2830.php).

United Nations Global Strategy for Women's and Children's Health

The 2010–2015 Global Strategy for Women's and Children's Health provided a road map to accelerate progress towards the achievement of MDGs 4 (reduce child mortality), 5 (improve maternal health) and 6 (combat HIV/AIDS, malaria and other diseases) by 2015 (www.who.int/pmnch/activities/advocacy/globalstrategy/en/).

Vienna Declaration and Programme of Action

The Vienna Declaration and Programme of Action is a human rights declaration adopted by consensus at the World Conference on Human Rights in 1993 in Vienna, Austria. The United Nations High Commissioner for Human Rights was created by this Declaration, endorsed by General Assembly Resolution 48/121 (www.ohchr.org/EN/ProfessionalInterest/Pages/Vienna.aspx).

WHA – World Health Assembly

The World Health Assembly is the supreme decision-making body for WHO. It generally meets in Geneva in May each year, and is attended by Delegations from all 194 Member States. Its main function is to determine the policies of the Organization (www.who.int/governance/en/).

WHO – World Health Organization

Founded in 1948, WHO's primary role is to direct and coordinate international health within the United Nations' system. WHO's main areas of work are health systems, promoting health through the life-course, non-communicable and communicable diseases, corporate services, and preparedness, surveillance and response (www.who.int/en/).

WHO Executive Board

The Executive Board is composed of 34 individuals technically qualified in the field of health, each one designated by a Member State elected to do so by the World Health Assembly. Member States are elected for three-year terms. The Board meets at least twice a year and its main functions are to give effect to the decisions and policies of the Health Assembly, to advise it and generally to facilitate its work (www.who.int/governance/eb/en/).

Working Group on the Right to Development

The Working Group was established by the Commission on Human Rights, in its Resolution 1998/72, and by the Economic and Social Council, in its decision 1998/269, with the mandate to 'monitor and review progress made in the promotion and implementation of the right to development as elaborated in the Declaration on the Right to Development' (www.ohchr.org/EN/Issues/Development/Pages/WGRightToDevelopment.aspx).

II

Freedom as the Foundation of Human Relations and Social Coexistence

Introduction

Religion has always been the subject of great consideration. This is seen in its regulation by domestic or international legal systems as well as in the mixed and even controversial interest elicited within the institutions of the international community. The choice of faith, and the consequent belonging to a religion, impacts every level of life, the social and political spheres. They play a formidable role in addressing the challenges our societies go through on a daily basis. Today, moreover, religion has taken on a renewed importance due to the complex relationship between the personal choice of faith and its public expression. Due to such implications, the choice, and the practice, of one's faith, must be free of constraints and coercion.

This is the doctrinal, legal and institutional *humus* of the interventions of the Holy See contained in this chapter, delivered to the various UN bodies responsible for human rights, especially during special debates on the right to religious freedom. A leitmotif of the interventions revolves around the idea that faith is a *religious fact* and an *institutional reality* intrinsically linked to it. The religious component is part of the personal identity of the believer. As such, its public dimension is ever pertinent to States and to the relations occurring among the larger family of nations. Hence, religious freedom, considered from the Christian perspective, fully belongs to those temporal matters which are to be considered, interpreted and used in the logic of dialogue and co-operation.[1]

By linking the contents of the numerous interventions with the methodology and content of international law of human rights, two aspects should be considered: the right to religious freedom and the right to non-discrimination on the basis of religion. This idea is put forward by the Second Vatican Council's Declaration *Dignitatis Humanae* which outlines some essential prerequisites: the unhindered ability of the human person to realize the need to rise above human matters and the possibility to keep this decision ongoing.[2]

The public dimension of religion – a practical reality formed by worship, teaching, training, institutional framework, organization and

[1] In this sense, cf. *Gaudium et Spes*, § 89.

[2] Similar considerations are found in the international instruments that have specifically been adopted by intergovernmental organizations since the Universal Declaration of Human Rights, e.g. the Declaration on the Elimination of All Forms of Intolerance and of Discrimination Based on Religion or Belief, adopted by the United Nations General Assembly on 25 November 1981 (UN Doc. A/RES/ 36/55).

relationships – paves the way to the complexity surrounding the inherent rights of the human person. Such a complexity results from the extensive contributions of history, doctrines, proclamations, as well as cultural and normative revolutions concerning these rights and other decisions which determine either their full or limited enjoyment or their complete denial. The example of discrimination on the grounds of religion is a case in point: we cannot simply denounce a generic discrimination, but we have to make a distinction between the one suffered by a person or by communities because of their choice of faith and the discrimination perpetrated by anyone – groups or even States – in the name of religion.

Protection and *limitations* are the two key elements surrounding any debate on religious freedom, a fundamental right because of its direct connection to the human person. In fact, it also serves a strategic role in evaluating and ensuring the proper attention and guarantee granted by the public authorities. This interpretation reflects the process of affirmation of human rights that has characterized the history of the last few centuries, placing the human person and his/her rights at the centre of reflections and of legal, political, cultural and religious actions. These very same reflections and actions, however, have revealed that the fundamental rights remain the best means of protection not only for the person per se, but for the indivisible unity proper to the human person: between the material and spiritual dimensions, between the individual and the collective dimension, between being a believer and being a citizen. Indeed, religious freedom raises the question of the *indivisibility* of human rights, which has become a guiding principle and fundamental assumption of the international law of human rights.

The interventions of the Holy See also reveal a different meaning of the right to religious freedom, repeatedly recalling the description and delimitation of its content. This is not to deprive the right of some of its components or to restrict its scope, but as a guarantee for its full protection and implementation, thereby preventing an erroneous – or at least partial – interpretation that can lead to other kinds of limitations. They seek to clarify the true sense and meaning of religious freedom while identifying those unessential elements which do not add any value to the right deriving from it. After all, a different interpretation would entail the possibility to determine arbitrarily what one should believe or even whether one can believe or not. Denial and indifference would inevitably lead to deleterious effects on the contents of faith or on the meaning of the religious message and, once again, on choosing a religion or being a member of a community of believers.

A second point relates to the exact understanding of religious freedom. It is not the assumption that all kinds of beliefs or forms of religion (or those claiming to be such) are equivalent. If this were the case, then religious freedom would be equivalent to the tolerance applied to the so-called forms of *new age*, even when confronted with behavior which is a manifest violation of rights and freedoms. This is an essential point in the current debate on the different interpretation of terms such as religion and belief. This is the case, for example, when traditional religions and new forms of beliefs, as well as theistic religions and non-theistic ones are equally treated in the domestic and international legal guarantees related to the right to freedom of religion.[3] This situation then evolves into concrete responses when governmental and intergovernmental bodies begin to claim that they can legislate on matters of religion. In this way, they trump the fundamental principle that the choice of one's faith as well as the religious practice of individuals and communities are the content of an inherent right which must never be confused with a concession passed by a State or by an international Institution.

Completing the big picture is the relationship between freedom of religion and freedom of creed or belief according to the meaning that religion and belief have come to acquire in the juridical context. Until the 1990s, the normative context placed religion and belief in close correlation (or rather in opposition) to allow supporters of state-atheism to justify their omissions or acts of intolerance towards religion and believers.[4] Currently, however, the expression 'freedom of belief' is considered an alternative to freedom of religion. The way has been paved for the idea that the right to freedom of belief or creed is no longer the equivalent of the freedom to profess and promote atheism, but rather a right not to profess any religion or belief, or to profess one's 'own', personal, individual beliefs system, expression used in international language, thus leading to a confrontation of different visions. This complex issue raises a recurring question in the interventions of the Holy See: is it just one of the signs of the growing secularization that has shifted the debate from

[3] Refers to the General Comment No. 22 (48), adopted by the Human Rights Committee, on Art. 18 of the International Covenant on Civil and Political Rights concerning freedom of religion (Doc. CCPR/C/21/Rev.1/Add. 4, 27 September 1993).

[4] All relevant international instruments on the issue deriving from Principle VII of the Helsinki Final Act (1975) of the Conference on Security and Cooperation in Europe, and from the UN Declaration on the Elimination of All Forms of Intolerance and of Discrimination Based on Religion or Belief (1981), are quite illustrative.

religion to spirituality as a vague attention to the sacred or is it a result of the clash of civilizations theory? This theory was much acclaimed in the wake of historic events such as the fall of the Berlin Wall in 1989 and the destruction of the New York Twin Towers in 2001 that introduced in the legal terminology concepts like Islamophobia and Christianophobia on the same level as the long-existing anti-Semitism.

Moving on to concrete situations, the interventions contained in this chapter show how the religious phenomenon is now pragmatically assimilated to 'lifestyles' that include a vague religious component made up of generic 'religious' practices, meanings and values. These lifestyles, however, are not rooted in a traditional religious/confessional identity. Rather, stress is placed on individual believers. On the other hand, there is ever-increasing consideration given to the *believing* dimension, to the *belonging* to a specific religious denomination, and to an ethical *behaving* that includes various elements pertaining to religions and beliefs. The objective is not to justify a right, but rather to legitimize the private dimension of religion with a new type of subject, the persons *believing without belonging* to a specific religion.

Similarly, another question concerns the conflict allegedly caused by the religious element, due to interpretations or visions inspired by the theory of the 'clash of civilizations' and thus entailing a negative meaning for religion and believers, as in the conflict between freedom of religion and freedom of expression. The stance of the Holy See is clear: the aim to preserve religion from the different forms of intolerance has led to identifying Islamophobia, anti-Semitism and – last chronologically speaking – Christianophobia as causes for intolerance towards individual believers as well as towards religious communities. This is evident when monitoring the new situations that have emerged during recent years in the international scenario, implying a negative take on religion, often seen as a cause of conflict. This has become a very heated debate which often lacks a 'positive' approach aimed at promoting the contents of the choice of faith and the consequent fundamental right to religious freedom. Indeed, the approach relating only to defamation of a religion runs the risk of omitting certain situations determined by State regulations which would be hardly compatible with international standards on human rights. This inevitably leads to the denial of freedom of worship, teaching, the use of religious symbols, the protection of places of worship, that is, all elements pertaining to the right to religious freedom. All in all, these considerations lead to one conclusion: the religious element may lose its precious value and its true meaning, turning religious freedom into a purely functional element for both the fundamental rights and for any approach dealing with religion.

Confronted with such a problematic scenario, the basic contents of a concept that apparently seemed acquired in theory as well as in practice are reaffirmed: freedom of religion is understood as the right of every person to profess their religion, according to the dictates of their conscience, either as an individual or in a community, free from any external coercion that can intervene or who think to have the right to intervene. Then, to affirm religious freedom as a fundamental right means to acknowledge the autonomy of the person not with respect to religion, but to all those who would like to limit his/her religious sentiment. For these reasons, a legal regulation – domestic as well as international – is required to provide effective guarantees without placing any coercion on the individual conscience.

Such a perspective is firmly rooted in the social doctrine of the Church. Religious freedom demands that no coercion be exerted on the human person in order to prevent her from following the dictates of conscience. This is reinforced in the very mission of the Church by the divine command: 'Go into the whole world and proclaim the gospel to every creature' (Mk 16:15). In fact, this is the invitation addressed to all Christians, called to spread the message of the Gospel to all nations, respecting the right to seek the Truth and to adhere to it freely. Here again the reference to freedom of religion as freedom of the human conscience must not to be hindered. Any form of apostolate or work to spread the Christian message must never utilize means that are incompatible with the spirit of the Gospel, rather this activity should ensure that everyone adheres to the faith manifesting a fully free consent, that is respectful of human dignity and freedom.

The interventions of the Holy See at the United Nations human rights bodies insist on the idea that religious freedom must be guaranteed for every person – not only to Christians. This right must also be recognized 'when they act in community' and set limits only to the extent that 'the just demands of public order are observed.'[5] This means a positive obligation to respect the right of religious communities to worship together with a power of self-organization to be enacted in the autonomous choice of religious leaders, priests, teachers, in the establishment of seminaries and religious schools or training for religious personnel, in the

[5] Second Vatican Council, Declaration on Religious Freedom, *Dignitatis Humanae*, § 4.

preparation and distribution of books and publications of religious content, as well as the possibility for believers to contribute – according to their religious views – to the life of society and to the international order. These provisions should be possible without having to obtain special authorizations, provided they do not fall within the limitations customarily prescribed by international law of human rights, summarized in the terms of public safety, order, health, morals or fundamental rights and freedoms of others.[6]

The justification of this lies in the fact that everyone has to make his own personal relationship with God in conformity with His law: 'In the depths of his conscience, man detects a law which he does not impose upon himself, but which holds him to obedience'.[7] For this reason, there is the duty to learn this law with increasing clarity and, for what concerns Christians, following the teaching of the Church and constantly conforming to the will of God. Respecting the right not to be hindered from following one's own conscience implies freedom of religion. This is the polar opposite of those mentalities which discriminate through coercive proselytism and forced conversions, forgetting that 'religious intolerance is at its height odious and offensive to the human person; with it, in fact man is deprived of his freedom to follow the dictates of his conscience: dictates that he considers supreme and sacred, even when, in good faith, he falls into error.'[8] Conscience, man's 'most secret core and his sanctuary, where he is alone with God, whose voice echoes in his depths',[9] becomes the point of reference and insuperable limit for every action concerning religious freedom.

Another area of investigation is contained in the question: from what assumptions does a correct vision of religious freedom stem? First, it stems from the human person's ability to choose freely to adhere to the principles, the doctrine, the ritual and operational elements of a 'community of believers', while being perfectly aware that those elements can also directly affect his life and, at the same time, the social context to which he belongs. This means overcoming the insidious idea of opposition between being a believer and being a citizen that can relativize the

[6] See the provisions of Art. 18.3 of the International Covenant on Civil and Political Rights.

[7] *Gaudium et Spes*, § 16.

[8] Second Vatican Council, Preparatory Scheme, 'De Libertate Religiosa', 19 November 1963, § 3, final para.

[9] *Gaudium et Spes*, § 16.

religious element, equating it, for example, only to rituals or unspecified forms of spirituality.

This is the context in which a negative obligation falls on public authorities: to refrain from preventing or limiting with laws, administrative acts or other forms of action, the freedom of believers to 'order their own lives in accordance with their religious principles'.[10] The relationship between religion and freedom has to be measured by the need for society not to hinder the exercise of that freedom. This implies, inter alia, that civil authorities refrain from forms of pressure to adhere to a religion to which the person has chosen not to adhere and that they do not prevent the profession of a religious faith that the person decides to profess. Such a profile is as timely as ever in the face of the widespread tendency to consider freedom of religion in 'negative' terms, thus widening the scope of the concept of discrimination. The result, in fact, is a reinterpretation of the relationship between freedom of religion and the principle of non-discrimination to assess how this fundamental principle of international law of human rights is actually applied to the freedom of religion, especially when considering the so-called indirect discrimination or measures having equivalent effect.[11]

This process, although originally an effort to give them additional protection – the so-called protection from intolerance – has resulted in the juxtaposition of the concepts of tolerance to the religion or belief. This has led to a totally negative view of religion which attempts to link the religious fact (and not only the phenomenon) to violence and war, through terrorism, xenophobia, nationalism, racism, anti-Semitism, exclusion, marginalization, discrimination of minorities, migrant workers and other vulnerable groups, intimidation and underdevelopment.[12] However, is it possible to connect the religious phenomenon merely to fundamentalism, violence or terrorism? And, to what extent are those groups that claim to be 'religiously inspired' actually intending to obscure the true meaning of religion and the freedoms connected therein? When dealing with these phenomena, national legal orders consider freedom of

[10] *Dignitatis Humanae*, § 4.

[11] The reference is to the debate on the alleged right publicly to criticize or to ridicule a religion/belief, as well as a religious leader. A similar approach also applies to issues that are more directly related to the legislative, administrative and regulatory measures typically adopted by the State which are reflected in the relationship between freedom of religion and non-discrimination, beginning with the consideration of freedom of religion in the constitutional guarantees.

[12] See Unesco, Declaration of Principles on Tolerance (1995), Preamble and Art. 1.

religion as a matter of public order, a category widely appreciated by the authority, as it offers high manoeuvring. A case in point is the reference to the secrecy of the proceedings, structure and members of the groups to invoke a restrictive intervention by the legal system as well as the potential negative effects on social coexistence of the ideas and manifestations stemming from them.

The statements delivered by the Holy See put forward some criteria to evaluate the effects of a widening or a generalization of the powers of domestic legal systems on the whole matter of freedom of religion. In other words, to what criterion should these limitations, imposed by the authority, respond: to the respect of the right to freedom of religion or to tolerance? And, again, does a fundamental right (at least according to international law) such as the right to religious freedom prevail over the forms of restriction imposed by domestic legal orders? Moreover, a proper reaction to these questions, referring to limitations on the exercise of fundamental rights, that religious freedom can only be identified by law, immediately denotes the tie among the three rights pertaining to 'intellectual freedom' (of religion, of conscience and of thought).[13] As a matter of fact, the boundaries – and therefore their restrictions – of these three rights have never been single-handedly outlined in an organic and sectoral way, because they still carry the overlapping of interpretations and tensions that led to their exclusion from the early 'declarations or charters' on human rights in the modern age.

Considering the current scenario, one sees a clear attempt to reduce freedom of religion to that of thought or even of opinion. As a result, there is a tendency to relegate religion to the mere subjective level, stripped of the social dimension in the name of respect for pluralism of thought and opinion. Likewise, restrictions on freedom of religion cannot be limited to mere tolerance. In fact, such an approach may determine that the 'increasing marginalization of religion ... that is taking place in some quarters, even in nations which place a great emphasis on tolerance',[14] forgets that the distinction between the right of religious freedom and the

[13] Such is provided for in Art. 18 of the Universal Declaration of Human Rights and later recalled by the International Covenant on Civil and Political Rights and by various Conventions adopted at the regional level, in particular the European Convention on Human Rights (1950) and the Inter-American Convention on Human Rights (1969).

[14] Pope Benedict XVI, Address in Westminster Hall, 17 September 2010, www.vatican.va/content/benedict-xvi/en/speeches/2010/september/documents/hf_ben-xvi_spe_20100917_societa-civile.html.

manifestation of that right has traditionally been the criterion to establish the degree of intervention in the sphere of religion by public powers.

Finally, the interventions by the Holy See reveal the way forward for another issue: the limitations that can be imposed on religious freedom. In other words, can the possibility to announce and spread the religious message be subjected to restrictions? While the right to religious freedom must be recognized in the legal system and proclaimed as a fundamental right, right limitations imposed by law can be applied for what concerns its exercise. Such limitations, however, depend on the situation and have to be put in place with the necessary political 'evaluation' to ensure 'the effective safeguard of the rights of all citizens and ... the peaceful settlement of conflicts of rights, also out of the need for an adequate care of genuine public peace, which comes about when men live together in good order and in true justice, and finally out of the need for a proper guardianship of public morality'.[15]

Obviously, there exist other aspects that indirectly exert limitations on the exercise of the right to religious freedom, as, for instance, the traditional historical and cultural ties of a religious community with a specific nation. These are the situations that allow a community to receive special recognition from a nation: such recognition should in no way give rise to discrimination towards 'other religious communities'.[16] There are notorious situations where the right to religious freedom is proposed in a different way with respect to its true nature. This is the case of the trend to incorporate religion into the wider concept of culture, as shown by the use of the term 'religions' to talk about existing *creeds* or *beliefs* in society that need to be harmonized: this, it is assumed, should be carried out through intercultural dialogue, thus considering religion in a purely instrumental way.[17]

Faced with these increasingly severe limitations, there must be an awareness of the essential relations between the religious community and the political community: the first has to meet the spiritual needs of the faithful, while the latter has to shape relations and institutions in

[15] *Dignitatis Humanae*, § 7. [16] Ibid., § 6.

[17] See e.g. the *Toledo Guiding Principles on Teaching about Religions and Beliefs in Public Schools*, adopted in 2007 by the Organization for Security and Cooperation in Europe. Quite emblematic is the decision of the United Nations General Assembly to institutionalize a dialogue between religions within the United Nations, affirming that 'mutual understanding and dialogue among religions constitute important elements of intercultural dialogue and of the culture of peace' (United Nations General Assembly, Resolution 61/221, 20 December 2006).

the service of the common good, beginning with respecting the religious freedom required to ensure the necessary independence to the religious community. This idea is reflected in the Encyclical *Centesimus Annus*: 'the Church respects the legitimate autonomy of the democratic order and is not entitled to express preferences for this or that institutional or constitutional solution'[18] and does not even have the task of evaluating political programmes, except for what concerns their religious or moral implications. This mutual autonomy, however, does not involve a total separation that excludes cooperation between the two communities. A correct understanding of religious freedom envisages a dimension that is at once individual and collective.[19]

Addressing the United Nations General Assembly on 18 April 2008, Pope Benedict XVI, while talking about the content of the right to freedom of religion, clearly deemed it 'inconceivable, then, that believers should have to suppress a part of themselves – their faith – in order to be active citizens. It should never be necessary to deny God in order to enjoy one's rights.'[20] A concept made explicit by Pope Francis in his speech at the United Nations General Assembly on 25 September 2015 recalling 'the painful situation of the entire Middle East, North Africa and other African countries, where Christians, together with other cultural or ethnic groups, and even members of the majority religion who have no desire to be caught up in hatred and folly, have been forced to witness the destruction of their places of worship, their cultural and religious heritage, their houses and property, and have faced the alternative either of fleeing or of paying for their adhesion to good and to peace by their own lives, or by enslavement.'[21]

The interventions presented in this chapter interpret and advance the Catholic social doctrine in an age when conflicts, integration processes, an ever-increasing human mobility, new and different technologies, the broader needs of peace and security, demand effective guarantees for

[18] Pope John Paul II, Encyclical Letter, *Centesimus Annus*, § 47.

[19] See Pope John Paul II, Letter to the Heads of State of the Nations who signed the Helsinki Final Act (1975) (1 September 1980), p. 4, https://w2.vatican.va/content/john-paul-ii/en/messages/pont_messages/1980/documents/hf_jp-ii_mes_19800901_helsinki-act.html. This vision includes the freedom of expression, teaching and evangelization, the freedom to manifest religion in public and the freedom to have one's own internal hierarchy and regulations.

[20] http://w2.vatican.va/content/benedict-xvi/en/speeches/2008/april/documents/hf_ben-xvi_spe_20080418_un-visit.html.

[21] http://w2.vatican.va/content/francesco/en/speeches/2015/september/documents/papa-francesco_20150925_onu-visita.html.

human rights. In a related development to the attention given to freedom of religion, the need to fight against racism and xenophobia has taken considerable energy. The rightful place of women in society, the persistence of slavery-like situations and new expressions of racial discrimination prompted several interventions oriented practically to implement the principle of equal dignity. This approach underlies the appeal of Pope Francis during the Meeting for Religious Liberty in Philadelphia, on 26 September 2015: 'Let us preserve freedom. Let us cherish freedom. Freedom of conscience, religious freedom, the freedom of each person, each family, each people, which is what gives rise to rights.'[22]

List of Statements

1 Freedom of Conscience and Expression of Religious Belief as Fundamental Human Rights

- THE POSITIVE ROLE OF BELIEVERS IN PUBLIC LIFE, 60th Session of the Commission on Human Rights – Item 11: *Civil and Political Rights, Sub-item (e): Religious Intolerance* (1 April 2004)
- RELIGIOUS FREEDOM: A TOUCHSTONE FOR THE OBSERVANCE OF THE OTHER FUNDAMENTAL RIGHTS, 61st Session of the Human Rights Commission – Item 11: *Civil and Political Rights* (1 April 2005)
- AVOID THE MISTAKES OF THE PAST: THE IMPERATIVE OF RELIGIOUS FREEDOM, 2nd Session of the Human Rights Council (21 September 2006)
- GUARANTEE SOCIAL COHESION THROUGH FREEDOM OF RELIGION, 6th Session of the Human Rights Council (14 September 2007)
- THE DENIGRATION OF RELIGIONS: AN OFFENSE TO PERSONAL AND SOCIAL JUSTICE, 4th Session of the Human Rights Council (22 March 2007)
- TODAY'S MARTYRS: VIOLENCE AGAINST RELIGIOUS MINORITIES, 9th Session of the Human Rights Council – Item 9: *Racism, Racial Discrimination, Xenophobia and Related Forms of Intolerance* (19 September 2008)
- FREEDOM OF RELIGION IS THE BEST PROTECTION AGAINST VIOLATIONS, 10th Session of the Human Rights Council – Item 3: *General Debate* (16 March 2009)

22 http://w2.vatican.va/content/francesco/en/speeches/2015/september/documents/papa-francesco_20150926_usa-liberta-religiosa.html.

- MEDIA AND RELIGION: THREATS AND OPPORTUNITIES, 12th Session of the Human Rights Council – Item 9: *Racism, Racial Discrimination, Xenophobia and Related Forms of Intolerance* (30 September 2009)
- AN URGENT NEED TO DELINEATE A POSITIVE AND OPEN SECULARITY, 13th Session of the Human Rights Council – Item 3: *General Debate* (12 March 2010)
- THE IMPORTANCE OF A POSITIVE INTERFAITH DIALOGUE, 13th Session of the Human Rights Council – Item 9: *Racism, Racial Discrimination, Xenophobia and Related Forms of Intolerance, Follow-Up and Implementation of the Durban Declaration and Programme of Action* (23 March 2010)
- RELIGION MUST NOT BE A CRITERION FOR DISCRIMINATION, 15th Session of the Human Rights Council – Item 9 (28 September 2010)
- RELIGIOUS FREEDOM AS A FUNDAMENTAL PATH TO PEACE, 16th Session of the Human Rights Council – General Segment (2 March 2011)
- FREEDOM OF RELIGION IN THE FIELD OF EDUCATION, 16th Session of the Human Rights Council – Item 3: *Interactive Dialogue* (10 March 2011)
- RELIGIONS ARE A RESOURCE, NOT A THREAT!, 19th Session of the Human Rights Council – High-Level Segment (1 March 2012)
- IT SHOULD NEVER BE NECESSARY TO DENY GOD TO ENJOY ONE'S RIGHTS, 20th Session of the Human Rights Council – Item 8: *Freedom of Religion* (3 July 2012)
- BLASPHEMY LAW: A PRETEXT FOR ACTS OF INJUSTICE AND VIOLENCE AGAINST RELIGIOUS MINORITIES, 21st Session of the Human Rights Council – Item 2: *Interactive Dialogue with the High Commissioner for Human Rights* (10 September 2012)
- THE STATE SHOULD NEVER IDENTIFY ITSELF WITH THE 'DOMINANT' COMMUNITY, 22nd Session of the Human Rights Council – Item 3: *Report of the Special Rapporteur on Freedom of Religion or Belief* (6 March 2013)
- THE SOCIAL CONTRIBUTIONS OF CHRISTIANS TO THE HUMAN FAMILY, 23rd Session of the Human Rights Council – Item 2: *Interactive Dialogue with High Commissioner* (27 May 2013)
- RELIGIONS MUST NOT BE MANIPULATED IN ORDER TO EXERT POWER, 25th Session of the Human Rights Council – Item 3: *Report of the Special Rapporteur on Freedom of Religion or Belief*, 12 March 2014
- THE NEED TO PROTECT AND DEFEND THE RIGHT TO RELIGIOUS FREEDOM WORLDWIDE, 27th Session of the Human Rights

Council – Item 2: *On the Opening Remarks of the High Commissioner for Human Rights* (8 September 2014)

- FREEDOM OF EXPRESSION VS. FREEDOM OF RELIGION, 28th Session of the Human Rights Council – Item 3: *Report of the Special Rapporteur on Freedom of Religion or Belief* (11 March 2015)
- THE RESPONSIBILITY TO PROTECT CHRISTIANS AND OTHER COMMUNITIES, PARTICULARLY IN THE MIDDLE EAST, 28th Session of the Human Rights Council – Item 3: *Report of the Special Rapporteur on Freedom of Religion or Belief* (13 March 2015)

2 Respecting Human Dignity and Condemning Violence against the Human Person

- TOWARDS THE ELIMINATION OF EVERY FORM OF RACISM, 60th Session of the Commission on Human Rights – Item 6: *Racism, Racial Discrimination, Xenophobia and All Forms of Discrimination* (22 March 2004)
- THE FOCUS ON THE PERSON MUST NOT BE A JUSTIFICATION FOR INDIVIDUALISM, 7th Session of the Human Rights Council – *Intercultural Dialogue on Human Rights* (18 March 2008)
- INTERACTION AND INTEGRATION MUST PREVAIL OVER RADICAL ASSIMILATION OR SEPARATION, 7th Session of the Human Rights Council – Item 9: *Racism, Racial Discrimination, Xenophobia and Related Forms of Intolerance, Follow-Up and Implementation of the Durban Declaration and Programme of Action* (19 March 2008)
- A CHANGE OF HEARTS TOWARDS OPENNESS, FRATERNITY AND SOLIDARITY, Durban Review Conference (20–24 April 2009)
- STATES NEED TO RESPECT ALL PERSONS BUT ALSO NEED TO REGULATE SOME ASPECTS OF SEXUAL BEHAVIOR, 16th Session of the UN Human Rights Council – Item 8: *General Debate* (22 March 2011)
- VIOLENCE AGAINST WOMEN: A TRAGIC REALITY, 17th Session of the Human Rights Council – Item 3: Interactive Dialogue (3 June 2011)
- DISCRIMINATORY LAWS, PRACTICES AND ACTS OF VIOLENCE MOTIVATED BY SEXUAL ORIENTATION AND GENDER IDENTITY, 19th Session of the UN Human Rights Council – Item 3: *Panel Discussion on Discriminatory Laws and Practices and Acts of Violence against Individuals Based on their Sexual Orientation and Gender Identity* (7 March 2012)
- THERE SHOULD EXIST NO 'MAJORITY' OR 'MINORITY', 19th Session of the Human Rights Council: *Rights of Persons Belonging to National or Ethnic, Religious and Linguistic Minorities* (14 March 2012)

- WE MUST NOT TOLERATE DISCRIMINATION AND VIOLENCE AGAINST WOMEN, 20th Session of the Human Rights Council – Item 3: '*Special Rapporteur on Violence against Women*' (26 June 2012)
- SERVILE MARRIAGE, A CONTEMPORARY FORM OF SLAVERY, 21st Session of the Human Rights Council – Item 3: *Interactive Dialogue with the Special Rapporteur on Contemporary Forms of Slavery* (13 September 2012)
- WE MUST VALUE AND UPHOLD THE TRANSCENDENT DIGNITY OF ALL PERSONS, 24th Session of the Human Rights Council – Item 3: *Contemporary Forms of Slavery* (12 September 2013)
- THE RIGHTS OF RELIGIOUS MINORITIES: AN ESSENTIAL PRECONDITION TO PEACE AND STABILITY, 6th Session of the Forum on Minority Issues (26 November 2013)
- PRESENTATION OF THE INITIAL PERIODIC REPORT OF THE HOLY SEE TO THE COMMITTEE ON THE CONVENTION AGAINST TORTURE, Committee on the Convention against Torture (5 May 2014)
- PROMOTING FAITH AND SHARED HUMAN VALUES TO ERADICATE MODERN SLAVERY, 27th Session of the Human Rights Council – Item 3: *Special Rapporteur on Contemporary Forms of Slavery* (9 September 2014)
- MEN AND WOMEN: A COMPLEMENTARITY IN EQUALITY, 29th Session of the Human Rights Council: *Full-Day Discussion on the Human Rights of Women* (19 June 2015)
- THE EFFECTS OF TERRORISM ON THE ENJOYMENT BY ALL PERSONS OF HUMAN RIGHTS AND FUNDAMENTAL FREEDOMS, 29th Session of the Human Rights Council: *Panel on the Effects of Terrorism on the Enjoyment by All Persons of Human Rights and Fundamental Freedoms* (30 June 2015)

1 FREEDOM OF CONSCIENCE AND EXPRESSION OF RELIGIOUS BELIEF AS FUNDAMENTAL HUMAN RIGHTS

THE POSITIVE ROLE OF BELIEVERS IN PUBLIC LIFE*

Mr Chairman,

The place of religions in society, and their desire to participate in public life at the service of the people, have been part of recent debates that have been provoked by political events and an increased pluralism in many countries of the world. Religion is an important dimension in the lives of individuals and peoples, and it is natural that it should play an active role in the public arena. In fact, the Universal Declaration of Human Rights (Art. 18) promotes religious freedom: 'Everyone has the right to freedom of thought, conscience and religion; this right includes freedom to change his religion or belief, and freedom, either alone or in community with others and in public or private, to manifest his religion or belief in teaching, practice, worship and observance.' I find it here opportune to emphasize that the right to religious freedom includes both an individual and an institutional dimension. The respect for the institutional dimension of religious freedom is necessary so as to guarantee full recognition and promotion of the individual aspect of the same right.

Any follower of any religion has the right, with no prejudice to the security and legitimate authority of the State, to be respected in his/her convictions and practices, in the name of religious freedom, which is one of the fundamental aspects of the freedom of conscience and an effective contribution to the common good of society. The international juridical instruments – treaties and declarations – have constantly affirmed the value and importance of religious freedom and, at the same time, provided protection against discrimination for all religious believers so that they may freely profess their faith, according to their conscience, their symbols and their tradition. Unfortunately, religious freedom continues to be violated in several places and there is an added dimension today of non-State groups taking upon themselves the initiative to discriminate and even use violence against religious minorities, in many cases with

* Statement delivered at the 60th Session of the Commission on Human Rights – Item 11: Civil and Political Rights, Sub-item (e): Religious Intolerance, 1 April 2004.

impunity. Places of worship and cemeteries are burnt down or vandalized and desecrated; believers are threatened, attacked and even killed, and their leaders are made a special target of discrimination. The ability to choose one's religion, including the right to change it, meets with great obstacles in some social contexts in direct violation of the guaranteed freedom of conscience.

The role of the Commission on Human Rights remains timely and necessary in the defense of religious freedom. Since 1987, a Special Rapporteur on freedom of religion or belief has been calling attention to the unfulfilled provisions of the Declaration on the Elimination of All Forms of Intolerance and of Discrimination Based on Religion or Belief. Such a precious service deserves sincere appreciation and should certainly continue to ensure that human rights norms concerning religious freedom become recognized and practiced by Member States. After all, 'Religious freedom, an essential requirement of the dignity of every person, is a cornerstone of the structure of human rights and for this reason an irreplaceable factor in the good of individuals and of the whole society ... an essential element for peaceful human coexistence ... The civil and social right to religious freedom, inasmuch as it touches the most intimate sphere of the spirit, is a point of reference for the other fundamental rights and in some way becomes a measure of them' (Pope John Paul II, Message for the Twenty-first World Day of Peace, 'Religious Freedom: Condition for Peace', 8 December 1987, § 1). This right, therefore, not only should not be violated by anyone, but believers at risk of discrimination and attacks must be protected, have a fair access to justice, and, if victimized, they should be compensated.

An emerging subtle form of religious intolerance is opposing the right of religion to speak publicly on issues concerning forms of behavior that are measured against principles of a moral and religious nature. While respecting a healthy sense of the State's secular nature, the positive role of believers in public life should be recognized. This corresponds, among other things, to the demands of a healthy pluralism and contributes to the building up of authentic democracy. Religion cannot be relegated to a corner of the private sphere of life and in this way risk losing its social dimension and its charitable action toward vulnerable people it serves without any distinction.

On the contrary, all religions can make a unique contribution to a peaceful living together by rejecting the violent plans and means of some of their members who cover their destructive goals under the guise of religion and by opening instead the way for interreligious dialogue. In the present circumstances, the way forward for a future of peace is no doubt that of mutual knowledge and understanding, of constructive dialogue and cooperation in the cause of peace. To attain this objective, however, the implementation of the right to religious freedom and practice, both for individuals and communities of faith, has to become a universal reality. At the same time, in the education process, at all levels, respect for these rights needs to be acknowledged and communicated thereby building a culture of reciprocal respect and of a positive appreciation for diversity in an environment where all human rights can flourish.

RELIGIOUS FREEDOM: A TOUCHSTONE FOR THE OBSERVANCE OF THE OTHER FUNDAMENTAL RIGHTS*

Mr Chairperson,

The unswerving commitment to religious freedom and to the elimination of all forms of religious intolerance is an important priority for the Delegation of the Holy See. My Delegation shares such a preoccupation with this Commission and it supports a continued engagement in highlighting often invisible or underplayed abuses with only a faint echo in the international arena. Based on the very dignity of the human person, and not on a concession by the State, is the right that no men or women should be forced to act against their convictions nor restrained from acting in accordance with their convictions in religious matters in private or in public, alone or in association with others.[1] The reaffirmation of this basic human right and its universal application is both timely and needed. It not only reflects the often-stated position of the Holy See; it underscores the requirements of the Universal Declaration of Human Rights (Art. 18) and the International Covenant on Civil and Political Rights and of the other accepted instruments on the free exercise of religion in society like the Declaration on the Elimination of All Forms of Intolerance and Discrimination Based on Religion or Belief. In fact, there seems to emerge the risk of underestimating that 'the social nature of the human person requires that individuals give external expression to internal acts of religion, that they communicate with others on religious matters,' especially with their religious authorities, that they may choose to change religion, that they may promote institutions, freely appoint their own ministers, access property for their own needs, and similar activities, of course, without any infringement of the rights of others.

This fundamental human right must remain among the issues of concern to the world community since its violation continues and even deteriorates in some cases with regard to both Christians and other religious groups, especially if their situation is that of a minority, as the Special Rapporteurs on freedom of religion and belief and on contemporary forms of racism, racial discrimination, xenophobia and related intolerance

* Statement delivered at the 61st Session of the Human Rights Commission – Item 11: *Civil and Political Rights*, 1 April 2005.

[1] Second Vatican Ecumenical Council, Declaration on Religious Freedom.

have pointed out. A policy of non-engagement seems acceptable in some places when Christian and other religious minorities are threatened or outright persecuted and in this way the indivisibility of human rights is weakened. 'The right to freedom of religion', observes Pope John Paul II, ' is so closely linked to the other fundamental human rights that it can rightly be argued that respect for religious freedom, is, as it were, a touchstone for the observance of the other fundamental rights.'[2]

The respect for religious freedom is key to a peaceful and constructive coexistence. The process of globalization we witness brings about an increased pluralism even in societies that have remained isolated for centuries and the growing phenomenon of migrations brings religions in a closer contact among themselves through the concrete expression and the behavior of their adherents. Without mutual respect and the State's commitment to an impartial and active implementation of the right to religious freedom the potential for destructive conflicts and the loss of freedom for society become unfortunately quite predictable. Then, to counteract any homogenizing tendency of globalization, the search for community has intensified and often religion is a major component of this effort. Extreme forms of secularism that don't acknowledge a public role of religion become socially counterproductive.

Mr Chairperson, to old prejudices and discriminatory laws the right to freedom of religions and belief is confronted with new challenges like the open hostility and even death met by religious persons engaged in the defense of human rights and like the deficit on religious tolerance toward several communities of Christians brought about by the War on Terror. Renewed vigilance and discernment are called for. The serious application of the existing instruments on the right to religious freedom and belief and a continued monitoring will facilitate that 'religious freedom be everywhere provided with an effective constitutional guarantee, and that respect be shown for the high duty and right of man freely to lead his religious life in society'.[3] States, in fact, are primarily responsible for the respect of these rights. General education and interreligious dialogue, however, will go a long way in making everyone aware of the critical importance of mutual respect and appreciation, and this at a moment when some non-State actors colour their unacceptable violent actions with religious ideals. Monitoring of the right to religious freedom will

[2] Address of Pope John Paul II to the Members of the Diplomatic Corps, Rome, 9 January 1989, § 6.

[3] Second Vatican Ecumenical Council, *Dignitatis Umanae*, § 15.

be more effective if accurate data could be systematically collected and professionally analyzed.

In conclusion, Mr Chairperson, this Delegation is convinced that 'together with religious freedom, all other freedoms develop and thrive'. Freedom of thought, conscience and religion is a right provided for by international human rights norms for individuals, communities and their institutional structures, three inseparable dimensions. The full implementation of this right is the challenge ahead for all of us.

AVOID THE MISTAKES OF THE PAST: THE IMPERATIVE OF RELIGIOUS FREEDOM*

Twenty-five years ago, the international community adopted by consensus the important Declaration on the Elimination of All Forms of Intolerance and of Discrimination Based on Religion or Belief.[1]

Today the implementation of this Declaration remains in many ways still a distant goal, a work in progress requiring concerted action to promote the standards of religious freedom recognized by the international community. In several countries intolerance and violent acts directed in particular at people and communities of different religions violate their rights in a variety of ways.

The Delegation of the Holy See observes that legal structures have not everywhere sufficiently evolved to protect religious minorities and their members, even when they are citizens of the countries concerned.

The rapid impact of the information and communication technologies gives new meaning to the global village beyond its economic networks. A plurality of ideas and cultures are brought closer and are mingled even in remote corners of the world, and the vast movements of migrants make them visible and concrete in daily life. What emerges is either a potential for fears and conflicts, or a new phase of mutual enrichment and respect that afford the opportunity to convey the contributions of all to more justice and a stable peace. An attitude of openness and mutual acceptance is therefore more urgent than any law tending to impose them, the education of the heart and the mind to recognize and value each person as an equal member of the human family. Communication media and textbooks should contribute in this effort and not stir up emotions with ambiguous or false messages that foster intolerance and close the minds to a future of coexistence.

To build such a future, a deeper understanding is needed: (1) of the fundamental role and contribution of religion in the lives of individuals

* Statement delivered at the 2nd Session of the Human Rights Council, 21 September 2006.

[1] The dignity and equality inherent in all human beings, a basic principle of the Charter of the United Nations, were seen as fundamentally violated when the right to freedom of thought, conscience and religion a person held and exercised 'either individually or in community with others and in public or in private, to manifest his religion or belief in worship, observance, practice and teaching' (Art. I, 1) is disregarded.

and communities; (2) of the differences among religions so that an honest and fruitful dialogue may take place; (3) of current geopolitics since regional and religious identities do not necessarily coincide, and this calls for a correction of perceptions.

Religion and the reason for religious tolerance are rooted in the person, believer or not. Focusing on ideologies rather than on people and communities of believers carries the risk of transforming religious claims into political self-interest.

Mr President,

In conclusion, allow me to use the words of Pope Benedict XVI to Representatives of Muslim Communities last year: 'The lessons of the past must help us to avoid repeating the same mistakes. We must seek paths of reconciliation and learn to live with respect for each other's identities. The defense of religious freedom, in this sense, is a permanent imperative.'[2]

[2] Apostolic Trip of Pope Benedict XVI to Cologne (Germany) on the occasion of the XX World Youth Day (18–21 August 2005), Audience to the Representatives of Muslim Communities.

GUARANTEE SOCIAL COHESION THROUGH FREEDOM OF RELIGION*

Mr President,

In current debates, there is a widely felt perception that the international community is confronted with the difficult task to balance freedom of religion, freedom of expression, respect of religious and non-religious beliefs and convictions, defamation of religion and members of a religion. The Special Rapporteurs on freedom of religion or belief and on Contemporary forms of racism, racial discrimination, xenophobia and related intolerance have illustrated well this complexity. How can one find a way forward?

The development of the protection and promotion of all fundamental rights, begun with the Universal Declaration of Human Rights (1948), shows that religious freedom can serve as an element of synthesis, as a bridge, among the diverse categories of human rights. The profession of a religion in public or in private is in fact a freedom that belongs not only in the area of civil and political rights – and therefore linked to freedom of thought, of expression and worship – but also in that of economic, social and cultural rights. Such a linkage is evident in the power of self-organization of religions, in the charitable action of individual members of faith communities and in the forms of solidarity carried out by religious institutions, among others, in the fields of health, education and formation. Moreover, the presence and influence of the principal world religions have often been a means of transcending the subjective limitations of the positivist juridical order with objective moral norms that serve the common good of all humanity.

Acknowledging to religious freedom the role of guaranteeing the interrelation among the different fundamental rights, it means that public powers should work in such a way that the profession of a religion should not limit civil rights or political and institutional participation nor should it ever be used to deny economic, social and cultural rights to individuals or to communities.

The principles and the rules for the protection of fundamental rights, that also through the action of the Human Rights Council, and its efforts to provide fair procedures and mechanisms, are in a process of

* Statement delivered at the 6th Session of the Human Rights Council, 14 September 2007.

consolidation as patrimony of the international community and of the various countries, give evidence that there is no contrast between religious freedom and freedom of expression: both belong to those intellectual faculties proper to the human person, to his/her action in the public and private spheres.

The reflection of the Council is challenged to consider the demands that today call for regulating the religious phenomenon before cases of discrimination and of real defamation of religions and members of a religion. But such demands show that international action, together with the internal initiatives of States, is called to guarantee a just balance in the exercise of these two rights, recognizing that the freedom of expressing a religious creed, when authentic, assumes a public function: it contributes to social cohesion and therefore to the peaceful living together of all people, minorities and majority, believers and non-believers, within the same country.

Mr President, in conclusion, the appropriate social and political context within which to promote and protect all human rights, including the profession of a religion or changing or rejecting it, implies the acceptance that human rights are interrelated and that international standards should be translated into judicial and legal national provisions for the equal benefit, protection and freedom of every person.

Thank you, Mr President.

THE DENIGRATION OF RELIGIONS: AN OFFENSE TO PERSONAL AND SOCIAL JUSTICE*

Mr President,

The notable increase of interest in religion for its impact on the lives of individuals and of societies around the world is a phenomenon that finds – rightly so – an echo also in the Human Rights Council. Abuse of rights of believers, even outright violence against them, State restrictions, undue impositions and persecution, public insult to religious feelings, unfortunately persist and call for remedy. The Delegation of the Holy See appreciates and fully supports the openness of the new Council to uphold a universal vision of human rights protection. A major contribution of the Council is an approach that is inclusive and consistent with existing provisions in human rights instruments and declarations that clearly support, among other rights, freedom of religion, of expression, of conscience, of worship in private and in public, and respect of religious convictions for believers of all faiths and for non-believers alike.

The Holy See Delegation observes with preoccupation the emergence of an apparent dilemma between respect due to religions and the right to religious freedom as if they were incompatible and mutually exclusive aspects. On the contrary, they are complementary values that cannot stand one without the other. The religious dimension of the human person, his attitude before transcendence and the consequent ethical demands, make up a concrete and fundamental manifestation of his or her capacity of free auto-determination. It is a basic reference point of personal and social behavior. Religions can offer, and in fact do offer, a solid foundation for the defense of the values of personal and social justice, for respect of others and of nature.

In the course of history, there have been sad episodes of religious fanaticism with tragic social results. Yet religions are among those social factors that, together with science, have more contributed to the progress of humanity through the promotion of cultural, artistic, social and humanitarian values. Therefore, any religion that preaches or condones violence, intolerance and hatred renders itself unworthy of the name. On the other hand, we cannot avoid noticing that besides pseudo-religious fanaticism there is evidence on occasions of a certain

* Statement delivered at the 4th Session of the Human Rights Council, 22 March 2007.

antireligious fanaticism that denigrates religion or, generally, the faithful of a religion, by attributing to them responsibility for violent actions done today or in the past by some members of that religion. The legitimate criticism of certain forms of behavior of followers of a religion should not turn into insult or unjust defamation nor into offensive mockery of its revered persons, practices, rites or symbols. Respect of the rights and dignity of others should mark the limit of any right, even that of the free expression and manifestation of one's opinions, religious ones included.

Respect for the human person and his or her dignity implies respect of his freedom in religious matters to profess, practice and publicly manifest one's religion without being mocked, injured, discriminated against. Respect of religion means respect of those who have chosen to follow it and practice it in a free and pacific way, in private and in public, individually or collectively. Offense to a religion, especially when it is that of a minority, brings about some coercion against its followers that will make it more difficult to profess, practice and manifest this religion in public.

The subject of religion and the subject of freedom is always the human person, whose dignity is at the origin of fundamental rights. The respect of any religion is based in the end on the respect that is due to all those who, in the exercise of their freedom, follow and practice it. Of course, such respect cannot imply contempt or attacks on the rights of people who do not follow the same religion or follow other convictions. In this way, the issue of respect due to religions should find its explicit foundation in the rights of religious freedom and freedom of expression. Consequently, the promotion of respect for the rights of freedom of religion and freedom of expression should not leave aside the respect of concrete religions, beliefs and opinions in which such rights are realized. One cannot consider the ridicule of the sacred as a right of freedom. In the full respect of the right of expression, mechanisms or instruments need to be developed, coherent with the human rights provisions, that would defend the message of religious communities from manipulation and would avoid a disrespectful presentation of their members.

Mr President,

In conclusion, a really democratic state values religious freedom as a fundamental element of the common good, worthy of respect and protection, and creates the conditions that allow its citizens to live and act freely. If the discussion focuses only on religious tolerance and defamation of religion, it limits the range of rights and the contribution that religions offer. In fact, the impression could develop that religion is tolerated on the base of cultural, ethnic, political circumstances, that could change or even turn into forms of coercion, and is not recognized as a fundamental human right inherent in every human person. A comprehensive approach, that sees respect of religion rooted in the freedom that every human person is entitled to enjoy in a balance of rights with others and with society, appears as the reasonable way forward.

Thank you, Mr President.

TODAY'S MARTYRS: VIOLENCE AGAINST RELIGIOUS MINORITIES*

Mr President,

In recent weeks, and in several geographical regions, the international community has witnessed an intensified expression of religious intolerance that violates the basic human rights of persons of one or another faith conviction. Places of worship have been set on fire and desecrated. Thousands of people have been forcibly uprooted, and their homes have been destroyed, family members wounded, and even killed, simply because they profess their own religion. Others have been detained on false accusations. Impunity for these crimes, as is often the case, gives the message that violent aggression against, and even the physical elimination of, people from a different faith conviction is acceptable. Sixty years ago, a solemn commitment was undertaken by the global community, through the Universal Declaration of Human Rights, to uphold and defend the belief that everyone has 'the right to freedom of thought, conscience and religion'. This right includes freedom to change his religion or belief, and freedom, either alone or in community with others and in public or private, to manifest his religion or belief in teaching, practice, worship and observance (Art. 18). The road to implementation of such a right remains long and arduous.

The Delegation of the Holy See is deeply concerned about the targeting of religious minorities, already suffering from social and political prejudices, and stereotyping, for discriminatory and violent behavior. This Delegation thus fully supports the reaffirmation, by the Human Rights Council, of the right to freedom of religion, conscience, belief and religious practice, in private and in public. It concurs also with the advice of the Special Rapporteur on Contemporary Forms of Racism, Racial Discrimination, Xenophobia and Related Intolerance, offered to this Council, to refocus its reflection away from the vague sociological concept of 'defamation of religions' to the juridical norm of non-incitement to national, racial or religious hatred, and to the rights well summed up in the International Covenant on Civil and

* Statement delivered at the 9th Session of the Human Rights Council – Item 9: *Racism, Racial Discrimination, Xenophobia and Related Forms of Intolerance*, 19 September 2008.

Political Rights (ICCPR).[1] In any society, the journey toward achieving mutual understanding, and peaceful and constructive coexistence, cannot be an isolated venture. The structural and institutional form of a society must be addressed if effective change is to be achieved. Such responsibility cannot be relegated to rhetorical statements but should instead be articulated at all the levels of action that can be undertaken by a State: within national legislation, the judicial system, the government, the educational system, the media, and faith communities themselves. In the inevitable pluralism that globalization introduces in every society, such concerted effort will bring about positive results.

As shown in the various Reports on the question of religion and human rights, prepared within the United Nations system, there are some legitimate concerns that underlie the call to address the issue of defamation of religions in tangible terms, but this should be done in a holistic, constructive and cooperative way. Indeed, a possible way forward can be found in building upon the UDHR, the ICCPR and the Declaration on the Elimination of All Forms of Intolerance and of Discrimination based on Religion or Belief, which the General Assembly adopted in 1981. A juridical and positive approach will avoid harmful, unintended consequences for society, and for members of minority religions, brought about by religious defamation laws where they are in place. For example, in several cases, blasphemy laws have been used as weapons against personal enemies or as an excuse to incite mob violence. Such actions result in polarizing religious communities, rather than in promoting tolerance. The Declaration on the Elimination of All Forms of Intolerance and of Discrimination Based on Religion or Belief, and the instruments on which it is based, could serve as a framework for a new treaty, or as a framework for developing a declaration on guidelines, standards and good practices. Thus the international community could move along a

[1] Art. 18: '1. Everyone shall have the right to freedom of thought, conscience and religion. This right shall include freedom to have or to adopt a religion or belief of his choice, and freedom, either individually or in community with others and in public or private, to manifest his religion or belief in worship, observance, practice and teaching. 2. No one shall be subject to coercion which would impair his freedom to have or to adopt a religion or belief of his choice. 3. Freedom to manifest one's religion or beliefs may be subject only to such limitations as are prescribed by law and are necessary to protect public safety, order, health, or morals or the fundamental rights and freedoms of others. 4. The States Parties to the present Covenant undertake to have respect for the liberty of parents and, when applicable, legal guardians to ensure the religious and moral education of their children in conformity with their own convictions.'

reassuring path to build a more serene human family while simultaneously addressing some major challenges facing us today. These include the urgent need to promote religious tolerance; to end religious discrimination by both State and civil society actors; to promote the practice of 'reasonable accommodation' of religious practices; to increase the capacity of protection of people from group violence; and to increase the capacity of the judicial systems to give defendants prompt and fair trials.

Thank you, Mr President.

FREEDOM OF RELIGION IS THE BEST PROTECTION AGAINST VIOLATIONS*

Mr President,

In her latest Report, the Special Rapporteur on Freedom of Religion and Belief informed the Human Rights Council that she 'regularly receives reports of violation of the rights of members of religious minorities and vulnerable groups to carry out their religious activities'. In many parts of the world, religious minorities, including Christian minorities, still face daily discrimination and prejudice. The Holy See expresses its concern on the increasing situations of religious intolerance and calls upon States to take all the necessary measures – educational, legal and judicial – intended to guarantee the respect of the right to freedom of religion and to protect religious minorities from discrimination.

At its first ever meeting on 'intolerance and discrimination against Christians', the Organization for Security and Cooperation in Europe (OSCE) emphasized that the denial of the rights of Christian communities is not only an issue where they form a minority, but that discrimination and intolerance may also exist where Christians are a majority in society. It seems to my Delegation that a number of States, that previously were committed to a balanced and healthy relationship between Church and State, are now increasingly siding with a new secularist policy that aims at reducing the role of religion in public life. In this regard, the Holy See calls upon these States to be inclusive and to recognize the important role religions can play within society. Religions, in fact, contribute to the promotion of moral and social values, which go beyond an individualistic concept of society and development, seeking the common good as well as the protection and the respect of human dignity.

Mr President,

Last autumn the Office of the High Commissioner for Human Rights (OHCHR) organized an experts' seminar on articles 19 and 20 of the International Covenant on Civil and Political Rights (ICCPR) as a contribution to a clarifying debate on some possible areas of complementary standards.

* Statement delivered at the 10th Session of the Human Rights Council – Item 3: *General Debate*, 16 March 2009.

Though the question concerning limitations to the Right to Freedom of Expression with a view to respecting the religious feelings of persons is a legitimate one – many States have those limitations in their laws, including Western States – the Holy See does not think that another international instrument is the right answer. My Delegation is of the opinion that the implementation of the universal principle of freedom of religion is the best protection; that each State should look into its own national legislation and should consider how it can encourage a frank but respectful discussion between members of the same religion, between representatives of different religions and persons who have no religious belief. One should, however, at all times keep in mind that the right to religious freedom is intrinsically related to the right to freedom of expression. Where followers of religions have no right to express their opinion freely, the freedom of religion is not guaranteed. Where persons are not allowed to engage in an honest discussion on the merits and/or flaws of a religion, the right to the truth is denied and the right to choose or change his/her religion or belief is seriously hampered.

Thank you, Mr President.

MEDIA AND RELIGION: THREATS AND OPPORTUNITIES*

Mr President,

For some time now, the international community has been searching for a balanced normative approach to the fundamental human rights of freedom of religion and belief, freedom of expression, and respect for all persons holding religious or different convictions. Resolutions and declarations are moving toward effective provisions for international protection and reaffirmation of the importance of dialogue. Such efforts are being undertaken with the aims of preventing social conflicts and the disparagement of individuals and groups of believers and avoiding marginalization of, or violence against, these groups. However, such a negative perspective risks losing sight of the critical importance of the positive aspects of religious freedom. Such freedom implies the protection of every person's right to choose, to profess and to disseminate individually, and in community, a belief according to his/her conscience, as stated in the Universal Declaration of Human Rights and in the other Human Rights instruments, with the corresponding obligation of States to protect this fundamental human right by means of an appropriate legal framework. The Delegation of the Holy See is of the opinion that the last report of the Special Rapporteur on Contemporary forms of racism, racial discrimination, xenophobia and related intolerance has taken a more positive approach to the issue. The questions of religious discrimination and incitement to religious hatred, and the sociological concept of 'Defamation of Religions', issues addressed in the latest Report, are better contextualized. The Rapporteur recommends anchoring the debate in the existing international legal framework, adding that in matters of belief rights, the human person should not be separated from her social relationship. 'The rights associated with religion are all the more in need of protection if they are considered to clash with a prevailing secular ideology or with majority religious positions of an exclusive nature. The full guarantee of religious liberty cannot be limited to the free exercise of worship, but has to give due consideration to the public dimension of religion, and hence

* Statement delivered at the 12th Session of the Human Rights Council – Item 9: *Racism, Racial Discrimination, Xenophobia and Related Forms of Intolerance*, 30 September 2009.

to the possibility of believers playing their part in building the social order.'[1]

The Delegation of the Holy See agrees, therefore, with the Special Rapporteur that only an integrated approach based on the full respect of the right to freedom of religion can be the answer in combating the old and new phenomenon of discrimination on the basis of religious conviction and practice. Aware that the increasing manifestations of religious intolerance are undermining the rights of all persons of any religion and belief and that practically all religious minorities are discriminated against around the world, my Delegation is convinced that a concerted solution is necessary. The consensus reached in the Durban Review Conference, for example, represents a fine balance between reaffirming the importance of freedom of expression and the need to curb hate speech. Particularly in this area that touches on deep emotions and on a personal and collective sense of identity, laws are not enough. A new outlook is required, one that takes into account the increased pluralism in most societies and the interconnectedness of a globalized world. Modern technology (especially through the means of social communication) can be an effective resource and can contribute to a clearer awareness of one's dignity and human rights. Thus the convergence of freedom of expression and the means of social communication is fundamentally positive. It is only a question of choice. Media can be used either to build and sustain the human community in all its economic, political, cultural, educational and religious aspects to the enrichment of people's well-being and spirituality or to injure the integral good of the person, to incite hatred, to marginalize and alienate people and to stereotype them based on race and ethnicity, sex, age and also religion. Indeed, in the relationship between the means of social communication and religion there are temptations on both sides. Media often ignore and marginalize religious doctrine, ideas, practices and experiences, and sentiments of religious persons are belittled and religion is judged by secular standards. Such a perspective can result in hostile treatment of legitimate religious groups. On the other hand, religion may negatively judge communication media and encourage religious exclusivism that foments disregard and hostility toward others.

[1] Address of Pope Benedict XVI at the Meeting with the Members of the General Assembly of the United Nations Organization, New York, 18 April 2008.

Freedom of expression is not only a right but also a duty that needs to be strengthened. The presumption should always be in favour of the possibility to exchange ideas and articulate opinions. Protecting the freedom of expression, however, is not an absolute obligation; normally it should be upheld for the good of society and also for the enjoyment of the freedom of religion and belief. But any form of incitement to hatred that affects the human person and his/her rights is unacceptable. When people are performing the social duty and right to inform, they are called to take into account principles of social ethics such as truth, solidarity, tolerance, fairness, principles that form the cornerstone of justice, equity, respect for privacy, subsidiarity. Media too should remain at the service of the person. It may be useful to underline in this context that the integral development of persons and their good cannot be realized apart from the common good of communities to which they belong. The common good, of which human rights are the grammar, should be understood as inclusive of the full range of physical, intellectual, emotional and spiritual goods. Thus, the person's innate social nature and religious feelings deserve the opportunity to grow and to be protected from abuse. Then, if the new technologies are to serve the good of individuals and of society, all users will avoid the sharing of words and images that are degrading of human beings, that promote hatred and intolerance, that exploit the vulnerable.

At this juncture, therefore, it is better to avoid a negative and limiting approach and insist rather on the positive aspects of the fundamental right to freedom of religion. The wise use of media and of educational systems and textbooks can teach mutual respect and appreciation. Moreover, initiatives of dialogue and efforts like that of the High Commissioner for Human Rights to attain a better understanding of Articles 19 and 20 of the ICCPR in the international law framework can go a long way toward promoting mutual understanding, sustaining freedom of religion, belief and conscience, and to preventing their disrespect. Civil authorities should contribute their part by guaranteeing the right to criticize the work of the media and by facilitating the participation of all, especially of ethnic groups and religious minorities, in the decision-making of communication policies.

In conclusion, Mr President, the road ahead points in the direction of comprehensive implementation of existing norms to protect freedom of religion and belief, of wise use of the freedom of expression, of greater sensitivity to the right to express religious convictions and, consequently, to demonstrate religious identity, both as an individual and in a group, in private and in public, in the common search for truth and peaceful coexistence. In this way, people come first since human rights belong to them and their communities rather than to abstract ideas, institutions or physical territories. In the same way, equality of treatment is preserved by protecting religious minorities from discriminatory legislation and practices. In the new digital arena, much can be achieved by encountering and knowing the traditions and values of each other, by creating a new mentality of understanding and respect, and by searching together for truth, goodness and beauty.

AN URGENT NEED TO DELINEATE A POSITIVE AND OPEN SECULARITY*

Mr President,

Three weeks ago, the Pontifical Council for Interreligious Dialogue and the permanent Committee of al-Azhar University for Dialogue among the Monotheistic Religions held the annual meeting of their Joint Committee for Dialogue in Cairo (23–24 February). In their joint declaration, the participants recommended paying 'greater attention to the fact that the manipulation of religion for political or other ends can be a source of violence', and avoiding 'discrimination on the basis of religious identity'.

Mr President, in a number of countries freedom of religion is not yet fully guaranteed. Recent surveys indicate that nearly 70 per cent of the world's 6.8 billion people live in countries with high restrictions on religion, the brunt of which often falls on religious minorities. The latter's rights are seriously violated, their freedom of worship hampered. In some regions followers of minority religions, that are not recognized by law, have to confess their faith in hiding and illegally, in fear of prison terms and persecution. In other places, while the right to freedom of religion is legally recognized, religious minorities are harassed and persecuted by members of the majority religion. Their properties are damaged, their houses of worship are destroyed, their lives severely threatened. These criminal acts are often committed with total impunity. Authorities stand idly by or are partisans in the conflict. Victims are forced to desist from reporting the injustice done to them for fear of further negative repercussions. Perpetrators harassing religious minorities feel encouraged by the silent collusion of State authorities and by a judicial system that is ineffective or partial. The limitation clauses in international instruments should not be used in a disproportionate manner to strike at the rights of religious and ethnic minorities and political opponents but only to protect and promote the human rights of all.

The Holy See calls therefore upon States to respect and promote the right to freedom of religion in all its aspects, through national legislation, including appropriate sanctions against violators to eradicate impunity effectively.

* Statement delivered at the 13th Session of the Human Rights Council – Item 3: *General Debate*, 12 March 2010.

Mr President, victims of discrimination and violent attacks have a right to obtain redress and compensation for the harm done to them by public or private agents. The State has the responsibility of protecting the fundamental human rights of all people in its territory. In order to obtain just redress, standard and objective methods should be laid down in national legislation for working out retribution and relief measures. As long as the State is not able or willing to provide effective legal protection for all its citizens, the continuous persecution of ethnic and religious minority communities will continue to afflict the world and to weaken the human rights of everyone.

Mr President, in his address to the members of the Diplomatic Corps last January, His Holiness Pope Benedict XVI underlined that 'sadly, in certain countries … one increasingly encounters in political and cultural circles, as well as in the media, scarce respect and at times hostility, if not scorn, directed towards religion … It is clear that if relativism is considered an essential element of democracy, one risks viewing secularity solely in the sense of excluding or, more precisely, denying the social importance of religion. But such an approach creates confrontation and division, disturbs peace, harms human ecology and, by rejecting in principle approaches other than its own, finishes in a dead end. There is thus an urgent need to delineate a positive and open secularity which, grounded in the just autonomy of the temporal order and the spiritual order, can foster healthy cooperation and a spirit of shared responsibility.'

Mr President, the way forward rests on an effective implementation of all human rights by recognizing and respecting the dignity of each human being, without distinction of ethnicity or religion; on rejection of all forms of discrimination on the ground of race, colour, sex or religion; on fair treatment in the courts; on an educational system that teaches peaceful coexistence built on mutual respect, solidarity and cooperation as means that promote a healthy social pluralism and a prosperous life for all members of our one human family.

Thank you, Mr President.

THE IMPORTANCE OF A POSITIVE INTERFAITH DIALOGUE*

Mr President,

Increasing instances of ridiculing religion, of lack of respect for religious personalities and symbols, of discrimination and killings of followers of minority religions, and a generalized negative consideration of religion in the public arena damage peaceful coexistence and hurt the feelings of considerable segments of the human family. These occurrences raise political and juridical questions regarding the way and the extent to which the implementation of human rights, and specifically the right to religious freedom, should protect people in their personal and collective exercise of faith and convictions. The protection of the right to religious freedom is particularly important since religious values are a bridge for and to all human rights; they allow the person to orient himself or herself to what is true and real. Human dignity, in fact, is rooted in the unity of the spiritual and material components of the person.

Belonging to a community, culture and religion is also part of the human experience – although these remain at the service of the integral development of the person – that constitutes the base of the universality of human rights. The legitimate concern, therefore, to prevent derision or insult to religions will have to take into account the interdependence – which comes from the natural relationship of the human person to others – between the individual and the community. Since belief systems are diverse and even in contrast among themselves, the justification for their respect will have to come from a universal foundation that is the human person. The obligations of society will derive accordingly. The UDHR and other human rights instruments provide a clear direction.

Pertinent legislation, therefore, should be oriented to achieve the common good and should be based on values, principles and rules that reflect human nature and are part of the conscience of the human family rather than on one or the other religion, while taking into account the full implications of freedom of expression and religion. The respect of everyone's right to religious freedom does not require the complete secularization of the public sphere or the abandonment of all cultural traditions nor does the respect of freedom of expression authorize lack

* Statement delivered at the 13th Session of the Human Rights Council – Item 9: *Racism, Racial Discrimination, Xenophobia and Related Forms of Intolerance, Follow-Up and Implementation of the Durban Declaration and Programme of Action*, 23 March 2010.

of respect for the values commonly shared by a particular society. A legislative framework that protects the common good and the equality of citizens in increasingly pluralistic societies implies that the normative systems applicable to believers must not be imposed on followers of other religions and on non-believers, otherwise human rights and the right to religious freedom can become a political tool for discrimination rather than a tool for ethical interpersonal relations. Nor can the State become an arbiter of religious correctness by deciding on theological or doctrinal issues: it would be the denial of the right to freedom of religion.

Present binding international and national juridical instruments, if properly applied, can remedy the gratuitous offenses to religions and belief through the enactment of measures that safeguard the common good and public order. Current debates on the convenience or inconvenience of new instruments to prevent discrimination and religious intolerance may offer the opportunity to revisit the proposal for a convention on freedom of religion. This task was left unfinished many years ago and it would bring together the arguments prompted by the new forms of societal pluralism and a more accurate understanding of human dignity.

The Delegation of the Holy See, on the other hand, is also convinced that a good road leading to peaceful coexistence is a more positive attitude towards religions and cultures. This can be achieved through an improved dialogue between the different faiths, a sincere promotion of the right to freedom of religion in all its aspects, and a frank and open discussion between representatives of the different belief-systems, as guaranteed by the right to freedom of expression.

Combating offensive attitudes towards religion by moving away from the universality provided by our common humanity and relying on the discretion of the State by introducing a vague concept of 'defamation' into the human rights system, do not support an effective and satisfactory solution. There is the additional real risk that the interpretation of what defamation entails may change according to the censor's attitude towards religion or belief, often at the tragic expense of minorities. This unfortunately is the case in those States that do not distinguish between civil and religious matters and identify with a particular religion, or with a certain sect within that religion, and interpret defamation according to the convictions of the religion or beliefs they adhere to, thus inevitably discriminating against those citizens who do not share the same convictions. The experience with national legislations that apply such concepts as 'defamation of religion' suggests that a possible international instrument on defamation of religion will only lead to further oppression of religious minorities, as can be verified in those countries.

Mr President, in conclusion, the Holy See calls upon the member-countries of this respected Council to transform these unfortunate incidents of religious intolerance and the culture that underlies them into an opportunity for a new engagement to dialogue and for the reaffirmation of the right and value of belonging to a community of faith or belief. Such individual choice, however, as the expression of personal fundamental human rights, always has to be exercised in the context of the common good.

RELIGION MUST NOT BE A CRITERION FOR DISCRIMINATION*

Mr President,

Religion has taken up greater visibility in the public arena in recent years. A widely spread anti-religious attitude, however, favors some manifestations linked to discrimination and prejudice, as the Special Rapporteur on contemporary forms of racism, racial discrimination, xenophobia and related intolerance has documented, and this raises complex questions of human rights. My Delegation would like to clarify the interplay and the contradiction between abstract claims and real violations of rights that appear in several instances of public discourse about religion.

The free expression of general or personal considerations in terms of public debate, or of cultural, philosophical and theological dialogue, cannot be regarded *tout court* as a form of defamation of religions, or as forms of incitement to hatred against a religion or a community of believers. Freedom of thought and expression, including freedom to criticize, when exercised within the limits of accuracy, fairness, respect, public morality and order, can be considered a gain of civilization to be protected as a common political and juridical patrimony of humanity, not only as a prerogative of a particular social context or a particular cultural tradition. The development and self-realization of the human person entails, as an essential component, the expression and sharing of her vision of reality. To deny this right would mortify one of the deepest aspirations of the human person and a key factor for the progress of all civilizations.

We must also distinguish the theoretical level, namely the abstract level of values and of philosophical or religious principles, from the existential level, i.e. the practical level where these values and principles affect individuals and communities of human beings. The focus of human rights should be on the human person and human communities. The State of law and human rights have as a mandate the protection and promotion of the dignity and fundamental rights and freedoms of individuals and communities of persons. The systems of values and principles, shared by individuals and communities of persons, are something good, also in the perspective of politics and law, but always if functional to the protection of individuals and communities of persons, not vice versa.

* Statement delivered at the 15th Session of the Human Rights Council – Item 9: 28 September 2010.

Respect for people and communities of persons then is not fulfilled by a mere 'preservation' or formal 'immunization' from criticism of the systems of values and principles, but by a substantive promotion and affirmation of fundamental rights and freedoms. Thus freedom of expression, including freedom to criticize, does not deny the rights of persons or communities of persons. It is rather an element of the rule of law which includes freedom of religion and belief, and the prohibition of discrimination based on religion or belief. In this context, attention should focus on the people and communities of persons to see how their rights are protected *de facto*, beyond the preservation of a given system of values or principles, cultural or religious, whether majority or minority.

The positions of extreme individualism and collectivism offer a partial view of the human person: the first leads her to isolation, the second cancels and absorbs her into the abstract idea of a social or ideological collectivity. These two perspectives do not allow for dialogue, rather make it impossible, because both counter the reality of human nature. The human being has its own uniqueness and originality but is open by nature to relationships with others. Only in these relationships is he fulfilled as a person. As the great civilizations of the world teach, the human person is a 'social being' that is fully realized only in the community, starting with the family up to all levels of society and thus to the national and international dimensions. In coherence with nature and human dignity, the community is not a limit to freedom and realization; on the contrary, it is the living space from which the person realizes and expresses her freedom, in which the person pursues her material, ethical and spiritual development, and in turn contributes to the development of the communities she belongs to, and ultimately to the entire human society.

When the social and communitarian dimension is denied, an essential component of the person is mortified and mutilated. History teaches us and documents the negative consequences when this aspect of the person is kept away or denied by ideology. When ideology reconstructs the human being as an abstraction, the dignity and human rights of the real person are radically violated and emptied of content from the inside. The road to the future, even in its religious dimension, passes through the understanding of the person and her natural vocation toward community, therefore through the full protection and full affirmation of human rights in their twofold and inseparable individual and communitarian dimensions.

The main responsibility of the State is the protection of its citizens and all persons, especially those under its jurisdiction. State laws must protect concrete persons even in their community requirements that are inseparable from the person. In the current debate levels are often confused so that ideologies are defended and the persons and communities of persons sometimes are not adequately protected. National legislation must be effective in protecting the rights of all persons within its jurisdiction. This implies that in the educational system, in the judicial system, in political participation, in access to employment, in a word, that in the civil and political society, religion must not be a reason for discrimination. 'Religion, in other words, is not a problem for legislators to solve, but a vital contributor to the national conversation.'[1] True defamation of a religion is when it is manipulated and transformed into an ideology of discrimination against concrete persons and communities of persons.

Mr President,

In conclusion, new forms of dialogue and education should be found to identify and promote shared values and universal principles, consistent with the dignity and social nature of the human person, directed to the common good and at building a society in which there is a concrete space for the rights and fundamental freedoms of persons and communities of persons. 'There are many areas in which the Church (all religions) and the public authorities can work together for the good of citizens … '[2] My Delegation agrees with that recommendation of the Special Rapporteur on contemporary forms of racism, racial discrimination, xenophobia and related intolerance, according to which we have to anchor the debate in the relevant existing international legal framework and thus ensure a peaceful future for all.

Thank you, Mr President

[1] Pope Benedict XVI, Address in Westminster Hall, 18 September 2010.
[2] Ibid.

RELIGIOUS FREEDOM AS A FUNDAMENTAL PATH TO PEACE*

Mr President,

At the heart of fundamental human rights is freedom of religion, conscience and belief: it affects personal identity and basic choices and it makes possible the enjoyment of other human rights. As the UN Declaration on the Elimination of Religious Discrimination recognises, the spiritual dimension of life is a vital part of human existence.[1] But an increased proliferation of episodes of discrimination and acts of violence against persons and communities of faith and places of worship in several different geographical regions of the world denies in practice the principle proclaimed in law. Religious strife is a danger to social, political and economic development. Religious conflict polarizes society, breaking the bonds necessary for social life and commerce to flourish. It produces violence, which robs people of the most fundamental right of all, the right to life. And it shows that seeds of distrust and bitterness that can be passed down through the generations. Often impunity and media neglect to follow such tragedies. A recent survey shows that out of 100 people killed because of religious hatred, 75 are Christian.[2] That concentration of religious discrimination should cause concern to all of us. But the Holy See's purpose in this intervention is to reaffirm the importance of the right to freedom of religion for *all* individuals, for *all* communities of faith, and for *every* society, in all parts of the world.

The State has the duty to defend the right to freedom of religion and it has therefore the responsibility to create an environment where this right can be enjoyed. As stated in the Declaration on Religious Discrimination and elsewhere, the State has to fulfil several duties in the everyday functioning of society. For example, the State must not practice

* Statement delivered at the 16th Session of the Human Rights Council – General Segment, 2 March 2011.

1 Declaration on the Elimination of All Forms of Intolerance and of Discrimination Based on Religion or Belief, General Assembly Resolution 36/55 (1981); e.g. fourth preambular para.

2 Cf. Aid to the Church in Need, Religious Freedom in the World – Report 2010; Conference, 'Persecution of Christians', organized by the Commission of the Bishops' Conferences of the European Community, the European Parliamentary Groups of the European People's Party and the European Conservatives and Reformists' Group on 10 October 2011.

religious discrimination – in its laws, in its policies, or by allowing *de facto* discrimination by public employees. It must promote religious tolerance and understanding throughout society, a goal that can be achieved if educational systems teach respect for all and judicial systems are impartial in the implementation of laws and reject political pressure aimed at ensuring impunity for perpetrators of human rights crimes against followers of a particular religion. The State should support all initiatives aimed at promoting dialogue and mutual respect between religious communities. It must enforce its laws that fight against religious discrimination vigorously, and without selectivity. The State must provide physical security to religious communities under attack. It must encourage majority populations to enable religious minorities to practice their faith individually and in community without threat or hindrance. The State must have laws that require employers to make 'reasonable accommodations' for an employee's religion.

Freedom of religion is a value for society as a whole. The State that protects this right enables society to benefit from the social consequences that come with it: peaceful coexistence, national integration in today's pluralistic situations, increased creativity as the talents of everyone are placed at the service of the common good. On the other hand, the negation of religious freedom undermines any democratic aspiration, favours oppression, and stifles the whole society that eventually explodes with tragic results. From this angle, as well, it is clear that freedom of religion and conviction is complementary and intrinsically linked to freedom of opinion, expression and assembly. Besides, an environment of real freedom of religion becomes the best medicine to prevent the manipulation of religion for political purposes of power grabbing and power maintenance and for the oppression of dissenters and of different faith communities or religious minorities. In fact, religious discrimination and strife are rarely, if ever, solely the product of differences in religious opinions and practices. Below the surface are social and political problems.

To reap the social benefits of religious freedom, specific measures need to be devised that allow the practical exercise of this right to flourish. Mr President, I would like to highlight some measures at the UN level. The Special Rapporteur on freedom of religion could be invited regularly to include information on persecution of religious groups. It would be helpful if the Office of the UN High Commissioner for Human Rights were to monitor the situation of governmental and societal restrictions on religious freedom and report annually to the Human Rights Council.

Article 20 of the Covenant on Civil and Political Rights,[3] which pertains to advocacy of religious hatred that incites religious discrimination, raises important questions, such as the relation between various rights, and about the best ways to achieve legitimate aims. Blasphemy laws are a case in point. The workshops mandated to study Article 20, and to propose good practices, are a step in the right direction.

I will conclude, Mr President, by calling attention to three false perceptions surrounding freedom of religion and belief. In the first place, the right to express or practice one's religion is not limited to acts of worship. It also includes the right to express one's faith through acts of charitable and social service. For example, providing health and education through religious institutions are important ways for people to live their faith.[4] Second, faith communities have their own rules for qualifications for religious office, and for serving in religious institutions, including charitable facilities. These religious institutions are part of civil society, and not branches of the state. Consequently, the limits that international human rights law places on States regarding qualifications on state office holding and public service do not apply automatically to non-State actors. As acknowledged by the Declaration on Religious Discrimination, freedom of religion entails the right of a religious community to set its own qualifications.[5] Religious tolerance includes respecting differences of opinions in these matters, and respecting the difference between a state and a religious institution. And, finally, there is a fear that respecting the freedom to choose and practice another religion, different from one's own, is based on a premise that all truth is relative and that one's religion is no longer absolutely valid. That is a misunderstanding. The right to adopt, and to change, a religion is based on respect for human dignity: the State must allow each person to freely search for the truth.

Mr President, the State has an ethical and legal obligation to uphold and make applicable the right to freedom of religion or conviction both because it is a fundamental human right and because it is its duty to defend the rights of its citizens and to seek the welfare of

[3] Art. 20: '1. Any propaganda for war shall be prohibited by law. 2, Any advocacy of national, racial or religious hatred that constitutes incitement to discrimination, hostility or violence shall be prohibited by law.'

[4] See, for example, Art. 6(b), Declaration on the Elimination of All Forms of Intolerance and of Discrimination Based on Religion or Belief.

[5] Art. 6(g), Declaration on the Elimination of All Forms of Intolerance and of Discrimination Based on Religion or Belief.

society. As His Holiness Pope Benedict XVI stated in addressing the diplomatic corps, religious freedom is 'the fundamental path to peace. Peace is built and preserved only when human beings can freely seek and serve God in their hearts, in their lives and in their relationships with others.'[6]

6 Address of Pope Benedict XVI to the Members of the Diplomatic Corps, 10 January 2011.

FREEDOM OF RELIGION IN THE FIELD OF EDUCATION*

Mr President,

The Special Rapporteur on freedom of religion or belief has addressed a very crucial and timely theme, the human right of freedom of religion in the context of and in relation to education. Modern States are built up, stand and develop, inter alia, on the pillars of education, health and social assistance. Besides, education seems to be an area that reacts with greater sensibility to cultural and demographic transformations that occur in society. At the same time, the transmission to new generations of a religion is a social enrichment worthy of preservation. Therefore the well-recognized right of parents to decide the type of religious education their children should receive takes precedence over any open or indirect imposition by the State. As Article 5.2 of the Declaration on the Elimination of All Forms of Intolerance and Discrimination Based on Religion or Belief unequivocally states: 'Every child shall enjoy the right to have access to education in the matter of religion or belief in accordance with the wishes of his parents, or, as the case may be, legal guardians, and shall not be compelled to receive teaching on religion or belief against the wishes of his parents or legal guardians, the best interest of the child being the guiding principle.' Similar language is in Article 18.4 of the International Covenant on Civil and Political Rights, as the Special Rapporteur has rightly underlined.

Education and freedom of religion or belief constitute a vast area of concern. The inter-relationship between the two is an evolving experiment in many ways, but fundamental rights cannot be transgressed: those relating to parents and those relating to believers themselves acting in community. On the other hand, while people should have the right to profess their religious ideas freely, this should be done within the limits imposed by the common good and a just public order, and, in every case, in a manner characterized by responsibility (*Compendium of the Social Doctrine of the Church*, 2004). The challenge of balancing rights of equal value is particularly obvious in preventing discrimination. The duty to guarantee an equal protection of rights should not be tainted by ideological positions that would consider a particular belief as intolerant while accepting that the State could force a religion to adopt a doctrine or

* Statement delivered at the 16th Session of the Human Rights Council – Item 3: *Interactive Dialogue*, 10 March 2011.

behavior that is against its own convictions. In this sense, public instruction should not treat the subject of religion in a way that leads to the rejection of the parents' preference and the advancement of an alternative set of beliefs. Finally, the assumption that a faith must change over time needs a cautious approach. While certain historical conditionings can be adapted to new circumstances, one has to avoid any form of relativism, on the one hand, and, on the other, undue interference in the internal life of faith communities that would violate the fundamental human right of freedom of religion.

In conclusion, Mr President, education and freedom of religion can reinforce each other. A fair presentation of different beliefs can prevent the stereotyping of other people's convictions, can open to dialogue and to respect of the inalienable dignity of every student, of every believer and of every person.

Thank you, Mr President.

RELIGIONS ARE A RESOURCE, NOT A THREAT!*

Madam President,

The implementation of human rights is a difficult challenge today, particularly with regard to the fundamental and inalienable right of every person to 'freedom of thought, conscience and religion or belief.' Among other elements, the evolving political situation, wrong perceptions of the role of religion, expediency and subtle ambiguities in the understanding of secularism lead to intolerance and even outright persecution of people because of their faith or religion. The freedom to manifest one's religion or belief in teaching, practice, worship and observance, which is guaranteed by human rights law and international instruments, is disregarded in several places in the world. Such stifling policies and practices place at risk the contribution of many citizens to social life and progress in their respective countries. The Holy See appreciates the regular attention of the Human Rights Council to this major issue as well as the related efforts and decisions taken by Special Procedures.

In many countries, however, the gap is growing between widely accepted stated principles, and their daily application on the ground. Serious research provides reliable data on current and repetitive patterns of gross violations of the right to freedom of religion. Christians are not the only victims, but terrorist attacks on Christians in Africa, the Middle East and Asia increased 309 per cent between 2003 and 2010. Approximately 70 per cent of the world's population lives in countries with high restrictions on religious beliefs and practices, and religious minorities pay the highest price. In general, rising restrictions on religion affect more than 2.2 billion people. The affected people either have lost the protection of their societies or have experienced some government-imposed and unjust restrictions, or have become victims of violence resulting from an impulsive bigotry.[1] The evidence shows that additional efforts are required from the international community in order to assure the protection of people in their exercise of freedom of religion and religious practice. Such actions are urgently required since in several countries the

* Statement delivered at the 19th Session of the Human Rights Council – High-Level Segment, 1 March 2012.

1 Ayaan Hirsi Ali, 'The War on Christians', *Newsweek*, 13 February 2012, p. 30 Cf. www.pewforum.org/Government/Rising-Restrictions-on-Religion.aspx. Also, Portes Ouvertes France, *Index Mondial de Persécution des Chrétiens*, 2011.

situation is worsening and since the factual reporting of such violations is underplayed, despite the fact, it should be highlighted in the pertinent Reports.

The Universal Declaration of Human Rights points to respect for the human dignity of all people as the foundation on which the protection of human rights is built. In the present circumstances, it is worth recalling that States should ensure that all their citizens have the right to enjoy freedom of religion individually, within the family, and as a community, and to participate in the public forum. Religious freedom, in fact, is not a derived right, or one granted, but a fundamental and inalienable right of the human person. A religious belief should not be perceived or considered as harmful or offensive simply because it is different from that of the majority. The task of the government is not to define religion or recognize its value, but to confer upon faith communities a juridical personality so that they can function peacefully within a legal framework. Respect for the religious freedom of everyone may be at stake in places where the concept of 'State religion' is recognized, especially when the latter becomes the source of unjust treatment of others, whether they believe in other faiths or have none.

Above the institutional considerations, the critical problem facing the promotion and protection of human rights in the area of religious freedom is the intolerance that leads to violence and to the killing of many innocent people each year simply because of their religious convictions. The realistic and collective responsibility, therefore, is to sustain mutual tolerance and respect of human rights and a greater equality among citizens of different religions in order to achieve a healthy democracy where the public role of religion and the distinction between religious and temporal spheres are recognized. In practical life, when managed in the context of mutual acceptance, the relations between majority and minority allow for cooperation and compromise and open the way for peaceful and constructive coexistence. But to achieve this desirable goal, there is a need to overcome a culture that devalues the human person and is intent on eliminating religion from the public life. Pope Benedict XVI has clearly described this situation when he writes: 'Sadly, in certain countries, mainly in the West, one increasingly encounters in political and cultural circles, as well in the media, scarce respect and at times hostility, if not scorn, directed towards religion and towards Christianity in particular. It is clear that if relativism is considered an essential element of democracy, one risks viewing secularity solely in the sense of excluding or, more precisely, denying the social importance of religion. But such an approach creates confrontation and division, disturbs peace, harms human ecology and, by rejecting in principle approaches other than its own, finishes in a dead end. There is thus an urgent need to delineate a positive and open secularity which, grounded in the just autonomy of the temporal order and the spiritual order, can foster healthy cooperation and a spirit of shared responsibility.'[2]

Madam President,

Religions are not a threat, but a resource. They contribute to the development of civilizations, and this is good for everyone. Their activities and freedom should be protected so that the partnership between religious beliefs and societies may enhance the common good. A culture of tolerance, mutual acceptance and dialogue is urgent. The educational system and the media have a major role to play by excluding prejudice and hatred from textbooks, from newscasts and from newspapers, and by disseminating accurate and fair information on all component groups of society. But lack of education and information, that facilitates an easier manipulation of people for political advantages, is too often linked to underdevelopment, poverty, lack of access to effective participation in the management of society. Greater social justice provides fertile ground for the implementation of all human rights. Religions are communities based on convictions and their freedom guarantees a contribution of moral values without which the freedom of everyone is not possible. For this reason, it becomes an urgent and beneficial responsibility of the international community to counteract the trend of increasing violence against religious groups and of a mistaken and deceptive neutrality that in fact aims at neutralizing religion.

Thank you, Madam President.

[2] Address of Pope Benedict XVI to the Members of the Diplomatic Corps for the Traditional Exchange of New Year Greetings, 11 January 2010.

IT SHOULD NEVER BE NECESSARY TO DENY GOD TO ENJOY ONE'S RIGHTS*

Madam President,

With deep concern, the Holy See Delegation calls attention to the widening gap between the commitment and the stated principles of the international community regarding freedom of religion, conscience and belief and the right to freedom of assembly, and the implementation of these fundamental human rights. The use of bombs and violent attacks against houses of worship and Christian communities at prayer have recently killed hundreds of innocent people in several countries. The persistence of such crimes and their geographical spread, the support in personnel and resources that fundamentalist groups provide them, their objective of destabilization of peaceful coexistence in mutual respect and collaboration, are as many reasons that should prompt a more effective response in terms both of public awareness and of preventive action.

Religious strife is a danger to social, political and economic development. Religious conflict in a polarized society breaks the ties that are necessary for social life and commerce to flourish. It produces violence which robs people of the most fundamental right of all: the right to life. It sows the seeds of distrust and bitterness that can be passed down through generations. Strife in one country can spill over and cause serious difficulties in other countries.

In a similar way, disappearances, arrests, detention, death threats and discrimination against converts and against individuals belonging to religious minorities or other faith communities are not uncommon all around the world. Violent attacks, statements and even school manuals inciting violence and killings of members of religious communities and religious minorities are on the news very often. Such threats to religious freedom profoundly affect human dignity. Limitations on the exercise of this right jeopardize personal identity, conscience and fundamental life choices, and they impair the enjoyment of other human rights.

Pope Benedict XVI has expressed his grave concern about such disturbing situations in various parts of the world, as a result of which 'it is impossible to profess one's religion freely except at the risk of life and personal liberty. In other areas, we see more subtle and sophisticated forms of

* Statement delivered at the 20th Session of the Human Rights Council – Item 8: *Freedom of Religion*, 3 July 2012.

prejudice and hostility towards believers and religious symbols.'[1] Christians represent the religious group that is subjected to religious persecution in the greatest numbers.

The transversal nature of religious freedom demands equal and effective protection under the law without discrimination for any person, but most especially for members of minority groups or persons who might be vulnerable to prejudice or discrimination for a variety of reasons. Thus the Vienna Declaration and Programme of Action proclaimed that 'persons belonging to minorities have the right to enjoy their own culture, to profess and practice their own religion ... in private and in public, freely and without interference or any form of discrimination.'[2]

Several other international human rights texts, General Assembly and Human Rights Council Resolutions[3] unambiguously state that 'everyone has the right to freedom of thought, conscience and religion or belief.' The freedom to manifest one's religion or belief in teaching, practice, worship and observance is also guaranteed. 'It is inconceivable that believers should have to suppress a part of themselves – their faith – in order to be active citizens. It should never be necessary to deny God in order to enjoy one's rights.'[4]

The ideals of religious freedom – in worship, practice and expression – are enshrined in the constitutions of most democratic States throughout the world. Such freedom is, moreover, a multi-faceted right, related, among others, to the rights to life and liberty.

In accord with the International Covenant on Civil and Political Rights, the Holy See Delegation recognizes that States are obligated to create and support infrastructural measures and favorable conditions to facilitate free and non-discriminatory development of religious communities and their members. Thus the right to religious freedom is not only an individual right but also constitutes a collective right for religious communities.[5]

1 Pope Benedict XVI's Message for the 2011 World Day of Peace, § 1.

2 Vienna Declaration and Programme of Action, Part. I, Art. 19.

3 General Assembly Resolution 36/55 of 25 November 1981, Declaration on the Elimination of All Forms of Intolerance and of Discrimination Based on Religion or Belief; Art. 18 of the International Covenant on Civil and Political Rights; Art. 18 of the Universal Declaration of Human Rights; Human Rights Council resolution 14/11 of 18 June 2010.

4 Pope Benedict XVI, Address to the General Assembly of the United Nations, 18 April 2008.

5 In this regard, it entails the right for such communities to govern themselves according to their own norms; the right to public worship; the right to instruct their

Madam President,

My Delegation acknowledges the correlation between social stability and recognition of human rights. Due to the unstable economic and political contexts in States throughout the world, it is essential that all human rights, and most especially the right to religious freedom, be protected. States must encourage the formation of collaborative networks that aim toward mutual understanding, promote interreligious dialogue and strengthen protection of religious groups through adequate and effective guarantees of religious freedom through access to legal systems that provide proportionate and adequate remediation and, when necessary, redress.

In the view of my Delegation, religious freedom cannot be restricted merely to freedom of worship. Also included in this fundamental freedom should be the right to preach, educate, receive new adherents, contribute to political discourse, as well as participate in public activities. Most importantly, the right to freedom of conscience must be upheld and protected. Believers should not be forced by governments to choose between conformity to governmental policies or legislation and faithfulness to religious tenets and beliefs. It also is important to respect the right of parents to a send their children to schools that reflect their beliefs. Compulsory, 'one-size-fits-all' educational systems can constitute a direct attack on the rights and duties of parents to assure the religious and ethical formation of their children. At the same time, all educational systems should promote respect and protection of people without any prejudice toward their respective religious beliefs or practices.

members in the practice of their faith; the right to select, educate, appoint, and transfer their own spiritual ministers: the right to construct buildings for religious purposes; the right to acquire and use funds or properties; the right to teach and witness to their faith publicly, whether by spoken or written word; and the right to hold meetings and to establish educational, cultural, charitable and social organizations, according to their respective motivations.

Madam President,

The Holy See Delegation would like to conclude by citing the Vienna Declaration, which calls 'upon all Governments to take all appropriate measures in compliance with their international obligations and with due regard to their respective legal systems to counter intolerance and related violence based on religion or belief…'[6]

Finally, we encourage every State to ensure, protect and promote the legitimate right of people to have, practice and to express their own religion or belief freely and without any type of coercion and violence and without the constant fear of becoming victims of anti-religious attacks that destroy their fundamental human rights.

Thank you, Madam President.

[6] Vienna Declaration and Programme of Action, Part II. Art. 22. The full citation reads: The Vienna Declaration calls 'upon all Governments to take all appropriate measures in compliance with their international obligations and with due regard to their respective legal systems to counter intolerance and related violence based on religion or belief… including practices of discrimination against women and including the desecration of religious sites, recognizing that every individual has the right to freedom of thought, conscience, expression and religion. The Conference also invites all States to put into practice the provisions of the Declaration on the Elimination of All Forms of Intolerance and of Discrimination Based on Religion or Belief.'

BLASPHEMY LAW: A PRETEXT FOR ACTS OF INJUSTICE AND VIOLENCE AGAINST RELIGIOUS MINORITIES*

Madam President,

Allow me to start by expressing my sincere gratitude to the High Commissioner for outlining in her intervention the human rights situations that require the Council's attention and the activities undertaken by her Office.

Madam President,

My Delegation wishes to thank the High Commissioner for her reference to the alarming situation of religious minorities in a number of regions and to the law against blasphemy which has recently been applied to Rimsha Masih. 'This is a girl who can neither write nor read, who collected garbage for a living, and found the fragments of the book (the sublime Quran) that were among the rubbish.'[1]

The Holy See Delegation regrets this new episode and reiterates the rejection to any act of violence and discrimination in the name of religion or against any religious group: 'the discrimination against human beings for religious motives and beliefs constitutes an offense to human dignity and a negation of the principles of the United Nations Charter.'[2]

My Delegation welcomes the steps taken by the Pakistani government for the physical protection of the girl accused and her family, as well as for the demonstrated effort for the clarification and solution of the case. At the same time, we would like to take this opportunity to underline the decision of President Asif Ali Zardari to grant the pardon to Madam Asia Bibi, a Christian woman who was sentenced to death in

* Statement delivered at the 21st Session of the Human Rights Council – Item 2: *Interactive Dialogue with the High Commissioner for Human Rights*, 10 September 2012.

1 Interview with Cardinal Jean-Louis Tauran, president of the Pontifical Council for Interreligious Dialogue, Radiovaticana, 25 August 2012, http://en.radiovaticana.va/storico/2012/08/29/her_name_is_rimsha_masih/en1-616655.

2 Declaration on the Elimination of All Forms of Intolerance and of Discrimination Based on Religion or Belief, proclaimed by the United Nations General Assembly on 25 November 1981 (Resolution 36/55), Art. 3, 'Everyone shall have the right to freedom of thought, conscience and religion. This right shall include freedom to have a religion or whatever belief of his choice, and freedom, either individually or in community with others and in public or private, to manifest his religion or belief in worship, observance, practice and teaching.' Cf. Universal Declaration of Human Rights (Art. 18); cf. International Covenant on Civil and Political Rights (Art. 18).

November 2010 on the same grounds. At the same time, we acknowledge the contributions and interest of the international community and of human rights advocates in both cases.

My Delegation, without undermining the principle of nonintervention and respect for national sovereignty, declares, however, that 'among the norms prejudicing the right of persons to religious freedom, particular mention must be made of the law against blasphemy in Pakistan: I once more encourage the leaders of that country to take the necessary steps to abrogate that law, all the more so because it is clear that it serves as a pretext for acts of injustice and violence against religious minorities.'[3]

Indeed, the existence of a civil law with religious character interpreted, sometimes, in a radical way by some intolerant groups, favors violent acts not only against Christians, but also against the religious minorities followers of the same religious denomination – object of the mentioned law – who are accused of heresy. Consequently, a separation between the political community and the religious community, a separation which benefits both communities, is required.

In order to combat religious intolerance, in theory and in practice, not only do we need the determination of the civil authorities, but also and primarily, that the religious leaders educate their believers to tolerance and mutual respect.[4] My Delegation acknowledges the efforts of many religious leaders in favor of an interreligious dialogue of peace and mutual tolerance.

In conclusion, the Holy See Delegation encourages 'the accompaniment of the full safeguarding of religious freedom and other humans rights by programs which, beginning in primary school and within the context of religious instruction, will educate everyone to respect their brothers and sisters in humanity.'[5] On not a few occasions, blind fundamentalism is the result of inadequate or little education, and the wrong association of certain decisions taken by the Western political communities with Christianity. Such interpretation does not reflect reality.

Thank you, Madam President.

[3] Address of Pope Benedict XVI to the Members of the Diplomatic Corps, Regia Hall, 10 January 2011.

[4] Ibid. 'I exhort everyone, political and religious leaders and persons of every walk of life, to set out with determination on the path leading to authentic and lasting peace, a path which passes through respect for the right to religious freedom in all its fullness.'

[5] Ibid. Cf. General Assembly Resolution A/RES/66/137, United Nations Declaration on Human Rights Education and Training, 16 February 2012.

THE STATE SHOULD NEVER IDENTIFY ITSELF WITH THE 'DOMINANT' COMMUNITY*

Mr President,

In today's world, because of their faith or belief, persons belonging to religious minorities experience various degrees of abuse that run from physical attacks to kidnapping for ransom, from arbitrary detention and obstacles in requesting registration, to stigmatization. Effective protection of the human rights of persons belonging to religious minorities is lacking or inadequately addressed even in the UN and international systems. Lately this worrying situation has caught the attention of some governments and segments of civil society. Thus awareness about this serious problem has become more evident. On the other hand, widespread discrimination affecting religious minorities persists and even increases.

The Special Rapporteur on Freedom of Religion or Belief has rightly focused his Report on the many human rights violations perpetrated against persons belonging to religious minorities. States may be directly involved through indifference toward some of their citizens or through the political will to marginalize, suppress or even eliminate communities with a different identity no matter how long they historically have been rooted in their own country. In some circumstances, non-State actors also take an active and even violent role by attacking religious minorities. The extensive indication of the variety of violations reported offers a realistic picture of today's oppression of religious minorities and should serve as a call to action.

However, the Report underplays the basic issue that minorities are defined either from the perspective of a 'majority' or from the perspective of other 'minorities'. Moreover, according to the Report the State should act in a neutral way in the recognition of religious groups. Indeed, the Report defines *individual persons* as holders of the right to freedom of religion and sees the goal of protection of religious freedom directed at 'ensuring the survival and continued development of the cultural, religious and social identity of the minorities concerned'.[1] It indicates

* Statement delivered at the 22nd Session of the Human Rights Council – Item 3: *Report of the Special Rapporteur on Freedom of Religion or Belief*, 6 March 2013.

[1] Human Rights Committee, General Comment No. 23 (1994) on the Right of Minorities (Art. 27), § 9.

individual protection of religious freedom as the way to achieve the protection of religious communities, a process that will not translate automatically in their protection. In fact, the Report itself shows very well that most violations of religious freedom occur at the religious group level.

While the State should enforce the universality of human rights by balancing freedom and equality, it often identifies itself with the 'dominant community' in a way that unfortunately relegates minorities to a second-class status, thus also creating problems for the religious freedom of individuals.

Individual freedoms and rights can be reconciled and harmonized with those of the community that wants to preserve its identity and integrity. There is no opposing dialectical process, but a necessary complementarity. The person should not become a prisoner of the community nor should the community become vulnerable simply because of the assertion of individual freedom. The Special Rapporteur rightly states that by stressing too narrow an understanding of equality, we may lose the diversity and specificity of freedom.

The legal recognition of a minority is the starting point for the necessary harmony between individual and group freedom. By adopting such a realistic approach to this issue the coexistence of communities is facilitated in a climate of relative tolerance. However, before such a realistic approach can be pursued, legal status must be granted to religious communities as is required by the innate human right of any person, which precedes and is binding on the State. We fully agree then with the Special Rapporteur's recommendation: 'What the State can and should do is create favourable conditions for persons belonging to religious minorities to ensure that they can take their faith-related affairs in their own hands in order to preserve and further develop their religious community life and identity.'[2] Only through respect for this balance can both peaceful coexistence and the advancement of all human rights be attained.

The State's role as guardian and enforcer of the freedom of religion not only for individuals but also for religious communities reveals that this balance is highly political. The secular State often is not neutral toward existing religious communities; not even in Western democracies where liberalism leads not so much to a neutral society but to one without a public presence of religion. But the State can preserve a religious identity provided it acts with neutrality and justice toward all religious groups in its territory. It can be added that the State should monitor violations of

[2] UN Doc. A/HRC/22/51. Summary.

freedom of conscience and the Rapporteur should address in this connection conscientious objection when it becomes impossible for a person to conform to the dominant social norms that are in contrast with moral dictates.

Mr President,

Religions are communities based on faith or belief, and their freedom guarantees a contribution of moral values without which the freedom of everyone is not possible. The recognition of the freedom of other religious communities does not reduce one's own freedoms. On the contrary, the acceptance of the religious freedom of other persons and groups is the cornerstone of dialogue and collaboration. Genuine freedom of religion bans violence and coercion, and it opens the road to peace and authentic human development through mutual recognition. The experience, and by now a tradition, of interreligious dialogue in Western societies proves the value of a reciprocal recognition of religious freedom.

Religious freedom is also a duty, a responsibility to be fulfilled by both individuals and religious groups. The recognition of the religious freedom of individuals and social groups implies that they should act by the same standards of the freedom they enjoy and such a condition justifies their presence as important and authentic actors in the public domain. To eclipse the public role of religion creates a society which is unjust since it would fail to take into account the true nature of the human person and would stifle the growth of authentic and lasting peace for the whole human family.

THE SOCIAL CONTRIBUTIONS OF CHRISTIANS TO THE HUMAN FAMILY*

Mr President,

My Delegation congratulates Madam High Commissioner for her presentation as well as for the activities of her office for the promotion, recognition and implementation of human rights.

Mr President,

The serious violations of the right to freedom of religion[1] in general, and the recent continuing discrimination and systematic attacks inflicted on some Christian communities in particular, deeply concern the Holy See. Credible research has reached the shocking conclusion that every year an estimate of more than 100,000 Christians are killed because of some relation to their faith.[2] Many others are subjected to forced displacement, to the destruction of their places of worship, to rape and to the abduction of their leaders – as recently happened in the case of Bishops Yohanna Ibrahim and Boulos Yaziji, in Aleppo (Syria).

Several of these acts have been perpetrated in parts of the Middle East, Africa and Asia, the fruit of bigotry, intolerance, terrorism and some exclusionary laws. In addition, in some Western countries,[3] where historically the Christian presence has been an integral part of society, a trend emerges that tends to marginalize Christianity in public life, to ignore

* Statement delivered at the 23rd Session of the Human Rights Council – Item 2: *Interactive Dialogue with High Commissioner*, 27 May 2013.

1 Cf. Universal Declaration of Human Rights (Art. 18); International Covenant on Civil and Political Rights (Art. 18).

2 www.noticiacristiana.com/sociedad/persecuciones/2011/06/cada-5-minutos-un-cristiano-muere-a-causa-de-su-fe-dice-un-estudio.html; 'World Christian Trends', paper presented at Notre Dame University, November 2012, by David B. Barrett and Todd M. Johnson (William Carey Library); David B. Barrett, George T. Kurian and Todd M. Johnson (eds), *World Christian Encyclopaedia*, 2nd edn, Oxford: Oxford University Press; Todd M. Johnson and Kenneth R. Ross (eds), *Atlas of Global Christianity*, Edinburgh: Edinburgh University Press.

3 Report 2012, Europe: 'Legal Restrictions Affecting Christians'; Gudrun Kugler, *Shadow Report on Intolerance and Discrimination against Christians in Europe*, Vienna: Observatory on Intolerance and Discrimination against Christians, 2010.

historic and social contributions and even to restrict the ability of faith communities to carry out social charitable services.[4]

Mr President,

The Human Rights Council has recognized that 'religion, spirituality and belief may and can contribute to the promotion of the inherent dignity and worth of the human person.'[5] The Christian religion, as other faith-communities, is 'at the service of the true good of humanity'.[6] In fact, 'Christian communities, with their patrimony of values and principles, have contributed much to making individuals and peoples aware of their identity and their dignity.'[7]

In this connection, my Delegation considers it useful to recall some pertinent data on the current services to the human family carried out in the world by the Catholic Church without any distinction of religion or race. In the field of education, it runs 70,544 kindergartens with 6,478,627 pupils; 92,847 primary schools with 31,151,170 pupils; 43,591 secondary schools with 17,793,559 pupils. The Church also educates 2,304,171 high school pupils, and 3,338,455 university students. The Church's worldwide charity and health care centers include: 5,305 hospitals; 18,179 dispensaries; 547 care homes for people with leprosy; 17,223 homes for the elderly, or the chronically ill or people with a disability; 9,882 orphanages; 11,379 crèches; 15,327 marriage counseling centers; 34,331 social rehabilitation centers and 9,391 other kinds

[4] Cf. 'In many countries Christians are deprived of fundamental rights and sidelined from public life; in other countries, they endure violent attacks against their churches and their homes. At times, they are forced to leave the countries they have helped to build because of persistent tensions and policies which frequently relegate them to being second-class spectators of national life. In other parts of the world, we see policies aimed at marginalizing the role of religion in the life of society,' Address of Pope Benedict XVI to the Members of the Diplomatic Corps, 9 January 2012; 'It even happens that believers, and Christians in particular, are prevented from contributing to the common good by their educational and charitable institutions,' Address of Pope Benedict XVI to the Members of the Diplomatic Corps, 7 January 2013.

[5] Durban Declaration and Programme of Action, World Conference against Racism, Racial Discrimination, Xenophobia and Related Intolerance, n. 8.

[6] Address of Pope Benedict XVI to the Members of the Diplomatic Corps, 8 January 2009.

[7] Pope Benedict XVI, Message for the Celebration of World Peace Day, 1 January 2011, § 7.

of charitable institutions. To such data about social action activity, there should be added the assistance services carried out in refugee camps and to internally displaced people and the accompaniment of these uprooted persons.[8]

Mr President,

Allow me to congratulate the Delegations, like that of Italy, that took the floor to defend the right to the freedom of religion of every person, and of Christians in particular, and to welcome the firm position of the Prime Minister of Bangladesh regarding proposals to introduce an anti-blasphemy law in her country. In conclusion, I wish to quote Pope Francis' hope that 'civil authorities everywhere respect the right to publicly express one's faith and to accept without prejudice the contribution that Christianity continues to offer to the culture and society of our time'.[9]

Thank you Mr President.

[8] www.fides.org/en/stats/32421VATICAN_WORLD_MISSION_DAY_CATHOLIC_CHURCH_STATISTICS_2012.

[9] Message on behalf of the Holy Father Francis to Cardinal Angelo Scola, on the occasion of the XVII centenary celebrations the Edict of Milan (that opened the way to religious freedom): 'delle autorità civili, sia ovunque rispettato il diritto all'espressione pubblica della propria fede e sia accolto senza pregiudizi il contributo che il cristianesimo continua ad offrire alla cultura e alla società del nostro tempo'.

RELIGIONS MUST NOT BE MANIPULATED IN ORDER TO EXERT POWER*

Mr President, as current conflicts show, the right to freedom of religion or belief is in urgent need of protection. It is often misinterpreted, as has become evident in certain judicial decisions. The Report of the Special Rapporteur on freedom of religion or belief helps in the analysis of its role and use in society and highlights its contribution to social cohesion, education and peaceful coexistence. It focuses on collective religious hatred and the Rapporteur seeks to find an understanding of the causes of that hatred, which seems to be generated by religion, and to identify in particular the responsibility of the State to prevent it.

Religious freedom should be protected not only in order to ensure a peaceful society, but also, primarily, because the human 'transcendent dignity must be acknowledged and protected as a universal good, essential to the building of societies directed toward human flourishing'.[1]

However, religions are incarnated in societies and cultures that may manipulate the religious message for specific and immediate goals such as group identity, political power, personal interest. In fact, certain actors may take it upon themselves to use religion, its symbols and language, for objectives other than their original purpose. In this context the State has the duty to prevent violations of human rights and incitement to hatred. It needs to act with justice and equity toward persons and religions without necessarily becoming itself areligious. As the legitimate authority aimed at fostering the common good of society, States hold a privileged position of responsibility to defend the freedom of religion and belief. Indeed, as the conclusion of the Report highlights, 'States must take an active role in promoting respect for everyone's freedom of thought, conscience, religion and belief'.[2]

In this context, my Delegation raises a word of caution regarding what the Report seemingly takes for granted, or assumes, that the position of the State in questions of religious liberty is 'neutral' or 'disinterested'. It would be naive to deny or ignore those all too common cases in which a secular 'authority' exercises judgment, indeed imposes its ideology, on situations that deal essentially with questions of religious liberty. Such an

* Statement delivered at the 25th Session of the Human Rights Council – Item 3: *Report of the Special Rapporteur on Freedom of Religion or Belief*, 12 March 2014.

[1] Cf. Pope Benedict XVI, Message of Peace, 2011, § 2.

[2] *Report of the Special Rapporteur on Freedom of Religion or Belief*, § 69.

ideology is really nothing less than a pseudo-form of 'religion' or 'belief' that limits the freedom of religious expression of others. Here arises a paradox: the 'disinterested', 'areligious', governing authority, in attempting to neutralize any 'traditional' religious expression, enters – intentionally or not – into an area that infringes upon religious freedom. Hence, we see cases in which people are punished and their fundamental rights violated by the so-called 'neutral' State authority in the name of non-discrimination because of a presumed infringement of religious tolerance in the way they express themselves, dress or wear religious symbols. These occurrences are becoming more common as courts and the State promote an ideological approach that sees religion more as a problem than as an essential element of human freedom.

Any sort of ideological imposition is reprehensible and poses an insidious threat to the very freedom of religion that should be fostered and defended. There is grave danger lurking when authorities ostensibly responsible for monitoring religious tolerance become completely intolerant to those who do not share their position.

'In many parts of the world, there seems to be no end to grave offences against fundamental human rights, especially the right to life and the right to religious freedom.'[3] The Report rightly confirms such offenses linked to collective hatred manifest in various forms, whether through physical violence, torture and abuse, or through disregard of the freedom of religion and religious institutions and their values and beliefs, and justified through a religious or ideological language.

Mr President,

The Holy See continues to insist upon respect for religious liberty and the autonomy of individuals to express freely their beliefs, in accord with just civil legislation and always with mutual respect for other convictions especially today in pluri-religious cultures and societies. This, however, does not entail reducing 'religious freedom' to a 'least common denominator' of practice and belief. On the contrary, it is desirable that religions interact among themselves, present their doctrines and sacred texts, accept constructive criticism. Freedom of conscience is based on reliable information provided by freedom of expression and personal formation. In this sense, the person should be free, in the civil realm, to follow

[3] Pope Francis' Message for the 2014 World Day of Peace, § 1.

his or her conscience in deciding matters related to profession of religion or belief.

While eradicating religious and ideological hatred is a noble goal, one must also realize the root cause is much more complex than what is proposed in the Report. 'Fear' is an important dimension underlying such hatred, but so too are ignorance of other religious beliefs and cultures and the simple reality of malice in the hearts of some who, notwithstanding efforts to find mutual understanding and trust, do not compromise in their obstinacy and hatred of others.

Facing today's numerous international problems, many of which have some religious component, the way forward is to find non-violent solutions through continued communal dialogue and patient efforts in view of reaching a greater mutual understanding.

Thank you, Mr President.

THE NEED TO PROTECT AND DEFEND THE RIGHT TO RELIGIOUS FREEDOM WORLDWIDE*

Mr President,

As the High Commissioner Mr Zeid Ra'ad Al Hussein begins his important mandate, the Holy See Delegation would like to congratulate him in this new and challenging role and to extend to him all the best as he moves forward.

The opening remarks of the High Commissioner underscore the wide array of ongoing human rights abuses, especially in those areas of civil and political conflict where violence has caused the killing of thousands of innocent people and displaced numerous others. Indeed, as the High Commissioner said, before such 'crimes against humanity', the international community must act to remove the root causes, not merely through words, but also by 'halting' these conflicts.

The High Commissioner's words clearly reveal the difficult task and grave responsibility placed before this Human Rights Council, and all States Parties, to defend and promote all human rights for all people. My Delegation would also like to highlight, among the rights listed in the opening statement, the need to protect and defend the right to religious freedom, which is clearly under attack in some parts of the world today. This is a fundamental human right based on the right of freedom of conscience. Experience shows that when this right is respected all other rights are as well. Furthermore, the right of citizenship has not been universally applied by some States, thus contributing to forced displacement and numerous abuses. There is the real risk that these people will be impeded in returning to their homes and property from which they have been forcefully eradicated, and not granted the protection and safety to live in peace in their cities and villages, as citizens with equal duties and rights.

The Holy See Delegation offers again its best wishes and support to the new High Commissioner in pursuing the high ideals of the Human Rights Council as set forth in the fundamental documents of the UN and in the Universal Declaration of Human Rights.

Thank you, Mr President.

* Statement delivered at the 27th Session of the Human Rights Council – Item 2: *On the Opening Remarks of the High Commissioner for Human Rights*, 8 September 2014.

FREEDOM OF EXPRESSION VS. FREEDOM OF RELIGION*

Mr President,

The international community is now confronted with a delicate, complex and urgent challenge with regard to respect for religious sensibilities and the need for peaceful coexistence in an ever more pluralistic world: namely, that of establishing a fair relationship between freedom of expression and freedom of religion. The relationship between these fundamental human rights has proven difficult to manage and to address on either a normative or institutional level. On the other hand, it should be recognized 'that the open, constructive and respectful debate of ideas, as well as interfaith and intercultural dialogue at the local, national and international levels, can play a positive role in combating religious hatred, incitement and violence'.[1] Failure in this effort is evident when excessive and irresponsible use of freedom of expression results in intimidation, threats and verbal abuse and these infringe upon freedom of religion and can sadly lead to intolerance and violence. Likewise, the Special Rapporteur on Freedom of Religion has focused on the violence committed 'in the name of religion',[2] and on its root causes.

Unfortunately, violence abounds today. If genocide means any act committed with the intent to destroy, in whole or in part, a national, ethnical, racial or religious group, as such,[3] then the international community as a whole is certainly witnessing a sort of genocide in some regions of the world, where the enslavement and sale of women and children, the killing of young men, the burning, beheading and the forcing into exile of people continue. In this context, the Delegation of the Holy See would like to submit to the joint reflection of the Human Rights Council that these and other unspeakable crimes are being committed against people belonging to ancient communities simply because their belief, social system and culture are different from the fundamentalist combatants of the so-called 'Islamic State' group. The appeal to religion in order to

* Statement delivered at the 28th Session of the Human Rights Council – Item 3: *Report of the Special Rapporteur on Freedom of Religion or Belief*, 11 March 2015.

1 Human Rights Council Resolution 16/18 on 'Combating intolerance, negative stereotyping and stigmatization of, and discrimination, incitement to violence and violence against, persons based on religion or belief', para. 5(h), p. 3.

2 Cf. UN Doc. A/HRC/28/66 paras. 3–82, pp. 3–18.

3 Cf. Articles II and III of the 1948 Convention on the Prevention and Punishment of Genocide.

murder people and destroy the evidence of human creativity developed in the course of history makes the ongoing atrocities even more repulsive and damnable. An adequate response from the international community, that should finally put aside sectoral interests and save lives, is a moral imperative.

Violence, however, does not stem from religion but from its false interpretation or its transformation into ideology. In addition, the same violence can derive from the idolatry of State or of the economy, and it can be an effect of secularization. All these phenomena tend to eliminate individual freedom and responsibility towards others. But violence is always an individual's act and a decision that implies personal responsibility. It is in fact by adopting an ethics of responsibility that the way toward the future can become fruitful, prevent violence and break the impasse between extreme positions, one which upholds any form of freedom of expression and the other which rejects any criticism of a religion. The risk of a double standard in the protection of human rights is never too far away. Some limits to freedom of expression are selectively imposed by law and accepted; meanwhile, systematic, provocative and verbally violent attacks on religion which hurt the personal identity of believers are endorsed.[4] Freedom of expression that is misused to wound the dignity of persons by offending their deepest convictions sows the seeds of violence. Of course, freedom of expression is a fundamental human right which is always to be upheld and protected; in fact, it also implies the obligation to say in a responsible way what a person thinks in view of the common good. Without this right, education, democracy, authentic spirituality would not be possible. It does not, however, justify relegating religion to a subculture of insignificant weight or to an acceptable easy target of ridicule and discrimination. Antireligious arguments even in the form of irony can surely be accepted, as it is acceptable to use irony about secularism or atheism. Criticism of religious thinking can even help dismantle various extremisms. But what can justify gratuitous insults and spiteful derision of the religious feelings and convictions of others who are, after all, equal in dignity? Can we make fun of the cultural identity of a person, of the colour of his skin, of the belief of his heart? A 'right to offend' does not exist. Criticism can produce good results if it takes into account that persons are more important than their convictions or their belief and that they have, simply because they are human beings, an innate right to be respected.

[4] Cf. UN Doc. A/HRC/25/34, para. 127.

The lack of an ethics of responsibility and fairness leads to the radicalization of positions when instead dialogue and mutual understanding are necessary to break the vicious circle of violence. The Constitution of the UNESCO reminds us that 'since wars begin in the minds of men, it is in the minds of men that the defenses of peace must be constructed.'[5]

Several mutually interdependent issues like freedom of religion, freedom of expression, religious intolerance, violence in the name of religion, come together in the concrete situations the world faces today. The way forward seems to be the adoption of a comprehensive approach that would consider these issues together in domestic legislation and deal with them in such a way that they may facilitate a peaceful coexistence based on the respect of the inherent human dignity and rights of every person. While opting to be on the side of freedom, the consequences of its exercise cannot be ignored and they should respect this dignity and, thus, build a more humane and more brotherly global society.

Thank you, Mr President.

[5] Constitution of the United Nations Educational, Scientific and Cultural Organization, 1945. Preamble.

THE RESPONSIBILITY TO PROTECT CHRISTIANS AND OTHER COMMUNITIES, PARTICULARLY IN THE MIDDLE EAST*

The Middle East is living in a situation of instability and conflict that recently have been aggravated. The consequences are disastrous for the entire population of the region. The existence of many religious communities is seriously threatened. Christians are now especially affected. These days even their survival is in question.

Efforts to build a better future for all are frustrated. We witness a situation where violence, religious and ethnic hatred, fundamentalist radicalism, extremism, intolerance, exclusion, destruction of the social fabric of whole societies and communities are becoming the features of a non-viable political and social model, endangering the very existence of many communities, the Christian community in particular.

Millions of people have been either displaced or forced to leave their ancestral lands. Those who stay in conflict zones or areas controlled by terrorist groups live under the permanent threat of human rights violations, repression and abuses. Both communities and individuals fall victim to barbaric acts of violence: they are deprived of homes, driven from their native lands, sold into slavery, killed, beheaded and burnt alive. Dozens of Christian churches and ancient shrines of all religions have been destroyed. The situation of Christians in the Middle East, a land in which they are living for centuries and have the right to remain, raises deep concerns. There are more and more reasons to fear seriously for the future of the Christian communities that have more than two thousand years of existence in this region, where Christianity has its full place, and began its long history. The positive contributions of Christians in the different countries and societies of the Middle East are well known and creative.

We are confident that governments, all civic and religious leaders in the Middle East, will join us in addressing this alarming situation by building together a culture of peaceful coexistence. In our globalized world, pluralism is an enrichment. The presence and the contributions of ethnic and religious communities reflect an ancient diversity and a common

* Statement sponsored by the Holy See, Lebanon and the Russian Federation and delivered by the Permanent Representative of Lebanon at the 28th Session of the Human Rights Council – Item 3: *Report of the Special Rapporteur on Freedom of Religion or Belief*, 11 March 2015.

heritage. A future without the different communities in the Middle East will run a high risk of new forms of violence, exclusion and the absence of peace and development.

We call upon the international community to support the deeply rooted historical presence of all ethnic and religious communities in the Middle East. Here world religions appeared, including Christianity. Now, they live a serious existential threat from the so-called 'Islamic State' (Daesh) and Al Qaeda, and affiliated terrorist groups, which disrupts the life of all these communities, and creates the risk of complete disappearance for the Christians. This support will help the countries of the region to rebuild healthy plural societies and sound political systems, ensuring human rights and fundamental freedoms for all. Therefore, we ask all States to reaffirm their commitment to respect the rights of everyone, in particular the right to freedom of religion, which is enshrined in the fundamental international human rights instruments.

2 RESPECTING HUMAN DIGNITY AND CONDEMNING VIOLENCE AGAINST THE HUMAN PERSON

TOWARDS THE ELIMINATION OF EVERY FORM OF RACISM*

Mr Chairman,

The wound of racism keeps returning to poison human relations. The forms taken by contemporary manifestations of racism are evident in spontaneous, officially tolerated or sometimes institutionalized behavior. In recent events intolerance, based on the idea of group superiority on the basis of the group's origin or attributed characteristics, provokes new violence and death, ethnic cleansing, refugee flows and untold misery. Racist behavior and self-affirmation become occasionally the cover for undemocratic hold on power and for a rationalized justification for corruption. It is not difficult to notice from the information networks that practically in all continents, with the increased mobility of people, immigrants, especially if in an irregular situation, find themselves exposed to attacks and forced marginalization as a result of prejudice, even when their presence is needed for economic and even demographic reasons. While race defines a human group in terms of immutable and hereditary traits, racist prejudice, which feeds racist behavior, can be applied by extension, with equally negative effects, to all persons whose ethnic origin, language, religion or customs make them appear different. In this way the right to full participation in society is denied to a variety of groups often set apart by the additional burden of great poverty.

The fight against racism remains therefore a contemporary commitment. Major positive steps have already been taken in recent decades in the effort to contain and eliminate prejudice and discrimination. The cornerstone remains the Universal Declaration of Human Rights with its principles of equality without distinction of any kind such as race, color, sex, language, religion, political or other opinion, national or social origin, property, birth or other status. These principles were further elaborated in other major instruments like the International Convention on the Elimination of All Forms of Racial Discrimination (1965), the Convention on

* Statement delivered at the 60th Session of the Commission on Human Rights – Item 6: *Racism, Racial Discrimination, Xenophobia and All Forms of Discrimination*, 22 March 2004.

the Elimination of All Forms of Discrimination against Women (1981) and the Declaration and Programme of Action of the World Conference against Racism, Racial Discrimination, Xenophobia and Related Intolerance held in Durban from 31 August to 8 September 2001.

The challenge now facing us is to implement the growing body of directives protecting human rights and aiming in particular at the elimination of every form of racism and related intolerance. To keep the political will focused on this major concern, the Working Groups established as a follow-up of the Durban Conference continue the search for concrete ways and means to achieve the objectives that the international community has set for itself in this regard. International instruments, national legislation, active forces of civil society, educational and religious institutions, as well as non-governmental organizations, by converging on the same goal in a comprehensive way, can defeat any persistent form of racism or at least contain their nefarious consequences.

The achievement of these objectives has to begin from an attitude of acceptance of the 'other' and of a genuine appreciation of the multiplicity of gifts that human groups and cultures contribute to the whole of the human family. This necessary positive outlook can come only from deep convictions to make the art of living together in peace and mutual respect a reality. A strategic tool in this regard is education, especially human rights education, that must go beyond the external expressions of a culture and reach out to the value system and the spiritual belief that sustain the identity of a people. Dialogue at this level will go a long way to eliminate the walls built by prejudice and historical circumstances. All major religions strive to inculcate this inner rooting of tolerant behavior and at the same time they provide encouragement to teach by example first of all. Together with education the role of the media is essential in forming a public opinion that is sensitive and respectful of the other. Care should be taken that selectivity of information may not lead to prejudice, in both the case of historical analysis and analysis of present political and ideological situations. On the other hand, a very positive service is provided by the media when they highlight successful best practices against racism.

In the search for adequate measures to protect people from racism, racial discrimination, xenophobia and related intolerance, inter alia, the Durban Declaration and Programme of Action recognizes 'the necessity for special measures or positive actions for the victims of racism, racial discrimination, xenophobia and related intolerance in order to promote their full integration into society'. Those measures 'should aim at correcting the conditions that impair the enjoyment of rights and the introduction of special measures to encourage equal participation of all racial and cultural, linguistic and religious groups in all sectors of society and to bring all onto an equal footing' (No. 108). Such a victim-centered approach calls for access to some mechanism of complaint and redress that will effectively respond also to the just expectations of the poorer and more marginalized people.

The consequences of racism, obvious in some extreme cases of open conflict and forced exile, are probably not sufficiently calculated for the more ordinary circumstances like in work situations, where the lack of equality of treatment and opportunity affects productivity negatively. In this as in other cases, a vicious circle develops as racism leads to vulnerability and marginalization and these conditions in turn are utilized to reinforce prejudice and racism.

In conclusion, Mr Chairman, the struggle against racism and all forms of intolerance stands a chance of success when human dignity and equality are recognized as the true foundation of social relations. The equal dignity of every person and of every human community provide a launching pad into the future that can stimulate the creativity of the international community to continue devising all practical measures necessary to achieve such a noble goal of eliminating all forms of racism and related intolerance and of promoting a fair and inclusive society.

THE FOCUS ON THE PERSON MUST NOT BE A JUSTIFICATION FOR INDIVIDUALISM*

Mr President,

The Delegation of the Holy See is grateful for and appreciates the initiative of the Human Rights Council to start an exchange of views and insights that try to arrive at the root of human rights. Prior to a specific articulation of rights, the search for a common point of departure appears necessary. The distinguished panellists have highlighted some starting points: a regional culture's expression, the concept of citizenship, a religious outlook. It is useful to recognize such differences in approach while asking if a deeper starting point may be necessary, a point that precedes differences, i.e. our common humanity. If the human person is the foundation, and the inherent dignity that all women and men possess, then we have a good base from where to move forward together.

The focus on the person, however, is not a justification for individualism. No person becomes a person unless they relate to others, a process that begins in the natural family. Therefore duties and responsibilities are not separable. To each right corresponds a duty. In this interaction of rights and duties and in the pursuit of the common good, communities are formed and protected.

The task then is to provide an enabling environment where the person can flourish without undue discrimination. Religious freedom, in many ways, is a symbol of this type of environment that sustains both individual persons and the community.

Perhaps the panellists may elaborate further their views on both the following questions: (1) how the source of rights in the person, as the Universal Declaration on Human Rights (UDHR) shows, in fact, guarantees the community; (2) how the pursuit of the common good, that embraces all social, civil, cultural and economic rights, can be the target of all development in human rights.

Such an exercise as today's panel can open the way for a fruitful dialogue that will overcome barriers and sustain reconciliation and a peaceful living together.

Thank you, Mr President.

* Statement delivered at the 7th Session of the Human Rights Council – *Intercultural Dialogue on Human Rights*, 18 March 2008.

INTERACTION AND INTEGRATION MUST PREVAIL OVER RADICAL ASSIMILATION OR SEPARATION*

Mr President,

The Delegation of the Holy See considers the continued involvement of the Human Rights Council with the problem of racism as timely and necessary. Unfortunately, discrimination based on race and perceived differences is still used to treat people in undignified ways and even to reduce them to enslavement. No corner of the world is exempt from experiences of racial discrimination, even though it has become a common conviction that racism, xenophobia and related forms of intolerance are condemned by customary law, by *ius cogens*, that all State and non-State actors are obliged to respect. The phenomenon of globalization has brought together previously remote people whose cultures and beliefs are quite different. At the same time, the resulting pluralization of societies has increased the risk of racism. In fact the lack of knowledge and the presence of unfamiliar traditions and customs tend to engender fear of the other person and the risk of rejection. But such fear must be overcome.

The way forward is not an abstract dialogue of civilizations, an insistent defense of communitarism, or an understanding of the individual cut off from any human relations. As the Report on Racism, Racial Discrimination, Xenophobia and Related Forms of Intolerance, Follow-Up and Implementation of the Durban Declaration and Programme of Action, observes, in the era of globalization, the State cannot be based exclusively on the idea of national identity. International human rights law clearly recognizes that the main function of the State is service to the human person, its life in community, and the promotion of the common good. The question of pluralism in contemporary societies and the fight against racism can find a solution in an environment where persons enjoy all human rights, civil and political as well as social, cultural and economic. It is not through radical assimilation or separation, but through interaction and integration on the base of the common values, as expressed by human rights, that genuine dialogue becomes possible. Tolerance alone does not suffice; everyone should acknowledge both the difference and

* Statement delivered at the 7th Session of the Human Rights Council – Item 9: *Racism, Racial Discrimination, Xenophobia and Related Forms of Intolerance, Follow-Up and Implementation of the Durban Declaration and Programme of Action*, 19 March 2008.

the equality with the other person in order to find solutions to the practical problems of living together.

As a first step, an encounter among persons calls for the knowledge and the positive will to share what is valuable. To achieve it, some requirements are necessary like 'freedom in investigating the truth, and – within the limits of the moral order and the common good – freedom of speech and publication ... [and] the right, also, to be accurately informed about public events'.[1] Secondly, in a frank dialogue, a sense of responsibility has to be present and the capacity to accept criticism directed at improving personal growth within the framework of human rights. More than insisting on a clash of civilizations and on *the phobia language*, that risk further polarizing positions, it is better to focus on the defense and promotion of human rights. A question can be raised of how a dialogue may be possible when, for example, migrants and asylum seekers are confined to a degraded existence and when minorities and groups of citizens are considered of inferior status even institutionally.

Religious intolerance has surfaced again as a contentious issue that should be addressed in the context of the indivisibility, interdependence and universality of human rights. There are groups identified by their ethnicity and a particular religion while others are only different because of their belief. The complexity of situations demands a collaborative and holistic approach among the Special Rapporteurs and other international mechanisms for a more effective impact and for an easier convergence on solutions. A common approach can be that of giving special attention to the victims of racial and/or religious discrimination, whose basic human rights are continuously denied even to the point of violent deprivation of life. For example, in some countries it is difficult for Christians publicly to profess their faith, since they are constrained by an imposition of invisibility. These factual data, if included, would make the Report on racism more objective and complete.

Racism and intolerance should be combated through concerted practical measures. Education, that favours mutual knowledge, that builds confidence and sustains the implementation of human rights, can serve as a critical vehicle for effective dialogue. Other concrete ways are the improvement of the United Nations early warning mechanisms related to this issue, the ratification of the Convention on the Elimination of All Forms of Racial Discrimination, the implementation of the Durban Declaration and Programme of Action, and the drafting by the Human

[1] Pope John XXIII, Encyclical Letter, *Pacem in Terris* (1963), § 12.

Rights Committee of a general comment on Article 20 of the International Covenant on Civil and Political Rights. Priority, however, should be given to a change of attitude so that the heart may be continually purified and no longer governed by fear or the spirit of domination, but by openness to others and solidarity. This is a fundamental role of religions that have the responsibility to offer a teaching that stresses the dignity of every human being and the unity of the human family.[2]

Thank you, Mr President.

[2] Cf. Pontifical Council for Justice and Peace, *The Church and Racism: Towards a More Fraternal Society*, Vatican City, 2001, p. 11.

A CHANGE OF HEARTS TOWARDS OPENNESS, FRATERNITY AND SOLIDARITY*

Mr President,

Allow me to express my congratulations on your election and wish you, the High Commissioner for Human Rights, and the entire Bureau success in leading this Conference to a positive conclusion.

Mr President,

The Delegation of the Holy See shares in the aspiration of the international community to overcome all forms of racism, racial discrimination and xenophobia in the awareness that 'all human beings are born free and equal in dignity and rights'[1] and are united in one human family. In fact, a just international community is properly developed when the natural desire of human persons to relate to each other is not distorted by prejudice, fear of others or selfish interests that undermine the common good. In all its manifestations, racism makes the false claim that some human beings have less dignity and value than others; it thus infringes upon their fundamental equality as God's children and it leads to the violation of the human rights of individuals and of entire groups of persons.

As party to the International Convention on the Elimination of All Forms of Racial Discrimination and to the common efforts of the United Nations and other relevant international organizations, the Holy See endeavours to assume fully its responsibility in accord with its proper mission. It is engaged in combating all forms of racism, racial discrimination, xenophobia and related intolerance in a spirit of cooperation. The Holy See actively participated in the Durban Conference of 2001 and, without hesitation, gave its moral support to the Durban Declaration and Programme of Action (DDPA) in the full knowledge that combating racism is a necessary and indispensable prerequisite for the construction of governance, sustainable development, social justice, democracy and peace in the world.

Today globalization brings people together, but spatial and temporal proximity does not of itself create the conditions for constructive

* Statement delivered at the Durban Review Conference, 20–24 April 2009.

[1] Universal Declaration of Human Rights, Art. 1.

interaction and peaceful communion. In fact, racism persists: the stranger and those who are different too often are rejected to the point that barbarous acts are committed against them, including genocide and ethnic cleansing. Old forms of exploitation give way to new ones: women and children are trafficked in a contemporary form of slavery, irregular immigrants are abused, persons perceived to be or who in fact are different become, in disproportionate numbers, the victims of social and political exclusion, ghetto conditions and stereotyping. Girls are forced into unwanted marriages; Christians are jailed or killed because of their beliefs. Lack of solidarity, an increased fragmentation of social relations in our multicultural societies, spontaneous racism and xenophobia, social and racial discrimination, particularly regarding minorities and marginalized groups, and political exploitation of differences are evident in everyday experience. The global impact of the current economic crisis affects, most of all, the vulnerable groups of society; this demonstrates how too often racism and poverty are inter-related in a destructive combination.

The Holy See is also alarmed by the still latent temptation of eugenics that can be fuelled by techniques of artificial procreation and the use of 'superfluous embryos'. The possibility of choosing the colour of the eyes or other physical characteristic of a child could lead to the creation of a 'subcategory of human beings' or the elimination of human beings that do not fulfil the characteristics predetermined by a given society. Moreover, increased security concerns and the consequent introduction of excessive measures and practices have created a greater lack of confidence among people of different cultures and have exacerbated the irrational fear of foreigners. The legitimate fight against terrorism should never undermine the protection and promotion of human rights.

Building on progress already made, our Durban Review Conference can be the occasion to set aside mutual differences and mistrust; reject once more any theory of racial or ethnic superiority; and renew the international community's commitment to the elimination of all expressions of racism as an ethical requirement of the common good, the attainment of which 'is the sole reason of existence of civil authorities'[2] at national, regional and international levels. Sharing resources and best practices in the concerted effort to implement the recommendations of the DDPA to eradicate racism is to acknowledge the centrality of the human person and the equal dignity of all persons. Such a task is the duty and responsibility of everyone. It is a clear example that doing what is right pays a

[2] Pope John XXIII, Encyclical Letter, *Peace on Earth*.

political dividend since it lays the foundation for a peaceful, productive and mutually enriching living together.

International covenants and declarations as well as national legislation are indispensable to create a public culture and to provide binding provisions capable of combating racism, racial discrimination, xenophobia and related intolerance. Without a change of heart, however, laws are not effective. It is the heart that must continually be purified so that it will no longer be governed by fear or the spirit of domination, but by openness to others, fraternity and solidarity. An irreplaceable role is played by education that shapes mentalities and helps to form consciences to embrace a more comprehensive view of reality and reject any form of racism and discrimination. Some educational systems should be reviewed so that every aspect of discrimination may be eliminated from teaching, textbooks, curricula and visual resources. The end process of such education is not only the recognition of everyone as having equal human worth and the elimination of racist thinking and attitudes, but also the conviction that States and individuals must take the initiative and make themselves a neighbour to all. Informal and general education plays a crucial role as well. Media, therefore, should be accessible and free of racist and ideological control as this leads to discrimination and even violence against persons of different cultural and ethnic background. In this way, educational systems and media join the rest of society in upholding human dignity which only a collective action of all sectors of society can protect and promote. In such a context of mutual acceptance, the right of access to education on the part of racial, ethnic and religious minorities will be respected as a human right that ensures the cohesion of society with the contribution of everyone's talents and capacities.

In the fight against racism, faith communities play a major part. The Catholic Church, for example, has not spared its best energies to strengthen its many scholastic institutions, to establish new ones, to be present in dangerous situations where human dignity is trampled upon and the local community is disrupted. In this vast educational network, it teaches how to live together and how to recognize that any form of racial prejudice and discrimination hurts the common dignity of every person created in the image of God and the development of a just and welcoming society. For this reason, it stresses that 'individuals come to maturity through receptive openness to others and through generous self-giving to them … In this perspective, *dialogue between cultures … emerges as an intrinsic demand of human nature itself, as well as of culture* … Dialogue leads to a recognition of diversity and opens the mind to the mutual acceptance and genuine collaboration demanded by the human family's basic vocation to unity. As such, dialogue is a privileged means for building *the civilization of love and peace*.'[3] The contribution of faith communities in combating racism and building a non-discriminatory society becomes more effective if there is a genuine respect of the right to freedom of religion as clearly enshrined in human rights instruments. Unfortunately, discrimination does not spare religious minorities, a fact that increasingly concerns the international community. The response to this legitimate concern is the full implementation of religious freedom for individuals and their collective exercise of this basic human right. While the right to freedom of expression is not a license to insult the followers of any religion, or stereotype their faith, existing mechanisms that provide legal accountability for incitement to racial and religious hatred should be used in the framework of human rights law to protect all believers and non-believers. National judicial systems should favour the practice of 'reasonable accommodation' of religious practices and should not be used to justify the failure to protect and promote the right to profess and freely practice one's religion.

The challenges ahead of us demand more effective strategies in combating racism, racial discrimination, xenophobia and related intolerance. These are evils that corrode the social fabric of society and produce innumerable victims. The first step for a practical solution lies in an integral education that includes ethical and spiritual values which will favour the empowerment of vulnerable groups like refugees, migrants and people on the move, racial and cultural minorities, people, prisoners of extreme poverty, or who are ill and disabled, and girls and women still stigmatized as inferior in some societies where an irrational fear of differences prevents full participation in social life. Secondly, in order to achieve coherence among the various structures and mechanisms designed to counteract racial attitudes and behavior, it is necessary to undertake a new examination aimed at making the various approaches more incisive and efficient. Thirdly, the universal ratification of major instruments against racism and discrimination, such as the International Convention on the Elimination of All Forms of Racial Discrimination and the International Convention on the Protection of the Rights of All Migrant Workers and Members of Their Families, will signal the political will of the international community to fight all expressions of racism. Finally, there is no substitute for fair national legislation that explicitly condemns all forms

[3] Pope John Paul II, Message for the Celebration of World's Day of Peace, 2001, § 10.

of racism and discrimination and enables all citizens to participate publicly in the life of their country on the basis of equality in both duties and rights.

Therefore, the work of this Conference has taken a step forward in combating racism, the reason for most countries to stay and join efforts for an outcome that responds to the need of eliminating old and new manifestations of racism. The Conference, as an international forum for the exercise of the right to freedom of expression, has unfortunately been used to utter extreme and offensive political positions that the Holy See deplores and rejects: they do not contribute to dialogue, they provoke unacceptable conflicts, and in no way can be approved or shared.

Mr President,

Eight years ago the countries of the world engaged themselves in a global commitment to combat racism through the adoption of the Durban Declaration and Programme of Action. This vision of change remains incomplete in its implementation, and so the journey must continue. Progress will be achieved through a renewed determination to translate into action the convictions reaffirmed at the present Conference 'that all peoples and individuals constitute one human family, rich in diversity' and that all human beings are equal in dignity and rights. Only then will the victims of racism be free and a common future of peace, ensured.

STATES NEED TO RESPECT ALL PERSONS BUT ALSO NEED TO REGULATE SOME ASPECTS OF SEXUAL BEHAVIOUR*

Mr President,

The Holy See takes this opportunity to affirm the inherent dignity and worth of all human beings, and to condemn all violence that is targeted against people because of their sexual feelings and thoughts, or sexual behaviors.

We would also like to make several observations about the debates regarding 'sexual orientation'.

First, there has been some unnecessary confusion about the meaning of the term 'sexual orientation,' as found in resolutions and other texts adopted within the UN human rights system. The confusion is unnecessary because, in international law, a term must be interpreted in accordance with its ordinary meaning, unless the document has given it a different meaning.[1] The ordinary meaning of 'sexual orientation' refers to feelings and thoughts, not to behavior.[2]

Second, for the purposes of human rights law, there is a critical difference between feelings and thoughts, on the one hand, and behaviour,

* Statement delivered at the 16th Session of the UN Human Rights Council – Item 8: *General Debate*, 22 March 2011.

1 Vienna Convention of the Law of Treaties, Art. 31(1): 'A treaty *shall* be interpreted in good faith in accordance with the *ordinary meaning* to be given to the terms of the treaty in their context and in the light of its object and purpose' (emphasis added).' Art. 31(4): 'A special meaning shall be given to a term if it is established that the parties so intended. These rules of treaty interpretation are based on customary international law, and are applicable to "soft law".'

2 Moreover, many publications have given definitions of 'sexual orientation', and all of the ones that we have seen are similar: they do not refer to behavior; they refer to sexual feelings and thoughts. E.g.:

(1) 'Sexual orientation means the general attraction you feel towards another person or persons.' Equality Commission (UK); see www.equalityhumanrights.com, under 'What does sexual orientation mean?'.

(2) 'Sexual orientation may be broadly defined as a preference for sexual partners ... ' International Labour Office, *ABC of Women Workers' Rights and Gender Equality*, 2nd edn, 2007, p. 167. A 'preference' is a mental-emotional state; it is not conduct.

(3) 'Sexual orientation refers to a person's sexual and emotional attraction to people ... ' Amnesty International, *Crimes of Hate, Conspiracy of Silence*, London: Amnesty International Publications, 2001, p. vii (emphasis omitted).

(4) '"Sexual orientation" refers to each person's capacity for profound emotional, affectional and sexual attraction to, and intimate and sexual relations'. Asia Pacific Forum, ACJ Report, 'Human Rights, Sexual Orientation and Gender Identity' (15th Annual Meeting, Bali, 3–5 August 2010), p. 8.

on the other. A state should never punish a person, or deprive a person of the enjoyment of any human right, based just on the person's feelings and thoughts, including sexual thoughts and feelings. But states can, and must, regulate behaviours, including various sexual behaviors. Throughout the world, there is a consensus between societies that certain kinds of sexual behaviors must be forbidden by law. Pedophilia and incest are two examples.

Third, the Holy See wishes to affirm its deeply held belief that human sexuality is a gift that is genuinely expressed in the complete and lifelong mutual devotion of a man and a woman in marriage. Human sexuality, like any voluntary activity, possesses a moral dimension: it is an activity which puts the individual will at the service of a finality; it is not an 'identity'. In other words, it comes from the action and not from the being, even though some tendencies or 'sexual orientations' may have deep roots in the personality. Denying the moral dimension of sexuality leads to denying the freedom of the person in this matter, and undermines ultimately his/her ontological dignity. This belief about human nature is also shared by many other faith communities, and by other persons of conscience.

And finally, Mr President, we wish to call attention to a disturbing trend in some of these social debates: people are being attacked for taking positions that do not support sexual behavior between people of the same sex. When they express their moral beliefs or beliefs about human nature, which may also be expressions of religious convictions, or state opinions about scientific claims, they are stigmatised, and worse – they are vilified, and prosecuted. These attacks contradict the fundamental principles announced in three of the Council's resolutions of this session.[3] The truth is, these attacks are violations of fundamental human rights, and cannot be justified under any circumstances. Thank you, Mr President.

[3] L.10 on freedom of opinion and expression; L.14 on freedom of religion or belief; L.38 on combating intolerance, negative stereotyping and stigmatization.

VIOLENCE AGAINST WOMEN: A TRAGIC REALITY*

Mr President,

The Delegation of the Holy See welcomes the second thematic report on violence against women, a topic of human rights concern that rightly has resulted in greater awareness among the general public and has strengthened the efforts of States to achieve just and equitable treatment of women.

As noted in the report, the root problem rests with a view of women that ignores or rejects their equal dignity. Notwithstanding the progress achieved, violence against women remains a tragic reality. Rape is used as a weapon of war during conflicts; girls are trafficked as merchandise; domestic workers at times are abused with impunity; young women are kidnapped, forced to convert and forced to marry; others are forced to abort. While violence occurs more frequently where poverty and social instability are prevalent, we also must recognize that some legal systems and traditions still condone it. Such negative and unequal treatment of women often causes long-lasting physical, psychological and social negative effects. There is still a long way to go in order to prevent violence against women and girls and to achieve effective equality everywhere.

As Pope Benedict XVI has remarked: 'There are places and cultures where women are discriminated against or undervalued for the sole fact of being women, where recourse is made even to religious arguments and family, social and cultural pressure in order to maintain the inequality of the sexes, where acts of violence are consummated in regard to women, making them the object of mistreatment and of exploitation in advertising and in the consumer and entertainment industry. Faced with such grave and persistent phenomena the Christian commitment appears all the more urgent so that everywhere it may promote a culture that recognizes the dignity that belongs to women, in law and in concrete reality.'[1]

Personal and structural forms of violence against women are often inter-related and demand assertive efforts to achieve their elimination. This phenomenon cannot be analyzed in isolation from the social context

* Statement delivered at the 17th Session of the Human Rights Council – Item 3: Interactive Dialogue, 3 June 2011.

1 Pope Benedict XVI, Address to the Participants in the International Convention on the Theme 'Woman and Man, The Human in its Entirety', Vatican City, 9 February 2008, www.vatican.va/holy_father/benedict_xvi/speeches/2008/february/documents/hf_ben-xvi_spe_20080209_donna-uomo_en.html.

in which it occurs. As it is noted by the Rapporteur, improvement in the standard of living and provisions of equal access to education will enable society to prevent additional occurrence of such violence. In fact, education itself can serve as a vehicle to create a mentality that supports and respects women.

Taking into account 'the fundamental anthropological truths of man and woman, the equality of their dignity and the unity of both, the well-rooted and profound diversity between the masculine and the feminine and their vocation to reciprocity and complementarity, to collaboration and to communion',[2] my Delegation considers that it is possible to improve the situation of women and to fight the scourge of violence, and to build a creative equality and a mutual respect that prevent any recourse to violence.

Thank you, Mr President.

[2] Ibid.

DISCRIMINATORY LAWS, PRACTICES AND ACTS OF VIOLENCE MOTIVATED BY SEXUAL ORIENTATION AND GENDER IDENTITY*

Mr Chairman,

The Holy See Delegation has noted with careful attention the Report on 'Discriminatory Laws and Practices and Acts of Violence against Individuals based on their Sexual Orientation and Gender Identity'. The Holy See has condemned repeatedly violence against people because of their perceived sexual differences. *The Catechism of the Catholic Church*, in fact, states: 'Every sign of unjust discrimination in regard [of homosexual persons] should be avoided.'[1] The teaching of the Catholic Church on this issue was authoritatively set forth in a 1986 letter to all the Catholic bishops throughout the world, as follows: 'It is deplorable that homosexual persons have been and are the object of violent malice in speech or in action. Such treatment deserves condemnation from the Church's pastors wherever it occurs. It reveals a kind of disregard for others which endangers the most fundamental principles of a healthy society. The intrinsic dignity of each person must always be respected in word, in action, and in law.'[2]

Sections III and IV of the Report cite numerous and lamentable examples of ways in which the dignity and human rights of persons have been transgressed because of their perceived sexual differences. These represent tragic incidents of how some human beings are treated by other members of the human family in a most inhumane manner. Most regrettably, examples of such unacceptable treatment on the basis of race, color, sex, language, religion, political or other opinion, national or social origin, property, birth or other status, can be listed in similar fashion. All such behavior, whether fomented between individuals, by social and cultural groups, or by the State itself, should be proscribed and sanctioned since it is not in conformity with the principle of universality enshrined in the Universal Declaration of Human Rights, which states that 'all human beings are born free and equal in dignity and rights.'

* Statement delivered at the 19th Session of the UN Human Rights Council – Item 3: *Panel Discussion on Discriminatory Laws and Practices and Acts of Violence against Individuals Based on their Sexual Orientation and Gender Identity*, 7 March 2012.

1 *Catechism of the Catholic Church*, London: Burns & Oates, 2003, § 2358.

2 Congregation for the Doctrine of the Faith, *Letter to the Bishops of the Catholic Church on the Pastoral Care of Homosexual Persons* (1986), § 10.

In this specific regard, the Report refers to the Vienna Declaration and Programme of Action that states: 'While the significance of national and regional peculiarities and various historical, cultural, and religious backgrounds must be borne in mind, it is the duty of States, regardless of their political, economic, and cultural systems, to promote and protect all human rights and fundamental freedoms.'[3]

Mr Chairman, it is the firm view of the Holy See that the grave problems of discrimination and violence toward the population upon which the Report focuses, or toward any other victimized groups or individuals, must be pursued on the basis of the principle of subsidiarity. Thus these problems should receive attention and effective action at the level of national and local governments, civil society, religious and cultural leaders. Such situations cannot be resolved by defining new categories, laws or policies that posit rights and privileges to special groups in society.

In Section II of her Report, entitled 'Applicable international standards and obligations', the Report advances compelling arguments, based in the Universal Declaration of Human Rights, to affirm the need for protection of the 'right to life, liberty and security of persons'. It further argues, on the basis of the Human Rights Committee general comment No. 6, that 'The State has an obligation to exercise due diligence to prevent, punish and redress deprivations of life, and to investigate and prosecute all acts of targeted violence.' My Delegation, however, finds both confusing and misleading the High Commissioner's decision to further develop her argumentation with an exclusive focus on those persons subjected to discrimination and violence on the basis of their perceived sexual differences. The rights cited by the High Commissioner are rights that should and must be universally respected and enjoyed; thus efforts to particularize or to develop special rights for special groups of people could easily put at risk the universality of these rights.

Moreover, the Holy See Delegation wishes to raise serious concern with the insertion of terms such as 'sexual orientation' and 'gender identity' which do not enjoy mention in binding documents of the United Nations and which are ambiguous in nature since they lack specific definition in international Human Rights instruments. In fact, my Delegation believes that the use of the term 'gender identity' was settled, in 1998, during the discussion leading up to the promulgation of the Statute of the International Criminal Court, which states, 'For purposes of this Statute, it is understood that the term "gender" refers to the two sexes, male and

[3] UN Doc. A/CONF.157/23, para. 5.

female, within the context of society. The term "gender" does not indicate any meaning different from the above.' Thus the Holy See notes that the categories 'sexual orientation' and 'gender identity' 'find no recognition or clear and agreed definition in international law'. Any requirement for States to take such terms into account in their efforts to promote and implement fundamental human rights could result in serious uncertainty in the application of law and undermine the ability of States to enter into and enforce new and existing human rights conventions and standards.[4]

In paragraph #68 of her Report, the High Commissioner rightly asserts that 'the Human Rights Committee has held that States are not required, under international law, to allow same-sex couples to marry.' She immediately proposes, however, that Sates have an obligation to 'ensure that unmarried same-sex couples are treated in the same way and entitled to the same benefits as unmarried opposite-sex couples.' In this regard, the Holy See expresses grave concern that, under the guise of 'protecting' people from discrimination and violence on the basis of perceived sexual differences, this Council may be running the risk of demeaning the sacred and time-honoured legal institution of marriage between man and woman, between husband and wife, which enjoyed special protection from time immemorial within legal, cultural, and religious traditions and within the modern human rights instruments, starting with the Universal Declaration of Human Rights, and extending to numerous other covenants, treaties and laws. Marriage contributes to society because it models the way in which women and men live interdependently and commit, for the whole of life, to seek the good of each other. The marital union also provides the best conditions for raising children; namely, the stable, loving relationship of a mother and a father; it is the foundation of the natural family, the basic cell of society. States confer legal recognition on the marital relationship between husband and wife because it makes a unique and essential contribution to the public good. If marriage were to be redefined in a way that makes other relationships equivalent to it, as has occurred in some countries and as the High Commissioner seems to be encouraging in her Report, the institution of marriage, and consequently the natural family itself, will be both devalued and weakened.

In conclusion, Mr Chairman, the Holy See Delegation condemns discrimination and violence against any human person, including those

[4] Cf. Statement of the Holy See to the 2008 United Nations General Assembly, discussion under Agenda item 64(b) entitled 'Promotion and Protection of Human Rights', UN Doc. A/63/635.

who are so targeted because of perceived sexual differences. We urge this Council, however, to preserve and maintain the universality of human rights and to fulfill its mandate to promote and monitor respect for the dignity of each and every human person. We raise serious concern with attempts to define new categories, introduce new terms, or posit new rights for special groups of people, within human rights law and instruments that already enjoy universal consensus. Such attempts pose a threat both to the universality of human rights, to national sovereignty, and to the social, cultural and religious institutions that are working to promote and attain the common good of all members of the human family.

THERE SHOULD EXIST NO 'MAJORITY' OR 'MINORITY'*

Madam President,

The 20th anniversary of the adoption of the UN Declaration on the Rights of Persons Belonging to National or Ethnic, Religious and Linguistic Minorities invites the international community to examine, with a more critical eye, the situation of minorities in the world, as the Report of the Independent Expert on Minority issues has rightly emphasized. The awareness of their own rights has greatly increased among the persons belonging to ethnic, religious and linguistic minorities, but, at the same time, the violations of these rights, on the part of States or of groups in society, have not ceased. Such problems are due either to indifference or to the political will to marginalize or to suppress, or even to eliminate, communities with a different ethnic or religious or linguistic identity. If a just participation by all is fostered in the governance of a State, all persons enjoying citizenship in its territory should have a right to be included. On the basis of such participation, peaceful coexistence, social development and prevention of conflicts will be the outcome.

Madam President,

The foundation upon which all existing communities in a State can cooperate constructively for the common good is well articulated in the Declaration, which affirms the 'inherent dignity and worth of the human person … [and] the equal rights of men and women and of nations large and small … without distinction as to race, sex, language or religion'.[1]

Distinct ethnic, religious or linguistic groups within a State can enrich its cultural and social life. The success of such contribution, however, is linked to the ability and duty of each respective group to be open to dialogue as 'individuals do not exist for themselves alone, but achieve their full identity in relation to others. The same can be said about groups of people. They indeed have a right to a collective identity that must be safeguarded, in accordance with the dignity of each member.'[2]

* Statement delivered at the 19th Session of the Human Rights Council: *Rights of Persons Belonging to National or Ethnic, Religious and Linguistic Minorities*, 14 March 2012.

1 Declaration on the Rights of Persons belonging to National or Ethnic, Religious and Linguistic Minorities, PP2 and PP1.

2 Pope John Paul II's Message for the 1989 World Day of Peace.

The Special Rapporteur might consider the usefulness of abolishing the concepts of 'majority' and 'minority' populations. Such development would be in accord with the foundational human rights principle that everyone is equal in rights and duties while also maintaining his right to associate with others in the preservation and development of cultural, religious and political identities and activities. This basic belief becomes the appropriate foundation of citizenship. A State in which all are partners through common citizenship, and which maintains laws and institutions that are at the service of everyone, can effectively carry out its responsibility to guarantee peace and promote the constructive contribution of all citizens. The selection of sectarian or ethnic or religious affiliation as criteria for belonging to a State runs contrary to the universality of human rights and lends itself to manipulation and abuses.

In a spirit of tolerance and mutual respect, educational programs that support a culture of dialogue, peace-building, democracy and pluralism can encourage a new start, in line with ongoing political, social and cultural changes in some regions of the world, and can open the way to a more peaceful future when the dignity of every person will be respected without such classifications as 'majority' and 'minority' but by virtue of our common God-given humanity.

Thank you, Madam President.

WE MUST NOT TOLERATE DISCRIMINATION AND VIOLENCE AGAINST WOMEN*

Madam President,

Violence against women remains an inescapable reality in too many places. Structures and attitudes of discrimination justify violence against women and impunity for their abuse too often perpetuates the problem. The daily fear of violence for attending school, the rape of a young girl with disabilities, and the forced marriage of a raped girl – each is a recent example that represents practices, laws and cultural conditioning and are manifestations of institutionalized and tolerated discrimination and violence against women. The Delegation of the Holy See thanks the Special Rapporteur for her efforts in promoting the advancement of women's rights. It is of the utmost importance that States establish mechanisms for the protection of women from discriminatory practices and perceptions in law and in practice in order to uphold human rights.

The Holy See acknowledges the unfortunate reality of discrimination and violence against women and recalls the words of Pope Benedict XVI: 'There are places and cultures where women are discriminated against or undervalued for the sole fact of being women ... where acts of violence are consummated in regard to women ... Faced with such grave and persistent phenomena the Christian commitment appears all the more urgent so that everywhere it may promote a culture that recognizes the dignity that belongs to women, in law and in concrete reality.'[1]

Madam President,

Times of political transition are prime opportunities to study the *de jure* and *de facto* condition of women. As we have seen throughout history and most recently in the Arab Spring in the Middle East and North Africa, these are times wrought with violence and instability.

Due to the destabilizing nature of political turmoil, the Holy See stresses the importance of women's roles in the family. 'The family is

* Statement delivered at the 20th Session of the Human Rights Council – Item 3: 'Special Rapporteur on Violence against Women', 26 June 2012.

1 Pope Benedict XVI, 'International Convention on Woman and Man, the "Humanum" in Its Entirety', 9 February 2008, www.vatican.va/holy_father/benedict_xvi/speeches/2008/february/documents/hf_benxvi_spe_20080209_donna-uomo_en.html.

the vital cell of society' and women, as equal participants in marriage as spouses and mothers, are fundamental to the preservation of the institution of family and, therefore, society.[2] 'Every social model that intends to serve the good of man must not overlook the centrality and social responsibility of the family', which includes all societies that are committed to the promotion and realization of human rights.[3] A consideration of women in the family cannot be ignored as it will supplement any attentive study of improvements in women's rights in the political, public, legal and social spheres.

It is essential to eliminate discrimination and violence through effective frameworks for the protection of women's rights and the empowerment of women in any context of political transition, economic crisis or otherwise. These structures must respond to the cross-cutting nature of sex-based discrimination against women including those with disabilities and those of particular religions or beliefs.

Madam President,

Unstable situations marked by violence present the risk of particularly aggressive behavior against the more defenseless groups of society. A grave concern of the Holy See is that the protection of women from violence be provided in these contexts, with special concern for women who are human rights defenders. Judicial impunity, cultural and social norms that tolerate discrimination and fail to address violent acts such as female infanticide or sex-selective abortion must be addressed and rejected.

It is necessary to construct a reality in which men and women are treated equally, viewed equally and freed from the undignified treatment of discriminatory practices. The dignity of each person, women and men, requires that just institutions and fair societies exist for its promotion.

[2] Second Vatican Ecumenical Council, Decree *Apostolicam Actuositatem*, § 11: AAS 58 (1966), p. 848.

[3] 'The Family, the Vital Cell of Society.' *Compendium of the Social Doctrine of the Church*, 2004, § 97.

Madam President,

Considering the 'well-rooted and profound diversity between the masculine and the feminine and their vocation to reciprocity and complementarity, to collaboration and to communion',[4] the Delegation of the Holy See reaffirms the intrinsic truth of the equal dignity of men and women and therefore the necessity to eliminate any discrimination and violence against women.

Thank you, Madam President.

[4] Pope Benedict XVI, 'International Convention on Woman and Man'.

SERVILE MARRIAGE, A CONTEMPORARY FORM OF SLAVERY*

Madam President,

The Holy See Delegation warmly welcomes Dr Gulnara Shahinian, Special Rapporteur on contemporary forms of slavery, including its causes and consequences.

Regrettably, women and children are usually the subject of slavery and its contemporary forms to a large extent, as they often have less personal and material means. We must denounce the existing discrimination and slavery on the grounds of belonging to other caste, religion, social class or ethnicity. The root causes for these new forms of slavery are manifold: poverty, lack of education, complicity of members of the family, pressure on the children, armed conflicts and violence, among others.

In addition, there exist sexual harassments and violence against the victims of the new forms of slavery. These problems are both the cause and the consequence of a deficit of education and a lack of self-esteem.

My Delegation regrets the existence of the so-called servile marriage in which one spouse is reduced to the condition of a mere object, on which it is possible to exercise some or all rights derived from ownership.

We must remember that all human beings have an inalienable and inherent dignity. No human being should be treated as an object or a commodity. Such attitude cannot be justified in any way, let alone for an eventual improvement in the economic or family situation. Child marriage, as indicated by the Special Rapporteur, implies that one spouse or both do not have the minimum marriageable age.

My Delegation welcomes the comments made by the Special Rapporteur on the need for a full and free consent to the marriage and the indication that there should be a minimum age to celebrate it, free and with full consent.

The social doctrine of the Church, about family and marriage: 'The family has its foundation in the free choice of the spouses to unite themselves in marriage, in respect for the meaning and values of this institution that does not depend on man but on God himself.' Marriage requires free consent, both from the man and the woman; therefore, forced, servile, by

* Statement delivered at the 21st Session of the Human Rights Council – Item 3: *Interactive Dialogue with the Special Rapporteur on Contemporary Forms of Slavery*, 13 September 2012.

correspondence or sham marriages (wife or husband married in order to legalize their immigration status) are also invalid.

In conclusion, my Delegation fully supports the efforts to combat and prevent forced marriage so as not to violate or limit the rights of any parties, husband and wife. We also support the increased investments in education for girls subjected to forced marriages or at risk, including those already married and pregnant.

My Delegation would like to encourage the international community and the Special Rapporteur to:

- Strengthen the efforts towards the eradication of corporal punishment, marriage without mutual full consent and domestic violence;
- Continue to improve health and education systems, giving access to all regardless of their economic, religious, social or ethnic background;
- Establish care programs for victims of servile marriages through education, shelter and medical or psychological support;
- Safeguard the family and marriage as the conjugal union between a man and a woman based on the free consent of the spouses.

Thank you, Madam President.

WE MUST VALUE AND UPHOLD THE TRANSCENDENT DIGNITY OF ALL PERSONS*

Mr President,

Modern day slave trade is a fast growing industry in our globalized world and it affects some 30 million persons. This criminal 21 billion-dollar-a-year industry is entrenched in almost all the supply chains providing food, clothes and electronics, to the world market. The products of our daily usage should remind us of the responsibility to be aware of how workers, who make our life more comfortable, are dealt with.

The Special Rapporteur on contemporary forms of slavery outlines effectively the challenges facing the international community and the initiatives needed to combat this practice which reduces human beings to mere tools for profit and poisons human society.

Today's slaves are children forced to work in hazardous and unhealthy conditions; they are women exploited in domestic work where the requirements of justice and of the 2011 Domestic Workers Convention (No. 189) – concerning decent work for domestic workers that entered into force a few days ago – are negated; they are women manipulated into sexual activity for tourists and other taskmasters; they are boys and men obliged to carry out dirty and dangerous jobs without any choice or rightful claims on their part. Many of these slaves remain imprisoned in their condition as a result of trafficking in persons on the part of criminal individuals and groups: all are victims whose plight is by now well documented, but not sufficiently addressed, as is the case of the migrants who disappear in the Sinai desert in their desperate journey towards freedom.

A culture of greed and total disregard of human dignity is at the root of the slavery phenomenon. First of all, it is a perversion of all ethical standards, 'an affront [to human dignity and] to fundamental values which are shared by all cultures and peoples, values rooted in the very nature of the human person'.[1] Moreover, this culture detaches freedom from the moral law with the consequence that the victims of contemporary slavery become a mere commodity in the market of consumerism.

* Statement delivered at the 24th Session of the Human Rights Council – Item 3: *Contemporary Forms of Slavery*, 12 September 2013.

1 Pope John Paul II, Letter to Archbishop Jean-Louis Tauran on the Occasion of the International Conference: 'Twenty-first Century Slavery: The Human Rights Dimension to Trafficking in Human Beings', Rome, 15 May 2002.

As the Special Rapporteur points out, progress has been made in combating slavery through juridical instruments, good practices and increased awareness of the many forms that this crime takes from debt bondage to servile marriage and from child slavery to domestic servitude.[2]

Mr President,

The Holy See is deeply concerned about the persistence of this social plague and, particularly through the activity of the Pontifical Council for the Pastoral Care of Migrants and Itinerant People, is committed to combating it in its various manifestations. Additionally, Christian faith-based groups have been on the forefront of this effort to reach out to victims of slavery and to provide them with an escape and a return to normal life by making available temporary shelter, counselling and legal advice. Thus, for example, in response to a strong appeal by Pope Francis, who stigmatized 'selfishness that continues in human trafficking, the most extensive form of slavery in this twenty-first century',[3] the Pontifical Academies of Sciences and Social Sciences, together with the World Federation of Catholic Medical Associations, are organizing a preparatory workshop to examine human trafficking and modern slavery.

To counteract the persistence of slavery some practical steps are called for: an updated national legislation, a public culture that values and upholds the transcendent dignity of every person, an effective judicial system that prevents slave masters from retaking control of their victims. Human security needs reinforcing and the root causes that make people vulnerable must be thoroughly addressed by promoting development, creating decent jobs, and facilitating access to education and health care. The Special Rapporteur reviews a series of good practices that would remedy this wound on the human family constituted by the various forms

[2] Several treaties have been enacted: The 1926 Slavery Convention or the Convention to Suppress the Slave Trade and Slavery; the ILO 1930 Convention Concerning Forced or Compulsory Labour or Forced Labour Convention (No. 29); The United Nations 1956 Supplementary Convention on the Abolition of Slavery, the Slave Trade, and Institutions and Practices Similar to Slavery; the 1957 ILO Abolition of Forced Labour Convention; the UN Convention against Transnational Organized Crime and the Protocol to Prevent, Suppress and Punish Trafficking in Persons, especially Women and Children. The UN Slavery Trust Fund on Contemporary Forms of Slavery was established in 1991 by the General Assembly.

[3] Pope Francis, *Urbi et Orbi Message*, Easter Sunday, 31 March 2013.

of modern slavery. As always, the challenge remains the implementation of human rights treaties and recommendations so that the collaboration of governments, the international community, the business sector and civil society may effectively advance the elimination of an evil that offends the dignity of every person.

THE RIGHTS OF RELIGIOUS MINORITIES: AN ESSENTIAL PRECONDITION TO PEACE AND STABILITY*

Madam Chairperson,

The topic of this Forum centered on guaranteeing the rights of religious minorities is both timely and necessary. Surveys related to religious minorities show that around the world attainment of such rights has been blocked or even has been reduced. Currently, in 51 per cent of all countries some limitation or restriction has been placed upon religious minorities and in 25 per cent of these countries, some or all religious minorities are classified as illegal. Furthermore, in 24.2 per cent of all countries, restrictions have been placed on building, leasing or repairing places of worship, while in 7.3 per cent of countries all such activities are completely prohibited. Restrictions placed on religious schools are found in 18.6 per cent of all countries, and this phenomenon is increasing.[1] The latest Pew Forum Report on Religion states: 'Globally, the share of countries with high or very high restriction on religion rose from 37% in the year ending in mid-2010 to 40% in 2011, a five-year high. Because some of the most restrictive countries are very populous, more than 5.1 billion people (74%) were living in countries with high government restrictions on religion or high social hostilities involving religion, the brunt of which often falls on religious minorities.'[2] Thus, in many parts of the world, religious minorities struggle merely to survive, and their future is tied to full respect of their rights. Therefore, in order to ensure the survival of religious minorities, we need to expand the discussion beyond the fundamental right to religious freedom, to that of guaranteeing all human rights of such groups. Recent events have shown how the identities of minorities are naturally linked to their sense of community, to the point that no peaceful political solution can be reached without addressing the religious dimension of the different minorities present in a country or region. The dramatic and horrendous civil war in Syria shows, beyond any doubt, that the respect and implementation of the rights of religious minorities are an essential precondition to peace and political stability.

* Statement delivered at the 6th Session of the Forum on Minority Issues, 26 November 2013.

1 Numbers taken from the dataset collected since 1990 by the Religion and State-Minorities Project (ARDA Project): www.thearda.com/ras/.

2 Pew Forum, 'Arab Spring Adds to Global Restrictions on Religion', 20 June 2013, p. 3.

Among religious minorities, Christian communities are under special threat,[3] especially in the Middle East, where they have existed for centuries and have developed a fair degree of peaceful coexistence, which now is deteriorating.[4] Members of the various Christian communities in Syria,[5] in Egypt,[6] in Iraq[7] and elsewhere are choosing exile over remaining in their ancestral lands where they are victims of untold violence, threats and an overall increase in discrimination.[8] The rights of these minorities are violated as a result of the lawlessness from wars, of prejudice, exclusion from public office, greed for their properties, and power plays. Without rapid changes, the presence of Christians in the Middle East, which has extended over the past two millennia, is no longer assured.

All religious minorities must be protected by respecting and upholding all the rights inherent in every person. In the experience of the Catholic communities, two approaches have proven effective: first, the recognition of the dignity of every person, and of her equal right and duty as any other citizen to participate in the social, cultural, political and economic life of the country; second, the implementation of practical steps, through education, dialogue and solidarity, that make possible productive coexistence.

The foundation for human relations in society and in any country that allows for practical initiatives of dialogue and friendship in today's pluralism of beliefs and life-styles is the common dignity shared by all as well as the gift of reason: 'In a globalized world marked by increasingly multi-ethnic and multi-religious societies, the great religions can serve as an important factor of unity and peace for the human family. On the basis of their religious convictions and their reasoned pursuit of the common good, their followers are called to give responsible expression to their commitment within a context of religious freedom. Amid the variety of religious cultures, there is a need to value those elements which foster

3 'In 2011 … harassment of Christians continued to be reported in the largest number of countries (105)', ibid., pp. 10–11. Christians were most subjected to government and social harassment in all countries.

4 Pew Forum, 'Religions on the Move: Religious Affiliation of International Migrants', 8 March 2012.

5 www.mei.edu/content/migration-syrian-christians.

6 http://weekly.ahram.org.eg/News/2402/24/The-Copts-flee-Egypt.aspx.

7 http://hal.archives-ouvertes.fr/docs/00/36/49/61/PDF/Chatelard_Iraqi_migration.pdf.

8 See the 'United States Commission on International Religious Freedom', Countries Reports: www.uscirf.gov/countries.html.

civil coexistence, while rejecting whatever is contrary to the dignity of men and women.[9] A practical aspect of the recognition of this common dignity is provided by the common citizenship that requires the State to prevent any discrimination based on religious conviction and its expression in private or in public with others. The State cannot imprison groups of citizens through archaic legal structures that more often facilitate their exploitation and abuse rather than their protection. The elimination of all barriers to the full enjoyment of citizenship becomes an urgent responsibility. Acceptance of diverse religious beliefs and groups should be seen as a normal experience. At the same time, when collective expressions of belief are accepted, the individual must be free to participate in society on the basis of equality of opportunities, duties and rights. Citizenship becomes the criterion for equal participation possibilities in the management of society.

The various recommendations of the Independent Expert on minority issues[10] are excellent, concrete and have all our support. Experience, however, indicates that such recommendations presuppose a modern, Western, secular State. On the other hand, the rights of religious minorities are highly dependent of the way States understand secularity and translate it into positive rights and policies. If the recommendations are to be more realistic the Forum should dedicate special attention to this issue. In line with the request for presentation of good practices that can help the protection of religious minorities, the Catholic experience has embraced a variety of initiatives:

- Promotion of interreligious meetings at the international and national level;
- Initiation of dialogue with specific religious communities;
- Acknowledgement and exchange, on a regular basis, of messages and good wishes for specific feasts observed by different religious communities as on the occasion of Ramadan, Purim, etc.;
- Education of millions of young people in Catholic schools that includes teaching mutual respect and rejection of manuals, textbooks, teaching, that promote hate;
- Encouragement, through the voice of the Pope, of public opinion that favours mutual respect and the formulation of just policies related to religious minorities.

[9] Pope Benedict XVI's Message for the 2011 World Day of Peace.

[10] UN Human Rights Council, Forum on Minority Issues. Sixth Session. Note by the Independent Expert on minority issues, Rita Izsak, on guaranteeing the rights of religious minorities. 3 October 2013, UN Doc. A/HRC/FMI/2013/2.

- Channelling of aid and services through Catholic programs open to serving all religious groups, since any poor or needy person is assisted without regard to race, language, religion or sex.

In conclusion, Madam Chairperson, it is well known that the international community has developed a significant number of instruments to guard against discrimination toward any religious group and to guide people toward the path of effective protection of persons and minorities professing a specific belief. Good practices are not lacking. Certainly the theme of the Forum is correct as it affirms that the rights of religious minorities extend beyond religious freedom, while, at the same time, that freedom remains of central importance to the life and identity of religious communities. The political will to recognize the equal human dignity and rights of all persons opens the way to a future without discrimination and persecution for religious people and communities and to a genuine and stable democracy.

PRESENTATION OF THE INITIAL PERIODIC REPORT OF THE HOLY SEE TO THE COMMITTEE ON THE CONVENTION AGAINST TORTURE*

Mr Chairperson, Members of the Committee,

Allow me, first of all, to extend cordial greetings to all the members of the Committee on the Convention against Torture and other Cruel, Inhuman or Degrading Treatment or Punishment. In the presentation of the Initial Report of the Holy See, I wish to introduce the members of our Delegation present for this interactive dialogue. With me this morning are Monsignor Christophe El-Kassis and Professor Vincenzo Buonomo, of the Secretariat of State of the Holy See, and Monsignor Richard Gyhra, Secretary of the Holy See Mission.

The Holy See acceded to the Convention against Torture (CAT) on June 22, 2002. It did so with the very clear and direct intention that this Convention applied to Vatican City State (VCS). In its capacity as the sovereign of Vatican City State, the Holy See provided an important 'Interpretative Declaration' that shows its approach to the CAT.[1] Such Declaration underlines the motives for accession to the Convention and expresses the moral support given to it, namely the defense of the human person as already indicated in the Universal Declaration of Human Rights.

For the Holy See, the Interpretative Declaration provides a necessary hermeneutic to understand the motives for acceding to the Convention and also for considering the implementation of the Convention by the legal order of Vatican City State which is the very exercise we are engaging in at this moment in the consideration of the Initial Report of the Holy See to the CAT.

In this sense, my Delegation deems it worthwhile to reiterate several of the more salient points of the Interpretative Declaration so as to properly frame the consideration and discussions of the Initial Report of the Holy See.

In the first place, the Interpretative Declaration lauds the Convention as a worthy instrument for the defense against acts of torture when it

* Presentation of the Initial Report to the Committee of the Convention against Torture, 5 May 2014.

1 In this sense, the Holy See acted in accord with the provisions of international law of treaties, in full compliance with those norms, as accepted by the other contracting Parties.

says: 'The Holy See considers the Convention against Torture and Other Cruel, Inhuman or Degrading Treatment or Punishment a valid and suitable instrument for fighting against acts that constitute a serious offence against the dignity of the human person.' In this sense, indeed, the Holy See wished to express the harmony of its own principles and vision of the human person with those ideals and practices set forth in the Convention against Torture.

Second, the Declaration elaborates more precisely the Holy See's position, in which the teaching of the Catholic Church clearly articulates its opposition to acts of violence and torture.[2]

Third, although the Convention applies to Vatican City State, the Holy See adds a crucial moral voice in its support through its teaching[3]

[2] Already in 1953, Pope Pius XII gave a clear condemnation of torture saying: 'Preliminary juridical proceeding must exclude physical and psychological torture and the use of drugs; first of all because they violate a natural right, even if the accused is indeed guilty, and secondly because all too often they give rise to erroneous results' (Address to the Sixth International Congress on Criminal Law, 3 October 1953). 'In recent times the Catholic Church has consistently pronounced itself in favor of unconditional respect for life itself and unequivocally condemned whatever violates the integrity of the human person, such as mutilation, torments inflicted on body or mind, attempts to coerce the will itself' (*Gaudium et Spes*, § 27. Cf. Pope John Paul II, *Veritatis Splendor*, § 80 and *Evangelium Vitae*, § 3). The Declaration also refers to the Code of Canon Law (1983), cc. 1397–8 and the *Catechism of the Catholic Church* (1995), §§ 2297–8, which 'enumerate and clearly identify forms of behavior that can harm the bodily or mental integrity of the individual, condemn their perpetrators and call for the abolition of such acts'. Following, and building upon, the teaching found in these fundamental documents of the Holy See, one should include the articulation found in the *Compendium of the Social Doctrine of the Church*, first published in 2004, which in treating the question of criminal interrogation states: 'the regulation against the use of torture, even in the case of serious crimes, must be strictly observed: "Christ's disciple refuses every recourse to such methods, which nothing could justify and in which the dignity of man is as much debased in his torturer as in the torturer's victim." International juridical instruments concerning human rights correctly indicate a prohibition against torture as a principle which cannot be contravened under any circumstances' (*Compendium of the Social Doctrine of the Church*, § 404).

[3] The Interpretative Declaration provides evidence of this unique contribution by offering examples from papal addresses and publications. On 14 January 1978, Pope Paul VI, in his last address to the diplomatic corps, after referring to the torture and mistreatment practised in various countries against individuals, concluded as follows: 'How could the Church fail to take up a stern stand ... with regard to torture and to similar acts of violence inflicted on the human person?' Pope John Paul II, for his part, did not fail to affirm that 'torture must be called by its proper name' (Cf. Pope John Paul II's Message for the 1980 World Day of Peace). He also expressed his deep compassion for the victims of torture and in particular for tortured women (see respectively, Pope John Paul II, World Congress on Pastoral Ministry for Human Rights, Rome, 4 July 1998; and Pope John Paul II, Message to the Secretary General

and through the following statement: 'In this spirit the Holy See wishes to lend its moral support and collaboration to the international community, so as to contribute to the elimination of recourse to torture, which is inadmissible and inhuman.'[4]

Finally, and not of least importance, the Interpretative Declaration insists that 'The Holy See, in becoming a party to the Convention on behalf of the Vatican City State, undertakes to apply it insofar as it is compatible, in practice, with the peculiar nature of that State.'[5] As such, in regard to the application of the Convention and any examination, questions or criticisms, or implementation thereof, the Holy See intends to focus exclusively on Vatican City State, respecting the international sovereignty of this State and the legitimate and specific authority of the Convention and of the Committee competent to examine State reports. Hence, my Delegation judges it useful to present, briefly yet clearly, the essential distinctions between Vatican City State and Holy See, as described in the Initial Report.[6]

The Holy See, as member of the international community, is related but separate and distinct from the territory of Vatican City State, over which it exercises sovereignty. Its international personality has never been confused with the territories over which it has exercised State sovereignty. In its present form, Vatican City State was established in 1929 to more

of the United Nations, 1 March 1993). To these could be added numerous other examples from the pontificates of Pope Benedict XVI and Pope Francis. For example, Benedict XVI, in speaking of the purpose of punitive institutions, declared: 'By their very nature, therefore, these institutions must contribute to the rehabilitation of offenders, facilitating their transition from despair to hope and from unreliability to dependability. When conditions within jails and prisons are not conducive to the process of regaining a sense of a worth and accepting its related duties, these institutions fail to achieve one of their essential ends. Public authorities must be ever vigilant in this task, eschewing any means of punishment or correction that either undermine or debase the human dignity of prisoners. In this regard, I reiterate that the prohibition against torture 'cannot be contravened under any circumstances' (Pope Benedict XVI, Address to the Participants in the Twelfth World Congress of the International Commission of Catholic Prison Pastoral Care, 6 September 2007).

4 Interpretative Declaration (The Holy See recognizes that its moral voice may assist the International Community in acting as an active agent in the promotion and defence of human rights. It willingly enters into the Convention against Torture with the principal intention of defending the inviolable rights of the human person and encouraging other Member States to do the same through adequate legislation and institutional practices which respect the life and dignity of the human person).

5 Ibid. 6 Holy See, Initial Report, §§ 4–6.

effectively guarantee the spiritual and moral mission of the Holy See. Therefore, colloquial references to the Holy See as the 'Vatican' can be misleading. In this sense, the Holy See, as mentioned, globally encourages basic principles and authentic human rights recognized in the CAT, while implementing it within the territory of Vatican City State in harmony with the Interpretative Declaration.

Having presented some of the essential points that should guide and assist our discussion, I now wish to give an overview of the Holy See's Initial Report.

The Initial Report of the Holy See, submitted to this Committee in December 2012, is divided into four parts: (1) Introduction, (2) General Information, (3) The Convention against Torture, and (4) Affirmation of the prohibition against torture and other cruel, inhuman or degrading treatment or punishment in the teachings and activities of the Holy See. Since much of the content of the Introduction has been already mentioned, as this provides a necessary guide to understanding the approach and perspective of the Holy See regarding the Convention, I shall proceed to the second part on 'General Information'.

Apart from presenting the essential distinctions and relations between the Holy See, Vatican City State and the Catholic Church, I wish to highlight several important elements presented within the section of 'General Information'. In particular, the first point of reference is the legal system of Vatican City State, that is autonomous in respect to the legal system of the Catholic Church. In fact, not all canonical norms are relevant for the governance of this territory. In relation to the topic of crime and punishment there are specific laws that criminalize illicit activities and provide for proportionate penalties in Vatican City State. The necessity of a penitentiary system, in this small territory, is minimal, especially considering certain aspects of the Lateran Treaty (Art. 22) which afford this territory the option of utilizing the judicial assistance of the Italian State if deemed necessary.

As noted in the section on Statistics, the small population of Vatican City State, while receiving roughly 18 million pilgrims and tourists annually, has a relatively tiny number of criminal and penal matters registered. It is also worth mentioning that the message of the various media services of the Holy See, disseminated in the major languages, reaches a truly international audience that makes it arguably one of the most effective moral voices in the world for human rights, including the position against torture and other cruel and inhuman punishments.

Turning now to the third part of the Initial Report, which addresses systematically each of the sixteen substantive articles of the CAT, my Delegation wishes to highlight several significant steps and improvements in Vatican City State to comply with the Convention, even since the consigning of the Initial Report in December 2012. In the first place, there is the modification of Vatican City State legislation with the promulgation of Pope Francis' Apostolic Letter on 11 July 2013, 'On the Jurisdiction of Judicial Authorities of Vatican City State in Criminal Matters', particularly Article 3, of Law No. VIII, which deals specifically with the Crime of Torture.[7] While the implementation of this basic law into the criminal and penal law of Vatican City State in some fashion touches upon different articles of the Convention, it is worth mentioning a few directly. In relation to Article 1 of the Convention, the new Vatican City State legislation integrates, practically verbatim, the definition of torture and cruel and inhuman punishment as supplied therein and, therefore, *de facto*, fulfills Article 4 of the Convention by its integration into the penal code and the establishment of appropriate penalties for such offenses. Paragraph 6 of the same article 3 of the amended Law VIII effectively restates article 15 of the Convention, prohibiting the use of any statement made as a result of torture to be considered as evidence.

[7] Holy See, *Supplementary Norms: Law VIII*, chapter I, *Crimes against the Person*, Art. 3: Torture. Full text follows:

(1) The public official having judicial, judicial police or law enforcement functions, as well as whoever performs in an official capacity a similar or analogous role, and whoever, under their instigation or with their consent or acquiescence, inflicts severe pain or suffering, whether physical or mental, on a person in order to obtain from him or a third person some information or a confession, or to punishing him for an act that he or a third person has committed, or is suspected of having committed, or to intimidate or coerce him or a third person, or for any other reason based on any kind discrimination, is punished with five to ten years' imprisonment.

(2) The penalty is increased by one-half if the offence results in serious injury or if it is committed against a minor. The penalty is doubled if the offence results in an injury of the utmost gravity.

(3) If, as an unintended consequence of the offence, the victim dies, the penalty shall be of no less than fifteen years' imprisonment.

(4) The offence does not exist when the pain or suffering arises from, is inherent to, or is caused by legitimate measures or sanctions.

(5) The offence is not justified by an order from a superior officer or a public authority, nor by a state of war or a threat of war, nor by internal political instability or any other exceptional circumstances.

No statement made under torture may be invoked or used as evidence in any proceedings, except against a person accused of torture, in order to prove that such a statement was made.

Also modified in July 2013, the amendments of Law IX address with greater specificity and clarity the questions of crimes, whether within or outside the territory of the State, of jurisdiction, of extradition, and of terms of sentencing.[8] The procedural and legislative changes seek to implement the principles contained in the Convention against Torture under Articles 3, 5 and 8. In particular, one should note the development on the question of extradition and also the denial thereof on the part of the Holy See if the requesting State practices torture or uses capital punishment.[9]

To summarize, the third part of the Holy See Report must be viewed through the updates offered by the recent modifications to the procedures and legislation of Vatican City State which are a significant improvement from previous legislation and enhance positively the contents of the Initial Report. In fact, my Delegation views this new legislation as a direct result of the Holy See's adhesion to the CAT. Therefore, I am sure the Committee will consider these new laws in the ensuing discussion and the eventual Concluding Observations.

The fourth part of the Initial Report, regarding the 'Affirmation of the prohibition against torture and other cruel, inhuman or degrading treatment or punishment in the teachings and activities of the Holy See', references the wide array of documents, proclamations, publications, radio and television programs by which the Holy See actively addresses not only followers of the Catholic Faith, but also the international community and all people of good will.[10]

In this way, the moral voice of the Holy See, while promoting and defending all authentic human rights, reaches the members of the Catholic Church in an attempt to foster an interior conversion of hearts to love God and one's neighbor. This love, in turn, should overflow into good practices at the local level in accordance with the laws of States. It should be stressed, particularly in light of much confusion, that the Holy

[8] Holy See, *Law IX: Amendments to the Criminal Code and the Code of Criminal Procedure.* Of particular relevance vis-à-vis the CAT are Articles 1–7 and 32–46.

[9] Cf. ibid., Chapter I, Art. 6 on 'Extradition'.

[10] In particular, the Holy See exercising its voice as a moral authority to the community of believers freely integrated into, and following, Catholic doctrinal and moral teaching, promotes the integral formation of the human person based on an accurate understanding of human dignity. This formation, while guided by Catholic principles, is primarily rooted in the education of the faithful, especially the young, which then also permeates all of society through the dedicated efforts of Catholic-inspired institutions, found throughout the world, as they fulfill their mission in the variety of fields from education, health care, penitentiaries, refugee camps, among others.

See has no jurisdiction – as that term is understood also under article 2.1 of the Convention – over every member of the Catholic Church. The Holy See wishes to reiterate that the persons who live in a particular country are under the jurisdiction of the legitimate authorities of that country and are thus subject to the domestic law and the consequences contained therein. State authorities are obligated to protect, and, when necessary, prosecute persons under their jurisdiction. The Holy See exercises the same authority upon those who live in Vatican City State in accordance with its laws. Hence, the Holy See, in respecting the principles of autonomy and sovereignty of States, insists that the State authority, which has legitimate competency, act as the responsible agent of justice in regard to crimes and abuses committed by persons under their jurisdiction. My Delegation wishes to emphasize that this includes not only acts of torture and other acts of cruel and inhuman punishments, but also all other acts considered as crimes committed by any individual who, notwithstanding affiliation with a Catholic institution, is subject to a particular State authority. The obligation and responsibility of promoting justice in these cases resides with the competent domestic jurisdiction.

To recapitulate this fourth part of the Report, it might be said that the measures employed by the Holy See to take effective legislative, administrative, judicial or other measures to prevent and to prohibit torture and to address its root causes to avoid future acts in this area are abundant. This manifests the Holy See's desire 'to lend its moral support and collaboration to the international community, so as to contribute to the elimination of recourse to torture, which is inadmissible and inhuman'.[11]

In line with above considerations, the Holy See assures this Committee of its continued implementation and promotion of the Convention against Torture. An analysis of the Concluding Observations offered in the reviews of other Member States suggests that an evolution in the interpretation of this document may raise some questions on the part of the States Parties. As Party to the CAT, the Holy See wishes, that in the application of the Convention to all appropriate new situations, all should remain within its specific area of concern that the CAT outlines.[12]

[11] Holy See, Interpretative Declaration.

[12] The caveat of the Holy See is twofold. First, for the sake of defending the competency, integrity and duty of the Committee to oversee the implementation of the Convention against Torture, it seems fair and prudent that the focus should remain upon the contents of the Convention. Second, the introduction of other themes, of which the Convention does not speak, effectively diminishes the original focus of the Convention and thus further jeopardizes the situations for those who are

My Delegation believes that the Holy See has fulfilled in good faith the obligations assumed under CAT, since it has integrated its values and principles into the legislation of Vatican City State according to the particular and unique nature of this State. In conclusion, allow me to underscore the singular role the Holy See has played, and will continue to play, in advocating on a global level the values and all human rights that safeguard the dignity of every person and which are a necessary component for friendly relations among peoples and peace in the world.

truly being abused, tortured and punished. As such, the purpose of the Convention, as it is being unfolded in the work of the Committee, runs the risk of not only being ineffective, but even counterproductive, with regard to its original, noble, intention.

PROMOTING FAITH AND SHARED HUMAN VALUES TO ERADICATE MODERN SLAVERY*

Mr President,

My Delegation thanks the Special Rapporteur on contemporary forms of slavery, including its causes and consequences, for her timely Report, both on the activities undertaken during the mandate of her predecessor, and on her own priorities during the period of 2014 to 2017.

Some shocking forms of contemporary slavery justifiably have attracted the attention of the media and the international community at large; these include massive kidnappings and sale of young girls under the false premises of religious teachings, as is done, for example, by Boko Haram in Nigeria or by the so-called Islamic State group in northern Iraq. Some 250,000 children are forcibly conscripted and even used as 'human shields' in the frontlines of armed conflicts. Without any intention to ignore or diminish concern for such shameful abuses of human dignity, Mr President, the Holy See takes note of the Special Rapporteur's stated intention to address the subtler forms of slavery that deserve specific attention, including the 5.7 million children who are victims of forced and bonded labour, domestic servitude, early, forced and servile marriage, child slave work and caste-based forms of slavery, which affect the lives of so many and are not confined to developing and poor countries.

While acknowledging the profit motive that selfishly motivates the demand for forced labour and other contemporary forms of slavery, the Special Rapporteur indicates additional important 'push' factors, including the increasing incidence of absolute poverty among many families affected by the economic crises, the lack of education, and illiteracy, long-term and apparently irreversible unemployment, which force people into informal-sector work without adequate pay or social protection, involuntary migration, and human trafficking.

The international community already has developed, and tries to implement, numerous international conventions and accords to protect against contemporary forms of slavery. My Delegation believes, however, that such instruments will not fully meet their aims if we do not simultaneously inspire broader political will and engage all members of society.

* Statement delivered at the 27th Session of the Human Rights Council – Item 3: *Special Rapporteur on Contemporary Forms of Slavery*, 9 September 2014.

We need to break the silence about this 'open wound on the body of contemporary society … ' and motivate 'men and women of good will who want to cry out, "Enough!"'.[1] Pope Francis takes each and every opportunity to denounce the 'many abominable forms of slavery [that] persist in today's world … '[2] Thus he has joined with leaders from other major religious traditions to promote the ideals of faith and of shared human values in order to eradicate modern slavery and human trafficking from our world and for all time.[3] Moreover, the Holy Father has announced that the theme, 'Slaves no more, but brothers and sisters', will be the title of the Message for the upcoming 48th World Day of Peace.

Mr President, to counter slavery effectively, the inviolable dignity of every person must be recognized above all: we are all equal members of the one human family and, therefore, we must reject any inequality, which would allow one person to enslave another. We are called to act everywhere with mutual love and generosity, thus leading to liberation and inclusion for everyone.[4]

[1] Address of Pope Francis to Participants in the International Conference to Combat Human Trafficking, Vatican City, 10 April 2014, http://w2.vatican.va/content/francesco/en/speeches/2014/april/documents/papa-francesco_20140410_tratta-persone-umane.html.

[2] Announcement of Pontifical Council for Justice and Peace: 'Slavery to be the theme of 2015 World Day of Peace', www.news.va/en/news/slavery-to-be-theme-of-2015-world-day-of-peace.

[3] Press Statement of 'Global Freedom Network', Vatican City, 17 March 2014, http://press.vatican.va/content/salastampa/en/bollettino/pubblico/2014/03/17/0182/00396.html.

[4] Announcement of Pontifical Council for Justice and Peace: 'Slavery to be the theme of 2015 World Day of Peace', www.news.va/en/news/slavery-to-be-theme-of-2015-world-day-of-peace.

MEN AND WOMEN: A COMPLEMENTARITY IN EQUALITY*

Mr President,

The Holy See Delegation is pleased to take part in this important full-day discussion on the Human Rights of Women as called for in Resolution 26/15, for the continued promotion, protection and support of women's human rights. There is still much to be done to arrive at the recognition of the equal human dignity that women possess and to acknowledging the necessary role that women play in society on the level of family and in social and political life. We are all too aware of the violations of women's human rights and dignity in many parts of the world, where they are subject to second-class social status or where they are victims of modern forms of slavery, including sex trafficking, early and forced marriages, lack of access to equal education, employment and wage discrimination, domestic violence and forced prostitution, among others.[1] Women and children are the most vulnerable in conflict situations wherein there is forced migration or displacement,[2] and in which, at times, they have been specifically targeted, kidnapped and systematically raped.[3] These ongoing abuses, coupled with the reality of new, modern, forms of slavery challenge the international community to continue to seek the path to realize the equal respect for women's dignity and the elimination of discrimination. This requires a renewed look at our social, political and cultural perspectives which, at times, incorporate a less than proper appreciation of women. As Pope Francis states, 'Think of the many forms of male dominance whereby the woman was considered second class. Think of the exploitation and the commercialization of the female body in the current media culture. And let us also think of the recent epidemic of distrust, skepticism, and even hostility that is spreading in our culture – in particular an understandable distrust from women – on the part of a covenant between man and woman that is

* Statement delivered at the 29th Session of the Human Rights Council: *Full-Day Discussion on the Human Rights of Women*, 19 June 2015.

[1] Cf. www.unwomen.org/en/what-we-do/ending-violence-against-women/facts-and-figures.

[2] Cf. www.un.org/en/letsfightracism/women.shtml.

[3] Intervention of the Permanent Observer of the Holy See to the UN, United Nations Security Council Open Debate on 'Women Peace Security', New York, 15 April 2015.

capable, at the same time, of refining the intimacy of communion and of guarding the dignity of difference.'[4]

Mr President,

The Holy See is most convinced that the fundamental equality of man and woman, and therefore the equality of their fundamental human rights, is rooted in the inviolable dignity of the human person. As such, any ideology or social policy, any culture that subjugates women, that relegates them to second class, or 'less than human', is in no way tolerable. To accept and to practice such a mentality is not only contrary to the equality of man and woman, but effectively demeans even the dignity of the male sex. The fundamental dignity, intrinsic to the human person, male and female, is such that to degrade one is necessarily a belittling of the other. This basic principle of equality stands as the foundation for properly understanding the complementarity of man and woman. The insistence upon the equality of sexes does not in any way inhibit the recognition of the distinction of them. On the contrary, the distinction of man and woman calls us to acknowledge uniqueness in their differences and a positive and mutual complementarity among them. '"Male" and "female" differentiate two individuals of equal dignity, which does not, however, reflect a static equality, because the specificity of the female is different from the specificity of the male, and this difference in equality is enriching and indispensable for the harmony of life in society.'[5] The path to overcoming discrimination, abuses of women's human rights and equality, should not be sought through the obfuscation of the complementarity in equality, but precisely in supporting it. 'We have not yet understood in depth what the feminine genius can give us, what woman can give to society.'[6]

The desire on the part of much of the international community to achieve an equal recognition of women's human rights should not fail to take into consideration the equality of every human person and the complementarity of man and woman. It may appear that any and every approach and perspective to bring about the desired equality and non-discrimination are equally effective. Approaches to attain equality and non-discrimination by eliminating the distinctions based on sex, cannot

[4] Pope Francis, General Audience, 22 April 2015.

[5] *Compendium of the Social Doctrine of the Church*, § 146.

[6] Pope Francis, General Audience, 15 April 2015.

fully respect and appreciate the inherent dignity of the human person. Ideologies that attempt to erase the distinction of man and woman to arrive at a 'non-gender common denominator' ultimately diminish the value of both the female and the male gender.[7] The approach should not attempt to find equal rights by way of eliminating the specificity of man and woman, but stressing their equality and their complementarity. As Pope Francis remarked: 'Modern contemporary culture has opened new spaces, new forms of freedom and new depths in order to enrich the understanding of this difference [between man and woman]. But it has also introduced many doubts and much skepticism. For example, I ask myself if the so-called gender theory is not, at the same time, an expression of frustration and resignation, which seeks to cancel out sexual difference because it no longer knows how to confront it … The removal of difference in fact creates a problem, not a solution.'[8] Extreme interpretations on both ends of the spectrum should be avoided. Either of reducing the character of womanhood to a merely social role or of the opposite extreme of 'emancipating' women from their unique and precious feminine attributes, proves to be a disservice to understanding the true role of woman and their indispensable characteristics and contributions to all levels and aspects of social life.

Mr President,

The Holy See Delegation remains optimistic that the international community will continue to strive to promote the human rights of women from an approach that is truly worthy and deserving of the human person. Much progress has already been made as witnessed by the growing number of women in important political and social roles such as Presidents, Heads of Government, Ministers, Members of Parliament, Ambassadors and many other professional positions. 'There is no doubt that we must do far more to advance women, if we want to give more strength to the reciprocity between man and woman. In fact, it is necessary that woman not only be listened to more, but that her voice carry real weight, a recognized authority in society.'[9]

Thank you, Mr President.

7 The interpretation of the term *gender* here is to be understood as set out in the Holy See's Final Statement at the Women's Conference in Beijing, 15 September 1995.

8 Pope Francis, General Audience, 15 April 2015.

9 Ibid.

THE EFFECTS OF TERRORISM ON THE ENJOYMENT BY ALL PERSONS OF HUMAN RIGHTS AND FUNDAMENTAL FREEDOMS*

Mr President,

The Holy See is grateful to the Human Rights Council for devoting a special panel of this 29th Session to discuss the effects of terrorism on the enjoyment of human rights and fundamental freedoms. In particular, we acknowledge the thorough and enlightening report of the Special Rapporteur. Terrorism is a terrible reality that is affecting all parts of the globe, destroying countless lives, threatening societies and annihilating cultures and their histories. Sadly, one must admit that the international community has not always been effective in preventing and curbing terrorism, especially in the Middle East and different parts of Africa. Since 2000, the world has witnessed a staggering 500 per cent increase in the number of victims of terrorist attacks. In particular, the past two years have seen a startling increase in the body count of innocent victims at the hands of ISIS and Boko Haram groups, among many others. In 2013, for example, 82 per cent of those victims were killed in just five countries: Iraq, Afghanistan, Pakistan, Nigeria and Syria. While considering the negative effects of terrorism on the enjoyment of human rights and fundamental freedoms, we should also be clear in our reasoning that these effects will continue, and indeed will become worse, if the causes of terrorism are not clearly and swiftly addressed by the national States concerned and the international community.[1]

Mr President,

The Holy See Delegation would like to denounce most especially terrorist acts carried out in the name of religion. As Pope Francis states, 'Religious fundamentalism, even before it eliminates human beings by perpetrating horrendous killings, eliminates God himself, turning him into a mere ideological pretext.'[2] Terrorism is a political means to

* Statement delivered at the 29th Session of the Human Rights Council: Panel on the Effects of Terrorism on the Enjoyment by All Persons of Human Rights and Fundamental Freedoms, 30 June 2015.

1 Cf. Global Report on Terrorism for 2013.

2 Address of Pope Francis to the Members of the Diplomatic Corps Accredited to the Holy See, 12 January 2015.

influence behavior and to reach objectives through fear. Acts of terrorism cause the destruction of human rights, political freedoms and the rule of law. Terrorism is the antithesis of the shared values and commitments which serve as the basis for peaceful coexistence domestically and internationally. Indeed, with the proliferation of terrorism and the impunity which its proponents enjoy, we can say that there is also a 'globalization of terrorism'. Developing from 'a subversive strategy typical of certain extremist organizations, aimed at the destruction of material goods or the killing of people, terrorism has now become a shadowy network of political collusion,'[3] in which antagonistic political powers are tempted to play a role by supplying resources of modern technology, advanced weaponry and financing to these terrorist organizations. A situation is thus created where the positive political will of the major players is required in order to address and resolve the problem of global terrorism and its disastrous effects.

Mr President,

The tragic humanitarian and social effects of terrorism are already well known. In the first place, the gravest violation is complete contempt for innocent human life, the basic right upon which all other human rights are founded. 'As such, there is an obligation on the part of the State to protect the right to life of every person within its territory and no derogation from this right is permitted, even in times of public emergency.'[4] Since terrorism does not recognize the dignity of its victims, there remains no other basis or logic by which the other fundamental rights and freedoms of the human person will be respected. As such, we see a sort of 'domino effect', namely, once you deny a person his/her right to life, you abuse other fundamental rights, including the right to freedom of belief and worship, the right to expression and freedom of conscience, the right to education and the right to be treated with equal dignity as any other citizen of a nation, despite difference in religion, social and economic status, language or ethnicity.

Due to the violence of new forms of terrorism and the breach of international humanitarian law, the international community faces the challenge of responding to the influx of refugees fleeing these troubled areas to find a safe haven. Those receiving countries must not only be

[3] *Compendium of the Social Doctrine of the Church*, § 513.
[4] OHCHR, 'Human Rights, Terrorism and Counter-Terrorism', Fact Sheet No. 32, p. 8.

lauded for their willingness to provide protection, but they too need the assistance of the international community to deal with the humanitarian crisis so as to avoid the eruption of further problems on their own soil. Terrorism also facilitates trafficking of persons and weapons, thus creating a black market for human commerce. Where terrorism has effectively taken hold, irreparable social and cultural damage has been done that will resonate through future generations. By destroying the infrastructure of cities and regions, especially by attacking government buildings, schools and religious institutions, terrorism literally brings a society to its knees. In addition, the demolition of cultural and ancient sites by terrorists threatens to annihilate the history of cultures and populations. Such destruction creates the breeding grounds for more violent extremism, thus continuing the vicious circle of violence propagating further violence.

Mr President,

Apart from the devastating social and humanitarian effects which, in reality, are much more immediate and concrete, the ongoing negative political effects of terrorism will continue to resonate, in many ways in an unforeseeable manner for generations yet to come. The political impact of terrorism is multifaceted and the parties occultly facilitating or supporting, financially or otherwise, terrorist activity for ulterior political agendas are not always so clearly identified. Nevertheless, it can hardly be doubted that terrorism has political effects and influences the political process, at least in democratic and partially democratic states. In addition to creating an environment of political instability for the countries and regions which suffer the most from terrorism, the political effect on a global level continues to grow. Governments throughout the world, in some cases using terrorism as an excuse, are preoccupied with national security and counterterrorism efforts, some of which also infringe upon the enjoyment of human rights and fundamental freedoms. This shows that the political instability and fragmentation caused by terrorism creates an equal and opposite reaction with serious political consequences. In this sense, collaborative effort on the part of the international community is all the more necessary. Efforts to reach a mutual approach to fighting terrorism must always give priority to the victims of terrorism; financial, political or ideological motives should never take precedence over coming to a unified vision as to how the plague of terrorism should be combated.

The most obvious way in which terrorism can influence the political process is by bringing about changes in public opinion, which governments then tend to take into account when formulating their policies. It can be very hard for governments to resist the pressure from public opinion for a strong reaction in the wake of a terrorist attack. The impact of terrorism on public opinion, however, is not as straightforward or predictable as one might imagine. There is no uniform public response to a terrorist attack. Nor do terrorist attacks necessarily change people's political opinions. The greater people's confidence in their own values, the less likely they are to change as a result of a major event, like a terrorist attack. Finally, the role and the power of media in forming and informing public opinion when addressing terroristic events are of the utmost importance.

Mr President,

The Holy See is deeply convinced that terrorism, especially those forms that derive from religious extremism, must be confronted with concerted political efforts by all players, especially by all the local and regional parties involved, as well as by the major international players, whose role is indispensable in negotiating and finding a viable solution, diplomatic or otherwise, to protect life and the future stability of the regions touched by terrorism. The response to terrorism cannot be merely by way of military action. Political participation, fair and just legal systems, and cutting all forms of public and private support for terrorism are means not only to respond, but also to prevent, terrorism. It is also important to remember the positive obligation that States have to undertake in order to protect their citizens and, where that is not possible, to collaborate with other regional authorities in order to address the threats posed by terrorist groups.

Thank you, Mr President.

EXPLANATORY NOTES

CEDAW – Convention on the Elimination of All Forms of Discrimination against Women

The CEDAW was adopted by the United Nations General Assembly on 18 December 1979, and entered into force as an international treaty on 3 September 1981 after the twentieth country had ratified it (www.un.org/womenwatch/daw/cedaw/text/econvention.htm).

CMW – International Convention on the Protection of the Rights of All Migrant Workers and Members of Their Families

The Convention was adopted by Resolution 45/158 of 18 December 1990 by the General Assembly of the United Nations (www2.ohchr.org/english/bodies/cmw/cmw.htm).

Declaration on the Elimination of All Forms of Intolerance and of Discrimination Based on Religion or Belief

This declaration was proclaimed by General Assembly Resolution 36/55 of 25 November 1981. It contains eight articles and has been considered a major international standard-setting instrument pertaining to the freedom of religion or belief (www.un.org/documents/ga/res/36/a36r055.htm).

Durban Declaration and Programme of Action (DDPA)

Adopted by consensus at the 2001 World Conference against Racism (WCAR) in Durban, South Africa, the DDPA is a comprehensive, action-oriented document that proposes concrete measures to combat racism, racial discrimination, xenophobia and related intolerance. It is holistic in its vision, addresses a wide range of issues, and contains far-reaching recommendations and practical measures. Although the DDPA is not legally binding, it has a strong moral value and serves as a basis for advocacy efforts worldwide (www.un.org/en/durbanreview2009/ddpa.shtml).

Durban Review Conference

The Durban Review Conference took place between 20 and 24 April 2009 in Geneva, Switzerland. It evaluated progress and reinvigorated actions and initiatives towards the goals set by the World Conference against Racism, Racial Discrimination, Xenophobia and Related Intolerance held in Durban, South Africa, in 2001 (www.un.org/en/durbanreview2009/).

High Commissioner for Human Rights

The High Commissioner for Human Rights is the principal human rights official of the United Nations. He heads the OHCHR and supervises the Human Rights Council at the United Nations Office in Geneva (www.ohchr.org/EN/AboutUs/Pages/HighCommissioner.aspx).

ICCPR – International Covenant on Civil and Political Rights

The ICCPR was adopted in 1966 by General Assembly Resolution 2200A. The Covenant elaborates further the civil and political rights and freedoms listed in the Universal Declaration of Human Rights (www.ohchr.org/en/professionalinterest/pages/ccpr.aspx).

ICERD – International Convention on the Elimination of All Forms of Racial Discrimination

The ICERD was adopted by General Assembly Resolution 2106 of 21 December 1965 and entered into force in 1969 (www.ohchr.org/EN/ProfessionalInterest/Pages/CERD.aspx).

ICESCR – International Covenant on Economic, Social and Cultural Rights

The ICESCR was adopted in 1966 by General Assembly Resolution 2200A. Together with the Universal Declaration of Human Rights and the ICCPR, the ICESCR makes up the International Bill of Human Rights (www.ohchr.org/EN/ProfessionalInterest/Pages/CESCR.aspx).

International Labour Organization (ILO)

The ILO was founded in 1919, in the wake of a destructive war, to pursue a vision based on the premise that universal, lasting peace can be established only if it is based on social justice. The ILO became the first specialized agency of the UN in 1946. The International Labour Organization (ILO) is the only tripartite UN agency with government, employer and worker representatives. This tripartite structure makes the ILO a unique forum in which the governments and the social partners of the economy of its 186 Member States can freely and openly debate and elaborate labour standards and policies (www.ilo.org/global/about-the-ilo/history/lang–en/index.htm).

ILO Domestic Workers Convention No. 189

On 16 June 2011, during the 100th International Labour Conference, the ILO tripartite system – governments, trade unions, and employers' associations – adopted the ILO Convention 189 Concerning Decent Work for Domestic Workers (Domestic Workers Convention, No. 189). This groundbreaking treaty establishes the first global standards for domestic workers and entered into force in 2013 (www.ilo.org/dyn/normlex/en/f?p=NORMLEXPUB:12100:0::NO::P12100_INSTRUMENT_ID:2551460).

Kidnapping of Bishops Yohanna Ibrahim and Boulos Yaziji

Syriac Orthodox Archbishop Yohanna Ibrahim and Greek Orthodox Archbishop Boulos Yazigi, were kidnapped by gunmen in April 2013 while they were returning from the Turkish border to their city of Aleppo, Syria. In the historic Joint Declaration of Pope Francis and Patriarch Kirill of Moscow and All Russia of February 2016, the two leaders also made an appeal for their prompt liberation.

OHCHR – Office of the United Nations High Commissioner for Human Rights

The OHCHR works to promote and protect the human rights that are guaranteed under international law and stipulated in the Universal Declaration of Human Rights of 1948. The office was established by the United Nations General Assembly on 20 December 1993 in the wake of the Vienna Declaration and Programme of Action (www.ohchr.org/EN/Pages/Home.aspx).

Pontifical Academy of Sciences

Originally founded in 1603, the Pontifical Academy of Sciences was given its current name and statutes by Pius XI in 1936. Its mission is to honor pure science wherever it may be found, ensure its freedom and encourage research for the progress of science (www.pas.va/content/accademia/en/about.html).

Pontifical Academies of Social Sciences

The Pontifical Academy of Social Sciences was established by John Paul II in 1994 with the aim of promoting the study and progress of the social sciences, primarily economics, sociology, law and political science, thus offering the Church those elements which she can use in the development of her social doctrine, and reflecting on the application of that doctrine in contemporary society (www.pass.va/content/scienzesociali/en/about.html).

Pontifical Council for Interreligious Dialogue

Instituted in 1964 on Pentecost Sunday by Pope Paul VI as Secretariat for Non-Christians, in 1988 it acquired its current name. The Pontifical Council for Interreligious Dialogue is the central office of the Catholic Church for the promotion of interreligious dialogue in accordance with the spirit of the Second Vatican Council, in particular the declaration '*Nostra Aetate*'. Its nature and goals are to promote respect, mutual understanding and collaboration between Catholics and the followers of others religious traditions; to encourage the study of religions; to promote the formation of persons dedicated to dialogue (www.pcinterreligious.org/).

UDHR – Universal Declaration of Human Rights

The Universal Declaration of Human Rights is a milestone document in the history of human rights. Drafted by representatives with different legal and cultural backgrounds from all regions of the world, the Declaration was proclaimed by the United Nations General Assembly in Paris on 10 December 1948, General Assembly Resolution 217A, as a common standard of achievements for all peoples and all nations. It set out, for the first time, fundamental human rights to be universally protected (www.un.org/en/universal-declaration-human-rights/).

United Nations Charter

The Charter of the United Nations was signed on 26 June 1945, in San Francisco, at the conclusion of the United Nations Conference on International Organization, and came into force on 24 October 1945. The Statute of the International Court of Justice is an integral part of the Charter (www.un.org/en/charter-united-nations/index.html).

UN Declaration on the Rights of Persons Belonging to National or Ethnic, Religious and Linguistic Minorities

The UN Declaration on the Rights of Persons Belonging to National or Ethnic, Religious and Linguistic Minorities was adopted by the UN Commission on Human Rights in its resolution 1992/16, and by the General Assembly in its resolution 47/135 in December 1992 (www.un-documents.net/a47r135.htm).

Vienna Declaration and Programme of Action

The Vienna Declaration and Programme of Action is a human rights declaration adopted by consensus at the World Conference on Human Rights in 1993 in Vienna, Austria. The United Nations High Commissioner for Human Rights was created by this Declaration, endorsed by General Assembly Resolution 48/121 (www.ohchr.org/EN/ProfessionalInterest/Pages/Vienna.aspx).

World Conference against Racism, Racial Discrimination, Xenophobia and Related Intolerance

The World Conference against Racism, Racial Discrimination, Xenophobia and Related Intolerance was held in Durban, South Africa, in September 2001. After intensive and often difficult deliberations on a number of issues, the Conference adopted a Declaration and Programme of Action that commits Member States to undertake a wide range of measures to combat racism and discrimination at the international, regional and national levels (www.un.org/WCAR/).

III

The Economy as a Means, Not an End

Introduction

The need for reconciling the requirements of policy sovereignty at the national level with the imperatives of an interdependent world economy is a long-standing challenge. In fact, it has been discussed for years and from many different angles and especially since the financial crisis of 1929. Keeping in mind that experience, the key objective of the architects of the Bretton Woods institutions was to design a post-war international economic structure that would prevent a recurrence of the opportunistic actions and damaging contagion that led to the breakdown of international trade and financial payments in the 1930s. Accordingly, such structures were expected to support the new policy goals of rising incomes, full employment and social security in the developed economies. Included were measures that sought to expand policy space for State-led industrialization and to increase the level and reliability of the multilateral financial support necessary to meet the needs of developing countries. Those results, due to their orientation toward developed countries, however, set the stage for the North–South conflicts of the post-Second World War period. In that context, the construction of a more development-friendly international economic order was a much slower and more uneven process after the war than the Bretton Woods architects had anticipated. It took the growing voices of newly independent developing countries in the late 1950s and early 1960s to shift multilateralism toward a more inclusive footing. This led to the creation of the United Nations Conference on Trade and Development (UNCTAD) in 1964, and to a subsequent broadening of the development agenda around a new international economic order.

At present, the international community continues to call for changes in the way the global economy is ordered and managed. Few would doubt that, during the last decades, new technologies have broken down traditional borders between nations and opened up new areas of economic opportunity, and that a less polarized political landscape has provided new possibilities for constructive international engagement. In addition, economic power has become more dispersed, mostly due to industrialization and rapid growth in East Asia, with corresponding changes in the workings of the international trading system. Yet today there are signs that this may be breaking down – evidenced by rapid increase in the polarization of the political landscape and the emergence of many disruptive non-State actors.

The linkage between these technological, political and economic shifts and a more prosperous, peaceful and sustainable world is not automatic. Indeed, growing global economic and power imbalances, increasing social and environmental challenges and persistent cyclical financial instability that results in full-blown crises, demand continuous analysis, reflection and debate by policymakers and leaders at all levels. Hunger, for instance, still remains a daily reality for hundreds of millions of people, particularly in rural communities, with children being the most vulnerable. The United Nations Food and Agriculture Organization (FAO) estimates that 842 million people, or roughly one in eight, suffered from chronic hunger in 2011–13, not getting enough food to lead active and healthy lives.[1] Pope Paul VI said during his famous speech to the United Nations General Assembly that the Church, while respecting the secularity and autonomy of temporal realities, 'has long experience in human affairs' and seeks to 'offer man her distinctive contribution: a global perspective on man and human realities'.[2]

The development of the social doctrine of the Church, especially since the innovative teaching found in the Encyclical Letter, *Rerum Novarum* (1891) of Pope Leo XIII, is a clear example of how the Holy See addresses new moral issues that affect the economy and social justice. Indeed, a double risk is contained in this development. First, enunciating abstract ethical principles and generic guidelines is often perceived as an irrelevant and impractical contribution. Second, the analysis of concrete cases and seeking practical and substantial answers may lead to the negative accusation of the Church meddling in the affairs of the State. The social doctrine of the Church and that of economic theory seem to have moved along two parallel but separate paths. In fact, the first has often enunciated rather precise and detailed principles on questions of economic and social relevance. However, there is no trace of these principles in

[1] This figure is lower than the 868 million reported with reference to 2010–12. The total number of undernourished has fallen by 17 per cent since 1990–92. Developing regions as a whole have registered significant progress towards the MDG 1 hunger target. If the average annual decline of the past 21 years continues to 2015, the prevalence of undernourishment will reach a level close to the target. Meeting it would require considerable and immediate additional efforts, www.fao.org/docrep/018/i3434e/i3434e.pdf.

[2] Pope Paul VI, Encyclical Letter, *Populorum Progressio*, 26 March 1967, § 13, http://w2.vatican.va/content/paul-vi/en/encyclicals/documents/hf_p-vi_enc_26031967_populorum.html.

economic manuals and not even in a magazine like the *Journal of Economic Literature* (*JEL*) of the American Economic Association whose aim is to list all the main contributions in economics.

Taking into account such risks, from her perspective the Holy See seeks to frame the context of the international crises, with their material and spiritual consequences, participating in the negotiating process inside the UN and its specialized agencies. Many causes led to the current financial and economic crisis. For example, the exponential and global increase in the emission of currency that started in the 1990s did not coincide with a more rapid production of income, even at current prices. This led to the formation of pockets of excessive liquidity and speculation bubbles that spawned a solvency and trust crisis that have spread ever since. This process can be summarized into three steps: in the early years of the Federal Reserve, international macroeconomic imbalances and the extremely accommodative monetary policy had favoured an increase in credit and private debt; banks and other intermediaries, seeking to maximize profits, had made extensive use of highly aggressive business models based on the use of innovative and risky financial instruments; the systems of regulation and supervision of financial markets had proved to be incapable of curbing such behaviors.

At the same time, we have witnessed the fragmentation of the production chain and the emergence of the *global value chain*, which resulted in a sudden and drastic change in the way in which production was organized on a global scale. The effects of the global economic crisis on the growth of the major world economic powers were extremely diversified. The reaction from the emerging countries, particularly China and India, was immediate and, after a slight GDP contraction and a sudden recovery, in 2010 the two Asian giants started to tap growth rates around 10 per cent. On the contrary, the crisis in the West was, and still is, of greater substance and duration, capable of almost nullifying an already slow growth. This crisis has highlighted the unsustainability of the existing development model. At the same time, the high social costs caused by the inevitable end of this model are difficult to be managed by parliamentary democracies.

Over the last 15 years we have witnessed substantial changes: in economic geography, in the weight of the actors, in the models of development and in the political-economic organizations that support them. Advanced countries are heavily indebted and their growth is slowing down, while the BRICs (Brazil, Russia, India, China) are now the true supporters of world growth, representing more than 16 per cent of the global GDP. This change has become evident in the last four years within the forum of the United Nations and, in particular, at the World Trade Organization. In April 2015, during the summit in New Delhi, the emerging markets, and in particular the BRICs, aware of their increased economic weight, showed a clear willingness to influence international governance by advancing their demands with their newly acquired authority, warning the developed world as never before. The recent entry of Russia into the World Trade Organization will further change the ability and political will of the BRICs to safeguard the multilateral trading system and influence a positive and balanced outcome of the Doha Round.

The attitude of Western countries in commercial negotiations has also radically changed. After a global recession, comparable to that of the 'Great Depression' resulting in the loss of about 30 million jobs and in a sharp rise in youth unemployment rates with the risk of a drift towards protectionism and the effects on their trade balances, the developed countries have tried to block all negotiations within the World Trade Organization. This attitude compromised the conclusion of the Doha Round negotiations whose aim was to put development at the heart of International Trade. This new Western obstructionist attitude emerged clearly during the thirteenth Ministerial Conference of the United Nations Conference on Trade and Development in April 2012 in Qatar. The final declaration of the Conference, Doha Manar,[3] on the other hand, was the first document approved by consensus at the multilateral level on an economic and commercial theme after the last economic and financial crisis and it recorded for the first time the redesigning of the relationship between 'the West and the Rest'.

The problems, however, extend beyond any technical solutions which may be proposed to remedy the dysfunctions. As Pope Francis has observed, the financial crisis 'makes us forget that its ultimate origin is to be found in a profound human crisis. In the denial of the primacy of human beings! We have created new idols. The worship of the golden calf of old has found a new and heartless image in the cult of money and the dictatorship of an economy which is faceless and lacking any truly humane goal.'[4]

[3] http://unctad.org/fr/PublicationsLibrary/iss2012d1_en.pdf.
[4] Pope Francis, Apostolic Exhortation, *Evangelii Gaudium*, § 55.

Over the last 15 years, the condition of many people living in poverty or near poverty has deteriorated as a result of processes that have displaced their livelihoods, severely impairing their ability to make a decent living. These processes include environmental degradation, violent conflict, forced resettlement, rapid fluctuations in the prices of commodities and agricultural products, stranded resources and natural disasters impacted by climate change, cyclical political and economic crises. The loss of benefits like insurance and pensions formally associated with employment in the developed world has further magnified the uncertainty and precariousness now faced by the middle class. In our globally interconnected world, people living in poverty are keenly aware from their exposure to mass and social media that their well-being is often determined by decisions of leaders and policymakers they have little opportunity to influence.

These profound political, economic and institutional crises open a new challenge for the social doctrine of the Church: renewing the semantics of the economy and finance.[5] This does not only mean that it has the duty to identify an intrinsic and autonomous ethics but that it should frame it in the context of other human activities. Economics and finance are not abstract concepts separated from the actors that are engaged in them in social, political, national and supranational contexts. In his Encyclical *Caritas in Veritate*, His Holiness Benedict XVI highlighted that 'the economic sphere is neither ethically neutral, nor inherently inhuman and opposed to society. It is part and parcel of human activity and precisely because it is human, it must be structured and governed in an ethical manner.'[6] Therefore, 'the economy needs ethics in order to function correctly – not any ethics whatsoever, but an ethics which is people-centered.' If economy and policy consider man in his integral dimension, rather than individual interests, they would help to overcome the crisis of confidence that involves both economic operators and institutions.

This renewed ethics implies the re-evaluation of work as an essential expression of human nature, as a means by which he can pursue self-realization, and not as a duty to be performed to obtain a salary with which to buy pieces of alternative life.

[5] M. Toso, *Per una riforma del sistema finanziario: Il contributo della dottrina sociale della Chiesa*, www.aclifai.it/_documenti/1331901841_Toso_2012_ELEA.pdf.

[6] Pope Benedict XVI, Encyclical Letter, *Caritas in Veritate*, § 36.

The ongoing financial crisis is the result of a fragmented cultural framework, which separates goods and values and denies a rationality that can coordinate different human scopes into a *telos* that orders them in relation to the perfect true and good, that is to say, to God. Economy and finance without reference to a human *telos* cannot fulfil the requirements of the common good: the network of social conditions that facilitate the achievement of human fullness.

Through the processes of de-industrialization and the transformation of towns, engaging less in 'factory' production and more in the production of services, the social structures and personal lives have deeply changed. We face a 'liquid modernity', as it has been called by sociologist Z. Bauman, that seems to have chosen uncertainty and nonlinearity as the principles on which it is based, contrary to what was accepted in the previous century. The 'solitude of the global citizen' and the widespread feeling of insecurity regarding the future, seem to be especially true among young people. The world economy, although growing, is not able to create enough jobs (jobless growth), in particular for young people. This phenomenon, far from being new, also occurs in emerging countries and in the developing world, where the creation of new jobs is still low compared to the high growth rates recorded by these economies. This is a symptom of a severe distortion in the prevailing economic conception that tends to consider the outcome of the production process (output) without considering the centrality of work in this process and in economic development. Development should instead be focused on job creation: 'the priority of work over capital places an obligation in justice upon employers to consider the welfare of the workers before the increase of profits. They have a moral obligation not to keep capital unproductive and in making investments to think first of the common good. The latter requires a prior effort to consolidate jobs or create new ones in the production of goods that are really useful.'[7]

The social doctrine of the Church reminds everyone of the duty to appreciate creation for what it is: a gift. The current crisis, thus, becomes an opportunity that, in the words of the Holy Father to the Diplomatic Corps, 'obliges us to re-plan our journey, to set ourselves new rules and to discover new forms of commitment, to build on positive experiences and to reject negative ones. The crisis thus becomes an opportunity for discernment, in which to shape a new vision for the future. In this spirit,

[7] Congregazione per la Dottrina della Fede, *Libertà Cristiana e Liberazione*, 1986, § 87.

with confidence rather than resignation, it is appropriate to address the difficulties of the present time.'[8] The Catholic Social Tradition has not been silent on the macro and global issues like the near collapse of the global financial system and its impact on development. The demands of the virtue of solidarity in response to countless victims and destructive consequences that have been left in the wake of the crisis have been articulated by a number of official voices. From admonitions about the 'globalization of indifference' that is a by-product of a system rooted in self-interest and fed by greed and dishonesty, Catholic Social Teaching has reiterated the need to keep the poor, the marginalized and the suffering at the centre of any reform agenda that is being proposed and debated by the G20 and the Financial Stability Board. This includes a close attentiveness to the deepening inequality across countries and regions that the current system has produced and a call for substantive adjustments and reforms to address the inherent corrosive tendencies of the system.

Solidarity's parallel principle of subsidiarity can be particularly helpful in examining the appropriateness of specific proposals, innovations and the processes chosen for their implementation. Subsidiarity is a reminder of the autonomy, richness and diversity of local communities where most families and people live each day. It shelters these communities from an invasive centralizing and homogenizing trend that shows a proclivity to a 'one-size-fits-all' approach that easily disregards the dignity, diversity and independence of these communities. While most frequently applied in the realm of politics, subsidiarity must also be respected and promoted when addressing the question of the appropriate size and authority of economic institutions and organizations.

'The law of profit alone cannot be applied to that which is essential for the fight against hunger, disease, and poverty.'[9] Led by the words of Saint John Paul II, the interventions and activities in the multilateral economic system demonstrate the wide variety of the contemporary economic and financial issues facing the world today. The motivation underlying these statements is to orient discussion regarding labour and related aspects of economic life towards the human person as the primary and central concern.

[8] Pope Benedict XVI, Encyclical Letter, *Caritas in Veritate*, § 21. Cf. Pontifical Council for Justice and Peace, 'Towards Reforming the International Financial and Monetary Systems in the Context of Global Public Authority', Rome, 24 October 2011.

[9] Pope John Paul II, Address to 'Jubilee 2000 Debt Campaign', 23 September 1999.

On the issue of intellectual property, in particular, the Holy See has consistently taught that there is a 'social mortgage' on all private property – a concept, which today must be also applied to 'knowledge'. Through both private and public investment, we have seen an incredible scientific advancement in the understanding and use of biological resources, the application of which, particularly in the medical, pharmaceutical and agricultural fields, holds great social value and potential to improve the lives of people. To continue incentivizing such innovation and to spread the benefits of these innovations widely, just legal frameworks for intellectual property protection play an essential role. In recognizing the value of intellectual property protection, the scope of its rights must always be measured in relation to greater principles of justice in the service of the common good.

The purpose of intellectual property rights and the effects of imbalances in its current system impacts traditional communities, developing countries and, in general, the common good. Through the statements delivered, a moral duty emerges to include developing countries in the benefits of new technological innovation in the research on genetic resources, particularly as these innovations pertain to essential elements of life and development, namely agriculture (food) and medicine (health). The patent regime for genetic resources must respect the rights of traditional communities, to both use and protect those genetic resources to which they have a claim, and to share in the benefits from their exploitation since their development derives, at least in part, from traditional knowledge that has been collectively accumulated over generations by those communities. The biological environment tends to be closely associated with the culture of traditional communities; it constitutes an integral factor of their identity and social cohesion. Native populations hold rights over the land and its fruits. These rights have to be protected, even where modern systems of property protection – both movable and immovable property as well as intellectual property – do not contain elements that allow such rights to be recognized and protected to a sufficient extent. Respect for the rights of traditional communities in regard to intellectual property protection of genetic resources requires a view of traditional knowledge as a common asset of that same community, which has grown with small, anonymous contributions over a great many generations.

Whatever agreements are made, they should guarantee the achievement of equitable economic participation in the benefits deriving from the commercial exploitation of biological resources and the promotion of effective means to ensure respect for the collective ownership of traditional knowledge. Research on genetic resources in advanced countries has developed new plants and seed varieties using, in part, the traditional knowledge of local communities in developing countries. Restrictions on the flow of this knowledge through intellectual property rights mechanisms have followed. This has resulted in the dependency of farmers on private firms and raised their expenditures on seeds, pesticides and fertilizers. The impact of such an industrialized, capital-intensive agriculture on traditional communities, biodiversity, and on developing countries, requires careful evaluation.[10] Agreements for access to both genetic resources and traditional knowledge related to these resources must be shaped by principles of justice, taking into account the relative positions of the various parties to the agreements.

Led by the principle of stewardship, which clearly emerges from the latest social Encyclical Letter of Pope Francis, *Laudato Si'*, the activities of the Holy See at the multilateral level have always pointed out a social aspect or dimension regarding how we use our knowledge and how we relate to our 'knowledge goods'. There is a moral duty not to treat as our absolute possession the legal rights acquired as a result of this knowledge nor to ignore the needs of, or impact on, others. The role of patents, if properly applied, would prevent an abuse in pricing by private companies and respond instead to the real needs of people, which represents an affirmation of the priority of the common good.

The social doctrine of the Church, as applied in the fields of patents, innovation and knowledge economy, shows the careful balance that is always necessary if the ultimate goal of creativity is the well-being of all the members of society and the implementation of effective solidarity.

List of Statements

1 Economy and Development: The Human Factor

- RE-ESTABLISH THE RIGHT HIERARCHY OF VALUES IN THE WORLD OF WORK, 92nd Session of the International Labour Organization Conference (8 June 2004)

[10] Pontifical Council for Justice and Peace, Trade, Development and the Fight against Poverty. Some Reflections on the Occasion of the World Trade Organization 'Millennium Round', 18 November 1999.

- A MORE EFFECTIVE SYSTEM OF INTERNATIONAL ECONOMIC COOPERATION FOR SHARED PROSPERITY, 11th Session of the United Nations Conference on Trade and Development, Sao Paulo, Brazil (13–18 June 2004)
- WHEN WORK IS ISOLATED FROM THE BROADER CONTEXT OF HUMAN RIGHTS, THE WORST FORMS OF EXPLOITATION TAKE OVER, 93rd Session of the International Labour Conference (7 June 2005).
- THE UNAVOIDABLE NECESSITY TO SHAPE A FAIR SYSTEM OF TRADE RULES, 6th Ministerial Conference World Trade Organization, Hong Kong, China (13–18 December 2005)
- THE ADOPTION OF THE CONSOLIDATED MARITIME LABOUR CONVENTION: IMPROVING FAIRNESS AND JUSTICE FOR ALL, 94th Session of the International Labour Conference (20 February 2006)
- DECENT WORK: THE WAY TO POVERTY ERADICATION, 95th Session of the International Labour Conference (8 June 2006)
- FULL EMPLOYMENT AND DECENT WORK FOR AN EQUITABLE AND SUSTAINABLE DEVELOPMENT, High-Level Segment of ECOSOC (5 July 2006)
- COMMITTED TO THE STRUGGLE FOR THE ERADICATION OF POVERTY AND HUNGER, United Nations Conference on Trade and Development Mid-term Review, Trade and Development Board, 23rd Special Session (5 October 2006)
- MAN'S FULFILLMENT AS A HUMAN BEING THROUGH WORK, 96th Session of the International Labour Conference (13 June 2007)
- ECONOMIC GROWTH BASED ON ABSOLUTE LIBERALIZATION IS NOT SUSTAINABLE, High-Level Segment of ECOSOC (4 July 2007)
- GLOBALIZATION: OPPORTUNITIES AND CHALLENGES FOR DEVELOPMENT, 12th Session of the United Nations Conference on Trade and Development, Accra, Ghana (20–25 April 2008)
- A RETHINKING OF THE DEVELOPMENT PARADIGM, United Nations Conference on Trade and Development, Trade and Development Board, 56th Session (18 September 2009)
- FROM POLITICAL WILL TO CONCRETE ACTION, 12th Session of the Human Rights Council – Item 3: *Promotion and Protection of All Human Rights, Civil, Political, Economic Social and Cultural Rights, including the Right to Development* (22 September 2009)

- DEVELOPMENT MUST ALSO INCLUDE SPIRITUAL GROWTH, 4th United Nations Conference on Least Developed Countries (LDCs), Istanbul, Turkey (9–13 May 2011)
- THE RESPONSIBILITY TO PROTECT THE YOUTH AND WOMEN FROM THE UNCERTAINTY OF WORKING CONDITIONS, 100th Session of the International Labour Conference (8 June 2011)
- A REVISION OF THE GLOBAL FINANCIAL AND COMMERCIAL ARCHITECTURE TO CORRECT DISTORTIONS, 13th Ministerial Conference of UNCTAD, Doha, Qatar (21–26 April 2012)
- THE FAILURE OF A 'ONE-SIZE-FITS-ALL' POLICY AS A RECIPE FOR GROWTH, 101st Session of the International Labour Conference (7 June 2012)
- TRANSNATIONAL CORPORATIONS AND HUMAN RIGHTS, 23rd Session of the Human Rights Council – Item 3: *Transnational Corporations and Human Rights* (31 May 2013)
- THE LAST CALL FOR THE CREDIBILITY OF THE MULTILATERAL TRADE SYSTEM, 9th Session of the Ministerial Conference of the World Trade Organization, Bali, Indonesia (4 December 2013)
- MESSAGE OF POPE FRANCIS ON THE OCCASION OF THE 103RD SESSION OF THE CONFERENCE OF THE INTERNATIONAL LABOUR ORGANIZATION (ILO): "BETTER WORK TO ENHANCE HUMAN DIGNITY", 103rd Session of the International Labour Conference (9 June 2014)
- PROTECT, RESPECT, REMEDY: THE REPORT OF THE WORKING GROUP ON THE ISSUE OF HUMAN RIGHTS AND TRANSNATIONAL CORPORATIONS AND OTHER BUSINESS ENTERPRISES, 26th Session of the Human Rights Council – Item 3: *Report of the Working Group on the Issue of Human Rights and Transnational Corporations and other Business Enterprises* (11 June 2014)
- 50TH ANNIVERSARY OF THE ESTABLISHMENT OF UNCTAD: PROSPERITY FOR ALL, 28th Special Session Trade and Development Board, 50th Anniversary of the Establishment of UNCTAD (17 June 2014)
- WHY TRADE MATTERS TO EVERYONE, message of H.E. Cardinal Peter K.A. Turkson on behalf of H.H. Pope Francis, 2014 World Trade Organization Public Forum (1–3 October 2014)
- THE VOCATION OF BUSINESS: CONTRIBUTE TO THE COMMON GOOD AND RESPECT HUMAN RIGHTS, 3rd Forum on Business and Human Rights: *High-level Discussion on Strengthening the Links between the Global*

Economic Architecture and the Business and Human Rights Agenda (3 December 2014)

- THE TRANSITION FROM THE INFORMAL TO FORMAL ECONOMY, 104th Session of the International Labour Conference (4 June 2015)
- THE EXPLOITATION OF FORCED LABOR IN THE GLOBAL SUPPLY CHAINS, 30th Session of the Human Rights Council – Item 3: *Special Rapporteur on Contemporary Forms of Slavery* (15 September 2015)
- THE RISKS OF THE POVERTY TRAP, General Council of the World Trade Organization (7 December 2015)
- MULTILATERALISM AT THE SERVICE OF THE INTEGRAL DEVELOPMENT OF THE HUMAN PERSON, 10th Session of the Ministerial Conference of the World Trade Organization, Nairobi, Kenya (16 December 2015)

2 Finance: The Golden Calf of Old Has Found a New and Heartless Image in the Cult of Money

- THE IMPACT OF THE GLOBAL ECONOMIC AND FINANCIAL CRISES ON THE UNIVERSAL REALIZATION AND ENJOYMENT OF HUMAN RIGHTS, 10th Special Session of the Human Right Council (20 February 2009)
- WHAT IS THE SOURCE OF VALUE?, 98th Session of the International Labour Conference (10 June 2009)
- THE WTO, THE MULTILATERAL TRADING SYSTEM AND THE CURRENT GLOBAL ECONOMIC ENVIRONMENT, 7th Session of the Ministerial Conference of the World Trade Organization (1 December 2009)
- ON THE REFORM OF THE GLOBAL FINANCIAL SYSTEM AND THE ECONOMIC MODELS, 13th Session of the Human Rights Council (3 March 2010)
- HUMAN RIGHTS AND FOREIGN DEBT: THE NEGATIVE IMPACT OF VULTURE FUNDS, 14th Session of the Human Rights Council – Item 3: *Interactive Dialogue on Human Rights and Foreign Debt* (2 June 2010)
- THE SUFFERING OF PEOPLE SHOULD NOT BE THE COEFFICIENT OF ADJUSTMENT OF THE ECONOMIC SYSTEM, 99th Session of the International Labour Conference (10 June 2010)
- GUIDING PRINCIPLES ON BUSINESS AND HUMAN RIGHTS: IMPLEMENTING THE UNITED NATIONS 'PROTECT, RESPECT AND REMEDY' FRAMEWORK, 17th Session of the Human Rights Council – Item 3: *General Debate* (3 June 2011)

- THERE IS NO FUTURE FOR THE ECONOMY UNLESS IT INVOLVES THE ETHICAL DIMENSION, 8th Session of the Ministerial Conference of the World Trade Organization (15–17 December 2011)
- FOREIGN DEBT VS. RIGHT TO DEVELOPMENT, 20th Session of the Human Rights Council: *Report on Guiding Principles on Foreign Debt and Human Rights* (11 June 2012)
- THE UNAVOIDABLE NECESSITY TO REBUILD THE LINKS BETWEEN EDUCATION AND WORK, 102nd Session of the International Labour Conference (12 June 2013)

3 Intellectual Property: Production and Inventive Activity for the Sake of the Common Good

- INGENUITY AND INTELLECTUAL PROPERTY MUST CONTRIBUTE TO THE DEVELOPMENT OF THE HUMAN FAMILY, 48th Series of Meetings of the WIPO General Assemblies (23 September 2008)
- PATENTABLE SUBJECT MATTER AND THE PATENTING OF LIFE FORMS, Trade-Related Intellectual Property Rights (TRIPs) Council at the World Trade Organization (8 June 2010)
- THE UNDULY RIGID ASSERTION OF THE RIGHT TO INTELLECTUAL PROPERTY, 48th Series of Meetings of the WIPO General Assemblies (21 September 2010)
- THE ULTIMATE GOAL OF INTELLECTUAL PROPERTY IS TO SERVE THE COMMON GOOD, 49th Series of Meetings of the WIPO General Assemblies (27 September 2011)
- THE MORAL RESPONSIBILITY TO CONCLUDE A TREATY FOR THE VISUALLY IMPAIRED, 50th Series of Meetings of the WIPO General Assemblies (1 October 2012)
- THE EXTENSION OF THE TRANSITIONAL PERIOD FOR LDCS: A CONCRETE EXAMPLE OF ACTING FOR THE COMMON GOOD, Trade-Related Intellectual Property Rights (TRIPs) Council at the World Trade Organization (11 June 2013)
- THE MARRAKECH DIPLOMATIC CONFERENCE: EMPOWERING THE BLIND, OR VISUALLY IMPAIRED PERSONS, AS A TOOL FOR RAISING THEIR ECONOMIC AND SOCIAL STATUS, Diplomatic Conference to conclude a Treaty to Facilitate Access to Published Works by Visually Impaired Persons and Persons with Print Disabilities, Marrakech, Morocco (18 June 2013)
- THE MARRAKECH AGREEMENT: A HISTORICAL RESULT, Diplomatic Conference to conclude a Treaty to Facilitate Access to Published

Works by Visually Impaired Persons and Persons with Print Disabilities, Marrakech, Morocco (27 June 2013)

- SCIENCE, TECHNOLOGY AND INNOVATION, AND THE POTENTIAL OF CULTURE FOR PROMOTING SUSTAINABLE DEVELOPMENT, High-Level Segment of the Economic and Social Council (4 July 2013)
- KNOWLEDGE ECONOMY: THE KEY DRIVER OF COMPETITIVENESS, 51th Series of Meetings of the WIPO Assemblies (24 September 2013)
- PUTTING OUR TALENTS AT THE SERVICE OF THE COMMON GOOD, 53rd Series of Meetings of the WIPO Assemblies (8 May 2014)
- THE LONG-STANDING IP PROTECTION RIGHTS VS. THE COMMON GOOD, 55th Series of Meetings of the WIPO Assemblies (5 October 2015)

1 ECONOMY AND DEVELOPMENT: THE HUMAN FACTOR

RE-ESTABLISH THE RIGHT HIERARCHY OF VALUES IN THE WORLD OF WORK*

Mr President,

The task of building a society which respects the human person and its work gives priority to the human ordering of social relationships over technical progress, necessary as the latter is. Such concern runs through the preparation documents of this 92nd International Labour Conference, especially the Report of the Director General who carefully highlights achievements and shortcomings as well as the strategic areas of future involvement demanded by the changing conditions of the world's economy.

In his call for a rediscovery of the meaning and value of work, Pope John Paul II has extended an invitation 'to address the economic and social imbalances in the world of work by re-establishing the right hierarchy of values, giving priority to the dignity of working men and women and to their freedom, responsibility and participation … [and] to redress situations of injustice by safeguarding each people's culture and different models of development'.[1]

Looking at the future, the projection that by the year 2015 there will be 3 billion people under the age of 25 makes the challenge of employment creation an issue already for now. The search for full employment is not only a legitimate preoccupation but an ethical commitment involving owners and management, financial institutions, the organization of trade, and workers. A joint effort has been the approach and the trademark of the ILO through its social dialogue of governments, employers and workers' representatives, a model that pioneered a method of society-building that has a fruitful proven track. The resulting economic system has a better chance to preserve the priority of work over capital and of the common good over private interest.

Job creation is the main road to personal and national development. The human person becomes the best capital with his/her creativity,

* Statement delivered at the 92nd Session of the International Labour Organization Conference, 8 June 2004.

1 Pope John Paul II, *Homily for the Jubilee of Workers*, 1 May 2000.

knowledge, relationships and spirituality. Working persons enrich society and foster ways of peace. Besides, the promotion of jobs in the poorer countries is also in the interest of the richer ones. If we take the case, for example, of agriculture, the readjustment and elimination of subsidies in developed countries will allow the employment of thousands, the growth of trade, the improvement of the national economy, in countries where agriculture is still the predominant way of life. As a consequence, the quality of life of everyone will benefit and forced displacement and international migration will no longer be an unavoidable necessity for survival. Besides, as noted in the Director General's Report, conflicts disrupt the achievements of set goals of development. But at the root of many conflicts is the lack of work and of a minimum earning capacity to escape poverty and live in dignity with one's family.

The interconnectedness of economic variables and actors on the global scene has been underlined in the important conclusions of the World Commission on the Social Dimension of Globalization. The Commission supports the ILO's strategic objectives and these, in turn, serve as a base for decent work. In this way, securing employment, with social protection, with adequate standards and rights at work, in a constructive tripartite social dialogue opened to other and new forces of civil society, recognizes that work is an expression of each person's dignity and identity and that it goes far beyond any quantitative measurable economic value.

It seems appropriate to emphasize that by preserving the priority of the person, globalization too becomes fair as it avoids leaving behind vulnerable groups, women and children in particular, migrant workers, seafarers and other categories of workers, and less developed populations. An important step in this direction has been the rapid entering into force of the Worst Forms of Child Labour Convention. Allow me, Mr President, to refer again to the social doctrine of the Church as presented by Pope John Paul II: 'A society depends on the basic relations that people cultivate with one another in ever widening circles – from the family to other intermediary social groups, to civil society as a whole and to the national community. States in turn have no choice but to enter into relations with one another. The present reality of global interdependence makes it easier to appreciate the common destiny of the entire human family, and makes all thoughtful people increasingly appreciate the virtue of solidarity.'[2]

2 Pope John Paul II's Message for the 2001 World Day of Peace, § 17.

Work that allows people to live a decent lifestyle requires today a concerted commitment to provide workers with sufficient education and training so they may have the skills needed to confront successfully the information revolution and the increasingly knowledge-based economy. Initiatives in this sense will protect them from poverty and social exclusion. Enhancing human capacity applies also to developing countries if they have to play their rightful role in world trade with the production of quality products. As Pope John Paul II has noted: 'It is not just a question of giving one's surplus to those in need, but of 'helping entire peoples presently excluded or marginalized to enter into the sphere of economic and human development. For this to happen … it requires above all a change of lifestyles, of models of production and consumption, and of the established structures of power which today govern societies.'[3]

In conclusion, Mr President, the just participation of all, individuals and states, in the building up of the future must lead to their fair share in the benefits resulting from decent work for all in the human family.

[3] Pope John Paul II, Encyclical Letter, *Centesimus Annus*, § 58.

A MORE EFFECTIVE SYSTEM OF INTERNATIONAL ECONOMIC COOPERATION FOR SHARED PROSPERITY*

Mr President,

The Holy See Delegation joins previous speakers in congratulating you and the bureau on the election to the guidance of this important Ministerial Conference on the 40th anniversary of the establishment of UNCTAD.

Forty years ago, the States participating in the first UN Conference on Trade and Development in Geneva expressed their determination 'to seek a better and more effective system of international economic cooperation, whereby the division of the world into areas of poverty and plenty may be banished and prosperity achieved by all'. They called for the abolition of poverty everywhere and they saw it as essential 'that the flows of world trade should help to eliminate the wide economic disparities among nations ... The task of development', they added, 'is for the benefit of the people as a whole'.[1] Today UNCTAD remains a valid instrument to achieve its initial aspirations and to promote development and dialogue between developed and developing countries. The goal of the present Conference shows the importance of enhancing coherence between national development strategies and global economic processes.

Globalization

Globalization is indeed a reality. Over the past fifteen years this process has been further accelerated by changes in international geopolitics and by the rapid fall in transport costs and, in particular, the spread of information and communication technologies. Many of the world's economies are increasingly integrated. With regard to advantages and challenges, costs and benefits, each society and each economy must come to terms with the global markets.

In fact, the importance of the economic dimension, based on market integration, is such that many international institutions consider it to be the salient feature of globalization. But globalization has other facets, such as the cultural and the ethical. Faced with problems like poverty,

* Statement delivered at the 11th session of United Nations Conference on Trade and Development, Sao Paulo, Brazil, 13–18 June 2004.

[1] Final Act of UNCTAD I, adopted on 15 June 1964. Preamble, 1, 4.

protection of the environment, security and the right to development, the global community is beginning to set itself common goals which are shared by all states and by civil society as a whole. The acceptance of the right to development, and the importance of everyone's participation as the means of achieving it, are some of the steps in the development of a common awareness of the ethical and cultural aspects involved in the process of integration. We must recognize that present gains are far below what might have been and that the dynamics of globalization have led to the marginalization, if not the impoverishment, of many people in the world. For these reasons, the different aspects of globalization, be they positive or negative, must be confronted by the various actors with shared responsibility. In different contexts globalization yields different results; these depend on the context. There are 'degrees of freedom' which are to be dealt with co-responsibly. As His Holiness John Paul II said: 'Globalization will be what people want it to be.'

Globalization and Poverty

Recent studies have shown that the number of people who live below the threshold of US$1 per day per capita has decreased since the eighties. This positive result has been attributed to the process of economic integration implemented by certain countries. There is, however, a marked regional imbalance. While some countries have significantly reduced their absolute number of people in poverty thanks to strong growth, in other regions, notably sub-Saharan Africa and Latin America, this number has increased. In overall terms the relation of economic openness to poverty reduction does not seem to be a robust one. But this cannot deny the fact that increased participation and integration represent the high road towards a more dignified life. Nevertheless, we must recognize that our understanding of the relation of economic integration to poverty reduction must be deepened and improved. The war to eradicate poverty has barely started.

Globalization and Inequality

It has been observed that economic integration has led to greater inequality. Inequality between countries has increased. The gap in pro capita income between the richest and the poorest has grown significantly and there is no indication that this trend will be reversed. Furthermore, the process is often associated with increased inequality within countries. We see countries with strong economic growth accompanied by growing inequality of income and an increasing gap between sectors of the population due to other aspects of poverty such as market access, health conditions, mortality – in particular child mortality – and education. Many economists have advanced the idea that inequality is a transient phenomenon which will yield to the achievement of grater homogeneity. Many data speak to the contrary be it in developing or developed countries.

Integration is not necessarily accompanied by increased participation, at all levels of society, in emerging opportunities which leads to greater social cohesion. Increased inequality, if permanent, leads to the firm exclusion of whole sectors of the population and may result in a structural dualism difficult to tear down once in place. An example is the marginalization of vast rural areas in developing countries. The increase in the numbers employed in the informal sector as compared to those in the formal sector in the urban zones of developing and less developed countries is an indication of structural problems which must be appropriately addressed.

This form of structural marginalization, besides violating human dignity and depriving people of their right to full participation in growth opportunities, has a second harmful effect. Recent analytical studies have shown that serious inequality reduces growth, thus creating a vicious circle which prevents many countries from staying apace with the complex dynamics of the global economy. Inequality is a violation of the potential to grow and thus leads to new forms of poverty.

Inequality is a source of conflict. The everyday denial of the possibility for mutual benefits deriving from the expectations generated by growing wealth leads to social unrest and violent confrontation. In certain cases and under certain conditions the acceptance of violence as a form of social expression has led to the terrorism which has characterized these past years.

In short, although it has been stressed that economic integration leads to increased growth and that therefore 'through growth, trade is good for the poor', we must be careful. It bears repeating that, in many countries, the elasticity of poverty to growth is low or non-existent. Therefore, opening up the economy is not, per se, an anti-poverty policy. We must develop an understanding of how trade integration policies can be real poverty reduction policies.

There is yet another dimension. The elimination of poverty is not merely a goal; it is also a means of ensuring sustainable growth. There is a causal nexus between poverty reduction and the capacity for growth and economic integration. Inverting the title of a World Bank report, it is possible to say 'poverty reduction is good for growth.' To this effect we must forcefully stress the importance of 'poverty eradication' as a common goal.

The link between the war on poverty and improved growth has a dual explanation. The first is the demand effect. Effective poverty reduction policies strengthen national markets which would otherwise be strangled and unable to generated growth thanks to the multiplier effect of increased activity. In the absence of a national market, economic integration and international opening up imply higher risks.

The second effect is linked to raising the human capital effect. By this is meant improving the capacity to participate in the opportunities offered by economic integration by an active population in a first stage and subsequently by the whole community. Together with infrastructure investment, investment in human capital is the decisive dimension to ensure sustainable, rather than volatile, growth.

The sole goal of development is not to make a person 'more productive' but rather to guarantee his dignity and improve his capacity to act freely. As a category, human capital is partial; nevertheless it defines succinctly the protagonist of development – the human person.

To speak of human capital and human resources means identifying the central element in the development process. Development is not only the elimination of poverty, but also better health and education, inclusion in society and the full enjoyment of civil and political rights. The economic, social, cultural and political dimensions of development are indissolubly linked. The nexus of these dimensions is the human person in all his relations.

If men and women are to become protagonists they need above all a family and social context in which they can be educated to meet the challenges of reality with responsibility. Development policies then should become more creative in taking these aspects into account. Of equal importance to guarantee balanced development is the gender issue. Dealing with gender issues means adopting policies and behavior patterns which ensure the full integration of women, particularly young women, in the social fabric thus guaranteeing them equality of rights and of access to education, health and growth. The empowerment of women contributes to change and brings about immediate results as regards effectiveness, income growth and enhanced investment in human capital.

All actors, national and international, public and private, can guarantee better success if in their common goal they embrace a concept of development which deals simultaneously with the microeconomic aspect of aid for the growth of individuals and of civil society and the national and international macroeconomic support policies.

At the international level, support policies include: renewing the flow of ODA, adopting more advanced forms of debt relief to ensure social development, adopting common rules to control the volatility of financial markets, reviewing trade rules on markets which are crucial to the development of the poorer countries. The private sector, on the other hand, should feel a greater awareness of its responsibility to become involved as a protagonist in the pursuit of this development goal.

In the present context of interdependence, States must engage in dialogue in order to identify the particular ways and means of their individual national development. Within this fine-tuning of the process, the basic responsibility rests with the individual government. Access to education and health, a better quality in public administration, good governance, education of public officials, are all elements indispensable to ensure a sustainable development.

It is not merely a matter of striking a balance between national and international responsibility but rather a matter of re-directing the joint action of the protagonists, simultaneously and coherently, towards the same, shared goal: development widely shared by all elements of society and an equitable and fair international trade system.

Mr President,

I cannot conclude without mentioning the fundamental and pioneering role played by UNCTAD during the last 40 years in carrying out its three-dimensional mandate. Without UNCTAD, dialogue and consensus-building between developing and developed countries would have been less rich, effective and fruitful (meaningful). In a world more and more interdependent, the role of UNCTAD remains more valid and necessary than ever if we want to maximize the advantages of globalization and minimize, if not eliminate, its perverse consequences. The Holy See takes advantage of this occasion to reaffirm its support for the revitalization of UNCTAD so that it may better honour its mandate and reach its objectives.

I would also like in this assembly to underline the importance of the role of the UNCTAD Secretariat and congratulate in particular the

Secretary General, Mr Ruben Recupero, for his commitment and dedication to the cause of global development. We are convinced, Mr President, that UNCTAD XI will be a decisive moment in the long and difficult journey of development.

Taken in this context, the role of UNCTAD, based on the three pillars of the mandate, the analysis of and research into the nexus between integration policies and social development and consensus-building and technical assistance, is once again a basic element in the achievement of the objectives which the international community has set itself.

WHEN WORK IS ISOLATED FROM THE BROADER CONTEXT OF HUMAN RIGHTS, THE WORST FORMS OF EXPLOITATION TAKE OVER*

Mr President,

The future that challenges and confronts the international community and individual countries is marked by an increasing awareness that only together we can make progress and find the right path toward a truly human life. The rapid pace of change may give rise to doubt and to the temptation of isolation and momentarily derail the move forward. But the process of globalization continues: making it inclusive and removing the obstacles that hinder its beneficial impact for all is the commitment that emerges from this 93rd International Labour Conference. Clearly the spirit of solidarity and of enterprise that flows from the unique tripartite collaboration of states, workers and employers shows a model of interdependence that can enrich other international organizations in this moment of search for reforms devoted to a more effective service to the whole human family.

The road towards a decent work for a decent life in a world where the globalization of solidarity is an active agenda starts indeed with young women and men and the promotion of their employment. There is a sense of urgency to find a response to the fact that globally less than half of the youth available for work had jobs in 2004 and that an estimated 59 million young people aged 15 to 18 years are in hazardous forms of work. Already John Paul II had asked during his visit to the ILO in 1982: 'Can we tolerate a situation in which many young people may find themselves without any prospect of one day getting a job and which, at the very least, could leave them with lifelong scars?'[1] In developing countries, lack of innovative technologies makes it difficult to translate research findings into productive initiatives. The priority to be given to education and formation, especially in a knowledge-based economy, is evident. At the same time, youth unemployment should be contextualized and the whole economic structure of developing countries needs to be sustained in its evolution and enabled to compete fairly in the world market. Decent jobs for young people have a critical payoff. Their creativity supported by an

* Statement delivered at the 93rd International Labour Conference, 7 June 2005.

[1] Pope John Paul II, Address to the International Labour Organization, 15 June 1982, § 12.

adequate technical culture and a sound sense of responsibility can make up for their limited experience and even open additional jobs through the micro enterprises they may launch with the granting of appropriate credit. The communities, where young people are not employed, lose hope. The creative energy of the young, not channeled toward productive goals, is dispersed and wasted. In fact, the risk is unfortunately real that lack of jobs and employment opportunities push the young into the destructive underworld of drugs, violence, criminal activities and even terrorism.

Speaking on May 1, 2005, to many workers attending his first Sunday audience, the new Holy Father Benedict XVI underlined how solidarity, justice and peace should be 'the pillars on which to build the unity of the human family'. He called on workers to witness in contemporary society the 'Gospel of work'. 'I hope', he added, 'that work will be available, especially for young people, and that working conditions may be ever more respectful of the dignity of the human person.'

The creation of decent work for all in a sustainable world has been a long-standing common base for a fruitful dialogue between the ILO and the social doctrine of the Church. It is the dignity of every human person that requires access to work in condition of personal security, health, fair remuneration, a safe environment. Work is a right and the expression of human dignity. My Delegation, therefore, sees unemployment as a 'real social disaster' and supports international organizations, employers, labour unions and governments to join forces, strengthen juridical norms of protection, promote the implementation of existing conventions. In such convergence of forces it is particularly significant to recall that the last official audience scheduled by the late Pope John Paul II, whose official visit to ILO and masterful Encyclical on human work, *Laborem Exercens*, remain a lasting contribution, had been for the ILO Director General. And much appreciated has been the presence of the Director General at the funeral of John Paul II and at the inauguration of Benedict XVI's ministry. There is a shared vision that work is the motor for development and poverty elimination, for unlocking the hidden resources of nature, for personal and professional fulfillment and family support, for social participation in the well-being of society.

As a popular saying goes, 'Think globally, act locally', fundamental principles and strategic objectives need to be embodied in the daily existence of people to make a difference. In the words of the Director General's Report, a common effort is demanded 'to maintain and increase this advocacy of a decent work perspective in economic and social policies locally, nationally and internationally', and to implement decent work country programs so as to move in this positive direction. However, a more determined outreach to the most vulnerable categories of workers is called for. Coherent action against forced labour, at the national level and in a collaborative mode with the international community can eradicate this most *indecent* work which should have no place in the modern world. The estimates provided for the first time at this Conference are their own commentary: Today, at least 12.3 million people are victims of forced labour worldwide. Of these, 9.8 million are exploited by private agents, including more than 2.4 million in forced labour as a result of human trafficking, a US$ 32 billion global business. Another 2.5 million are forced to work by the State or by rebel military groups.[2] Obviously the human person is treated as an instrument of production, his or her freedom and dignity violated, the rights that flow from work stifled. When work is isolated from the broader context of human rights, the worst forms of exploitation take over.

An important sign of the continued dynamism of the ILO is its persevering commitment to focus on forced labour as well as on all segments of the world of work that are most marginalized. The workers of the sea have not been forgotten. For fishermen, a much needed instrument that holds the potential for improving the life of 90 per cent of these most forgotten people, is the convention hopefully to be approved and opened for ratification at this Conference. It is difficult, and therefore a greater achievement, to produce a convention that will take into consideration in a balanced way very different situations that go from the small fisher that fishes with a net from his wooden boat for sustenance to the commercial fishing vessels, some so sophisticated as to be a processing factory on the waves of the sea. Fishing is a complex and also dangerous profession with high occupational accidents, deaths and injuries. The proposed convention: 'Work in the fishing sector', and its Recommendations, can make all kind of professional fishing safer and a decent workplace.

For the first time, an integrated approach and framework is proposed for the protection of workers against injuries and sickness related to their work. The combination of norms, clear lines of responsibility and mechanism for compliance should strengthen prevention and increase the well-being of workers and their productivity. It is a dramatic realization

[2] International Labour Office, A Global Alliance against Forced Labour, Report I (B) International Labour Conference, 93rd Session 2005, p. 10.

to read that fatal and non-fatal accidents are estimated at 270 million and that some 160 million workers suffer from work-related diseases.[3] An instrument dealing with renewed commitment with occupational safety and health seems really timely and opportune.

Mr President, new questions and problems are always arising as the economy, technological advances and the globalized organization of society evolve. Work remains central in building up the future. But the protagonist of his work is the human person and safeguarding his dignity and centrality in all new realities is the best guarantee for a more just and peaceful world.

[3] International Labour Organization, Promotional Framework for Occupational Safety and Health, 93rd Session 2005, p. 3

THE UNAVOIDABLE NECESSITY TO SHAPE A FAIR SYSTEM OF TRADE RULES*

The Delegation of the Holy See wishes to express its gratitude to the Chief Executive of the Hong Kong Special Administrative Region, to the Secretary for Commerce, Industry and Technology, and to the people of Hong Kong for the kind welcome extended and to congratulate them on the excellent arrangements that have been made for this Conference. Equal appreciation goes to the Chairman of the General Council and to the Director General of the WTO for their efforts throughout this preparatory period.

The Hong Kong conference takes place at a moment when several tensions are challenging world nations, threatening the precarious economic political and social balance achieved so far. But 'the Holy See is confident', as Pope Benedict XVI says, 'that a sense of responsibility and solidarity with the most disadvantaged will prevail, so that narrow interests and the logic of power will be set aside.'[1] The Doha Round of negotiations offers an occasion to pursue the common good of the entire human family, in particular by taking into account that 'the vulnerability of rural areas has significant repercussions on the subsistence of small farmers and their families if they are denied access to the market.'[2]

The Holy See advocates an equitable and participatory multilateral system of trade relations directed to attaining and developing the common good. A spirit of solidarity among all countries and people should overcome the tireless competition for achieving and defending privileged positions in international trade. Protectionism too often protects already privileged segments of society. Effective multilateralism, on the other hand, is an inclusive process that sees liberalization as having a social mortgage because at the core of all social and economic relations, and hence of trade relations, is the human person, with dignity and inalienable human rights. Therefore, a rule-based trade system or, better, a fair system of trade rules is indispensable.

A fair system of trade rules should be shaped according to the level of economic development of the Member States and give explicit support and special and differential treatment to the poor. When the positions of

* Statement delivered at the 6th Ministerial Conference World Trade Organization, Hong Kong, China, 13–18 December 2005.

[1] Pope Benedict XVI at the 33rd Conference of FAO, 24 November, 2005.

[2] Ibid.

the contracting parties are excessively unequal, the consent of the parties does not suffice to guarantee the justice of their contract: 'trade relations can no longer be based solely on the principle of free, unchecked competition, for it very often creates an economic dictatorship. Free trade can be called just only when it conforms to the demands of social justice'.[3] A fair system of trade rules can be considered as an international public good. Without a fair system of trade rules, vulnerable people in all countries, including developed ones, will be 'locked in a poverty trap'. In fact for many poor countries confronted with trade liberalization the major cost is that they are not able to reap the benefits of the new opportunities offered in the new scenario. In our perspective of a development-oriented trade system, seen as having not only economic but also ethical values, aid and assistance are fundamental instruments, while the basic method of work is the commitment of every country and every person to assume responsibility for their future.

Trade has the capacity to deliver an efficient allocation of resources. Yet, trade cannot by itself be the solution to every social problem of developing countries. The removal of artificial restraints on the flow of goods and services can, in the short-term, bring about adjustment costs that have a destructive impact on the lives of the poor. International trade rules should enable governments to adopt the measures necessary to reduce the social costs of trade liberalization. Indeed the global gain from trade liberalization should allow for 'compensating losers'.

This approach is in line with the concern to put the human being at the centre of any development and trade strategy, recognising that only by raising an individual's capabilities, enabling every person and social group to make the most of the opportunities created by trade liberalization, will it be possible to implement a truly mutually beneficial fair trade. Therefore a development strategy that is mutually beneficial entails a double responsibility for both rich and poor countries. Rich countries have the duty to assist poor countries by helping them to create the economic, social and institutional pre-conditions that are necessary to participate in international trade on an equal footing. On the other hand, poor countries have the duty to implement the structural reforms that are necessary to achieve this goal. A bridge stands up on two pillars: both are necessary. In this case, a wider engagement of developed countries in building a development-oriented system of rules and giving all the necessary assistance, and least developed countries' and developing countries'

[3] Cf. Paul VI, *Populorum Progressio*, § 59.

responsibility in making the necessary institutional changes, are the two pillars of a sustainable trade system.

Trade opening is a real opportunity for developing countries and an essential element of the development process; however, it is not per se a sufficient condition for pulling countries out of poverty. They need to be equipped in order to take this opportunity. Without appropriate infrastructure for access to markets, human capital and capacity building, it is very unlikely that any country could benefit from trade. This is why we agree with the position of those who say that a great effort is necessary to develop both inside and outside the WTO, in line with the integrated framework approach, technical assistance and a wide 'aid for trade' initiative. This initiative should be country-specific, recognizing that countries at different levels of development can make different commitments, that is with the flexible approach typical of the Special and Differential Treatment experience; it should be based on a preliminary monitoring of the bottlenecks and weaknesses that confront participation in international trade. A generous Aid for Trade initiative should be predictable, specific, monitored and country-driven. In this regard, consideration should be given for an 'Aid for Trade Fund' to provide developing countries with the finances needed to address adjustment costs arising from the Doha negotiations as well as their supply side constraints. Indeed, weak economies urgently need support for improving their supply capacity and trade-related infrastructure in order to be able to translate improved market access into increased exports.

Mr Chairman,

The international trading system should guarantee a true *partnership* based on equal and reciprocal relations among rich and poor countries. This necessitates the recognition of the right of all people to have effective control over choices that regard their future. The WTO system should encourage participation of all States, above all of the most disadvantaged, in the negotiation process. Among other advantages, this would forestall the establishment of hidden privileges. Trade rules should be negotiated by all, in the interest of all, and adhered to by all, avoiding closed-door decision-making that lacks the transparency and democracy necessary for the participation of the weak and voiceless. It could be interesting to consider the possibility that a percentage of the Official Development Assistance (ODA) given to poor countries be used to support small farmers in developed countries with the view to facilitate opening access to their markets and cutting subsidies that distort trade. The benefits that would result for developing countries would be larger, stable and leading to their self-reliance.

Free trade is not an end in itself but rather a means for better living standards and the human development of people at all levels. The universal destination of the goods of the earth requires that the poor and marginalized should be the focus of particular concern.[4] Trade exchanges should enable all people to have access to these goods. Thus, essential services such as health, education, water, and food are not normal goods since citizens cannot choose not to use them without harm to themselves and high social costs for society.[5] These public goods often require government intervention in markets to ensure equitable access to them.[6] It is the task of the State to provide for the defense and preservation of common goods which cannot simply be addressed by market forces. There exist important human needs which escape the market logic. There are goods which due to their very nature cannot and must not be bought or sold[7] In a very special way, the movement of professionals and workers, a phenomenon of increasing importance that contributes in a critical way to the production of wealth, cannot be planned and managed within only market considerations.

In today's world, where the knowledge economy is becoming such an essential requirement, the concern for the TRIPS Agreement takes on new significance. While there is a need to protect intellectual property rights as an incentive for innovation and technology creation, it is also important to ensure broad access to technology and knowledge especially for low-income countries. The new goods derived from progress in science and technology are key to world trade integration. Improved technology and know-how transfer from the developed countries is then necessary for the less developed countries to catch up and gain international trade competitiveness.

[4] Cf. *Compendium of the Social Doctrine of the Church*, § 182.

[5] Cf. Pope John Paul II, at FAO Headquarter, 5 December 1992, § 4. We realize that 'food aid can do much good for recipient countries. However, it should not be used by donor countries so as to result in commercial displacement of food commodities. In the long term, food security problems will not be solved by increasing food aid dependency of entire populations' that should 'receive an education that prepares them to provide healthy and sufficient foodstuffs on their own'.

[6] Cf. *Trade Justice, Catholic Social Justice Series*, 54 (2005).

[7] Cf. *Centesimus Annus*, § 40.

Further, any amendment to the Doha Declaration on the TRIPS Agreement and Public Health should be respectful to the Decision of 30 August 2003 on the Implementation of Paragraph 6. This Decision assured to poor countries access to the means for the production and importation of essential drugs needed to face the main pandemics suffered by their populations. It balanced the two important objectives of intellectual property rules: creating incentives for innovation and spreading the benefits of the innovations as widely as possible. However, the 30 August Decision is being weakened by regional and bilateral agreements containing 'TRIPS plus' variants, which are more onerous for poor developing countries.

The ministerial meeting in Hong Kong could provide not only an important chance to restore confidence in the Doha Development Round, but also to restore full credibility and legitimacy of the WTO system and to have the public at large understand its value. Despite all its functioning constraints, the WTO remains unique in its kind of international organizations as a member-driven one with an ambitious policy of inclusion. The mechanism of an effective Dispute Settlement Body (DSB) is evidence of a guarantee of the equality of all countries in front of the law, regardless of their economic power and it protects virtually all Member States from unfair, unilateral commercial actions.

This Ministerial Conference has the potential to be remembered as a milestone in the establishment of a socially just international trading-system. The more the rights and needs of the poor and the weak are taken into account, the greater becomes the possibility for justice and peace in our world, indispensable conditions for sustainable development and for all alleviation of poverty. These two goals constitute the common ambition we aspire to and for which we promote fair trade.

Thank you, Mr Chairman.

THE ADOPTION OF THE CONSOLIDATED MARITIME LABOUR CONVENTION: IMPROVING FAIRNESS AND JUSTICE FOR ALL*

Mr Chairperson,

The Holy See Delegation takes this opportunity to join its voice to that of numerous other Delegations in highlighting the significance of this Conference. Three reasons in fact point out the importance of the present occasion. It underscores the truly historical opportunity presented by this Tenth Maritime Session of the International Labour Conference (ILO). It gives a chance to welcome the proposed Consolidated Maritime Labour Convention as an indispensable tool of decent work. It proves once again the value of tripartite negotiations and cooperation to ensure a successful and timely outcome. Allow me to add that the word 'historical' is not a rhetorical expression, but the definition of an achievement made possible thanks to the spirit of dialogue and the quality negotiations which have prevailed, thus enabling the conference to reach a consensus even on the more difficult provisions. The challenge that now remains is to formalize the good work already done.

Life at sea will still be difficult and dangerous for the world's 1.25 million seafarers, but we are confident that the adoption of this comprehensive convention on maritime labour standards, while not eroding existing seafarers' rights, will provide the appropriate environment for the emergence of a new maritime world order that will provide 'opportunities for women and men to obtain decent and productive work, in conditions of freedom, equity, security and human dignity', as the Report of the Director General has stated.[1] Indeed, a globalized maritime world is fast developing with ships linking the four corners of the world and crews increasingly made up of persons from culturally and religiously diverse nationalities. Therefore before these developments the logical step is to provide the proper environment and the just standards and sufficient security so that each human face is fairly and, hopefully, warmly recognized for the personal worth and inalienable dignity he or she has and for the professional contribution he or she makes to maritime work.

* Statement delivered at the 94th Session, International Labour Conference, 20 February 2006.

1 International Labour Conference, 94th (Maritime) Session, 2006: Report of the Director General on developments in the maritime sector, Geneva: ILO, 2006, p. 7.

Various international and national organizations and many individuals inspired by their Christian faith or by a genuine sense of human solidarity, and specifically reaching out to the People of the Sea, are working for a globalization with a human face, where benefits accrue to everyone without exclusion of any category of people. For decades they have been offering their precious services to seafarers on land and on merchant, fishing and passenger vessels. Permit me to refer to one example, the Apostleship of the Sea of the Catholic Church and to the ecumenical network of non-profit Christian organizations, that includes the Apostleship of the Sea, the International Christian Maritime Association (ICMA) representing 526 seafarers' centers and 927 chaplains in 126 countries. From this collective experience comes a strong encouragement to reaffirm maritime welfare and the well-being of the People of the Sea by adopting fair and forward-looking standards and the Convention at the center of concern of this Conference. The whole maritime industry will have a better future with healthier, more satisfied and qualified, and adequately protected seafarers and their families.

Five years ago the ILO moved a joint resolution by the representatives of International Seafarers and Ship Owners, a resolution supported by governments, to create a new Maritime Labour Convention. Those farsighted delegates pointed out that the shipping industry is the world's first global industry and that it requires global labour standards applicable to an entire industry and such that they can safeguard the rights, welfare and human dignity of all seafarers. By doing so they acknowledged that those same seafarers by their own labour are the bedrock of this very important and very successful industry and that the human element must be its priority.

Mr Chairperson,

The concept of 'fair trade' is progressing slowly but surely in many parts of the world. Sea transport being an essential part of international trade, has the time not come to extend this notion of 'fair trade', or even better of a fair system of trade rules, to maritime transport, fishing and other categories alike? Has the time not come to provide to maritime workers social security and protection? What the Holy Father Benedict XVI writes in his recent first Encyclical applies as well to the world of the sea: 'there can never be room for a poverty that denies anyone what is needed for a dignified life.'[2]

[2] Pope Benedict XVI, Encyclical Letter, *Deus Caritas Est*, § 20.

The Delegation of the Holy See, therefore, wishes to commend all delegates and the ILO personnel for their commitment and hard work over the last five years to develop this Consolidated Maritime Labour Convention and congratulates them and the dedicated staff of this Organization for bringing the maritime world to this decisive point of change. A change which, if adopted, and ratified early, and implemented effectively at the national level, will bring great benefits to the lives of millions of people over time and be an example of good practice to the whole industrialized world. The proposed new instrument has taken into account today's globalized economy and it shows a positive side of it, that the previously mentioned Encyclical expresses in this way: 'Concern for our neighbour transcends the confines of national communities and has increasingly broadened its horizon to the whole world' (§ 30).

At this crucial moment all delegates have a chance to enlarge the horizon of solidarity by adopting the proposed Consolidated Maritime Labour Convention. In doing so, the globalized maritime industry will move forward towards improved fairness and justice for all.

Thank you, Mr Chairperson.

DECENT WORK: THE WAY TO POVERTY ERADICATION*

Mr President,

The international community has committed itself in a solemn way to promote 'full and productive employment and decent work for all, including for women and young people'.[1] The strategic role of work in combating poverty and the quality of work, within its social context, bear directly on the dignity of the human person even before they serve as indispensable tools of development. The Delegation of the Holy See notices with satisfaction that decent work, not only as a notion, but as a strategic agenda, is now at the forefront of any discussion on eradicating poverty and that a convergence of efforts is under way for its implementation. The task, however, is far off from reaching its target. The liberalization of finance and trade and the ongoing process of globalization have produced much wealth, but plenty of evidence shows growing disparities among and within countries in reaping the benefits of this increased wealth. If the measure of decent work is adopted, it becomes clear that too many people remain excluded from enjoying it because they are indecently exploited or are altogether out of work. People not sufficiently qualified to board the globalization train or whose capacity and talents are utilized to propel forward the global economy without their sharing in the accruing benefits, are in the tens of millions: undocumented migrants working in agriculture, in manufacturing, in domestic service; women in the textile industry working in unhealthy conditions and with miserable salaries; workers labelled by their race, caste or religion that are relegated to the marginal jobs of society without a chance for upward mobility; exploited workers in export processing zones and all over the world, workers being paid less and less who must work more and more to earn a decent salary. A case can be made, it has been observed, that inequality and poverty are the overriding moral issues of the twenty-first century. Thus a globalization that fosters economic growth without equity blocks access to decent work and calls into question the current functioning of the international structures created to facilitate the flow of ideas, capital, technology, goods and people for the common good.

* Statement delivered at the 95th Session, International Labour Conference, 8 June 2006.

1 United Nations General Assembly, Resolution 60/1: 2005 World Summit Outcome, n. 47.

The importance of work is evident above all in the formation of a person's humanity. Not consumption, but the capacity to create new things, situations, expressions, marks the vitality of a person, her/his self-expression. The personal imprint given through work brings about satisfaction and the will to grow, to give and contribute in a positive way to social coexistence. If work is lacking or is indecent, it is the person that is stifled and pushed into a crisis and a person in crisis is easily tempted by anti-social and destructive behaviour. From the primacy of the ethical value of human labour follows 'a logical sequence of priorities: of the person over work, of work over capital, of the universal destination of goods over the exclusive right to private ownership of the means of production',[2] in a word, of the human being over enterprises, increased stock market value, material possessions. The changed perspective that decent work for all entails, calls for a renewed emphasis on the dignity of every person and on common good by placing them at the center of all labour activities and policies.

Mr President,

The initiatives of solidarity undertaken to promote the implementation of the Decent Work Agenda at the local level are effective forms of cooperation that give credibility to this Agenda. In past decades, the ILO has developed a rich body of labour standards; they remain the main road through which the international community can achieve a progressive improvement of the quality of work and of the rights of workers. At the same time, this unique dimension of the ILO requires today a convergence of efforts with other international agencies and a coherence of plans and actions so that the complexity of the economy and social relations may not frustrate or delay the global goal of decent work.

Two steps taken in this context add an encouraging dimension to the concrete implementation of decent work objectives. The first concerns the 1999 Worst Forms of Children Labour Convention (§ 182) and the recent good news that for the first time the number of children bound to work in the world has been reduced by 11 per cent between 2000 and 2004, passing from 248 to 218 million. The prospect that children may be taken out of agricultural work or quarrying, that they may not be trafficked for forced prostitution, that they may be able to go to school

[2] Cf. Pope John Paul II, Encyclical Letter, *Laborem Exercens*, §§ 12–20.

and grow up with hope, should redouble the determination of governments, employers, unions, the civil society to aim at a total elimination of child labour. The second step regards the hopefully soon to be adopted Convention and Recommendation on a Framework for Occupational Safety and Health. A safe and healthy working environment is an integral component of decent work, especially if we keep in mind that 270 million work accidents are registered every year and 160 million people suffer illnesses related to work and accidents and illnesses causing the death of about 5,000 workers daily.[3] The patient development of labour standards, when the political will and the collaboration of all segments of society are present, becomes an effective tool that gives results and changes the world of work for the better.

Mr President,

In conclusion, the fast-evolving process of globalization impacts directly on the organization of production and of work and continues to demand adaptation and imagination to sustain decent work. But work will be really decent if, as Pope Benedict XVI has reminded workers on the occasion of last May 1st, the human person 'is subject and protagonist of work'. In fact, work is of primary importance for any woman and man's 'fulfilment and the development of society, and this is why it is necessary that it always be organised and developed in full respect of human dignity and at the service of the common good'.[4]

[3] Cf. Bureau international du travail, Conférence internationale du travail, 93rd session, 2005. Report IV (1): 'Cadre promotionnel pour la sécurité et la santé au travail', p. 1.

[4] Cf. Pope Benedict XVI's Homily of 19 March in *L'Osservatore Romano*, 20–21 March 2006, p. 7.

FULL EMPLOYMENT AND DECENT WORK FOR AN EQUITABLE AND SUSTAINABLE DEVELOPMENT*

Mr President,

The goal of equitable development regularly pursued by the UN Economic and Social Council (ECOSOC) has taken a new and timely turn in the present session. ECOSOC focuses on a theme that is both timely and strategic: 'Creating an environment at the national and international levels conducive to generating full and productive employment and decent work for all, and its impact on sustainable development'. The Delegation of the Holy See fully endorses this agenda that highlights the central place of the human person, the value of human work and that points out the way to overcome chronic poverty and marginality. Decent work, in fact, entails a quality of life that goes beyond production: it is a dimension of the person himself, who gives work its highest value.

People looking and hoping for a job, who find themselves out of work, are at an all-time high with the consequent serious risk that the fight against poverty and the achievement of the Millennium Development Goals will be frustrated and that this frustration may provoke disorderly behavior and, surely, a less secure world. Already in 1967 Pope Paul VI had stated: 'Development is the new name of peace' (*Populorum Progressio*). It may be now the occasion to ask why much direct financial assistance and technology exchange have not been as effective as planned and to reconsider the relationship between development and the broader goals of international cooperation.

If individuals and the different groups and associations which make up society take on a primary responsibility in the economy in a healthy subsidiarity, this local involvement can propel the economy forward. At the grass root level it is the creation of new jobs that puts the economy in motion. Active participation in work unclenches the creative capacities and energies of each person within the specific moment and level of development of a country. Step by step poverty is reduced, emigration becomes an option instead of a necessity, social standards begin to develop, people are lifted out of a vicious circle of misery and indecent conditions of life. It becomes clear that 'the primary basis of the value of work is the human person as such' (Pope John Paul II, *Laborem Exercens*, 6).

* Statement delivered at the High-Level Segment of ECOSOC, 5 July 2006.

To obtain this goal for societies in the grip of unemployment, assistance for capacity building will have to be adapted to the level of development of each country. In this way, a waste of resources will be avoided. Donors will see their solidarity fruitful for the receiving countries and, in the long run, also for themselves. In our present interconnectedness, to the necessity of preparing products for the global market corresponds the responsibility to help the people of the least developed societies to have the training and the know-how that allow them a fair chance to compete. A realistic partnership gives priority to the choices based on local possibilities of labour intensive economic initiatives managed with honesty and responsible competence and leading out of a stifling status quo. Such a job-creating approach prevents the unintended effect of some official development assistance that ends up by enriching a small group of corporations or small group of persons who then incline to block democratization and even to tolerate corruption.

When the process of transformation of society takes hold, decent work contributes another important dimension, that of a sense of future that is hopeful and that gives the possibility to recover personal protagonism and self-respect, and that favors a more integrated social structure. In fact the family can be supported, children are not forced to work and instead can accede to education, the values of organization and participation are learned. On this basis, work serves as a major element in the self-fulfillment of each woman and man.

The way forward, then, appears to be the political acceptance of conditions that allow for local labour-intensive employment and this creation of jobs fights poverty and sets in motion social change. In the context of today's globalization, however, while wealth increases, the gap between rich and poor persists. A convergence or coherence among international actors in the economic and development arena can multiply the results in job creation, and this implies a better coordination of financial investment policies, of agricultural reforms and access to markets, of good governance. A progressive elimination of external debt will then result as a consequence of this strategy. If the Doha trade round negotiations fail to conclude with some positive agreements, the world's poor and hungry will pay most of the price and the chance for their growth, their development and for decent work will vanish for a long time. The courage and political imagination to make the needed compromises can lead instead to a renewal of common action and show a concrete commitment to the elimination of global poverty which is still a scandal and a threat to peace and security. At this juncture in history when the international family of nations wants to promote 'better standards of life in larger freedoms', special interests of agencies and of countries should give way to the opportunity of a coherent action for the common good, for a fair share by all in trade, in decision-making, and in the benefits of development.

Work and development call for a change in focus and priorities so that the enabling environment of peace, dialogue, respect of subsidiarity and participation may allow for the growth of decent work and ultimately the development of every person. The proposed 'Decade for Full and Productive Employment and Decent Work for All' could serve as a period of reflection and action on these priorities. The rules of the economy and trade, the technical progress we daily witness, the political engagement for a just international order: all these are components of an enabling environment geared to safeguard the dignity and creativity of every human person and ensure a future of justice and peace for the entire human family.

COMMITTED TO THE STRUGGLE FOR THE ERADICATION OF POVERTY AND HUNGER*

Mr President,

The Delegation of the Holy See expresses its sincere appreciation for the steady action of UNCTAD in favor of development, especially of the least developed countries and of Africa, the often forgotten continent. In fact, in its historic commitment and in its action UNCTAD has carried out the UN Charter's objective to promote social progress and better standards of life.

Lately the world economy grew at a fast rate. More wealth has been produced. In 2006, the growth rate is expected to be close to 4 per cent even if interest rates and oil prices have been rising. However, the good performances of the world economy and the benefits of globalization are not equally distributed among and within countries. The significant growth of recent years is not yet consolidated and several poor countries, mainly in Africa, are still at the margin of the development process.

In recent years a number of initiatives have been implemented to alleviate poverty and to enhance growth prospects in LDCs: the launching of the Millennium Development Goals, the work of implementation of the Doha agenda, various debt reduction initiatives and the new Official Development Assistance commitments, to name the most important: all aimed at giving a decisive contribution to poverty reduction and elimination while at the same time they raised great expectations among people in developing countries.

Good will and good planning notwithstanding, concrete results so far have been disappointing. The Doha agenda had a big setback in Cancun and the more recent ministerial conference in Hong Kong has not so far produced a clear agreement on the issues that are crucial for poor countries, such as agricultural subsidies in developed economies. At present Sub-Saharan African countries are not expected to meet any of the targets of the MDG by the required date (2015). Besides, less than half of the eligible countries have succeeded so far in obtaining the maximum debt relief possible. Realistically, then, the UNCTAD's 2006 Trade

* Statement delivered at the UNCTAD Mid-term Review, Trade and Development Board, 23rd Special Session, 5 October 2006.

and Development Report calls for a 'fundamental reorientation of policy' and for a 'policy innovation' in order to have a 'new focus on poverty reduction'.

The UNCTAD Mid Term Review provides the opportunity to refocus the development effort by reaffirming the spirit of Sao Paulo: 'We are committed to the struggle for the eradication of poverty and hunger. Policy instruments and measures, at the national and international levels, should be adopted ... to encourage the creation of opportunities for the poor women and men of the world to have access to jobs and to stable and adequate remuneration.' The realization of this commitment has been pursued by UNCTAD through the three pillars of its action: research and policy analysis, consensus building and technical cooperation, a core of competences proven to be effective for developing countries.

It is crucial that research and policy analysis be completely independent and accessible also to LDC. Moreover, policy prescriptions following from research should be tailored in terms of both objectives and timing to the needs and capabilities of poor countries.

With respect to consensus building, UNCTAD has a unique role, being a knowledge-based institution, and as such it should be at the heart of a process that creates among multinational institutions a consensus centered on development.

Regarding technical cooperation, it is important that UNCTAD increases its participation in country-level development programs with other UN and multinational organizations in order to improve efficiency in its actions and to implement on the ground its role in consensus building.

In pursuing its objectives, UNCTAD should envision development as referred to the human person rather than to the economy in general. In fact, any development strategy has to recognise that its true goal is uplifting the worth and dignity of any woman and man. While these values can be enhanced by raising economic standards, the economic dimension doesn't exhaust them. A person's value and dignity lies in being open to others and in developing in action.

Any policy-oriented strategy therefore is called to take into account that human capital is central in any development program. Only educated people can make the most of the opportunities created by globalization. Education has a much broader meaning than just schooling: it implies the introduction of the individual to the full understanding of reality beginning from his/her traditions and culture.

Thus development initiatives should involve much more local communities. A stronger participation of these communities witnesses not only a proactive involvement of people in the development process but also it reduces the risk that globalization proceeds at the expense of local traditions.

If civil society actors and local communities participate in the design and organization of aid and development packages, a solution may become available in resolving the 'democratic deficit' of the current globalization process.

The fact that the human person is not an island, but a network of relations should make us cautious about recent discussions on labour mobility. In the case of temporary labour migrations, the effects of this experience on family and on societies of countries of origin and countries of destination will have to be carefully analyzed.

Aid and development packages should be oriented at increasing opportunities for individuals and communities. In this context, the Aid for Trade initiative is certainly a big step forward since it allows access to the potential benefits of globalization and trade integration to several countries and peoples.

With the person at the center of development and development at the center of the international community agenda, the next step can be what the latest LDC report states: a 'development-driven approach to trade rather than a trade-driven approach to development'. This new relationship implies a policy shift to 'place production and employment at the heart of efforts to reduce poverty'.

On the other hand, poor countries need to be equipped to make the most of the opportunities coming their way. Besides enhancing human capital, efforts should be conveyed to three well-known areas:

Health: poor countries, especially in sub-Saharan Africa, still suffer from terrible sanitary conditions. Without a drastic reduction in mortality rates and increase in life-expectancy there will not be the possibility for poor people to take the opportunities offered them.

Infrastructure: lack of infrastructures is at present one of the most pressing problems for poor countries, especially in Africa. Without a proper infrastructural framework peoples and governments cannot have access to international markets therefore losing all the potential benefits of trade.

Institutions: several poor countries lack the institutional structure needed to accompany the development process. Lack of property rights and widespread corruption are major factors that hamper development.

A strong moral aspect cannot be underestimated: people receiving aid cannot allow corruption to destroy the trust of the population in donor countries.

Mr President,

If we truly care about persons and peoples and their development, the eradication of poverty will not remain a mirage, but a reachable goal.

MAN'S FULFILLMENT AS A HUMAN BEING THROUGH WORK*

Mr President,

Even today, the pursuit of social justice remains a most challenging ideal and an operational task for the International Labour Organization (ILO) as it continues to develop up-to-date standards and to influence policy in the world of work within the evolving global economy. In this regard, the Delegation of the Holy See acknowledges shared objectives with the ILO. It fully supports the combined action of workers, employers and governments to make decent work for sustainable development a collective goal within the international community as well as a priority in national programs. Much of the restlessness and many of the conflicts that torment our society are rooted in the lack of jobs, in employment which lacks decent work conditions or living wages, and in unjust economic relations. The timely agenda of this Conference rightly addresses old and new forms of discrimination, social protection, the new context of work and its impact on individual workers and their families, and related themes. In fact, work, enterprise and the global arena of financial investments, trade and production should be rooted in a creative, cooperative, and rule-based effort at the service of the human person, of every man and woman, and of their equal dignity and rights. It is the human dimension of work that needs to be valued and protected; moreover, an enabling environment must be created so that personal talents are invested for the common good.

In recent years changes have been brought about in the fields of economy, technology and communications that have transformed the face of work and the conditions of the labor market, at times in dramatic ways. Obviously, the international system is evolving under the weight of an ageing population in some regions, of outsourcing, of the gap between needed skills and an educational system still incapable of preparing people with skills to meet such demands, of the search for balance between fair policy space and an effective multilateralism, of the demand for greater flexibility and mobility. One emerging tendency appears to favor more individualistic relations between enterprise and employees. These latter would protect their own rights on the base of their skills

* Statement delivered at the 96th Session of the International Labour Conference, 13 June 2007.

and entrepreneurial ability. These developments may be calling on us to rethink current forms of solidarity. Although workers may no longer find themselves in physical proximity with each other, solidarity remains crucial and indispensable if founded on our common humanity that links all types of work.

In turn, 'through work man not only transforms nature, adapting it to his own needs, but he also achieves fulfillment as a human being and, indeed, in a sense, becomes "more a human being"' (Pope John Paul II, *Laborem Exercens*, 9). In a way, the world of labor has overturned the old practice: now work tends to take precedence over capital and real wealth is found in the knowledge, in the human and relational capacities of workers, in their creativity and ability to confront new situations. At the same time, even in the face of such new approaches to work, exploitation is possible in the form of overwork, excessive flexibility and stiff competition that make family life and personal growth impossible.

The new globalized context of work makes it evident that a person working with and for other persons progressively reaches out to the whole human family. Through his work a person is opened to an increasingly universal dimension and, in this way, can 'humanize' globalization and thus, by keeping the human person at the center of this process, can provide an ethical measure against its negative aspects. Therefore the universalization of labor standards should not be considered a burden on trade agreements but rather a concrete support for the human rights of workers and a condition for more equitable competition on the global level. At the same time this universalization will not leave workers and their families only at the 'mercy' of economic forces beyond the control of national policies. The mechanisms needed to implement such an approach can vary from special international funds for the protection of workers to a normative, incremental application of standards and, in this way, can promote and carry on the historic achievement of organized labor. As the world is confronted with a globalization that increases wealth but is not equitable in its distribution, social goals cannot be left out of the picture. A policy of convergence between social and economic policies seems better suited to stimulate the creation of new employment opportunities and advance decent work, both of which still elude too many people.

The urgent necessity of creating new jobs is rightly recognized as the first means to prevent discrimination and poverty. With an estimated 195 million men and women unable to find work last year and with

1.4 billion people holding jobs that did not pay enough to lift them above the US$2 a day poverty line, the responsibility of the international community and of governments is put to the test to ensure both an enabling economic environment and the availability of decent work. The Second Global Report on Discrimination under the follow-up to the ILO Declaration on Fundamental Principles and Rights at Work rightly highlights some categories of workers that deserve special attention in the new market circumstances: women still remaining without equal pay for equal work and in need of fairness in career advancement; people with disabilities; the tens of millions of migrants, a major component of productivity in the global economy; young and old workers; people living with HIV and AIDS; working parents searching for better measures to reconcile responsibilities to both work and family; the masses of rural poor without practically any safety net; children forced too early into the labor market.

Within this somewhat somber picture, the proposal of a Convention and Recommendation Concerning Work in the Fishing Sector represents a sign of major progress. It is estimated that some 40 million people worldwide work in the fishing industry; 1.5 million of these are industrial or deep-sea fishers, while the rest are traditional coastal fishers. The harsh reality of the work environment for fishers, their confined space in the fishing vessels and their vulnerability; their long working hours causing excessive fatigue that can result in serious occupational accidents; the exploitation of children in deep-sea diving who are exposed to injuries and death; and the excessive long periods away from the family; these and similar other considerations have prompted careful negotiations that hopefully will now be brought to conclusion with an additional instrument of protection. In fact, the proposed Convention and Recommendation can also provide the basis for the elimination of abuse and discrimination inflicted on industrial fishers through the illegal, unreported and unregulated fishing on distant water vessels within the system of open registry. Inter-related issues of justice, safety and health demand a concerted response to the legitimate claim by fishers that their rights be protected and that their quality of life be advanced. Solidarity cannot extend, of course, to permit over-fishing or to causing damage to ocean life. Such solidarity should instead help fishers and countries that, due to lack of resources, sell their fishing rights to richer countries with evident threat to the survival of small and coastal fishers and consequent destruction of the fish habitat.

Mr President,

The instruments of protection become the expression of solidarity at a global level, especially for the large number of people without work or without decent work. A simpler lifestyle and a more equitable sharing of the resources of the planet are needed. The Holy Father Benedict XVI has recently remarked: 'It is not possible to continue using the wealth of the poorest countries with impunity, without them also being able to participate in world growth' (Address to New Ambassadors, June 1, 2007). The new horizon of the social question is now the world because the human person is at its center as protagonist of an integral development, which is the new name of peace. Through the adoption of Decent Work as a development paradigm for the multilateral system, locally adapted and implemented in Decent Work Country Programs, workers, employers and governments, acting together, can give concrete form to this vision for a better future.

Thank you, Mr President.

ECONOMIC GROWTH BASED ON ABSOLUTE LIBERALIZATION IS NOT SUSTAINABLE*

Mr President,

The continued effort to address the plight of people trapped in poverty and to search for new ways and means to free them from its destructive consequences remains essential if the international community wants to achieve truly integral human development. The Delegation of the Holy See believes that the question of poverty 'should be given the highest attention and priority, for the sake of poor and rich countries alike'.[1] The process of globalization has brought us to a new historic moment in the evolution of the economy. The worldwide impact of communication technology and the instant dissemination of information pre-socialize the poor, the young in particular, to expectations of a more decent and humane life-style, to which they are entitled. When such anticipations are frustrated, society faces a risk of violent reactions and peace is endangered for all.

Wealth has increased in recent decades lifting millions of persons out of extreme poverty as a result of the opening of markets, of scientific and technological progress, and the circulation of capital. Life-expectancy has improved on every continent, literacy rate has increased, and also democracy is now more widespread than it was thirty years ago. Regrettably evidence shows the persistence of areas of poverty in different geographical regions and among segments of population within countries. In the fight against poverty the fact cannot be ignored that, instead of declining, the number of people living on less than US$2 a day grew to 1.37 billion and an estimated 854 million people worldwide are undernourished. In several regions of Africa and Asia, life-expectancy is almost half of that in rich countries and illiteracy reaches high levels. Thus attainment of the Millennium Development Goals remains an urgent task. Based on current trends, it appears that most developing countries will fail to meet the majority of these goals by 2015. The reaffirmed partnership in the search for and in the action to achieve greater equity requires the political will to reexamine in depth the reasons why developing countries are facing such difficulties with meeting these goals.

* Statement delivered at the High-Level Segment of ECOSOC, 4 July 2007.

1 Pope Benedict XVI to the Chancellor of Germany Angela Merkel, 16 December 2006.

Poverty elimination demands an integration between the mechanisms that produce wealth and the mechanisms for the distribution of its benefits at the international, regional and national levels. Exclusion from technological and economic progress, even within the same national community, leads to entrenchment, not elimination, of poverty. An approach to economic growth based on absolute liberalization proves to be socially and, in the long run, economically non-sustainable. In a context of globally increasing wealth and availability of goods, a more systematic and comprehensive analysis is needed to understand how existing methods of trade and mechanisms of production should be modified in order to lift people out of poverty.

The 'big push' that generous donors had envisioned with carefully thought out plans has not yielded all the concrete results expected. Nor has the advantage provided by the cancellation of external debt always resulted in greater access to education, health and social services. The question to be posed is not whether but how additional aid should be given. The projects of multilateral institutions and developed countries aimed at reducing poverty and improving growth in poor regions, like the Millennium Development Goals, the Highly Indebted Poor Countries Initiative and the Poverty Reduction Strategy, have made some limited progress. More recently Decent Work Country Programs proposed by the International Labour Organization and supported by the ECOSOC 2006 Ministerial Declaration aim at generating employment opportunities and decent work. In fact, with employment opportunities a community can be taken out of poverty in a stable and sustainable way. Work is the only possibility for a community to generate its own value added that pays the way out of poverty. Then, empirical evidence shows that foreign aid, while improving living conditions for some individuals, has not been enough to end national-level poverty. Perhaps it is necessary to direct aid to more targeted and less generic projects that can bring about tangible, measurable and empowering change in the daily life-experience of individuals and families and in the social fabric of the community. Directing aid to the creation of jobs would fall within this approach. Such effective aid requires multiple channels of distribution and should reach the basic infrastructure of communities that is assured not only by governments but also by community-based organizations and institutions, including those sponsored by faith-groups, such as schools, hospitals and clinics, community centers, and youth training and recreation programs. In particular, education is a long-term economic investment for everyone, and health provides a durable character to that investment. An educated person can be fully aware of his/her worth and dignity and that of every human being and can act accordingly. The value of education goes beyond its relationship with health. Consider the most important feature of the person: being relational with others. Educated people can establish among themselves social relations not based on force and abuse but on respect and friendship. In such an environment, it is easier to reduce corruption, one of the plagues of poor countries, and to improve respect for law and property rights, crucial for the positive functioning of an economic system. This form of public–private partnership not only delivers services but it helps change mentality and disposition toward development without losing respect for local culture and tradition. Changing mentality at the local level becomes a winning strategy in the fight against poverty.

In order to promote development at the macroeconomic level it seems necessary to reinforce the productive capacity of the poorer countries by means of investment in technical formation; this allows for competition in today's knowledge-based economy and gives support to enterprises that create new jobs and decent work. In this regard, trans-national corporations carry a particular responsibility to facilitate the transfer of technology, sponsor capacity building in management, and enable local partners to provide more employment opportunities. Foreign investors need to contribute to the overall development of the country in which they establish operations; this is particularly relevant for those engaged in the extraction industry and other short-term commercial enterprises. On their part, governments need to assure conditions that are favorable to ethical investment, including a well-functioning juridical system, a stable system of taxation, protection of the right to property, and an infrastructure that allows access by local producers to regional and global markets. Corruption has a strong moral relationship with foreign aid. Although it is very difficult to condition foreign aid on such factors as corruption and democracy, nevertheless we have to consider that aid flows are based primarily on voluntary efforts by people in donor countries. Such trust could be destroyed by repeated misuse of aid flows by corrupt governments in receiving countries. Keeping the above observations in mind, it appears logical that the allocation of national resources should give priority to building social capital over military expenses. It is striking to note that worldwide military expenditures exceed US$ 1,118 billion each year, a sum far higher than the global investment for human development. Together with foreign aid, corporate transfer of resources, cancellation of external debt for the poorer countries, the increasing flows of migrations wisely managed can contribute to the elimination of poverty.

Mr President,

The Holy See has repeatedly insisted that, while the governments of poorer countries have a responsibility with regard to good governance and the elimination of poverty, 'the active involvement of international partners is indispensable. It is a grave and unconditional moral responsibility, founded on the unity of the human race, and on the common dignity and shared destiny of rich and poor alike, who are being drawn ever closer by the process of globalization.'[2] Working toward this goal in a coherent use of resources and strategies should allow all people to become 'the artisans of [their] destiny'.[3] New international binding agreements to regulate the exploitation of natural resources, to report stolen public funds, to limit the arms trade, to eliminate distorting subsidies in agriculture, and similar initiatives, will go a long way to translate into concrete decisions the often stated goal of solidarity. But concrete persons are the motor of development. Eradication of poverty is a moral engagement. The various religions and cultures see its achievement as a most important task that frees people from much suffering and marginalization, that helps them to live peacefully together, and that provides individuals and communities the freedom to protect their dignity and actively contribute to the common good.

Thank you, Mr President.

[2] Ibid. [3] Pope Paul VI, Encyclical Letter, *Populorum Progressio*, § 65.

GLOBALIZATION: OPPORTUNITIES AND CHALLENGES FOR DEVELOPMENT*

Mr President,

At the outset, my Delegation expresses it appreciation for the great organization and hospitality provided by the people and Government of Ghana for this UNCTAD's Ministerial Conference.

Mr President,

The world's economy has witnessed a period of remarkable success that has included in its benefits also several developing countries. This global positive achievement is a signal that with a concerted effort and a generous political will it is not impossible to reach the Millennium Development Goals (MDGs). The Delegation of the Holy See rejoices at such progress and supports UNCTAD's continued role in sustaining it. At the same time, the evidence of an uneven distribution of wealth among countries and segments of population within them cannot be ignored. The 'bottom billion' is not a statistic, but women and men who are members of our human family and thus entitled to share in the economic process so they too may live with dignity.

The road ahead is still long. As the findings of UNCTAD's research point out, 'with the end of 2007, we have already passed the halfway mark to the 2015 target deadline for the reduction of poverty and we are still far from achieving the Millennium Development Goals (MDGs). The GDPs per capita of rich countries are about 5–7 times more than the world average, while the GDPs per capita of the poorest countries are about 3–6 per cent of the world average. These figures fuel concerns of increasing concentration of income and wealth and the magnitude of the inequality, raising question on the responsiveness of poverty reduction to economic growth.'[1]

'Addressing the opportunities and challenges of globalization for development' is the theme of this 12th Ministerial Conference. The insight of His Holiness Pope Benedict XVI that globalization, 'also

* Statement delivered at the 12th Session of the United Nations Conference on Trade and Development, Accra, Ghana, 20–25 April 2008.

[1] UNIFEM, 11 January 2008.

needs, in addition to a foundation of shared values, an economy capable of responding effectively to the requirements of a common good which is now planetary in scope,' converges with the objectives of this Conference.[2]

The Delegation of the Holy See appreciates the work undertaken by UNCTAD and its Secretariat and is convinced that the key added value it contributes comes from the appropriate balance among its three pillars: Research and Analysis, Consensus building and Technical assistance. Among these, the independence of analysis gives UNCTAD a competitive advantage that is particularly important in helping developing countries to design policy strategies and actions. Then, the 4 themes chosen by delegates for the 12th Conference reflect well the preoccupation which must be ours. Finding the right response to these themes is crucial to allow the world to reach the MDGs in 2015.

The high level of expertise present at this Conference provides an exhaustive overview of current challenges. This Delegation therefore will focus its communication on a few issues, the crucial role played by the human person in development, and this in an African perspective. Three topics are therefore highlighted: the role of the African entrepreneur, the rural world and the eradication of poverty, human mobility and its relation to development.

Development is centered on, and oriented to, the human person who acts in a web of relations that fulfill his/her primary and original aspirations: the desire for truth, for love, for beauty and for justice. The heart of development is found in this vision; it concerns everyone, irrespective of the level of wealth, the country of origin or the specific culture. In fact, development, more than a target to be reached, is a path to be pursued. Genuine development is realized where persons are enabled to achieve their most fundamental desires and needs. It is successful when it recognizes the central role played by the human person, man and woman, through their work and their creativity. Prior to technical aspects, the human dimension should point out the way forward and remain the ultimate goal. Authentic development is multidimensional and should promote all physical and spiritual aspects of people's lives, 'every person and the whole person'.[3] As a common task of all people, it calls for inclusiveness and the active participation of less developed countries that cannot

[2] Pope Benedict XVI's Message for the 2008 World Day of Peace, § 10.
[3] Paul VI, Encyclical Letter on the Development of Peoples, 1967.

be relegated to the passive role of recipients of development policies and projects designed elsewhere.

At the center of development and the indispensable resource for any economy, the human person is also the key for a new chance for Africa. Entrepreneurs can provide success for the continent through the innovative quality of their entrepreneurial initiatives, which, in turn, require a realistic 'enabling environment'. This enabling environment includes good infrastructures and predictable regulations. The tax regime must be fair and clear. A reliable dispute settlement institution must be enforced. The development of such an institutional setting is the main responsibility of governments, with the support of donors, but also of the civil society. Institutions are shaped by individuals and the proper development of an equitable and efficient institutional setting is therefore a collective responsibility of any society. This responsibility includes ensuring peace, education and health, but also economic development.

Access to credit remains an issue particularly significant for the informal sector which represents an important part of the economy in LDCs. Access to credit includes the condition that rates be affordable. Microfinance institutions may be very helpful provided that they have themselves a fair access to credit via commercial banks. In developing countries foreign firms have a particularly important task: that of contributing to technological diffusion, of elevating production and work standards and of assisting local entrepreneurs. In this way they play a positive role in making globalization more human.

Moreover, respect for the necessary sense of equity calls for guaranteeing equality of opportunity for every entrepreneur on the international market. This could require the relaxation of some constraints that at present are limiting the degree of competitiveness of domestic enterprises in LDCs, compared to their counterparts in advanced economies. In particular the issue of non tariff barriers to trade (rules of origins, adoption of standards, etc.) should be carefully analyzed in order to be non-discriminatory against the poorest countries

Not to be overlooked is that promoting entrepreneurship, especially at the beginning of the development process, is one of the major channels of job creation. The realisation of an 'enabling environment' can allow both the creation of new jobs and the improvement in the quality and dignity of work. Work plays a crucial part in the life of every person who, as a protagonist, shows that the dignity of work interfaces with the dignity of the human person. Through work people participate in their own development and in the production and exchange of goods and services and thus in the life of the society where they live as essential players for its development.

The achievement of high quality and dignity of work cannot be separated from the issue of health and education. This is true particularly in Africa where in some countries diseases and illiteracy are hampering the development of entire societies. Education is crucial for work not only because it allows for the improvement of the quality of the goods and services that are produced but also because it provides the foundations of work relations and working conditions.

Addressing development and poverty eradication in Africa cannot ignore the predominant importance of its rural world. In Africa, the majority of the poor live in rural areas (three in every four people in developing countries) and most of them depend on agriculture for their livelihood. Half of the very poor living in rural areas are tied to very small farms. Improving life conditions in rural areas tackles poverty directly.

For years many farmers around the world were complaining of the low price of commodities which did not cover basic costs of production and did not permit a decent life for their families. Today, there is a new scenario in place. The increased price level for many soft commodities could have a positive impact on the revenue of several farmers in poor countries. At the same time low-income populations can suffer from higher prices of staple food. The difficulties will be particularly high for net importing countries. Here the poorest farmers whose production is just enough to cover the needs of their family could not reap the benefits of the higher farm gate prices. In order to address this new situation the reduction of distorting subsidies in advanced economies should be accompanied by reforms in the poorest countries aimed at increasing agricultural production in a sustainable way. These reforms should not be limited to technical improvements in the productive processes but also include new organizational structures that could allow small and individual farmers to be more efficient and competitive. Some good initiatives are already working and need to be promoted (e.g., the Comprehensive Africa Agriculture Development Programme supported by the Global Donor Platform for Rural Development).

On the other hand, sustainability implies that the success of the development of local agricultures should be linked with preserving the environmental equilibrium that in Africa is particularly delicate.

The people living in rural areas courageously confront adverse conditions and, at times, real catastrophes that call for the solidarity of all. At the same time the dignity often displayed by the poor in such adverse conditions should be a lesson for us all. Looking always for more money, for a constant accumulation of goods, as it is often observed in richer population, can stir up an inordinate race that blinds people to the necessities of the poor and the respect of their dignity as well as obfuscate respect for God's creation. Some attitudes are not sustainable, are unfair to the poorest in all countries, and should be counteracted by a simpler life-style.

Mr President,

Placing the human person at the center of economic concerns helps the international community to correctly manage the growing modern phenomenon of human mobility. Migration affects the lives of millions of people and millions of families. Many villages receive a decisive portion of their revenues from remittances sent home by migrants. While now migration contributes to the globalization process as well as increasing because of it, it clearly plays an economic role as a factor of development. At the same time, migration has become a controversial political and social issue. However, to reduce migrants to a functional role of the economy and downplay their human rights will prove in the end a failing policy for development. In this century of migrations, the research and analysis capability of UNCTAD would be welcomed to build up a sort of 'common ethic of emigration' for developing and developed countries. In LDCs an increasing share of emigrants is composed of skilled people. The reason for this migration is known: limited employment possibilities, poor working conditions, low levels of pay and political instability while, at the same time, the demand for skilled people increases in developed countries often confronted with the ageing of their population. The 'brain drain' caused by such migration could be particularly costly for the poorest countries: 'development needs the talents of Africans.'[4] Thoughtful proposals have been put forward to make the flow of migration fruitful for both countries of origin and countries of destination. They are to a large extent based on the concept of temporary movement. While recognizing that educated persons working in more developed countries can gain additional skills and experience that can be placed at the benefit of the country of origin, it is crucial that these people may find on their return the conditions for putting into action with profit their newly acquired

[4] As rightly stated by the Secretary General of UNCTAD, Dr Supachai in the 2007 LDC Report.

competence and experience, and that their human rights be safeguarded all along the process of emigration, foreign residence and return, to make emigration a win–win situation for development and coexistence.

In conclusion, Mr President, the objectives of the Conference will be reached for the benefit of the world's community if the spotlight is kept on the centrality of the human person in development and on the duty of solidarity that comes from the awareness that the family of nations is one where every individual and every country enjoy equal dignity. Although presently confronted with a slowdown of the world economy, that could trigger some fears about the future, we should, however, keep in mind that ultimately the human person has an innate resource in being created for the fulfillment of the common good and thus always open to the future with an outlook, not of fear, but full of hope.

Thank you, Mr President.

A RETHINKING OF THE DEVELOPMENT PARADIGM*

Mr Chairman,

The more than one-year-old global economic and financial crisis continues to severely affect both advanced and developing countries. Its impact on employment levels has been especially painful and is expected to worsen during the coming months. While weak signs of a recovery can be spotted in advanced economies, several developing countries still find themselves in the midst of strong recession. Due to the limited size of their financial and credit systems, poor countries did not initially suffer the direct impact of the financial crisis that principally hit the more advanced economies. However, the developing countries now are suffering indirectly from the global economic consequences caused by the financial crisis.

Developing countries are indeed more heavily dependent on the external sector than are industrialised countries, where the internal market forces generally play the major role in determining total demand. It is the composition of their exports that makes developing countries particularly vulnerable to the current global crisis. In fact, the exports of poor countries are heavily specialised either in commodities or in low-skill manufacturing goods. The contraction of global demand thereby has exerted a strong impact on the economies of such countries and has placed them in an extremely difficult situation.

Moreover, developing countries are severely constrained in attempts to develop a policy response to the crisis. Advanced countries generally have responded to the crisis with a strong intervention by the State, either through automatic stabilizers or through exceptional spending, mostly financed with public debt. In developing countries, this type of policy action is challenged, on the one hand, by the low impact of government spending on the overall economy, and, on the other hand, by the difficulty in gaining access to international financial markets.

External aid has a crucial importance during the current critical phase. For a number of developing countries, aid is the only source of foreign financing. Advanced economies, therefore, should be aware that reduction of official aid can exacerbate poverty in developing countries.

* Statement delivered at the UNCTAD Trade and Development Board 56th Session, 18 September 2009.

Unfortunately, past experiences show that aid flows from donor countries tend to suffer a significant contraction during crisis periods. UNCTAD and multilateral institutions should make every effort to ensure that donors fulfill their promises by maintaining the levels of aid to which they previously committed themselves, even during this phase of adverse economic conditions.

The limited amount of resources presently available could constitute an incentive for both donors and recipients to enhance the efficiency of internal and external income distribution policies that often are criticized for their ineffectiveness. As his Holiness Pope Benedict XVI says in the Encyclical *Caritas in Veritate*: 'A more devolved and organic system of social solidarity, less bureaucratic but no less coordinated, would make it possible to harness much dormant energy, for the benefit of solidarity between peoples' (§ 60).

Mr Chairman, UNCTAD's Least Developed Countries (LDC) Report calls for a 'rethinking of the development paradigm'. One of the key policy actions suggested is to rethink the role of the State in promoting development in LDCs. While it is not possible to neglect the crucial role played by the State in economic development, we should be aware of the fact that institutions alone, even if they are well designed, cannot ensure the achievement of the desired goals. In the words of Pope Benedict XVI, 'In reality, institutions by themselves are not enough, because integral human development is primarily a vocation, and therefore it involves a free assumption of responsibility in solidarity on the part of everyone' (*Caritas in Veritate*, § 11).

Focusing on the vocational nature of economic development, we should keep in mind that it presupposes the exercise of responsible freedom by both individuals and groups of peoples. Policies and institutions, therefore, should be designed to ensure human freedom, but such freedom also should be exercised within the limits of individual responsibility in the context of the human family. This premise has several direct and practical consequences. For example, while agriculture represents a critical issue that is slowing down the Doha Development Round negotiations, the experience of the poorest countries has demonstrated that, during the current economic crisis, food shortages and hunger continue to claim a significant number of victims each year.

Freedom and solidarity, then, should guide advanced economies to take decisive steps toward the elimination of trade barriers on agricultural products. Nevertheless, since the majority of poor countries have already duty-free access to European and American agricultural markets through the Everything But Arms initiative and the African Growth and Opportunity Act, agricultural liberalization is not the most decisive economic policy that can be implemented. During recent years, UNCTAD repeatedly has stressed that the major problem confronting poor countries is the poor productivity of their agricultural sectors, which, in fact, has developed into a chronic deficiency in LDCs. As stressed by the latest Least Developed Countries Report: 'Without a significant agricultural surplus, food security will remain precarious and diversification of the national economy into manufacturing and other sectors will be undermined by rising food prices and wage costs.'

In this context, national governments should give priority to the increase of agricultural productivity within their development policies, while advanced economies should take up the responsibility of providing knowledge and technology to implement them. As stated in *Caritas in Veritate*: 'This can be done by investing in rural infrastructures, irrigation systems, transport, organization of markets, and in the development and dissemination of agricultural technology that can make the best use of the human, natural and socio-economic resources that are more readily available at the local level, while guaranteeing their sustainability over the long term as well. All this needs to be accomplished with the involvement of local communities in choices and decisions that affect the use of agricultural land' (§ 27).

In conclusion, Mr Chairman, freedom, solidarity and responsibility are the pillars by which, we believe, it would be possible to build a new paradigm of economic development, one that is centered on the unconditional value of the human person. In the context of the unprecedented challenges posed by the current economic crisis, we support the UNCTAD proposal of rethinking the development paradigm and believe that it would be important not only to redefine the role played by the State in the economic domain, but also to give a human component to development policies irrespective of the financial and other constraints affecting least developing countries.

FROM POLITICAL WILL TO CONCRETE ACTION*

Mr President,

The current financial crisis is showing the degree of global interdependence of national economies. It risks also jeopardizing the efforts of the international community to meet the Millennium and other development goals in many countries.

Moreover, it could bring about a reduction of the public and private funding of national social safety nets and undermine thereby the enjoyment of human rights not only by the poorest and weakest segments of the population, but also by other groups negatively affected by the crisis. A key factor to mitigate the adverse effects of the crisis, we believe, is placing the human person at the center of economic and social policies at the international and national levels.

The Holy See Delegation views the current debate on the right to development within this Council and its mechanisms as an opportune occasion to strengthen the international commitment on the operationalization of this right and to transform this political willingness into concrete action. Achieving development is not only a matter of eliminating material poverty, but also of principles and values guiding economies and societies in all countries irrespective of their per capita income level. Furthermore, risks of a deterioration of the economic and social situation are present in most countries, including in high-income countries, due to the rising number of the population suffering new forms of poverty, social exclusion and marginalization. Needless to say, these economic and social inter-country inequalities risk being significantly increased by the financial crisis. For these reasons, my Delegation notes with interest the work that is being accomplished by the Task Force aiming at creating a list of right-to-development criteria and operational sub-criteria around three main components: human-centered development, an enabling environment, and social justice and equity. We believe that a global agreement on these criteria could constitute a fundamental step not only towards the operationalization of the 1986 Declaration, but also in the direction of the systematic consideration of the human person and its inherent rights and dignity in the elaboration of development policies at all levels.

* Statement delivered at the 12th Session of the Human Rights Council – Item 3: *Promotion and Protection of All Human Rights, Civil, Political, Economic Social and Cultural Rights, including the Right to Development*, 22 September, 2009.

In the context of the development process, the human person is not only a receiver of aid but also the real actor of his or her integral development and of the relations among peoples and persons. As restated in the recent Encyclical *Caritas in Veritate*: 'Man is the source, the focus and the aim of all economic and social life' (§ 25). We support the Task Force's approach of a comprehensive human-centered development that implies the indivisibility and interdependence of all human rights as well as the relevance, not only of development outcomes, but also of the development realization process and of its sustainability. My Delegation believes also that the cultural component of the right to development defined in the 1986 Declaration cannot be complete without including the ethical and spiritual dimensions of the person. These qualitative dimensions should be reflected among the human-centered criteria of this right that are being elaborated by the Task Force.

The Task Force view of the duty of States to create, individually and collectively, an enabling environment for the realization of the right to development should be endorsed. States therefore are called to remove obstacles to development due to the violation of human rights and the international community to support the development process, especially in the poorest countries. In this context, the principle of subsidiarity is particularly relevant. Solidarity and subsidiarity can be viewed as complementary. While the former relates to the mobilization of financial and human resources for development, the latter helps to identify the most appropriate level of decision-making and intervention. The principle of subsidiarity can therefore be seen as a cross-cutting criterion for the creation of the enabling environment to the right to development. It allows the participation of the beneficiaries of aid in the process of development through the responsible use of their freedom and talents.

Finally, we support the adoption of criteria of social justice and equity that imply moral imperatives prompting action for the protection of human rights and for an equitable sharing of benefits from development, including, among others, access to food, housing, education, health and employment. We follow with interest as well the overall work of the Task Force and Working Group aiming at identifying operational right-to-development criteria and dialoguing with existing poverty reduction, debt transfer, technology transfer and other global partnerships. We believe that such work is laying the groundwork for States and the international community to concretely reduce economic and social disparities, too often a cause of violations of human dignity and human rights.

DEVELOPMENT MUST ALSO INCLUDE SPIRITUAL GROWTH*

Mr President,

First of all my Delegation would like to thank the Government of Turkey for the effective organization of this timely and important conference and for the great hospitality of the Turkish people.

Mr President,

The LDCs' development paradigm implemented over the past years has proven ineffective. Since the early 2000s the continued growth (7 per cent per year from 2002 to 2007) in many LDCs has not translated into an improved situation for the people. The number of very poor people has actually increased (more than 3 million per year from 2002 to 2007). In 2007, 59 per cent of the population in African LDCs was living on less than US$1.25 per day.

Currently the growth in many of these countries comes primarily from the exploitation and export of natural resources, especially mineral reserves, while growth across other sectors is not robust or consistent. Unfortunately the growth that is realized in the extractives sector is the subject of many controversies on revenue distribution and local community impact, and only creates a significant number of jobs in the exploratory and build-up phase of the project but very few that are long-term. This correlates with ILO research that shows the labor force in LDC countries increasing by 2.5 per cent per year but the opportunities for employment are not commensurate with either the robust growth or the demand for employment. The impact of these limited employment opportunities is experienced particularly by the young and those who are entering the work force for the first time. The success stories are found in countries that have created some productive capacities such as horticulture, in the cases of Uganda and Ethiopia. Ghana and Kenya that are not LDCs have also shown good performance in this area.

The analysis of this current reality in the LDC group has led UNCTAD, in its Least Developed Countries Report 2010, to propose a new

* Statement delivered at the 4th United Nations Conference on Least Developed Countries, Istanbul, Turkey, 9–13 May 2011.

international development architecture that calls for a more comprehensive approach to the challenges of development. It should be noted that at the session of the UNCTAD's Trade Development Board (TDB) dedicated to LDCs, the majority of the groups were in favour of the proposed new international architecture for development. Several groups also insisted on the need to include specific considerations for post-conflict management situations, the reconstruction of infrastructures and agricultural production, while others have insisted that regional approaches to these issues be considered.

The Holy See supports this new approach and will focus its intervention on three themes.

The First Theme Looks at the Pillars of 'Integral Human Development'

In the Encyclical Letter, *Caritas in Veritate*, that was released in June 2009, Pope Benedict XVI reviews the foundational teaching on development that was presented in the Encyclical Letter of Pope Paul VI, *Populorum Progressio* ('On the Progress of Peoples'), in 1967: 'development cannot be limited to mere economic growth. In order to be authentic, it must be complete: integral, that is, it has to promote the good of every man and of the whole man.'[1] It is important that we recall this foundational teaching on the nature of development and recover its central truth as we reflect on the specific challenges that the LDCs present at this ministerial conference.

Since 1967 numerous theories and approaches to development have been proposed and tested and this has resulted in a much deeper understanding of the complex and evolving challenges that any consideration of this topic presents. It remains, however, true that there are still millions who have little or no access to the goods and benefits that development offers. An honest evaluation of the progress that has been made is reflected in the words of the Holy Father who writes that 'progress, remains an open question, made all the more acute and urgent by the current economic and financial crisis. If some areas of the globe, with a history of poverty, have experienced remarkable changes in terms of their economic growth and their share in world production, other zones are still living in a situation of deprivation comparable to that which

[1] Pope Paul VI, Encyclical Letter, *Populorum Progressio*, § 14.

existed at the time of Paul VI, and in some cases one can even speak of a deterioration.'[2]

In numerous other evaluations, including the aforementioned UNCTAD report, we have been reminded that a comprehensive and inclusive framework for international development is essential if any enduring results are to be achieved. In the Catholic Social Teaching tradition the pillars for such a framework have been evolved and been identified as follows: respect for human dignity; protection of human rights; care of creation; participation in community, subsidiarity and solidarity. Other pillars that are judged to be constitutive of an integral development plan are education; natural resource exploitation; agriculture; manufacturing; trade; financial services; infrastructure and technology.

As we continue to reflect on the specific challenges which development presents in LDCs it remains imperative that these pillars serve as a guide in our efforts to promote and sustain an approach to development that is integral and authentically human.[3]

The Second Theme Deals with the Kind of Growth Necessary for 'Integral Human Development'

Any approach to the challenge of development must recognize that 'the development of individuals and peoples depends partly on the resolution of problems of a spiritual nature. Development must include not just material growth but also spiritual growth.'[4] Too often the use of quantifiable metrics and economic criteria to measure such realities as gross domestic product or the narrow horizon of stock market growth fails to capture the full measure of what it means to be human, fails to appreciate the transcendent dimension of the person and therefore what it takes to promote the development of the whole person.

Growth therefore that promotes 'integral human development' is one that is inclusive of the pillars already mentioned above and evaluated by how well it promotes sustainable development and communities, creates decent jobs, alleviates people's poverty and protects the environment.

[2] Pope Benedict XVI, Encyclical Letter, Caritas in Veritate, § 33.

[3] Ibid., § 23 Pope Benedict reiterates this approach when he writes: 'Many areas of the globe today have evolved considerably, albeit in problematical and disparate ways, thereby taking their place among the great powers destined to play important roles in the future. Yet it should be stressed that progress of a merely economic and technological kind is insufficient. Development needs above all to be true and integral.'

[4] Ibid., § 7.

A model of growth that includes these objectives will build a domestic economic and commercial cycle that is sustainable, respects the environment and promotes development. Among the necessary elements in this growth model, especially in LDCs, are a vibrant agriculture sector and job creation across a number of sectors that will engage the large number of people who are entering the employment sector.

In LDCs, for example, the agricultural value added for workers rose three times more slowly than the GDP per capita over the last 20 years. At the same time, LDCs' dependence on imported food commodities has greatly increased (multiplied by 3 between 2000 and 2008). As a result it is among the 2.5 billion people dependent on agriculture for their daily sustenance that one finds most of the people who suffer from malnutrition and hunger.

Any growth model that is adopted therefore must recognize and strengthen the central role of agriculture in economic activity; thereby reducing malnutrition in rural areas and increasing production per person in order to enhance local, regional or national food independence.

Investments to improve productivity are required in the areas of seeds, training, sharing of tools for cultivation and of the means for marketing. Structural changes are also demanded according to the specificity of individual states. For example, we must ensure security of land tenure for farmers, especially for those with small landholdings. The customary right of land ownership may be reconsidered. A clear property right gives the farmer the opportunity to pledge his land in exchange for seasonal credit to purchase necessary inputs. In addition, the aim of land tenure has now become increasingly important in the face of the expansion of the phenomenon of land grabbing. In Sub-Saharan Africa, 80 per cent of the land is occupied by poor who have no land title.

Across all sectors of society from agriculture to manufacturing to delivery of services we must remember that decent work 'expresses the essential dignity of every man and woman in the context of their particular society: work that is freely chosen, effectively associating workers, both men and women, with the development of their community.'[5] Work is not a commodity. Decent work gives everyone the opportunity to use his own talents and to be creative; it is a motor of sustainable growth at the service of the common good and so it must be a central objective of the new architecture. The final goal, then, is the creation of a 'work

[5] Ibid., § 63.

that makes it possible for families to meet their needs and provide schooling for their children, without the children themselves being forced into labor; work that permits the workers to organize themselves freely, and to make their voices heard; work that leaves enough room for rediscovering one's roots at a personal, familial and spiritual level; work that guarantees those who have retired a decent standard of living.'[6]

The Third Theme to be Kept in Mind is the Role of the State in Promoting 'Integral Human Development'

The number of institutions, agents and actors in the development space has increased exponentially over the years. The official development commitments of governments alongside those of voluntary organizations have been substantial during that time. They have now been joined and in some instances are dwarfed by the presence of such actors as corporations, private foundations and private investors. There is, we believe, a need and room for all of these actors for they can bring different perspectives, modes of operating and can thereby make unique contributions to the development that is needed in LDCs.

In this environment, however, the role of the state and of regional, international and global authorities is critical and must be supported and respected. Combined with the Catholic perspective on the responsibility of the state to guarantee public order and promote the common good, these bodies must play a pivotal role in orchestrating and directing LDC development. This can be especially challenging in a post-conflict context and especially so in a 'failed state' situation.

The teaching of our tradition, when it comes to the responsibility of governments to enact the legal framework and rules so that financial and commercial activities fulfill their social purpose and function smoothly, has consistently asserted a positive role for a limited government, that is neither libertarian nor collectivist. It became clear during the 2008 financial crisis that the market does not naturally contain in itself the ingredients for an automatic correction of errors and would have led to a collapse of the financial and economic system if the States had not acted. The rescue of the banks, necessary as it has been, did not prevent the painful impact of the crisis on the population since ultimately the correction of the market's vagaries is carried out to the detriment of

[6] Ibid.

populations, states have a duty to intervene pre-emptively to avoid such suffering. 'The articulation of political authority at the local, national and international levels is one of the best ways of giving direction to the process of economic globalization. It is also the way to ensure that it does not actually undermine the foundations of democracy.'

While recognizing the benefits of free trade to promote development and therefore the urgency to close the gap in the Doha Development Round, in the implementation of the commitments taken of a duty-free, quota-free access to the market for the LDCs, adequate measures should be taken to protect farmers against price volatility which has a strong impact on food security for several reasons: high prices make food unaffordable for the poor and temporarily low prices give farmers the incorrect information on needed seedlings after harvest for the following year. To prevent price volatility or at least weaken its impact, local food crops need to be protected against sudden disruptions in international prices. For example, the establishment of regional stockpiles of raw food (cereals, oil, sugar) can have a twofold benefit: these stocks can be sold at an affordable price in case of shock and they can play a moderating role against the volatility of local prices.

The 'developmental state' plays a unique and key role in the development of a country and with other regional and international authorities is expected to coordinate appropriate and constructive plans. In addition to the tasks already mentioned above, the responsibility of mobilizing the domestic resources that are regarded as a critical component of stable financing for government priorities and development needs has been identified as essential. This is a tedious and complicated undertaking, especially where no basic framework or infrastructure exists to advance such an objective. Alongside the other resources like FDI (Foreign Direct Investment), ODA (Official Development Assistance) and remittances from local citizens working abroad, these domestic resources will play an essential role in any development plan.

(a) Corporations. The presence of private corporations in communities, societies and countries continues to grow and they have a far-reaching impact wherever they are located. Their influence on development, depending on their size and footprint, in local communities and across broad sections of society can be significant and should be monitored and evaluated by the state. They should also be expected to fulfill their obligations as good corporate citizens by keeping in mind according to the Holy Father that, 'business management cannot concern itself only with the interests of the proprietors, but must also assume responsibility for all the other stakeholders who contribute to the life of the business: the workers, the clients, the suppliers of various elements of production, the community of reference.'[7]

(b) Private Finance and Development. The presence of private finance institutions and actors, such as private equity and hedge funds, in countries and regions across the world, continues to increase. Facilitated by the continued expansion and integration of all aspects of the global financial system, their presence presents a unique set of challenges in LDCs. It is important that LDCs be in a position to benefit from their presence and assure that their activities are making a contribution to lasting development.

Once again Pope Benedict reminds all actors in this space, and this applies especially to those investors in LDCs, that, 'What should be avoided is a speculative use of financial resources that yields to the temptation of seeking only short-term profit, without regard for the long-term sustainability of the enterprise, its benefit to the real economy and attention to the advancement, in suitable and appropriate ways, of further economic initiatives in countries in need of development. It is true that the export of investments and skills can benefit the populations of the receiving country. Labour and technical knowledge are a universal good. Yet it is not right to export these things merely for the sake of obtaining advantageous conditions, or worse, for purposes of exploitation, without making a real contribution to local society by helping to bring about a robust productive and social system, an essential factor for stable development.'[8]

In conclusion, Mr President, LDCs continue to face enormous challenges as they search for the resources and the path to development for their citizens. There remains no easy formula for success but the promise of solidarity can be a foundation for the renewal of commitment by those who have wrestled with this challenge for decades and a guidepost for the new actors in this space. There are numerous different and essential roles and responsibilities for the successful implementation of the development process in the LDCs. Thus, the Holy See anticipates a new Programme of Action for the LDCs for the coming decade. Now is the time to translate into concrete action the commitments that have been

[7] Ibid., § 34. [8] Ibid., § 40.

made in these days. The future well-being of the LDCs depends to a great extent upon the spirit of gratuitousness that motivates our common efforts. Working together in a coordinated and cooperative fashion, the institutions and actors from all sectors can and must support the efforts of all LDCs to achieve their goals as members of the one human family.

THE RESPONSIBILITY TO PROTECT THE YOUTH AND WOMEN FROM THE UNCERTAINTY OF WORKING CONDITIONS*

Mr President,

The Delegation of the Holy See congratulates the ILO for its steadfast service to social development through the collaborative action of workers, employers and governments. This 100th Conference is evidence of this fruitful approach in the pursuit of the common good. These are critical and challenging times for developed countries as they are slowly emerging from a financial crisis of unprecedented depth whose consequences are evident across all sectors of societies. These impacts are especially obvious in the acute and prolonged levels of unemployment that men and women in many countries are suffering. Social and economic safety nets have been stretched to the breaking point and austerity programs entail severe cuts in the basic services that citizens, especially the elderly, children and the poor have come to rely on.

Old formulas for recovery and economic growth are proving less certain in a globally integrated economic environment and sovereign governments in most instances have not been able to find a formula for economic growth that restores jobs and includes new employment opportunities for the millions who are looking for work. Despite the fact that the majority of macroeconomic indicators seem to have recovered to pre-crisis levels, the labour market is still suffering: unemployment rates remain high and show no sign of recovery in the short term and the long-term prognosis is uneven.

The experience of a weak economic recovery that brings with it very few new job opportunities is a reality in some countries while a robust stock market recovery with only mediocre job creation is the situation in a number of other countries. Moreover, a recovery in labour markets at the global level has been uneven, with moderate improvement being delivered in developing and emerging countries but raising unemployment in advanced economies. In the advanced economies space the unemployment problems remain particularly acute as they account for

* Statement delivered at the 100th Session of the International Labour Conference, 8 June 2011.

55 per cent of the total increase in the world's unemployment that occurred between 2007 and 2010 while accounting only for 15 per cent of the world's labour force.

The enduring high rates of unemployment are accompanied by another critical factor in the current economic condition: the absence of any sustained increase of employment opportunities. The world economy, albeit growing at a steady level, is not able to create a sufficient number of jobs. This is true not only in advanced economies but also in emerging markets such as China and India where employment elasticity is extremely low, despite the two-digit growth rates in output.

This is a structural problem that was already identified well before the outbreak of the crisis and was known as jobless growth. A sustained repetition of this paradigm will lead to severe strain on those searching for meaningful work and on the attendant social unrest in local communities. We must do our very best to avoid this scenario.

Youth Unemployment

An area of critical concern is the impact of unemployment on young people in different communities across the world. In fact, some 78 million young people in the 15–24 age group were unemployed in 2010, a rate 2.6 times that of adult unemployment. Youth unemployment is a common problem in every country; however, it is particularly acute in the developed world. It is somewhat ironic that post-industrial economies characterised by an ageing population are not able to create enough meaningful and decent work opportunities to meet the needs and the expectations of their young people who comprise a much smaller percentage of the population.

Youth unemployment has a wider and deeper impact that affects society as a whole. It is well documented that people who are underemployed, who become redundant or become unemployed early in their working years, can easily become demoralised, lose confidence in their abilities and in their employment prospects and find themselves trapped in a spiral of social exclusion. Documented evidence of how the financial crisis has resulted in unprecedented levels of youth unemployment has raised the spectre of a 'lost generation' of young people who have dropped out of the job market. The uncertainty over working opportunity and conditions, when it becomes endemic, tends to 'create new forms of psychological instability, giving rise to difficulty in forging coherent life-plans, including that of marriage. This leads to situations of human decline, to say nothing of the waste of social resources. In comparison with the casualties of industrial society in the past, unemployment today provokes new forms of economic marginalization, and the current crisis can only make this situation worse'.[1]

Women's Employment

The second area of vulnerability is constituted by women. Despite the significant progress that has been made in recent decades in reducing women's discrimination in the workplace, women continue to be penalized in the labour market with restricted access to several jobs. Their economic activity, hence, is by no means restricted to working for a salary: their unpaid work – which does not enter GDP statistics – contributes in a crucial way to personal, societal and national well-being. If it is true, and not mere rhetoric, that human resources are the most precious among economic resources, the economic role of women should be taken more seriously than it is usually done. In OECD countries the employment rate of women is on average 20 per cent below that of men with this gap reaching 30 per cent in countries such as Italy or Japan. In addition, women's wages are consistently lower by 20 per cent to 30 per cent and they continue to constitute a much larger percentage of those who are filling low-paid jobs. However, one of the greatest cross-cutting discrimination realities that still exist is the fact that labour markets remain so inflexible and find it difficult to reconcile the work model and schedule with the responsibilities for childcare and the care of other dependants that many in the workforce carry. Generating and taking care of new generations is the human activity which is closest to economic investment, and the family itself is a sort of 'relational' investment. As a firm is the observable outcome of risky human actions and interactions, namely an investment that implies personalized and durable relations, so is the family. As the firm is understood as a 'unit' of some kind, with a 'common good' of its own, so it is of the family. Hence, supporting women's contribution to economic and societal well-being should obviously include affordable childcare facilities, flexible working arrangements, job sharing, maternity and parental protection, but it would also require revaluing the

[1] Pope Benedict XVI, Encyclical Letter, *Caritas in Veritate*, § 25.

'common good' dimension of women's investment in generation – that is, in meaningful and durable relationships which open the new generations to the quest for beauty, for sense, for meaning – which are undoubtedly the most significant drivers to human, economic and societal innovation and progress.

Domestic Workers

Another group of people calling for special attention are domestic workers and ILO is providing a timely response through a new instrument of protection carefully designed and presented for approval at this conference. The growth of domestic work as a service sector is particularly strong in developed countries and has been fuelled by several factors: significant demographic changes such as ageing populations, decline in the welfare provisions provided by governments, increasing labor force participation by women, and the challenges of balancing the responsibilities of working life and family life in urban areas.[2]

The adoption of a new Convention on domestic work is made essential by the experience of the persistent exclusion of these workers from even the basic labor protections. Domestic workers, in many countries, are living in miserable conditions and often remain excluded from labor laws and collective bargaining agreements. This endemic exclusion from adequate social protection deprives them of the security that 'decent work' deserves and requires. This is even more problematic, given that many of these domestic workers are migrant women, who leave their family in order to economically sustain it; they provide care for their employer's children or elderly, in exchange for a wage that can improve the material quality of life of their own families, which they can seldom visit. This pattern creates a sort of 'global care chain' which is structurally built on the disruption of basic family relationships for all women involved. The medium- and long-term consequences of such disruption deserves more attention within a 'relational' approach to the economic situation of women, as it is well known that families play a crucial role in providing social capital for human and economic development, especially in low-income countries.

Decency emphasizes the need both to understand and ground the ultimate significance of work. Work is not only toil and effort, which results

[2] Asha D'Souza, *Moving towards Decent Work for Domestic Workers: An Overview of the ILO's Work*, Geneva: International Labour Organization, 2010.

in services, activities or production, but also an opportunity for people to transform reality and fulfill their personal vocations.

Pope John Paul II defined work as a 'hard good' emphasizing the need to put effort and passion in what is man's primary activity. It is good not only in the sense that it is useful or something to enjoy; it is also good as being something worthy, that is to say, something that corresponds to man's dignity, that expresses this dignity and increases it.[3]

In this 100th session of the International Labour Conference we must reaffirm the importance of a new governance based on the principle of subsidiarity and tripartitism that gives the ILO an edge in integrating 'real world' knowledge about employment and work. In a globally integrated financial system that is characterized by speed, mobility and flexibility, the voice and advocacy of those who protect and promote the rights of workers and the dignity of labour is essential. As Pope Benedict says: 'In the global era, the economy is influenced by competitive models tied to cultures that differ greatly among themselves. The different forms of economic enterprise to which they give rise find their main point of encounter in commutative justice. Economic life undoubtedly requires contracts, in order to regulate relations of exchange between goods of equivalent value. But it also needs just laws and forms of redistribution governed by politics, and what is more, it needs works redolent of the spirit of gift.'[4]

The challenge is laid out before all actors – public and private – who are charged with ensuring that our burgeoning and mercurial global economic system adheres to fundamental principles of justice which prioritize the needs of the most vulnerable in a way that respects individual and corporate activity within the overarching principle of the global common good. The ILO is very well situated to ensure that this process of re-assessment and reform of the global financial system remains rooted in the concerns of the smallest and most vital units that make up modern society: the family, the workplace, the community. As mentioned by Benedict XVI, 'economic life must be understood as a multi-layered phenomenon.' Without excluding the essential roles of market and state, 'civil society' may be an essential voice to advance the good of all.[5] The

3 Pope John Paul II, Encyclical Letter, *Laborem Exercens*, § 27.

4 *Caritas in Veritate*, § 37.

5 'Today we can say that economic life must be understood as a multi-layered phenomenon: in every one of these layers, to varying degrees and in ways specifically suited to each, the aspect of fraternal reciprocity must be present. In the global era, economic activity cannot prescind from gratuitousness, which fosters and disseminates

Holy See brings a rich tradition that is matched by its experience across the globe and across the centuries; journeying with organizations such as the ILO, it forges an ever-expanding communion that favours the good of everyone and of all peoples.

solidarity and responsibility for justice and the common good among the different economic players … Solidarity is first and foremost a sense of responsibility on the part of everyone with regard to everyone, and it cannot therefore be merely delegated to the State,' ibid., § 37.

A REVISION OF THE GLOBAL FINANCIAL AND COMMERCIAL ARCHITECTURE TO CORRECT DISTORTIONS*

Mr President,

At the outset, my Delegation wishes to warmly thank the Government of Qatar and the city of Doha for hosting this Ministerial Conference.

The last Conference in Accra took place at the beginning of the financial crisis whose profound consequences are still felt today. Since the 1990s, money and credit instruments worldwide have grown more rapidly than the accumulation of wealth, even adjusting for inflation. The higher growth of global financial markets relative to the real economy was not only due to the financial sector liberalization, but also to the existence of monetary and financial markets of a predominantly speculative sort. Such disproportionate growth of financial markets caused the formation of pockets of excessive liquidity and speculative bubbles, which in the late 2000s turned into a series of solvency and confidence crises, resulting in the 2008 financial crisis. As Pope Benedict XVI precisely pointed out in his social Encyclical, *Caritas in Veritate*, the roots of this crisis are not only economic and financial but above all moral in nature. Given the complexity of the economy, the importance of ethical and cultural factors cannot be overlooked or underestimated. Recognizing the primacy of being over having and of ethics over the economy, the world's peoples ought to adopt an ethic of solidarity to fuel their action.

The 2008 crisis marked a turning point for the world economy. In particular, the subsequent global economic recession has eliminated at least 30 million jobs around the world:[1] it negatively affected the social situation in many countries, in particular those with large segments of the population that are poor or not effectively protected by social safety nets. The enjoyment of fundamental economic and social rights by countless persons has been compromised, including the right to food, water, decent work, education and health.

* Statement delivered at the 13th Ministerial Conference of UNCTAD, Doha, Qatar, 21–26 April 2012.

[1] J. Somavia, ILO Director General, The Global Jobs Crisis: The G-20 must act now to avoid a lost decade, Statement, 2 November 2011, www.ilo.org/global/about-the-ilo/press-and-media-centre/statements-and-speeches/WCMS_166696/lang–en/index.htm.

Clearly the consequences of the crisis go far beyond the financial domain, extending to the economic, social and cultural spheres. For these reasons, the international community cannot let the financial system continue being a source of global economic instability; it must urgently take measures to prevent the outbreak of other financial crises in the future.

One of the most significant lessons we learned during this period is that all countries, developed and developing alike, can pay serious social, political and economic costs if the financial markets are left to regulate themselves. Engaging in financial activity cannot be reduced to making profit; it must also include the promotion of the common good among those who lend, those who borrow and those who work.[2] Economic and financial actors, both at the international and national levels should recognize that self-regulation of the market and agreements limited to reconciling the interests of the most powerful countries are not enough and they must take into account that they are at the service of man.

The Holy See, on several occasions and in different fora, has called attention to the urgency of a new and profound reflection on the meaning and objectives of the economy and of a far-sighted revision of the global financial and commercial architecture in order to correct problems of functioning and distortions. This revision of international economic rules should be integrated in a new global model of development.

A genuinely human-centered economic and social development is based not only on economic principles, such as free market, profit and human behavior, but also on the value of the human being and on ethical principles, real commitment, inclusive governance and social equity. The centrality of the human person in the development process implies, also, the promotion of intermediate bodies – the family in particular – and different social communities where the person lives.[3]

This approach includes the goal of the economy as functional to the full development of the person and to the creation of community where equity and solidarity prevail. As the world becomes increasingly interconnected, a major goal of economic integration is to serve as a tool for the creation of one world community. While this goal needs time,

[2] Relating to the 1929 crisis, Pope Pius XI observed that: 'it is obvious that not only is wealth concentrated in our times but an immense power and despotic economic dictatorship is consolidated in the hands of a few, who often are not owners but only the trustees and managing directors of invested funds which they administer according to their own arbitrary will and pleasure' (*Quadragesimo Anno*, § 105).

[3] 'As a spiritual being, the human creature is defined through interpersonal relations', Pope Benedict XVI, *Caritas in Veritate*, § 53.

effort and patience to be reached, local and national economies can be stepping stones in this direction.

A major theme of the current conference is a 'call for new ideas that spur stable growth and reduce inequality'. Mr President, the Holy See shares the same concerns on economic development but stresses that the really 'new idea' is the implementation of authentic development: the one that puts the human person at its centre.

With the human person at the center, growth and development strategies become comprehensive and sustainable. They can be truly comprehensive because they share a universal principle and they can be sustainable because they call for the effective participation of the person as the true protagonist of development.

Naturally this strategy introduces an ethical principle in the development process. 'The economy needs ethics in order to function correctly – not any ethics whatsoever, but an ethics which is people-centered' (*Caritas in Veritate*, § 45). Ethics are not external to the economy; they are intrinsic to it since the economy is the result of the collective action of groups of human persons. 'Thus every economic decision has a moral consequence' (*Caritas in Veritate*, § 37). An economy does not have a sustainable future if it does not take into account the ethical dimension because ultimately it would negate its own origins.

Several important consequences derive from this premise. I will refer to some of them. A human-centered development process needs to be employment-oriented. During the last decade the world economy has not been able to create sufficient employment opportunities for its population. In advanced economies we have witnessed what has been called a jobless growth and, even in the more dynamic emerging economies, employment elasticities have been extremely low despite a two-digit growth rate in output.

The negotiating text rightly observes that people everywhere share similar needs, aspirations and desires. Development is the tension toward the fulfillment of these desires. As such, development is not just an economic concept, but rather a universal dimension that concerns every person. In this context, the Holy See Delegation would like to add that the underlying principle of any truly human needs-based economic policy is that goods, services, labour and financial markets cannot be analyzed separately from the full breadth of human aspirations that include together with important material aspirations also aspirations to cultural, social and political flourishing. Human labour, in particular, makes it possible for each person to share in the common endeavor of improving the human condition. Indeed, the aim of the economy is to serve an integral human development, and not vice versa.

The Holy See has repeatedly stated that work is not only toil and effort, resulting in activities, production and wages, but also an opportunity for man to transform reality and to fulfill his personal vocation. John Paul II reminded us that work 'is not only good in the sense that it is useful or something to enjoy; it is also good as being something worthy, that is to say, something that corresponds to man's dignity, that expresses this dignity and increases it. A working man becomes … "more a human being"'.[4] This is why development should be aimed primarily at fostering employment opportunities.

A second consequence deals with development strategies; they need to be addressed to the entire society without excluding any segment. In this respect, the informal sector and its workers deserve a special mention. This sector occupies millions of people across the world and includes heterogeneous economic productive groups. However, these persons labor at times under unregulated working conditions, without social protection and often with too low wages. Addressing the needs of the people working in this sector should become a priority of national governments and international organizations, and therefore there should be allocated financial resources adequate to the size of this sector.

A third consequence calls attention to the central role of education in development. If young minds, the future of our society, are not sufficiently prepared, millions will not be able to enter the labour market of tomorrow. Education enables the accumulation of human capital which is a decisive determinant of economic growth. Moreover, higher human capital facilitates the adoption of new technologies and fosters innovative activities that are in great need in developing countries. Most importantly, an educated person can be fully aware of one's pivotal role in the development process and can therefore provide a more responsible contribution to economic development. For these reasons, all possible efforts should be made to help developing countries invest more effectively in their educational systems and constantly evaluate their quality.

The international community should also promote innovative economic policies, and if needed adequately fund them through development aid, aimed at fulfilling the needs of the poorest and marginalized

[4] Pope John Paul II, Encyclical Letter, *Laborem Exercens*, § 9, www.vatican.va/holy_father/john_paul_ii/encyclicals/documents/hf_jp-ii_enc_14091981_laborem-exercens_en.html.

segments of the world population. Given the productive, technological and scientific capacities of the world economy in the twenty-first century, the international community cannot wait until the end of the current global economic crisis, or until the transition of least developing countries into emerging economies, in order to fulfill the fundamental human rights that millions of people are still not enjoying, in particular, but not exclusively, in Africa.

A fourth consequence shows the necessity to reduce the excessive volatility of food commodity prices and to support commodity-dependent developing countries in formulating sustainable and genuine democratic national development strategies. This area of trading has consequences on the daily nutrition and life of the poorest people in the world, and carries therefore a strong ethical dimension. Whether this trading will be further regulated or not, it needs to be taken into account by States and economic actors involved in trading, including financial institutions, and multinational and national corporations. Commodities are unique in that they touch directly the fundamental rights to food and water of the human person.

Moreover, for the promotion of development, it is important to recognize the benefits of free trade and, therefore, the urgency to implement the commitments already taken regarding a duty-free quota-free market access for the LDCs. In addition, adequate measures should be taken to protect farmers against price volatility since it has a strong impact on food security: high prices make food unaffordable for the poor and temporarily low prices give farmers the incorrect information on needed seedlings after harvest for the following year.

A final consequence aims to reconnect finance, including from a regulatory point of view, with the real economy in support of truly human-centered and sustainable development. The Holy See Delegation suggests that UNCTAD, through its technical expertise and research activities in the area of macroeconomic finance, could contribute, in collaboration with other relevant United Nations agencies and financial international organizations and regulators, to reflect on this point.

Such a reflection could provide a greater ability to adopt policies and binding rules that are aimed at achieving the common good at the local, regional and world levels. As Pope Paul VI stated, 'such international collaboration among the nations of the world certainly calls for institutions that will promote, coordinate and direct it, until a new juridical order is firmly established and fully ratified. We give willing and wholehearted support to those public organizations that have already joined in promoting the development of nations' (*Populorum Progressio*).

The dynamic mix of new realities and the continuing importance of international cooperation underscore UNCTAD's role as an institution that continues to place interdependence at the heart of its integrated approach to trade and development, and to serve as a valuable forum for a comprehensive dialogue between developed and developing countries. The role of this Organization as a place for frank and open discussion should be encouraged and further developed, especially in view of the magnitude of the challenges facing the global community and the opportunities for all countries to address persistent and emerging development concerns.

Furthermore, this Organization should play a crucial role in continuing its research and analysis on the international financial and monetary systems and price volatility of commodities as well as on other key development areas such as employment, education and the informal sector. In these areas as well it should provide developing countries with innovative technical assistance. Finally, UNCTAD should consider, within its areas of competence, contributing to improve the coherence and governance of the international monetary, financial and trade systems, including a more effective participation of developing countries.

Mr President,

The economic crisis has shown that previous economic models no longer correspond to reality. We can read this economic crisis also as an opportunity to rethink the economy, taking into account the needs of all levels of society and finding 'new models'. Therefore, if this Conference signals the political will to make progress at least in some of the objectives listed in the final document, it will be a decisive step towards the creation of an international economic, trading and financial system based on the principle of social justice. In this respect, ethical values, such as transparency, honesty, solidarity and responsibility, cannot be ignored: they preserve a person-centered goal in any economic activity, prevent crises caused by greedy speculation and provide a comprehensive approach that does not separate the social consequences from economic and environmental decisions. Moreover, an additional step that ensures success in the long run is the inclusion of the dimension of gratuitousness and of the logic of gift as an expression of fraternity and involvement of the entire human family, both as a protagonist of economic development and as the primary objective of trade and economic activity.

In conclusion,

the outcome of this UNCTAD XIII Ministerial Conference must place the proper focus on actions toward achieving human, economic and social development, those aspects which build up the foundation of sustainable development. The Delegation of the Holy See hopes that the result of this Conference will not only be successful, but also innovative and forward-looking and that the commitments that emerge will move the world and humanity forward so as to truly contribute to the spiritual and material well-being of all people, their families and their communities.

THE FAILURE OF A 'ONE-SIZE-FITS-ALL' POLICY AS A RECIPE FOR GROWTH*

Mr President,

The Delegation of the Holy See joins previous speakers and expresses its appreciation to Director General Mr Juan Somavia, as he concludes his mandate, for his precious service and his able leadership and extends congratulations to the new Director General Mr Guy Ryder. We look forward to a continued collaboration as the International Labour Organization addresses work and its impact on the economy and society in the best interest of every human person and for the just progress of every country.

The financial and economic crisis has generated a widespread sense of frustration as the aspiration for decent work appears to many people totally unreachable. In fact half of the world's workers, more than a billion and half persons, hold on to a vulnerable job. More than 200 million people are officially unemployed, among them 80 million young persons. A quick recovery doesn't seem realistic. A long period of stagnation risks causing more unemployment and social instability. It is safe to say that, in recent years, several of the paradigms that we were accustomed to are no longer valid and should to be reassessed.

The first paradigm is related to what constitutes the engine of growth of the world economy. During the last 25 years more than half of the world's economic growth has been contributed by the advanced economies while the emerging markets' share has been around 40 per cent. During the 2008–2009 crisis, on the other hand, emerging markets contributed almost 90 per cent of the world's growth and served as growth engines. The advanced economies, Europe in particular, are still struggling to deal with the debt problem inherited from the financial crisis and have not entered a solid period of recovery. The high growth of some emerging economies during the last decade has allowed the lifting of several million people out of poverty. It has been an unprecedented step toward poverty reduction. But in too many developing countries growth is not happening. In fact, in terms of per capita income, they are now as far behind advanced economies as they were thirty years ago.

* Statement delivered at the 101st Session of the International Labour Conference, 7 June 2012.

The second paradigm that has been challenged by the crisis is the assumption of a 'one-size-fits-all' policy as a recipe for growth. The experience of some of the BRIC economies shows that it is possible to consistently grow at high rates by following unconventional policies.

Mr President, the Holy See, on several occasions and in different fora, has stressed that the effective idea needed to implement true development is centering it on the human person. It is by putting the human person at the center that growth and development strategies can be inclusive and sustainable. They can be inclusive because they share this universal principle and they are sustainable because they call for the real participation of the person as the true protagonist of development. As His Holiness Pope Benedict XVI said in *Caritas in Veritate*, 'As a spiritual being, the human creature is defined through interpersonal relations.'

Several important consequences follow from this premise. First of all, development needs to be employment-oriented. During the last decade the world economy has not been able to create sufficient employment opportunities. In particular, the current crisis has led to a substantial increase in youth unemployment rates, reversing earlier favorable trends. That the global youth unemployment rate increased to a greater degree than the adult unemployment rate supports the classic premise that youth are more vulnerable to economic shocks. Young people are the 'first out' and 'last in' during times of economic recession. Youth unemployment and underemployment impose heavy social and economic costs, resulting in the loss of opportunities for economic growth, erosion of the tax base which undermines investment in infrastructure and public services, increased welfare costs, unutilized investment in education and training, and with the possibility of social instability and conflict, increased levels of poverty, crime and substance abuse. Too many young people are employed in informal work while those in formal work are subjected to insecure employment conditions and to the constant pressure of subcontracting, which brings lower wages and lack of protection in the area of social security, preventing many from leading a decent life.

Work is more than a job. It implies exertion and fatigue to produce and achieve good results, but also the ability to transform reality and fulfill a personal vocation. Thus, work expresses and increases man's dignity.[1] There is a practical advantage as well in this approach. The *subjective, personal* dimension in work affects the actual *objective* result in all activities, but especially in services, in research and technological innovation; that

[1] Cf. Pope John Paul II, Encyclical Letter, *Laborem Exercens*, § 27.

is, in those economic activities that promote knowledge and true wealth creation, human and social development.

A second consequence deals with social protection, a right of all to social security and to a standard of living adequate for the health and well-being of themselves and their family. Healthy and safe working conditions, wage protection, decent working hours, are all measures to be taken into account according to national circumstances. The global market and today's profoundly changed environment have stimulated first and foremost, on the part of rich countries, a search for areas in which to outsource production at low cost with a view to reducing the prices of many goods, increasing purchasing power and thus accelerating the rate of development in terms of greater availability of consumer goods for the domestic market. These processes have led to a *downsizing of social security systems* as the price to be paid for seeking greater competitive advantage in the global market, with consequent grave danger for the rights of workers, for fundamental human rights and for the solidarity associated with the traditional forms of the social State. Systems of social security can lose the capacity to carry out their task, both in emerging countries and in those that were among the earliest to develop, as well as in poor countries. Here budgetary policies, with cuts in social spending, often made under pressure from international financial institutions, can leave citizens powerless in the face of old and new risks. Such powerlessness is increased by the lack of effective protection on the part of workers' associations. Through the combination of social and economic change, trade union organizations experience greater difficulty in carrying out their task of representing the interests of workers, partly because governments, for reasons of economic utility, at times limit the freedom or the negotiating capacity of labour unions. Hence traditional networks of solidarity have more and more obstacles to overcome. In reforming and redesigning social security systems it is important that an adequate importance is given to the family. The family is not only the center of personal relations of individuals but also a strong responsibility for those who are the primary source of income for their next of kin. In such cases the loss of a job can become an economic tragedy as well as a loss of opportunities for young people.

The mobility of labor, associated with a climate of deregulation, is an important phenomenon with certain positive aspects: it can stimulate wealth production and cultural exchange. Nevertheless, uncertainty over working conditions caused by mobility and deregulation, when it becomes endemic, tends to create new forms of psychological instability, giving rise to difficulty in forging coherent life-plans, including marriage. This leads to situations of human decline, to say nothing of the waste of social resources. In comparison with the casualties of industrial society in the past, unemployment today provokes new forms of economic marginalization, and the current crisis can only make this situation worse. Being out of work or dependent on public or private assistance for a prolonged period undermines the freedom and creativity of the person and his family and social relationships, causing great psychological and spiritual suffering.

In conclusion, Mr President, the path forward to an effective recovery presupposes a new vision and strategic investments to provide employment and to sustain enterprises. Priority given to work shows that the economy remains at the service of man and society within an ethical horizon that guarantees its proper role. Confidence becomes possible again as well as a sense of solidarity that embraces the victims of the crisis, first, but extends to society at large. The primary capital to be safeguarded and valued is the human person in his or her integrity: 'Man is the source, the focus and the aim of all economic and social life.'[2] Good decisions are necessary in order to move toward a post-crisis phase of the globalization of the economy and of work. But only a corresponding 'ethical interaction of consciences and minds'[3] will give rise to integral development where the human person, at the center of labor relations, journeys with hope toward a better future.

[2] *Gaudium et Spes*, § 63.
[3] Pope Benedict XVI, Encyclical Letter, *Caritas in Veritate*, § 9.

TRANSNATIONAL CORPORATIONS AND HUMAN RIGHTS*

Mr President,

The urgency of the call to increased Corporate Social and Environmental Responsibility was elevated to a new pitch for all stakeholders when the news about the collapse of a garment factory on the outskirts of Dhaka on 24 April spread rapidly around the world. The loss of more than 1,100 young lives coupled with the untold pain of their relatives, and the suffering and crushed dreams of hundreds more is a reminder of corrective actions that need to be undertaken by all corporations that participate in a global supply chain process that relies continually on the contribution of workers. The images of that disaster are also a reminder of the interdependence that globalization has brought about in transnational economic activity.

Deeply moved by the tragic case of Dhaka, Pope Francis expressed his concern about conditions where 'People are less important than the things that give profit to those who have political, social and economic power.' Pointing to the core issues that are often present in factory life today he said that 'Not paying a just [wage], not providing work, focusing on balance sheets, only looking at making personal profit, that goes against God!', while describing the conditions in which the workers lost their lives as 'slave labour'.[1]

Numerous challenges have emerged throughout the evolution of industrialization and its attendant mass production processes over the last three hundred years. Governments, civil society, unions, shareholders and corporations sometimes cooperatively and at other times in adversity have worked to decrease the negative impacts of those realities. However, still in our own day the number of human lives that are lost or severely crushed as a result of unsafe working conditions remains too great.

In recent years various initiatives have been undertaken by different stakeholders to address some of the remaining challenges that exist in the predominant supply chain business model that cuts across nearly all business sectors. They have successfully brought some level of scrutiny to the

* Statement delivered at the 23rd Session of the Human Rights Council – Item 3: *Transnational Corporations and Human Rights*, 31 May 2013.

[1] Cf. Homily of Pope Francis for the feast of St Joseph the Worker, in the Chapel of Domus Sanctae Marthae, on 1 May 2013 (cf. *L'Osservatore Romano*, Thursday–Friday, 2–3 May 2013, p. 6).

policies and more importantly the practices that needed to be changed. These stakeholders from both the public and private sectors from civil society and from the faith-based investment community deserve to be applauded for their achievements to protect human dignity, promote human rights and safeguard the environment.

As recently as 2009, in the Encyclical, *Caritas in Veritate*, Pope Benedict XVI reminded us all that 'among those who sometimes fail to respect the human rights of workers are large multinational companies as well as local producers' (§ 22). It remains important for all, therefore, to recognize labour standards as an integral and important part of corporate social responsibility. Freedom of association, the elimination of all forms of forced and compulsory labour, the abolition of child labour and the effective elimination of discrimination in employment and payment must be respected and enforced in all jurisdictions.

Another important aspect of the work that remains to be done in this arena is a more complete and deliberate consensus about the role and responsibility of corporations in society. While a great number of people and corporate leaders have successfully moved beyond the view that the maximization of profit is the sole reason and purpose for corporations, the support and adoption of the legal framework that can serve as a foundation for this new vision is still in its infancy. The search for a consensus that will provide the desirable balance between the role and responsibility of governments and the public sector and at the same time the space for private corporations to make their valuable contributions to the common good continues. We must sustain our commitment to that search and allow it to produce appropriate and different but clear solutions for the varying situations, cultures and regions that exist across the world.

The endorsement by the UN Human Rights Council in June 2011 of the Guiding Principles on Business and Human Rights was an important milestone. It was followed in November 2011 by the release of 'The Corporate Responsibility to Respect Human Rights: An Interpretive Guide' by the Office of the High Commissioner for Human Rights. Thus the commitment to implementation became evident. The foundational platform that calls states to protect, corporations to respect and all stakeholders to remedy past abuses of human rights is both clear and welcome.

The collaborative and inclusive process that led to the adoption of these important policies by the United Nations was a clear indication that all stakeholders, some of whom previously had been on opposite sides in the many debates related to the issues addressed in these commitments, were ready both to embrace the social commitment of corporations and to create the tools and mechanisms that would facilitate the fulfillment of such responsibilities. The ongoing commitments by different stakeholders to the due diligence that is integral to the promotion of human rights are making an important contribution to the strategic work that is now being accomplished.

Corporate social responsibility is not only necessary because both international organizations and public opinion are increasingly demanding that private companies take a greater role in promoting well-being wherever they operate but also because it is an issue of social justice.

The Holy See takes this opportunity to recall the responsibility of transnational corporations and other business enterprises to respect human rights. Proper regulation can contribute to the promotion of and respect for human rights and to the common good of all. Every business, regardless of its size or number of employees, where it has been established in the country of installation or operation, should support, respect and protect internationally proclaimed human rights within their sphere of influence.

Greater transparency by all corporations is also needed so that all stakeholders have the information required to make well-founded judgments about the ways in which human rights are respected and protected. Consumers also will benefit from increased transparency and be in a better position to make informed judgments about their purchasing choices. In that way they can reward companies that are proactive in respecting human rights and avoid those who only give lip service to that priority. Better certifications and international standards can also help to address this global challenge by establishing a clear benchmark and framework for monitoring those who respect human rights and social corporate responsibility.

In conclusion, Mr President, with the images of the factory collapse in Bangladesh still before the eyes of the world, we wish to make a special appeal for the establishment, promotion and exchange of good and innovative practices gleaned from a wide variety of actors, in both the public and private sectors, so that a more robust respect for human rights will become a priority for all corporations. The achievement of these goals will benefit people everywhere and support the universal common good. Responsible business practices that respect human rights and protect the environment will support a more sustainable and inclusive economy.

Thank you, Mr President.

THE LAST CALL FOR THE CREDIBILITY OF THE MULTILATERAL TRADE SYSTEM*

Mr President,

First of all, my Delegation would like to thank the Government of Indonesia for the effective organization of this timely and important conference and for the generous hospitality of the Indonesian people.

Mr President,

Five years after the onset of the global financial crisis, the world economy still struggles in hope of returning to a strong and sustained growth path. The rate of world output, which was 2.2 per cent in 2012, is projected at a similar rate in 2013. As in previous years, developed countries are expected to show the poorest performance, with an approximate increase of 1 per cent in gross domestic product (GDP).[1] Developing countries are expected to grow by between 4.5 per cent and 5 per cent in 2013, as in 2012. This growth has been driven more by domestic demand than by exports, as external demand from developed economies has remained weak. Economic activity in many developed countries and a number of emerging market economies is still suffering from the impact of the financial and economic crisis and from the unsustainable financial processes and domestic and international imbalances that led to it.

Experience and economic research show that financial crises have a long-lasting impact on the economy. Not only the balance sheets of financial institutions are heavily affected, but also those of the government and of the private sector suffer heavily. In several advanced economies, this has resulted in an unprecedented increase in government debt and poses a severe constraint on future growth prospects. Moreover, the restrictive fiscal policies, which often are implemented in order to cope with the debt, have, in turn, worsened the already precarious economic condition of several countries.

While a minority is experiencing exponential growth in wealth, the gap is widening to separate the vast majority from the prosperity enjoyed by those happy few. This imbalance is the result of ideologies

* Statement delivered at the 9th Session of the Ministerial Conference of the World Trade Organization, Bali, Indonesia, 4 December 2013.

[1] Cf. UNCTAD Trade and Development Report, http://unctad.org/en/PublicationsLibrary/tdr2013_en.pdf.

that defend the absolute autonomy of the marketplace and of financial speculation. Consequently, there is an outright rejection of the right of States, charged with vigilance for the common good, to exercise any form of control. A new tyranny is thus born, invisible and often virtual, which unilaterally and relentlessly imposes its own laws and rules. An even worse development is that such policies are sometimes locked in through trade rules negotiated at the WTO or in bilateral or regional FTAs. Debt and the accumulation of interest also make it difficult for countries to realize the potential of their own economies and keep citizens from enjoying their real purchasing power. To all this, we can add widespread corruption and self-serving tax evasion, which have taken on worldwide dimensions. The thirst for power and possessions knows no limits. In this system, which tends to devour everything which stands in the way of increased profits, whatever is fragile, like the environment, is defenseless before the interests of a deified market, which become the only rule.

In this setting, the promotion of trade could have a positive impact on several economies and thus set the stage for a stronger recovery and for a return to pre-crisis growth, as the weak internal demand can be supported by the external component. Each meaningful economic decision made in one part of the world has repercussions everywhere else; consequently, no government can act without regard for shared responsibility. As we have experienced over the last few years, it is becoming increasingly difficult to find local solutions for major global problems that overwhelm local politics with difficulties to be resolved. If we really want to achieve a healthy world economy, what is needed at this juncture of history is a more efficient way of interacting, which, with due regard for the sovereignty of each nation, ensures the economic well-being of all countries, not just of a few.

The Bali package has the potential to be a vital step towards the creation of something new by WTO, something that can lead to other new opportunities – to innovation in our approach to multilateral negotiations. A balanced and fair trade facilitation agreement clearly is within reach. It could be the first multilateral trade agreement produced by the WTO; moreover, this trade facilitation deal could represent the most significant development delivered so far by the WTO. It is well known that there are significant economies of scale that can be realized in this domain. Many time-saving techniques, such as computerized container scanning, are only available in high-volume ports; in addition, the marginal value of investment in trade facilitation may be higher when trade volume is large, since cost savings are passed on to a larger quantity of goods. Thus this has the potential of generating a virtuous circle where more efficient trade facilitation stimulates trade, and in turn trade improves trade facilitation.

A trade facilitation agreement, therefore, is as close to a 'win–win' condition as can exist in the real world. Both developed and developing countries would benefit, and the gains will be larger for the latter. By some estimates, a trade facilitation agreement is estimated to reduce costs for developed countries by 10 per cent, but, for developing countries, by 14 per cent. In fact, at its core, trade facilitation is about connecting countries – their farmers and businesses – to the global economy. This is most important for small and medium-sized businesses that have the drive to succeed but lack the resources to maneuver through red tape. However, developing countries alone should not bear the costs of technological improvements to facilitate trade. A requirement that developing countries choose between funding vital education, health care, or transportation programs in order to fund trade facilitation technology is unjust. Developed countries, which will share in the benefits, must share in the costs.

As we have seen over the last three months, agreement is also reachable on additional development issues such as a monitoring mechanism for the implementation of special and [differential] provisions, and new guidelines on rules of origin and, last but not least, the concerns of certain developing countries about food security.

The volatility of food prices in recent years has caused great harm to farmers, in both the global North and South. The complexity and cost of operating grain reserves is well known. However, the lack of insurance against market failure could result in enormous costs for emergency assistance. Worse yet, such a crisis could cost lives – lives lost to hunger as an immediate consequence, and lives blighted for several generations by the effects of malnutrition on fetal development. In recent years the Holy See consistently has expressed concern about food security, as stated by Pope Francis in His Message for the World Food Day: 'an invitation to rethink and renew our food systems from a perspective of solidarity, overcoming the logic of unbridled exploitation of creation and orienting better our commitment to cultivate and look after the environment and its resources, to guarantee food security and progress towards sufficient and healthy food for all'. The 'text on public stockholding for food security purposes' follows along the same lines[2] and could represent a good

[2] Doc. JOB/TNC/29.

basis for the future negotiation in the post-Bali Agenda. We invite all delegates to support and finalize an agreement that would provide a more secure, stable and equitable access to food for countries that need it.

Mr President, the Bali conference occurs after a long series of failed Ministerial Conferences. We are collectively responsible for making it a successful conference. For too many years, multilateral negotiations have been stalled by a limited amount of issues that are effectively impeding the success of the whole package.

As a result, many countries opted to liberalize trade through Regional or Bilateral Trade Agreements. The number of such agreements has increased exponentially during the last 15 years. Currently there is a clear tendency to further enlarge these RTAs to form mega-regional trade agreements such as the Transatlantic Trade and Investment Partnership, or the Trans-Pacific Partnership. Certainly, the enlargement of regional trade agreements is a step towards further trade liberalization but we have to bear in mind that these agreements inevitably threaten the desirability reaching an agreement on a truly multilateral basis. In fact, by entering a regional trade agreement a country reduces the incentives to extend its efforts on trade liberalization at a multilateral level. Most importantly, we know that only the multilateral system is a clear, equitable system that provides effective guarantees for small and poor countries that tend to be penalized in a Regional Trade Agreement where it is asymmetric. Among the most damaging concessions developing countries make in regional and bilateral agreements are those enhancing the monopolies on life-saving medicines,[3] which reduce access and affordability and those that provide excessive legal rights to foreign investors, limiting the policy space for nations to promote sustainable and inclusive development.[4]

[3] See, e.g., 'All Costs, No Benefits: How TRIPS-Plus Intellectual Property Rules in the US–Jordan FTA Affect Access to Medicines', Oxfam Briefing Paper No. 102, 21 March 2007, www.oxfam.org/sites/www.oxfam.org/files/all%20costs,%20no%20benefits.pdf.

[4] See, e.g., UNCTAD, 'Towards a New Generation of International Investment Policies: UNCTAD's Fresh Approach to Multilateral Investment Policy-Making', IIA Issues Note No. 5, July 2013, http://unctad.org/en/PublicationsLibrary/webdiaepcb2013d6_en.pdf.

Mr President,

In conclusion, we all should be aware of the fact that we currently find ourselves at a crossroad in multilateral trade negotiations and probably in shaping the future for the WTO. Two contradictory paths could be taken at this crossroad.

In one, we fail to deliver a meaningful post-Bali Agenda. In this way not only will we lose yet another opportunity, but also many offers of flexibility, for this package will disappear for an indeterminate period of time. In this scenario, the role and the credibility of the WTO itself will inevitably start to be questioned. How can we ask individuals and firms to believe in a multilateral framework that in a period of almost 20 years has yet to reach the closure of the first negotiation round? The loss of the WTO as a negotiating forum, of course, would have the greatest impact on the smallest and the poorest economies. Big countries will always have options. Fair or unfair, that is a reality. As Pope Francis urged in his Apostolic Exhortation 'The need to resolve the structural causes of poverty cannot be delayed, not only for the pragmatic reason of its urgency for the good order of society, but because society needs to be cured of a sickness which is weakening and frustrating it, and which can only lead to new crises. Welfare projects, which meet certain urgent needs, should be considered merely temporary responses. As long as the problems of the poor are not radically resolved by rejecting the absolute autonomy of markets and financial speculation and by attacking the structural causes of inequality,[5] no solution will be found for the world's problems or, for that matter, to any problems. Inequality is the root of social ills.'[6]

The second path, to be taken as we exercise our common responsibility, will result in a more hopeful scenario. Over the last months some progress has been made on the Doha agenda and new proposals have been put on the table. It is possible, therefore, to bring about, through this conference a turnaround in trade talks, so that the WTO can regain its central role in addressing new problems, tackling new opportunities, and, most importantly, in promoting more free and equitable trade, not as an end unto itself, but as one of many tools to end poverty for all.

[5] This implies a commitment to 'eliminate the structural causes of global economic dysfunction', Address of Pope Benedict XVI to the Diplomatic Corps, 8 January 2007: AAS 99 (2007), § 73.

[6] Pope Francis, Apostolic Exhortation *Evangelii Gaudium*, § 202, www.vatican.va/holy_father/francesco/apost_exhortations/documents/papa-francesco_esortazione-ap_20131124_evangelii-gaudium_en.html#_ftnref173.

MESSAGE OF POPE FRANCIS ON THE OCCASION OF THE 103RD SESSION OF THE CONFERENCE OF THE INTERNATIONAL LABOUR ORGANIZATION (ILO): 'BETTER WORK TO ENHANCE HUMAN DIGNITY'*

To Mr Guy Ryder, Director General of the International Labour Organization

At the dawn of creation, God made man the steward of his handiwork and charged him to cultivate and protect it. Human labor is part of that creation and continues God's creative work. This truth leads us to consider work as both a gift and a duty. Indeed, labor is not a mere commodity but has its own inherent dignity and worth. The Holy See expresses its appreciation of the ILO's contribution to upholding the dignity of human work in the context of social and economic development through discussion and cooperation between governments, laborers and employers. Such efforts serve the common good of the human family and promote the dignity of workers everywhere.

This Conference has been convened at a crucial moment of social and economic history, one which presents challenges for the entire world. Unemployment is tragically expanding the frontiers of poverty (cf. Address to the *Centesimus Annus Pro Pontifice* Foundation, 25 May 2013). This is particularly disheartening for unemployed young people who can all too easily become demoralized, losing their sense of worth, feeling alienated from society. In working for greater opportunities for employment, we affirm the conviction that it is only 'through free, creative, participatory and mutually supportive work that human beings express and enhance the dignity of their life' (*Evangelii Gaudium*, 192).

Another grave and related issue confronting our world is that of mass migration: the sheer numbers of men and women forced to seek work away from their homelands is a cause for concern. Despite their hopes for a better future, they frequently encounter mistrust and exclusion, to say nothing of experiencing tragedies and disasters. Having made such sacrifices, these men and women often fail to find dignified work and fall victim to a certain 'globalization of indifference'. Their situation exposes them to further dangers such as the horror of human trafficking, forced

* Message delivered at the 103rd Session of the International Labour Conference, 9 June 2014.

labor and enslavement. It is unacceptable that, in our world, slave labor has become common coin (cf. Message for World Day of Migrants and Refugees, 24 September 2013). This cannot continue! Human trafficking is a scourge, a crime against the whole of humanity. It is time to join forces and work together to free its victims and to eradicate this crime that affects all of us, from individual families to the worldwide community (cf. Address to the New Ambassadors Accredited to the Holy See, 12 December 2013).

It is also time to reinforce existing forms of cooperation and to establish new avenues for expanding solidarity. This calls for: a renewed insistence on the dignity of every person; a more determined implementation of international labor standards; planning for a focused development on the human person as its central actor and primary beneficiary; a re-evaluation of the responsibilities of international corporations in the countries where they operate, including the areas of profit and investment management; and a concerted effort to encourage governments to facilitate the movement of migrants for the benefit of all, thus eliminating human trafficking and perilous travel conditions. Effective cooperation in these areas will be greatly assisted by defining future Sustainable Development Goals. As I recently expressed to the Secretary General and Chief Executives of the United Nations: 'Future sustainable development goals must therefore be formulated and carried out with generosity and courage, so that they can have a real impact on the structural causes of poverty and hunger, attain more substantial results in protecting the environment, ensure decent work for all, and provide appropriate protection for the family, which is an essential element in sustainable human and social development.'

Dear Friends, the social teaching of the Catholic Church supports the initiatives of the ILO which aim to promote the dignity of the human person and the nobility of human labor. I encourage you in your efforts to face the challenges of today's world in fidelity to these lofty goals. At the same time, I invoke God's blessing on all that you do to defend and advance the dignity of work for the common good of our human family.

FRANCIS

PROTECT, RESPECT, REMEDY: THE REPORT OF THE WORKING GROUP ON THE ISSUE OF HUMAN RIGHTS AND TRANSNATIONAL CORPORATIONS AND OTHER BUSINESS ENTERPRISES*

Mr President,

The Delegation of the Holy See welcomes the document developed by the working group in elaborating the Guiding Principles on Business and Human Rights. While the unanimous endorsement of the Guiding Principles by the Human Rights Council signaled a strong global political commitment, targeted efforts have been necessary in order to effectively disseminate them worldwide to all stakeholders.

Since 2011, the Working Group has supported dissemination and implementation efforts by reaching out to new audiences, multipliers and catalysts. It has also contributed to the provision of a space for constructive dialogue on progress and challenges around the implementation of the Guiding Principles, both internationally and regionally; to the construction of a stronger business and human rights regime, including through the development of national action plans on business and human rights; and to the enhancement of the understanding of the notion of effective remedy for adverse human rights impacts linked to business activities.

Despite the significant efforts made to implement the Guiding Principles, key challenges remain: these include broadening dissemination, reaching scale in implementation, building trust between stakeholders and overcoming barriers to effective remedy. The difficulties are many: both at the level of organizational applications and legal implications and at the level of understanding the meaning and benefits of the principles themselves. But the main claim seems now to have gained a wide agreement: businesses have to recognize human rights as the binding framework of their activities. Thus, the Holy See Delegation welcomes the opportunity of taking another step in addition to the Working Group efforts to promote the Guiding Principles.

The ability of international corporations to partially escape territoriality and carve for themselves an existence 'in between' national

* Statement delivered at the 26th Session of the Human Rights Council – 3: *Report of the Working Group on the Issue of Human Rights and Transnational Corporations and other Business Enterprises*, 11 June 2014.

legislation is rightly one of the concerns of the international community. Their mobility in terms of their country of incorporation, management, production, and financial flows allows them to navigate national legislations, take advantage of regulatory arbitrage and choose the jurisdictions that may offer the best return in terms of profits. Pope Francis, in his Apostolic Exhortation 'The Joy of the Gospel', and other religious leaders in the international community have repeatedly pointed out that profit cannot be the only rationale of business activity. Transnational corporations are part of the human family and as such their activity should abide by the standard of human rights.[1]

Another point of concern to the international community is the *inherent complexity* of the transnational corporations regarding their diverse operating models (*modus operandi*) which makes them very hard to monitor and supervise. The resulting absence of robust and timely transparency makes it very difficult to measure *compliance with rules and legislations. Human rights violations all too often occur out of utter neglect* toward consequences that would have been foreseeable had anyone cared to think about them. These sorts of 'neglects' are not casual, but systemic. They are the rational result of a systemic exclusion of the vulnerable in the logic of economic activities. Pope Francis describes this reality as follows: 'It is no longer simply about exploitation and oppression, but something new. Exclusion ultimately has to do with what it means to be, a part of the society in which we live; those excluded are no longer society's underside or its fringes or its disenfranchised – they are no longer even a part of it. The excluded are not the "exploited" but the outcast, the "leftovers".'[2]

The death of over 1,100 innocent workers in the collapse of the Rana Plaza garment factory in Bangladesh last year was egregious but unfortunately the very tip of an iceberg. The violation of human rights in the workplace is a daily life experience for tens of thousands of people across the world especially in jurisdictions with lax enforcement of laws and regulations. In this sense my Delegation shares the conclusion of the Report on the priority to 'review access to remedy for victims of

[1] Pope Francis, Apostolic Exhortation, *Evangelii Gaudium*, § 56 and n. 204. Archbishop Justin Welby, 'Good Banks': Transcript of Archbishop Justin Welby's speech of 12 June 2013, 'The City and the Common Good: What Kind of City Do We Want?', St Paul's Institute, London.

[2] *Evangelii Gaudium*, § 54.

business-related adverse human rights impacts, including legal and practical barriers to accessing courts, and the availability and effectiveness of State-based non-judicial mechanisms'.

Another significant challenge to a State-driven International order and the application of the Guiding Principles is the emergence of transnational corporations as *global players* with multiple centers of operation. The size of their operation, their numbers of workers, their financial flows allow them not only to be 'just another player in the market,' but to shape significantly laws and rules, markets and societies to their own advantage and purpose. That corporations have a *social role* through the 'social license to operate' that is granted to them by societies through their government agencies is not some novelty but unfortunately a forgotten dimension of modern business school curricula. Both the Church and the international community assert that, beside legitimate profit, economic enterprise *must work for the common good.* For globalization to be true to humanity, these corporations have to abide by the standard of human rights and must assume their share of responsibility toward the common good.[3]

Mr President,

The Delegation of the Holy See is aware that there are no easy solutions for addressing the multifaceted and complex challenges of business and human rights, or for providing the effective remedy and accountability that victims are legitimately seeking as a matter of urgency. Addressing those challenges and effectively managing business-related human rights risks requires sustained attention and a 'smart mix' of regulatory and policy approaches and incentives. The constructive and welcome engagement of all stakeholders in international economic and commercial matters will help to achieve an integral development and solidarity which is grounded in a vision of the future that guarantees an equitable distribution of resources and is responsive to the interdependence of people.[4]

The Commentary to the Foundational Principle 11 states the universality of human rights and therefore the responsibility of corporations operating at transnational levels: 'The responsibility to respect human rights is a global standard of expected conduct for all business

[3] Ibid., §§ 203 and 205.

[4] Cf. *Compendium of the Social Doctrine of the Church*, § 373.

enterprises wherever they operate. It exists independently of States' abilities and/or willingness to fulfill their own human rights obligations, and does not diminish those obligations. And it exists over and above compliance with national laws and regulations protecting human rights.'[5] By stressing that their responsibility stems directly from human rights, the Guiding Principles underline that the mandatory nature of this responsibility is ultimately a moral one, and they also express one of the major difficulties in the application of the guidelines: how can we convince international corporations to rise up willingly to this responsibility if no national legal obligation binds them to do so?

A binding instrument would raise moral standards and change the way international corporations understand their role and activities. In this regard, it has been proposed that the synergy between public sector corporations and private ones could constitute another emerging form of economic enterprise which cares for the common good without giving up profits.[6]

Mr President,

The Guiding Principles are an important instrument in setting up a framework for the activity of Transnational Corporations. The responsibility to respect human rights stems from the recognition that businesses have a social function that cannot be reduced only to the production and distribution of goods and services. As important actors within a

[5] OHCHR, 'Guiding Principles on Business and Human Rights: Implementing the Human Nations "Protect, Respect and Remedy" Framework', Geneva: United Nation Publishing Service, 2012, p. 13: HR/PUB/11/4.

[6] 'When we consider the issues involved in the relationship between business and ethics, as well as the evolution currently taking place in methods of production, it would appear that the traditionally valid distinction between profit-based companies and non-profit organizations can no longer do full justice to reality, or offer practical direction for the future. In recent decades a broad intermediate area has emerged between the two types of enterprise … This is not merely a matter of a "third sector", but of a broad new composite reality embracing the private and public spheres, one which does not exclude profit, but instead considers it a means for achieving human and social ends. Whether such companies distribute dividends or not, whether their juridical structure corresponds to one or other of the established forms, becomes secondary in relation to their willingness to view profit as a means of achieving the goal of a more humane market and society … Without prejudice to the importance and the economic and social benefits of the more traditional forms of business, they steer the system towards a clearer and more complete assumption of duties on the part of economic subjects' (*Caritas in Veritate*, § 41).

globalized world they bear a responsibility to abide by, and to promote human rights in their own domain of activity. While the Guiding Principles can improve the integration of the priority of the human person and the environment in international economic activity, only a binding instrument will be more effective in advancing this objective.

50TH ANNIVERSARY OF THE ESTABLISHMENT OF UNCTAD: PROSPERITY FOR ALL*

Mr President Mr Secretary General of the United Nations, Mr Secretary General of UNCTAD,

At the outset, the Holy See wishes to warmly thank you and the UNCTAD for organizing this special event on UNCTAD's 50th anniversary. Events such as this provide us an opportunity to reflect on past accomplishments. More importantly, they should also serve as occasions to stimulate our thinking about the future. In this way, inspired by the past, informed by the present, and motivated by the challenges of the future, we can truly make a difference. The Holy See is one of the 'founders' of UNCTAD and, since 1964, has been present at all its General Conferences and principal activities.

The Holy See strongly supported the original inspiration of UNCTAD that created a global trading system friendly to the development of poor countries. This system facilitates regional trade and corrects asymmetries between different trade partners, with special concern for trade in raw materials and food. At the same time, it should be said that the critical evaluation of the evolution of the Global Economy conducted by UNCTAD and many of its insights relating to trade and development were quite helpful in the development of the social doctrine of the Church concerning relations with countries, Notwithstanding the conclusion of the Uruguay Round of international trade negotiations in 1994, which moved most of the international trade discussion and agreement to the WTO, UNCTAD has remained the most important think-tank and political advocate of the least developed countries (LDCs) and other countries with particular needs, and as such it continues to enjoy the deep esteem of the Holy See and continues to be an inspiration for its international positions.

Emerging from the flames of the most destructive war in history, humanity for the first time possessed the power to render itself extinct. The United Nations was therefore created for a very basic reason: peaceful coexistence. Yet the United Nations flourished because it transcended this very basic objective. The United Nations also became an instrument

* Statement delivered at the 28th Special Session Trade and Development Board, 50th Anniversary of the Establishment of UNCTAD, 17 June 2014.

for a better world. Its aspirations were, and are, noble. One objective particularly stands out: 'to promote social progress and better standards of life in larger freedom'.

This objective called for a global economic system, which would give to all peoples the opportunity to realize their full human potential. To accomplish such aims, UNCTAD was created in 1964, at a time when a large part of the world's population had shed the bonds of colonialism and attained independence. With this expansion in the community of nations came a stronger voice for what was to become the community of developing nations. From its inception UNCTAD was the strongest multilateral voice available for the community of developing nations, a constant provocation to reform the global economic system so as to ensure that it would truly benefit all of humanity.

UNCTAD, therefore, exists with one simple but quite challenging goal: to make the global economic system work for every person. This is clearly captured in UNCTAD's motto today: 'Prosperity for all'. This is a short, but engaging statement. Prosperity leads to empowerment. Empowerment leads to opportunity. Opportunity leads to advancement. And this leads to even greater prosperity, which serves to reinforce the virtuous circle. 'Prosperity for all' has a particular decisive importance today, especially in the context of a global society that is becoming ever more uneven, and in which, in spite of the economic convergence of developed, emerging and poor countries, inequalities between rich and poor are becoming an unbridgeable abyss.

Mr President,

My Delegation would like to recall a theme which has been often discussed in UNCTAD: the role that UNCTAD can play in shaping the future. We maintain that what the world needs now, more than ever, is a new culture of fair multilateral relations based on a new culture of cooperation and international brotherhood. This should be the permanent role of UNCTAD, to be an opportunity and a place for a renewed and effective dialogue on development.

I believe that Secretary General Dr Kituyi has taken important steps in this direction through the creation of the Geneva Dialogues. This important initiative opens a necessary space for high-level discussion and debate on key development-related issues without the formalities of the intergovernmental process. Yet this is not to undermine the heart of UNCTAD which is its intergovernmental machinery. Rather, my Delegation sees this initiative as an important step to inject new life into the intergovernmental machinery by introducing an opportunity to discuss important issues that may not yet be ready for the negotiating table. Through an informal dialogue and constructive engagement, perhaps more progress can be achieved in arriving at a consensus on the key development issues of the day. This new culture affecting diplomacy and multilateral relations can perhaps be one of the major accomplishments of the golden jubilee: it is the way to the future where solidarity promotes the prosperity of the entire human family. Thank you.

WHY TRADE MATTERS TO EVERYONE*

Trade is nearly as ancient as humanity and plays a central role in the development and flourishing of peoples. Like music, it is one of the great international languages!

In our globalizing world, benefits surely flow from a more open trading environment – economic growth, innovation, employment opportunities, cultural enrichment. Trade can be an agent of development. Trade tariff barriers contributed to the economic and political catastrophes between the two world wars of the last century. By contrast, dismantling protectionist measures and outlawing unfair preferences can help to create a more level playing field, including for the world's poorest countries. Still, the successes of modern business activity, including international trade, 'even if they have reduced poverty for a great number of people – this is the great concern of Pope Francis – have often led to widespread social exclusion'.[1]

For all freedom comes with responsibility. All liberty comes with a corresponding duty of justice. This is certainly true of the free movement of goods and services that underpins our system of international trade. 'Free trade', said Pope Paul VI, 'can be called *just* only when it conforms to the demands of social justice.'[2] And justice is not served when trading partners are in unequal positions – in such a case, the 'virtue' of competition deteriorates into the 'vices' of economic manipulation and dictatorship.

Trade is unbalanced and unjust when it adds to the landscape of social exclusion – when it transgresses anyone's dignity anywhere in the world; when it neglects the common good of the whole of humanity; when it worsens the distribution of income; when it fails to create sustainable employment; when, worse, it takes advantage of human trafficking and modern slavery; and when in effect it bars the poor, the weak, and the vulnerable from participating in economic life. Such a trading system cannot be justified when it protects or even enhances the ability of large corporations to cut corners, avoid paying taxes and discard workers rather than supporting the ability of the poor and marginalized to earn

* Message of H.E. Cardinal Peter K. A. Turkson, President of the Pontifical Council for Justice and Peace on behalf of H.H. Pope Francis, delivered at the 2014 World Trade Organization Public Forum, 1–3 October 2014.

1 Pope Francis, Message to the World Economic Forum, Annual Meeting at Davos-Klosters, 17 January 2014.

2 Pope Paul VI, Encyclical Letter, *Populorum Progressio*, § 59.

a decent living and live in dignity. It cannot be defended when it runs roughshod over basic human rights, refusing to hear the cries of the poor who toil long hours for scandalously low pay in unsafe working conditions. It cannot be defended when it treats the natural environment as yet another resource to be plundered, rather than a precious gift to be stewarded prudently and wisely, including with self-restraint.

In short, trade can only matter to everyone when it benefits everyone, and when no one is discarded or 'thrown away'. For this, we need a wide sense of responsibility on the part of all. Business must fulfill its true role as a noble vocation, prioritizing the global common good ahead of narrow self-interest. The WTO has an important role to play in forging a fairer system of international trade – one that puts service ahead of mastery.

In conclusion, may I extend to this year's WTO Public Forum the prayerful wish of Pope Francis: 'From such openness to the transcendent, a new political and business reality can take shape, one capable of guiding all economic and financial activity within the horizon of an ethical approach that is truly humane.'[3]

Cardinal Peter K.A. Turkson
President, Pontifical Council for Justice and Peace

[3] Pope Francis, Message to the World Economic Forum, Annual Meeting at Davos-Klosters, 17 January 2014.

THE VOCATION OF BUSINESS: CONTRIBUTE TO THE COMMON GOOD AND RESPECT HUMAN RIGHTS*

Allow me to begin by thanking the organizers of the Third United Nations Forum on Business and Human Rights for the opportunity to convey some observations and Pope Francis' perspective on the relationship of business and human rights, an aspect of the social doctrine of the Catholic Church that the Holy See offers as his contribution to the current debate.

Mr President,

The interplay of business and human rights offers a good opportunity to further humanize the economy. The international community is engaged in this task and companies, civil society, political representatives, have worked in the direction of enhancing awareness that respect of human rights in the long run is also good business. Among the practical steps taken are the Guiding Principles on Business and Human Rights. The Principles have been widely endorsed, signaling a strong political commitment. Targeted efforts, however, are still indispensable in order to spread them successfully worldwide to all stakeholders. Besides, experience shows that further steps are required in the construction of a stronger business and human rights regime, including the development of national action plans on business and human rights and effective remedies to those business practices whose violation of human rights produces negative consequences. The financial crisis has demonstrated the difficulty of relying on business to voluntarily self-regulate. In particular, weak and poor States suffer the consequences of an asymmetry in the international system where the business companies' rights are backed up by hard laws and strong enforcement mechanisms while their obligations are backed up only by soft laws like voluntary guidelines. Then, 'there are numerous people, especially immigrants, who, compelled to work "under the table", lack the most basic juridical and economic guarantees.'[1] Another concern regards the ability of international corporations to partially escape

* Statement delivered at the 3rd Forum on Business and Human Rights: *High-level Discussion on Strengthening the Links between the Global Economic Architecture and the Business and Human Rights Agenda*, 3 December 2014.

1 Pope Francis, Address to Participants in the World Congress of Accountants, Rome, 14 November 2014.

territoriality and carve for themselves an 'in between' existence that evades national legislation. Their mobility in terms of their country of incorporation, management, production and financial flows allows them to navigate national legislations, take advantage of regulatory arbitrage and choose the jurisdictions that may offer the best return in terms of profit. But profit cannot be the only rational goal of business activity, as Pope Francis and other religious leaders tell us. When human rights are neglected, a systemic exclusion of the vulnerable comes about. The Pope points out that a new development occurs: 'It is no longer simply about exploitation and oppression, but something new. Exclusion ultimately has to do with what it means to be a part of the society in which we live; those excluded are no longer society's underside or its fringes or its disenfranchised – they are no longer even part of it. The excluded are not the 'exploited' but the outcast, the 'leftovers'.[2] Against this background, a binding instrument would raise moral standards, change the way international corporations understand their role and activity, and help clarify the extraterritorial obligations of States regarding the acts of their companies in other countries. In this regard, it has been proposed that the synergy between public sector corporations and private ones could constitute another emerging form of economic enterprise which cares for the common good without giving up profit.[3]

Mr President,

Significant progress has been achieved in different areas of life that have improved people's well-being: health care, education, communications. Modern business activity has played a fundamental

[2] Pope Francis, Apostolic Exhortation, *Evangelii Gaudium*, § 53.

[3] Pope Benedict XVI, *Caritas in Veritate*, § 46: 'When we consider the issues involved in the relationship between business and ethics, as well as the evolution currently taking place in methods of production, it would appear that the traditionally valid distinction between profit-based companies and non-profit organizations can no longer do full justice to reality, or offer practical direction for the future. In recent decades a broad intermediate area has emerged between the two types of enterprise ... This is not merely a matter of a 'third sector', but of a broad new composite reality embracing the private and public spheres, one which does not exclude profit, but instead considers it a means for achieving human and social ends. Whether such companies distribute dividends or not, whether their juridical structure corresponds to one or other of the established forms, becomes secondary in relation to their willingness to view profit as a means of achieving the goal of a more humane market and society .... Without prejudice to the importance and the economic and social benefits of the more traditional forms of business, they steer the system towards a clearer and more complete assumption of duties on the part of economic subjects.'

role in bringing about these changes by stimulating and developing the immense resources of human intelligence. But, we are still confronted with problems like environmental degradation, violent conflicts, forced resettlement, the rapid fluctuation in the prices of commodities and agricultural products, stranded resources and natural disasters impacted by climate change, and cyclical political and economic crises. The loss of benefits like insurance and pensions typically associated with employment in the developed world has further magnified the uncertainty and precariousness now faced by the middle class. In our globally interconnected world, people living in poverty are keenly aware, from their exposure to mass and social media, that their well-being is often determined by decisions made by leaders and policymakers they have little opportunity to influence. At the root of this situation is an individualistic ideology, one described by Pope Francis as 'an economy of exclusion and inequality' (*Evangelii Gaudium*, 53). It rests on the 'presumption' that human beings are naturally selfish and on the automatic ability of a free market, unhindered by regulations, to generate increased efficiency and aggregate growth. This ideology describes the future not in terms of uncertainty but in terms of risk based on probability. The consequences of any action may be rationally assessed and the bottom line is determined by profit maximization.

Certainly, business enterprises are crucial for issues of sustainability not only because they are fundamental pillars of the private sector, but also because they can satisfy many human needs through the provision of goods and services. They have a social responsibility where, through the 'social licence to operate' that is granted to them by their government, they must work not only for their legitimate profit, but also for the common good while abiding by human rights standards.

In fact, what is needed is a renewed, profound and broadened sense of responsibility. The total commitment of all the relevant players, particularly companies, is essential: 'given that large multinational companies have become important economic and political actors influencing both international relations and economic and social development, they play a very significant role in addressing global societal challenges. Therefore, a better understanding is needed of how multinational companies integrate within both the traditional international and domestic environments to create shared value.'[4]

[4] www.ohchr.org/Documents/Issues/Business/ForumSession2/Events/2Dec.XI.2-BocconiUniversity_researchproposal.pdf.

First of all, we need to take into account, as Pope Francis clearly states, that: 'Business is a vocation, and a noble vocation, provided that those engaged in it see themselves challenged by a greater meaning in life.'[5] The international business community can count on many men and women of great personal honesty and integrity, whose work is inspired and guided by high ideals of fairness, generosity and concern for the authentic development of the human family. Pope Francis continues: 'Economy and finance are dimensions of human activity and can be occasions of encounter, of dialogue, of cooperation, of recognized rights and of services rendered, of dignity affirmed in work. But in order for this to happen, it is necessary to always place man with his dignity at the center, countering the dynamics that tend to homologize everything and place money at the apex. When money becomes the end and the motive of every activity and of every venture, then the utilitarian perspective and brute logic – which do not respect people – prevail, resulting in the widespread collapse of the values of solidarity and respect for the human being. Those working in various capacities in economy and finance are called to make choices that promote the social and economic well-being of the whole of humanity, offering everyone the opportunity to pursue his/her own development.'[6]

The Holy See strongly believes that a new political and business mentality can take shape, one capable of guiding all economic and financial activity within the horizon of an ethical approach that does not exclude but transcends profit. The Pope warns that 'it is not enough to give practical answers to economic and material questions. It is necessary to generate and cultivate ethics of economy, of finance and of employment; it is necessary to maintain the value of solidarity – this word which today risks being taken out of the dictionary – solidarity as a moral approach, an expression of attention to others in all their legitimate needs.'[7]

We are asked, above all, to build a meaningful future for the generations to come. 'If we want to deliver to future generations an improved environmental, economic, cultural and social patrimony, which we inherited', says Pope Francis, 'we are called to assume the responsibility of working for the globalization of solidarity. Solidarity is a demand that

[5] Pope Francis, Apostolic Exhortation, *Evangelii Gaudium*, § 203.

[6] Pope Francis, Address to Participants in the World Congress of Accountants, Rome, 14 November 2014.

[7] Ibid.

arises from the same network of interconnections which develop with globalization.[8]

In conclusion, the interplay of human rights and the economy, the business world in particular, will become more productive when they move forward on a double track. First, the current situation of inequality and of exclusion which affects too many people, must be addressed with urgency and effectiveness. Second, a peaceful and creative society is possible when the economy is placed within a context where human persons have priority, are free to contribute their talents and their dignity is properly recognized.

[8] Ibid.

THE TRANSITION FROM THE INFORMAL TO FORMAL ECONOMY*

Current Economic Situation

Mr President,

Economic inequalities persist and are increasing on every continent: a situation that creates more unemployment and widens the social inequities that are among the most powerful causes of instability in many societies, including some where peace is threatened or has already been undermined.[1] The turbulence of our times – economic, social and political – makes the achievement of social justice very much an agenda for today. Thus, in 2014, 1 per cent of the global population held 48 per cent of the world's wealth, leaving the remaining half to the 99 per cent of the people.[2] The challenge of bringing unemployment and underemployment back to 2008 pre-crisis levels now appears as daunting a task as ever. ILO's World Economic Outlook confirms these trends: the world risks plunging from a jobless recovery into a period characterized by rising unemployment. To meet the expectation of new labour market entrants, an additional 280 million jobs need to be created by 2019 to close the unemployment gap. It appears unlikely, however, that the world economy will be able to either deliver or sustain such job creation. Youth, especially young women, are disproportionately affected. Almost 74 million young people (aged 15–24) were looking for work in 2014. The youth unemployment rate is on average three times higher than that of their adult counterparts. Increased youth unemployment is common to all regions. It is occurring despite the trend of improvements in educational achievement and thus it increases skill mismatches and fuels social discontent. This becomes a push factor for dramatic migration flows and for an increase in volunteers who join extremist violent groups. The Holy See, as a solution to this situation, proposes the need for increased solidarity and cooperation among all the members of the international

* Statement delivered at the 104th Session of the International Labour Conference, 4 June 2015.

[1] The International Labour Organization unanimously adopted the ILO Declaration on Social Justice for a Fair Globalization on 10 June 2008.

[2] Oxfam Report available at https://www.oxfam.org/en/pressroom/pressreleases/2015–01–19/richest-1-will-own-more-all-rest-2016.

community and the multiplication of efforts to improve economic and social conditions in the countries of origin of migrants.

Rising unemployment is a major factor, which drives the mounting inequalities and should be addressed through carefully designed labor markets and tax policies. Employment should not be considered simply as a means for obtaining profit, but above all a goal that affects man and his dignity. If there is no work, this dignity is wounded! In fact, anyone who is unemployed, or even underemployed, suffers personal frustration, and risks becoming a victim of marginalization or even social exclusion.[3]

Labor Protection in a Changing World

Therefore, labor protection measures, such as a minimum wage, the amount of hours and maternity protection standards, should be strengthened, even though they may have cost implications for an enterprise in the short term. However, in the long term, such measures can encourage enterprises to invest in technological and organizational improvements in order to offset increased costs, which can, in turn, spur productivity growth. A safe and motivating working environment, a mutually beneficial flexible work organization, and giving workers a fair share of the accrued benefits, are elements known to improve the competitiveness and productivity of enterprises.[4] As acknowledged also by the World Bank, there is a current need for better regulation of labor markets in the interest of prosperity and equity.[5]

Over the past three decades, significant transformations in the global economy have gone hand in hand with institutional changes in the world of work, which has been reshaped by globalization. Today, much of international trade involves buyers and suppliers operating within an ever-expanding global supply chain. All this has implications for workers' welfare.[6] The promotion of increased employment as a means of eradicating poverty should not be viewed as an issue that could be

[3] Cf. Pope Francis, Address of Pope Francis to the Managers and Workers of the Terni Steel Mill and the Faithful of the Diocese of Terni-Narni-Amelia, Italy, 20 March 2014.

[4] ILO: Conclusions concerning the promotion of sustainable enterprises, International Labour Conference, 96th Session, Geneva, 2007.

[5] World Bank: World Development Report 2013: Jobs (Washington, DC, 2012).

[6] At its 319th Session (2013), the Governing Body selected the item 'Decent work in global supply chains' with a view to a general discussion at the 105th Session (2016) of the International Labour Conference.

compromised: 'Labor ... is not a mere commodity. On the contrary, the worker's human dignity in it must be recognized. It therefore cannot be bought and sold like a commodity.'[7] Technological advancements, such as the expansion of the Internet, have facilitated long-range communication, thus reinforcing established centers and further marginalizing peripheries. This phenomenon has accelerated changes in the production process and in work. Despite increasing efficiency in production and widening the availability of services for customers, the demand for workers to continue for prolonged periods has grown in many sectors and occupations.

It is well known that economic progress should not be measured solely by the Gross Domestic Product (GDP). To the contrary, the well-being of a nation should be measured by a series of indicators linked to social protection systems, including access to quality services, education, decent work, adequate, safe and nutritious food, adequate housing, personal safety, and basic income security, as well as the enjoyment of a safe, clean, healthy and sustainable environment. The 2008 ILO Declaration on Social Justice for a Fair Globalization reaffirmed the importance of these constitutional objectives of the ILO.[8] Labor protection is grounded in the ILO's founding values: labor is not a commodity, improving conditions of work is central to social justice and to a country's prosperity, universal and lasting peace.

The Holy See Delegation believes that poverty eradication requires a specific and concerted commitment by governments, employers and workers' organizations, the private sector and civil society. This commitment is grounded in human dignity, human rights and solidarity. It should result in concrete measures for protecting workers and their families from risks, such as unemployment, injury and illness. Since the development of employment-creating initiatives is intimately linked with the promotion of entrepreneurship, policies aimed at promoting the development of Small and Medium Enterprises (SMEs) are crucial for economic recovery.

SMEs are the privileged environment where the creativity, industriousness and self-promotion of workers can be tested and developed. However, they are often characterized by suboptimal labor standards where employment quality is lower and is associated with the creation of informal jobs. It is therefore important that the promotion of SMEs occurs

[7] Pope Pius XI, Encyclical Letter, *Quadragesimo Anno*, § 83.

[8] The International Labour Organization unanimously adopted the ILO Declaration on Social Justice for a Fair Globalization on 10 June 2008.

within a regulatory framework that favors the spread of sustainable labor standards.

Transition from the Informal to Formal Economy

Mr President,

The informal economy is a major challenge for workers' rights, in particular for their social protection and decent working conditions. As highlighted by the Director General in his Report, 'globally, half of the labour force is working and producing in the informal economy. Although the informal economy is largest in the developing countries, informality continues, and is even growing, in the industrialized countries.'[9]

The 'informal economy' includes all economic activities not adequately covered by formal arrangements as well as informal work which can be carried out across all sectors of the economy both in public and private spaces. Most people enter the informal economy not by choice, but as a consequence of lack of opportunities in the formal economy, or because the institutional development does not allow the emergence of a sufficiently developed formal sector.

While the informal economic activity represents a promising sign of economic growth and development, it raises some ethical and legal questions. Some workers and economic units in the informal economy can have a large entrepreneurial potential if transition to the formal economy is facilitated. The significant increase in job opportunities in the context of informal activities is caused by low skills and lack of specialization of a large number of local workers and by a disorderly growth in formal economic sectors. In some countries, excessive regulation may also exert pressure on small entrepreneurs to remain or to move to the informal sector. Large numbers of people are thus forced to work under seriously distressing conditions and in situations that lack the rules necessary to safeguard their rights. Levels of productivity, income and living standards are extremely low and often inadequate for guaranteeing the minimum level of subsistence to workers and their families.

The Holy See Delegation considers it of the utmost importance that the ILO Member States take appropriate measures to promote a

[9] Guy Ryder, 'The future of work centenary initiative', International Labour Conference, 104th Session, 2015, Doc. ILC.104/DG/I.

gradual transition from the informal to the formal economy. National circumstances and laws should be taken into account. The transition of workers and economic units from the informal to the formal economy should respect workers' fundamental rights and ensure opportunities for income security, livelihoods and entrepreneurship. At the same time it should promote the creation, preservation and sustainability of decent jobs in the formal economy while preventing informalization of formal economy jobs.

In particular, these measures should take into account the following factors: (a) the diversity of causes, characteristics and circumstances of workers and economic units in the informal economy, their different needs of protection and the need to address such diversity with a case-by-case approach; (b) the necessity of effective measures to promote transition from the informal to the formal economy and to prevent and sanction deliberate evasion from the formal economy which aims at avoiding taxation, social and labor laws and regulations; (c) the need to eradicate child labor, often associated with higher level of informality and still sadly widespread in some regions. The ILO's 2015 Report on Child Labour indicates that the number of minors at work has been reduced from 246 million in 2000 to 168 million, a figure that still requires additional efforts, especially if we consider that 22,000 boys and girls every year lose their lives in work accidents.[10]

The transition from informal to formal economy will take time. In order to be effective, the cost of transition should be shared among all stakeholders who participate in the production process. Associations of informal workers and producers should be favoured as they are a crucial instrument of representation and shared participation.

Trade and the Informal Economy

A powerful instrument to foster this transition is openness to international integration which, under appropriate policies, could favour the local adoption of internationally accepted standards. Labour provisions are increasingly included in bilateral and regional trade agreements.

As of June 2013, fifty-eight trade agreements included labor provisions and about 40 per cent include conditions. This implies that compliance

[10] Available at www.ilo.org/ipec/Campaignandadvocacy/wdacl/2015/lang–en/index.htm.

with labor standards entails economic consequences in terms of an economic sanction or benefit. The remaining 60 per cent of trade agreements include labor provisions exclusively promotional in nature. While these provisions do not directly link compliance to economic consequences, they provide a framework for dialogue, cooperation, and/or monitoring. This approach is found mainly in the European Union. There is, however, the risk that labor provisions contained in preferential trade agreements may divert trade towards less demanding partners, with an unintended belittling of ILO standards

The Holy See underscores the necessity that the ILO Standards should not be weakened but serve as a basis for all current and future bilateral and plurilateral agreements.

Conclusion

Mr President,

The transition from informal to formal employment is a delicate process that should recognize the rights of everyone, particularly of the most vulnerable, people who are left out and marginalized. The challenge is to reduce inequality, to support the transition to greater protection in the formal economy and to maintain the priority of labor rights for everyone in trade agreements.

The considerations that moved the founders of the ILO to make social justice the ultimate goal of this organization, the everyday business of which is the world of work, established a nexus and responsibility that remain unchanged nearly 100 years later. Consequently, when governments, employers and workers come together at the ILO to seek consensus, they should always be guided by the requirements of social justice. Coherence requires that the future work of the centenary initiative should also relate to the future of social justice.

Allow me to conclude with the words of Pope Francis: 'We can no longer trust in the unseen forces and the invisible hand of the market. Growth in justice requires ... programs, mechanisms and processes specifically geared to a better distribution of income, the creation of sources of employment and an integral promotion of the poor ... '[11] Only in this way can economic growth be truly inclusive.

[11] Pope Francis, Apostolic Exhortation, *Evangelii Gaudium*, § 204.

THE EXPLOITATION OF FORCED LABOR IN THE GLOBAL SUPPLY CHAINS*

Mr President,

My Delegation thanks the Special Rapporteur for her thought-provoking Report on contemporary forms of slavery, including its causes and consequences.

At the present time, 35.8 million people[1] experience the deprivation of one of the fundamental and universal rights: the right to be free from slavery in all its numerous forms. According to ILO data, 5.5 million of the 20.9 million persons in forced labor are children, with up to 15 per cent of those working in supply chains.[2] As the Special Rapporteur underlines, even if globalization has created unprecedented opportunities, 'the demand for cheap labor meets a ready supply of workers from vulnerable groups: indigenous peoples, minorities, those considered to be from the "lowest castes" and migrants, especially those in an irregular situation.'[3]

Sectors with a high risk of contemporary forms of slavery using supply chains, include agriculture, construction, mining and the textile industry. These often 'rely on temporary or migrant labor and are characterized by complex contracting and subcontracting chains which make the victims dependent on their exploiters',[4] especially 'in countries where labor regulations fail to comply with international norms and minimum standards, or, equally illegally, in countries which lack legal protection for workers' rights'.[5] Such enslavement is accomplished by blackmail and threats made against workers and their loved ones, by the confiscation of their identity documents, through physical violence, and by forcing them to live clandestinely or in disgraceful living and working conditions.

* Statement delivered at the 30th Session of the Human Rights Council – Item 3: *Special Rapporteur on Contemporary Forms of Slavery*, 15 September 2015.

1 The Global Slavery Index 2014, Walk Free Foundation, available at www.globalslaveryindex.org/.

2 Urmila Bhoola, Report of the Special Rapporteur on contemporary forms of slavery, including its causes and consequences, 8 July 2015.

3 Ibid., point B, 'Causes and prevalence of contemporary forms of slavery in supply chains and examples of sectors at risk', p. 19.

4 Ibid.

5 Pope Francis' Message for the 2015 World Day of Peace, 'No longer slaves, but brothers and sisters'.

However, there are many other forms of slavery which go beyond the exploitation of forced labor of the supply chain: a great number of people, many of whom are minors, are also forced into prostitution, or to become sex slaves. Women are forced into marriage or sold for arranged marriages and bequeathed to relatives of their deceased husbands without any right to give or withhold their consent. There are also persons, minors and adults alike, who are made objects of trafficking for the sale of organs, for recruitment as soldiers, for begging, for illegal activities such as the production and sale of narcotics or for disguised forms of cross-border adoption. This old inhuman phenomenon of man's subjugation by man, is rooted, today as in the past, in 'a notion of the human person which allows him or her to be treated as an object, deprived of their freedom, sold and reduced to being the property of others and treated as a means to an end'.[6]

Frequently, the victims of human trafficking and slavery are taken in by false promises of employment, while looking for a way out of a situation of extreme poverty or they are forced by debt bondage. However, beyond poverty, many other causes help to explain contemporary forms of slavery. Among these, we can find underdevelopment and exclusion, and also corruption, greed, armed conflicts, violence, criminal activity and terrorism. The task of the international community is to 'recognize that we are facing a global phenomenon which exceeds the competence of any one community or country' and 'in order to eliminate it, we need a mobilization comparable in size to that of the phenomenon itself.'[7] National and international efforts should be committed to prevention, to victim protection, to the legal prosecution of perpetrators, working for victims' psychological and educational rehabilitation in order to reintegrate them into the society where they live or from which they have come.[8] States should ensure that their own legislation truly respects the dignity of the human person in the areas of migration, employment, adoption, the movement of businesses offshore and the sale of items produced by slave labor, seeking the most suitable modalities to punish those who are complicit in this inhuman trade.[9]

Intergovernmental organizations, in keeping with the principle of subsidiarity, are called to coordinate initiatives for combating the transnational networks of organized crime which oversee the

[6] Ibid. [7] Ibid. [8] Ibid.

[9] Pope Francis, Address to the Participants in the Plenary Session of the Pontifical Academy of Social Sciences, 18 April 2015.

trafficking of persons and the illegal trafficking of migrants.[10] In this regard, the many efforts of the Catholic Church, especially on the part of religious communities, to counter the modern form of slavery could be used as a best practice for other institutions and agencies.

Mr President,

It is necessary for the international community to cast off the relativistic culture where one person takes advantage of another, treating others as mere objects, imposing forced labor on them or enslaving them to pay their debts. We must overcome the 'globalization of indifference' to their plight, transforming it through a renewed sense of solidarity and fraternity.

Thank you, Mr President.

[10] Pope Francis' Message for 2015 World Day of Peace, 'No longer slaves, but brothers and sisters'.

THE RISKS OF THE POVERTY TRAP*

Mr President,

My Delegation wishes to extend its sincere gratitude to you, Mr Chair, for convening this meeting and providing me with an opportunity to share our views on current WTO issues. I also join other Delegations in thanking the Director General of the WTO for his comprehensive report this morning on various areas of our common concern.

Mr President,

The Holy See is confident that, in Nairobi, a sense of responsibility and solidarity with the most disadvantaged will prevail, so that narrow interests and the logic of power will be set aside. In this regard, in his recent address to the UNON, Pope Francis affirmed that 'while recognizing that much has been done in this area, it seems that we have yet to attain an international system of commerce which is equitable and completely at the service of the battle against poverty and exclusion. Commercial relationships between States, as an indispensable part of relations between peoples, can do as much to harm the environment as to renew it and preserve it for future generations.'[1] It must not be forgotten that the vulnerability of rural areas, if they are denied access to the market, has significant repercussions on the subsistence of small farmers and their families.

The Holy See recognizes the benefit of an equitable and participatory multilateral system of trade relations directed to attaining and developing the common good. A spirit of solidarity among all countries and peoples should replace the ceaseless competition that aims to achieve and defend privileged positions in international trade. Protectionism too often favors already privileged segments of society. Effective multilateralism, on the other hand, is an inclusive process which acknowledges that at the core of all social and economic relations, and hence of trade relations, is the human person, with inherent dignity and inalienable human rights. Therefore, a rules-based trade system or, better yet, a fair system of trade rules, is indispensable. It is no coincidence that as the rule of law

* Statement delivered at the General Council of the World Trade Organization, 7 December 2015.

[1] Pope Francis, Address to UNON, Nairobi, 26 November 2015.

in trade has spread, average tariffs have fallen dramatically. In fact, they have been cut in half. Average applied tariffs were 15 per cent in 1995. Today they stand at less than 8 per cent and trade volumes have more than doubled.

This Organization provides a forum for policy dialogue and information sharing, where members can monitor each other's practices and regulations to ensure that agreements are being observed. This process of monitoring trade policies, underpinned by a clear system of common rules and obligations, was pivotal in ensuring that the financial crisis of 2008 was not followed by an outbreak of protectionism as we saw in the 1930s. Multilateralism has a development value. In this twentieth year of the WTO, we should seek to strengthen multilateral trade. The GATT/WTO has played an important role in strengthening multilateralism. It has promoted an inclusive and open rules-based and non-discriminatory trading system and it has contributed to rapid economic growth. The legal and policy framework of the WTO remains a bulwark against protectionism. For those who cynically question the effectiveness of the WTO, we should ask them why is it that over 30 new Members, now accounting for approximately 20 per cent of the WTO membership, acceded since 1995? The WTO has contributed to the enhanced welfare in these Members and to growth in the global economy.

In his last Encyclical Letter, Pope Francis reminded us that: 'inequity affects not only individuals but entire countries; it compels us to consider an ethics of international relations. A true "ecological debt" exists, particularly between the global North and South, connected to commercial imbalances with effects on the environment, and the disproportionate use of natural resources by certain countries over long periods of time.'[2] Therefore, a fair system of trade rules should be shaped according to the level of economic development of the Member States and give explicit support and special and differential treatment to the poorest countries. When the levels of development of the Members are excessively unequal, the consent of the parties may not be sufficient to guarantee the justice of their agreement: 'trade relations can no longer he based solely on the principle of free, unchecked competition, for it very often creates an economic dictatorship. Free trade can be called just only when it conforms to the demands of social justice.'[3] Moreover, the question of justice in today's trade rules is problematic because such

[2] Pope Francis, *Laudato Si'*, § 51.

[3] Pope Paul VI, Encyclical Letter, *Populorum Progressio*, § 59.

rules tend to grant more privileges to those who possess more economic power.

A fair system of trade rules is an international public good that can play a major role in the promotion of sustainable development and the alleviation of poverty, as has been recognized in the United Nations' 2030 Agenda for Sustainable Development. Without a fair system of trade rules, vulnerable people in many developing and developed countries will be 'locked in a poverty trap'. This approach is in line with the concern to put the human person at the center of any development and trade strategy, recognizing that only by promoting individuals' capabilities, by enabling every person and every social group to make the most of the opportunities created by trade liberalization, will it be possible to implement a truly mutually beneficial fair trade. Opening access to new markets offers a real opportunity for developing countries and is an important element of the development process; however, it is not per se a sufficient condition for lifting countries out of poverty. The international trading system should guarantee a true partnership based on equal and reciprocal relations among rich and poor countries. Free trade is not an end in itself but rather a means for better living standards and the human development of people at all levels. The Doha Development Agenda in this sense represents a significant multilateral attempt to trade and development interests of those developing Members so as to heal the imbalance codified in the rules.

Mr President,

In conclusion, the Delegation of the Holy See reiterates its hope that the consensus reached on the proposal of extension and non-violation complaints at the TRIPs Council, over the past weeks, represents an important sign by the World Trade Organization in preparation for the next Ministerial Conference. The Holy See Delegation remains confident that a sense of common responsibility, as shown in the decisions adopted, will bring us to reach a historic result in Nairobi. In this regard, before the Assembly of the UNON, last Thursday, the Holy Father expressed his desire that: 'the deliberations of the forthcoming Nairobi Conference will not be a simple balancing of conflicting interests, but a genuine service to the care of our common home and the integral development of persons, especially those in greatest need.' In the context of a 'family of nations' those countries economically more developed can provide assistance that will allow for attainment of the development which corresponds to our shared human dignity. Precisely because people have been endowed with the same extraordinary dignity no one should be reduced to living without the benefits of trade.

Thank you, Mr President.

MULTILATERALISM AT THE SERVICE OF THE INTEGRAL DEVELOPMENT OF THE HUMAN PERSON*

The Delegation of the Holy See wishes to begin by expressing thanks and congratulations to President Minister of Foreign Affairs, Amina Mohamed, and to the people of Kenya for the warm welcome and excellent arrangements that have been made for this occasion. My Delegation extends its appreciation also to the Chairman of the General Committee and the Director General for their tireless efforts in preparation for the Conference. This Tenth Ministerial Conference of WTO represents a time of hope. But for this hope to be realized, all present must remain faithful to the promises and commitments made to the poor in Doha. There has been less than satisfactory progress in the areas of trade for the poorest countries. As recalled by Pope Francis in his recent visit to UNON: 'while recognizing that much has been done in this area, it seems that we have yet to attain an international system of commerce which is equitable and completely at the service of the battle against poverty and exclusion. Commercial relationships between States, as an indispensable part of relations between peoples, can do as much to harm the environment as to renew it and preserve it for future generations.'[1]

On this occasion of the 20th anniversary of the WTO, we observe that in the evolution of the talks over the last years there is a sense of detachment from the issues that are perceived as relevant by specialists and by the general public. The high hopes following the launch of the Doha round of negotiations rapidly gave way to disillusions and disappointments. After years of lengthy negotiations, these hopes have been revived by the Bali agreement, only to be subsequently dashed by the difficulties in implementing the Bali package.

We clearly live in unprecedented times. Globalization is shaping and changing the world economy at a speed that is totally unexpected; some countries, in particular emerging economies, are experiencing social and economic changes that are of an order of magnitude far larger than previous historical experiences. This is certainly positive as most of those transformations are for the better and have allowed millions of poor individuals to be lifted out of poverty; however, these developments expose

* Statement delivered at the 10th Session of the Ministerial Conference of the World Trade Organization, Nairobi, Kenya, 16 December 2015.

[1] Pope Francis, Address to UNON, Nairobi, 26 November 2015.

the limits of the WTO and other multilateral institutions. They appear slow to adapt to change and are characterized by a decision-making process that is too lengthy and cumbersome.

In particular, there is the risk that the WTO, by focusing its efforts on negotiating details of complex trade agreements, could miss the point of the most relevant issues. The widespread implementation of regional trade agreements, some of which resemble multilateral agreements on a small scale, is a testimony of the fact that where the multilateral approach fails, alternatives are pursued.

Such rules have been among the guiding principles of GATT's negotiations and subsequently of the WTO, but over time they seem to be lost among the endless details of trade agreements. We therefore hope for the WTO to rediscover and re-emphasize its basic principles as stated in the preamble of the agreement that established the WTO: 'Recognizing that their relations in the field of trade and economic endeavour should be conducted with a view to raising standards of living, ensuring full employment and a large and steadily growing volume of real income and effective demand, and expanding the production of and trade in goods and services, while allowing for the optimal use of the world's resources in accordance with the objective of sustainable development, seeking both to protect and preserve the environment and to enhance the means for doing so in a manner consistent with their respective needs and concerns at different levels of economic development.'

The Holy See hopes for a change in this approach, that it would be more aimed at fostering inclusion and development of people in an increasingly interdependent world.

We encourage all member countries to simplify WTO procedures, guided by the principles of solidarity and the centrality of the human person, in order to reach a stronger and more inclusive participation.

Those same principles and rules should be effectively adopted by member countries which need to comply with their individual actions to the general principles of limited sovereignty. It is important that this concern be shared among all members at all levels. This concern, in fact, had already been raised by Pope Benedict XVI: 'Unfortunately, too much confidence was placed in those institutions, as if they were able to deliver the desired objective automatically. In reality, institutions by themselves are not enough, because integral human development is primarily a vocation, and therefore it involves a free assumption of responsibility in solidarity on the part of everyone' (*Caritas in Veritate*, § 11).

Modernizing multilateralism could therefore be achieved by rediscovering the roots of the multilateral ideal, which is ultimately based on the fact that all human beings are united by a common humanity rooted in the dignity of the human person. Following this premise, both individual actors and multilateral institutions can work together with the goal of reaching the common good.

Regionalism and Multilateralism

As stressed above, during the last decades, there has been a proliferation of regional and bilateral trade agreements conducted in parallel with negotiations at the multilateral level. A few weeks ago, twelve of the largest trading nations in the world reached agreement on the Trans Pacific Trade Partnership; similarly, the US and the EU are in advanced stages of negotiations to close the deal on the Transatlantic Trade and Investment Partnership, a deal that contains a large set of measures aimed at significantly reducing tariffs and non-tariff barriers significantly.

Regional Trade Agreements (RTAs) have several advantages: by respecting Article 24 of GATT, they are a step nearer trade liberalisation; moreover, they can provide a framework that allows developing countries a gradual adjustment to the increased degree of competition implied by free trade; finally, they can be a valuable instrument to develop South–South trade which could be a crucial element in the development of several developing countries.

However, there are several risks associated with RTAs. The most relevant is that they risk being interpreted as a substitute to multilateral negotiations. In a sense, this is a case where pluralism is interpreted as being opposed to multilateralism and where the particular good is seen as opposed to the common good.

The Holy See strongly stresses the importance of recognizing a primacy of multilateral agreements over bilateral and regional ones. Despite its limits and its complexity, the multilateral framework gives pluralism a universal dimension and facilitates inclusive dialogue. More specifically, in a multilateral framework, weaker and smaller countries are better safeguarded than in a regional and bilateral setting where the counterparts are large and strong countries. In such asymmetric settings, advanced economies inevitably have more bargaining power with respect to LDCs, with the result that the latter are not able to grasp fully the benefits of the agreements.

Rules of Origin

Rules of Origin have prevented LDCs from grasping the full benefits of preferential trade agreements. These rules set requirements that are difficult to meet by developing countries. Such rules are often considered to be overly restrictive and inflexible, making it difficult for LDCs to take full advantage of the preferences they are granted.

In several cases, LDCs are collectively able to meet the requirements set by the Rules of Origin of developed countries; however, individually they fail to do so. Since the Bali conference, LDCs have been advocating on several occasions the need for a multilateral framework for reforming the design and implementation of rules of origin by advanced economies in preferential trade agreements. Efforts should be increased in order to reach an agreement by the Nairobi conference. Particular attention should be given to the possibility of tailoring the definition of Rules of Origin according to the level of development and industrialization of the country or to the possibility that requirements for LDCs should be binding collectively and not individually.

More generally, advanced economies should multiply their efforts to design preferential treatments for LDCs which are effectively accessible to them. All too often, in fact, preferential treatments remain only on paper and are not effectively used by LDCs because they lack the tools and the possibilities to comply with them. A more effective dialogue between LDCs and preference-granting countries should be encouraged in order to maximise the possibility for the former to take the most of the benefits of trade.

Agriculture

The agriculture sector plays an important role in the economy of most LDCs, accounting for 24 per cent of the GDP and more than a third of employment in LDCs. A key negotiating priority has therefore been to support reform of agriculture rules including market access, domestic support and export competition.

Accomplishing the main objectives of the agriculture negotiations, i.e., substantial improvements in market access, phasing out of all forms of export subsidies and substantial reductions in trade-distorting domestic support, would constitute a positive outcome for LDCs, which remain vulnerable to the effects of trade-distorting agricultural policies followed by other Members. WTO Members have recognized the special needs of

LDCs by providing them with specific flexibilities. However, the simple removal of agricultural subsidies in developed countries is not enough and may produce negative consequences for the poor. Therefore, the reduction of distorting subsidies should be accompanied by international support aimed at increasing agricultural production in an inclusive and sustainable way. In this respect, the example of cotton with its dual track approach of addressing simultaneously the trade and development aspects has been a unique and successful initiative by the WTO and could potentially constitute an example for other products.

Service Waiver

Following the 2013 Bali decision on the operationalization of the services waiver, negotiations have progressed in identifying the tools to be applied in this context. Among such tools, emphasis has been given to the expansion of the access for temporary movement of workers under Mode 4 of GATS. Regarding negotiations on temporary migrant workers, special attention should be given to the selectivity of those measures. Selective measures often result in large brain drains from LDCs which in turn may hinder the accumulation of human capital and growth in these countries. Greater effort should be put in finding tools that accompany the service waiver with the development of the service sector in LDCs that could potentially employ returning migrants.

More generally, the temporary movement of workers is part of a global phenomenon of international movement of peoples (due to a variety of economic, environmental and political causes, including violent conflict) of such large proportions that is reshaping the societies of whole countries and regions. However, great care should be taken when dealing with this issue, discriminating against economic migrants. As stated by Pope Benedict XVI: ‘Obviously, these labourers cannot be considered as a commodity or a mere workforce. They must not, therefore, be treated like any other factor of production. Every migrant is a human person who, as such, possesses fundamental, inalienable rights that must be respected by everyone and in every circumstance’ (*Caritas in Veritate*, § 62). The fundamental nature of the human being has therefore to be at the center of any negotiation dealing with migration and labor movement.

Trade and Development: An Ecological Approach

It is well known that trade is intimately connected with development as it is one of the most robust and effective channels for enhancing economic growth. In discussing trade policies all countries should be aware that we are all part of the same human community and we all make use of the same global resources. 'Whether believers or not, we are agreed today that the earth is essentially a shared inheritance, whose fruits are meant to benefit everyone' (*Laudato Si'*, § 93).

The recent Encyclical Letter of Pope Francis is rich with suggestions and indications on this theme. Here we offer to the debate two specific issues. The first is the importance of the environmental dimension of the policies implemented. 'It is essential to seek comprehensive solutions which consider the interactions within natural systems themselves and with social systems. We are faced not with two separate crises, one environmental and the other social, but rather with one complex crisis which is both social and environmental. Strategies for a solution demand an integrated approach to combating poverty, restoring dignity to the excluded, and at the same time protecting nature' (*Laudato Si'*, § 139).

The second is the importance of labour. In implementing policy actions to tackle the current economic challenges, we need to bear in mind that the first objective should be the increase of employment. Labour enhancing policies are not only important for the development of countries and regions, but mostly for the development of the talents that each human being has. 'We were created with a vocation to work. The goal should not be that technological progress increasingly replace human work, for this would be detrimental to humanity. Work is a necessity, part of the meaning of life on this earth, a path to growth, human development and personal fulfillment. Helping the poor financially must always be a provisional solution in the face of pressing needs. The broader objective should always be to allow them a dignified life through work' (*Laudato Si'*, § 128).

These are clearly challenging issues that require an enormous effort in coordinating the initiatives of different multilateral institutions; however, they can be the beginning of a new approach to trade and development centered on an integral ecology respecting both human and social dimensions.

Mr President,

In conclusion, the Holy See Delegation remains confident that a sense of common responsibility, as shown in the previous Ministerial Conference, will bring us to reach a historic result in Nairobi. In this regard, before the Assembly of the UNON the Holy Father expressed his desire that: 'the deliberations of the forthcoming Nairobi Conference will not be a simple balancing of conflicting interests, but a genuine service to the care of our common home and the integral development of persons, especially those in greatest need.' In the context of a 'family of nations' those countries economically more developed can provide assistance that will allow for attainment of the development which corresponds to our shared human dignity.

2 FINANCE: THE GOLDEN CALF OF OLD HAS FOUND A NEW AND HEARTLESS IMAGE IN THE CULT OF MONEY

THE IMPACT OF THE GLOBAL ECONOMIC AND FINANCIAL CRISES ON THE UNIVERSAL REALIZATION AND ENJOYMENT OF HUMAN RIGHTS*

As we are daily reminded by the media, the world financial crisis has created a global recession causing dramatic social consequences, including the loss of millions of jobs and the serious risk that, for many of the developing countries, the Millennium Development Goals (MDGs) may not be reached. The human rights of countless persons are compromised, including the right to food, water, health and decent work. Above all, when large segments of a national population see their social and economic rights frustrated, the loss of hope endangers peace. The international community has a legitimate responsibility to ask why such a situation developed; whose responsibility it is; and how a concerted solution can lead us out of the crisis and facilitate the restoration of rights. The crisis was caused, in part, by problematic behavior of some actors in the financial and economic system, including bank administrators and those who should have been more diligent in monitoring and accountability systems; thus they bear much responsibility for the current problem. The causes of the crisis, however, are deeper.

Reflecting, at that time, on the 1929 crisis, Pope Pius XI observed that: 'it is obvious that not only is wealth concentrated in our times but an immense power and despotic economic dictatorship is consolidated in the hands of a few, who often are not owners but only the trustees and managing directors of invested funds which they administer according to their own arbitrary will and pleasure' (*Quadragesimo Anno*, § 105). He also noted that free competition had destroyed itself by relying on profit as the only criterion. There are economic, juridical and cultural dimensions of the present crisis. To engage in financial activity cannot be reduced to making easy profits, but also must include the promotion of the common good among those who lend, those who borrow and those who work. The lack of an ethical base has brought the crisis to low-, middle- and

* Statement delivered at the 10th Special Session of the Human Right Council, 20 February 2009.

high-income countries alike. The Delegation of the Holy See, Mr President, calls for renewed 'attention to the need for an ethical approach to the creation of positive partnerships between markets, civil society and States' (Pope Benedict XVI).

The negative consequences, however, exert a more dramatic impact on the developing world and on the most vulnerable groups in all societies. In a recent document, the World Bank estimates that, in 2009, the current global economic crisis could push an additional 53 million people below the threshold of US$2 a day. This figure is in addition to the 130 million people pushed into poverty in 2008 by the increase in food and energy prices. Such trends seriously threaten the achievement of the fight against poverty in the Millennium Development Goals by 2015. Evidence indicates that children, in particular, will suffer the most from economic hardship, and a strong increase in the infant mortality rate in poor countries is forecast for 2009.

It is well known that low-income countries are heavily dependent upon two financing flows: foreign aid and migrant remittances. Both flows are expected to decline significantly over the next months, due to the worsening of the economic crisis. Despite the official reaffirmation of commitment by donors to increase Official Development Assistance (ODA) in accord with the Gleneagles agreement, currently most donors are not on track to meet their targets for significant scale-up of ODA by 2010. Moreover, the most recent figures reveal a slowing down of aid flows. This results in worry that a possible direct effect of the global economic crisis will be a major reduction of aid to the poor countries. On the other hand, remittances from migrant workers already have been reduced significantly. This threatens the economic survival of entire families who derive a consistent share of their income from the transfer of funds by relatives working overseas.

The Delegation of the Holy See, Mr President, would like to focus on a specific case in this crisis: its impact on the human rights of children, which exemplifies, as well, what is symptomatic of the destructive impact on all other social and economic rights. At present, some important rights of poor people are heavily dependent on official aid flows and on workers' remittances. These include the right to health, education and food. In several poor countries, in fact, educational, health and nutritional programs are implemented with the help of aid flows from official donors. Should the economic crisis reduce this assistance, the successful completion of these programs could be threatened. By the same token, in many poor regions, entire families can afford to have their children educated and decently nourished due to remittances received from migrants. If the reduction of both aid and remittances continue, it will deprive children of the right to be educated, creating a double negative consequence. Not only will we prevent children from the full exercise of their talent that, in turn, could be put to use for the common good, but also the preconditions will be established for long-range economic hardship. Lower educational investment today, in fact, will be translated into lower future growth. At the same time, poor nutrition among children significantly worsens life-expectancy by increasing both child and adult mortality rates. The negative economic consequences of this go beyond the personal dimension and affect entire societies.

Mr President, let me mention another consequence of the global economic crisis that could be particularly relevant for the mandate of the United Nations. All too often, periods of severe economic hardship have been characterized by the rise in power of governments with dubious commitments to democracy. The Holy See prays that such consequences will be avoided in the present crisis, since they would result in a serious threat for the diffusion of basic human rights for which this institution has so tenaciously struggled.

The last fifty years have witnessed some great achievements in poverty reduction. Mr President, these achievements are at risk, and a coherent approach is required to preserve them through a renewed sense of solidarity, especially for the segments of population and for the countries more affected by the crisis. Old and recent mistakes will be repeated, however, if concerted international action is not undertaken to promote and protect all human rights and if direct financial and economic activities are not placed on an ethical road that can prioritize persons, their productivity and their rights over the greed that can result from a fixation on profit alone.

WHAT IS THE SOURCE OF VALUE?*

Mr President,

For 90 years the International Labour Organization has been a protagonist and witness of social progress. Today it confronts another major challenge through its tripartite system of concertation: it is called to play a critical role in confronting the consequences of the current economic crisis on workers, their families and the entire human community, especially on the most vulnerable groups, not least among them the workers of the informal economy and those who lose the right to social protection by losing their job. In fact, 'those whose voice has least force in the political scene are precisely the ones who suffer most from the harmful effects of a crisis for which they do not bear responsibility'.[1] The global economy is experiencing its deepest downturn in 50 years: the world GDP is expected to shrink by 1.5 per cent in the current year and the forecasts for the next years point to only a mild and gradual recovery. After the financial turbulence of the past year, it is now the real economy that is hit hard. The consequences on the labor market are particularly worrying. ILO forecast an increase in world unemployment to over 7 per cent in 2009 up from 5.7 per cent in 2007. In absolute terms this would increase the number of jobless persons by 50 million. Thus, the Global Jobs Pact becomes an ethical requirement.

The poorest economies have been hit hardest during the last two years, first and momentarily by the increase in food prices, and later by the adverse effects of the economic crisis. In these countries, even persons able to retain a job could be exposed to extreme poverty. Forecasts speak of tens of millions of people who could fall into extreme poverty in the poorest regions in the world, mainly in Sub-Saharan Africa. The search for employment has also become more complicated for the young entering the labor market; their expectations challenge society to devise new measures to allow them to lend their energy and capacities to the growth of the economy.

The current economic and financial crisis demands effective measures to address and change the behaviors, practices and misjudgments

* Statement delivered at the 98th Session of the International Labour Conference, 10 June 2009.

1 Pope Benedict XVI, Letter to British Prime Minister Mr Gordon Brown ahead of the G20 Summit, 30 March 2009.

that led to it. It has shown the frailty of financial wealth and the uncertain role that capital has in our economies. In a period where markets are attributing so little value to financial wealth and are emphasizing the risk associated to capital, a crucial question emerges: what is the source of value? What has true value?

In this context, an essential reply emerges, and it is exactly what the social doctrine of the Church has always stressed: while being complementary to capital, labor has an intrinsic priority over capital. Labor proceeds from the person; is an inherent expression of personal identity; and ultimately finds its source of value in the richness and depth of the person: 'there is no doubt that human work has an ethical value of its own, which clearly and directly remains linked to the fact that the one who carries it out is a person.'[2]

Therefore, labor has value not only because it produces a valuable object nor because it has a definitive meaning in itself, but because it is an act of the person. As stated by John-Paul II, 'in the final analysis it is always man who is the purpose of the work, whatever work it is that is done by man – even if the common scale of values rates it as the merest "service", as the most monotonous even the most alienating work.'[3] This productive work is at the base of the real economy rather than speculation that is prompted solely by greed for profit.

Mr President,

Over the years ILO has placed much emphasis on the notion of decent jobs. We can say that decent work is at the center of ILO policy and initiatives. However, in the ILO jargon, decency is mainly related to the provision and realization of standards in terms of safety, wages, health, environment, and similar rights. In this respect, there is a risk that by putting the emphasis on standards we restrict the notion of work to the task that has to be performed. This approach not only restricts the definition of decency but also limits the notion of work to its objective dimension: what is produced, how it is produced and in what way it is produced.

While the Holy See praises all the efforts that are aimed at improving working conditions, especially of the poor, as well as the introduction of new standards, like the proposed instrument for the protection of

[2] Pope John Paul II, Encyclical Letter, *Laborem Exercens*, § 6. [3] Ibid.

domestic workers, it stresses the need to recognize that a work-centered strategy has to put the person, not the task, at the center of the production process. If this is done, then decency acquires a new importance and a more profound meaning because it is linked directly to the person and his dignity. In fact, it is the dignity of the person that provides the basis for setting standards that make a job decent.

Work, then, acquires a new subjective dimension in addition to the objective one. Since the person is the primary subject to undertake work activity, the subjective dimension of work emerges as a more important and complete aspect that allows the self-realization of the person as an individual and, most importantly, in her relation to society. In the majority of cases, work is not just an act of the person directed to personal interests, but also a social act whereby men and women work with, and relate to others.

The recognition that the value of the work lies in the dignity of the person allows the notion of work to be inserted in a wider and more profound context that sustains it. As a result of this approach, when losing his job an individual can experience economic difficulties and hardships but does not lose his dignity.

Mr President,

The recognition of these essential features of human work has two strategic implications for dealing with the current crisis and defining a strategy for economic recovery.

In implementing policy actions to tackle the global economic slowdown, the first objective should be the preservation and protection of employment. The general consensus on the priority of labor over capital notwithstanding, when an economic crisis calls for restructuring, all too often employment reduction is the first action undertaken. A conclusion could be drawn that labor is not the most crucial and important factor but, on the contrary, is a major obstacle to economic efficiency. The truth is that labor not only is a decisive factor in economic efficiency but also is a crucial element of social stability. Thus we need to be aware of the risk that the resumption of employment may arrive too late after the economic recovery since this would pose serious socio-economic problems. For millions of men and women the loss of job becomes a source of economic hardship for the entire family, thus dangerously widening the economic and social impact of the crisis. In addition, when unemployed, individuals tend to lose and waste their skills, further reducing the likelihood of finding a new job and ultimately depleting the overall human capital of society.

Decent work, then, is the main road to overcome the current crisis, a strategy that as well can create the conditions for a stable and lasting economic development. We must bet on the person's creative work and on her/his talents.

The world is populated by millions and millions of persons who can put their talents and ideas at the service of economic recovery. Every person, irrespective of race, sex and religion, has gifts that can be employed in and contribute to the world of work. The task of the governments and of economic institutions is to create the conditions under which these talents can be put to the best use. Society is challenged to do its best to prevent the dissipation and loss of such talents, even through new creative forms of participation in the system of production.

In several developing countries, many millions of individuals are still trapped by hunger and extreme poverty. Often these persons are so overwhelmed by their basic needs (food, safety, health, etc.) that they are incapable of putting their talents to work. For this reason, even if the current economic condition is not favorable, official aid flows to poor countries should not be reduced since they represent a crucial share of national income and a decisive element in allowing them to look at the future with brighter hope. Global solidarity pays back high returns for the global economy. For this reason, several local Churches have taken the initiative of launching special loan and solidarity funds in support of workers who have lost their job so they may not lose their dignity and their human rights.

The second element in the strategy to overcome the crisis should be to design policy initiatives that give particular attention to sustaining small and medium-sized enterprises. SMEs in fact are by far the predominant form of enterprise in advanced economies as well as in developing countries and as such they account also for a large share of employment. Most importantly, SMEs are the cradle of the entrepreneurial initiative and the context where millions of persons contribute their talents and skills for the realization of their desires and the achievement of the common good.

Two aspects appear critical for SMEs: the first is the provision of credit. At present SMEs appear to be particularly penalized by the severe credit crunch that has characterized domestic and international financial markets. Efforts should be invested in finding the most suitable instruments and initiatives to alleviate credit restrictions and to support these firms in the difficult road to economic recovery.

The second aspect is linked to the labor market. Currently, in the majority of countries employment protection legislation is designed primarily for large firms while small firms are excluded from many policy initiatives. As a consequence, economic viability of SMEs appears to be the precondition for any effort aimed at preserving employment. In other words, in the case of small firms, employment insurance is indispensable to their economic viability.

Mr President,

The concerns raised in recent years about a 'jobless growth' are now evolving into fears that the coming years will be characterized by 'labor-intensive restructuring' and a 'jobless recovery'. We must act decisively and in a timely way in order to prevent this occurrence. If we succeed, we can transform the economic crisis into an opportunity to reaffirm the centrality of the human person in labor relations; to encourage a life-style of sobriety, solidarity and responsibility; to direct all economic activities to the common good. The crisis will be reined in, as the Holy Father has observed, if all forces of society will seek 'to offer security to families and stability to workers and, through appropriate regulations and controls, to restore ethic to the financial world'.[4]

[4] Pope Benedict XVI, Letter to British Prime Minister Mr Gordon Brown ahead of the G20 Summit, 30 March 2009.

THE WTO, THE MULTILATERAL TRADING SYSTEM AND THE CURRENT GLOBAL ECONOMIC ENVIRONMENT*

Mr Chairman,

The current economic crisis has heavily impacted the poor of the world. On several occasions it has prompted the Holy See to call the attention of States and international organizations to its dramatic consequences, high unemployment in particular. This Seventh Session of the Ministerial Conference of the World Trade Organization is an important opportunity to renew the commitment of the international community for concerted action to lead developed and developing countries on the road to recovery and growth. The recent social Encyclical of Pope Benedict XVI, *Caritas in Veritate*, presents an extensive analysis of the present global economic environment and offers some practical indications for fair solutions. My Delegation would like to invite you to a thoughtful reflection on this major statement and its articulate vision of development. This document reaffirms that every country has a right to define its own economic model, but within an inclusive and fair globalization where solidarity, investments, trade, technology transfer, capacity building and knowledge sharing are put at the service of a development with a new face. Such a new model of development is based on the centrality of the person, recognizing that each human being has a dignity, desire for freedom and fulfillment of his/her deepest aspirations in all economic mechanisms.

In today's complex international scene, there are many and overlapping actors and causes affecting both underdevelopment and development. As a result, difficulties in the functioning of multilateral institutions are increasing and particularistic solutions to a common problem are adopted. The current state of trade talks is a clear example of this phenomenon. The slow progress of the Doha Round of negotiations has spurred the growth of several Preferential Trade Agreements (PTAs) as an alternative route for achieving trade liberalization. It is certainly true that in principle PTAs that meet the full spirit of Article 24 of GATT constitute a step toward global free trade; however, it is also well known that when PTAs are asymmetric, involving advanced economies and developing countries, they could backfire for the latter countries. Therefore,

* Statement delivered at the 7th Session of the Ministerial Conference of the World Trade Organization, 1 December 2009.

given the development goal of current trade negotiations, we must recognize that the interests of the poorest countries are better safeguarded within the rules of the multilateral trading system. In this respect the present Ministerial Conference represents a unique opportunity to relaunch trade negotiations.

Moreover, the confirmation of the centrality of the multilateral system is a crucial opportunity to reaffirm that a truly pluralistic approach based on the cooperation of each single member could allow the achievement of the common good by respecting the dignity of every single person as a member of the one community of the human family.

The multilateral trading system and trade liberalization have stimulated economic growth worldwide, including in least developed countries (LDCs). But disparities in the level of development continue within and among nations. Besides, the financial crisis is likely to have a considerable adverse effect on international trade as well. The Doha Round of multilateral trade negotiations has not been concluded, jeopardizing a continued dynamic expansion in the exports of developing and transition economies. However, important positive agreements have been reached in the process. It is therefore crucial that every effort is made in order to allow the realization of these benefits so that new resources could be made available to the development particularly of the poorest countries.

'If the market is governed solely by the principle of the equivalence in value of exchanged goods', observes Pope Benedict XVI, 'it cannot produce the social cohesion that it requires in order to function well. *Without internal forms of solidarity and mutual trust, the market cannot completely fulfill its proper economic function.*'[1] Thus, what kind of 'equivalence of value' can propose the billion men, women and children who suffer from hunger and deprivation? Their income is too low to be even noticed by the market; but if the market does not see them, it cannot respond to their needs. In this case 'economic activity cannot solve all social problems through the simple application of *commercial logic*.' The 'bottom billion' cannot be left out of the picture. It seems evident that the market cannot rely only on itself. It 'needs to be *directed towards the pursuit of the common good*, for which the political community in particular must also take responsibility'.[2] In this setting, the Aid for Trade initiative, launched at the last Ministerial Conference, has proved to be able to combine market mechanisms with the need of solidarity, making good progress since its launch. Moreover, if the promises made during the G20

[1] Ibid., § 35 [2] Ibid., § 36.

meeting held last April will be fulfilled, additional important resources will be made available. However, several poor countries have not been able to fully exploit the potential benefits of this initiative. We should make every effort to extend these potential gains to the countries that most need them.

Given the recent FAO Conference on Food Security and the critical issue represented by agriculture in current trade talks, allow me to raise the point that the market, such as it is sometimes promoted, cannot answer, for example, the problem of malnutrition and hunger in the world without recourse to non-market values like solidarity and trust.

It is well known that in several countries the State takes the initiative to acquire foodstuff on the market for the most underprivileged. These products are subsidized and resold at low prices, a procedure that in a way inserts the poorest people in the market since their need is translated into solvent request and becomes perceptible by the market. This approach, however, represents a high cost for the State not sustainable in particular for many of the least advanced countries. Here solidarity between rich and poor countries finds a logical role to play. The ensuing benefit affects also the economy because the decrease of social inequality prevents 'the progressive erosion of "social capital": the network of relationships of trust, dependability, and respect for rules, all of which are indispensable for any form of civil coexistence'.[3]

Indeed, as recently stressed by a WTO report, world agricultural exports have almost tripled over the last twenty years and the amount of food that is actually globally produced is technically able to satisfy the current demand. 'Hunger is not so much dependent on lack of material things as on shortage of social resources, the most important of which are institutional. What is missing, in other words, is a network of economic institutions capable of guaranteeing regular access to sufficient food and water for nutritional needs, and also capable of addressing the primary needs and necessities ensuing from genuine food crises, whether due to natural causes or political irresponsibility, nationally and internationally. The problem of food insecurity needs to be addressed … by investing in rural infrastructures, irrigation systems, transport, organization of markets, and in the development and dissemination of agricultural technology that can make the best use of the human, natural and socio-economic resources that are more readily available at the local level, while guaranteeing their sustainability over the long term as well. All this needs to

[3] Ibid., § 32.

be accomplished with the involvement of local communities in choices and decisions that affect the use of agricultural land.[4] In this way a more generous and appropriately diversified Aid for Trade can make a real difference.

The increase in agricultural productivity at the local level of the poorest countries would allow not only the increase of the overall supply of food but could also contribute to the stabilization of commodity prices that would be less dependent on climate change. This latter aspect could significantly reduce the level of uncertainty that severely harms farmers whose incomes are excessively exposed to the high variability in food prices. The success of this effort would bring about an improvement in the income of rural populations where many of the world's poor are concentrated, thus contributing to resolve the problem of hunger.

Moreover, investing in agriculture will have a multiplier effect as agriculture plays a multi-functional role not only in the production of food, but also as a place of life and of socialization, an instrument for protection of the environment and shaper of the landscape. In all, the attention to agriculture and its relationship to trade success comes when primacy is given to the human person.

Mr Chairman,

In conclusion, if this Conference signals the political will to make progress in monitoring and surveillance to disputes, accessions, Aid for Trade, technical assistance and international governance, it will be a decisive step towards the creation of an international trading system based on the principle of social justice. Indeed social ethics like transparency, honesty, solidarity and responsibility cannot be ignored: they preserve a person-centered goal in any economic activity, prevent crises caused by greedy speculation and provide a comprehensive approach that does not separate the social consequences from economic and environmental decisions. But there is an additional step that ensures success in the long run, the inclusion of the dimension of gratuitousness and the logic of gift as an expression of fraternity and involvement of the entire human family both as a protagonist of development and as the primary objective of trade and economic activity.

[4] Ibid., § 27.

ON THE REFORM OF THE GLOBAL FINANCIAL SYSTEM AND THE ECONOMIC MODELS*

Mr President,

My Delegation joins previous speakers in expressing our condolences and solidarity to the people of Chile for the victims of the recent earthquake.

Mr President,

The Delegation of the Holy See wants to restate its conviction that the perspective of human rights provides a positive contribution for a solution to the current financial crisis. Even though some signs of recovery seem visible, the crisis continues to aggravate the conditions of millions of people in their access to the basic necessities of life and has adversely compromised the retirement plans of many. This situation, therefore, calls for new regulations and a sound global system of governance that ensures a sustainable and comprehensive path to development for all. In the establishment of new regulations and reliable governance there exists a unique opportunity to address the root causes of the crisis and to affirm an integrated approach to the implementation of all economic, social, civil and political human rights as outlined in the Universal Declaration of Human Rights.

United Nations reports give plenty of evidence regarding the many negative consequences of the financial crisis: the scandal of hunger, the growing inequality worldwide, millions of unemployed people and millions of others reduced to extreme poverty, institutional failures, lack of social protection for countless vulnerable persons. These imbalances, the Holy Father reminds us in the recent Encyclical *Caritas in Veritate*, 'are produced when economic action, conceived merely as an engine for wealth creation, is detached from political action, conceived as a means for pursuing justice through redistribution'.[1] Equity and justice are essential criteria in the management of the world economy.

The enjoyment of human rights becomes possible when States translate principles into law and make change on the ground a reality. While the State is the first actor in the implementation of human rights,

* Statement delivered at the 13th Session of the Human Rights Council, 3 March 2010.

1 Pope Benedict XVI, Encyclical Letter, *Caritas in Veritate*, § 36.

it cannot fail to collaborate with all other players in its own civil society and with the international community, interconnected and interdependent as we are in today's globalized world. In fact, the common goal is the protection and respect of human dignity that binds together the entire human family, a unity rooted on the four basic principles of the centrality of the human person, solidarity, subsidiarity and the common good. In this context, the review of the Human Rights Council should aim also at making change on the ground a reality and the concrete implementation of human rights, its priority.

Mr President,

An important message conveyed by Pope Benedict XVI in *Caritas in Veritate* in this moment of economic crisis is the invitation to overcome the obsolete dichotomy between the economic, social and ecological spheres. Markets and freedom are important requirements in building a healthy society, but the context within which they operate is global and must include the universal principles of honesty, justice, solidarity and in addition the principles of 'reciprocity and gift'.[2] The focus of concern in the reform of the financial system, and the economic models that are operative in government programs and corporate policies, should shift from goods and services to the persons who are recipients of these services; in this way, they have access to the resources to improve their position in life and thus place their talents at the service of their local community and the universal common good. The social doctrine of the Church has always pursued such a goal with special care for the more vulnerable members of society. In fact, by giving priority to human beings and the created order that supports them on their earthly journey, we can modify the rules that govern the financial system to serve concrete change, to move away from old habits of greed that led to the present crisis, and to promote effective integral development and the implementation of human rights since 'the primary capital to be safeguarded and valued is the human person in his or her integrity' (*Caritas in Veritate*, § 25).

[2] Ibid. 'The great challenge before us, accentuated by the problems of development in this global era and made even more urgent by the economic and financial crisis, is to demonstrate, in thinking and behaviour, not only that traditional principles of social ethics like transparency, honesty and responsibility cannot be ignored or attenuated, but also that in *commercial relationships* the *principle of gratuitousness* and the logic of gift as an expression of fraternity can and must *find their place within normal economic activity*. This is a human demand at the present time, but it is also demanded by economic logic. It is a demand both of charity and of truth.'

HUMAN RIGHTS AND FOREIGN DEBT: THE NEGATIVE IMPACT OF VULTURE FUNDS*

Mr President,

Let me start by thanking the independent expert for his report presented to the Council. The report draws attention to the negative impacts of 'vulture fund' activities on international debt relief efforts and on the capacity of indebted poor countries that have benefited from debt relief to create the necessary conditions for the realization of human rights. It also examines the measures and proposals designed to combat these speculative investors.

The sharp contraction of the global economy that began in the second half of 2008 and accelerated into the first quarter of 2009 doesn't appear to be slowing down. The economic situation is still fragile and prospects are still uncertain in all regions of the world. The financial crisis was harsher in the developed countries and consequently its effects have been felt most severely there, but the subsequent collapse of aggregate demand in those countries is still working its way through the global economy and in particular on the least developed countries. The international community cannot ignore this fact; while reaffirming the principle that debts must be repaid, ways must be found that do not compromise the 'fundamental right of peoples to subsistence and progress'.[1] The economy is not above the priority of human rights since it is at the service of the human person and the common good.

The voluntary nature of international debt relief schemes has created opportunities for vulture funds to acquire defaulted sovereign debt at vastly reduced prices and then seek repayment of the full face value of the debt through litigation, seizure of assets or political pressure. The goal of such activities is to obtain high returns at bargain prices regardless of the ethical consequences of such actions. The so-called vulture fund activities complicate sovereign debt restructuring by causing inequitable burden sharing among creditors, and undermine trade and investment relations of the countries that they target.

* Statement delivered at the 14th Session of the Human Rights Council – Item 3: *Interactive Dialogue on Human Rights and Foreign Debt*, 2 June 2010.

[1] Pope John Paul II, Encyclical Letter, *Centesimus Annus*, § 35: AAS 83 (1991), p. 838; cf. also the document *At the Service of the Human Community: An Ethical Approach to the International Debt Question*, published by the Pontifical Commission 'Iustitia et Pax'.

The debt of the developing countries must be placed in a broader context of economic, political, human rights and technological relations concerns as well as of international collaboration in pursuing the objectives of the common good. This interdependence calls for a new and more comprehensive concept of solidarity which respects the equal dignity of all peoples. Solidarity implies an awareness and acceptance of co-responsibility for the causes and the solutions relative to international debt. Co-responsibility will help to create or restore relations based on trust between nations (creditors and debtors) and between the various actors (political authorities, commercial banks, international organizations) for cooperation in the search for solutions. Thus mutual trust is an indispensable value which must be constantly renewed.

While we support the solution proposed in the report, our Delegation would like to ask the independent expert what form of State control and preventive measures in the financial market could impede the emergence of manipulative strategies that damage the Heavily Indebted Poor Countries (HIPCs).

THE SUFFERING OF PEOPLE SHOULD NOT BE THE COEFFICIENT OF ADJUSTMENT OF THE ECONOMIC SYSTEM*

Mr President,

The effects of the financial and economic crisis have globally damaged the welfare of families and individuals. Timid, uneven and uncertain signs of recovery notwithstanding, the impact of this recession has stifled progress in poverty reduction, increased unemployment in developed countries and every household has suffered setbacks in low-income countries. In 2015, 20 million more people in Sub-Saharan Africa, and 53 million more people globally, will find themselves in extreme poverty.[1] While there is general agreement on the need for structural reforms, vested interests must not lay most of the burden on wage earners, rural people and already marginalized groups in society. Economic mechanisms without ethical criteria will not lead to constructive solutions.

The crisis can open a new perspective on the role of markets and on the role of the State. The food crisis of 2008 has shown that countries lacking basic food supplies could not simply rely on the forces of the market to ensure food for their people. Several export countries responded with protectionism and speculation resulting from the perception of shortage. Countries heavily dependent on food import witnessed serious protests. Thus a certain degree of self-sufficiency and a better regulation of the commodities markets became a logical conclusion.

The 2009 financial crisis has shown that financial markets are not self-regulating. Greed prevented the interruption of a process whose systemic risks had been foreseen by many. Financial measures and the assurance provided by States and Central Banks saved the banking system and avoided financial meltdown but were not capable of preventing the subsequent serious economic crisis that has resulted in a significant increase of unemployment and precariousness and has affected the most vulnerable persons and countries. Another result has been the enormous amount of

* Statement delivered at the 99th Session of the International Labour Conference, 10 June 2010.

[1] The crisis will likely have serious costs as measured by several human development indicators: 1.2 million more children under five and 265,000 more infants will die between 2009 and 2015; 50,000 more students will not complete primary education in 2015; 100 million fewer people will have access to safe drinking water in 2015. Cf. World Bank, *Global Monitoring Report 2010: The MDGs after the Crisis*.

public debt generated, especially by major advanced economies. In industrialized countries, in coming years, gross public debt will exceed 100 per cent of GDP thus raising sustainability issues. Governments, weakened by the level of their debt, feel obliged by the financial markets to reduce it. Public budgets and growth will be affected: taxes will increase, buying power will decrease and unemployment will grow. The weak economic recovery runs the risk of being jeopardized.

This is a delicate condition for major advanced economies, since the process of fiscal consolidation will constrain economic growth. Recent experience shows that the adjustment coefficient is the level of employment, the buying power of people and their ability to feed, educate and care for themselves. Justice demands that the suffering of people should not be the coefficient of adjustment of the economic system. While the merits of open markets in the creation of wealth should be acknowledged, some additional and internationally coordinated action, as well as the development of some means of common governance, appear necessary. We need to keep in mind that work is more than wages; it is the means to self-fulfillment and the way to achieve one's life project.

The Delegation of the Holy See fully supports the aim of the ILO to give priority to persons and their work in the search for innovative and dynamic policies aimed at removing structural impediments to the recovery of the economy. The attention to domestic workers and the positive vote taken on a new binding instrument for their protection express preference for the most vulnerable members of society. Domestic workers are doubly at risk. First, they come from the most disadvantaged segments of society with very limited resources for protection. Extreme necessity pushes them to take up any job available, even though, in more than a few cases, conditions at work are very hard. Second, the ambience of their employment is open to exploitation. Women and girls constitute the majority within this category of workers. Often they lack juridical and social protection, fair remuneration, limits on the amount of hours they are expected to work, a guarantee for a weekly period of rest, safeguards during times of illness or for maternity. When abuses occur, there is no appeal and the only option is to escape and thus to lose salary due as well as employment. On many occasions, within the privacy of the domestic walls, the dignity of domestic workers is violated. Physical and sexual harassment are not uncommon. Racial and religious identities expose these workers, especially women, to heavy discrimination.

If the domestic worker is an immigrant, especially if without proper documentation and/or a labour contract, his/her vulnerability is much greater. But we should consider that this is one of the few sectors of the economy where immigrant workers are complementing and not substituting indigenous workers, since typically they accept jobs that the latter are unwilling to assume. In many poor countries, young girls are engaged in domestic work and their own families see their service as a normal contribution to family survival. On the other hand, domestic workers assume a critical role, especially in Western societies, where life-style and demographic changes demand their presence. They become an important presence in the family since they manage the household, care for the elderly and for the children and thus allow mothers and daughters to pursue careers and active roles in society. Another important contribution offered by domestic workers is found in the remittances that they send home and that benefit families and local development. The opportunity and necessity of a new binding norm, an International Convention on Domestic Workers, appears undeniable: it will promote opportune national legislation for their protection, support their rights of association, of collective negotiation, and of union representation. An education campaign already should start to make domestic workers, as well as employers, aware of reciprocal duties and rights. This widening horizon on the world of work offers both a challenge and new possibilities, as the social Encyclical of Pope Benedict XVI, *Caritas in Veritate*, states: '*labour unions* – which have always been encouraged and supported by the Church ... Looking to wider concerns than the specific category of labour for which they were formed, union organizations are called to address some of the new questions arising in our society ... The global context in which work takes place also demands that national labour unions, which tend to limit themselves to defending the interests of their registered members, should turn their attention to those outside their membership, and in particular to workers in developing countries where social rights are often violated. The protection of these workers ... will enable trade unions to demonstrate the authentic ethical and cultural motivations that made it possible for them, in a different social and labour context, to play a decisive role in development.'[2]

As part of this widening of horizons in the struggle for a global implementation of decent work, attention should focus on other categories of workers in need of protection: the masses of still unorganized workers, rural workers, and unemployed youth. The rights of unorganized workers are too often ignored, and, as a result, their security in the

[2] Pope Benedict XVI, Encyclical Letter, *Caritas in Veritate*, § 64.

workplace, their protection from unjust firing, and their entitlement to at least a minimum salary are not respected. Rural workers, in particular, are left out of the range of attention. Not always ready to confront market forces because of lack of training or lack of information, due to the current crisis, they risk being deprived of public support for technical capacity-building or for trade. These are badly needed measures responding to readjustment policies that proved to be counter-productive. Thus some of these policies should be revised, and an allowance made for an incremental opening of borders for homogeneous groups of countries, for as long as they can improve their productivity and their capacity to profit from the market. In 92 countries, agriculture represents more than 75 per cent of the GDP; between 2 billion and 2.5 billion persons derive their income from agriculture. This sector of the economy is a source of work, of food, of social networks, of emancipation of women, and of protection (or degradation) of the environment. By creatively supporting work in this sector, malnutrition and poverty can be reduced and eventually eliminated, and such workers integrated in the global economy.

Finally, child labor and youth unemployment call for a concerted response. More than 215 million children are constrained to work, many in dangerous conditions. The number of unemployed youth has increased by 8.5 million between 2008 and 2009, the largest year-on-year increase in the last 10 years, and by more than 10 million since 2007. Wasted capacities and frustration can have disastrous social consequences for the future.

Mr President,

The economic crisis can become an opportunity. The complexity of the situation makes it difficult to make appropriate choices. If, however, the recovery is comprehensive in its embrace of all workers, renews the tripartite dialogue that is at the core of the ILO mission, and gives priority to people and their talents, then a step forward will be taken in the pursuit of justice by the international community. In this approach, A Global Jobs Pact indeed will reduce the time lag between economic recovery and a recovery with decent work opportunities. If a reduction in military expenses is added to these efforts, rather than the 6 per cent increase in such expenses that occurred in 2009, more resources can be channeled toward the recovery of truly decent jobs. Men and women, workers, employers and entrepreneurs, constitute the best resources available; their intelligence, creativity and energy can develop new jobs and sustain innovation if their freedom is not detached from the responsibility to prevent the emergence of financial speculation at the expense of the real economy and of greed destructive of jobs and savings.

In conclusion, good decisions are necessary in order to move toward a post-crisis phase of the globalization of the economy and of work. But only a corresponding 'ethical interaction of consciences and minds' will give rise to integral development[3] where the human person is at the center of labour relations, confident to journey toward a better future.

[3] Ibid., § 9.

GUIDING PRINCIPLES ON BUSINESS AND HUMAN RIGHTS: IMPLEMENTING THE UNITED NATIONS 'PROTECT, RESPECT AND REMEDY' FRAMEWORK*

Mr President,

With regard to human rights as they relate to business, the Delegation of the Holy See welcomes the work and contributions of the UN Special Representative of the Secretary General on business and human rights and endorses the Guiding Principles on Business and Human Rights Framework. The process of developing the Framework and Guiding Principles has been open to all stakeholders. Moreover, substantial input has been provided by civil society groups working with communities that, either directly or indirectly, have been negatively impacted by corporate practices. As a work in progress, this document serves as a base to continue an important dialogue on business and human rights among all relevant stakeholders. The Framework does not answer all questions and dilemmas related to this field, but it does provide a foundation for further work to develop over time.

The Framework makes a positive contribution by creating a standard whereby companies are expected to adopt comprehensive human rights policies; assess, on an ongoing basis, the potential and current impact on human rights that is exerted by their operations and throughout their supply chains; to integrate their analysis and findings into respective company policies and culture; and to openly monitor and report on their performance.

The focus is on the prevention of human rights violations in the first place, and on remediating any violations that have been caused directly or indirectly. This approach is consistent with that outlined by Pope Benedict XVI in his recent Encyclical where he states that 'business management cannot concern itself only with the interests of the proprietors, but must also assume responsibility for all the other stakeholders who contribute to the life of the business: the workers, the clients, the suppliers of various elements of production, the community of reference'.[1] In view of the size and reach of multinational and global corporations and the influence and impact that their operations have on millions of people across

* Statement delivered at the 17th Session of the Human Rights Council – Item 3: *General Debate*, 3 June 2011.

[1] Pope Benedict XVI, Encyclical Letter, *Caritas in Veritate*, § 40.

the globe, the recognition of this multi-layered and multi-dimensional responsibility becomes ever more urgent and essential. TNCs bear a significant responsibility to respect and promote human rights and to support integral development that enhances the quality of life in the LDCs.

Regrettably, TNCs have failed to measure up to this standard on numerous occasions, have violated established rules and regulations, and thus have caused exceptional damage. Evidence of such failures can be found in the manufacturing sector when workers have been deprived of a living wage, when safety and security measures have not been observed, and especially when forced or child labor has been tolerated. The extractives and energy sectors, for example, remain particularly susceptible to a corporate culture that operates without sufficient regard for the rights of indigenous and local communities and deprives these same communities of safe water, food and livelihoods. In other instances, in order to circumvent social and environmental laws, some TNCs have resorted to the practice of sub-contracting without adequately monitoring the policies and practices of their business partners. In countries where governments lack the resources to monitor these companies, it must be recognized and enforced that the principal contractor carries responsibility for assuring that subcontracting partners observe and respect such rules.

The new Guiding Principles that aim at operationalizing the 'Protect, Respect and Remedy' Framework make a major contribution to clarifying the role of the State's duty to protect human rights and establish policies and mechanisms to hold companies accountable for human rights violations. The Principles clearly articulate the role of companies to respect human rights by, at a very minimum, avoiding adverse impact on human rights that may be caused through their various activities. These Principles also describe and promote the avenues required by individuals and communities in order to remedy any human rights abuses caused by corporations. Also necessary are a more effective mechanism of enforcement and surveillance as well as a clearly stated commitment by companies to respect the laws and regulations of the countries where they are operating. In this manner, TNCs will assure their compliance with the demands of their social contract and license to operate and to behave as good corporate citizens.

A strong and effective follow-up mechanism is needed in order to ensure that the full benefit of the work completed thus far will be brought to fruition. It should include the possibility of receiving communications and undertaking investigations, and of making recommendations and providing expert advice. Expertise and good practice in the field of human rights is constantly improving. Therefore, when designing follow-up mechanisms, we should aim not simply to preserve outcomes to date, but also to ensure that these will stay relevant and will be developed further. The Guiding Principles provide for such an approach, since they call upon States to periodically assess the adequacy of laws requiring business enterprises to respect human rights, to be transparent and accountable in their negotiations and contracts especially with weaker and under-resourced jurisdictions where they operate, and to be especially attentive to the needs of vulnerable populations – women, children, indigenous peoples and people living in conflict zones. In addition capacity building is necessary and should be initiated by offering technical expertise to those who need it most.

Mr President,

Looking at the future, we hope that the increased protection and promotion of human rights by TNCs, operating within a sound ethical framework, can promote a globalization that has a human face and a sustainable framework. The implementation of these Guiding Principles should be located in a multi-stakeholder process and based on the principle of subsidiarity. It should involve all business actors, such as national and local governments, labour unions, consumer associations, grass-roots organizations of the civil society, companies and investors. It should establish the necessary structures, for example, judicial and non-judicial remedies, to address the human rights issues that emerge. Such structures will be an important component of a future that is rooted in justice, especially for the individuals and communities most immediately affected by corporate abuse. The constructive and welcome engagement of all stakeholders in international economic and commercial matters will help to achieve an integral development and solidarity which is grounded in a vision of the future that guarantees an equitable distribution of resources and is responsive to the interdependence of people.[2] By accepting these principles and supporting the proposed Framework, the United Nations and the Human Rights Council can provide the leadership that will assist TNCs, civil society, investors and States to promote the common good of the human family.

[2] Cf. Pontifical Council for Justice and Peace, *Compendium of the Social Doctrine of the Church*, § 373.

THERE IS NO FUTURE FOR THE ECONOMY UNLESS IT INVOLVES THE ETHICAL DIMENSION*

Mr Chairman,

The Holy See Delegation extends its congratulations to the Russian Federation, Montenegro, Samoa and Vanuatu for their accession to the World Trade Organization.

Mr Chairman,

The eighth Ministerial Conference of the WTO takes place at unprecedented times for the world economy. The recovery from the financial crisis of 2008 lasted only a few months and there are already clear signs of a slowing down of economic activity in advanced and emerging economies. If these signs are confirmed, the world risks plunging into a double-dip recession which could entail prolonged periods of stagnation and high unemployment.

The economic situation in advanced economies and in Europe is the reason for particular concern. The debt crisis is forcing several European countries to implement tough fiscal policies, with the risk of worsening the economic cycle. In these cases the weakest are penalized the most, in particular young adults, who experience an unemployment rate at the highest level in decades, and the poor confronted with a strong increase in inequality in all countries.

Evidence from the recent financial crisis has shown us that trade has been an effective tool in helping a rapid recovery. Now the primary challenge WTO faces is to sustain this approach and discourage countries to give in to the temptation of protectionism that promises to deliver some illusory short-run benefits while preventing more conspicuous long-term gains.

An additional burden could be imposed on the shoulders of the young and of the poor if they are deprived of such an effective tool for improving the economy as an open trade.

In this context, the Delegation of the Holy See would like to recall the ethical foundation of trade. Ethics is not an external element of the economy and the economy does not have a future if it does not take

* Statement delivered at the 8th Session of the Ministerial Conference of the World Trade Organization, 15–17 December 2011.

into account the ethical dimension. The economy functions not only through self-regulation of the market and much less through agreements limited to reconciling the interests of the most powerful countries, but it needs also to take into account that it functions at the service of man. The production of resources and goods and their strategic management require a sense of ethics and of the common good since without them the economy becomes naive, cynical and destined to failure. In fact, every economic decision has a moral consequence. The economy needs an ethical perspective centered on the person and able to offer sure points of reference to new generations. Economic and commercial activities oriented to development should be able to reduce poverty effectively and to alleviate the suffering of the most unprotected. On several occasions the Holy See has called attention to the urgency of a new and profound reflection on the meaning and objectives of the economy and of a far-sighted revision of the global financial and commercial architecture in order to correct problems of functioning and distortions. This revision of international economic rules must be integrated in the framework of a new global model of development. In reality, it is required by the planet's ecological state of health, and, above all, by the cultural and moral crisis of man, and the symptoms have been evident everywhere for a long time. As Pope Benedict XVI states: 'taking care of the needy means not just giving bread to the hungry, but also letting yourself ponder the causes why the other person is hungry.' Only with the acceptance of effective rules that protect the management of the economy in an ever more interdependent world will our efforts be directed toward the pursuit of the common good.

Despite the seriousness of the general economic condition and despite the strong need for improving trade, we observe that trade negotiations are at an impasse. This stalemate has lasted for several years and there is no sign that the current round of negotiations will be concluded in the near future. There is a concrete risk that the entire Doha Development Round may end in failure, jeopardizing all the efforts devoted to the promotion of development through trade.

However, looking at the work conducted during the last years, as the 'Easter package' clearly shows, significant progress has been made in several areas, and an agreement can be within reach. In other critical areas such as agriculture, positions are distant and a solution does not seem to be close.

During the current year serious attempts have been conducted in order to reach an agreement on a smaller set of issues – the so-called

LDC plus package – in order to take a step forward toward the implementation of the Doha Development Agenda. Despite the failure of this new attempt, the Delegation of the Holy See supports the adoption of a pragmatic approach and the consolidation of the progress made so far. This option ensures that countries will reap the trade liberalization benefits that, in some areas, remain significant. If the opportunity is missed, the poor will end up paying the highest cost.

The success of the Aid for Trade initiative gives evidence of the potential benefits deriving from trade and, on the other hand, of the cost of inaction. In fact, lack of decision seems to turn into an effective tool through which several countries are pursuing protectionist policies.

Another positive achievement is given by the group of countries whose accession has so significantly advanced that they are at the threshold of completion. The creation of an 'Accessions Commitments Database' allows Members, acceding governments and the Secretariat to rapidly and efficiently retrieve information on 'commitment language' for all completed accessions under Article XII of the Marrakech Agreement. Ensuring transparency and predictability in the accession process remains a key priority for the Membership and the Secretariat. In this sense my Delegation, appreciating all the efforts made by the Director General and the Secretariat, underlines the need for enhanced technical assistance and capacity building to help LDCs to complete their accession process, implement their commitments and become integrated into the multilateral trading system.

One area where progress will deliver significant and tangible benefits to poor and developing countries is that of the Rules of Origin (ROO). Negotiations to harmonize non-preferential rules of origin were launched sixteen year ago, but an agreement has not been reached so far. A solution to this problem will determine a significant step toward a more stable clear and predictable set of rules for trade talks. Transparency and predictability are particularly valuable for developing countries which are much penalised by the complexity of the current set of rules.

Preferential Rules of Origin should be amended in favour of poor countries. Often, for these economies, the potential benefits deriving from the margin of preferences are not captured because of the presence of strict ROO. In practice, ROO go against the realization of comparative advantages since poor countries tend to specialize in very simple activities characterized by low added value. If advanced economies wish to use trade as an effective tool to lift countries out of poverty they need to recognize that giving poorer countries a margin of preference is not enough without rules of origin that allow these economies to really exploit the preferences.

Mr Chairman, after years of standstill, the Ministerial Conference provides an opportunity to start taking tangible steps toward the implementation of the Doha Development Agenda. WTO members must 'think big' in order to conclude a broad deal, otherwise the risk of the marginalization of the multilateral trading system will become real. A positive conclusion of the Round will represent a win–win situation: a chance for developed countries to strengthen the confidence in the multilateral trading system, to guard against the rise of protectionism, and to boost the global economy while reducing its asymmetries; a chance for newly emerging economies to lock in those benefits permanently while avoiding new trade arrangements that may well exclude them; last but not least, a chance for the poorest developing countries to realize the gains of the Doha Development Agenda promised long ago.

Mr Chairman, to sum up, the human family has not been created to serve the market, but the market to serve the human family. If this principle is respected, even though times are difficult, fear will give way to hope.

FOREIGN DEBT VS. RIGHT TO DEVELOPMENT*

Madam President,

The Holy See strongly supports the Report's assertion that human rights as well as the rules of justice and ethics apply to all economic and social relations, including foreign debt obligations. Human rights criteria for evaluating foreign debt can be an important tool for moving development from the narrow 'economic' or material understanding to one based on integral human development, one that promotes 'the development of each man and of the whole man'.[1] This recognizes the 'right to development'[2] grounded in the humanity of each and every person, from conception to natural death, regardless of their age, nationality, race, religion, ethnicity, sex and disability status. At the same time, we acknowledge the role that corruption has played and continues to play in aggravating the problem of debt obligations in many less developed countries.

A people-centered ethics is one that is grounded in a view of the human person which emphasizes human dignity, the basis of human rights, for human rights are those rights that spring from what it means to be human. All just economic activity respects this human dignity. Wealth and debt must serve the common good. If justice is violated, wealth and debt become instruments of exploitation, especially of the poor and marginalized. But unjust, and especially exploitative, economic transactions are invalid and must be made just, even if each party agreed to the legal terms of the exchange, as may happen when the rich lend to the poor. For many years now all have come to recognize that 'the heavy burden of external debt ... compromises the economies of whole peoples and hinders their social and political progress'.[3]

Foreign debt is just a symptom of the lack of justice in the flow of capital in the world.[4] 'The debt question is part of a vaster problem: that of the persistence of poverty, sometimes even extreme, and the emergence of new inequalities which are accompanying the globalization process. If the aim is globalization without marginalization, we can no longer

* Statement delivered at the 20th Session of the Human Rights Council: *Report on Guiding Principles on Foreign Debt and Human Rights*, 11 June 2012.

1 Pope Paul VI, Encyclical Letter, *Populorum Progressio*, § 14.

2 General Assembly Resolution 41/128 of 4 December 1986.

3 Pope John Paul II noted in his World Peace Day Message of 1998, § 4, www.vatican.va/holy_father/john_paul_ii/messages/peace/documents/hf_jp-ii_mes_08121997_xxxi-world-day-for-peace_en.html.

4 Ibid.

tolerate a world in which there live side by side the immensely rich and the miserably poor, the have-nots deprived even of essentials and people who thoughtlessly waste what others so desperately need. Such contrasts are an affront to the dignity of the human person.'

Thus, in evaluating foreign loans consideration should be given to: (1) reducing unethical loan practices; and (2) better aligning foreign loans with authentic human development. If both the loan process and the loan use have to respect human rights there is a much better chance that the money from the loan will promote development and the necessary environment for the enjoyment of human rights. Many of the barriers to development arise because the human costs and benefits of economic activities are not given adequate, or any, weight in the decision-making process. 'Human costs always include economic costs, and economic dysfunctions always involve human costs',[5] and the consequent violation of human rights.

While institutionalizing the inclusion of human rights into the cost and benefit calculations will present challenges, we would like to remind the Council that every past improvement in human rights and expansion of participation and inclusion faced the same challenge. In a few words, financial relationships that increase inequality and do not promote income convergence are 'contrary to justice'.[6]

Along with the Report, and most objective observers, the Holy See recognizes that loans to developing countries have at times promoted inequality and have become barriers to development rather than serving as tools to promote development. Often this is due to changes in outside economic circumstances which can turn a good and just loan arrangement into a barrier to development and a vehicle for exploitation. One such change in outside circumstances that the Report addresses and responds to relates to fluctuations in currency values.

The Holy See supports the new principle for transparency in foreign loans at all levels and by all actors (borrowers, lenders and international agencies) in order to lessen the chance of the grave mistakes that were made in the past, when corruption led to secret loans for dubious purposes, taken out by lenders not interested in the common good, with the poor in developing countries bearing the burden. We support this

[5] Pope Benedict XVI, Encyclical Letter, *Caritas in Veritate*, § 32, www.vatican.va/holy_father/benedict_xvi/encyclicals/documents/hf_ben-xvi_enc_20090629_caritas-in-veritate_en.html.

[6] Cf. Aquinas ST, II, II, q. 78.

reform and encourage efforts to correct the injustices of past loans with more aggressive debt remission.

The Holy See hopes that 'the process of debt cancellation and reduction for the poorest countries will be continued and accelerated. At the same time, these processes must not be made conditional upon structural adjustments that are detrimental to the most vulnerable populations.'[7] The Holy See supports the Human Rights Council's call to end conditionality in debt cancellation and renegotiation, and supports its call to respect the sovereignty and right of each country to independently plan its own development strategies and not be forced by outside agencies or governments to pursue policies which are more in the interest of the lending nations than the common good of the developing nations. Furthermore, programs for debt cancellation or relief should not result in insurmountable obstacles to future responsible borrowing that may be critically necessary for the long-term development and prosperity of the country at risk.

Greater transparency will also help in preventing the building up of unsustainable levels of debt by developing nations. In both developing and developed countries the lack of transparency in the accumulating of debt has added to economic uncertainty in the world financial system. The Guiding Principles on Foreign Debt and Human Rights move in the direction of a concrete solution. Sovereign debt cannot be viewed as an exclusively economic problem. It affects future generations a well as the social conditions that allow the enjoyment of human rights of vast numbers of people entitled to the solidarity of the whole human family.

Thank you, Madam President.

[7] From the Address of Pope Benedict XVI to the Members of the Diplomatic Corps accredited to the Holy See, 8 January 2007.

THE UNAVOIDABLE NECESSITY TO REBUILD THE LINKS BETWEEN EDUCATION AND WORK*

Crisis and Impact on Youth and Women

Mr President,

This conference takes place in particularly adverse economic conditions. The recovery from the global financial crisis is very slow. At the end of 2012, five years after the outbreak of the global financial crisis, the total number of jobless was almost 200 million. Since 2007, some 39 million people dropped out of the labor market as job prospects proved unattainable thus opening a global gap of 67 million jobs lost.[1] A moderate growth in the labor market is expected for 2013–2014, but this will be insufficient to alleviate the crisis. Advanced economies have been hit hardest. The regions that avoided an increase in unemployment, on the other hand, have experienced deterioration in job quality, since at-risk employment and the number of workers living below or very near the poverty line increased. Additionally, there has been a global 'spill-over' of new recession conditions in Europe. The length and depth of the labour market crisis is worsening labor market mismatches, contributing to the increased incidence of unemployment.

Youth remains particularly affected by the crisis. Globally, some 73 million young people currently are unemployed and by 2014 another half million are likely to be pushed into unemployment. The unemployment rate among youth is predicted to increase from 12.6 per cent in 2012 to 12.9 per cent by 2017. Policy- and decision-makers need to take additional steps to recover from the second dip in the job market. Ways to deal with these challenges include overcoming uncertainty to increase investment and job creation; coordinating stimuli for global demand and more employment; addressing labour market mismatches and promoting structural change; and increasing efforts to promote long-term youth employment. Innovative solutions call for steady employment for everyone so that economic growth and well-being are not

* Statement delivered at the 102nd Session of the International Labour Conference, 12 June 2013.

[1] International Labour Organization, *Global Employment Trends 2013*, Geneva: ILO, 2013, p. 10, www.ilo.org/wcmsp5/groups/public/–dgreports/–dcomm/–publ/documents/publication/wcms_202326.pdf.

disconnected.[2] This urgency becomes more evident if we keep in mind that the economic crisis has been preceded by a period of jobless growth. A dramatic shift is needed in the current policy approach in order to fight the structural challenges of unemployment.

Work Builds Community

Work is the primary sphere where the links between the person, the economy and the environment are built, the first step toward their reconstruction, and where social and economic relations are nourished. The first link that we need to consider is the intergenerational link. We have stressed that youth unemployment is becoming a major emergency, especially in advanced economies, particularly in Europe, where, in some countries, youth unemployment rate is close to 50 per cent. The same countries are engaged in a reform of their welfare system to enable them to cope with population ageing. This can result in an intergenerational conflict since the old generation is lengthening its permanence in employment while the new generation faces increasing difficulties in entering the labor market. Policies and institutions need to address this conflict and, in this framework, a key role has to be assumed by the family. The family, in fact, is the primary sphere where potential intergenerational conflicts of interest can be solved and recast. Thus labour market policies have to take into account the role of the family within society. In this regard, in addition to policies that favour youth employment, it is necessary to implement policies aimed at promoting women's participation by facilitating the conciliation between work and family.

Education and Work

It is necessary to rebuild the links between education and work. Youth unemployment has a twofold implication. On the one hand, it highlights the inability of the economy to generate enough job opportunities for the new generations. On the other hand, it points out the difficulties of the education system in generating the qualifications and skills needed in the labor market. The education system is the cornerstone of any development strategy. It is, in fact, the primary source of human capital, which

2 Pope Benedict XVI, Encyclical Letter, *Caritas in Veritate*, § 32: AAS 101 (2009), pp. 666–7.

is the most effective engine of economic growth. More importantly, educated individuals become fully aware of the worth of all persons and of the value of work, not because of what it produces but because of who undertakes it. Without this subjective dimension, there would be no concern for the dignity of work, and only the economic dimension would be seen as relevant. However, the education system also has some crucial tasks, not only to make the most of the talent of each individual but also to effectively convey them toward skills and expertise useful in the labor market. If this is achieved, then the education system can effectively contribute to the reduction of mismatches in the labor market and increase the employability of younger generations.

Links within the population also need to be rebuilt. Prolonged periods of unemployment demoralize individuals, depreciate human capital, and ultimately lead to social exclusion. We should aim, therefore, at increasing employment opportunities for individuals at risk of marginalization and social exclusion. In this respect, social partners and trade unions could play a particularly decisive role.

Work: The Way Out of Poverty

Mr President,

Experience shows that work is the way out of poverty for poor households and that the expansion of productive and decent employment is the way economies grow and diversify. For countries at all levels of development, an adequate supply of jobs is the foundation of sustained and growing prosperity, inclusion and social cohesion. Where jobs are scarce or available jobs leave households in poverty, there is less growth, less security, and less human and economic development. In the current weak and turbulent international economic environment, job creation is the most pressing global development priority. As the United Nations and the global community debate the development agenda for the coming decades, jobs should take center stage.

The social dimension of work has always been emphasized by the Catholic Church. For this reason, it is of serious concern, first, that over the next ten years, 45 million to 50 million new jobs will be needed each year just to keep up with the growth of the world's working-age population and to reduce the unemployment caused by the crisis; second, that a wave of technological innovation is altering the capacity of modern manufacturing and the ability of service activities to generate jobs; third, that within and across countries, widening inequalities in income and opportunity are weakening the social and political fabric of our societies and are fuelling a downward cycle of economic, political and social uncertainty. If the ambitious goal of creating sufficient new jobs is to be realized, one prior condition is to take a fresh outlook on work that is based on ethical principles and spiritual values, which give dignity to workers in their service to the family and society.

Good Practices

Countries that achieved major job creation and poverty alleviation, for example, in Asia and Latin America, addressed the structural factors underlying poverty and underemployment. Policies included extensive social protection with active support for diversification of their economies, inclusive access to finance and employment-friendly macroeconomic policies that fostered both investment and consumption. Similar policies were the critical ingredients of short-term responses to the global financial and economic crisis, with well-designed social protection systems playing a leading role in enhancing resilience, stabilizing aggregate demand and protecting the most vulnerable groups.

It is necessary to integrate these objectives into a new global framework that will shape policy and mobilize international development assistance. As the external economic environment becomes less stable and supportive, progress rests increasingly on domestic policies that foster job-friendly and poverty-reducing growth. While the specific circumstances, priorities and needs of each country may differ, employment and livelihood objectives should be core objectives of all national development strategies, with ample space left to national policy design and adaptation. Such policies also could mobilize international development assistance. Low-income countries need support for the investments in infrastructure that create jobs in the short run and in skills and innovation that raise productivity and income of workers over the medium term. Development assistance could help kick-start nascent efforts to establish nationally defined social protection floors and launch labor market programs to address the special needs of women, youth and vulnerable people. Knowledge assistance would be as important as hard financial support, if not more.

Conclusions

Mr President,

The worldwide financial and economic crisis has highlighted a grave deficiency in the human perspective, thus reducing man to only one of his needs, namely, that of consumption. Worse yet, nowadays, human beings themselves are considered as consumer goods which can be used and thrown away. The problem of unemployment, in particular, is very often caused by a purely economic view of society, which seeks self-centered profit, outside the bounds of social justice. Within the economy links between individuals, firms and policies need to be rebuilt. All too often policies are aimed at addressing the needs of businesses without considering the needs of workers, and vice versa. We must promote the conditions for a recovery built on substantial job creation in order to establish a new social pact that puts the person and work at the center of the economy. This can be accomplished by following the principle of subsidiarity that allows each individual and each business to be the protagonist of the development of the entire society. In this respect, given its tripartite nature, the ILO can play a decisive role. The social dimension of work needs to prevail through disinterested solidarity and the return to person-centered ethics that renew the world of work.[3]

[3] Address of Pope Francis to the Non-Resident Ambassadors to the Hoy See: Kyrgyzstan, Antigua and Barbuda, Luxembourg, and Botswana, Clementine Hall, 16 May 2013.

3 INTELLECTUAL PROPERTY: PRODUCTION AND INVENTIVE ACTIVITY FOR THE SAKE OF THE COMMON GOOD

INGENUITY AND INTELLECTUAL PROPERTY MUST CONTRIBUTE TO THE DEVELOPMENT OF THE HUMAN FAMILY*

Mr President,

The Delegation of the Holy See joins previous speakers and expresses its congratulations to you for your able leadership and to our new Director General Dr Francis Gurry. It looks forward to a renewed and dynamic service of the World Intellectual Property Organization (WIPO) as it advances knowledge in the best interest of every human person and for the just progress of every country.

The Holy See is particularly attentive to the ethical and social dimensions that in a unique way flow from, affect and mark out the human person and her action. It certainly recognizes in intellectual property the characteristic value of innovation and of creativity, of intelligence in all its aspects. At the same time, in any undertaking of thought and action, in every scientific, technical or juridical approach, intellectual property is called to respect creation both in the area of knowledge and discovery and in the recognition of the nature of things: matter, intellect, living beings and, above all, the human person.

Human ingenuity is multifaceted, resourceful and capable of finding responses to the challenges that confront the human family. The constant request to register new patents evidences such ingenuity and their regulation requires a balanced norm so that the impact on the economy may be beneficial, as well, to the poorer countries and may value their specificity and identities. In fact, all countries contribute unique gifts stemming from their economic, social, cultural and spiritual traditions.

Among the various important areas of concern that engage the committed staff of WIPO, some new debates are of particular interest to this Delegation:

* Statement delivered at the 48th Series of Meetings of the WIPO General Assemblies, 23 September 2008.

- the possibilities and the implications of international protection of genetic resources, traditional knowledge, folklore and cultural expressions;
- the requirement of a legal implementation of copyrights and related issues concerning the protection of the rights of broadcasting organizations;
- and, above all, the process that has allowed the organization of the work in such a way that it now can take into account the expectation of development together with the requirements of norms and technologies related to intellectual property.

In conclusion, Mr President, with our renewed congratulations to the new DG, and thanks to his predecessor, Dr Kamil Idris, it has to be stated that, through its creativity and sense of solidarity, WIPO can, and has the responsibility to, contribute in a major way to the strengthening of a peaceful and more equitable international community.

Thank you.

PATENTABLE SUBJECT MATTER AND THE PATENTING OF LIFE FORMS*

Mr President,

I join previous speakers and congratulate you on your election.

On the issue of Article 27.3(b), Patentable Subject Matter, the Delegation of the Holy See wishes to provide some comments and raise some additional concerns.

Article 27.3(b) allows Members to exclude from patentability plants and animals, but not micro-organisms, and allows Members to exclude from patentability biological processes which are essential for the production of plants and animals, but not non-biological or microbiological ones. The rationale behind this provision is to reinforce the international protection of patents and other intellectual property rights (IPRs) on non-biological and microbiological life developments by linking such protection to the general legal framework on trade of other goods and services. Such protection, however, should be promoted fairly and in full accord with the development objectives established by article 7 of TRIPS, with the provisions of Article 8 related to the political freedom of States to protect public health and nutrition, and to promote the public interest in sectors of vital importance to their socio-economic and technological development, and with provisions of Article 27.2, which allows members to 'exclude from patentability inventions, the prevention within their territory of the commercial exploitation of which is necessary to protect public order or morality, including to protect human, animal or plant life or health or to avoid serious prejudice to the environment'.

The patenting of life forms could sometimes serve as a tool to support biotechnologies that are problematic both from an ethical point of view and from the point of view of a 'development-friendly' intellectual property system.

In relation to human life, Article 4 of the Universal Declaration on the Human Genome and Human Rights states that: 'The human genome in its natural state shall not give rise to financial gains,'[1] while

* Statement delivered at the Trade-Related Intellectual Property Rights (TRIPs) Council at the World Trade Organization, 8 June 2010.

1 UN Doc. A/53/152 of 9 December 1998; United Nations Educational, Scientific and Cultural Organization (UNESCO), Records of the General Conference, 29th Session, Paris, 21 October–12 November 1997, Resolution 6.

Article 21 of the Council of Europe Convention for the Protection of Human Rights and Dignity of the Human Being with Regard to the Application of Biology and Medicine states that: 'The human body and its parts shall not, as such, give rise to financial gains.'[2] In the same regard, the United Nations Declaration on Human Cloning[3] acknowledges the ethical concerns that certain applications of rapidly developing life sciences may raise with regard to human dignity, human rights and the fundamental freedoms of individuals, and calls States to adopt all measures necessary to protect adequately human life in the application of life sciences. Thus, the TRIPS agreement, other WTO rules, and all other international, regional and bilateral trade and IPR agreements should not reduce the ability of States to govern the aspects of IPR related to human life and dignity.

Mere commercial control of production and distribution of new life forms could affect both food security and development prospects of poor countries. Private monopolistic rights should not be imposed over those biological resources, from which the basic food and medicine requirements of human life are derived. An inclusive approach to IPR should not ignore the major economic, environmental and ethical concerns about the patenting of life, since such action would exert a negative impact on consumer rights, biodiversity conservation, environmental protection, indigenous rights, scientific and academic freedom, and, ultimately, the economic development of many developing countries insofar as it depends on new technologies.

In 2007, the United Nations adopted a Declaration on the Rights of Indigenous Peoples which recognizes, in Article 31, that 'indigenous peoples have the right to maintain, control, protect and develop their cultural heritage, traditional knowledge and traditional cultural expressions, as well as the manifestations of their sciences, technologies and cultures, including human and genetic resources, seeds, medicines, knowledge of the properties of fauna and flora, oral traditions, literatures, designs, sports and traditional games and visual and performing arts' and the 'right to maintain, control, protect and develop their intellectual property aver such cultural heritage, traditional knowledge and traditional cultural expressions'. When opportune and feasible, the WIPO/GRTKF (Genetic

[2] Council of Europe, ETS No. 164, Oviedo, 4 April 1967.

[3] UN Doc. A/RES/59/280, Resolution adopted by the General Assembly on 8 March 2005.

Resources, Traditional Knowledge and Folklore) developments and conclusions should be acknowledged within the context of the TRIPS rules.

Among agents of development, there is a significant concern about patenting of varieties of seeds that are genetically engineered. An unlimited application of patent procedures to biological, scientific and technical developments could be harmful to both traditional and modern methods of research and production, especially with regard to new varieties that are beneficial in the developing world. Concentration of seed ownership could threaten the autonomy of local farmers, who are forced to buy seeds every season from a handful of companies with whom they have little power to negotiate competitive prices. Ownership of intellectual property rights to seeds could seriously jeopardize the practice of saving seeds in order to trade or replant them during the next season. Most small and medium-scale farmers routinely save seeds, and an important portion of world population depends on the continued financial stability of farmers who do so. The international community should render due attention to concerns about the concentration of technology and resources in food production by a small group of entities and companies that are driven by purely commercial goals. Special attention also should be given to intellectual property protection of seeds discovered by individual farmers – both from developed or developing countries – and to the rights of indigenous peoples to the traditional use and ownership of those plants that are essential to their livelihoods and cultures.

The main goal of the international community should be to promote the common good. Moreover, international trade rules and negotiations should aim toward the good of all, especially of those people who are poor and vulnerable, should ensure both the means for human sustenance, such as food, water, medicines, health environment, etc., and the means for the cultural, social and spiritual development of people.

Discussions about the international protection of intellectual property rights and about the scope and consequences of Article 27, 3.b, also should be guided, in all sincerity, by the promotion of the common good and of human dignity, as it is rightly stated in the Declaration, the Final Act, the Preamble and the Annex 1C of the Agreement of Marrakech.

THE UNDULY RIGID ASSERTION OF THE RIGHT TO INTELLECTUAL PROPERTY*

Mr President,

The Delegation of the Holy See greatly appreciates that the focus of attention of this High-Level Segment of the 48th Series of Meetings of the WIPO's General Assemblies is directed to the critical issues of innovation, growth and development: enhanced creativity opens new concrete options for all.

The *raison d'être* of the protection system of intellectual property is the promotion of literary, scientific or artistic production and, generally, of inventive activity for the sake of the 'common good'. Thus protection officially attests the right of the author or inventor to recognition of the ownership of his work and to a degree of economic reward. At the same time it serves the cultural and material progress of society as a whole. According to Article 27 of the Universal Declaration of Human Rights, 'Everyone has the right to the protection of the moral and material interests resulting from any scientific, literary or artistic production of which he is the author.' In the end, intellectual property protection recognizes the dignity of man and his work that becomes an expression of, and a contribution to, the growth of the individual personality and to the common good.

Economists recognize several mechanisms through which intellectual property rights (IPRs) may stimulate economic development: these are interdependent so that a broad view of incentives associated with IPRs is appropriate. They devote much attention to this issue, but evidence to date is fragmented and somewhat contradictory, in part because many of the concepts involved have not yet been measured. A stronger system of protection could either enhance or limit economic growth. While strengthening IPRs has potential for enhancing growth and development in the proper circumstances, it might also raise difficult economic and social costs. Indeed, developing economies could experience net welfare losses in the short run because many of the costs of protection could emerge earlier than the dynamic benefits. This situation explains why it is often difficult to organize a convergence of interests in favor of reform of intellectual property in developing countries.

* Statement delivered at the 48th Series of Meetings of the WIPO General Assemblies, 21 September 2010.

The adoption of stronger IPRs in developing countries is often defended by claims that this reform will attract significant new inflows of technology, a blossoming of local innovation and cultural industries, and a faster closing of the technology gap between developing and developed countries. It must be recognized, however, that improved IPRs by itself is highly unlikely to produce such benefits.

The increase of benefits deriving to countries from IPRs depends on their ability to absorb and develop technologies and new products. In this context, three issues are critical for development purposes. First, it is clear that the ability to adapt new technologies to local industrial uses is improved if it meets with high levels of education and an adequate qualified human capital. Thus, there are important pay-offs in providing access to technical training and secondary or university education. Second, the absorption of foreign technologies to enhance productivity, in a critical way, depends on the Research and Development (R&D) performance of local enterprises. This observation points to the importance of developing an effective technology policy for promoting technical change in domestic enterprises. Such programs could include technology demonstration projects, information sharing through conferences, the encouragement of research, joint ventures and improved linkages between public research institutes and enterprises.

Third, in many countries a relevant problem is the inability of research institutes to bring their inventions to market in a useful way. Stronger IPRs alone would help in this context, but so also would development contracts between institutes and enterprises with defined ownership shares and increased flexibility for researchers to form new business concerns. Last but not least, it is also important for countries to encourage the development of financial markets in such a way that they become capable of managing the significant risks involved in technology development.

Mr President,

These few observations want to underline the conviction that the main goal of the international community in developing a fair regime of intellectual property rights should aim toward the good of all, the pursuit of more equitable international relations, especially with regard to poorer and more vulnerable people. Of this goal we are reminded by Pope Benedict's latest Encyclical Letter: 'in the context of immaterial or cultural causes of development and underdevelopment, we find these same patterns of responsibility reproduced. On the part of rich countries there is excessive zeal for protecting knowledge through an unduly rigid assertion of the right to intellectual property, especially in the field of health care. At the same time, in some poor countries, cultural models and social norms of behavior persist which hinder the process of development.'[1]

[1] Pope Benedict XVI, Encyclical Letter, *Caritas in Veritate*, § 22.

THE ULTIMATE GOAL OF INTELLECTUAL PROPERTY IS TO SERVE THE COMMON GOOD*

Mr Chairman,

Let me start by presenting you our congratulations on your election as the chair of the General Assembly and I extend them to your two vice chairs. My Delegation is confident that under your leadership we will be able to reach a positive outcome.

Allow me also to express our support for the efforts of the Director General and his staff in encouraging innovation and creativity over the last year in all the regions of the world, while promoting a balanced and effective international intellectual property system.

In this and in other fora, the Holy See has argued that intellectual property deserves protection since it creates incentives for innovation. Such protection, however, must be tempered to allow the spreading of the benefits of innovation as widely as possible. The very creative and innovative impact that IP rights provide should aim primarily *at serving the common good of the human community*. Individual persons and associations are called to contribute to the cultural, economic, political and social life of the civil community to which they belong. Since all human beings should contribute to society, special attention is required to make possible also the participation of the most disadvantaged. For this reason the poor should be helped 'to acquire expertise, to enter the circle of exchange, and to develop their skills in order to make the best use of their capacities and resources'.[1] Education is the critical strategy to achieve this goal. In fact, it endows needy people with the basic knowledge which enables them to express their creativity and develop their talents. In this way they become active protagonists for their future and no longer merely passive elements in the social order where the human person 'must be and must continue to be, its subject, its foundation and its end'.[2]

Since the last Assemblies, meaningful and hopeful progress has taken place in various substantive sectors of the Organization, such as the

* Statement delivered at the 49th Series of Meetings of the WIPO General Assemblies, 27 September 2011.

[1] Pope John Paul II, Encyclical Letter, *Centesimus Annus*, § 34, www.vatican.va/edocs/ENG0214/__P6.HTM.

[2] Pope Pius XII, Radio Message, Christmas Eve, 1944: AAS 37 (1945), p. 12.

Standing Committee on the Law of Patents (SCP), WIPO's Intergovernmental Committee on Intellectual Property and Genetic Resources, Traditional Knowledge and Folklore (IGC). The Strategic Realignment Program (SRP) has been refined and its progressive implementation shared through informative briefings offered by the Secretariat.

A major success of the Organization has occurred in the Standing Committee on Copyright and Related Rights (SCCR). After ten years of a stand-off, a positive and cooperative engagement by Delegations has led to the SCCR's recommendation to resume the failed 2000 Diplomatic Conference on a treaty for the protection of audiovisual performances. My Delegation looks forward as well to reaching an agreement on the visually impaired and on people with print disabilities. This agreement will make a significant contribution in mitigating the difficulty faced by more than 284 million visually impaired people worldwide,[3] about 90 per cent of whom live in developing countries.[4] These are people with limited access to education and culture, not because they lack thirst for knowledge or because they lack aspiration to play their part in the material and cultural welfare of the world community, but because of their disability.

The rapid development of technology in the area of the media is surely one of the signs of advancement in today's society; it is also a challenge for the Member States of this Organization that have to undertake a particular effort to face it. The Holy See, as a practical demonstration of its commitment and recognizing the lead role played by copyright, has updated its legislation in this field by adopting a new law.[5] Such a decision shows the significant role played by intellectual property in this State.

During the last biennium, the Intergovernmental Committee on Intellectual Property and Genetic Resources, Traditional Knowledge and Folklore (IGC) undertook a tremendous effort toward the development of an international protection instrument and during the last session it has elaborated a proposal for a renewal of its mandate. The Holy See remains engaged in this Committee and would like to underline a few elements:

- intellectual manifestations of tradition or folklore deserve recognition, first, because they constitute a means of constructing and projecting the identity of the members of the community concerned and, second,

[3] www.who.int/mediacentre/factsheets/fs282/en/. [4] Ibid.
[5] Law on the protection of copyright and related rights, March 2011 n. CXXXII.

because they are a common asset of that same community, which has grown by small, anonymous contributions over many generations;

- many biological resources bearing great economic and social usefulness are located in territories inhabited since time immemorial by native communities within the jurisdiction of countries other than those where industrial development of genetic material takes place and patents are obtained. Those native communities already have some knowledge and make use of some of the biological properties protected by patents. Indigenous communities' ancestral concern for the soil needs to be considered: it generates a right to its use and usufruct. This right extends also to the plants and animals of a territory. Consequently, the biological environment tends to be closely associated with the culture of local people, and constitutes an integral factor of their identity and social cohesion. Native populations' rights over the land and its fruits exist, and have to be protected, even where modern systems of property protection – both movable and immovable property such as intellectual property – do not foresee their recognition and protection to a sufficient extent.[6]

Mr Chairman,

I would like to conclude by reaffirming the right to private property and in particular to intellectual property. This right is under a 'social mortgage', for the satisfaction of essential human needs. It has an intrinsically social function, which is justified precisely by the principle of the universal destination of goods.[7] The universal destination of goods represents the sum total of social conditions which allow social groups and their individual members to arrive at their own fulfillment. The common good, however, is realized if solidarity prevails. In our globalized world, an equitable relationship with others is a must since we are all really responsible for all.

Thank you.

6 WIPO/GRTKF/IC/1/7 Cf. ILO, C-169, Arts. 13–18. Cf. Pontifical Council 'Justice and Peace', 'Towards Better Land Distribution – The Challenge of Agrarian Reform', Vatican City 1997, para. 11; Pontifical Council 'Justice and Peace', Indigenous Peoples in the Teaching of John Paul II, Vatican City 1993, p. 22.

7 Pope John Paul II, Encyclical Letter, *Sollicitudo Rei Socialis* (1987), § 42.

THE MORAL RESPONSIBILITY TO CONCLUDE A TREATY FOR THE VISUALLY IMPAIRED*

Mr Chairman,

First of all, the Holy See Delegation presents congratulations for your re-election as the Chair of the General Assembly; it extends them to your two vice-chairs. It deeply appreciates the work you carried out between the last session and now in trying to reach an agreement on a number of issues. We are confident that under your leadership we will be able to arrive at a positive outcome during this session, as we did in the last one.

Allow me also to express our appreciation to the Director General and his staff for the enormous effort put in place in encouraging innovation and creativity over the last year in all the regions of the world, while promoting a balanced and effective international intellectual property system. We would also like to thank the International Bureau of WIPO for the hard work in the preparation of this meeting.

Since the last Assemblies, significant and positive progress has taken place in various substantive sectors of the Organization. The conclusion of the Beijing Treaty represents an important milestone toward closing the gap in the international rights system for audiovisual performers and it has reflected the collaborative nature of the multilateral process. In line with this substantial result and with the enormous effort put in place by all Delegations during the last sessions of the Standing Committee on Copyright and Related Rights (SCCR), my Delegation looks forward to reaching an agreement on an international legally binding instrument on limitations and exceptions for visually impaired persons with print disabilities.

Visually impaired individuals have access to only 5 per cent of published books in developed countries. In poorer countries the percentage is closer to 1. At a time when technology brings massive amounts of information to households and businesses, it is a shocking fact that even in the most developed countries in the world, less than 5 per cent of information is available in usable formats such as audio, large print and Braille.

* Statement delivered at the 50th Series of Meetings of the WIPO General Assemblies, 1 October 2012.

Article 27 of the Universal Declaration of Human Rights recognizes to all individuals the right to freely participate in the cultural life of the community and to enjoy the arts. This is a copyright issue that has a clear human rights dimension: the need to ensure that copyright is not a barrier to equal access to information, culture and education for people with print disabilities and other reading disabilities.

Pope John Paul II in his Encyclical Letter, *Laborem Exercens* stated that 'It would be radically unworthy of man, and a denial of our common humanity, to admit to the life of the community, and thus admit to work, only those who are fully functional. To do so would be to practice a serious form of discrimination, that of the strong and healthy against the weak and sick.'[1] Since all persons are called to contribute to society, it is a basic requirement to create an international instrument that could help poor and disabled persons to develop their skills in order to make the best use of their capacities and resources both for personal fulfillment and their own contribution to society.

The Holy See recognizes that intellectual property protection is necessary for progress and for the just compensation of researchers and producers. At the same time, it recalls that the primary goal of new knowledge is the service of *the common good of the human community*. This common good must be served in its fullness, not according to a reductionist vision that subordinates it only to the advantage of some people; rather, it is to be based on a logic that leads to the acceptance of greater responsibility. 'The common good corresponds to the highest of human inclinations,[2] but it is a good that is very difficult to attain because it requires the constant ability and effort to seek the good of others as though it were one's own good. The distribution of created goods, which, as every discerning person knows, is laboring today under the gravest evils due to the huge disparity between the few exceedingly rich and the unnumbered property-less, must be effectively called back to and brought into conformity with the norms of the common good, that is, social justice.'[3]

In conclusion, the Delegation of the Holy See would like to emphasize the ethical and social dimensions that in a unique way flow from,

[1] Pope John Paul II, Encyclical Letter, *Laborem Exercens*, § 22: AAS 73 (1981), p. 634.

[2] Saint Thomas Aquinas places 'knowledge of the truth about God' and 'life in society' at the highest and most specific level of man's '*inclinationes naturales*' (*Summa Theologiae*, I–II, q. 94, a. 2: Ed. Leon, 7.170).

[3] Pope Pius XI, Encyclical Letter, *Quadragesimo Anno*, § 197.

affect and mark out the human person and her action. In any undertaking of thought and action, in every scientific, technical or juridical approach, intellectual property is called to respect creation both in the area of knowledge and discovery and in the recognition of the nature of things: matter, intellect, living beings, and, above all, the human person.

Mr Chairman,

Let me assure you that you can count on the constructive cooperation and support of this Delegation.

Thank you, Mr Chairman.

THE EXTENSION OF THE TRANSITIONAL PERIOD FOR LDCS: A CONCRETE EXAMPLE OF ACTING FOR THE COMMON GOOD*

Mr President,

I join previous speakers in congratulating you on your election and for the positive outcome just reached on the extension until 1 July 2021, of the Transitional period under Article 66.1 of the TRIPs Agreement. The Observer Delegation of the Holy See to the World Trade Organization (WTO) appreciates the humanitarian and ethical dimensions taken into account in these negotiations.

The least developed countries represent the poorest and weakest segment of the international community. They are populated by more than 880 million people (approximately 12 per cent of world population), but account for less than 2 per cent of world GDP and approximately 1 per cent of global trade in goods.[1] The low level of socio-economic development in such countries is characterized by weak levels of technical expertise and of institutional capacity, low and unequally distributed income and scarcity of domestic financial resources. In past years, the development paradigm implemented in these LDCs has proven ineffective. Since the early 2000s, the continued growth in many LDCs (7 per cent per year between 2002 and 2007) has not translated into an improved quality of life for the people. The number of very poor people actually has increased (more than 3 million per year from 2002 to 2007). In 2007, 59 per cent of the population in African LDCs was living on less than US$1.25 per day.

LDCs continue to be characterized by multiple structural constraints that include low per capita income, low levels of human development and extreme vulnerabilities to external shocks. LDCs are home to more than 50 per cent of the one billion people who live in extreme poverty. According to the 2012 UNCTAD report on LDCs, these countries should prepare for a relatively prolonged period of uncertainty, with

* Statement delivered at the Trade-Related Intellectual Property Rights (TRIPs) Council at the World Trade Organization, 11 June 2013.

1 www.unaids.org/en/media/unaids/contentassets/documents/unaidspublication/2013/JC2474_TRIPS-transition-period-extensions_en.pdf (last consulted 6 June 2013).

possible escalation of financial tensions and real economic downturn.[2] As underlined in the Istanbul Program of Action, least developed countries are most 'off-track' in the achievement of the internationally agreed development goals. Their productive capacity is limited, and they have severe infrastructure deficits.[3] In 2011, of the 34 million people living with HIV worldwide, some 9.7 million lived in LDCs. Of these, 4.6 million were in need of antiretroviral treatment; however, only 2.5 million were receiving it.[4]

Up to one-half of those deprived of treatment were expected to die within 24 months.[5] In the 49 countries designated as LDCs by the United Nations, non-communicable disease burdens are rising much faster than in higher income countries.

The flexibility agreed in TRIPS Article 66.1 was accepted in recognition of the economic, financial and administrative constraints preventing LDCs from immediate observance of all the obligations set out in the TRIPS Agreement. This was an acknowledgement that LDCs have special needs and requirements, including the need for flexibility to create a viable technological base. Besides, the 2005 extension experience shows the impossibility to predict when LDCs will be classified as developing countries. The extension of the transition period under Article 66.1 to 1 July 2021, is in line with the overarching goal of the Istanbul Programme of Action (IPoA). The latter plans 'to overcome the structural challenges faced by least developed countries in order to eradicate poverty, achieve internationally agreed development goals and *enable graduation from the least developed country category*'.[6] This goal is expected to be achieved through national policy actions and international support. Graduation from the category of least developed countries (LDCs) has always been among the ultimate objectives of the previous three decennial Programs of Action for LDCs. However, the IPoA was the first to include a clearly articulated, time-bound and concrete objective of enabling LDCs

[2] http://unctad.org/en/PublicationsLibrary/ldc2012overview_en.pdf.

[3] Istanbul Plan of Action (para. 4) UN Doc. A/CONF.219/3, http://ldc4istanbul.org/uploads/IPoA.pdf.

[4] TRIPS Transition Period Extensions for Least Developed Countries, UNDP and UNAIDS Issues Brief, p. 13 (February 2013).

[5] Michel Sidibé, UNAIDS Executive Director, Report to 31st UNAIDS Programme Coordinating Board, December 2012, www.unaids.org/en/media/unaids/contentassets/documents/speech/2012/12/20121211_SP_EXD_31st_PCB.pdf.

[6] Istanbul Plan of Action (para. 27), UN Doc. A/CONF.219/3, http://ldc4istanbul.org/uploads/IPoA.pdf.

to meet the criteria for graduation.[7] The Program set the highly ambitious target that half of the LDCs should be able to meet graduation criteria by the end of the decade.

Mr President,

A well-designed intellectual property system must balance the private rights of inventors with the public needs of society. International intellectual property rules reflect this premise: the stated Objectives of TRIPS include the assertion that 'the protection and enforcement of intellectual property rights should contribute to the promotion of technological innovation and to the transfer and dissemination of technology, to the mutual advantage of producers and users of technological knowledge and in a manner conducive to social and economic welfare, and to a balance of rights and obligations'.[8]

The Delegation of the Holy See urges all Member States, therefore, to bear in mind that the main goal of the international community in developing a fair regime of intellectual property rights should aim toward the good of all and the pursuit of more equitable international relations, especially with regard to poorer and more vulnerable people. This goal reminds us of the Pope's words: 'in the context of immaterial or cultural causes of development and underdevelopment, we find these same patterns of responsibility reproduced. On the part of rich countries there is excessive zeal for protecting knowledge through an unduly rigid assertion of the right to intellectual property, especially in the field of health care. At the same time, in some poor countries, cultural models and social norms of behaviour persist which hinder the process of development.'[9]

In conclusion, Mr President, the consensus reached on the proposal of extension represents an important sign by the World Trade Organization, especially in anticipation of the next Ministerial Conference in Bali. The Holy See Delegation hopes that a sense of common responsibility, as shown in the decision adopted, will bring us all to support such extension as an accelerated step toward the human and economic progress of least developed countries.

Thank you, Mr President.

[7] Graduation from the list of LDCs is based on a systematic review and assessment of socio-economic progress of least developed countries based on three criteria: per capita income and two composite indices (Human Asset Index and Economic Vulnerability Index).

[8] Art. 7 TRIPs Agreement.

[9] Pope Benedict XVI, Encyclical Letter, *Caritas in Veritate*, § 22.

THE MARRAKECH DIPLOMATIC CONFERENCE: EMPOWERING THE BLIND, OR VISUALLY IMPAIRED PERSONS, AS A TOOL FOR RAISING THEIR ECONOMIC AND SOCIAL STATUS*

Mr President,

As we gather to show the solidarity of the world family to all visually impaired, at the outset, my Delegation wishes to warmly thank the Government of Morocco and the city of Marrakech for hosting this Diplomatic Conference.

Some 285 million people are visually impaired worldwide according to estimates of the World Health Organization and approximately 90 per cent of them live in developing countries. Only 1 per cent of the books in developing and least developed countries, however, are available in formats accessible to blind people. In the developed countries as well visually impaired individuals have access to only 5 per cent of published books. Such a situation has been appropriately called a 'book famine'. In fact, many visually impaired learners and university students in developing countries lack access to textbooks.

The Universal Declaration of Human Rights recognizes the right of all individuals to freely participate in the cultural life of the community and to enjoy the arts (Art. 27). This Conference is mandated to deal with a copyright issue that has a clear human rights dimension: the need to ensure that copyright is not a barrier to equal access to information, culture and education for people with print, reading and related disabilities, 'giving people a variety of opportunities to discover their potential, understand their environment, discover their rights and take total control of their destiny'.[1] This objective implies access to knowledge and skills needed to develop a person's capacity to shape her future.

Twenty or thirty years ago little could be done about the 'book famine'. Printing braille books was time-consuming and resource-intensive. Technology has brought about important changes. Today

* Statement delivered at the Diplomatic Conference to conclude a Treaty to Facilitate Access to Published Works by Visually Impaired Persons and Persons with Print Disabilities, Marrakech, Morocco, 18 June 2013.

1 Divine Chris Boame, Coordinator Inclusive Education Programme, Krachi East and West Districts, Ghana Educational Empowerment of the Blind and Persons with Low Vision In Ghana, A Shared Responsibility, www.afri-can.org/workshops/Ghana %20articles/Divine.doc.

visually impaired people can read books on computers using text-to-speech technology, magnification, by means of so-called braille displays, or by listening to normal audio books. Now every book on the planet can quite easily be made accessible to blind users; instead of the 1 per cent or 5 per cent access of the past, today's technical capacity allows close to 100 per cent. Our goal, then, is not just a treaty, but rather a treaty that will resolve obstacles to access.

While new technologies make it possible to imagine a world where visually impaired persons can access a broad variety of documents just as sighted people can do, the out-of-date legal environment is a barrier. The protection of intellectual property is an important value, which we must respect. However, there is a social mortgage on all property, including intellectual property. The very creative and innovative thrust that the intellectual property rights system offers, exists primarily to serve the common good of the human community.

At the national level, some countries have limitations and exceptions in copyright laws to enable accessibility for persons with reading disabilities without the permission of copyright owners. These provisions, however, vary considerably from country to country. They are often quite restrictive or focused only on older technologies such as raised paper braille. As a consequence, the total number of accessible resources is very low, particularly in smaller market countries. This Marrakech Diplomatic Conference represents a historic opportunity for the international community to give a concrete answer to most practical issues at the global level.

The exercise, therefore, of the exceptions and limitations permitted under the treaty must not be impeded or negated by other disciplines such as technological protection measures and contract law. We also caution against the introduction of new obligations that override sovereign discretion by WIPO Member States apropos of how national governments create other exceptions and limitations in order to address public interest needs. Accordingly, it is critical that the discussions focus on existing approaches already recognized under the Berne Convention as consistent with the three-step test, specifically fair use and fair dealing, whether in place of or in addition to specific limitations and exceptions in national law.

Mr President,

The primary goal of the copyright system is the dissemination of creative works to enhance the common good. Copyright has never been an end in itself. Increasingly, technological developments have strained the capacity of copyright law to limit the ways in which the public accesses creative works.

As stated by Pope John Paul II, in his Encyclical Letter, *Laborem Exercens*, 'It would be radically unworthy of man, and a denial of our common humanity, to admit to the life of the community, and thus admit to work, only those who are fully functional. To do so would be to practise a serious form of discrimination, that of the strong and healthy against the weak and sick.'[2] Since all persons are called to contribute to society, it is fundamental to create an international instrument that could give even to impaired people a variety of opportunities to discover their potential, understand their environment, discover their rights and put to the best use their talents and resources both for personal fulfilment and for their contribution to society.

This common good must be served in its fullness, not according to a reductionist vision subordinated only to the advantage of some people; rather, it is to be based on a logic that leads to the acceptance of a comprehensive responsibility. 'The common good corresponds to the highest of human inclinations,[3] but it is a good that is very difficult to attain because it requires the constant ability and effort to seek the good of others as though it were one's own good. The distribution of created goods, which, as every discerning person knows, is labouring today under the gravest evils due to the huge disparity between the few exceedingly rich and the unnumbered property-less, must be effectively called back to and brought into conformity with the norms of the common good, that is, social justice.'[4]

[2] Pope John Paul II, Encyclical Letter, *Laborem Exercens*, § 22: AAS 73 (1981), p. 634.

[3] Saint Thomas Aquinas places 'knowledge of the truth about God' and 'life in society' at the highest and most specific level of man's '*inclinationes naturales*' (*Summa Theologiae*, I–II, q. 94, a. 2: Ed. Leon, 7.170).

[4] Pope Pius XI, Encyclical Letter, *Quadragesimo Anno*, § 58.

Mr President,

A positive decision on this issue would result in an important sign not only from the World Intellectual Property Organization, but from all the international community. My Delegation hopes that a sense of common responsibility should urge us all to ensure that what has been achieved during the past months will not be lost. In this way, this Diplomatic Conference can arrive at a positive decision for the good of our entire human family.

During the upcoming two weeks, negotiations will challenge all participants to demonstrate sufficient flexibility in view of an achievable compromise that strengthens the international common good and overcomes particular positions. Empowering the blind, or visually impaired persons, is vital for raising their economic and social status. It becomes, therefore, a shared responsibility to help making such empowerment succeed for the benefit in particular of the many groups in society that have a stake in this process. Policymakers are called to adopt a pragmatic approach; service providers, an effective implementation; and the labour market, to remove all forms of discrimination. In conclusion, Mr President, everyone has to rise sufficiently above national interests to see that a new treaty of solidarity with all visually impaired can and should be concluded as a message of hope for them and a sign of responsibility by the international community.

THE MARRAKECH AGREEMENT: A HISTORICAL RESULT*

Mr President,

The Delegation of the Holy See joins previous speakers and expresses its satisfaction for the successful achievement of a Treaty to Facilitate Access to Published Works for Persons Who Are Blind, Visually Impaired, or Otherwise Print Disabled. It warmly thanks the Government of Morocco and the city of Marrakech for hosting this Diplomatic Conference as well as the WIPO's team, led by the Director General Francis Gurry, and everyone who has contributed to a smooth and constructive task.

The international community has shown the way forward. Looking at the future, a lesson emerges from the process of negotiations and the political will to reach out to visually impaired people. It is a deep sense of human solidarity with victims of disabilities and the openness to their full participation in the life of society. As new priorities are debated for the post-2015 development concerns, placing the needy at the center will provide the right approach and it confirms that success is effective when the human family is seen as one.

Mr President,

It took some years of hard work to arrive at this happy conclusion. The result, however, shows not only a sense of balance and respect for all interested parties, but also a substantive achievement. Such achievement makes a difference in the daily life of the beneficiaries of this Treaty: their quality of life can be improved by their easier access to a vast field of knowledge that will enrich them personally and make them more useful to society.

At the same time this historic Treaty becomes a strong signal that multilateralism not only is alive, but that it can serve well as an effective system for the concrete implementation of the common good through the responsible involvement of all parties in any negotiations undertaken.

Allow me, Mr President, to conclude by quoting from a recent message by Pope Francis to an association of blind and visually impaired people. The Holy Father wished this association well and, for the human

* Concluding remarks delivered at the Diplomatic Conference to conclude a Treaty to Facilitate Access to Published Works by Visually Impaired Persons and Persons with Print Disabilities, Marrakech, Morocco, 27 June 2013.

and spiritual promotion of its constituency, invited it to 'spread always the culture of encounter, of solidarity, of acceptance of people with disabilities, not only by asking for just social measures, but also by promoting their active participation in the life of society'.[1] The Holy See, prompted by the words of the Holy Father and by the humanitarian dimension and the potential benefit for tens of millions of visually impaired persons, has decided to immediately sign and it looks forward to a wide ratification of the new Treaty.

[1] www.vatican.va/holy_father/francesco/messages/pont-messages/2013/documents/papa-francesco_20130611_audiomessaggio-ciechi_it.html (last consulted 26 June 2013).

SCIENCE, TECHNOLOGY AND INNOVATION, AND THE POTENTIAL OF CULTURE FOR PROMOTING SUSTAINABLE DEVELOPMENT*

Mr President,

The international community is searching for new models of development that can fight poverty and improve the quality of life more effectively. In this ECOSOC Substantive Session, 'Science, technology and innovation, and the potential of culture for promoting sustainable development' have been chosen as the instruments for a systemic reform and a new way forward. Undoubtedly, for the overall achievement of human development science, technology and innovation (STI) are key elements. They have helped many areas of the world to evolve considerably and take their place in the global context. The discovery of new medicines, for example, has lengthened the average lifespan of entire regions and provided immunity from contagious diseases. Progress of a merely economic and technological kind, however, is insufficient. 'Development needs above all to be true and integral',[1] such as to embrace all the aspirations of the human person who remains its best resource and indispensable protagonist.

STI are critical dimensions of human knowledge and progress. At the same time, they carry a social mortgage that finds expression in solidarity with poorer individuals and countries and in a lifestyle based on human relations that take precedence over technical mechanisms, as useful as these are. The importance of culture rests on the fact that it speaks of the intelligence of rational beings enabling them to understand and order the world that surrounds them. Besides, knowledge is the result of an incredible amount of observation, analysis and reflection accumulated over centuries and that have become a common patrimony. That is why intellectual property protects an invention for only an agreed period of time after which it becomes public and remains at the service of all. Certainly science and technology are powerful instruments of change. In the last decades the world wide web has created a true revolution. An ever-increasing mass of information, documents, statistics and art expressions is uploaded every day, and for the most part it can be accessed freely. But

* Statement delivered at the High-Level Segment of the Economic and Social Council, 4 July 2013.

[1] Pope Benedict XVI, Encyclical Letter, *Caritas in Veritate*, § 23.

the spread of data and information through IT technologies cannot be automatically equated to a transmission of knowledge whose modality plays a role more important now than ever before. In fact, human culture expresses the way we live together as human beings. Without culture no human being accesses the full possession of faculties like speech, reason and even freedom.[2] The importance of culture as a vehicle of our common humanity can never be overstressed. The relationship between culture and development has to be considered, therefore, in a dialectic and not in a deterministic way. Cultural changes are in fact both a cause and an effect of social and economic change. Culture includes both the system of values, norms, preferences and the level of knowledge acquired through the educational system. It follows that culture is a strategic resource for an effective human development which must include the improvement of human dignity, individual, social, and political freedom, i.e. of human rights.[3] Culture in fact is not just an end in itself or the delivery of new products, but a way to express interpersonal relations, which constitute the fundamental dimension of human beings.

Even if STI all belong to the field of human knowledge, there is no simple and linear link between them. Technology is not only an application of science. 'Technology enables us to exercise dominion over matter, to reduce risks, to save labour, to improve our conditions of life ... Technology is the objective side of human action.'[4] It is a specific knowledge that accounts for how to achieve a specific objective result.

[2] 'Man comes to a true and full humanity only through culture, that is through the cultivation of the goods and values of nature. Wherever human life is involved, therefore, nature and culture are quite intimately connected one with the other', *Gaudium et Spes*, § 53.

[3] 'In these conditions, it is no cause of wonder that man, who senses his responsibility for the progress of culture, nourishes a high hope but also looks with anxiety upon many contradictory things which he must resolve ... How is the dynamism and expansion of a new culture to be fostered without losing a living fidelity to the heritage of tradition. This question is of particular urgency when a culture which arises from the enormous progress of science and technology must be harmonized with a culture nourished by classical studies according to various traditions', *Gaudium et Spes*, § 56.

[4] 'Technology is a profoundly human reality, linked to the autonomy and freedom of man. In technology we express and confirm the hegemony of the spirit over matter ... Technology enables us to exercise dominion over matter, to reduce risks, to save labour, to improve our conditions of life. It touches the heart of the vocation of human labour: in technology ... man recognizes himself and forges his own humanity. Technology is the objective side of human action whose origin and *raison d'être* is found in the subjective element: the worker himself.' Pope Benedict, XVI, Encyclical Letter, *Caritas in Veritate*, § 69.

The difference between science and technology is that techniques actually become embedded in real objects or procedures. Thus, by its own nature, technology tends to be protected by intellectual property rights and is consequently a source of power and money. The rationale behind technology, science and innovation is not the same and public policies should avoid equating them.

The Report of the UN Secretary General on 'Science, technology and innovation' rightly states their relevance for development as supported by strong evidence from development economics. Public policies should foster science and research, promote a friendly environment for technological development and facilitate a culture of innovation. Private–public partnerships are also welcomed and necessary to meet the growing cost of research and innovation. On the other hand, we cannot simply assume that STI will automatically lead to positive socio-economic gains. Technology and innovation are not neutral: their outcome will vastly depend on what they are used for. Most importantly, we need not surrender to the idea that science has embedded a notion of self-determination according to which whatever can be done is feasible. 'When technology is allowed to take over, the result is confusion between ends and means, such that the sole criterion for action in business is thought to be the maximization of profit, in politics the consolidation of power, and in science the findings of research. Often, underneath the intricacies of economic, financial and political interconnections, there remain misunderstandings, hardships and injustice. The flow of technological know-how increases, but it is those in possession of it who benefit, while the situation on the ground for the peoples who live in its shadow remains unchanged: for them there is little chance of emancipation.'[5]

Mr President, two conclusions emerge. First, there is a need for an ethically responsible use of technology. Second, in the use and development of STI, forms of solidarity are required that are truly favourable to the poorest countries. In this way, the promotion of scientific knowledge in developing countries and the transfer of technologies to them becomes a moral component of the common good.

Often the development of peoples is considered a matter of financial engineering, the freeing up of markets, the removal of tariffs, investment in production, and institutional reforms – in other words, a purely technical matter. All these factors are of great importance, but we have to ask why technical choices made thus far have yielded rather mixed results.

[5] Pope Benedict XVI, Encyclical Letter, *Caritas in Veritate*, § 71.

We need to think hard about the cause. Development will never be fully guaranteed through automatic or impersonal forces, whether they derive from the market or from international politics. 'Development is impossible without upright men and women, without financiers and politicians whose consciences are finely attuned to the requirements of the common good.'

The international community is entering a critical phase of redefining sustainable development in its three pillars – economic, environmental and social – as an effective way to combat poverty and improve the lives of people worldwide. Investing in education and innovation opens the way toward a future of greater equality and prosperity as they sustain growth, employment and distribution, but with an indispensable condition, that the human person with her dignity, aspirations and fundamental rights be placed at the center of all policies and programs.

KNOWLEDGE ECONOMY: THE KEY DRIVER OF COMPETITIVENESS*

Madam President,

The Delegation of the Holy See would like to congratulate you on your election to chair the General Assembly. We welcome the two new vice-chairs as well and thank the outgoing chair and vice-chair for all the hard work over the past year. My Delegation is confident that under your leadership we will be able to reach a positive outcome during this session, as we did in the previous ones.

Allow me also to express our appreciation to the Director General and his staff for the enormous efforts over the last year in maintaining the Organization's rightful place as the global IP authority. After the Beijing momentum, we now have the Marrakech spirit that has led to a new treaty, the Marrakech Treaty to Facilitate Access to Published Works for Persons Who Are Blind, Visually Impaired, or Otherwise Print Disabled, and that should stimulate further creative collaboration.

In fact, over the last year our Organization has shown the way forward to the international community. The process of negotiations and the political will to reach out to visually impaired people have provided a lesson that enables us to look at the future with greater confidence. The lesson is a deep sense of human solidarity with victims of disabilities and the acceptance of their full participation in the life of society. As new priorities are debated for the post-2015 development concerns, placing the needier persons at the center of plans and programs will ensure the right approach and confirm that success is effective when the human family is seen as one.

Economic indicators show that in the last 20 years the decisive factors in productivity have shifted from land and capital to know-how, technology and skill and that the wealth of the industrialized nations is based much more on this kind of the ownership than on natural resources. The words of John Paul II remain pertinent and timely: far too many people still 'have no possibility of acquiring the basic knowledge which would enable them to express their creativity and develop their potential, and have no way of entering the network of knowledge and intercommunication which would enable them to see their qualities appreciated

* Statement delivered at the 51th Series of Meetings of the WIPO Assemblies, 24 September 2013.

and utilized'.[1] Knowledge and innovation have played a crucial role in development from the beginnings of human history. But with globalization and the technological revolution of the last few decades, knowledge has clearly become the key driver of competitiveness and is now profoundly reshaping the patterns of the world's economic growth and activity.

A well-designed intellectual property system must balance the private rights of inventors with the public needs of society. International intellectual property rules reflect this premise: the stated Objectives of TRIPS include the assertion that 'the protection and enforcement of intellectual property rights should contribute to the promotion of technological innovation and to the transfer and dissemination of technology, to the mutual advantage of producers and users of technological knowledge and in a manner conducive to social and economic welfare, and to a balance of rights and obligations.'[2] The primary goal of intellectual property is not an allocative efficiency, but the support of a democratic culture. A human being is truly human only if he is master of his own actions and the judge of their worth, only if he is the architect of his own progress.[3]

Madam President,

In conclusion, let us assure you that you can count on the constructive spirit and support of the Holy See during these Assemblies.

Thank you, Madam President.

[1] Pope John Paul II, Encyclical Letter, *Centesimus Annus*, § 33.
[2] Art. 7 TRIPs Agreement.
[3] Pope Paul VI, Encyclical Letter, *Populorum Progressio*, § 34.

PUTTING OUR TALENTS AT THE SERVICE OF THE COMMON GOOD*

Madam President,

The Delegation of the Holy See joins previous speakers and expresses its sincere congratulations to you and to the Chair of the Coordination Committee for the integrity and transparency manifested throughout the entire election and confirmation process of the WIPO's Director General for the next term. We would like as well to express warmest appreciation to Dr Francis Gurry on his re-election and confirmation for a second term as Director General.

The Holy See expects that this Organization will continue to be led in the right direction and stands ready to cooperate. Many areas of the globe today have seen considerable development, and even if this was achieved through different strategies and is marked by persisting challenges, each of these areas is taking its place among the powers destined to play a key role in the future. However, progress of a merely economic and technological kind is insufficient. Development needs to be integral. The mere fact of emerging from economic backwardness, though positive in itself, does not resolve the complex issues of human advancement. This does not happen for the countries spearheading such progress, nor for those already economically developed and not even for those that are still poor. All these countries can suffer not only through old forms of exploitation, but also from the negative consequences of an uneven growth characterized by inequality.

The Holy See recognizes the role of the protection system of intellectual property in promoting the literary, scientific or artistic production and, generally, the inventive activity for the sake of the 'common good'. At the same time it emphasizes the ethical and social dimensions that in a unique way involve the human person and her action. All too often, as Pope John Paul II observed, 'the fruits of scientific progress, rather than being placed at the service of the entire human community, are distributed in such a way that unjust inequalities are actually increased or even rendered permanent.'[1] The Holy See has constantly highlighted, in this and in other fora, that there is a 'social mortgage' on all private

* Statement delivered at the 53rd Series of Meetings of the WIPO Assemblies, 8 May 2014.

[1] Pope John Paul II, Address to 'Jubilee 2000 Debt Campaign', 23 September 1999.

property including 'intellectual property' and 'knowledge'. The historical Treaty to Facilitate Access to Published Works for Persons Who Are Blind, Visually Impaired, or Otherwise Print Disabled, signed last year in Marrakech, shows that the law of profit alone should not place undue limits on what is essential for education and for the fight against hunger, disease and poverty.

The World Intellectual Property Indicators in 2013 show that during the current term of the Director General, the Patent Cooperation Treaty, the Madrid system and the Hague system have achieved excellent results. The distribution of IP filing activity varied across income groups. For the period 2007–2012, patent, trademarks and industrial designs saw a shifting trend in filing activity from high-income to middle-income countries. Still the majority of patent filings occurred at the IP offices of high-income countries (64.5 per cent) while lower-middle-income and low-income countries represented together 3.2 per cent[2] of patent activity worldwide. Our challenge for the next years is to translate into reality our common goal: an accessible and efficient intellectual property system that provides benefits for all. Human imagination is resourceful and capable of finding responses to the challenges that confront the human family. All countries contribute unique gifts coming from their economic, social, cultural and spiritual traditions. Putting our 'talents' at the service of the common good will assist us in facing current and future challenges.

Among the various important areas of concern that this body is called to address, some new debates are of particular interest to this Delegation:

- reaching an agreement on a text of an international legal instrument which will ensure the effective protection of genetic resources, traditional knowledge, traditional cultural expressions and folklore;
- moving forward in the negotiation on the Treaty on the Protection of Broadcast Organizations, taking into account current rapid technological developments;
- and, above all, the ratification and entry into force of the Marrakech Treaty to Facilitate Access to Published Works for Persons Who Are Blind, Visually Impaired, or Otherwise Print Disabled.

[2] www.wipo.int/export/sites/www/ipstats/en/wipi/2013/pdf/wipo_pub_941_2013_highlights.pdf.

In conclusion, Madam President

Allow me to renew the Holy See's congratulations to the Director General for his re-election and restate our will to collaborate with him and the Secretariat during this new term.

Thank you, Madam President.

THE LONG-STANDING IP PROTECTION RIGHTS VS. THE COMMON GOOD*

Mr President,

The Delegation of the Holy See would like to congratulate you on your election to chair the General Assembly. We welcome the two new vice-chairs as well and thank the outgoing chair and vice-chair for all their hard work over the past year. My Delegation is confident that under your leadership we will be able to reach a positive outcome during this session, as we did in the previous ones.

Allow me also to express our appreciation to the Director General and the Secretariat for the preparation of these Assemblies and for the substantial outcomes achieved by WIPO in recent years, in particular in relation to work concerning global IP services. The steady growth of applications and the expansion of membership cannot be achieved without proper responses to the evolving demands from the real world.

The context in which intellectual property (IP) operates in the contemporary world is vastly different from the one in which IP was born. The new context has changed the position of IP both in the economy and in society. Over the past few decades, the center of wealth creation has been shifting from tangible assets or physical capital to intangible assets or intellectual capital or, as the OECD calls it, knowledge-based capital.

We live in a global knowledge economy and the key to future progress is to excel at turning what we discover and learn into marketable new products and technologies. As clearly shown by the Global Intellectual Property Reports, innovation adaptation and the use of these new technologies are the primary drivers of growth within international economies.

Through both private and public investments, we continue to see incredible scientific advancement in the understanding and use of biological resources, the applications of which hold great social value and potential to improve the lives of people, particularly in the medical, pharmaceutical and agricultural fields. To continue incentivizing such innovations and to spread the benefits of these innovations widely, just legal frameworks for intellectual property protection play an essential role. Yet, while we recognize the value of intellectual property protection, the scope of

* Statement delivered at the 55th Series of Meetings of the WIPO Assemblies, 5 October 2015.

those rights must always be measured in relation to greater principles of justice in service of the common good. However, nowadays, the fruits of scientific progress, rather than being placed at the service of the entire human community, are distributed in such a way that inequalities are actually increased. The law of profit alone cannot be applied to that which is essential for the fight against hunger, disease and poverty.[1]

WIPO is also making a significant contribution to IP information sharing and dissemination through its work related to global IP infrastructure. The contribution to society from the invention to be patented does not consist only of the invention as such, but also of the provision of technical information related to that invention. The global patent system needs continued improvement towards increased transparency and efficiency. International enterprises can be caught unaware of existing patent rights in various markets, while inventors and researchers need access to a fully articulated and comprehensive database of patent claims. A comprehensive database would lower search costs for inventors and examination offices.

While WIPO needs to follow the principles and objectives set in the Organization's Convention, this has to be done in a manner that continues responding to the ever-changing realities of the international community. This means that the Organization has to continue to work at the service of the real world, which is formed by innovators, creators and especially the users of the IP system and IP information. The Secretariat and the Member States should revive the normative work in a functional and responsible manner that could be accepted across the system and through which we can fulfill our responsibility as a member of the global community.

The present-day intellectual property rights system is built on long-standing and traditional concepts of protection and designed for an era before the technological revolution. Classic copyrights cannot be sustained in this modern digital world and the 'one-size-fits-all' approach of patent rules is no longer viable for the cross-industry complexities of the new technology development. The Organization is called to face major challenges and offer a place for bridging the gap between the prevalent trade-oriented approach and the broader implications of intellectual property regulation. In this sense, the renewal of the mandate for the Intergovernmental Committee on Intellectual Property and Genetic

[1] Pope John Paul II, Address to 'Jubilee 2000 Debt Campaign', 23 September 1999.

Resources, Traditional Knowledge and Folklore (IGC) could represent a strong signal.

Mr President,

In conclusion, let us assure you that you can count on the constructive spirit and support of the Holy See during these Assemblies.

Thank you, Mr President.

EXPLANATORY NOTES

Berne Convention for the Protection of Literary and Artistic Works

The Berne Convention deals with the protection of literary and artistic works and the rights of their authors. It is based on three basic principles and contains a series of provisions determining the minimum protection to be granted, as well as special provisions available to developing countries that want to make use of them. The three basic principles are the following: (a) Works originating in one of the Contracting States (that is, works the author of which is a national of such a State or works first published in such a State) must be given the same protection in each of the other Contracting States as the latter grants to the works of its own nationals (principle of 'national treatment'); (b) Protection must not be conditional upon compliance with any formality (principle of 'automatic' protection); (c) Protection is independent of the existence of protection in the country of origin of the work (principle of 'independence' of protection). If, however, a Contracting State provides for a longer term of protection than the minimum prescribed by the Convention and the work ceases to be protected in the country of origin, protection may be denied once protection in the country of origin ceases (www.wipo.int/treaties/en/ip/berne/summary_berne.html).

CDIP – Committee on Development and Intellectual Property

The CDIP was established by the WIPO General Assembly in 2008 with a mandate to: develop a work-program for implementing the 45 adopted Development Agenda recommendations; monitor, assess, discuss and report on the implementation of all recommendations adopted; and for that purpose to coordinate with relevant WIPO bodies; and discuss IP- and development-related issues as agreed by the Committee, as well as those decided by the General Assembly. The Committee reports and makes recommendations annually to the General Assembly. It is composed of all WIPO Member States and is open to the participation, as observers, of all intergovernmental and non-governmental organizations with permanent observer status in WIPO, and of other IGOs and NGOs admitted by the Committee on an ad hoc basis (www.wipo.int/policy/en/cdip/).

DDA – The WTO Doha Development Agenda

The Doha Round is the most recent round of trade negotiations among the WTO membership. Its aim is to achieve major reform of the international trading system through the introduction of lower trade barriers and revised trade rules. The work program covers about 20 areas of trade. The Round is also known semi-officially as the Doha Development Agenda as a fundamental objective is to improve the trading prospects of developing countries. The Round was officially launched at the WTO's Fourth Ministerial Conference in Doha, Qatar, in November 2001. The Doha Ministerial Declaration provided the mandate for the negotiations, including on agriculture, services and an intellectual property topic, which began earlier. In Doha, ministers also approved a decision on how to address the problems developing countries face in implementing the current WTO agreements (https://www.wto.org/english/tratop_e/dda_e/dda_e.htm).

Distortion

When prices are higher or lower than normal, and when quantities produced, bought, and sold are also higher or lower than normal – i.e. than the levels that would usually exist in a competitive market (https://www.wto.org/english/thewto_e/whatis_e/tif_e/agrm3_e.htm).

DSB – Dispute Settlement Body

The dispute settlement is the central pillar of the multilateral trading system, and the WTO's unique contribution to the stability of the global economy. Without a means of settling disputes, the rules-based system would be less effective because the rules could not be enforced. The system is based on clearly defined rules, with timetables for completing a case. First rulings are made by a panel and endorsed (or rejected) by the WTO's full membership. Appeals based on points of law are possible (https://www.wto.org/english/thewto_e/whatis_e/tif_e/disp1_e.htm).

Export Competition

Term used in these negotiations to cover export subsidies and the 'parallel' issues, which could provide loopholes for governments' export subsidies – export finance (credit, guarantees and insurance), exporting state trading enterprises, and international food aid (https://www.wto.org/english/thewto_e/whatis_e/tif_e/disp1_e.htm).

GATT – General Agreement on Tariffs and Trade

Formed in 1947 and signed into international law on 1 January 1948, GATT remained one of the focal features of international trade agreements until it was replaced by the creation of the World Trade Organization on 1 January 1995. The foundation for GATT was laid by the proposal of the International Trade Organization in 1945; however, the ITO was never completed (https://www.wto.org/english/thewto_e/whatis_e/tif_e/disp1_e.htm).

GATS – General Agreement on Trade in Services

The GATS is a treaty of the World Trade Organization that entered into force in January 1995 as a result of the Uruguay Round negotiations. The treaty was created to extend the multilateral trading system to the service sector, in the same way the General Agreement on Tariffs and Trade provides such a system for merchandise trade (https://www.wto.org/english/tratop_e/serv_e/gatsqa_e.htm).

GDP – Gross Domestic Product

The GDP is the monetary value of all the finished goods and services produced within a country's borders in a specific time period. Though GDP is usually calculated on an annual basis, it can be calculated on a quarterly basis as well. GDP includes all private and public consumption, government outlays, investments and exports minus imports that occur within a defined territory (www.investopedia.com/terms/g/gdp.asp#ixzz40XZFTQ9b).

IGC – WIPO's Intergovernmental Committee on Intellectual Property and Genetic Resources, Traditional Knowledge and Folklore

Established in 2000, WIPO's Intergovernmental Committee on Intellectual Property and Genetic Resources, Traditional Knowledge and Folklore (IGC) is a forum where WIPO Member States discuss the intellectual property issues that arise in the context of access to genetic resources and benefit-sharing as well as the protection of traditional knowledge and traditional cultural expressions (the terms 'traditional cultural expressions' and 'expressions of folklore' are used interchangeably in WIPO discussions). The IGC holds formal negotiations with the objective of reaching agreement on one or more international legal instruments that would ensure the effective protection of genetic resources, traditional knowledge and traditional cultural expressions. Such an instrument or instruments could range from a recommendation to WIPO members to a formal treaty that would bind countries choosing to ratify it (www.wipo.int/export/sites/www/tk/en/resources/pdf/tk_brief2.pdf).

ILC – International Labour Conference

The Member States of the ILO meet at the International Labour Conference, held every year in Geneva, Switzerland, in the month of June. Each Member State is represented by a Delegation consisting of two government delegates, an employer delegate, a worker delegate, and their respective advisers. (Employer and Worker delegates are nominated in agreement with the most representative national organizations of employers and workers.)

Every delegate has the same rights, and all can express themselves freely and vote as they wish. So it happens that worker and employer delegates sometimes vote against their government's representatives or against each other. This diversity of viewpoints, however, does not prevent decisions being adopted by very large majorities, or in some cases even unanimously (www.ilo.org/ilc/AbouttheILC/lang–en/index.htm).

International Labour Organization (ILO)

The ILO was founded in 1919, in the wake of a destructive war, to pursue a vision based on the premise that universal, lasting peace can be established only if it is based on social justice. The ILO became the first specialized agency of the UN in 1946. The International Labour Organization is the only tripartite UN agency with government, employer and worker representatives. This tripartite structure makes the ILO a unique forum in which the governments and the social partners of the economy of its 186 Member States can freely and openly debate and elaborate labour standards and policies (www.ilo.org/global/about-the-ilo/history/lang--en/index.htm).

ILO Domestic Workers Convention No. 189

On 16 June 2011, during the 100th International Labour Conference, the ILO tripartite system – governments, trade unions and employers' associations – adopted the ILO Convention 189 Concerning Decent Work for Domestic Workers (Domestic Workers Convention, No. 189). This groundbreaking treaty establishes the first global standards for domestic workers and entered into force in 2013 (www.ilo.org/dyn/normlex/en/f?p=NORMLEXPUB:12100:0::NO::P12100_INSTRUMENT_ID:2551460).

IPRs – Intellectual Property Rights

IPRs are the legal rights given to creators of intellectual property. IPRs usually give the creator of intellectual property the right to exclude others from exploiting the creation for a defined period of time. Intellectual property laws provide the incentives that foster innovation and creativity, and strive to ensure that the competitive struggle is fought within certain bounds of fairness. The protection of IPRs contributes significantly to technological progress and the competitiveness of businesses. Intellectual property shall include the rights relating to: literary, artistic and scientific works; performances of performing artists, phonograms and broadcasts; inventions in all fields of human endeavour; scientific discoveries; industrial designs; trademarks, service marks and commercial names and designations; protection against unfair competition; and all other rights resulting from intellectual activity in the industrial, scientific, literary or artistic fields (www.wipo.int/export/sites/www/about-ip/en/iprm/pdf/ch2.pdf).

IMF – International Monetary Fund

The International Monetary Fund is an international organization created for the purpose of standardizing global financial relations and exchange rates. The IMF generally monitors the global economy, and its core goal is to strengthen economically its member countries. Specifically, the IMF was created with the intention of: (1) Promoting global monetary and exchange stability; (2) Facilitating the expansion and balanced growth of international trade; (3) Assisting in the establishment of a multilateral system of payments for current transactions (www.imf.org/external/about.htm).

MVT – The Marrakech Treaty to Facilitate Access to Published Works for Persons Who Are Blind, Visually Impaired, or Otherwise Print Disabled

The MVT is the latest addition to the body of international copyright treaties administered by WIPO. It has a clear humanitarian and social development dimension and its main goal is to create a set of mandatory limitations and exceptions for the benefit of the blind, visually impaired and otherwise print disabled (VIPs). It requires Contracting Parties to introduce a standard set of limitations and exceptions to copyright rules in order to permit reproduction, distribution and the availability of published works in formats designed to be accessible to VIPs, and to permit exchange of these works across borders by organizations that serve those beneficiaries. The Treaty clarifies that beneficiary persons are those affected by a range of disabilities that interfere with the effective reading of printed material. The broad definition includes persons who are blind, visually impaired, or reading disabled or persons with a physical disability that prevents them from holding and manipulating a book (www.wipo.int/treaties/en/ip/marrakesh/summary_marrakesh.html).

MFN – Most Favoured Nation

Under the WTO agreements, countries cannot normally discriminate between their trading partners. Grant someone a special favour (such as a lower customs duty rate for one of their products) and you have to do the same for all other WTO members (https://www.wto.org/english/thewto_e/whatis_e/tif_e/fact2_e.htm).

National Treatment

Imported and locally produced goods should be treated equally – at least after the foreign goods have entered the market. The same should apply to foreign and domestic services, and to foreign and local trademarks, copyrights and patents. This principle of 'national treatment' (giving others the same treatment as one's own nationals) is also found in all the three main WTO agreements, although once again the principle is handled slightly differently in each of these (https://www.wto.org/english/thewto_e/whatis_e/tif_e/fact2_e.htm).

Paris Convention for the Protection of Industrial Property

This Convention applies to industrial property in the widest sense, including patents, trademarks, industrial designs, utility models (a kind of 'small-scale patent' provided for by the laws of some countries), service marks, trade names (designations under which an industrial or commercial activity is carried out), geographical indications (indications of source and appellations of origin) and the repression of unfair competition (www.wipo.int/treaties/en/ip/paris/summary_paris.html).

SCCR – Standing Committee on Copyright and Related Rights

The SCCR was set up in the 1998–1999 biennium to examine matters of substantive law or harmonization in the field of copyright and related rights. The Committee is composed of all Member States of WIPO and/or of the Berne Union; and, as observers, certain Member States of the United Nations which are non-members of WIPO and/or the Berne Union, as well as a number of intergovernmental and non-governmental organizations. The Standing Committee formulates recommendations for consideration by the WIPO General Assembly or a Diplomatic Conference (www.wipo.int/policy/en/sccr/).

SCP – Standing Committee on the Law of Patents

The SCP was created in 1998 to serve as a forum to discuss issues, facilitate coordination and provide guidance concerning the progressive international development of patent law. By dealing with clusters of interlocking issues rather than working in isolation on single issues, it is intended to provide Member States with an effective mechanism for setting priorities and allocating resources, and ensure the coordination and continuity of interrelated, ongoing work. The Committee is composed of all Member States of WIPO and/or of the Paris Union. As observers, certain Member States of the UN, who are not members of WIPO and/or the Paris

Union, as well as a number of accredited intergovernmental and non-governmental organizations also participate in the SCP (www.wipo.int/policy/en/scp/).

SCT – Standing Committee on the Law of Trademarks, Industrial Designs and Geographical Indications

The SCT was created in 1998 to serve as a forum to discuss issues, facilitate coordination and provide guidance on the progressive development of international law on trademarks, industrial designs and geographical indications, including the harmonization of national laws and procedures (www.wipo.int/policy/en/sct/).

TRIPs – The WTO Agreement on Trade-Related Aspects of Intellectual Property Rights

The TRIPs agreement is the Uruguay Round agreement covering the protection and enforcement of intellectual property rights. Intellectual property rights were a key area of concern for the USA during the Uruguay Round negotiations. From the perspective of the USA, the TRIPs Agreement was a major achievement of the Uruguay Round. The TRIPs Agreement incorporates by reference most of the substantive provisions of two earlier multilateral IPR conventions: the Paris Convention for the Protection of Industrial Property (1967) (covering patents, trademarks, trade names, utility models, industrial designs and unfair competition) and the Berne Convention for the Protection of Literary and Artistic Works (1971) (covering copyrights). The TRIPs Agreement applies to all WTO Members; it explicitly covers patents, trademarks, copyrights and related rights, geographical indications, layout designs (topographies) of integrated circuits (usually called semiconductor mask works in the USA), industrial designs and undisclosed information (trade secrets) (https://www.wto.org/english/tratop_e/trips_e/intel2_e.htm).

UNCTAD Conference

The Conference with the highest decision-making body of UNCTAD is the quadrennial conference, at which Member States make assessments of current trade and development issues, discuss policy options and formulate global policy responses. The conference also sets the organization's mandate and work priorities. The conference is a subsidiary organ of the United Nations General Assembly; the conferences serve an important political function: they allow intergovernmental consensus building regarding the state of the world economy and development policies, and they play a key role in identifying the role of the United Nations and UNCTAD in addressing economic development problems (http://unctad.org/en/Pages/Meetings/UNCTAD-Conferences.aspx).

UNCTAD Trade and Development Board

In between the quadrennial Conferences, the Trade and Development Board oversees the activities of the organization. It meets in Geneva in a regular session and up to three times a year in executive sessions to deal with urgent policy issues, as well as management and institutional matters (http://unctad.org/en/Pages/Meetings/TDB.aspx).

Vulture Funds

There is no international legal regime that governs cases of state 'insolvency' or 'bankruptcy'. When a state defaults on its sovereign debts, it has to start, on its own initiative, a process of restructuring its foreign debt, which entails complex and protracted negotiations with a range of very different types of creditors, including private commercial creditors. According to Cephas Lumina, former Independent Expert, 'vulture funds' are: 'private commercial entities that acquire, either by purchase, assignment or some other form of transaction, defaulted or distressed debts, and sometimes actual court judgements, with the aim of achieving a high return. In the sovereign debt context, vulture funds (or "distressed debt funds", as they often describe themselves) usually acquire the defaulted sovereign debt of poor countries on the secondary market at a price far less than its face value and then attempt, through litigation, seizure of assets or political pressure, to seek repayment of the full face value of the debt together with interests, penalties and legal fees.'[2]

The WIPO Development Agenda

The WIPO Development Agenda ensures that development considerations form an integral part of WIPO's work. The effective implementation of the Development Agenda, including the mainstreaming of its

[2] UN Doc. A/HRC/14/21, 29 April 2010, para. 8.

recommendations into our substantive programs, is a key priority. The adoption of the Development Agenda was an important milestone for WIPO. The Agenda was formally established by WIPO's Member States in 2007, in a decision which included the adoption of 45 Development Agenda recommendations, grouped into six clusters, and the establishment of a Committee on Development and Intellectual Property (CDIP) (www.wipo.int/ip-development/en/agenda/).

WTO General Council

The General Council is WTO's highest-level decision-making body in Geneva, meeting regularly to carry out the functions of the WTO. It has representatives (usually ambassadors or equivalent) from all member governments and has the authority to act on behalf of the ministerial conference, which only meets about every two years (https://www.wto.org/english/thewto_e/gcounc_e/gcounc_e.htm).

WTO Ministerial Conference

The WTO Ministerial Conference is the topmost decision-making body, which meets at least once every two years. The Ministerial Conference can take decisions on all matters under any of the multilateral trade agreements (https://www.wto.org/english/thewto_e/whatis_e/tif_e/org1_e.htm).

IV

The Quest for Peace

Introduction

Largely unknown to the general public, the activity of the Holy See in the field of disarmament, security and arms control has had some considerable achievements. It has often encouraged – and continues to encourage – the international community 'to be resolute in promoting effective disarmament and arms control negotiations and in strengthening international humanitarian law by reaffirming the preeminent and inherent value of human dignity and the centrality of the human person'.[1] A question, however, can be raised asking why and on what basis of legitimacy the Holy See should be present in international fora since it has not possessed an army for some 150 years.

Without aiming at an exhaustive overview of the activity of the Holy See in the area of disarmament, this introduction should serve as a starting point and an invitation to deepen the knowledge of this experience and to promote commitment to serve the noble cause of peace through disarmament. From the Catholic perspective, this involvement is not a luxury but part of a person's identity and responsibility to be a peacemaker.

If the Holy See opted for an observer status at the United Nations, she made a different choice in the field of disarmament. In the wake of the Second World War that left the world with millions of dead, wounded and disabled persons, and with massive destruction of infrastructures, Europe found itself in a state of despair and disorientation. Besides the obvious need for economic and political reconstruction, there was a parallel urgent need for a moral recovery and the foundation of a 'new world order' based on respect for human dignity and fundamental human rights.

Today, economic and political reconstruction seems to have been achieved, and the financial and economic crisis partly overcome. States, however, continue to increase their military capabilities to meet new and asymmetrical challenges in an increasingly dangerous world that led Pope Francis to warn of a 'piecemeal World War III'. Instead of pursuing much needed domestic or international development programmes, which are reduced in favour of military expenditure and weapons renewal, several countries are indeed pursuing military modernization and boosting military budgets in spite of persisting economic inequalities. Hundreds of new aircraft, tanks and missiles are rolling off assembly lines, and tens

[1] www.unog.ch/80256EDD006B8954/%28httpAssets%29/42E72A73A7F63697C125756D003EAD09/$file/HolySee.pdf

of thousands of troops are taking part in bloody wars or war games and parades to show a country's military readiness.

In this context the Holy See, inspired by the teaching of universal brotherhood and of justice and peace between men and peoples contained in the Gospel, desired to make its contribution to initiatives like disarmament which promote security, mutual trust and peaceful co-operation in relations between peoples,[2] and considered it a moral obligation to join the international community as an active key player in the creation and shaping of appropriate mechanisms and negotiated treaties that limit and regulate the use of arms. In this way it responds to the expectations of people suffering and struggling because of armed conflicts and widespread violence, and aims at progressively de-weaponizing security. In particular, the Holy See has taken a strong position on the elimination of nuclear weapons, with a view to banning them once and for all, by adopting 'the ethic of responsibility' to replace 'the ethic of fear'.

The Holy See has acceded to and ratified practically all the instruments relating to arms control and disarmament: for instance, the Holy See acceded to the Treaty on the Non-Proliferation of Nuclear Weapons (NPT) on 25 February 1971,[3] to the Biological Weapons Convention (BWC) on 7 January 2002,[4] to the Convention on Prohibitions or Restrictions on the Use of Certain Conventional Weapons Which May Be Deemed to Be Excessively Injurious or to Have Indiscriminate Effects (CCW) on 22 July 1997,[5] and it ratified the Chemical Weapons Convention (CWC) on 12 May 1999,[6] the Convention on the Prohibition of the Use, Stockpiling, Production and Transfer of Anti-Personnel Mines and on their Destruction on 17 February 1998,[7] and the Convention on Cluster Munitions (CCM) on 3 December 2002.[8] Additionally, the Holy See is a Member State of the Organization for Security and Co-operation in Europe since 25 June 1973 and is a State Party to the International Atomic Energy Agency (IAEA) since 29 July 1957.

[2] http://disarmament.un.org/treaties/a/npt/holysee/acc/washington.
[3] Ibid.
[4] http://disarmament.un.org/treaties/a/bwc/holysee/acc/washington.
[5] https://treaties.un.org/pages/ViewDetails.aspx?src=TREATY&mtdsg_no=XXVI-2&chapter=26&lang=en.
[6] www.opcw.org/news/article/holy-see-ratifies-the-chemical-weapons-convention/.
[7] www.unog.ch/80256EE600585943/%28httpPages%29/6E65F97C9D695724C12571C0003D09EF?OpenDocument.
[8] https://treaties.un.org/Pages/ViewDetails.aspx?src=TREATY&mtdsg_no=XXVI-6&chapter=26&lang=en.

Three main objectives are recurrent and central to the position of the Holy See in the field of disarmament, as it results clearly from the statements included in this chapter.

First, the defence of human dignity and the centrality of the human person is a priority with special concern for the victims of armed conflicts. An authentic peace is only possible if 'the dignity of the human person is promoted at every level of society, and every individual is given the chance to live in accordance with this dignity.'[9] The position of the Holy See is rooted in the social doctrine of the Church and it goes beyond the mere discussion on weapons to draw attention on their effects and their humanitarian consequences relying on scientific, technical and strategic data.[10]

Second, even assuming that a state has the right, if not the duty, to defend and protect its population and ensure its safety, it does not mean that everything is acceptable in the conduct of hostilities. In armed conflicts there exist certain fundamental ethical, humanitarian and legal principles that must be adhered to by everyone, with no exceptions. The failure to preserve peace should not give rise to actions that are equivalent to war crimes, genocide and crimes against humanity: it is in such despicable events that the Holy See advocates for a minimum of humanity in situations where we witness an obvious failure. The Holy See has often taken a stance against the abuses of human rights in conflict situations and delivered Statements to various Special Sessions of the Human Rights Council, which can be held at any time to address human rights violations and emergencies, provided that at least one-third of the Member States request so.[11]

[9] http://w2.vatican.va/content/john-paul-ii/en/messages/peace/documents/hf_jp-ii_mes_08121994_xxviii-world-day-for-peace.html.

[10] See for instance the following statements: 'The Need to Provide Assistance to the Innocent Witnesses of a Wrong Approach to Security' (2004); 'Consideration of the General Status and Operation of the Anti-Personnel Mine Ban Convention: Assisting the Victims' (2007); 'Dublin Diplomatic Conference on Cluster Munitions: The Priority Must Revolve Around Human Dignity, Prevention and Assistance to Victims' (2008); 'The Need to Create Adequate Structures to Provide Assistance to Victims and their Reintegration in Society' (2009); and 'Assistance to Victims Stems from the Centrality of the Human Person and Form His/Her Inalienable Dignity' (2012).

[11] Cf., for example, 'The Confusion between the Military Interests and the Humanitarian Urgency' (2010); 'May Peace Triumph Over Division and Umbrage in Syria' (2011); 'We Must Strengthen Our Efforts to Restore Peace in the Democratic Republic of the Congo' (2008); 'The Urgency to Respond to the Deteriorating of the Political and Humanitarian Crisis in the Central African Republic' (2014); 'The

Third, peace and security are not preserved only by military means. As Pope Paul VI eloquently observed: 'development is another name for peace'.[12] Education, health, social justice, political participation and regional and international cooperation are in fact elements indispensable for the national and international security and peace. Therefore, it is not reasonable nor useful to invest excessively in the military, and squander resources that are more necessary for the development and vital needs essential to the development of people, with a great and inevitable suffering of the most vulnerable and poor.[13] Disarmament itself is also essential for stability and security: in fact, increasing or renovating the military of a State will inevitably lead to regional and even international destabilization and possibly conflict, in what has been called the 'security dilemma', where actions by a state intended to heighten its security, such as increasing its military strength or making alliances, can often lead other states to respond with similar measures, producing a sort of endless spiral.[14]

The above-mentioned objectives are not sufficient for the Holy See. It must work as well in collaboration with other state actors, international organizations such as the ICRC, and with civil society organizations in order to transform these objectives into practical binding rules,[15] respected in time of war and in time of peace, in the quest of a true global peace, which is not merely and negatively defined as 'the absence of war' and 'reduced solely to the maintenance of a balance of power between enemies'. Rather, for the Holy See, peace is 'founded on a correct understanding of the human person' and 'requires the establishment of an order based on justice and charity'[16] in order to preserve potential victims from paying the price of human short-sightedness.

Need to Create the Conditions of a Stable and Immediate Peace in the Occupied Palestinian Territory including East Jerusalem' (2014).

12 http://w2.vatican.va/content/paul-vi/en/encyclicals/documents/hf_p-vi_enc_26031967_populorum.html.

13 See, for instance, 'The Futility of War as a Means to Resolve Disagreements: We Must Pursue the Way of Dialogue among all the People in Syria' (2012) and 'Peace, the *sine qua non* for the Enjoyment of all Human Rights' (2013).

14 See, for instance, 'Violence Only Begets Further Violence: The Appalling Report of the Independent International Commission of Inquiry on the Syrian Arab Republic' (2013); and 'Geneva II Conference: Dialogue as the Only Way Forward' (2014).

15 Cf. the statement, 'The Contributions of Non-Governmental Actors to a Strong and Credible Legal Instrument' (2008).

16 www.vatican.va/roman_curia/pontifical_councils/justpeace/documents/rc_pc_justpeace_doc_20060526_compendio-dott-soc_en.html (15 February 2015).

In this connection, three examples better illustrate the engagement of the Holy See in the field of disarmament:

1. Since the Second Vatican Council and Pope John XXIII's Encyclical *Pacem in Terris*, the Holy See has advocated in favour of general nuclear disarmament. Despite some limited progress, nuclear proliferation and the risks that the possession of these weapons entails is considerable. The Holy See has partnered with a coalition of States, NGOs (International Campaign to Ban Nuclear Weapons), the ICRC and the Societies of the Red Cross and Red Crescent to revive the debate on nuclear disarmament from a new perspective: the humanitarian consequences of a nuclear detonation whether intentional or accidental. The Holy See is at the forefront of this initiative. Three major conferences have been held in Oslo (Norway, March 2013), Nayarit (Mexico, February 2014) and Vienna (Austria, December 2014). Addressing this last Conference in Vienna, which gathered about 160 countries and 900 participants, the Holy Father – through a message, called for total nuclear disarmament.[17] The Holy See also issued a solid background paper[18] which basically set the tone of the Vienna Conference on the Humanitarian Impact of Nuclear Weapons, held 8–9 December 2014. The paper questions the ethical foundations of nuclear deterrence: the mere possession of nuclear weapons is per se immoral, and not just their use.
2. Another concern of the Holy See is the use of explosive weapons in highly populated areas. For the first time in the history of mankind, the world population is more urban than rural and therefore it is very likely that armed conflict will increasingly take place in urban contexts, which has been proved by recent conflicts in the Middle East, Africa and Europe. Under such conditions, it is almost impossible to respect international humanitarian law, in particular the distinction between military and civilian targets, the rule of proportionality, etc. The humanitarian consequences of conflicts in urban areas are catastrophic and the conditions for a decent life are no longer possible: civilians are not just collateral damage but become the overwhelming majority of casualties and wounded with a widespread and systematic

[17] See the statement, 'The Ethical and Humanitarian Consequences of Nuclear Weapons' (2014).

[18] www.paxchristi.net/sites/default/files/nuclearweaponstimeforabolitionfinal.pdf (16 February 2015).

destruction of economic, educational and health infrastructures.[19] In every consideration of the overwhelming numbers of violent conflicts, especially when intertwined political, religious or civil issues interface and exacerbate the hatred among the belligerents and reconciliation seems to become even more difficult, the Holy See has been striving with various partners, particularly NGOs, to sensitize the international community to this new situation and to encourage a multilateral reflection in order to find concrete and suitable solutions.

3. In certain instances, the Holy See is also committed to the monitoring and careful evaluation of breakthroughs in military technology which may potentially cause conflicts to escalate if certain advanced weapons fall into the wrong hands or are not secured by States. Prevention, therefore, is undoubtedly the best option.[20] In recent years, scientific and technological progress in the field of robotics have proceeded at a blistering pace. Several countries have long initiated research programmes to develop military applications which are completely autonomous systems and would be able to perform military operations without human intervention, as far as to take the decision to kill. Proponents of such systems argue that a robot has no feelings and is therefore less subject to hatred or revenge; another argument in favour is that it would be just as capable as a human being to respect international humanitarian law, if not more. The Holy See spoke out and delivered some interventions on the ethical implications related to robotics in general, and in particular for military use, and expressed its deep concerns in relation to the use of drones and the troubling ethical consequences for users and victims alike. While acknowledging that, in many fields, autonomous technology may indeed prove beneficial to humanity, the application of autonomy to weapons technology is entirely distinct. The decision regarding the life and death of human beings can never be left to a machine, regardless of the degree of perfection the machine may have. On top of a large number of practical problems related to drones, it has to be kept in mind that conflicts will always have a political and human dimension, which cannot be avoided without risking the dehumanization of the human person. As the use of weaponized drones in armed conflicts and other

[19] See, for instance, 'The Urgency of an Adequate Response to the Humanitarian Consequences of Cluster Munitions' (2008).

[20] Cf. 'The Need to Promote a Culture of Prevention through the Adoption of New Legal Instruments' (2004).

international hostile actions has increased exponentially in recent years, the ethical and humanitarian concerns remain more than ever relevant, and in fact become more and more compelling as the use of this lethal weapon increases.[21]

In a world with increasing explosions of violence, the search for peace remains a priority goal of the Holy See and of the international community. Peace is indispensable for development and resources available should be directed to improve the quality of life of people everywhere. It is always the human person that should be at the centre of concern.

List of Statements

1 Promoting the Right to Peace and the End to Armed Conflicts

- RESTORE PEACE IN THE DEMOCRATIC REPUBLIC OF THE CONGO, 8th Special Session of the Human Rights Council on the situation of human rights in the East of the Democratic Republic of the Congo (28 November 2008)
- THE UMPTEENTH EPISODE OF VIOLENCE IN THE ISRAELI–PALESTINIAN CONFLICT: THE ATTACK AGAINST THE HUMANITARIAN FLOTILLA SAILING TO GAZA, 14th Session of the Human Rights Council, Urgent Debate on the Israeli raid on the flotilla sailing to Gaza (1 June 2010)
- PREVENT VIOLENCE THROUGH DIALOGUE BETWEEN ALL PARTIES INVOLVED IN THE LIBYAN ARAB JAMAHIRIYA, 15th Special Session on the Situation of Human Rights in the Libyan Arab Jamahiriya (25 February 2011)
- MAY PEACE TRIUMPH OVER DIVISION AND UMBRAGE IN SYRIA, 18th Special Session of the Human Rights Council on Syria (2 December 2011)
- THE AGGRAVATION OF THE SYRIAN CONFLICT: PROVIDE HUMANITARIAN ASSISTANCE TO DISPLACED PERSONS, 21st Session of the Human Rights Council – Item 4: *Interactive Dialogue with the Independent International Commission of Inquiry on the Syrian Arab Republic* (17 September 2012)

[21] Cf. 'The Humanitarian and Ethical Implications of the Use of Weaponized Drones and their Impact on Civilians' (2013); 'The Need for the CCW to Address the Drone Issue before it Becomes a Destabilizing Force' (2014).

- SYRIA: THE FUTILITY OF WAR AS A MEANS TO RESOLVE DISAGREEMENTS, 19th Session of the Human Rights Council – Urgent Debate on Syria (28 February 2012)
- A DURABLE AND ACCEPTABLE SOLUTION IN SYRIA THROUGH PEACEFUL NEGOTIATIONS, at the 23rd Session of the Human Rights Council – *Urgent Debate on the Deteriorating Situation of Human Rights in the Syrian Arab Republic and the Recent Killings in Al Qusayr* (29 May 2013)
- PEACE, THE SINE QUA NON FOR THE ENJOYMENT OF ALL HUMAN RIGHTS, 23rd Session of the Human Rights Council – Item 5: Report of the Intergovernmental Working Group on the Right to Peace (7 June 2013)
- VIOLENCE ONLY BEGETS FURTHER VIOLENCE: THE APPALLING REPORT OF THE INDEPENDENT INTERNATIONAL COMMISSION OF INQUIRY ON THE SYRIAN ARAB REPUBLIC, 24th Session of the Human Rights Council – Item 4: *Interactive Dialogue with the Independent International Commission of Inquiry on the Syrian Arab Republic* (16 September 2013)
- THE DETERIORATING OF THE POLITICAL AND HUMANITARIAN CRISIS IN THE CENTRAL AFRICAN REPUBLIC, 20th Special Session of the Human Rights Council on the Human Rights Situation in the Central African Republic (20 January 2014)
- GENEVA II CONFERENCE ON SYRIA: DIALOGUE AS THE ONLY WAY FORWARD, International Conference on Syria (Geneva II), Montreux, Switzerland (22 January 2014)
- THE PRIMACY OF INTERNATIONAL LAW OVER UNILATERAL INITIATIVES, 25th Session of the Human Rights Council on the situation in Ukraine (26 March 2014)
- A STABLE AND IMMEDIATE PEACE IN THE OCCUPIED PALESTINIAN TERRITORY INCLUDING EAST JERUSALEM, 21st Special Session of the Human Rights Council on the human rights situation in the Occupied Palestinian Territory including East Jerusalem (23 July 2014)
- THE RESPONSIBILITY TO PROTECT CHRISTIANS AND OTHER RELIGIOUS MINORITIES IN IRAQ AGAINST THE SO-CALLED "ISLAMIC STATE", 22nd Special Session of the Human Rights Council on the human rights situation in Iraq in light of abuses committed by the Islamic State in Iraq and the Levant and associated groups (1 September 2014)
- CLOSENESS AND SOLIDARITY TO ALL THE PEOPLE OF UKRAINE, 28th Session of the Human Rights Council on the situation in Ukraine (26 March 2015)

- BOKO HARAM: CRIMES IN THE NAME OF RELIGION ARE NEVER JUSTIFIED, 23rd Special Session of the Human Rights Council on the Situation of Human Rights in Nigeria – Boko Haram (1 April 2015)
- FEAR, MISTRUST, AND DESPAIR CAUSED BY POVERTY AND FRUSTRATION IN BURUNDI, 24th Special Session of the Human Rights Council on Burundi (17 December 2015)

2 Disarmament and Arms Control

2.1 Weapons of Mass Destruction (Nuclear Weapons, Biological Weapons Convention)

- THE IMPORTANCE OF THE BIOLOGICAL WEAPONS CONVENTION, 6th Review Conference of the States Parties to the Biological Weapons Convention (20 November 2006)
- MESSAGE OF POPE FRANCIS ON THE OCCASION OF THE VIENNA CONFERENCE ON THE HUMANITARIAN IMPACT OF NUCLEAR WEAPONS, Conference on the Humanitarian Impact of Nuclear Weapons, Vienna, Austria (8 December 2014)
- THE ETHICAL AND HUMANITARIAN CONSEQUENCES OF NUCLEAR WEAPONS, Conference on the Humanitarian Impact of Nuclear Weapons, Vienna, Austria (9 December 2014)

2.2 Conventional Weapons

2.2.1 Anti-Personnel Landmines Convention

- ASSISTANCE TO THE INNOCENT WITNESSES OF A WRONG APPROACH TO SECURITY, Convention on the Prohibition of the Use, Stockpiling, Production and Transfer of Anti-Personnel Mines and on their Destruction: *Standing Committee on Victim Assistance and Socio-Economic Reintegration* (10 February 2004)
- CONSIDERATION OF THE GENERAL STATUS AND OPERATION OF THE CONVENTION: ASSISTING THE VICTIMS, 8th Meeting of States Parties to the Convention on the Prohibition of the Use, Stockpiling, Production and Transfer of Anti-Personnel Mines and on their Destruction, Dead Sea, Jordan (21 November 2007)
- EXTEND THE TIME LIMITS PROVISIONS OF ARTICLE 5 OF THE ANTI-PERSONNEL LANDMINES CONVENTION, 9th Meeting of States Parties to the Convention on the Prohibition of the Use, Stockpiling, Production and Transfer of Anti-Personnel Mines and on their Destruction (24 November 2008)

2.2.2 Convention on Cluster Munitions

- NOTE OF THE HOLY SEE ON CLUSTER MUNITIONS, Note released by the Holy See (May 2007)
- DUBLIN DIPLOMATIC CONFERENCE ON CLUSTER MUNITIONS: HUMAN DIGNITY, PREVENTION, AND ASSISTANCE TO VICTIMS, Dublin Diplomatic Conference on Cluster Munitions, Dublin, Ireland (19 May 2008)
- THE CONTRIBUTIONS OF NON-GOVERNMENTAL ACTORS TO A STRONG AND CREDIBLE LEGAL INSTRUMENT, concluding statement, Dublin Diplomatic Conference on Cluster Munitions, Dublin, Ireland (30 May 2008)
- THE SIGNING OF THE CONVENTION ON CLUSTER MUNITIONS: THE LARGE NUMBER OF VICTIMS IS THE MOST VALID ARGUMENT FOR COOPERATION, signing of the Convention on Cluster Munitions, Oslo, Norway (3–4 December 2008)
- A FAIR AND EQUITABLE FINANCING FOR AN EFFECTIVE IMPLEMENTATION OF THE CONVENTION ON CLUSTER MUNITIONS, 1st Review Conference of the Convention on Cluster Munitions (CCM), Dubrovnik, Croatia (7 September 2015)

2.2.3 Convention on Certain Conventional Weapons

- A CULTURE OF PREVENTION THROUGH THE ADOPTION OF NEW LEGAL INSTRUMENTS, 7th Session of the Group of Governmental Experts of the States Parties to the Convention on Prohibitions or Restrictions on the Use of Certain Conventional Weapons Which May Be Deemed to Be Excessively Injurious or to Have Indiscriminate Effects (8 March 2004)
- THE CALL FOR A MORATORIUM ON THE USE OF CLUSTER MUNITIONS WHILE AN APPROPRIATE INSTRUMENT IS ADOPTED, 11th Session of the Group of Governmental Experts of the States Parties to the Convention on Prohibitions or Restrictions on the Use of Certain Conventional Weapons Which May Be Deemed to Be Excessively Injurious or to Have Indiscriminate Effects (4 August 2005)
- THE RATIFICATION OF PROTOCOL V ON THE EXPLOSIVE REMNANTS OF WAR: THE HOLY SEE'S ENCOURAGEMENT AND COMMITMENT TO THE FAMILY OF NATIONS, Meeting of the States Parties to the Conventions on Prohibition or Restrictions on the Use of Certain Conventional Weapons Which May Be Deemed to Be Excessively Injurious or to Have Indiscriminate Effects (24–25 November 2005)

- UNITED WE STAND, DIVIDED WE FALL: THE NEED TO FURTHER NEGOTIATE AN INSTRUMENT ON CLUSTER MUNITIONS AND THEIR HUMANITARIAN CONSEQUENCES, 3rd Review Conference of the High Contracting Parties to the Convention on Certain Conventional Weapons (7 November 2006)
- THE URGENT NEED FOR THE CCW TO NEGOTIATE AN EFFECTIVE TEXT CENTERED ON THE HUMAN PERSON, Group of Governmental Experts of the States Parties to the Convention on Prohibitions or Restrictions on the Use of Certain Conventional Weapons Which May Be Deemed to Be Excessively Injurious or to Have Indiscriminate Effects (19 June 2007)
- THE URGENCY OF AN ADEQUATE RESPONSE TO THE HUMANITARIAN CONSEQUENCES OF CLUSTER MUNITIONS, Group of Governmental Experts of the States Parties to the Convention on Prohibitions or Restrictions on the Use of Certain Conventional Weapons Which May Be Deemed to Be Excessively Injurious or to Have Indiscriminate Effects (14 January 2008)
- ASSISTANCE TO VICTIMS AND THEIR REINTEGRATION IN SOCIETY, CCW Group of Governmental Experts on Protocol V on Explosive Remnants of War (22–24 April 2009)
- THE CONFUSION BETWEEN THE MILITARY INTERESTS AND THE HUMANITARIAN URGENCY, Conference of the High Contracting Parties to the Convention on Certain Conventional Weapons (25–26 November 2010)
- THE NEED TO AVOID UNJUST AND INEFFICIENT COMPROMISES, 4th Review Conference of the Convention on Prohibitions or Restrictions on the Use of Certain Conventional Weapons Which May Be Deemed to Be Excessively Injurious or to Have Indiscriminate Effects (14 November 2011)
- A DILIGENT AND COMPLETE IMPLEMENTATION OF PROTOCOL V IS OUR MORAL RESPONSIBILITY, 6th Review Conference of the States Party to Protocol V of the Convention on Prohibitions or Restrictions on the Use of Certain Conventional Weapons Which May Be Deemed to Be Excessively Injurious or to Have Indiscriminate Effects (12–13 November 2012)
- ASSISTANCE TO VICTIMS: THE CENTRALITY OF THE HUMAN PERSON AND HIS/HER INALIENABLE DIGNITY, Meeting of the States Parties to the Convention on Prohibitions or Restrictions on the Use of Certain Conventional Weapons Which May Be Deemed to Be Excessively Injurious or to Have Indiscriminate Effects (15–16 November 2012)

- THE HUMANITARIAN AND ETHICAL IMPLICATIONS OF THE USE OF WEAPONIZED DRONES AND THEIR IMPACT ON CIVILIANS, Annual Meeting of the High Contracting Parties to the Convention on Prohibitions or Restrictions on the Use of Certain Conventional Weapons Which May Be Deemed to Be Excessively Injurious or to Have Indiscriminate Effects (14 November 2013)
- MACHINES CAN NEVER TRULY REPLACE HUMANS IN MORAL DECISIONS OVER LIFE AND DEATH: THE ACCOUNTABILITY VACUUM, Meeting of Experts on lethal autonomous weapons systems of the High Contracting Parties to the Convention on Prohibitions or Restrictions on the Use of Certain Conventional Weapons Which May Be Deemed to Be Excessively Injurious or to Have Indiscriminate Effects (13 May 2014)
- THE MORAL DUTY OF INTERNATIONAL COOPERATION AND COMPLIANCE WITHIN THE FRAMEWORK OF PROTOCOL V, 8th Conference of High Contracting Parties to Protocol V of the Convention on Prohibitions or Restrictions on the Use of Certain Conventional Weapons Which May Be Deemed to Be Excessively Injurious or to Have Indiscriminate Effects (10 November 2014)
- THE NEED FOR THE CCW TO ADDRESS THE DRONE ISSUE BEFORE IT BECOMES A DESTABILIZING FORCE, Meeting of the States Parties to the Convention on Prohibitions or Restrictions on the Use of Certain Conventional Weapons Which May Be Deemed to Be Excessively Injurious or to Have Indiscriminate Effects (13 November 2014)
- THE IMPORTANCE OF A SERIOUS AND HONEST IMPLEMENTATION OF PROTOCOL V, 9th Conference of High Contracting Parties to Protocol V of the Convention on Prohibitions or Restrictions on the Use of Certain Conventional Weapons Which May Be Deemed to Be Excessively Injurious or to Have Indiscriminate Effects (9 November 2015)
- THE CHALLENGES FOR INTERNATIONAL HUMANITARIAN LAW IN A GLOBALIZATION OF INDIFFERENCE, Meeting of the States Parties to the Convention on Prohibitions or Restrictions on the Use of Certain Conventional Weapons Which May Be Deemed to Be Excessively Injurious or to Have Indiscriminate Effects (12 November 2015)

1 PROMOTING THE RIGHT TO PEACE AND THE END TO ARMED CONFLICTS

RESTORE PEACE IN THE DEMOCRATIC REPUBLIC OF THE CONGO*

Mr President,

The daily reports on human suffering in the North Kivu district of the Democratic Republic of the Congo are deeply troubling to the Delegation of the Holy See. Death, rape, lootings, forced recruitment and displacement of the civilian population have become a daily reality in that country. The international community cannot stand idly by but needs to speak out clearly. In fact, with a view to the growing consensus behind the responsibility to protect, it is of the utmost importance for the international community to restore the rule of law and to search for the common good.

The Holy See condemns the large-scale occurrence of serious violations of human rights and of humanitarian law. It deplores the recruitment of children and adolescents as soldiers. It is alarmed by the many cases of torture and other cruel, inhumane and degrading treatment, including the frequent occurrence of sexual violence against women and girls by all parties to the conflict. The international community needs to act swiftly in the face of these grave infringements of human rights.

Moreover, the Holy See denounces the illicit trade in weapons, and in particular of small arms and light weapons in the DRC. They increase the intensity of violence and threaten the lives and the integrity of an unacceptable number of innocent people.

The Congolese Bishops issued a Statement saying that the Congolese people 'are living through a genuine human tragedy that, as a silent genocide, is being carried out under everyone's eyes'.[1] While the Holy Father, Benedict XVI, called upon all to 'collaborate to restore peace in

* Statement delivered at the 8th Special Session of the Human Rights Council on the situation of human rights in the East of the Democratic Republic of the Congo, 28 November 2008.

[1] Conférence Épiscopale Nationale du Congo, Déclaration du Comité permanent des évêques sur la guerre dans l'Est et dans le Nord-Est de la RD Congo, La RD Congo pleure ses enfants, elle est inconsolable, 13 November 2008, www.cenco.cd/presidencenco/messagenov2008.htm.

that land, too long a land of martyrdom, respect for the legal rights and above all the dignity of every person'.[2]

The latest figures show that about 2 million people are forcibly displaced in the DRC. Their right to food, water, decent work, adequate housing, education and health is seriously jeopardized. Many of those displaced end up in camps, where they can be assisted by the international aid organizations. Others, however, are less fortunate and cannot be reached by humanitarian agencies because of ongoing fighting between the different factions. It was recently reported that about 200,000 people are living in the bush and little is known about their situation.

A positive step has been allowing the ICRC to carry out its humanitarian mandate. In the same spirit, international humanitarian and human rights organizations and agencies should be welcomed to carry out their respective roles to eliminate suffering of people. Moreover, international organizations and in particular the African Union should strengthen their efforts to achieve a peaceful solution to the crisis in the DRC.

My Delegation calls upon the warring parties in the Democratic Republic of Congo to respect the ceasefire that has been reached, and to comply with the Peace agreements that have been signed in the past. The people of Congo, like all the people of our planet, have a 'sacred right to peace'.[3] In order to achieve a stable peace it has to be based upon dialogue and reconciliation as peace can only be achieved through justice.

Thank you Mr President.

2 Pope Benedict XVI, After the Angelus of 9 November 2008, www.vatican.va/holy_father/benedict_xvi/angelus/2008/documents/hf_ben-xvi_ang_20081109_en.html.

3 United Nations General Assembly, Declaration on the Right of Peoples to Peace, UN Doc. A/39/51 (1984), p. 1.

THE UMPTEENTH EPISODE OF VIOLENCE IN THE ISRAELI–PALESTINIAN CONFLICT: THE ATTACK AGAINST THE HUMANITARIAN FLOTILLA SAILING TO GAZA*

Mr President,

With profound sadness the Holy See Delegation notes that the unsettled situation in the Middle East remains a source of tragic events. The latest loss of life caused by the use of force in the Israeli attack in international waters against the humanitarian flotilla of ships sailing to the Gaza Strip unfortunately adds another link in the long chain of conflicts and confrontations that produce suffering and tensions for the Palestinian population and the population of Israel.

To the families of the new victims goes our solidarity and condolences. It is hoped that recent and past victims may encourage a wide understanding that violence does not lead to enduring peace, but that dialogue, respect of rights and mutual acceptance do.

To make an effective dialogue possible, a full, impartial and transparent investigation into the latest incident, based upon international law and international humanitarian law, is necessary.

While all the facts are ascertained, it is clear that the humanitarian needs of the people of Gaza are not met and all parties involved and the international community have a responsibility to cooperate so that the fundamental human rights of those persons are implemented.

As the Holy See has previously stated, it is always opposed to the use of violence from whatever side it may come. Violence makes even more difficult the search for peaceful solutions, the only ones that can build a future of constructive coexistence.

My Delegation calls once again upon all parties involved to come to a durable solution of the Israeli–Palestinian conflict through negotiation, leading to a two-State solution, with Israel and an independent Palestinian State living side by side in peace and security.

Thank you Mr President.

* Statement delivered at the 14th Session of the Human Rights Council, Urgent Debate on the Israeli raid on the flotilla sailing to Gaza, 1 June 2010.

PREVENT VIOLENCE THROUGH DIALOGUE BETWEEN ALL PARTIES INVOLVED IN THE LIBYAN ARAB JAMAHIRIYA*

Mr President,

The Delegation of the Holy See follows the political and social developments that are unfolding in some countries of North Africa with great attention and concern. The current crisis in the Libyan Arab Jamahiriya, however, is particularly worrying because of the unwarranted loss of human lives, the targeting of civilians and of peaceful protesters, and the indiscriminate use of force.

In the present circumstances it becomes urgent to reaffirm that the primary responsibility of the State is the protection of its citizens and the respect of their human rights and fundamental freedoms, such as the freedom of assembly, and to serve the legitimate aspirations of its people.

In fact, this Delegation supports any effort aiming at bringing together in honest dialogue all parties involved, demonstrators and Authorities of the Libyan Arab Jamahiriya, to prevent any further escalation of violence, of revenge and of intimidation. Violence only leads to a humanitarian catastrophe. Especially vulnerable in this crisis are asylum seekers, refugees and irregular immigrant workers from Sub-Saharan Africa, who risk being made a scapegoat of accumulated frustrations.

Mr President, the Delegation of the Holy See expresses its condolences to the Libyan people and to the families of the victims of this bloodshed and prays for the recovery of the wounded. Let us pray that peace may soon prevail and allow a renewed society to look with hope to a future where human rights and the innate dignity of every person are respected.

Thank you, Mr President.

* Statement delivered at the 15th Special Session on the Situation of Human Rights in the Libyan Arab Jamahiriya, 25 February 2011.

MAY PEACE TRIUMPH OVER DIVISION AND UMBRAGE IN SYRIA*

Madam President,

The Delegation of the Holy See follows with great concern the dramatic and growing episodes of violence in Syria which have caused many victims and grave suffering. On this occasion I wish to reiterate the repeated appeals of the Holy Father to the faithful to pray that the effort for reconciliation may prevail over division and resentment,[1] and to the Authorities and all the citizens to spare no effort in the search for the common good and in the acceptance of legitimate aspirations for a future of peace and stability.[2]

Madam President,

The events which have occurred in the past months in Syria have been born from the desire for a better future of economic well-being, justice, freedom and participation in public life and they point to the urgent necessity of real reforms in social, economic and political life. It is nevertheless highly desirable that these developments do not take place through intolerance, discrimination or conflict, and even less through violence, but rather through absolute respect for truth, for coexistence, for the legitimate rights of individuals and groups, as well as for reconciliation. Such principles must guide leaders while taking account of the aspirations of civil society as well as the instances of the international community.[3]

Madam President,

The Delegation of the Holy See expresses its condolences to the families of the victims and prays for the recovery of the wounded. May peace soon prevail and allow a renewed society to look with hope to a future where the innate dignity of every person is respected.

* Statement delivered at the 18th Special Session of the Human Rights Council on Syria, 2 December 2011.

1 Post-Angelus Appeal, 7 August 2011.

2 Appeal at the conclusion of the Regina Caeli prayer, 15 May 2011.

3 Cf. Speech of the Holy Father Pope Benedict XVI to the Ambassador of Syria to the Holy See on the occasion of the presentation of Credential Letters, 9 June 2011.

THE AGGRAVATION OF THE SYRIAN CONFLICT: PROVIDE HUMANITARIAN ASSISTANCE TO DISPLACED PERSONS*

Madam President,

The Report of the Independent International Commission of Inquiry on the Syrian Arab Republic and other sources of information document all too well the results of months of violence in that country: thousands of victims, some estimate 30,000, have lost their lives and many others who have been wounded; city neighbourhoods destroyed; more than a quarter of a million made refugees; 1.2 million internally displaced people; classes cancelled indefinitely for tens of thousands of children. Above all, social trust and civil coexistence have been broken. This violent conflict shows the futility of war as a means to resolve disagreements. It is appropriate that this Council should adopt the perspective of the victims in its resolve to promote human rights and to uphold humanitarian law. Respect for the fundamental rights of the victims of this conflict is, in fact, the road that can lead to healing human relations and to peace, an indispensable prerequisite for negotiations and an effective response to the expectations of the people for a democratic new beginning.

The Holy See has been following the worsening of the conflict in Syria with great attention and deep concern given the risk of destabilization in the entire region and the total disregard for the civilian population; has reiterated its rejection of violence from whatever source it may come; and regrets the loss of so many human lives and family tragedies. The voice of the Holy Father Benedict XVI, a pilgrim of peace in the area, has condemned without any ambiguity the use of violence: 'Even though it seems hard to find solutions to the various problems that affect the region', he said, 'we cannot resign ourselves to violence and to the aggravation of tensions. The commitment to dialogue and to reconciliation must be a priority for all the parties concerned and must be supported by the international community.'[1] A stable peace in the Middle East is an important benefit for the whole world. With God's gift of peace, local people can use their talents for the development and progress of their

* Statement delivered at the 21st Session of the Human Rights Council – Item 4: *Interactive Dialogue with the Independent International Commission of Inquiry on the Syrian Arab Republic*, 17 September 2012.

1 Angelus, Sunday, 9 September 2012.

countries, enjoy their right to a decent life there, and avoid the misery and suffering of forced uprooting and exile.

Solidarity with the people of Syria and, by extension, with the whole of the Middle East, implies that the international community should put aside selfish interests and support the political process for a cessation of violence and for an orderly and inclusive participation of all groups in the management of the country as citizens of equal dignity and responsibility. An additional requirement appears urgent in order to make solidarity effective and genuine and to provide humanitarian assistance to all displaced people and other victims of bombardment and indiscriminate destruction, especially to children. Then, to the importation of arms: the firm and common will for peace and the importation of ideas for reconciliation should be substituted. Furthermore, journalists should report on this situation with fairness and complete information so that public opinion may more easily grasp the futility of violence and how in the long run it does not benefit anyone. Media, too, can help build a culture of peace and point at the benefits of reconciliation.

The wave of protests, peaceful on the part of most of the participants, that have characterized what has been called the Arab Spring, stemmed from the deep desire, especially of younger people, for greater freedom, better employment, a real participation in public life. To frustrate these aspirations through the manipulation of power and forms of control will have a lasting damage and miss a historic opportunity for progress.

Madam President,

The people of Syria and the Middle East deserve support and solidarity in their moment of need. The promotion of all human rights is an effective and indispensable strategy for the success of their struggle for peace and social coexistence.

Thank you, Madam President.

SYRIA: THE FUTILITY OF WAR AS A MEANS TO RESOLVE DISAGREEMENTS*

Madam President,

The Delegation of the Holy See follows with great concern the dramatic and growing episodes of violence in Syria which have caused many victims and grave suffering. As we debate the continuing serious crisis in that country, I wish to reiterate the repeated appeals of His Holiness Pope Benedict XVI, and, in particular, that of 12 February last for an urgent end to the violence and bloodshed unfolding in Syria.[1] On that occasion, His Holiness called for every party to the conflict to give priority to the way of dialogue, of reconciliation and of commitment to peace. We must not succumb to the logic of violence, where violence begets further violence. It is never too late to refrain from violence!

Madam President,

My Delegation expresses its solidarity with the victims of violence and appeals for urgent humanitarian and medical assistance to relieve the sufferings of all those wounded and injured.

Madam President,

The Holy See extends a hand of friendship to all the people of Syria, of whatever religion or ethnic background, confident that all Syrians share the same common values of dignity and justice for all regardless of creed or ethnicity. Syria has a long history of peaceful coexistence among her diverse religious and ethnic communities. The Delegation of

* Statement delivered at the 19th Session of the Human Rights Council – Urgent Debate on Syria, 28 February 2012.

1 'Dear Brothers and Sisters, I am following with deep apprehension the dramatic and escalating episodes of violence in Syria. In the past few days they have taken a heavy toll of victims. I remember in prayer the victims among whom are several children, the injured and all those who are suffering the consequences of an ever more worrying conflict. In addition, I renew a pressing appeal to put an end to violence and bloodshed. Lastly, I invite everyone – and first of all the political Authorities in Syria – to give priority to the way of dialogue, of reconciliation and of the commitment to peace. It is urgently necessary to respond to the legitimate aspirations of the different members of the nation, as well as to the hopes of the international community, concerned for the common good of the society as a whole and for the region.' Appeal of His Holiness Pope Benedict XVI, 12 February 2012.

the Holy See appeals to the Syrian people not to lose sight of this heritage in responding to the legitimate aspirations of the different members of the nation. Syria, no less than any nation, is a member of the family of nations, and so the international community is right to be concerned for the peace and stability of the region.

Madam President,

The Delegation of the Holy See remains convinced that regional and multilateral organizations are an important instrument in promoting peace and stability in the world, an instrument which is ever more valuable in times of crisis, and for that reason welcomes the various initiatives in favour of peace through the path of dialogue and reconciliation. The primary responsibility, however, rests with the people of Syria and for that reason I renew the Holy Father's appeal to the Syrian people 'to give priority to the way of dialogue, of reconciliation and of commitment to peace'.

Thank you, Madam President.

A DURABLE AND ACCEPTABLE SOLUTION IN SYRIA THROUGH PEACEFUL NEGOTIATIONS*

Mr President,

Violence in Syria has proven once again that it is the terrain of the violation of all human rights. Lives have been destroyed by the tens of thousands; a million and a half persons have been forced to flee abroad as refugees; more than four million people have lost their homes; and civilians have been targeted by warring parties in total disregard of humanitarian law. This enormous national tragedy risks intensifying regional and global conflicts, to transform ambitions for political power into ethnic and religious fundamentalist confrontations, to melt down the entire country.

The way forward is not by a military intensification of the armed conflict but by dialogue and reconciliation, a process that the proposed diplomatic conference can help to promote, if the political will is there to sustain it. An immediate ceasefire will stop the bloodshed, a useless and destructive tragedy that mortgages the future of Syria and the Middle East. As Pope Francis said: 'How much blood has been shed! And how much suffering must there still be before a political solution to the crisis will be found?'[1] The Holy See all along has insisted that only peaceful negotiations will lead to an acceptable solution of the crisis and that participation in an eventual government and in positions of responsibility by representatives of all citizens can ensure a constructive and lasting peaceful coexistence of all component communities of Syrian society.

Children in refugee camps and in conflict areas, traumatized and forcibly deprived of their rights, suffer the most of the consequences of violence, and call for generous solidarity on the part of the international community. Only in this way can they and their families hope again for a normal existence. In particular unaccompanied minors deserve specific attention and assistance to prevent them falling victim to trafficking and other forms of exploitation.

Silencing the guns is the priority. Besides, the necessity of overcoming any pessimism there may be concerning the achievement of successful

* Statement delivered at the 23rd Session of the Human Rights Council – *Urgent Debate on the Deteriorating Situation of Human Rights in the Syrian Arab Republic and the Recent Killings in Al Qusayr*, 29 May 2013.

1 Pope Francis, *Urbi et Orbi Message*, Easter Sunday, 31 March 2013.

negotiations should be seen against the deaths caused daily by the use of guns – a price too great the people of Syria have already paid. This moral responsibility is unavoidable, and it calls for a rejection of personal revenge and of inordinate ambitions of dominance by any group.

In conclusion, Mr President, the Holy See Delegation restates its call for negotiations and for putting an end to violence. People should take precedence over power and revenge. Their unspeakable suffering must not be ignored by any of the parties involved as they are all called to act now for peace, reconstruction and a new beginning of human relations based on human rights and the common interest of the one human family.

Thank you, Mr President.

PEACE, THE SINE QUA NON FOR THE ENJOYMENT OF ALL HUMAN RIGHTS*

Mr President,

Peace, being one of the deepest desires of the human heart, is a right that everyone should enjoy and a situation that makes the integral human development. Peace is the condition that makes all other rights possible. The realization of the fundamental rights eventually leads to a true peace based on freedom, justice and brotherhood. The UN Charter, the Universal Declaration of Human Rights and several other international instruments express in a virtuous dialectic this deep and necessary link between peace and human rights. Consequently, the threat of war should be eliminated, and rightfully the African Charter on Human and Peoples' Rights states: 'All peoples shall have the right to national and international peace and security' (Art. 23(1)).

Defining peace by the absence of war would mean reducing it to a negative value. Peace is built day by day within the family, at school and within society. Without solid economic, political, cultural and spiritual foundations, peace is a mirage to naive minds. Those who want to base peace exclusively on strength and on the balance of power are wrong. One has only to read the history of the twentieth century and contemplate the reality of recent conflicts that this Council often examines. Peace cannot be imposed by the number of weapons amassed, neither by how sophisticated they are, nor by their cruelty. If peace had been settled by military power, numerous peoples would not have suffered so many wars, death, ruin and destructive hatred. Peace is another name for development. Peace is best served by the schools we build, by the health facilities we establish, and by open prospects for the future for younger generations.

* Statement delivered at the 23rd Session of the Human Rights Council – Item 5: *Report of the Intergovernmental Working Group on the Right to Peace*, 7 June 2013.

Mr President,

It is a commonplace to say that our world is much more interdependent than ever. But this reinforces our belief that the human family is one and that all men and all women share the same dignity. Violence, injustice and the thirst for power – within societies and among nations – merely increase the risk of wars and conflicts. Someone's peace and security cannot be ensured without peace and security of others. Our world does not lack resources but suffers from injustice. Divisions seem increasingly deeper and the search for peace more and more elusive. The opposite of peace is more than war. It is fear. In this sense, fear is the common denominator between rich and poor, between developed and developing countries, between military powers and those who are less privileged.

Mr President,

War is the failure of human beings and of the humane. War is the illusion that we can defend or build a healthy and better society, inflicting untold suffering on others. By destroying the other, we destroy the humane. No one emerges unscathed from a conflict or from an experience of violence. Peace is less spectacular, more patient and more respectful of the differences, more modest. Yet, only those values are able to build a truly humane society.

The establishment of an open intergovernmental working group with the task of initiating the official codification of the human right to peace was a wise decision that we hope will bear fruit in an effective declaration, shared by all.

In the construction or restoration of peace, historical and contemporary examples teach us that non-violence, as a doctrine and as a method, was and remains the most appropriate way of mediation and reconciliation in order to renew human, social and political ties, in favor of the common good and a lasting peace.

VIOLENCE ONLY BEGETS FURTHER VIOLENCE: THE APPALLING REPORT OF THE INDEPENDENT INTERNATIONAL COMMISSION OF INQUIRY ON THE SYRIAN ARAB REPUBLIC*

Mr President,

The Report of the Independent International Commission of Inquiry on the Syrian Arab Republic vividly portrays the ongoing tragedy in that country and the enormous suffering of its people. Violence reduced to a rule of life by all parties in the conflict generates all sorts of crimes and multiplies the suffering of families and individuals without distinction. Violence also has forced millions of Syrians to abandon their homes and to seek protection in refugee camps. Well over a million children are uprooted.

The Holy Father Francis in particular and the Holy See are deeply worried by the large-scale destructive mood that prevails instead of reason and a minimal respect of human dignity. The Holy Father's initiative to pray and fast for peace found a vast response among persons of every persuasion in the world and they listened well to his lament when he said: 'As if it were normal, we continue to sow destruction, pain, death. Violence and war lead only to death … Violence and war are never the way to peace!'

Most people of our world want peace. The cessation of violence is urgent to meet such aspiration as well as to allow humanitarian assistance to begin healing the dangerous situation of a population without medicines and adequate food and shelter. No military solution is a viable option for the conflict in Syria. Besides, the supply of arms only fuels this conflict and should be stopped.

The first step taken, after the unconscionable and criminal use of chemical weapons, to place these instruments of death under international control, can become the positive beginning of a process whereby all parties involved on the ground together with their allies will dialogue and jointly search for a political settlement.

* Statement delivered at the 24th Session of the Human Rights Council – Item 4: *Interactive Dialogue with the Independent International Commission of Inquiry on the Syrian Arab Republic*, 16 September 2013.

Mr President,

The difficulties involved for a diplomatic solution to the bloody crisis in Syria seem insurmountable, but the way of dialogue and a rebuilding of trust are the only reasonable options to put an end to suffering and destruction.

Justice and Peace are not mutually exclusive and both can be pursued together so that impunity is not tolerated and reconciliation made possible.

In conclusion, Mr President, enough suffering has been visited on the Syrian people, especially on minorities like Christians. All fundamental human rights have been cruelly disregarded and the common people have paid the price.

The Delegation of the Holy See encourages all parties to pursue negotiations in a constructive dialogue that may provide a ray of hope to the People of Syria and courage to move into a peaceful future.

Thank you, Mr President.

THE DETERIORATING OF THE POLITICAL AND HUMANITARIAN CRISIS IN THE CENTRAL AFRICAN REPUBLIC*

Mr President,

The Delegation of the Holy See is grateful for the initiative taken by the Council to urgently review the human rights situation in the Central African Republic. The social and political situation in the country is deteriorating on a daily basis and has resulted in utter disrespect for the rights to life and dignity of countless children, women and men. The first-hand, direct testimony of the Catholic bishops of the country confirms it as they write: 'For the most part, the country has plunged into desolation; the roads are not maintained; the hospitals have been destroyed or have been deprived of medicines and trained staff; persons living with HIV/AIDS no more have access to antiretroviral medicines; schools are no longer standing … murder has become a banal and trivial act; we are falling into a culture of violence and death.'[1]

My Delegation welcomes the decision to expedite the appointment of an Independent Expert on Human Rights in the Central African Republic. An objective analysis of the situation is urgent. Some voices in the international community claim that a religious war is under way. Religious leaders in the country, however, inform us that there are no clear-cut confessional lines among the conflicting parties. They maintain that the seeds for the present conflict were sown many years ago and are related to a constant cycle of exploiting the poorest sectors of society, of corruption among the most powerful, and of impunity for crimes committed especially when they were directed against the most vulnerable. Mr President, placing the blame on religion for the conflict situation in the Central African Republic merely deflects the attention and energy of the international community and the citizens of the country itself from dealing with the true roots of the problem.

In fact, leaders of the major faith traditions in the country are urging their respective followers to set aside the desire for vengeance, to avoid any

* Statement delivered at the 20th Special Session of the Human Rights Council on the Human Rights Situation in the Central African Republic, 20 January 2014.

1 'Reconstruisons Ensemble Notre Pays: Dans La Paix!', Message des évêques de Centrafrique aux fidèles chrétiens, aux hommes et aux femmes de bonne volonté, 8 January 2014.

inducements toward political or economic corruption, to engage in the reconstruction of national unity and to initiate a process of rebuilding the social fabric of society and of seeking reconciliation on the levels of inter-personal relationships, local communities and of the nation as a whole.

Integral human development is the best strategy to restore and preserve the enjoyment of human rights in conflict-torn countries such as the Central African Republic. For this reason, the Delegation of the Holy See urges this Council to promote a prompt, expanded and effective engagement of the international community, of the African Union in particular, in responding to the political and humanitarian crisis in the country and to assure ongoing provision and monitoring of development cooperation in order to avoid a recurrence of the conflicts that have led to the present-day crisis. Allow me to conclude with the recent words of Pope Francis: 'I think above all of the Central African Republic, where much suffering has been caused as a result of the country's tensions, which have frequently led to devastation and death … I express my hope that the concern of the international community will help to bring an end to violence, a return to the rule of law and guaranteed access to humanitarian aid, also in the remotest parts of the country.'[2]

Thank you, Mr President.

[2] www.vatican.va/holy_father/francesco/speeches/2014/january/documents/papa-francesco_20140113_corpo-diplomatico_en.html.

GENEVA II CONFERENCE ON SYRIA: DIALOGUE AS THE ONLY WAY FORWARD*

Mr Secretary General,

Representatives of the Syrian population and of the international community come together today, at this Geneva II Conference, to take concrete steps towards a peaceful future for the Syrian people and the Middle East. Confronted with the indescribable suffering of the Syrian people, a sense of solidarity and common responsibility prompts us to engage in a dialogue which is based on honesty, mutual trust and concrete steps. Dialogue is the only way forward. There is no military solution to the Syrian crisis. The Holy See is convinced that violence leads nowhere but to death, destruction and no future.

My Delegation is happy to contribute to this critical process, in itself a sign of a political will that gives priority to negotiations over guns, to people over inordinate power. For this reason all religious leaders, in particular, converge on this conviction that violence has to stop because too much suffering has been inflicted on all the people of Syria and on the entire region. Recent meetings of religious representatives of different confessions have reconfirmed this constructive approach that is based on the equal dignity of every person created in the image of God and open to others.

The time has come to take concrete steps to implement the good intentions expressed by all parties to the current conflict. In this context, the Holy See renews its urgent appeal to all the parties concerned for the full and absolute respect for humanitarian law and offers the following proposals:

(a) As invoked by all men and women of good will, an immediate cease-fire without preconditions and the end to violence of all kinds should become a priority and the urgent goal of these negotiations. All weapons should be laid down and specific steps should be taken to stop the flow of arms and arms funding that feed the escalation of violence and destruction to leave room for the instruments of peace. The money invested in arms should be redirected to humanitarian assistance. The immediate cessation of violence is in the interest of

* Statement delivered at the International Conference on Syria (Geneva II), Montreux, Switzerland, 22 January 2014.

all. It is a humanitarian imperative, and represents the first step to reconciliation.

(b) The cessation of hostilities should be accompanied with increased humanitarian assistance and the immediate start of reconstruction. Millions have been displaced and are in life-threatening situations. Family life has been disrupted. Educational and health facilities have been destroyed or made inoperative.

(c) The war brought about the economic collapse of many regions of Syria. Reconstruction efforts should start together with negotiations and should be sustained by the generous solidarity of the international community. In this process, young people should be given a preferential consideration so that through their employment and work they may become protagonists for a peaceful and creative future for their country.

(d) Community rebuilding calls for dialogue and reconciliation sustained by a spiritual dimension. The Holy See strongly encourages all religious faiths and communities in Syria to reach a deeper mutual knowledge, a better understanding and a restoration of trust.

(e) It is important that regional and international powers favor the ongoing dialogue and that regional problems be addressed. Peace in Syria could become a catalyst of peace in other parts of the region, and a model of that peace that is so urgently needed.

Beyond the tragedies of the current crisis, new opportunities and original solutions for Syria and its neighbors can come about. A just approach would be to recognize that the existence of cultural, ethnic and religious diversity and pluralism should not be a negative factor or, worse, an inevitable source of conflict, but rather the possibility for every community and individual to contribute their gifts to the common good and the development of a richer and more beautiful society. There is a role for everyone where citizenship provides equal participation in a democratic society with equal rights and duties. In this way no one is forced to leave his country because of intolerance and the inability to accept differences. In fact, the equality assured by common citizenship can allow the individual to express for himself and in community with others the fundamental values all persons hold indispensable to sustain their inner identity. Such an understanding and development of society opens the way to a durable and fruitful peace.

Mr Secretary General,

Since the Syrian crisis began, the Holy See has been following its developments with deep concern and has consistently advocated that all parties involved commit themselves to the prevention of violence and to the provision of humanitarian assistance to all victims. The voice of the Holy Father has been raised on numerous occasions to remind people of the futility of violence, inviting a negotiated resolution of problems, calling for a just and equitable participation of everyone in the life of society. Together with an invitation to pray for peace, He has promoted an active response on the part of Catholic organizations and institutions to the emerging needs. Memorable endures the Holy Father's proposal for a Day of Prayer and Fasting for peace in Syria and the Middle East that was received worldwide with an overwhelmingly positive response.

Allow me to conclude by echoing the words of Pope Francis: 'I ask each party in this conflict to listen to the voice of their own conscience, not to close themselves in solely on their own interests, but rather to look at each other as brothers [and sisters] and decisively and courageously to follow the path of encounter and negotiation, and so overcome blind conflict.' 'It is neither a culture of confrontation nor a culture of conflict which builds harmony within and between peoples, but rather a culture of encounter and a culture of dialogue; this is the only way to peace.'

Mr Secretary General,

The people of Syria have lived together in peace throughout history, and can do so again.

THE PRIMACY OF INTERNATIONAL LAW OVER UNILATERAL INITIATIVES*

Mr President, first of all, the Holy See wishes to express its closeness to all the people of Ukraine in this time of crisis.

As it has emphasized on other occasions, the Holy See recognizes and supports the special role of the United Nations and its bodies in promoting peace and peaceful coexistence among nations. These international institutions have the task of ensuring respect for certain indispensable principles, necessary for building and maintaining the international order. These include the freedom and territorial integrity of each nation, fidelity to agreements undertaken and the defence of the rights of minorities.

These international bodies were established because of the need to ensure peace and respect for fundamental human rights, which are also the presuppositions for the common good of humanity.

One of the specific ways of giving concrete expression to the common good and human dignity at the international level is the determination of the just proportion and weight to be given to perceived national interests, given that these interests are inter-relational and may never be considered absolute. To promote and defend them, not only is it never right to harm the legitimate interests of other States, but there is also an obligation to promote and defend the common good of all peoples (cf. Statement of the Permanent Observer of the Holy See at the 64th Session of the United Nations General Assembly, 6 May 2010).

Thus, the Holy See considers that, for the good of the international order, national interests, including the rights of minorities and respect for territorial integrity, should be resolved through internationally accepted procedures, rather than by the unilateral initiatives of any particular country.

With regard to the specific situation of Ukraine, the Holy See stands by the international community, as expressed in this august Assembly, in its efforts to reach a solution of this crisis through dialogue and concord. It, accordingly, calls on all Parties involved to respect the principles of international law, to ensure the protection of the common good, to

* Statement delivered at the 25th Session of the Human Rights Council on the situation in Ukraine, 26 March 2014.

abstain from any initiatives which innovate, or attempt to innovate the situation at the expense of the international order, and to avert at all costs the danger of bloodshed and loss of life, resolving disputes exclusively by dialogue and diplomatic means.

Thank you, Mr President.

A STABLE AND IMMEDIATE PEACE IN THE OCCUPIED PALESTINIAN TERRITORY INCLUDING EAST JERUSALEM*

Mr President,

As the number of people killed, wounded or uprooted from their homes continues to increase in the conflict between Israel and some Palestinian groups, particularly in the Gaza Strip, the voice of reason seems submerged by the blast of arms. Violence will lead nowhere either now or in the future. The perpetration of injustices and the violation of human rights, especially the right to life and to live in peace and security, sow fresh seeds of hatred and resentment. A culture of violence is being consolidated, the fruits of which are destruction and death. In the long run, there can be no winners in the current tragedy, only more suffering. Most of the victims are civilians, who by international humanitarian law, should be protected. The United Nations estimates that approximately 70 per cent of Palestinians killed have been innocent civilians. This is just as intolerable as the rockets and missiles directed indiscriminately toward civilian targets in Israel. Consciences are paralyzed by a climate of protracted violence, which seeks to impose a solution through the annihilation of the other. Demonizing others, however, does not eliminate their rights. Instead, the way to the future lies in recognizing our common humanity.

In his Pilgrimage to the Holy Land, Pope Francis demanded that the present unacceptable situation of the Israeli–Palestinian conflict be brought to an end.[1] 'For the good of all', he said, 'there is a need to intensify efforts and initiatives aimed at creating the conditions for a stable peace based on justice, on the recognition of the rights of every individual and on mutual security. The time has come for everyone to find the courage to be generous and creative in the service of the common good, the courage to forge a peace which rests on the acknowledgement by all of the right of two States to exist and to live in peace and security within internationally recognized borders.'[2] The legitimate aspiration to security, on one side, and to decent living conditions, on the other, with access to the normal means of existence like medicines, water and jobs,

* Statement delivered at the 21st Special Session of the Human Rights Council on the human rights situation in the Occupied Palestinian Territory including East Jerusalem, 23 July 2014.

[1] Address of Pope Francis in Bethlehem, 25 May 2014. [2] Ibid.

for example, reflects a fundamental human right, without which peace is very difficult to preserve.

The worsening situation in Gaza is an incessant reminder of the necessity to arrive at a cease-fire immediately and to start negotiating a lasting peace. 'Peace will bring countless benefits for the peoples of this region and for the world as a whole,' adds Pope Francis, 'and so it must resolutely be pursued, even if each side has to make certain sacrifices.' It becomes a responsibility of the international community to engage in earnest in the pursuit of peace and to help the parties in this horrible conflict reach some understanding in order to stop the violence and look to the future with mutual trust.

Mr President,

The Delegation of the Holy See reiterates its view that violence never pays. Violence will only lead to more suffering, devastation and death, and will prevent peace from becoming a reality. The strategy of violence can be contagious and become uncontrollable. To combat violence and its detrimental consequences we must avoid becoming accustomed to killing. At a time where brutality is common and human rights violations are ubiquitous, we must not become indifferent but respond positively in order to attenuate the conflict which concerns us all.

The media should report in a fair and unbiased manner the tragedy of all who are suffering because of the conflict, in order to facilitate the development of an impartial dialogue that acknowledges the rights of everyone, respects the just concerns of the international community and benefits from the solidarity of the international community in supporting a serious effort to attain peace. With an eye to the future, the vicious circle of retribution and retaliation must cease. With violence, men and women will continue to live as enemies and adversaries, but with peace they can live as brothers and sisters.[3]

Thank you, Mr President.

[3] Words of Pope Francis, Vatican Gardens, 8 June 2014.

THE RESPONSIBILITY TO PROTECT CHRISTIANS AND OTHER RELIGIOUS MINORITIES IN IRAQ FROM THE SO-CALLED 'ISLAMIC STATE'*

Mr President,

In several regions of the world there are centers of violence – Northern Iraq in particular – that challenge the local and international communities to renew their efforts in the pursuit of peace. Even prior to considerations of international humanitarian law and the law of war, and no matter what the circumstances, an indispensable requirement is respect for the inviolable dignity of the human person, which is the foundation of all human rights. The tragic failure to uphold such basic rights is evident in the self-proclaimed destructive entity, the so-called 'Islamic State' group (ISIS). People are decapitated as they stand for their belief; women are violated without mercy and sold like slaves on the market; children are forced into combat; prisoners are slaughtered against all juridical provisions.

The responsibility of international protection, especially when a government is not able to ensure the safety of the victims, surely applies in this case, and concrete steps need to be taken with urgency and resolve in order to stop the unjust aggressor, to re-establish a just peace and to protect all vulnerable groups of society. Adequate steps must be taken to achieve these goals.

All regional and international actors must explicitly condemn the brutal, barbaric and uncivilized behavior of the criminal groups fighting in Eastern Syria and Northern Iraq.

The responsibility to protect has to be assumed in good faith, within the framework of international law and humanitarian law. Civil society in general, and religious and ethnic communities in particular, should not become an instrument of regional and international geopolitical games. Nor should they be viewed as an 'object of indifference' because of their religious identity or because other players consider them to be a 'negligible quantity'. Protection, if not effective, is not protection.

The appropriate United Nations agencies, in collaboration with local authorities, must provide adequate humanitarian aid, food, water,

* Statement delivered at the 22nd Special Session of the Human Rights Council on the human rights situation in Iraq in light of abuses committed by the Islamic State in Iraq and the Levant and associated groups, 1 September 2014.

medicines and shelter to those who are fleeing violence. This aid, however, should be a temporary emergency assistance. The forcibly displaced Christians, Yazidis and other groups have the right to return to their homes, receive assistance for the rebuilding of their houses and places of worship, and live in safety.

Blocking the flow of arms and the underground oil market, as well as any indirect political support, of the so-called 'Islamic State' group, will help put an end to the violence.

The perpetrators of these crimes against humanity must be pursued with determination. They must not be allowed to act with impunity, thereby risking the repetition of the atrocities that have been committed by the so-called 'Islamic State' group.

Mr President,

As Pope Francis stressed in his letter to Secretary General Ban Ki-moon, 'the violent attacks … cannot but awaken the consciences of all men and women of good will to concrete acts of solidarity by protecting those affected or threatened by violence and assuring the necessary and urgent assistance for the many displaced people as well as their safe return to their cities and their homes.' What is happening today in Iraq has happened in the past and could happen tomorrow in other places. Experience teaches us that an insufficient response, or even worse, total inaction, often results in further escalation of violence. Failing to protect all Iraqi citizens, allowing them to be innocent victims of these criminals in an atmosphere of empty words, amounting to a global silence, will have tragic consequences for Iraq, for its neighboring countries and for the rest of the world. It will also be a serious blow to the credibility of those groups and individuals who strive to uphold human rights and humanitarian law. In particular, the leaders of the different religions bear a special responsibility to make it clear that no religion can justify these morally reprehensible and cruel and barbaric crimes, and to remind everyone that, as one human family, we are our brothers' keepers.

CLOSENESS AND SOLIDARITY TO ALL THE PEOPLE OF UKRAINE*

With reference to the Statement made by this Permanent Mission at the 25th Session of the Human Rights Council on March 26, 2014, the Holy See reiterates its closeness and solidarity to all the people of Ukraine, whose country continues to be affected by the present conflict.

With this intervention, the Holy See intends to stress once again the urgent need to respect international legality regarding Ukraine's territory and borders, as a key element for ensuring stability at both the national and the regional levels, and to re-establish law and order based on full respect for all fundamental human rights.

In this regard, the Holy See welcomes the steps taken to enforce the ceasefire, which is intended as an essential condition to arrive at political solutions exclusively through dialogue and negotiation. At the same time, it emphasizes the crucial need for all parties to implement the decisions taken by common agreement, acknowledging in this context the efforts made by the UN, the Organization for Security and Cooperation in Europe (OSCE) and other relevant organizations with reference to the Package of Measures for the Implementation of the Minsk Agreements.

The Holy See holds that the full adherence of all parties to the provisions of said Agreements is a prerequisite for all further efforts to improve the humanitarian and human rights situation in the affected territories, by, first of all, bringing an end to the loss of human life, acts of violence and other forms of abuse. It should also include the release of all hostages and illegally held persons and ensure unfettered access by all legitimate actors to provide humanitarian assistance in those areas.

At the same time the Holy See is concerned about the social emergency facing the population living in the areas affected, who suffer from poverty, hunger, insecurity and health risks. It is also concerned about injured and displaced persons and families suffering from the loss of loved ones. In this urgent situation, the Holy See is committed to offering its assistance through its institutions and requests the charitable organizations of the Catholic Church to intensify and coordinate their efforts to provide assistance to the people of Ukraine. The Holy See also wishes to express its confidence in the solidarity of the international community.

* Statement delivered at the 28th Session of the Human Rights Council on the situation in Ukraine, 26 March 2015.

BOKO HARAM: CRIMES IN THE NAME OF RELIGION ARE NEVER JUSTIFIED*

Mr President,

The ongoing violence, persecution and murder at the hands of the Boko Haram group especially in Nigeria, but also in Cameroon, Benin, Chad and Niger, present serious transgressions under international law, including war crimes and crimes against humanity which require an urgent and effective response from the involved States, together with the solidarity of the international community. With the merciless acts of this terrorist group, we are witnessing the continued development and dissemination of a radical and ruthless type of extremism inspired by an ideology which attempts to justify its crimes in the name of religion. Furthermore, with the recent explicit allegiance of Boko Haram to the so-called Islamic State group (ISIS), one cannot be blind to the fact that such extremist groups are growing like a cancer, spreading to other parts of the world and even attracting foreign militants to fight in their ranks.

Nigeria, in particular, has 'had to confront considerable problems, among them new and violent forms of extremism and fundamentalism on ethnic, social and religious grounds. Many Nigerians have been killed, wounded or mutilated, kidnapped and deprived of everything: their loved ones, their land, their means of subsistence, their dignity and their rights. Many have not been able to return to their homes.'[1] These crimes perpetrated at the hands of Boko Haram have been continuing with impunity and, as witnessed in the last 12 months, have only increased in their intensity and destructive effects. As Pope Francis noted, the tragedy faced in Nigeria at the hands of these extremists 'is a scourge which needs to be eradicated, since it strikes all of us, from individual families to the international community.'[2]

Crimes in the 'name of religion' are never justified. Massacring innocent people in the name of God is not religion but the manipulation of religion for ulterior motives. In fact, 'believers, both Christians and Muslim, have experienced a common tragic outcome, at the hands of people

* Statement delivered at the 23rd Special Session of the Human Rights Council on the Situation of Human Rights in Nigeria – Boko Haram, 1 April 2015.

1 Pope Francis, Letter to the Bishops of Nigeria, 17 March 2015.

2 Pope Francis, Discourse to the Members of the Diplomatic Corps Accredited to the Holy See, 12 January 2015.

who claim to be religious, but who instead abuse religion, to make of it an ideology for their own distorted interests of exploitation and murder.'[3]

Mr President,

Notwithstanding the military efforts of the Nigerian government to stop these terrorists, even with the recently formed alliance of a Multinational Joint Task Force composed of neighboring countries also threatened by Boko Haram, the extremists continue their fury of violence, creating ever more instability in Western Africa. Such a situation clearly poses a dangerous uncertainty to the whole region and even beyond. Without swift, decisive and combined action on the part of the Nigerian government, its bordering countries, the African Union and the United Nations, the serious threat of violence will only continue to jeopardize the lives of millions of civilians throughout that region.

It appears that the time is ripe for the international community to assist in bringing an end to the violence, which has caused numerous civilian victims. Before such violations of international human rights and humanitarian laws, we cannot afford to have a posture of indifference that would lead to the widening contagion of violence and also set a dangerous precedent of 'non-action' in response to such horrific crimes.

The Holy See encourages an international collaborative effort to address this crisis situation with urgency so as to prevent the extension of Boko Haram and other terrorist groups and their strategy of inflicting suffering on the local people and to destabilize Africa even further.

Thank you, Mr President.

[3] Pope Francis, Letter to the Bishops of Nigeria, 17 March 2015.

FEAR, MISTRUST, AND DESPAIR CAUSED BY POVERTY AND FRUSTRATION IN BURUNDI*

Mr President,

Given the urgent concerns being raised at the international level regarding the human rights situation in Burundi, my Delegation is grateful for your timely action in convening this Special Session. The present crisis, and the obstacles to the exercise of human rights in this country, evoke past tensions that have affected this and other countries in the Great Lakes region. Those tensions, like their tragic consequences, have never been adequately addressed despite subsequent recovery and reconciliation initiatives.

Mr President,

The Holy See Delegation sincerely hopes that this Council, in close consultation and collaboration with other intergovernmental bodies with appropriate mandate and responsibility in this regard, will take immediate action to:

1. put in place international efforts that guarantee an end to wanton violence and prevent arms trafficking;
2. promote effective, objective, open and transparent efforts at reconciliation, dialogue and peace-building;
3. assure unbiased mediation of the conflict and establish monitored democratic processes that include all sectors of the population;
4. build conditions that will allow the safe and voluntary return of refugees.

Above all, let us keep our deliberations aimed at preserving and defending human rights in Burundi, recalling the words of Pope Francis: 'In the work of building a sound democratic order, strengthening cohesion and integration, tolerance and respect for others, the pursuit of the common good must be a primary goal. Experience shows that

* Statement delivered at the 24th Special Session of the Human Rights Council on Burundi, 17 December 2015.

violence, conflict and terrorism feed on fear, mistrust, and the despair born of poverty and frustration.'[1]

Thank you, Mr President.

[1] Pope Francis, Address during Meeting with Authorities and Diplomatic Corps during Visit to Nairobi, Kenya, 25 November 2015, http://w2.vatican.va/content/francesco/en/speeches/2015/november/documents/papa-francesco_20151125_kenya-autorita.html.

2 DISARMAMENT AND ARMS CONTROL

2.1 Weapons of Mass Destruction (Nuclear Weapons, Biological Weapons Convention)

THE IMPORTANCE OF THE BIOLOGICAL WEAPONS CONVENTION*

Mr President,

At the outset, my Delegation wishes to congratulate you on your election as President of this important Conference.

The prohibition of biological weapons is the linchpin in building peace and security for the entire human family. After the failure of the 5th Review Conference on Biological Weapons, the States Parties to the Biological Weapons Convention are confronted with a challenge whose stakes are so important for the whole of humanity that only a success is feasible. It is a shared responsibility to strengthen the norms that this Convention continues to remind. Not all taboos are to be eradicated. Quite the contrary. Some of them are the necessary condition for life in society or for life itself. Using life to destroy life, using science to spread death instead of curing disease and suffering should remain the absolute taboo. In addition to its illusive nature, the very idea of using biological weapons to win a war should remain in the domain of the unthinkable.

These intuitions and convictions have long resided in the collective conscience and unconsciousness of humanity. If, at certain times in history, the temptations to break this salvific taboo were enormous, the revolution in the field of life sciences and biotechnology combined with certain suicidal tendencies make us fear the worst for the whole of humanity, even for those who think they can profit from the use of biological weapons. It is urgent that practical measures at national, regional and international levels be taken to prevent the irreparable. Bioterrorism can only be countered by a collective will and joint action in the fields of safety and of biosecurity.

The universalization of the Convention should be a priority. No State should stay out of it under any pretext. This should result in a

* Statement delivered at the 6th Review Conference of the States Parties to the Biological Weapons Convention, 20 November 2006.

seamless and good faith cooperation beyond the economic interests of any party.

In the joint efforts of States Parties and to take into account, among others, the risks of the dual use of life science, all stakeholders involved in research, industry, management or control should join forces. Scientists, universities, industries, government agencies, international agencies should all together feel responsible for the use of biotechnology to promote life and an integral human development from which all countries should benefit through responsible research and industry and, of course, through international cooperation. Here I would like to emphasize the importance of the ethical training of students and researchers in the field of life sciences. Codes of conduct should be developed, disseminated and respected by all those involved in this field. The ethical convictions are a prerequisite that could successfully ground laws and control of the States and of the relevant international organizations.

For the Convention not to remain a dead letter, it is necessary for States Parties to favor transparency and the adoption of trust-building measures. No State alone is capable of winning the war against the proliferation of biological weapons. Transparency is the best way to build confidence gradually. However, a fundamental question remains: what to do when trust is lacking? States Parties have the duty to put in place a number of measures to mutually show their good faith and their strict compliance with obligations.

Mr President,

The Convention on Biological Weapons is an essential component of security and even of the survival of humanity. States Parties have the means to succeed. They showed it in 2002 when they found solutions accepted by all in order to break the impasse. The 6th Review Conference should represent a new starting point. It should be possible to find the framework and mechanisms to continue discussions, exchanges and negotiations on a regular basis. It is vital that the process initiated in 2002 remains alive and effective. There are significant risks and challenges. Only our common will is able to avoid and overcome them.

Thank you Mr President.

MESSAGE OF POPE FRANCIS ON THE OCCASION OF THE VIENNA CONFERENCE ON THE HUMANITARIAN IMPACT OF NUCLEAR WEAPONS*

To His Excellency Mr Sebastian Kurz, Federal Minister for Europe, Integration and Foreign Affairs of the Republic of Austria, President of the Conference on the Humanitarian Impact of Nuclear Weapons

I am pleased to greet you, Mr President, and all the representatives from various Nations and International Organizations, as well as civil society, who are participating in the Vienna Conference on the Humanitarian Impact of Nuclear Weapons.

Nuclear weapons are a global problem, affecting all nations, and impacting future generations and the planet that is our home. A global ethic is needed if we are to reduce the nuclear threat and work towards nuclear disarmament. Now, more than ever, technological, social and political interdependence urgently calls for an ethic of solidarity (cf. John Paul II, *Sollicitudo Rei Socialis*, para. 38), which encourages peoples to work together for a more secure world, and a future that is increasingly rooted in moral values and responsibility on a global scale.

The humanitarian consequences of nuclear weapons are predictable and planetary. While the focus is often placed on nuclear weapons' potential for mass-killing, more attention must be given to the 'unnecessary suffering' brought about by their use. Military codes and international law, among others, have long banned peoples from inflicting unnecessary suffering. If such suffering is banned in the waging of conventional war, then it should all the more be banned in nuclear conflict. There are those among us who are victims of these weapons; they warn us not to commit the same irreparable mistakes which have devastated populations and creation. I extend warm greetings to the *Hibakusha*, as well as other victims of nuclear weapons testing who are present at this meeting. I encourage them all to be prophetic voices, calling the human family to a deeper appreciation of beauty, love, cooperation and fraternity, while reminding the world of the risks of nuclear weapons which have the potential to destroy us and civilization.

Nuclear deterrence and the threat of mutually assured destruction cannot be the basis for an ethics of fraternity and peaceful coexistence

* Message delivered to the Conference on the Humanitarian Impact of Nuclear Weapons, Vienna, Austria, 8 December 2014.

among peoples and states. The youth of today and tomorrow deserve far more. They deserve a peaceful world order based on the unity of the human family, grounded on respect, cooperation, solidarity and compassion. Now is the time to counter the logic of fear with the ethic of responsibility, and so foster a climate of trust and sincere dialogue.

Spending on nuclear weapons squanders the wealth of nations. To prioritize such spending is a mistake and a misallocation of resources which would be far better invested in the areas of integral human development, education, health and the fight against extreme poverty. When these resources are squandered, the poor and the weak living on the margins of society pay the price.

The desire for peace, security and stability is one of the deepest longings of the human heart. It is rooted in the Creator who makes all people members of the one human family. This desire can never be satisfied by military means alone, much less the possession of nuclear weapons and other weapons of mass destruction. Peace cannot 'be reduced solely to maintaining a balance of power between enemies; nor is it brought about by dictatorship' (*Gaudium et Spes*, § 78). Peace must be built on justice, socio-economic development, freedom, respect for fundamental human rights, the participation of all in public affairs and the building of trust between peoples. Pope Paul VI stated this succinctly in his Encyclical *Populorum Progressio*: 'Development [is] the new name for peace' (§ 76). It is incumbent on us to adopt concrete actions which promote peace and security, while remaining always aware of the limitation of short-sighted approaches to problems of national and international security. We must be profoundly committed to strengthening mutual trust, for only through such trust can true and lasting peace among nations be established (cf. Pope John XXIII, *Pacem in Terris*, § 113).

In the context of this Conference, I wish to encourage sincere and open dialogue between parties internal to each nuclear state, between various nuclear states, and between nuclear states and non-nuclear states. This dialogue must be inclusive, involving international organizations, religious communities and civil society, and oriented towards the common good and not the protection of vested interests. 'A world without nuclear weapons' is a goal shared by all nations and echoed by world leaders, as well as the aspiration of millions of men and women. The future and the survival of the human family hinges on moving beyond this ideal and ensuring that it becomes a reality.

I am convinced that the desire for peace and fraternity planted deep in the human heart will bear fruit in concrete ways to ensure that nuclear weapons are banned once and for all, to the benefit of our common home. The security of our own future depends on guaranteeing the peaceful security of others, for if peace, security and stability are not established globally, they will not be enjoyed at all. Individually and collectively, we are responsible for the present and future well-being of our brothers and sisters. It is my great hope that this responsibility will inform our efforts in favor of nuclear disarmament, for a world without nuclear weapons is truly possible.

From the Vatican, 7 December 2014
FRANCISCUS PP.

THE ETHICAL AND HUMANITARIAN CONSEQUENCES OF NUCLEAR WEAPONS*

Nuclear weapons are a global problem. They affect not just nuclear-armed states, but other non-nuclear signatories of the Non-Proliferation Treaty, non-signatories, unacknowledged possessing states and allies under 'the nuclear umbrella'. They impact future generations and the entire planet that is our home. The reduction of the nuclear threat and disarmament require a global ethic. Now more than ever the facts of technological and political interdependence cry out for an ethic of solidarity in which we work with one another for a less dangerous, morally responsible global future. The response that the international community gives will affect future generations and our planet.

We all know the risks of nuclear weapons, not least that of the instability they cause. Is it reasonable to think that the balance of terror is the best basis for the political, economic and cultural stability of our world?

The status quo is unsustainable and undesirable. If it is unthinkable to imagine a world where nuclear weapons are available to all, it is reasonable to imagine a world where nobody has them. Moreover, this is our reading of the letter and the spirit of the NPT.

Some positive steps have been made towards the goal of a world without nuclear weapons (NPT, CTBT, START, NEW START, etc.). The Holy See, however, still thinks that these steps are limited, insufficient and frozen in space and time. The institutions that are supposed to find solutions and new instruments are deadlocked. The actual international context, including the relationship between nuclear weapons States themselves, does not lead to optimism.

The world faces enormous challenges (environmental problems, migration flows, military conflicts, extreme poverty, regular economic crises, etc.). Only cooperation and solidarity among nations is able to confront them. To continue investing in expensive weapon systems is paradoxical. In particular, to continue investing in the production and the modernization of nuclear weapons is not logical. Billions are wasted each year to develop and maintain stocks that will supposedly never be used. Can one justify such a high cost only for reasons of status?

* Statement delivered at the Conference on the Humanitarian Impact of Nuclear Weapons, Vienna, Austria, 9 December 2014.

The term national security often comes up in discussions on nuclear weapons. It seems that this concept is used in a partial and biased manner. All States have the right to national security. Why is it that the security of some can only be met with a particular type of weapon whereas other States must ensure their security without it? On the other hand, reducing the security of States, in practice, to its military dimension is artificial and simplistic. Socio-economic development, political participation, respect for fundamental human rights, strengthening the rule of law, cooperation and solidarity at the regional and international level, etc. are essential to the national security of States. Is it not urgent to revisit in a transparent manner, how States, especially nuclear weapons states, define their national security?

We are now witnessing a renewed awareness after two decades lost to the cause of nuclear disarmament. During the last decade of the Cold War, Churches, NGOs, academia, think tanks and popular movements were committed to a world without nuclear weapons. The goal, the intentions and arguments remain valid even if the international context has changed.

The 'humanitarian initiative' is a new hope to make decisive steps towards a world without nuclear weapons. The partnership between States, civil society, the ICRC, International Organizations, and the UN is an additional guarantee of inclusion, cooperation and solidarity. This is not an action of circumstance. This is a fundamental shift that meets a strong quest of a large number of the world's populations which would be the first victims of a nuclear incident.

The Holy See, ever since the emergence of the nuclear era, advocates the abolition of these weapons which are seemingly without any military logic. Since the Encyclical *Pacem in Terris* of Pope John XXIII (1963), the Holy See continues to question the ethical basis to the so-called doctrine of nuclear deterrence. Ethical and humanitarian consequences of the possession and use of nuclear weapons are catastrophic and beyond the rational and reasonable.

This Delegation is aware that the goal of a world without nuclear weapons is not easy to achieve. For this, all energies and commitments are necessary. They are even more necessary in this time of international tensions. The role of churches and religious communities, civil society, academic institutions is vital to not let hope die, to not let cynicism and realpolitik take over. An ethics based on the threat of mutual assured destruction is not worthy for future generations. Only an ethic rooted in solidarity and peaceful coexistence is a great project for the future of humanity.

2.2 Conventional Weapons

2.2.1 Anti-Personnel Landmines Convention

ASSISTANCE TO THE INNOCENT WITNESSES OF A WRONG APPROACH TO SECURITY*

Allow me, Madam Co-Chair, to briefly address the issues of assistance to the victims of anti-personnel mines and, in particular, of their indispensable re-integration in a normal socio-economic life. In Asia and Africa I have personally seen the ravages caused by anti-personnel mines on the bodies of fleeing refugees and of working women and men in border villages. Such mines are a source of inhuman suffering.

The Holy See gives capital importance to the Ottawa Convention, to its implementation as a means of prevention and to its requirement to assist the victims of these dreadful weapons. In fact, the central point of the Convention is preventing that persons may become innocent victims of this vile, murderous and useless arm. And when there has been the lack of knowledge, of ability or of will to take political decisions or practical measures to prevent production and dissemination of anti-personnel mines, national authorities and the international community have no right to avoid their respective responsibility for a comprehensive treatment of the tragic consequences mines cause.

We must not make the victims of mines victims also of oblivion and discrimination or victims of a condescending type of assistance. Mines victims are citizens and full members of their community. They have the right to be effectively associated in the elaboration and implementation of both rehabilitation and socio-economic re-integration policies. A practical understanding of solidarity implies that special attention should be granted to those men and women who need it so that in turn they may play an active role in promoting a pacified and fraternal humanity.

Victims of anti-personnel mines are innocent witnesses of a wrong approach to security. A large number of countries have realized that anti-personnel mines, besides their inhuman and devastating effects in the long run, are a useless arm. They give the illusion of an artificial security. In

* Statement delivered at the Convention on the Prohibition of the Use, Stockpiling, Production and Transfer of Anti-Personnel Mines and on their Destruction: Standing Committee on Victim Assistance and Socio-Economic Reintegration, 10 February 2004.

most cases the citizens of the country that employs this arm are those who suffer most its disastrous consequences. The universalization of the Convention is the recognition that the suffering and the broken lives of the victims are by far a price too high for a semblance of security. For this reason, on the agenda of the forthcoming First Review Conference of the Convention in Nairobi the plight and a program of assistance to victims of anti-personnel mines should take a prominent place in the reflection.

It must be acknowledged that substantial progress has been achieved in this area. Millions of mines have been destroyed. States, volunteers and faith-communities have provided invaluable assistance to maimed and traumatized victims. Much remains yet to be done, Madam Co-Chair. The greatest risk is the temptation of discouragement before the enormity of the task. Neither the destruction of the stocks nor de-mining challenges should make us forget the victims who will need a sustained national commitment and an always renewed international solidarity for some long years.

Healing entire populations of the consequences of war and armed conflicts, especially the people that have been most affected and victimized, is the best investment in building up true security and a durable peace.

CONSIDERATION OF THE GENERAL STATUS AND OPERATION OF THE CONVENTION: ASSISTING THE VICTIMS*

Mr President,

The Holy See Delegation would like to express its appreciation to Your Royal Highness, to the people and Government of Jordan for the excellent way you organized this meeting. My Delegation expresses also its support to your efforts that the peoples and States of the Middle East region could draw benefit from joining the Landmine Ban Convention.

Mine Ban Treaty and Mine Ban action continue to make progress towards eradicating antipersonnel landmines. But significant challenges remain in some areas; survivor and victim assistance being one of them.

Victim assistance, as per Article 6 of the treaty, stands out as a core component of mine action and an obligation of States Parties under the Convention. Ten years after the entry into force of the Mine Ban Treaty, measures are yet to be taken to ensure the much needed survivor assistance. In the meantime, funding has become less than needed for many mine action programs.

The survivor and victim assistance activities should be a priority for both States Parties and non-States Parties to the Convention, especially those involved in conflicts. Often, conflicts, capacity and financial constraints and lack of continued international support stifle the Victims Assistance Programs.

Although survivor assistance is the prime responsibility of an affected State, consistent and long-term support by the international community is needed. Victims' assistance is a basic human rights issue. Therefore, the Holy See, through its Pontifical Council for Health Care Workers and various institutions and humanitarian organizations, is providing continuous assistance to a number of landmine victims and survivors.

* Statement delivered at the 8th Meeting of States Parties to the Convention on the Prohibition of the Use, Stockpiling, Production and Transfer of Anti-Personnel Mines and on their Destruction, Dead Sea, Jordan, 21 November 2007.

Mr President,

The Holy See is particularly concerned about the ongoing tragic situation of mine survivors and victims. Last Sunday, 18 November, addressing a large crowd of pilgrims and visitors gathered in St Peter's Square in Rome for the noon Angelus blessing, His Holiness Pope Benedict XVI added his voice in support of all victims of landmines and conveyed his good wishes to those participating in this meeting of States Parties. In his message, the Pontiff expressed the 'heartfelt best wishes and encouragement for a good outcome of the Conference so that these ordnances that continue to make victims, including many children, are completely banned'.

Mr President,

It is essential to put always the human person, the victims, their families and communities at the center of our activities and concern. It is true that all the articles of the Convention are interconnected. But the main concern of all obligations should remain the human person.

To put the victims at the center of our work means to make available financial and especially human resources in order to create the necessary conditions which enable victims to fully occupy their legitimate place in society. The common effort of all actors should aim to open the way to every victim, as a free person endowed with dignity and worth, to fully play his/her social, economic and political role in the society. To translate this principle into reality, the victim assistance dimension should remain our priority and be very high on our agenda.

In order to avoid discrimination between victims, it is imperative to seek a lasting coordination to harmonize all assistance activities within the framework of the antipersonnel landmines convention, the Protocol V annexed to the CCW, the future instrument on Cluster Munitions and the Action Plan related to small arms and light weapons, etc.

The victims – all victims – have rights and it is imperative to respect these rights, starting with the right to life, human dignity and security. The compassion dimension and human closeness is also of importance to victims and constitutes an invaluable support, especially during the difficult moments of this human tragedy that landmine victims face, in many cases, alone and in the face of general indifference.

Mr President, the success of our convention will be measured by our ability to respond properly also to the challenges of the rehabilitation and reintegration of all landmine victims and survivors, and thus to offer them credible hope for a better future.

Thank you.

EXTEND THE TIME LIMITS PROVISIONS OF ARTICLE 5 OF THE ANTI-PERSONNEL LANDMINES CONVENTION*

Mr President,

The secret of the success of the Ottawa Convention and, more recently, of the Convention on Cluster Weapons, is best illustrated by the multiple and successive failures and blockages in other fields of disarmament. This gives us a proper frame of reference so that success does not turn into lethargy and achievements into memories of the past.

The key to all this is the centrality of the human person. Disarmament for disarmament, or supremacy of the rule of force, are the recipe for endless negotiations. The Ottawa Convention is a pioneer since it was able to evaluate the effects of a specific weapon on individuals and communities and to respond to this in the most appropriate way. Of course, this is important in provisions concerning assistance to victims. However, the centrality of the human person is evident also in the rest of the articles of the Convention, including the one dealing with the destruction of stocks and, in particular, in the context of Article 5 on de-mining.

Mr President,

The success of the 9th Meeting of States Parties will be evaluated in a special way by its ability to deal effectively with the issue of extension of the deadlines provided in Article 5.

If we want that there will be no more new victims, it is imperative to proceed in de-mining the areas affected as soon as possible. The most effective and least costly remedy is prevention. Not just financially but, especially, in human terms. How can we assess the death of people or human suffering? How can we compare the broken destinies of individuals, families and communities with the resources needed to initiate and ensure a complete de-mining of villages, roads and fields? In a certain way, de-mining is the other side of victim assistance.

For this reason, the question of the extension of the deadlines should be taken with the utmost seriousness. It is important to analyze the reasons why some States Parties are not able to complete on time the task

* Statement delivered at the 9th Meeting of States Parties to the Convention on the Prohibition of the Use, Stockpiling, Production and Transfer of Anti-Personnel Mines and on their Destruction, 24 November 2008.

imposed by the Convention. While the primary responsibility is that of the States Parties concerned, it is also that of all States Parties to the Convention. Each one has to play its own role: it is up to the affected countries to present, in transparency, feasibility plans and to redouble efforts to complete the work already begun; it is up to donor countries to respond positively to the needs of States Parties whose economic, financial and technical resources, in this time of international crisis, are not enough to enable them to honor their obligations in the field of de-mining. It is up to all States Parties to the Convention to address this issue in a clear and constructive atmosphere, where cooperation must remain the key word. Cooperation is the hallmark of the Ottawa Convention and should remain so. For the first time we make decisions in this field. We should think about not setting precedents that could contradict the spirit of the Convention or make its implementation difficult. After one year from the 2nd Review Conference and from the eve of the signing ceremony of the Convention on Cluster Munitions, the methods and the decision-making mechanisms of the Convention should keep and respect the original inspiration.

We must do this, not only because the Convention is a legally binding instrument, but, especially, for current victims, their families and communities. We must do it also because there must not be any more victims of anti-personnel mines.

Thank you for your attention!

2.2.2 Convention on Cluster Munitions

NOTE OF THE HOLY SEE ON CLUSTER MUNITIONS*

Ever since cluster munitions were conceived and produced, from the Second World War onwards, this weapon has enjoyed an acknowledged attractiveness among military personnel and it underwent rapid development between the 1950s and the 1970s. However, the first efforts in the 1970s to propose more or less radical limitations indicate clearly that the problems posed by this weapon were identified relatively early. The multiplicity of actors (about thirty producer countries, some tens of possessor and potential user countries, and, for some time now, the entry upon the scene of non-State players), can only make the situation more problematic. The fifty or so years which have elapsed provide enough distance and a sufficiently precise picture to formulate an objective judgment on the nature of this weapon and its use.

Cluster munitions raise a grave humanitarian question. The particularly insidious nature of this weapon is in fact contrary to human dignity, which is at the basis of humanitarian law. Since their effects are indiscriminate, cluster munitions violate in particular the principles of necessity and distinction. The massive use of cluster munitions in recent years, especially because of their capability of covering large areas (footprint) at a relatively low cost, has resulted in a large quantity of explosive remnants of war. For long periods after the cessation of conflicts, all this poses a serious obstacle for the return of evacuated, displaced or refugee populations to their dwelling places and for access to places where they exercise their socio-economic activities. Clearly, this also poses serious problems for peacekeeping operations and sometimes for political reconciliation and reconstruction. Numerous countries have been deeply affected by cluster munitions and will still need many years before they will be freed from this handicap. This is apart altogether from mentioning the high cost in human life, especially among children. In relation to the latter, it is difficult to understand the military objective behind the attractive design for children other than the desire to do damage in excess of the stated military objectives.

Already a large number of countries, the International Committee of the Red Cross, several international organizations and a large number

* Note released by the Holy See, May 2007.

of NGOs, brought together under the leadership of the 'Cluster Munitions Coalition', have recognized the grave humanitarian question posed by cluster munitions, which should not be considered a legitimate conventional weapon. This analysis demands rapid and appropriate action in order to remedy this deficiency in international law. The solution can only come from cooperation among all the actors, governments, international organizations, civil society, producer countries, user countries, affected countries, developed or developing countries, etc. These actors cannot limit themselves to tackling the consequences of the problem but should also reflect on the causes.

The Holy See appreciates and supports the decisions already taken by several countries to ban, limit the use of or institute moratoria with regard to cluster munitions in general or certain types of cluster munitions in particular.

This awareness encourages moving forward and not remaining content with dogmatic affirmations about the legitimacy of cluster munitions. All weapons banned today or whose use is regulated have at some time been considered legitimate. To prove the compatibility of cluster munitions with international humanitarian law is in the first place incumbent on those who use them or wish to have them in their weapon stores. The proof cannot be reduced to a declaration of legitimacy. It is imperative on the part of those who advocate the military usefulness of cluster munitions to acquire reliable information and to publish the data which they possess concerning the immediate consequences during hostilities and the post-conflict consequences. The overwhelming majority of victims of cluster munitions are civilians and especially children who make up a third of the victims. The argument of collateral damage is unacceptable given the proportion of civilian casualties during the conflict and given the suffering and consequences for the entire population of the affected areas in the period following the cessation of hostilities.

A critical attitude remains essential with regard to the possibility of technological improvement which, it is claimed, would lead to the production of cluster munitions with failure rates of 1 per cent or 2 per cent. In the first place, these rates can never be demonstrated: laboratory tests or tests during maneuvers in peace time never correspond to use on the battlefield, since the failure rate depends as much on technological characteristics as on environmental ones. The recent conflicts where cluster munitions of the latest generation, which have systems which should limit failure rates to 1 per cent, never functioned as promised. The rate of non-exploded devices is much higher by far and the humanitarian consequences for civilian populations just as disastrous as in previous conflicts. On the other hand, even were one willing to accept the argument regarding the reliability rate, it is still the case that the most recent conflicts have demonstrated that hundreds of thousands and even millions of cluster munitions have been used: 1 per cent failure means many innocent victims, a large number of unexploded devices and areas which remain affected for many years. The problem is clearly very complex and cannot be envisaged from a merely technical point of view, but it is necessary to adopt a humanitarian approach based principally on human dignity.

On the basis of these observations, the Holy See supports every process and every effort aimed at achieving the ideal, rational and reasonable objective of banning the production, possession, transfer and use of cluster munitions, of destroying stocks, of initiating a collective effort based on international cooperation to clean up areas affected and to assist persons and communities who have become victims of these weapons. The CCW seems to be the most suitable forum for negotiating a possible treaty on condition that three essential elements are respected: the adoption of a substantial mandate to permit adequate tackling of the problems caused by cluster munitions; the adoption of a time frame for negotiation; negotiation in good faith of an effective and applicable text far removed from lowest common denominator approaches. To do nothing or to limit oneself to formal action incapable of protecting civilian populations in the best possible way will not lend more credibility to the CCW. Credibility arises from treating problems in a serious, effective and productive fashion.

The Holy See reiterates what its Delegation stated at the end of the meeting of the CCW Third Review Conference on 17 November 2006: 'Since the humanitarian dimension of this question is so serious, and demanding an urgent response, it is understandable and worthwhile that all additional initiatives that can be taken to move forward the process towards an international agreement be encouraged.' The example of the Ottawa Convention, the result of a distinct though not separated CCW negotiation, encourages us to set out on a path which is difficult and demanding but, at the same time, exhilarating. The easiest thing would be to do nothing. But a facile approach is costly in terms of names and faces. The cost is the name and face of each of the victims of these pernicious weapons. By displaying an added value for multilateralism, the two processes can be complementary and can mutually reinforce each other without excluding the possibility of convergence at a further stage in the negotiations. A process outside of the framework of the CCW should in any case respect certain requirements such as an approach which is transparent, inclusive and as wide as possible.

Being highly complex, the process, the objective of which is to tackle the humanitarian problem posed by cluster munitions, should also tackle a series of questions including the definition of cluster munitions and the criteria for such a definition, the scope of the instrument and the adoption of effective measures to monitor its implementation, the adoption of clear measures regarding responsibility and assistance in the area of mine-clearance in the contaminated areas, measures concerning the ban on the use of these weapons and the destruction of existing stocks, aspects relating to cooperation and international assistance for persons and communities who are victims of cluster munitions.

We are encouraged to favour this option by the growing awareness also of some producer countries that are beginning to question themselves; this heartens us in the defence of a demanding ethical and humanitarian norm in the area of the compatibility of weapon systems with international humanitarian law. Some of these countries have already taken the decision to remove certain kinds of cluster munitions from their stocklists; others have already begun to replace, once and for all, cluster munitions with other kinds of weapons.

It would be understandable that, due to difficulties to find an immediate one-off solution, a transitory period to reach the objective of a total ban might be envisaged. But it would be imperative to strengthen the regulation of use during this transitory period, for example, by immediately banning certain types and by scrupulously respecting the rules of distinction and necessity. And, above all, by holding to a strictly defensive understanding with regard to the use of cluster munitions for the exclusive protection of the national territory. These are essential elements for immediately placing at the center of our attention the recognition of the fundamental value of human dignity which must provide the foundation for all efforts and processes which seek to strengthen international humanitarian law.

DUBLIN DIPLOMATIC CONFERENCE ON CLUSTER MUNITIONS: HUMAN DIGNITY, PREVENTION, AND ASSISTANCE TO VICTIMS*

Mr President,

The Delegation of the Holy See is particularly honoured to take the floor at the start of this Diplomatic Conference. It is happy to see the fruition of the concerted efforts of a large number of actors to take to a positive conclusion a process that seeks greater security and protection. We need to move beyond a reductive and narrow vision that would give the illusion that protection comes only through arms, specifically, those we are engaged to ban.

First of all, the Delegation of the Holy See would like to express its satisfaction at seeing you, Mr Ambassador, presiding over the proceedings of this meeting and facilitating the negotiations toward a strong and operational agreement. The Holy See offers Ireland its support and is available to join forces in building together a more human, more secure and more cooperative world.

Mr President,

This Dublin Conference is the result of the awareness that a concrete, credible and effective action is needed to respond to a problem that has lasted too long. For years, NGOs, ICRC and various countries have raised the issue of cluster munitions without success at first. Our satisfaction is great now. No one today denies the existence of humanitarian problems linked with cluster munitions, the urgency of a collective action and the indispensable effort to translate these concerns into a targeted development of international humanitarian law. The different partners of the Oslo Process and the States Parties to the Convention on Certain Conventional Weapons (CCW) are in agreement on this urgency. No doubt important differences still exist concerning an appropriate response. The Holy See, however, cannot but insist on the priority of human dignity, of the interests of the victims, the priority of prevention and stability, and on the concept of security based on the lowest level of armaments. Peace

* Statement delivered at the Dublin Diplomatic Conference on Cluster Munitions, Dublin (Ireland), 19 May 2008.

transcends by far the framework of military considerations. Peace is not just the absence of war.

Human rights, development, social and political participation, justice, cooperation, this and similar concepts, take a critical role in a modern definition of authentic peace. Security relying only on arms and force is ephemeral and an illusion. Cluster munitions illustrate perfectly the point. Even so-called victories prove to be lasting defeats for the civil population, for development, for pacification, for stability. Decades after the utilization of cluster munitions, peace preserves a bitter taste with thousands of victims, socio-economic development stifled, considerable human and financial resources wasted.

The chance for a decision is given us here and now. In a globalized and more and more interdependent world, the problems of some are the problems of all: of rich and poor countries; of developed and developing countries; of countries producing and exporting cluster munitions and countries that import them; user and non-user countries. What is not done today will have to be done tomorrow, with a supplement of suffering, of economic costs and of deeper wounds to heal.

Understandably, some countries will face greater difficulties in implementing the commitments that will derive from the future instrument. Make no mistake, however: affected countries and victims are those that have paid and keep paying the most exorbitant price. Those who have to renounce these types of arms, those who have to give up exporting them, those obliged to destroy their stocks, those who will be engaged in de-mining and decontamination activities, those who will invest resources for the victims, their families and communities, all people involved in the various humanitarian activities, will have to make also some efforts. Such efforts should be considered by the political and military leadership, and by the people of their countries, as a necessary but quite rewarding participation in the construction of a more peaceful and more secure world, where everyone enjoys greater security.

In this as in other contexts, cooperation and partnership are essential for success. A partnership among States, United Nations, international organizations, the Committee of the Red Cross and the NGOs is the secret of a common success and an indispensable element to reach the object of the future instrument. Victims should have a privileged place in this plan; their role should be an active one from start to finish. In the negotiations under way, every player should find its appropriate place, so that support for the Convention to be adopted may result complete, strong and operational. Everyone is needed in the implementation of this project. Let us work hand in hand as partners to meet now the challenge of the adoption and tomorrow: that of implementation.

Mr President,

True, States have a right to defend peace, security and the stability of peoples under their responsibility. But this can be better achieved without recourse to the arms race and to war. In his address before the United Nations General Assembly in 1965, Pope Paul VI reminded the Community of Nations of the challenge of peace without recourse to arms: 'One cannot love with offensive arms in hand. Arms, above all terrible arms that modern science has provided, even before causing victims and destruction, generate bad dreams, nourish bad feelings, bring about nightmares, lack of trust, bad decisions; they required enormous expenses; they block solidarity projects and useful work; they distort the psychology of peoples. Till men will remain weak, unstable and even mean as he often shows to be, defensive arms will unfortunately be necessary. But you, your courage and your quality prompt you to study the means to ensure international life without recourse to arms: here is a goal worthy of your efforts, here is what people are awaiting from you, here is what must be reached!'

Mr President,

The eyes of peoples, of victims, of affected countries are focused on this Diplomatic Conference, and all await from us a courageous decision, as Pope Benedict XVI reminded the world yesterday. The world awaits an act of faith in the human person and his highest aspirations to live in peace and security, a commitment to make solidarity the most splendid expression of the unity of the human family and of its common destiny. I am convinced, Mr President, that at the closing of this Conference all participants will leave as winners and satisfied to have made the right choice.

Thank you, Mr President.

THE CONTRIBUTIONS OF NON-GOVERNMENTAL ACTORS TO A STRONG AND CREDIBLE LEGAL INSTRUMENT*

Mr President,

The protection and care of the victims of cluster munitions, the prevention of their suffering, and the addition of a related new chapter in international humanitarian law, have been clear and compelling objectives of the Holy See from the very beginning of the process that has led to this Diplomatic Conference. These goals have been achieved.

The success of the Conference is due to the convergent efforts of all participants whose good will and their primary concern for the dramatic condition of many victims, and the victims' families and communities, have moved them to take decisive action.

My Delegation recognizes with great appreciation the invaluable contribution of everyone and wants to underline in particular the leadership role that you Mr President have effectively exercised with the support of your capable team and the full weight of the Irish Government.

Among the many voices raised in the world on behalf of the victims of cluster munitions, of peace and development in the countries affected but stifled by these terrible weapons, there has been that of Pope Benedict XVI who called for 'a strong and credible international instrument'.

Moving along this path, many countries as well as non-governmental organizations and individuals have engaged with determination and a sense of solidarity and compassion in hard work for a Convention on Cluster Munitions. The process has steadily progressed from Oslo, to Lima, to Vienna, to Wellington and finally to Dublin.

Mr President,

Among the positive results reached allow me to highlight three of them. First, the new Convention opens up a wider care for victims of cluster munitions by including their families and communities. It also calls on the sense of solidarity of the international community to assume responsibility for their psychological and material assistance and for the clearance of the territories contaminated by these munitions.

* Concluding statement delivered at the Dublin Diplomatic Conference on Cluster Munitions, Dublin, Ireland, 30 May 2008.

Second, the new Convention recognizes 'the specific role and contribution of relevant actors' (Article 5.2(c)). Indeed many actors are providing care to the victims as well as human, financial and technical cooperation in the different activities called for by this Convention: States Parties, United Nations bodies, international organizations, the International Committee of the Red Cross and the civil society. In this connection, we would like to put on record our understanding and interpretation of Article 5.2(c): when a State Party develops a national plan and budget to carry out assistance activities according to the Convention 'with a view to incorporating them within the existing national disability, development and human rights frameworks and mechanisms', it shall guarantee the pluralism that is inherent in any democratic society and the diversity of relevant non-governmental actors. This respectful form of coordination of the various activities of governmental and non-governmental actors is in line with what the Preamble states (PP 10).

Third, the new Convention is an achievement in itself but also a positive message to pursue efforts by the international community in the overall disarmament and arms control negotiations. The task is not concluded. In fact, now begins the challenge of implementing this instrument and directing material and human resources towards works of peace, solidarity and development.

Mr President,

The Delegation of the Holy See cannot conclude without stating once again how much it values the spirit of partnership shared with the members of the Core Group and of all other Delegations, the International Committee of the Red Cross, and the Cluster Munitions Coalition.

The spirit of partnership has sustained the process successfully concluded, a success that was not assured when a handful of States started it. That same spirit can ensure an equally successful implementation and a hopeful future for victims and affected countries.

Thank you, Mr President.

THE SIGNING OF THE CONVENTION ON CLUSTER MUNITIONS: THE LARGE NUMBER OF VICTIMS IS THE MOST VALID ARGUMENT FOR COOPERATION*

Mr President,

This Conference is another concrete step to translate our common resolve into action, to tackle a huge humanitarian problem and to make sure that, in the future, the cluster munitions will never be a cause of human suffering. My Delegation thanks you, Mr President, for your commitment and your achievements from the very beginning of this common effort. I would like to thank Norway as well for hosting this meeting. This is another sign of a long and generous commitment in the field of IHL. The Holy See is proud to be your partner and is determined to continue, with you and all our friends: States Parties, Signatories, international organizations, ICRC, and the civil society, until we succeed definitively in solving the problem of cluster munitions.

The best way to solve this problem is to prevent new victims and new contaminated areas. Prevention is easier than remedy and more cost-effective. The Holy See appeals to all States outside the Convention to consider joining the global effort and our common determination. Valid arguments for such a cooperation have been on the table for many years. The most convincing one is the fact of the big numbers of victims with names and faces, and the reality of many families and communities affected by their suffering. All of them still bear unspeakable consequences years after the end of conflicts.

Allow me, Mr President, to mention very briefly three other areas:

1. Our Convention is still young but it has vigor and moral resources. The determination of all actors should remain strong. After showing strong resolve in Dublin when we adopted this treaty, all of us, we should continue to show domestically the same will to implement all our obligations in good faith.
2. After a few years of reflection and debate, it is the time to put together the means necessary for the life of the Convention. An Implementation Support Unit (ISU), with secured and predictable finances, should be the next step to help all of us to make the Convention more effective

* Statement delivered at the signing of the Convention on Cluster Munitions, Oslo, Norway, 3–4 December 2008.

and universal. All States Parties need to share the burdens in a just and equitable manner.

3. Mr President, IHL is not a cold body of rules written for the past. IHL has to evolve and to become more protective of the civilian populations. In time of crisis and conflicts, IHL should never be weakened or a bargaining chip among States or within a State in the public debate.

In conclusion, let me thank you again, Mr President, and reiterate the readiness of the Holy See to work with all partners and friends to make the promising start a full success for all affected and non-affected persons, communities and countries.

Thank you, Mr President.

A FAIR AND EQUITABLE FINANCING FOR AN EFFECTIVE IMPLEMENTATION OF THE CONVENTION ON CLUSTER MUNITIONS*

Madam Chair,

This first review Conference marks an important date for the Convention on cluster munitions. In this regard, I would like to express the appreciation of the Holy See Delegation to you, Madam Chair, and to Croatia for all the good work and the commitment for a successful outcome of this meeting and a new start in the implementation of the obligations that all the States Parties accepted in order to prevent the devastating consequences of cluster munitions and to make up for the mistakes of the past. Please also allow me to congratulate Costa Rica for its commitment and leadership, in particular for what concerns the universalization of the Convention.

From the very beginning, the combined efforts and partnerships between the different stakeholders made the CCM an exemplary instrument. It is important to recall and keep in mind the fundamental principles of this Convention: to place the human person, in particular the victims, at the center of our concerns; to continue strengthening the standards; to focus on prevention; not to evade responsibilities and take concrete measures in the implementation of the obligations contracted; to grant the administrative and financial resources to achieve the goals of the Convention.

At present, the greatest challenge for the Convention is to acquire the administrative and financial resources allowing for an effective and efficient implementation. This is a collective responsibility and the burden should be shared fairly. In order to finalize the work we have begun, a concrete follow-up to our commitments is very important. It is also essential to engage in a sincere cooperation between the countries affected and donors. Each State Party, each partner of the Convention, must be involved and contribute to the proper functioning of the Convention and its bodies. Our meeting today is called to decide upon the financing of the Support Unit and the structure of future meetings. It would be absurd to recur to models that do not function, like the ones we are familiar with in other contexts which greatly affect our work. The States Parties to the

* Statement delivered at the 1st Review Conference of the Convention on Cluster Munitions (CCM), Dubrovnik, Croatia, 7 September 2015.

CCM took on commitments before ensuring the financing sources. We all share the responsibility to devise a fair and equitable model so as not to repeat the unfortunate experience of the Anti-Personnel Land Mines Convention.

The issue of financing is of paramount importance. It has direct implications on the operations and on the effective implementation of the CCM. The universalization of the Convention and of its standards is a priority. The assistance to the countries affected is essential. A balanced and dynamic structure is required to implement the goals of the Convention. For all these reasons, we need a competent, efficient, stable and lasting Support Unit.

The Holy See Delegation is confident that the States Parties to the Convention will carry out their responsibility – individually and collectively – in order to prevent cluster munitions becoming a threat to the life of populations and an obstacle for the socio-economic development of the regions that experienced wars.

As it has always been from the beginning of the Oslo process, the Holy See is firm and determined to contribute to the success of this humanitarian challenge. The work is far from being completed. We all need to make the right decisions in order to prevent the dangers of cluster munitions. We owe it to the victims of the past and to prevent further victims.

Thank you, Madam Chair.

2.2.3 Convention on Certain Conventional Weapons

A CULTURE OF PREVENTION THROUGH THE ADOPTION OF NEW LEGAL INSTRUMENTS*

Mr President,

As we begin the seventh session of the Group of Governmental Experts, the Delegation of the Holy See would like to offer some methodological comments of a general nature in order to share with you, Mr President, and with the Delegations of the States Parties some reasons for satisfaction and also to raise some questions regarding the present status and the future of the CCW.

The Holy See expresses its appreciation for the positive results of the negotiations and for the adoption of a Fifth Protocol regarding explosive remnants of war. This is a step in the right direction. But some crucial issues remain to be solved in order to prevent the recurrence of victims and the damages of past wars. These victims remind us constantly of the exorbitant cost of any war in general and of the consequences of the choice and use of some arms in particular. The Holy See is also encouraged by the renewal of the mandate of the Group of Experts. Other problems equally important such as those of explosive remnants of war are yet to receive adequate attention from the States Parties.

The multilateral negotiations of arms control or of disarmament still remain slow and long, and results are reached almost always on the basis of the lowest common denominator. On the contrary, the production of new conventional arms follows the most advanced and the most rapid scientific and technological discoveries. The result is that these arms are more and more devastating and cause useless human suffering for much longer periods of time than the conflicts themselves. Cluster bombs, which are increasingly being used in armed conflicts, illustrate tragically this worrying reality. In this context, States Parties should pay particular attention to this type of sub-ammunition, bearing in mind its traumatizing and devastating effects on civilian populations as well as the negative socio-economic consequences both during and after hostilities.

* Statement delivered at the 7th Session of the Group of Governmental Experts of the States Parties to the Convention on Prohibitions or Restrictions on the Use of Certain Conventional Weapons Which May Be Deemed to Be Excessively Injurious or to Have Indiscriminate Effects, 8 March 2004.

Mr President, the Holy See is involved in a great number of countries of all the regions, in initiatives concerning victims of armed conflicts and their families, including victims of anti-personnel mines and explosive remnants of war. I do not need to describe the frustration and discouragement of thousands of volunteer workers who are obliged to repeat over and over again the job that has already been done and, in some cases, have to watch the sufferings of the victims without any form of action. It seems to me inappropriate to limit our work and decisions to the quest solely for remedial measures. Prevention is surely less costly in terms of human lives and socio-economic damage. A culture of prevention is the most appropriate in order to ensure a security which is based on justice, trust and cooperation between States. For that reason, the right equilibrium should be that of an armament maintained at the lowest level and whose effects would bring about minimal suffering and damages. There is no need to add to the failure of war in resolving problems or to its success in causing as many victims and as much unhappiness as possible.

Mr President, the Holy See is prepared to work with you and with all States Parties in promoting a culture of prevention and adopting new instruments which will spare us the efforts that are needed to continually heal the useless sufferings which are caused by these devastating weapons.

Thank you, Mr President.

THE CALL FOR A MORATORIUM ON THE USE OF CLUSTER MUNITIONS WHILE AN APPROPRIATE INSTRUMENT IS ADOPTED*

Mr Chairperson,

Since the Second World War, the use of cluster munitions in about twenty conflicts in Asia, Africa, Europe, the Middle East and Latin America has left us enough perspective, information and experience to make an objective judgment based in terms of international humanitarian law and of a strictly pragmatic point of view on the consequences of the use of an entire category of weapons. Humanitarian organizations, United Nations agencies and development agencies have unanimously recognized the need for a serious reflection on the legitimacy of the use of cluster munitions. There are thousands of dead, injured and disabled victims of cluster munitions. The return of refugees is hindered and so is the development of numerous regions, contaminated by unexploded cluster munitions.

Some countries have come to realize that the failure rate of cluster munitions is so high that they decide to remove from their military inventories certain categories of cluster munitions whose use would pose serious humanitarian problems, disproportionate to the military gain. Such choices of precaution and responsibility are to be welcomed. It is in this spirit that my Delegation understands the European Parliament's resolution adopted in 2004 which calls for an immediate moratorium on the use, stockpiling, production and transfer or export of cluster munitions.

Mr Chairperson,

A pause for reflection is needed. However, it would be insufficient and inadequate to limit our reflection to the question of improving the accuracy of cluster munitions knowing that these weapons, by their design, are not precision weapons. On the contrary, they are dispersed over large areas, making it very difficult, if not impossible, to respect the principle of distinction between military and civilian targets, particularly in densely populated areas. Moreover, even if we could improve the accuracy

* Statement delivered at the 11th Session of the Group of Governmental Experts of the States Parties to the Convention on Prohibitions or Restrictions on the Use of Certain Conventional Weapons Which May Be Deemed to Be Excessively Injurious or to Have Indiscriminate Effects, 4 August 2005.

of cluster munitions, the consequences of their use would still remain sufficiently grave to undertake a thorough discussion on the nature of these weapons – not only on the quality of manufacturing but on the technological means for their improvement. The lack of accuracy and the high rate of unexploded bomblets must make us question the legitimacy of this weapon.

Mr Chairperson,

In conclusion, the Holy See believes that consultations in this field are more than necessary and should begin without further delay, and include States, NGOs, the UN, ICRC and all those involved in humanitarian de-mining action. However, while awaiting the results of such consultations, the international community cannot and should not simply quantify the victims and damage caused by cluster munitions. If, for various reasons, it is not possible to find an immediate agreement on the definitive ban on the production and use of these weapons, the Holy See strongly supports the idea of a moratorium on the use of cluster munitions during the whole period of the proposed consultations, while awaiting the adoption of an appropriate international instrument.

Thank you, Mr Chairperson.

THE RATIFICATION OF PROTOCOL V ON THE EXPLOSIVE REMNANTS OF WAR: THE HOLY SEE'S ENCOURAGEMENT AND COMMITMENT TO THE FAMILY OF NATIONS*

Mr President,

First of all I would like to express the satisfaction of the Holy See for the excellent work you have carried out to advance the objectives of the Convention on Prohibitions or Restrictions on the Use of Certain Conventional Weapons Which May Be Deemed to Be Excessively Injurious or Have Indiscriminate Effects (CCW).

The Holy See acknowledges the positive steps already taken within the framework of the CCW in order to reduce the disastrous consequences caused by certain conventional weapons. We are, however, still too far from reaching the goals that the States Parties have set for themselves.

The many victims of mines other than antipersonnel mines (MOTAPM), of explosive remnants of war, of sub-munitions, just to give some examples, are a daily reminder of the necessity to adopt appropriate measures in response to the humanitarian challenge that no longer needs to be demonstrated. The evidence is easily found by looking at the thousands of victims, at the handicapped, at the infected regions, at the stunted development, at the lack of security and at the fear engendered. This blacklist is very familiar to humanitarian NGOs, to development agencies and to governments.

Mr President,

In the context of the CCW, the Holy See supports the negotiation as early as possible of a substantial instrument capable of responding effectively to the concrete humanitarian risks of MOTAPM.

At the same time, the Holy See appeals again for a moratorium on the utilization of sub-munitions and for a period of serious reflection in order to evaluate this category of arms in the light of international humanitarian law. To this effect, my Delegation finds it necessary to adopt a specific mandate to study this question.

* Statement delivered at the Meeting of the States Parties to the Conventions on Prohibition or Restrictions on the Use of Certain Conventional Weapons Which May Be Deemed to Be Excessively Injurious or to Have Indiscriminate Effects, 24–25 November 2005.

Mr President,

The Holy See is happy with the adoption of the Protocol V on the Explosive Remnants of War even though it would have preferred a stronger instrument. After its competent authorities have examined this Protocol, the Holy See has now taken the decision to ratify it as it waits for its entry into effect as soon as possible.

On this occasion, the following declaration of the Holy See has been made with reference to its notification of consent. 'In acceding to the Protocol on Explosive Remnants of War (ERW) annexed to the Convention on the Prohibitions or Restrictions on the Use of Certain Conventional Weapons Which May Deemed to Be Excessively Injurious or to Have Indiscriminate Effects (CCW), adopted on November 28, 2003, at the Meeting of the States Parties to the CCW, the Holy See, as it did on 16 June 1997, when it acceded to the Convention and to its first four Protocols, "in keeping with its proper nature and with the particular condition of Vatican City State, intends to renew its encouragement to the international community to continue on the path it has taken for the reduction of human suffering caused by armed conflicts."

With the approval of the Fifth Protocol, the CCW is confirmed as a "forward-looking living instrument" of international humanitarian law, intended to address the problems arising from modern armed conflicts and to improve its effectiveness for the protection of civilians and combatants in such situations.Although one could have wished for a greater incisiveness in the Protocol in responding to the problems originating from the ERW, the adoption of this instrument represents an important multilateral tool for the control of arms for humanitarian reasons, capable of calling States to responsibility for the ERW and for damages caused by them.

In keeping with its own commitment to encouraging the development and implementation of humanitarian law on the part of all States and in all circumstances, the Holy See is convinced that the Fifth Protocol signifies a further step along the path of the international community's journey of concretely promoting the culture of life and of peace, based upon the dignity of the human person and the primacy of the rule of law, through a responsible, honest and consistent cooperation of all the members of the community of nations.'

Thank you, Mr President.

UNITED WE STAND, DIVIDED WE FALL: THE NEED TO FURTHER NEGOTIATE AN INSTRUMENT ON CLUSTER MUNITIONS AND THEIR HUMANITARIAN CONSEQUENCES*

Mr President,

The Holy See Delegation warmly welcomes your election to the Presidency and expresses its appreciation for the excellent preparatory work that you and your team have carried out for weeks. Your success is the success of all. The Holy See will do everything in her power to support your efforts and to come out from this review Conference with tangible results for men and women and for all populations affected by wars and conflicts.

The success we aim at, Mr President, will be measured by the impact that our decisions will have on the everyday lives of a number of people in conflict zones. The different items on the agenda are closely interrelated. The universalization of the Convention, the respect for contracted obligations, the sponsorship program and the scrupulous implementation of the agreements adopted by the various Protocols to the Convention should hold together as a whole, not only in theory, but also as a shared commitment of all States Parties. In armed conflicts and their wake of misery and suffering, there are no winners and losers. We either all win or lose. Past and recent history constantly reminds us. What seems to be a victory today will be a defeat tomorrow.

Mr President,

The CCW, despite its limitations and failures, continues to offer invaluable services to reduce, if not eliminate, the effects of certain inhumane weapons. This Convention should retain its dynamic, developing and flexible character. It would be damaging and artificial to reduce this Convention and its protocols to what has been achieved so far. New weapons are devised and produced. It is important that the discussions and negotiations go together with the military progress to ensure that these new weapons meet the criteria imposed by the Convention and its protocols and to see if there is a need to negotiate new instruments where existing agreements no longer meet the new military standards.

* Statement delivered at the 3rd Review Conference of the High Contracting Parties to the Convention on Certain Conventional Weapons, 7 November 2006.

In this framework, the Holy See welcomes the negotiation, adoption, and entry into force of Protocol V, although its text could have been more incisive and adapted to the various catastrophic situations created by the remnants of war. It is now the duty of States to make this Protocol useful, effective and operational.

The adoption of Protocol V must not divert from other emergencies. Mines different from the anti-personnel ones keep causing heavy humanitarian problems for many people, for peacekeeping operations and for humanitarian organizations that are active in pre- and post-conflict fields. The Holy See hopes that a substantial and solid agreement on a new Protocol will be achieved by the end of this Conference.

Mr President,

A review Conference does not concern only the past or the present but it has also to address the future. Otherwise, it risks being stuck and discrediting itself. In such an evolving world, especially in the field of technologies and their military applications, the CCW has the duty to examine the nature and the use of certain weapons. Even if we do not want the CCW to become a permanent forum with a permanent secretariat, it is neither possible nor desirable to discard new negotiations.

The Holy See has already and repeatedly called for the start of negotiations on the issue of cluster munitions that pose serious humanitarian problems during and after conflicts. For this reason, we hope that the review Conference will adopt a specific mandate to negotiate on this topic. The CCW cannot be indifferent to such a serious problem that will eventually have to be addressed sooner or later. We owe this to yesterday's and today's victims and to the potential victims of tomorrow. While waiting for these negotiations to bring appropriate and effective solutions, the Holy See, once again, calls for a moratorium on the utilization of these munitions.

In the context of technological development and production of new weapons systems, a thorough examination of the issue of laser weapons is necessary.

Mr President!

The challenges faced by the CCW are considerable but the States Parties have the means to identify whether a political will among them exists and whether the interests of the most vulnerable populations are taken into account. Why cannot legitimate national security be ensured without jeopardizing the life and development of large populations? War and conflicts are always, even as a last resort, a failure. We should not add the irreparable to the failure. The CCW should respect its role as guardian of what is left of humanity in situations of violence and suffering. This review Conference is the occasion to recall CCW's fundamental purpose and to draw its practical consequences. This is the price of the meaningfulness and relevance of the CCW.

Thank you, Mr President.

THE URGENT NEED FOR THE CCW TO NEGOTIATE AN EFFECTIVE TEXT CENTERED ON THE HUMAN PERSON*

Mr Chairman,

Recently, the issue of cluster munitions and of a necessary response to serious humanitarian problems, which they continue to create, largely occupied a great number of actors who have clearly understood the urgency and seriousness of this issue. This urgency and seriousness proceeds less than a tactical or strategic military calculation or than commercial considerations, as it is a vision that puts the human person at the center of the deliberation and of the action that follows.

This urgency and seriousness should be perceived collectively by the Convention on Conventional Weapons (CCW) and lead it to the decision long awaited by individuals, families, communities and countries who are affected by and who are the witnesses, dead or alive, of the ravages of this weapon – a weapon that we do not need to demonstrate any further that should no longer exist in the arsenals of armies that have a concern to respect international humanitarian law. States Parties have the necessary perspective to understand the nature and the use of this weapon. We have deliberated enough and the time for well-informed and well-founded decisions has come.

Mr Chairman,

The Holy See has diffused last May a note that explains its position on this issue. Let me highlight a few points that I consider important for our meeting this week.

This session of the Group of Governmental Experts is crucial and it stands at a crossroads. The objective is no less than an adequate response to a serious humanitarian problem and, at the same time, the credibility of the CCW, which should result in an effective and concrete action to the question posed by cluster munitions.

As the Holy See has said recently, if the CCW wants to deal with the problem that occupies us this week, three conditions are necessary: the adoption of a substantial mandate to be able to deal appropriately with

* Statement delivered at the Group of Governmental Experts of the States Parties to the Convention on Prohibitions or Restrictions on the Use of Certain Conventional Weapons Which May Be Deemed to Be Excessively Injurious or to Have Indiscriminate Effects, 19 June 2007.

the problems generated by cluster munitions; the adoption of a temporal framework of the negotiation; negotiation, in good faith, of an effective and applicable text, far from the lowest common denominator trails. To do nothing or merely a formal action, unable to best protect civilians, will not give any credibility to the CCW. Credibility comes from treating problems in a serious, efficient and productive way.

Mr Chairman,

The Holy See has supported and reiterates its support for all processes and all efforts seeking to achieve the ideal, rational and reasonable objective to prohibit the production, possession, transfer and use of cluster munitions, to destroy stockpiles, to initiate a collective effort based on international cooperation in order to clean up affected areas and to assist individuals and communities, victims of these weapons. The process that began in Oslo, and continued in Lima, is moving in the right direction and it could well be complementary to the work of the States Parties to the CCW. With the added value of multilateralism, the two processes can be complementary and reinforce each other, without excluding the possibility of convergence at a later stage of the negotiations.

Mr Chairman,

The Group of Governmental Experts, and subsequently the States Parties, have necessary and sufficient time to make the right decisions before the end of this year. The Holy See can only appeal to all States Parties, international organizations and civil society to join efforts and to adopt a demanding and ambitious approach that can solve the problem of cluster munitions once and for all.

We do understand that, because they cannot find an immediate solution, we may consider a transitional period to achieve the goal of a total ban. However, it would be imperative, during this transitional period, to strengthen the regulation on their use, through, for example, an immediate ban on certain types of weapons and a strict respect for the rules of distinction and need, and, above all, a strictly defensive concept of the use of cluster munitions, accepted only for the exclusive protection of national territory. It is essential to put, hereon, at the center of our attention, the recognition of the fundamental value of human dignity, which should be the fundamental aspect of all efforts and all processes that seek to strengthen international humanitarian law.

Thank you, Mr Chairman.

THE URGENCY OF AN ADEQUATE RESPONSE TO THE HUMANITARIAN CONSEQUENCES OF CLUSTER MUNITIONS*

Mr President,

First, I would like to congratulate you on your election to the Presidency and assure you of my Delegation's support.

In his speech to the diplomatic corps accredited to the Holy See held last Monday, Pope Benedict XV 'encouraged the adoption of appropriate measures to tackle the humanitarian problem posed by cluster munitions'.

For his part, the Secretary for Relations with States reiterated the position of the Holy See in his speech to the General Assembly of the United Nations, last October, saying that a quick response to the problem of cluster munitions has become an ethical imperative knowing the high cost in human lives, the majority of whom are civilians and, especially, children.

Mr President, I would not repeat here the Holy See's position because it has already been explained several times, including last May in a detailed note which was widely distributed. However, let me emphasize three points that I think are important for our deliberations at this very point of the crucial debate that the international community is conducting in different fora, which we wish will be fruitful and complementary.

1. It is not a coincidence that the intervention of the Pope was made immediately before our meeting today, and some weeks before the Wellington Conference. Our deliberations will be judged by the practical results that will or will not make a difference to thousands of people and dozens of countries.

   The Holy See Delegation was pleased that the States Parties to the CCW have recognized the urgency of an adequate response to the humanitarian problems caused by cluster munitions. To be credible, the recognition of this urgency should have a translation into our deliberations and in the conclusion of the negotiations and, in good faith, in a possible instrument that adequately addresses the challenges faced by the States Parties to the CCW.

* Statement delivered at the Group of Governmental Experts of the States Parties to the Convention on Prohibitions or Restrictions on the Use of Certain Conventional Weapons Which May Be Deemed to Be Excessively Injurious or to Have Indiscriminate Effects, 14 January 2008.

2. The participation of producers, users and stockpilers to the current efforts is obviously important. The Holy See can only welcome seeing the commitment of many countries, and of these categories, within the CCW as within the Oslo process. However, it is also crucial to consider that many countries can also become producers, users and stockpilers. Proliferation risks, in this field as in others, are far from being negligible. Quite the contrary. The use of these weapons by non-State actors in recent conflicts should lead us to be vigilant and determined to act urgently. Prevention, among other things, should be the common point of concerted action between the existing producers and users and those who are still not complying.
3. Experience has shown that the prohibition of some categories of weapons made, in good faith, through the negotiations on international instruments, never put national security in danger. The real danger comes rather from the stockpiling of weapons and from the trend to rely only on weapons to ensure national or international security. Development, mutual trust, prevention, creation of the conditions for a dignified life, are the parameters without which there cannot be any security or stability.

The assertion of the military necessity for cluster munitions seems unacceptable. A simple question should be answered: how is it that, since the first use of cluster munitions, we have not been able to respect the rules of international humanitarian law – in particular, the one on the distinction between civilian and military?

In addition, invoking the financial constraints to refuse or postpone measures that the States Parties to the CCW have called urgent, seems inadmissible if we seriously look at the volume of military budgets of each ones.

Mr President,

If war has a grasp, peace has one also. And, in all cases, it is more modest by far. Preserving life, creating conditions for a dignified life for entire populations, ensuring security and stability at the lowest level of armaments, etc., are exciting challenges. CCW will come out grown and more credible if the States Parties will collectively address these challenges.

Thank you, Mr President.

ASSISTANCE TO VICTIMS AND THEIR REINTEGRATION IN SOCIETY*

Madam Coordinator,

At the outset, I would like to express to you the Holy See's satisfaction and appreciation for the excellent preparation and conduction of our work. I would also like to state my satisfaction with the decision to organize this meeting of experts to accelerate the implementation of the obligations we have all undertaken by ratifying Protocol V, in the attempt to connect, in principle and practice, international humanitarian law and human rights. By strengthening international humanitarian law with the adoption of Protocol V, States Parties reaffirm that the dignity of the human person is inalienable and that at the core of the Protocol should remain the survivors and the victims of explosive remnants of war. Prevention and assistance are the two pillars of the Protocol. Allow me, Madam Coordinator, to develop some features on the issue of victim assistance. On this issue, I will be satisfied to insist on three dimensions:

1. All victims of conflicts, and of different categories of weapons and ammunition, have the right to receive assistance without discrimination. However, the brought aid should be tailored and specific. This should not, in any case, lead to the exclusion of people or groups of people, direct or indirect victims, and let them live on the margins of society. A successful assistance is the one that allows victims to recover a dignified place in society. A dignified place means above all to be treated as a full person: autonomous, active and participating in building a prosperous and solidary society.

   The Holy See, through its institutions involved in the action in favour of the victims of mines, munitions, explosive remnants of war, tries to help in bringing the affected people, in dozens of countries, back to the maximum of normality. The normality of being a schoolboy, a student, a peasant, a worker, a craftsman or an independent professional; that of being a father or a mother of a family; that of being a full member of the society in which they live. To do this, education and training are the ideal means on the path of social, economic and political reintegration.

* Statement delivered at the CCW Group of Governmental Experts on Protocol V on Explosive Remnants of War, 22–24 April 2009.

The victims of explosive remnants of war should not be also victims of discrimination. They do not expect help to survive, but rather the establishment of conditions that will allow them to be full members of the societies in which they live and where they will be able to give their contribution to prosperity and peace, because they are the first to achieve in their flesh and in their existence what is the nature of conflicts and their consequences. That said, we should not forget the size of compassion and human proximity that are so important for the victims and that represent a valuable support, especially in the most difficult phases of this human tragedy experienced by the victims, that are left, in many cases, all alone and in general indifference. Victim assistance is therefore a matter of dignity, rights, justice and brotherhood.

2. The second dimension that I would like to raise is that of partnership. The first responsibility is the one of the State in supporting the victims. However, the overwhelming majority of countries affected by explosive remnants of war are developing countries and are therefore unable to meet their obligations without international assistance. For this reason, donor countries have an important role to play. Anyway NGOs and religious communities, located in the most remote areas, should also contribute. The Holy See, rich with decades of experience in this field, thinks that, at least so far, the most fruitful model, on a national level, is that of a partnership between the three main actors: the specialized agencies, the public sector and the private sector.

   This partnership on the national level should be completed by another partnership among governments, UN agencies, international organizations and civil society. Of course, we should not forget the victims and their representative organizations as essential components from the analysis of the situation through the definition of appropriate policies to the implementation of adopted plans.

3. The third dimension is the one that is taught us by the long-time experience in the field. The great models and the most generous theoretical reflections remain empty if they do not have an impact on victims' daily lives. For this the following concrete measures are essential:
   (a) to ensure adequate regular budgets for assistance to victims, above all, providing qualified human resources;
   (b) to create the necessary structures for physical and psychological rehabilitation;

(c) to create educational and training structures to enable the social, economic and political reintegration of victims;
(d) to practice a realistic policy of assistance, taking into account not only the direct victim himself, but also his family and the local community. It is at this level that the exclusion can be best avoided.

Experience has shown us that whenever these four elements were provided cumulatively, the integration of the victims was a success for the victims themselves and for society in general.

In conclusion, the Holy See is pleased that victim assistance becomes an essential component of several legally binding instruments such as Protocol V, the Ottawa Convention and the Convention on Cluster Munitions. Although Member States to these instruments are different, common sense suggests searching for harmonization and synergy that will avoid the unnecessary dispersion of resources and that will be beneficial to all stakeholders and, first and foremost, to the victims themselves. This is important not only as a matter of efficiency, but specifically to avoid discrimination between different categories of victims.

The Delegation of the Holy See is confident that victims' assistance will remain the priority for States Parties to Protocol V.

Thank you, Madam Coordinator.

THE CONFUSION BETWEEN THE MILITARY INTERESTS AND THE HUMANITARIAN URGENCY*

Mr President,

The Holy See Delegation would like to congratulate you on your election and it gives you its support to achieve the expectations of our people, men and women, who are victims of armed conflicts. It is our collective responsibility to create the conditions needed to protect them better. The CCW is one of the fora that should play a credible role in meeting these pressing expectations. The CCW is not a world apart. It is a tool to support humanitarian objectives.

The protection of civilians in times of war and armed conflicts has accompanied mankind throughout its history, but, with varying degrees of acceptability of the suffering inflicted. However, what is new is the awareness that security is not just military. The so-called balance between military and humanitarian considerations is almost impossible to be defined and to be determined before seeing the results of a military action. After what number of dead, wounded and disabled can we talk about unacceptable military behavior? After how many destructions of infrastructures, livelihood sources and traumas can we begin to say that the balance is broken? If any military action has the only purpose of national defense, then it must incorporate a paramount humanitarian dimension, which should take into account immediate and post-conflict consequences. The defense of national security interests cannot and should not justify everything.

In this perspective, the work of the Group of Governmental Experts of the CCW, that has been working for several years on the question of cluster munitions, was not able to find an adequate response to the humanitarian problems caused by these weapons, precisely because of the confusion between military interests and humanitarian emergency. This Delegation considers that the Group's President's current text is far from meeting the urgency expressed by the mandate. I would like to take this opportunity to thank Mr Gary Domingo for his commitment, his dynamism and his availability to move the negotiations forward in the right direction.

* Statement delivered at the Conference of the High Contracting Parties to the Convention on Certain Conventional Weapons, 25–26 November 2010.

The costs of armed conflicts, beyond the human cost which is impossible to evaluate, are exorbitant. It is always more judicious, and wiser, to prevent than to repair. This Delegation has always advocated a precautionary approach. In this perspective, I would to highlight the particular importance of having a restrictive approach on the transfers of cluster munitions. The proposal to negotiate an agreement on the transfers presents an evident humanitarian interest and it would be a pity not to proceed, in one way or another, in the direction of this proposal.

In conclusion, Mr President, I would like to call all States Parties to the CCW to initiate a collective reflection to reform and better adapt this institution, after thirty years of its creation. It is time to draw the consequences, as all the countries in the world have done in many fields, of the deep changes of last decades, which have had an evident effect on many disarmament entities and on how they work. The 2011 Review Conference is the most appropriate opportunity to make the necessary decisions that will make the CCW even more credible and more effective in its ongoing efforts to better protect people of all countries that are in situations of armed conflicts.

Thank you, Mr President.

THE NEED TO AVOID UNJUST AND INEFFICIENT COMPROMISES*

Mr President,

After 30 years from its adoption, today deliberations resume on the Convention on Certain Conventional Weapons (CCW) in the context of the Fourth Review Conference. The Holy See Delegation would like at the outset to express its satisfaction at seeing you, Mr President, directing our work to make this meeting a success for the promotion of international humanitarian law.

Since the Third Review Conference, some positive steps have been taken in the right direction and now it is important to preserve the momentum and make them productive in the coming years. Allow me to just mention the most important of these achievements: the efforts undertaken for the universalization of the Convention; the sponsorship program to support increased participation in the work of the Convention; the creation of the support unit and its commitment to make implementation more sustained and efficient; the successful initiatives to make Protocol V and Amended Protocol II more operational.

However, this Delegation regrets that an agreement has not been reached concerning mines other than antipersonnel mines (MOTAPM) and, like all other States Parties, it notes the absence of a consensus on this issue. But the fact that this item is maintained on the agenda of the Convention encourages raising it again with the hope that an agreement will soon be possible since a majority of players continues to consider that MOTAPM remain a significant threat to civilian populations. In the context of this Review Conference, it seems important to reflect in a special way on Protocol III on incendiary weapons. Since the adoption of this protocol, important developments have taken place and it would be useful to revisit this issue in order to improve and strengthen the protection of civilians from the harmful effects of this category of weapons.

* Statement delivered at the 4th Review Conference of the Convention on Prohibitions or Restrictions on the Use of Certain Conventional Weapons Which May Be Deemed to Be Excessively Injurious or to Have Indiscriminate Effects, 14 November 2011.

Mr President,

Let me now raise another important point of our work program, that of cluster munitions. During the last five years, the CCW has devoted much effort, time and financial resources to respond to the humanitarian risks caused by these weapons. Already during the Third Review Conference in 2006, the Holy See, with five other partners, had presented a document calling for the adoption of a negotiating mandate for a new protocol on cluster munitions. Unfortunately, this was not accepted by a number of Delegations. It is only after this negative conclusion that my Delegation decided to cooperate with a large number of countries to find a satisfactory humanitarian solution outside the framework of the CCW. It was no longer acceptable to see the number of victims increase, polluted areas barred from the most basic economic activities. It was necessary to ensure prevention and remedy. This is precisely what the Convention on Cluster Munitions has adequately achieved.

Despite the adoption of the Convention on Cluster Munitions, this Delegation continued to support efforts to find a supplementary agreement in the framework of the CCW on the same issue. It was required, however, that the new instrument was compatible with the spirit and letter of the Convention on Cluster Munitions. In reality, the two instruments, the Oslo Convention and the proposed Protocol VI, have two completely different definitions and two completely different scopes. The red line for this Delegation is the international humanitarian law already in force; weakening it would be a betrayal of the aspirations of peoples to reduce the impact of armed conflicts and it would also be contrary to the objectives of the CCW. For these reasons, I would like, Mr President, to express the disappointment of my Delegation at the text which is presented under the responsibility of the Chairman of the Group of Governmental Experts on the issue of cluster munitions. In addition to the lack of consensus on the text in question, it is clear that the eventual adoption of the draft Protocol would set an unacceptable precedent, as it would for the first time endorse an instrument that weakens the provisions of international humanitarian law already adopted in an international instrument signed or ratified by a majority of countries.

In an unstable international situation and in an uncertain world, international humanitarian law remains an essential safety measure not to be weakened. The multiple internal conflicts where cluster munitions have been used or may be used are many. The responsibility of the CCW to protect civilian populations rests on its ability to comply with the provisions of international humanitarian law and even in strengthening them. On the contrary, weakening the international humanitarian law would discredit this Convention. The call by the President of the International Committee of the Red Cross in the context of the negotiation of the CCW on cluster munitions is just, powerful, and in continuity with the tradition of the defence of humanitarian values. This Delegation has heard this call and fully agrees with it.

Mr President,

The CCW has an important place and role in the international system that seeks to reduce the impact of indiscriminate weapons on civilian populations, on the development and implementation of the conditions that allow an exit from war situations. To accomplish its objectives, the CCW should find a strong consensus to meet current challenges. The choice of convenient or unjust and inefficient compromises is a serious risk that will deprive the CCW of credibility. This institution has many strengths and there is still time to make the CCW a tool to promote international humanitarian law in the field of conventional arms control.

Thank you, Mr President.

A DILIGENT AND COMPLETE IMPLEMENTATION OF PROTOCOL V IS OUR MORAL RESPONSIBILITY*

Mr President,

At the outset, allow me to congratulate you on your election to preside over this 6th Review Conference.

Recent conflicts in various regions of the world confirm the urgent need for a renewed and strong response to the problem of the explosive remnants of war. Protocol V should be one important element of the international effort to prevent real humanitarian tragedies, and to constitute a remedial answer where prevention was not possible. The Holy See Delegation is very much concerned about many situations where ERW are not only posing a safety problem for the local population, but also a national and regional security problem. A huge amount of explosive weapons are not monitored, not recorded, and not secured. Some of them fell into the hands of terrorist groups and criminal gangs. Some others went to the population at large and constitute now and in the future a big risk for the stability of countries and a permanent cause for eventual criminal or political violence. The credibility of Protocol V is at stake: the diligent and complete implementation of the provisions of this protocol should be our common goal. This is the only way to protect the civilian population, and in some cases the national community as a whole, from the consequences of explosive remnants of war and in particular the huge amount of abandoned stocks.

Mr President,

In such cases, time is of the essence. In a situation of conflict, States are required to record the use and abandonment of explosive weapons. They are also required to share the information after the conflict has ended. Any hesitation in this regard has a very negative humanitarian consequence. It means more victims and bigger economic and social costs, and long-term hampering of development. The third phase should start as soon as possible to secure the abandoned stocks and to clean the polluted areas. International cooperation, where needed, is a moral responsibility.

* Statement delivered at the 6th Review Conference of the States Party to Protocol V of the Convention on Prohibitions or Restrictions on the Use of Certain Conventional Weapons Which May Be Deemed to Be Excessively Injurious or to Have Indiscriminate Effects, 12–13 November 2012.

During the negotiation of this protocol, it was not possible to have a provision about the user's responsibility. The provision on international cooperation should remain strong because it is the right thing to do, but also because it is so important for the universalization of the protocol. In almost all recent conflicts, States Parties and non-States Parties to the Protocol were involved. This fact makes implementation more difficult. But this should never be an excuse not to implement fully Article 4 of the protocol. In this context, the Holy See shares the concerns of the International Committee of the Red Cross and other partners in the NGO's community concerning the lack of total or partial implementation of Article 4 which is the cornerstone of this instrument. Without respecting the provision of this article, the rest of the protocol is almost impossible to achieve.

Mr President,

The Holy See understands and supports protocol V and the CCW in general as a concrete expression of the dignity of the human person and as a necessary application of international humanitarian law. Our reading of the provisions of the disarmament instruments in general, including protocol V, is based on a humanitarian approach where the human person is the center of attention, and the subject of protection. Civilian populations must be protected in all circumstances. We have to admit that in recent and current conflicts, the civilian populations were not protected and international humanitarian law was merely a set of non-respected rules. This is the challenge for all of us to make protocol V effective in protecting the civilian populations from the consequences of explosive weapons during conflicts and after the conflicts have ended. The civilians should not have to pay twice for the absence of a secure, free and peaceful environment.

ASSISTANCE TO VICTIMS: THE CENTRALITY OF THE HUMAN PERSON AND HIS/HER INALIENABLE DIGNITY*

Mr President,

The history of humanity, written or oral, has often been one of wars and conflicts. The most obvious narrative is that of armed conflicts, in which priority is given to ethnic, religious or national interests regardless of huge human costs. Civilians, who are not directly involved in the conflict and all those who can be grouped under the concept of innocent bystanders, have remained forgotten during the conflicts and often in the history books. Yet another narrative exists despite its more modest character. It is not less effective and promising. This is the parallel story that focuses on the protection of civilians and of those who do not participate directly in a conflict. In a nutshell, it is the history of the human conscience that refuses to allow the suffering inflicted on innocent people. The most ancient sources of the history of humanity reflect the fundamental idea that, in military conflicts, 'the right of parties to choose means and methods of warfare is not unlimited': not all are acceptable.

More recently, since the nineteenth century, we have seen the latter trend growing and taking the form of a body of law that any party to an armed conflict must respect. This trend culminated in the Geneva Conventions on international humanitarian law that subsequently several multilateral instruments have tried to develop and strengthen. International humanitarian law has come to represent a minimum of humanity in situations of extreme violence and of failure to prevent it.

It is clear, however, that despite legal, political and humanitarian provisions, civilians in urban areas continue to be by far the first victims of armed conflicts. Such a fact, while it does not imply that the principles of international humanitarian law are inadequate or unnecessary, raises the fundamental issue of the needless and unacceptable suffering imposed on the civilian population.

To illustrate this reality, it is enough to look closely at the statistics related to victims of conflicts that the world has known since the 1950s. Whether in international or local conflicts, the overwhelming majority

* Statement delivered at the Meeting of the States Parties to the Convention on Prohibitions or Restrictions on the Use of Certain Conventional Weapons Which May Be Deemed to Be Excessively Injurious or to Have Indiscriminate Effects, 15–16 November 2012.

of the dead, injured or disabled are civilians and damages primarily affecting the civilian infrastructure and the basic resources of subsistence of entire populations. Although incomplete and limited, statistical data provide sufficient information to tell the story of inadmissible and useless suffering and demonstrate that the fundamental principles of international humanitarian law often are not respected. They are sufficiently strong and convincing to allow the rejection of the so-called collateral damage excuse. A declaration of international humanitarian law principles is not enough, nor is recourse to formal arguments. The reality on the ground should be the compelling argument to document compliance or non-respect of binding international humanitarian law.

The concept of 'Unacceptable Harm to Civilians', born when 46 States adopted a Declaration in 2007 which was the starting point of the Oslo process on cluster munitions, is of great relevance in strengthening and making international humanitarian law more operational. This concept neither weakens nor contradicts the principles of international humanitarian law. But it requires each party to an armed conflict, State actors or non-State actors, to take into account the principles of international humanitarian law as well as those of human rights. For the first time, in the Convention on Cluster Munitions, assistance to victims is considered a human right. It is a remarkable development in the field of international law and in the relationship between international humanitarian law and human rights.

Formal legality is not the only condition of acceptability that goes beyond the principle of proportionality that would give priority to military advantage. An operation or a military attack could be formally consistent with the principle of proportionality, but unacceptable in the light of current standards in the perception of human dignity and human rights. The notion of acceptability also can be connected to the concept of 'cumulative effect', as presented by the International Tribunal for the Former Yugoslavia in the Kupreškić case: attacks that, per se, are in the grey zone of legitimacy but could be considered illicit in light of their cumulative effect against the civilian population.

A few years ago, researchers, NGOs, international organizations and some governments embarked on an effort to rethink the protection of civilians who face the consequences of military activities in armed conflicts. Instead of dealing with each particular type of weapons, as was the case for the Convention on Certain Conventional Weapons (CCW), the concept of explosive weapons and their effects, rather than technology, was put at the center of reflection.

Explosive weapons constitute a broad category of weapons (bombs, mortar ammunition, grenades, rockets, missiles, improvised explosive devices (IEDs), car bombs, etc.) not explicitly prohibited under international humanitarian law and that probably never will be. Now, however, many voices are raised to question the use of these weapons in populated areas and call for the protection of civilians living there. This view is shared by the United Nations Secretary General,[1] the Chairman of the International Committee of the Red Cross,[2] the United Nations Institute for Disarmament Research[3] and NGOs.[4]

Experience shows that the use of explosive weapons in populated areas has most often caused a significant number of victims, major destruction of socio-economic infrastructures, severe psychological trauma and the hindrance of development for many years. Children and women are particularly affected. These results cause hatred and socio-political wounds that are difficult to heal. In the case of internal or international conflicts, they make reconciliation more difficult, if not impossible, and they become a contradiction when international operations to restore or maintain peace and to win over the hearts and minds of local people are undertaken.

The acceptability of military losses diminishes considerably, especially in some countries. The governments, whose armed forces are engaged in armed conflicts, take very seriously public opinion on the issue of casualties among their troops. But, unfortunately, this is not always the case with respect to disproportionate losses of civilians not belonging to the same national community. This poses a problem of principle and a practical problem: first, the dignity of the human person is not conditioned by language, religion, nationality or geopolitics; second, the suffering and useless and superfluous injury are unacceptable anywhere and under any circumstances.

The consideration of the issue of explosive weapons is recent, but it carries already the promise of fruitful results for the protection of

1 Security Council, Report of the Secretary General on the Protection of Civilians in Armed Conflict, UN document S/2010/579, 11 November 2010, paras. 48–51.

2 See 'Sixty years of the Geneva Conventions and the decades ahead', 9 November 2009, www.icrc.org/eng/resources/documents/statement/geneva-convention-statement-091109.htm; Statement of 22 November 2010 by Yves Daccord, Director General of the ICRC, in Security Council, UN document S/PV.6427, provisional, p. 10.

3 UNIDIR, Discourse on Explosive Weapons (DEW) Project, www.unidir.org.

4 Richard Moyes, *Explosive Violence: The Problem of Explosive Weapons*, London: Landmine Action, 2009.

civilians in populated areas. The road ahead, however, may be long. In fact, it is a lifelong commitment that should be passed on from one generation to another with the goal of always better protecting and minimizing the number of victims to the utmost. Meanwhile, interim steps are indispensable to build a strong and convincing argument to prompt the international community to consider protection of civilians as necessary and urgent, especially in populated areas given the rapid urbanization of the world. All those who already have spoken on the issue highlight four elements:

1. It is essential to better define the conceptual framework and the basic terminology so that these may be better understood and accepted by the different actors.
2. Even though enough data are available to say, with sufficient confidence, that the use of explosive weapons raises a problem for the protection of civilian populations in urban areas, we also need more transparency in the collection and analysis of data on the part of all actors and of States themselves in the first place. The States actually have to give factual proof that they meet their obligations in the field of international humanitarian law. One can only regret that States do not undertake a systematic collection of data on civilian victims and that, when they do, such data are not usually published.
3. States should publish the political declarations concerning the rules of utilization of explosive weapons in general and, in particular, in the urban areas. The fact of publishing documents of this type would strengthen the notion of responsibility of the State before their own people and the international community.
4. The users of explosive weapons must also recognize their responsibility towards the victims, in one way or another. Already several legal instruments make assistance to victims a fundamental element of the obligations agreed on by States (the Ottawa Convention, CCM, Protocol V). Assistance to victims is a human right, a humanitarian and political commitment, and it stems from the centrality of the human person and from her inalienable dignity, which constitutes the ethical base of international humanitarian law.

In conclusion, one can affirm with sufficient confidence that it is impossible to use explosive weapons in populated areas and maintain a position of respect for the principles of international humanitarian law that would result in protection of civilians. Sadly, law alone cannot eradicate war, armed conflicts and armed violence from human history. These conflicts are evidence of the failure of humanity in its collective effort to build peaceful civilizations. It is essential to adopt an approach that goes beyond formal legality to reach the goal of a minimal, if not a zero, acceptability and tolerance of the suffering imposed on innocent people.

Mr President,

For all these reasons, the CCW is required to embark on a continued discussion on the effects of explosive weapons in populated areas, and to make the appropriate decisions to promote the protection of civilian populations in an effective manner.

THE HUMANITARIAN AND ETHICAL IMPLICATIONS OF THE USE OF WEAPONIZED DRONES AND THEIR IMPACT ON CIVILIANS*

Mr President,

The Holy See Delegation would like to express its satisfaction on your election as president of this meeting and to thank you for the excellent preparatory work.

Mr President,

Lethal autonomous weapons and drones, although distinct, share much the same humanitarian implications and raise several questions of grave ethical concern. Most critical is the lack of ability for pre-programmed, automated technical systems to make moral judgments over life and death, to respect human rights, and to comply with the principle of humanity. These questions will grow in relevance and urgency as robotic technology continues to develop and continues being utilized. With this concern in mind, I take the opportunity to express our support for your initiative, Mr President, that envisions the adoption of a mandate to start thinking about these important and urgent matters. Indeed advantage should be taken of all relevant contributions from all fields, particularly those of international humanitarian law and human rights law.

On this occasion, allow me to address the issue of drones and to propose some reflections related to the ethical dimension of these systems.

The use of weaponized drones in armed conflicts and other international hostile actions has increased exponentially in the last several years. Social, political, economic and military factors may have changed the equation for some decision-makers regarding the use of weaponized drones, but the ethical and humanitarian concerns remain relevant, and in fact have become more compelling as their use increases. The development of weaponized drone technology and its more frequent military application represents a notable change in the conduct of hostile action. From a user's standpoint, the ability to operate remotely, even from a

* Statement delivered at the Annual Meeting of the High Contracting Parties to the Convention on Prohibitions or Restrictions on the Use of Certain Conventional Weapons Which May Be Deemed to Be Excessively Injurious or to Have Indiscriminate Effects, 14 November 2013.

computer halfway around the world, greatly reduces risks to the user's own military personnel and it extends the strategic reach to the point of enabling it to deal with perceived threats around the world.

Consideration has to be given, however, in addition to international law and the law of war, to the humanitarian and ethical implications of the use of weaponized drones as well as to other questions related to human rights law. Armed drones – like any other weapon – are and should always be subject to the rules and moral principles these juridical instruments impose.

It is difficult to assess the precise impact on civilians of the use of weaponized drones, due in part to the lack of transparency in reporting, but it is indisputable that large populations live in constant fear of their strikes. Credible sources report a high number of casualties in the civilian population. Thus, if the economics of drones may make sense to the budgets, it is ethically imperative that those cost savings not be the only costs considered. Costs to civilian life and property, as well as the psychological and economic cost of living in constant fear of future mistaken strikes, should not be ignored.

Some additional pressing questions should worry the international community. When a weaponized drone is piloted from thousands of miles, who bears the responsibility for humanitarian violations in its use? When vital data related to the use of weaponized drones is withheld from scrutiny, how can compliance with international law, international humanitarian law and ethical standards be verified?

Weaponized drones are useful precisely because they take a number of important functions out of the hands of human beings, increasing accuracy and decreasing risks to life and limb for military personnel. Yet the increasing involvement of a pre-programmed machine in several steps of the targeting and attacking process further blurs the question of who is accountable when something goes wrong. Clear accountability is essential to upholding the laws and norms of international humanitarian law.

Furthermore, it is essential to understand and lay out the criteria to identify legitimate targets and distinguish targets from innocent civilians. The lack of military risk and supposed accuracy of surveillance and targeting by weaponized drones may make operators and commanders more willing to execute strikes with greater risk to civilians: greater transparency and clearer accountability in their use is critical.

Decisions over life and death are uniquely difficult decisions, a heavy responsibility for a human being, and one fraught with challenges. Yet it is a decision for which a person, capable of moral reasoning, is uniquely suited. An automated system, pre-programmed to respond to given data inputs, ultimately relies on its programming rather than on an innate capacity to tell right from wrong. Thus any trend toward greater automation of warfare should be treated with great caution. But even in the limited automation of 'human-in-the-loop' drone systems, there lies the potential for removing the essential human component from the process. Human decision-makers involved should be trained, well informed and should dispose of reasonable and sufficient time to be in a position to make sound ethical decisions.

The emerging class of remote operators of robotic weapons systems such as drones have not necessarily been given such training or adequate time to deliberate as they make decisions on the screen which affect life and death thousands of kilometers away. This procedure has ethical implications for the civilian cost at the receiving end of the drones, but it also adversely affects the operator. A study showed that nearly 30 per cent of drone pilots experience what the military calls 'burnout', defined by what the military describes as 'an existential crisis'.

In this context of dehumanized warfare, with remotely operated weapons and low risk on one side, a key ethical question thus is whether this lowers the threshold of conflict, making it seem more attractive to enter into war. Considering this question, with the near inevitability in modern warfare of massive civilian casualties, should give pause.

A final ethical consideration to explore briefly is the threat of proliferation of sophisticated drone technology. The need to account for ethical considerations and set a strong precedent for restricting their use becomes much more urgent when considered in light of the ongoing and accelerating proliferation of these weapons around the world. Any precedent set by failing to account now for all humanitarian and ethical considerations in the use of drones becomes an increasing danger as drone technology proliferates further.

Mr President,

As we enter this new era of technology in warfare, it is essential that all actors stop to consider all relevant questions related to the use of drones. Respect for life, respect for human rights and avoiding dehumanization are our collective challenge.

MACHINES CAN NEVER TRULY REPLACE HUMANS IN MORAL DECISIONS OVER LIFE AND DEATH: THE ACCOUNTABILITY VACUUM*

Mr President,

Let me first commend you for the good preparation for this very important meeting, even if the mandate is simply to discuss in an informal setting emerging concerns around new technologies which would not only impact on the way of conducting war but more importantly would question the humanity of our societies in relying on machines to make decisions about death and life.

In 2013, this Delegation expressed its deep concerns in relation to the use of drones and the troubling ethical consequences for users and victims alike.

While in many fields autonomous technology may indeed prove beneficial to humanity, the application of autonomy to weapons technology is entirely distinct: it seeks to place a machine in the position of deciding over life and death. We are most troubled by emerging technologies of autonomous weapon systems which may move beyond surveillance or intelligence-gathering capabilities into actually engaging human targets. Good intentions could be the beginning to a slippery slope. When humanity is confronted with big and decisive challenges – from health to the environment, to war and peace – taking time to reflect, relying on the principle of precaution, and adopting a reasonable attitude of prevention are far more suitable than venturing into illusions and self-defeating endeavors.

Autonomous weapon systems, like any other weapon system, must be reviewed and pass the IHL examination. Respect for international law, for human rights law, and IHL is not optional. The Holy See supports the view that autonomous weapon systems have, like drones, a huge deficit which cannot be addressed only by respecting the rules of IHL. To comply, these systems would require human qualities that they inherently lack. The ethical consequences of such systems if deployed and used cannot be overlooked and underestimated.

* Statement delivered at the Meeting of Experts on lethal autonomous weapons systems of the High Contracting Parties to the Convention on Prohibitions or Restrictions on the Use of Certain Conventional Weapons Which May Be Deemed to Be Excessively Injurious or to Have Indiscriminate Effects, 13 May 2014.

The increasing trend of dehumanization of warfare compels all nations and societies to reassess their thinking. The prospect of developing armed robots designed to engage human targets has the potential of changing the fundamental equation of war. Taking humans 'out of the loop' presents significant ethical questions, primarily because of the absence of meaningful human involvement in lethal decision-making.

Mr President,

For the Holy See the fundamental question is the following: can machines – well-programmed with highly sophisticated algorithms to make decisions on the battlefield in compliance with IHL – truly replace humans in decisions over life and death?

The answer is no. Humans must not be taken out of the loop over decisions regarding life and death for other human beings. Meaningful human intervention over such decisions must always be present.

Decisions over life and death inherently call for human qualities, such as compassion and insight, to be present. While imperfect human beings may not perfectly apply such qualities in the heat of war, these qualities are neither replaceable nor programmable. Studies of soldiers' experiences support that human beings are innately averse to taking life, and this aversion can show itself in moments of compassion and humanity amidst the horrors of war.

Programming an 'ethical governor' or 'artificial intelligence' to enable autonomous weapon systems to comply technically with the law of war in the areas of distinction and proportionality, even if possible, is not sufficient. The fundamental problem still exists: a lack of humanity, a lack of meaningful involvement by human beings in decisions over the life and death of other human beings. The human capacity for moral reasoning and ethical decision-making is more than simply a collection of algorithms. The human factor in decisions over life and death can never be replaced.

It is already extremely complex to apply the rules of distinction and proportionality in the context of war. Distinguishing combatant from civilian, or weighing military gain and human suffering, in the heat of war, is not reducible to technical matters of programming. Meaningful intervention by humans, with our unique capacity for moral reasoning, is absolutely essential in making these decisions.

Part of the justification for developing these weapons may be the idea that 'if we don't develop this technology, someone else will'. The development of complex autonomous weapon systems is likely out of the reach of smaller States or non-State actors. However, once such systems are developed by larger States, it will not be extremely difficult to copy them. History shows that developments in military technology, from crossbows to drones, give the inventing side a temporary military advantage. The inevitable widespread proliferation of these weapon systems will fundamentally alter the nature of warfare for the whole human family.

Minimizing the risks to its own forces is understandable and legitimate. However, with no casualties or tales of horror from one side, the domestic political cost of waging war becomes less significant. This represents an important deterrent to overly hastened military action, and is a deterrent that should not be lightly disregarded.

Autonomous weapon systems technology makes war too easy and removes its reliance on soldierly virtues. Several military experts and professionals, who consider killing people a most serious matter, are deeply troubled by the idea of delegating these decisions to machines. Obviously these voices value the potential of robots to assist in bomb disposal, evacuation of the wounded, or surveying a battle scene, but the potential for robots to completely replace soldiers on the field remains of grave concern to them.

Furthermore, the delegation of the human decision-making responsibilities to an autonomous system designed to take human lives creates an accountability vacuum that makes it impossible to hold anyone sufficiently accountable for violations of international law incurred by an autonomous weapon system.

It is exactly these concerns that call for a multilateral approach to questioning the development and implementation of autonomous weapon systems. As in the case of actions like the Protocol on Blinding Laser Weapons, it is imperative to act before the technology for autonomous weapon systems progresses and proliferates, before such weapons fundamentally alter warfare into an even less humane, less human, affair.

Mr President,

In conclusion, it is important to recognize that meaningful human involvement is absolutely essential in decisions affecting the life and death of human beings, to recognize that autonomous weapon systems can never replace the human capacity for moral reasoning, including in the context of war, to recognize that development of autonomous weapon systems will ultimately lead to widespread proliferation, and to recognize that the development of complex autonomous weapon systems which remove the human actor from lethal decision-making is short-sighted and may irreversibly alter the nature of warfare in a less humane direction, leading to consequences we cannot possibly foresee, but that will in any case increase the dehumanization of warfare.

Thank you, Mr President.

THE MORAL DUTY OF INTERNATIONAL COOPERATION AND COMPLIANCE WITHIN THE FRAMEWORK OF PROTOCOL V*

Mr President,

I would first like to congratulate you on your assumption of the presidency and for all the preparatory work to make our meeting as productive as possible.

The CCW and its Protocols, including Protocol V, are intended to be an important part of the fabric of international humanitarian law which is not an end in itself but a means to protect civilians in armed conflicts. The most perfect instruments would be useless if their implementation had no concrete consequences for men and women living in areas of armed conflict. We are all aware that the adoption of a number of instruments in the disarmament field was only possible at the level of the lowest common denominator. 'Realism' invoked to convince those who want more robust instruments is the promise of implementation in good faith which would be an invaluable service to countries in conflict.

Mr President,

Protocol V did not escape this logic. For the sake of credibility and to keep the door open for negotiating and adopting other instruments in the future, it is incumbent upon all States Parties to take seriously the implementation of this instrument in both its preventive dimension as well as in its remedial dimension. The many recent conflicts in the Middle East, Africa, North Africa, Europe, remind us of our responsibilities regarding explosive remnants of war and abandoned ordinances. Apart from the safety of civilians, we are witnessing national and regional destabilization because of the lack of safety and security of stocks, that the international community is unable or not prepared sufficiently to prevent. The States Parties have the responsibility to avoid Protocol V becoming a text unable to prevent and remedy. In this context, the implementation of Article 4 of the Protocol is all the more necessary. Without strict respect for this article, other provisions of this Protocol would be impossible to meet. We

* Statement delivered at the 8th Conference of the High Contracting Parties to Protocol V of the Convention on Prohibitions or Restrictions on the Use of Certain Conventional Weapons Which May Be Deemed to Be Excessively Injurious or to Have Indiscriminate Effects, 10 November 2014.

continue to share with the ICRC, other States Parties and various NGOs the same concern about the Article 4 implementation.

It is true that the primary responsibility is that of the affected State. But international cooperation is also an obligation. Almost all current conflicts involve national, regional and international actors, State actors and non-State actors. It must also be borne in mind that the majority of countries in conflict are developing countries which do not always have sufficient means to overcome the consequences of armed conflict on their soil.

Mr President,

The success of the partnership between States, international organizations and NGOs in several areas of disarmament is well established. CCW, including Protocol V, has always opened its door to the participation of civil society and its organizations. We all profit from the professionalism and expertise of these organizations. We believe they should continue to have a place and a voice in this place, and a role to play in international cooperation in the prevention and remedy of damages caused by explosive remnants of war.

Mr President,

Wars and armed conflicts are always a failure of politics and of humanity. IHL should keep this essential human dimension to make coexistence possible nationally and internationally. When the international community fails to preserve peace, it should not accept a second failure. Protocol V is a modest attempt to prevent innocent people from becoming victims once the conflict is over. Compliance is not only a legal obligation. It is in the first place a moral duty towards the people and a political duty to restore peace.

I thank you, Mr President.

THE NEED FOR THE CCW TO ADDRESS THE DRONE ISSUE BEFORE IT BECOMES A DESTABILIZING FORCE*

Mr President,

First of all, I would like to congratulate you on your assumption of the presidency and for the preparatory work to make this meeting as productive as possible.

Mr President,

In the context of this annual meeting of the CCW, I would like to raise several important issues that the CCW, it seems to me, should consider.

First, I thank the French Presidency for the excellent work that has enabled the informal meeting of last May to conclude the work on the lethal autonomous weapons systems. It is a matter of great importance to my Delegation and it is larger than the scope of the CCW where our primary interest is the development and respect for international humanitarian law. The automation of war and therefore the risk of its dehumanization should prompt States Parties toward a deeper reflection and eventually to a decision to enact the indispensable measures that are necessary. A consideration merely from the military viewpoint would be artificially reductive. A global approach is indispensable: scientific, legal, cultural, economic, ethical, and humanitarian. The Holy See stated its position on this question at the informal meeting. I will not repeat it now. But I would like only to reaffirm our wish that the mandate regarding this topic be renewed taking into account the importance of preserving an official trace of the statements, documents, debates and discussions.

Mr President,

The second question I would raise is the use of explosive weapons in populated areas. Today we witness numerous conflicts, an overwhelming majority of which unfold in urban areas. With growing urbanization of the world population, the tendency for urban wars will increase.

* Statement delivered at the Meeting of the States Parties to the Convention on Prohibitions or Restrictions on the Use of Certain Conventional Weapons Which May Be Deemed to Be Excessively Injurious or to Have Indiscriminate Effects, 13 November 2014.

How to protect the civilian populations? What should we do to safeguard civil infrastructures, indispensable for the livelihood of large communities? Is the current international humanitarian law sufficient? If not, how do we complete it and adapt it? What is certain, from the observations and data presently available, is that civilian populations are the first victims of conflicts. In many cases, they have no protection. Millions of refugees and displaced people, a majority of them civilian victims, a great number women and children; total or partial destruction of numerous urban centers; total disorganization of social, academic, economic and political life; the exacerbation of hatred and of feelings of revenge that makes the re-establishment of peace and national reconstruction more difficult, if not impossible. It seems to me that an essential question touches all States Parties: does the CCW have something to say and do in such a situation? For the credibility and the integrity of the Convention and for the respect of the numerous victims, I would like to suggest that we put this question on the agenda of the CCW.

Mr President,

The third and last question that I would like to raise is that of the use of armed drones. The Holy See has intervened in the meeting of 2013 dedicating its statement exclusively to the topic of armed drones. The fact of having adopted a mandate regarding the lethal autonomous weapons systems does not dispense the CCW from discussing in an appropriate manner the complex question of the use of armed drones. We are witnessing a certain proliferation of this technology and a growing use of it in various conflicts. The challenges are multiple and related to international humanitarian law, to human rights, and to international law. The ethical implications are not insignificant. The choice of indifference in relation to this question is counter-productive. The fact of not addressing problems at the right moment can have disastrous consequences and make them almost insoluble, as experience in other domains teaches us. There is still time for the CCW to become interested in drones before they become an additional source of greater destabilization when the international community needs more than ever stability, cooperation and peace.

I thank you, Mr President.

THE IMPORTANCE OF A SERIOUS AND HONEST IMPLEMENTATION OF PROTOCOL V*

Mr President,

At the outset, the Holy See Delegation would like to congratulate you on your election and we look forward to working with you to make our meeting a success in preventing and reducing the suffering of whole populations living in conflict areas.

Several military conflicts are unfolding in different regions of the world, from Europe to the Middle East to Africa, and the world is watching passively or even ignoring cynically. The humanitarian consequences of these conflicts are horrendous: hundreds of thousands of dead and injured, millions of refugees, whole generations sacrificed. The parties to different international instruments of international humanitarian law developed to face these kinds of situations, at the least to minimize the humanitarian suffering, seem very little willing to live up to their responsibility.

This annual meeting of States Parties to Protocol V of the CCW is an opportunity to have an honest review of the relevance of this treaty in the real world. It is legitimate to ask the simple question: what did Protocol V change for entire populations living in conflict areas? Are these populations better protected from the explosive remnants of war? Are any preventive measures taken by the parties to the conflicts to reduce the harm caused to the civilian populations, especially the weakest ones: children, women, elderly, disabled people?

Too many countries are plagued with explosive remnants of war from old and new conflicts. The extensive use of ammunition with high failure rates is resulting in a large number of victims and preparing for a humanitarian catastrophe in the future. Abandoned weapons are another concern leading to arms trafficking, terrorist attacks, destabilizing factors that open the way for new conflicts. This issue was a big problem in the last years and is now a reason to worry about the future in many regions and for many populations.

* Statement delivered at the 9th Conference of the High Contracting Parties to Protocol V of the Convention on Prohibitions or Restrictions on the Use of Certain Conventional Weapons Which May Be Deemed to Be Excessively Injurious or to Have Indiscriminate Effects, 9 November 2015.

In this area, States Parties to Protocol V have a special responsibility. It is not a secret that several States Parties, during the negotiations and the adoption of this Protocol, were seeking a stronger treaty able to respond effectively to the root causes and the consequences of explosive remnants of war. Notwithstanding the weakness of this instrument, this Delegation hoped and is still hoping that a serious and honest implementation of Protocol V would make a difference in the lives of affected populations. What remains is to overcome the many qualifiers and ambiguities and to embark on a real and effective cooperation between affected countries and users of weapons. Beyond the letter of treaties, legally weak or strong, all actors have a shared responsibility to protect each and every human person out of a shared common dignity, out of an ethical responsibility and out of caring for the future of a peaceful and stable world order.

Mr President,

The legacy of the present conflicts should not make whole populations hostage of the explosive remnants of war and abandoned weapons. A serious implementation of Protocol V will help to keep a glimpse of hope to prevent additional victims. It is of great importance that Protocol V be an effective element making possible reconstruction, reconciliation and development once conflicts are over.

Mr President, I thank you.

THE CHALLENGES FOR INTERNATIONAL HUMANITARIAN LAW IN A GLOBALIZATION OF INDIFFERENCE*

Mr President,

My Delegation congratulates you on your election and wishes you every success in leading our work.

In a deteriorated international context, armed conflicts and security tensions on all continents are the cause of thousands of deaths, millions of refugees, destruction, misery and unspeakable suffering. International structures, institutions, treaties and conventions, which are supposed to prevent or at least mitigate the consequences of these tragedies, seem paralyzed. The great, generous and ambitious ideas at the basis of our international system seem to have lost much of their attraction and their dynamism. International humanitarian law and the law of war are no longer accepted, at least in practice, as the indisputable norm of any armed conflict. Economic globalization that would have the unity of the human family as foundation, and cooperation as its objective, to promote solidarity and a peaceful and just world, is unfortunately feeding a 'globalization of indifference'. The most obvious expressions of such indifference are the collective selfishness and cynical realism which exclude the weakest and sacrifice human persons on the altar of short-term interests of power.

Mr President,

In this context and in the framework of the CCW, an alarming development seems to be gaining ground. The respect and promotion of international humanitarian law are increasingly ignored and violated. Just look at what is happening in today's armed conflicts. At best, the humanitarian principles have become a mesmerizing litany. The Holy See is alarmed by these developments that can only lead to more violence, misery and suffering. The Holy See associates itself with the responsible and urgent warning launched recently by the United Nations Secretary General and the President of the International Committee of the Red Cross. The description they make of the continued erosion of, and the non-compliance with, the rules of international humanitarian

* Statement delivered at the Meeting of the States Parties to the Convention on Prohibitions or Restrictions on the Use of Certain Conventional Weapons Which May Be Deemed to Be Excessively Injurious or to Have Indiscriminate Effects, 12 November 2015.

law is alarming. The two senior leaders judge the current situation as unacceptable. They see that the world is at a crossroads and that all State and non-State actors have the duty to engage to 'renew a contract for humanity' that should benefit millions of people affected by armed conflicts.

The challenges of peace and respect of international humanitarian law are also the challenges of the CCW. If it wants to preserve some credibility, it should make a real contribution to development, respect and promotion of international humanitarian law. It has a mandate and the means to do so. But the political will and a more ambitious vision of priorities are also required. Surely, military means are not the preferred way to ensure peace and protect civilians; rather, it is the respect of an ethic of brotherhood and solidarity; the pursuit of an international policy based on justice, dialogue and cooperation; the guarantee of the dignity of the person and of the ensuing rights. Great principles cannot ensure fair and peaceful order if they are not effectively translated into practice. The practical implementation of international humanitarian law is the indispensable minimum against the inhumanity of war and armed conflict.

Mr President,

The Holy See considers that the CCW can and must make a contribution in this direction. Three urgent issues are on the agenda of the CCW and its protocols. Now is the time to act, because the lives of thousands of people are at risk. It is also about the future of the next generations. It is also about the security and stability of all countries, increasingly interconnected. The Holy See proposes to put in place a Group of Governmental Experts on lethal autonomous weapon systems (LAWS), another one on the use of explosive weapons in populated areas and a third group for the revision of the protocol on incendiary weapons. These are not new issues for the CCW. What is happening on the ground in many conflicts is unacceptable. The CCW bears a part of the responsibility with regards to these negative developments and to providing solutions in areas of its competence.

Mr President,

In a renewed awareness of the seriousness of the situation of international humanitarian law, the CCW is called to fulfill its role, in partnership with the ICRC, international organizations and the civil society active in this area. Allow me, Mr President, to conclude with this quote from the speech of Pope Francis to the General Assembly of the United Nations last September. He says:

> Without the recognition of certain incontestable natural ethical limits and without the immediate implementation of those pillars of integral human development, the ideal of 'saving succeeding generations from the scourge of war' and 'promoting social progress and better standards of life in larger freedom', risks becoming an unattainable illusion, or, even worse, idle chatter which serves as a cover for all kinds of abuse and corruption … War is the negation of all rights and a dramatic assault on the environment. If we want true integral human development for all, we must work tirelessly to avoid war between nations and peoples. To this end, there is a need to ensure the uncontested rule of law and tireless recourse to negotiation, mediation and arbitration.

I thank you, Mr President.

EXPLANATORY NOTES

APLC – Anti-Personnel Landmines Convention

The 1997 Convention on the Prohibition of the Use, Stockpiling, Production and Transfer of Anti-Personnel Mines and on their Destruction is the international agreement that bans antipersonnel landmines. It is usually referred to as the Ottawa Convention or the Mine Ban Treaty. The Convention was concluded by the Diplomatic Conference on an International Total Ban on Anti-Personnel Land Mines at Oslo on 18 September 1997 (www.un.org/disarmament/convarms/landmines/mineban/).

BWC – Biological Weapons Convention

The Convention on the Prohibition of the Development, Production and Stockpiling of Bacteriological (Biological) and Toxin Weapons and on their Destruction, commonly known as the Biological Weapons Convention (BWC) or Biological and Toxin Weapons Convention (BTWC), opened for signature in 1972 and entered into force in 1975. The BWC effectively prohibits the development, production, acquisition, transfer, stockpiling and use of biological and toxin weapons and is a key element in the international community's efforts to address the proliferation of weapons of mass destruction (www.unog.ch/bwc).

CCM – Convention on Cluster Munitions

The CCM was concluded by the Dublin Diplomatic Conference on Cluster Munitions at Dublin on 30 May 2008. The Convention is the result of the Oslo process, a diplomatic process that included States, civil society, the International Committee of the Red Cross as well as the United Nations (www.unog.ch/ccm).

CCW – Convention on Certain Conventional Weapons

The Convention on Prohibitions or Restrictions on the Use of Certain Conventional Weapons Which May Be Deemed to Be Excessively Injurious or to Have Indiscriminate Effects as amended on 21 December 2001 (CCW) is usually referred to as the Convention on Certain Conventional Weapons. It is also known as the Inhumane Weapons Convention. The purpose of the Convention is to ban or restrict the use of specific types of weapons that are considered to cause unnecessary or unjustifiable suffering to combatants or to affect civilians indiscriminately. The structure of the CCW – a chapeau Convention and annexed Protocols – was adopted in this manner to ensure future flexibility (www.unog.ch/ccw).

CCW Protocol IV on Blinding Laser Weapons

Protocol IV on Blinding Laser Weapons was negotiated and adopted on 13 October 1995 during the First Review Conference of the States Parties to the Convention on Certain Conventional Weapons and entered into force on 30 July 1998 (www.unog.ch/ccw).

CCW Protocol V

The most recent of the Protocols annexed to the Convention, Protocol V on Explosive Remnants of War, was adopted on 28 November 2003 and entered into force on 12 November 2006. The Protocol, which is the first multilaterally negotiated instrument to deal with the problem of unexploded and abandoned ordnance, is intended to eradicate the daily threat that such legacies of war pose to populations in need of development and to humanitarian aid workers operating in the field to help them (www.unog.ch/ccw).

CTBT – Comprehensive Nuclear-Test-Ban Treaty

The Comprehensive Nuclear-Test-Ban Treaty (CTBT) bans nuclear explosions by everyone, everywhere: on the Earth's surface, in the atmosphere, underwater and underground. Many attempts were made during the Cold War to negotiate a comprehensive test ban, but it was only in the 1990s that the Treaty became a reality. The CTBT was negotiated in Geneva between 1994 and 1996 (https://www.ctbto.org/the-treaty/).

Geneva II Conference on Syria

The Geneva II Conference on Syria took place on 22 January 2014 in Montreux and continued 23–31 January 2014 in Geneva with the aim of finding a solution to the civil war in Syria.

ICRC – International Committee of the Red Cross

Established in 1863, the ICRC's exclusively humanitarian mission is to protect the lives and dignity of victims of armed conflict and other situations of violence and to provide them with assistance. It directs and coordinates the Red Cross and Red Crescent Movement's international relief activities during armed conflicts (https://www.icrc.org/).

Independent International Commission of Inquiry on the Syrian Arab Republic

The Independent International Commission of Inquiry on the Syrian Arab Republic was established on 22 August 2011 by the Human Rights Council through resolution S-17/1 adopted at its 17th Special Session with a mandate to investigate all alleged violations of international human rights law since March 2011 in the Syrian Arab Republic. The Commission was also tasked to establish the facts and circumstances that may amount to such violations and of the crimes perpetrated and, where possible, to identify those responsible with a view of ensuring that perpetrators of violations, including those that may constitute crimes against humanity, are held accountable (www.ohchr.org/EN/HRBodies/HRC/IICISyria/Pages/IndependentInternationalCommission.aspx).

Intergovernmental Working Group on the Right to Peace

The Intergovernmental Working Group was established at the 20th session of the Human Rights Council in 2012 by Resolution 20/15, with the task of progressively negotiating a draft United Nations declaration on the right to peace (www.ohchr.org/EN/HRBodies/HRC/RightPeace/Pages/WGDraftUNDeclarationontheRighttoPeace.aspx).

NEW START – New Strategic Arms Reduction Treaty

NEW START is a treaty to reduce nuclear weapons between the United States of America and the Russian Federation. It was signed on 8 April 2010 in Prague and, after ratification, entered into force on 5 February 2011. It is expected to last at least until 2021. NEW START is the replacement of START.

NPT – Non-Proliferation Treaty

The NPT is a landmark international treaty whose objective is to prevent the spread of nuclear weapons and weapons technology, to promote cooperation in the peaceful uses of nuclear energy and to further the goal of achieving nuclear disarmament and general and complete disarmament. The Treaty represents the only binding commitment in a multilateral treaty to the goal of disarmament by the nuclear-weapon States. Opened for signature in 1968, the Treaty entered into force in 1970. On 11 May 1995, the Treaty was extended indefinitely. A total of 190 parties have joined the Treaty. To further the goal of non-proliferation and as a confidence-building measure between States Parties, the Treaty establishes a safeguards system under the responsibility of the International Atomic Energy Agency (www.un.org/disarmament/WMD/Nuclear/NPT.shtml).

Special Sessions of the Human Rights Council

Pursuant to paragraph 10 of General Assembly Resolution 60/251, and in accordance with rule 6 of the rules of procedure of the Human Rights Council, the Council 'shall hold special sessions, when needed, at the request of a member of the Council with the support of one third of the membership of the Council' to address human rights violations and emergencies (www.ohchr.org/EN/HRBodies/HRC/Pages/Sessions.aspx).

START – Strategic Arms Reduction Treaty

START is a treaty between the United States of America and the Union of Soviet Socialist Republics on the limitation and reduction of strategic nuclear stockpiles. Signed on 31 July 1991, it entered into force on 5 December 1994. It expired on 5 December 2009.

UNIDIR – United Nations Institute for Disarmament Research

The UNIDIR is an autonomous, voluntarily funded organization that is embedded within the United Nations. Its mission is to help the international community identify and solve disarmament and security-related problems (www.unidir.ch/).

Vienna Conference on the Humanitarian Impact of Nuclear Weapons

The Vienna Conference on the Humanitarian Impact of Nuclear Weapons was held in Austria, 8–9 December 2014, and consolidated a set of substantive and strong conclusions with respect to the humanitarian consequences of nuclear weapons, the risks associated with the existence of these weapons, as well as the legal and moral dimensions of this weaponry (www.bmeia.gv.at/en/european-foreign-policy/disarmament/weapons-of-mass-destruction/nuclear-weapons-and-nuclear-terrorism/vienna-conference-on-the-humanitarian-impact-of-nuclear-weapons/).

V

Solidarity with all Humanity

Introduction

In the course of its representation activities at the global level, the Holy See focuses much of its concern on the plight of the most poor and vulnerable members of society, those who often are marginalized from access to social protection, care and enjoyment of rights and dignity. Thus the principle of solidarity inspires much of the representational activity of the Holy See within the multilateral organizations. This principle has deep roots in the Judaeo-Christian Scriptures, in the lived witness of Jesus and in the practical Tradition of works of charity and justice during the past two millennia. The Holy See strives to bring the direct, grassroots knowledge and experience of local Catholic Church communities in virtually every part of the world to the global institutions that are committed to advance peace, harmony and respect for all persons and families. In so doing, the Holy See proposes the principle of solidarity as the key to making today's world a better place to live, where all persons, without distinction, are treated with equal dignity.

St John Paul II urgently articulated the need for solidarity when he noted at the dawn of the Third Millennium:

> Our world is entering the new millennium burdened by the contradictions of an economic, cultural, and technological progress which offers immense possibilities to a fortunate few, while leaving millions of others not only on the margins of progress but in living conditions far below the minimum demanded by human dignity. How can it be that even today there are still people dying of hunger? Condemned to illiteracy? Lacking the most basic medical care? Without a roof over their heads?[1]

This same Pope insisted that sweeping changes must be made among individuals, governments and entire societies:

> It is not merely a matter of 'giving from one's surplus,' but helping entire peoples … presently excluded or marginalized to enter into the sphere of economic and human development. For this to happen, it is not enough to draw on the surplus goods which in fact our world abundantly produces; it requires above all a change of life styles, of models of production and consumption, and of the established structures of power which today govern society.[2]

As he envisioned, through the lens of solidarity, a more just and inclusive world of the future, Pope Francis detailed the actions which must be

[1] Pope John Paul II, *Novo Millennio Ineunte*, § 50.
[2] Pope John Paul II, Encyclical Letter, *Centesimus Annus*, § 58.

undertaken, with serious commitment, transparency and accountability, by States and the entire global family:

> In the case of global political and economic organization, much more needs to be achieved, since an important part of humanity does not share in the benefits of progress and is in fact relegated to the status of second-class citizens. Future Sustainable Development Goals must therefore be formulated and carried out with generosity and courage, so that they can have a real impact on the structural causes of poverty and hunger, attain more substantial results in protecting the environment, ensure dignified and productive labor for all, and provide appropriate protection for the family, which is an essential element in sustainable human and social development. Specifically, this involves challenging all forms of injustice and resisting the 'economy of exclusion', the 'throwaway culture' and the 'culture of death' which nowadays sadly risk becoming passively accepted.[3]

The interventions of the Holy See contained in this Chapter reveal her active participation at the multilateral level. Be it at the World Health Organization, at the international conferences of the Red Cross, or at the Human Rights Council of the United Nations, the Holy See has always decried the disparity among nations and the many situations of inequality, poverty and injustice, which 'are signs not only of a profound lack of fraternity, but also of the absence of a culture of solidarity'.[4]

Motivated by such belief, the Holy See never fails to raise concerns about those who experience the greatest suffering in the face of humanitarian emergencies: those living in extreme poverty, those excluded from the mainstream of society, who cannot count on well-developed economic and social infrastructure to fulfil their basic physical and emotional needs and to protect them from threats to physical and family well-being, and to life itself. Another serious preoccupation frequently expressed by the Holy See is that of the 'long-term' and 'forgotten' emergencies that do not receive sufficient attention from the international community, or sufficient resources and political will to facilitate adequate responses to the human and environmental suffering caused by them.[5]

While recognizing international humanitarian law as an important, invaluable, non-negotiable and still relevant instrument, the Holy See frequently urged the development of practical actions to effectively

[3] Pope Francis, Address to the UN System Chief Executive Board for Coordination, Vatican City, 9 May 2014, http://w2.vatican.va/content/francesco/en/speeches/2014/may/documents/papa-francesco_20140509_consiglio-nazioni-unite.html.

[4] Pope Francis' Message for the 2014 World Day of Peace.

[5] Cf. 'The Need to Defend Human Dignity and Promote Humanitarian Law' (2003).

implement such international legislation at the operational level and to encourage the political will for global adherence to such life-saving commitments. In this regard, in addition to recognizing the need for education on the legal technicalities of applying international humanitarian law, the Holy See has appealed for education on the ethics and principles on which such legislation is based and on the consequent formation of conscience that will assure its implementation in a universal and non-discriminatory manner.[6]

The Holy See duly acknowledges the primary duty of States to assure protection and assistance to those affected by humanitarian emergencies within their respective borders. It notes, however, that increasingly complex factors influence both the causes and results linked to natural and human-made emergencies in today's world. It rejects the tendencies of some States to impose biased or repressive measures against those affected by such disasters. Thus the Holy See calls for the international community to maintain its vital and indispensable role in assisting national authorities to respond to crises and, where these are unable to do so, to provide access to emergency and life-saving regional and international resources. It also notes the key role played by religious organizations in providing unbiased and holistic assistance to those affected by the wide range of humanitarian emergencies.[7]

One of the recurrent preoccupations of the Holy See concerns the need to assure the achievement of the right to health and to promote just public health policies and the highest attainable standards of health care. In this regard, the interventions of the Holy See have been rooted in its uncompromising belief in the sanctity of human life from conception to natural death. With equal determination, the Holy See has insisted on the unique dignity of each and every human person without regard to sex (male/female), or social, economic, ethnic, political or religious status.[8] These beliefs and values constitute the foundation of its advocacy to place the human person at the centre of all health care policy and decisions. Thus, the Holy See consistently has maintained that failure to do so results in a social system that comprises a person's absolute right to life and basic health care on the basis of the ability to pay, and on other subjective decisions that sacrifice life and health in exchange for short-term social, economic and political advantage.

[6] Cf. 'The Need to Reawaken Public Conscience' (2011).
[7] Cf. 'Together for Humanity' (2009).
[8] Cf. The Right of Everyone to the Enjoyment of the Highest Attainable Standard of Physical and Mental Health (2008).

A major focus of the Holy See's defence of the right to life relates to the attempts of some governments and health care agents to promote abortion as an acceptable, or even advisable, 'solution' to health care crises of both pregnant women and the children they carry in their wombs. In this regard, the Holy See rejects all such claims and insists that abortive procedures and abortifacient medicines violate the life of the defenceless, unborn child. It insists further that human rights are universal and indivisible and one cannot seek to safeguard one right by violating the most basic right of the child – that of life itself. The Holy See frequently points to scientific evidence that the majority of complications during pregnancy and labour are caused by the lack of medical skills, of hygiene and of antibiotics, rather than by any 'threat' posed by the unborn child to the life of the mother.

Much emphasis is placed by the Holy See on the right of everyone to the highest attainable standards of physical and mental health. This is in full accord with the Constitution of the World Health Organization. In a similar vein, due recognition has been given to the fact that this same Constitution recognizes the definition of 'health' as extending beyond medical interventions and social determinants to include a 'state of complete physical, mental and social well-being and not merely the absence of disease or infirmity'.[9] At the same time, faithful to its grounding in Catholic Church doctrine, the Holy See also maintains that access to spiritual assistance should be included among those conditions that guarantee the full enjoyment of the right to health.[10] There is no such provision in the World Health Organization Constitution but it is included as an essential component in the World Health Organization definition of Palliative Care.[11]

In efforts to promote universal health coverage, the Holy See urges that fundamental values, such as equity, human rights and social justice, be integrated into explicit policy objectives. It also calls for greater global

9 Preamble to the Constitution of the World Health Organization as adopted by the International Health Conference, New York, 19 June–22 July 1946; signed on 22 July 1946 by the representatives of 61 States (Official Records of the World Health Organization, No. 2, p. 100) and entered into force on 7 April 1948.

10 Charter for Health Care Workers, § 40, Pontifical Council for Health Pastoral Care, Vatican City, 1995, www.healthpastoral.org/pdffiles/Charter_06_Chapter2.pdf.

11 'Palliative care is an approach that improves the quality of life of patients and their families facing the problem associated with life-threatening illness, through the prevention and relief of suffering by means of early identification and impeccable assessment and treatment of pain and other problems, physical, psychosocial and spiritual', www.who.int/cancer/palliative/definition/en/.

solidarity and commitment to development assistance for health, since most low-income countries need the support of the international community, especially of high-income countries and other development partners, in order to overcome the funding shortfalls in this essential component of assuring the well-being of their respective population.[12] In addition to provision of funding, an appeal is made for more advanced countries to make available their experience and technology to less developed countries.[13] While recognizing the prerogative of private industry to intellectual property rights and to profit, the Holy See also reminds commercial enterprises, especially manufacturers of pharmaceuticals and diagnostic tools, to respect the flexibilities made available to governments in order to make life-saving medicines and diagnostics available, accessible and affordable throughout the world, and not simply to a 'select few' in high-income nations.[14] One group particularly deprived of access to medicines is that of children, since many essential medicines have not yet been developed in appropriate formulations or dosages specific to paediatric use.

Moreover, the Holy See tenaciously insists that the inequalities, both between countries and within countries, and between racial and ethnic groups, represent another key obstacle to achieving the internationally articulated goals in public health.[15] It frequently highlights the tragic fact that in many regions of the world women continue to receive poorer-quality health care. The Holy See also pledges to steadfastly maintain its service and accompaniment of the poorest people in Africa, since this continent continues to bear an inequitable burden in morbidity and mortality caused by preventable and treatable diseases.[16] Looking towards the future, the Holy See has joined other nations in their appeals to prioritize health in the next generation of global development goals. It has articulated this task before the international community as that of describing health objectives in an appropriate and convincing way.[17]

12 Cf. 'Sustainable Health Financing Structures and Universal Coverage' (2012).

13 Pope John Paul II, Address to the 14th International Conference Organized by the Pontifical Council for Health Care Workers, 19 November 1999, § 5.

14 Cf. 'The Need for Universal Access to Medicines and Diagnostic Tools' (2010); 'Key Elements to Guarantee Access to Medicines' (2013); 'The Primacy of the Right to Health Over the Focus on Profit' (2015).

15 Cf. 'The Rural Urban Divide: Re-Prioritize Investment in Healthcare' (2015).

16 Cf. 'We Must Not Forget Africa' (2007).

17 Cf. 'Prioritizing Health in the Next Generation of Development Goals' (2013).

The Holy See frequently calls attention to the fact that among civil society organizations assuring health care within various national systems the programs sponsored by the Catholic Church and other faith-based organizations stand out as key stakeholders. World Health Organization officials have acknowledged that such organizations 'provide a substantial portion of care in developing countries, often reaching vulnerable populations living under adverse conditions'.[18] However, despite their excellent and documented record in the fields of community-based and primary health care, pandemic diseases, prevention and control of non-communicable diseases, faith-based organizations do not receive an equitable share of the resources designated to support global, national and local health initiatives.[19]

Another grave concern expressed by the Holy See revolves around the growing numbers of elderly persons who are experiencing serious challenges, such as poverty, food insecurity, homelessness, poor access to needed social protection, to health care and other needed services, as well as increasing isolation, institutionalization and discrimination. Given changes in family and social demographics, fewer young people are available, or willing, to provide family assistance and care to the elderly. There is a tendency to tolerate a 'throwaway' approach to senior and other vulnerable members of families and local communities.[20] Thus Pope Francis has noted with grave concern: 'The victims of this [throwaway] culture are precisely the weakest and most fragile human beings – the unborn, the poorest, the sick and elderly, the seriously handicapped, etc. – who are in danger of being "thrown away", expelled by a system that must be efficient at all costs.'[21]

The Holy See encourages the international community to move beyond a view that characterizes elderly people as a 'financial burden', or as 'non-contributing members' of society, to the recognition that such

18 Kevin De Cock, 'Faith-based organizations play a major role in HIV/AIDS care and treatment in sub-Saharan Africa,' as quoted in press release by the World Health Organization, 9 February 2007, www.un.org/apps/news/story.asp?NewsID=21511&Cr=hiv&Cr1=aids.

19 Cf. 'Health Care Personnel in the Catholic Church' (2008).

20 Cf. 'The Need for States to Create the Proper Conditions to Allow the Elderly to Make their Contributions to Society' (2014).

21 Address of Pope Francis to a Delegation from the Dignitatis Humanae Institute, Clementine Hall, 7 December 2013, http://w2.vatican.va/content/francesco/en/speeches/2013/december/documents/papa-francesco_20131207_istituto-dignitatis.html.

persons are an important resource contributing lived and practical experience, relational maturity and deep wisdom to the younger generations. This more positive view of the elderly could and should form the basis for strategies and plans to protect and include the elderly in mainstream community and family life.[22]

Finally, the Holy See did not fail to take note of the significant number of indigenous peoples in all parts of the world (130 million in 90 countries) and acknowledged the 2014 World Conference on Indigenous Peoples as a significant opportunity to foster greater interest and respect for these communities and a unique opportunity to reaffirm the Declaration on the Rights of Indigenous Peoples. The Holy See maintains that all initiatives related to these peoples should be inspired and guided by the principle of respect for their identity and culture, including specific traditions, religious beliefs and ability to decide their own development in cooperation with national governments.[23] The Holy See notes the problematic relations between some transnational companies and indigenous groups especially in the area of extractive industries. It urges models of authentic human development that respect the fundamental rights, including labour rights and the culture of indigenous peoples as well as natural environmental resources. It also appeals for reconciliation between these peoples and the societies presently living on their traditional lands.

In conclusion, as the world continues to witness persistent and new humanitarian emergencies, solidarity should not be a mere feeling of vague compassion but 'a firm and persevering determination to commit oneself to the common good; this is to say, to the good of all and of each individual, because we are all really responsible for all.'[24] A case in point is the need for universal access to health care, which is one of the leitmotifs of the Holy See's pronouncements at the World Health Organization: indeed, it should be the goal of the international community to enable everyone to access health services without running the risk of financial hardship in doing so. Solidarity with all humanity comes from an absolutely binding and supernatural ethic; this is why it is not simply an option, but a moral duty.

[22] Cf. 'The Social Role of Older Persons: Give Space to the Elderly to Give Space to Life' (2013).

[23] Cf. 'The Need to Directly Include Indigenous Peoples in the Decision-Making Processes' (2014).

[24] Saint John Paul II, Encyclical Letter, *Sollicitudo Rei Socialis* (1987), § 38.

List of Statements

1 Humanitarian Emergencies: Ensuring an Adequate Response

- DEFEND HUMAN DIGNITY AND PROMOTE HUMANITARIAN LAW, 28th Conference of the International Committee of the Red Cross and Red Crescent (2–6 December 2003)
- A HOLISTIC CONCEPT OF HEALTH: THE HOLY SEE'S RESERVATIONS TO THE AGENDA FOR HUMANITARIAN ACTION, concluding session of the 28th Conference of the International Committee of the Red Cross and Red Crescent (2–6 December 2003)
- THE EMBLEM DEBATE: THE NEED TO RESPECT AND ACKNOWLEDGE THE NEUTRALITY, UNITY AND HUMANITY OF THE MOVEMENT, Diplomatic Conference on the Emblem of the Red Cross and Red Crescent Movement (5–6 December 2005)
- TOGETHER FOR HUMANITY, 30th International Conference of the Red Cross and Red Crescent (26–30 November 2007)
- THE HUMAN PERSON MUST ALWAYS BE AT THE CENTER OF HUMANITARIAN ASSISTANCE, Humanitarian Affairs Segment of the UN Economic and Social Council (20 July 2009)
- THE NEED TO REAWAKEN PUBLIC CONSCIENCE, 31st International Conference of the Red Cross and Red Crescent (28 November–2 December 2011)
- PREVENTION OF NATURAL AND MAN-MADE DISASTER, A COLLECTIVE RESPONSIBILITY TO PRESERVE OUR COMMON HOME, 2015 Humanitarian Segment of the Economic and Social Council (19 June 2015)
- THE CONTINUED EROSION AND NON-COMPLIANCE WITH INTERNATIONAL HUMANITARIAN LAW, 32nd International Conference of the Red Cross and Red Crescent (8–10 December 2015)

2 Right to Health and Access to Medicines

- WE MUST NOT FORGET AFRICA, 60th World Health Assembly (14–23 May 2007)
- PROGRESS REPORT ON THE GLOBAL PLAN AND STOP TB STRATEGY, 60th World Health Assembly: item 12.6 – Report on Progress with Global Plan and Stop TB Strategy as well as pending resolution for World Health Assembly Consideration (17 May 2007)
- THE RIGHT OF EVERYONE TO THE ENJOYMENT OF THE HIGHEST ATTAINABLE STANDARD OF PHYSICAL AND MENTAL HEALTH, 7th

Session of the Human Rights Council, Item 3: *Promotion and Protection of All Human Rights, Civil, Political, Economic, Social and Cultural Rights, including the Right to Development* (11 March 2008)

- RESPECT FOR THE DIGNITY OF THE HUMAN PERSON IN ALL HEALTH-RELATED CARE, 61st World Health Assembly (22 May 2008)
- PRIMARY HEALTH CARE AND HEALTH SYSTEM STRENGTHENING, 124th Meeting of WHO Executive Board – Provisional agenda item 4.5: 'Primary Health Care, including Health System Strengthening' (19–27 January 2009)
- HUMAN ORGAN AND TISSUE TRANSPLANTATION, 124th Meeting of WHO Executive Board – Provisional agenda item 4.12: 'Human Organ and Tissue Transplantation' (19–27 January 2009)
- HEALTH CARE PERSONNEL IN THE CATHOLIC CHURCH, 62nd World Health Assembly (18–27 May 2009)
- IMPACT ON HEALTH AND HEALTH CARE DURING THE GLOBAL ECONOMIC CRISIS, 62nd World Health Assembly (18–27 May 2009)
- CUTBACKS IN INTERNATIONAL AND PUBLIC HEALTH: A SHORT-TERM FINANCIAL BENEFIT VS. THE LONG-TERM HUMAN COST, 2009 High-Level Segment of the Economic and Social Council (9 July 2009)
- MONITORING THE ACHIEVEMENTS OF THE HEALTH-RELATED MILLENNIUM DEVELOPMENT GOALS, 63rd World Health Assembly (17–21 May 2010)
- UNIVERSAL ACCESS TO MEDICINES AND DIAGNOSTIC TOOLS, 14th Session of the Human Rights Council – Item 3: *General Debate* (8 June 2010)
- SUSTAINABLE HEALTH FINANCING STRUCTURES AND UNIVERSAL COVERAGE, 65th World Health Assembly (21–26 May 2012)
- PRIORITIZING HEALTH IN THE NEXT GENERATION OF DEVELOPMENT GOALS, 66th World Health Assembly (20–28 May 2013)
- KEY ELEMENTS TO GUARANTEE ACCESS TO MEDICINES, 23rd Session of the UN Human Rights Council – Item 3: *Report of the Special Rapporteur on the Right to Health* (28 May 2013)
- EFFECTS OF CLIMATE CHANGE ON HEALTH, 67th World Health Assembly (19–24 May 2014)
- THE PRIMACY OF THE RIGHT TO HEALTH OVER THE FOCUS ON PROFIT', 2015 Social Forum of the Human Rights Council (18 February 2015)
- THE RURAL URBAN DIVIDE: RE-PRIORITIZE INVESTMENT IN HEALTH CARE, 68th Assembly of the World Health Organization (20 May 2015)

- SECURING THE REALIZATION OF THE RIGHT TO HEALTH THROUGH ACCESS TO MORE AFFORDABLE MEDICINES, World Trade Organization's Trade-Related Intellectual Property Rights Council (6 November 2015)

3 The Rights of Elderly Persons

- THE RIGHT TO HEALTH OF OLDER PERSONS, 18th Session of the Human Rights Council on the *Thematic Study on the Realization of the Right to Health of Older Persons* (16 September 2011)
- THE SOCIAL ROLE OF OLDER PERSONS: GIVE SPACE TO THE ELDERLY TO GIVE SPACE TO LIFE, 24nd Session of the Human Rights Council – Items 2 & 3: *Promotion and Protection of the Human Rights of Older Persons* (13 September 2013)
- ALLOW THE ELDERLY TO MAKE THEIR CONTRIBUTIONS TO SOCIETY, 27th Session of the Human Rights Council – Item 3: *Report of the Independent Expert on the Promotion and Protection of Human Rights of Older Persons* (15 September 2014)
- THE QUALITY OF OUR SOCIETIES IS MEASURED BY THE ATTENTION TO THE ELDERLY, 30th Session of the Human Rights Council – Item 3: *Independent Expert on the Rights of Older Persons* (16 September 2015)

4 Promoting the Rights of Indigenous Peoples

- THE NEED TO DIRECTLY INCLUDE INDIGENOUS PEOPLES IN THE DECISION-MAKING PROCESSES, 27th Session of the Human Rights Council – Item 3: *General Debate* (17 September 2014)
- THE SYSTEMATIC VIOLATIONS OF INDIGENOUS PEOPLES' HUMAN RIGHTS AND THEIR TRADITIONAL KNOWLEDGE AND FOLKLORE, 30th Session of the Human Rights Council: *Annual Half-Day Panel Discussion on the Rights of Indigenous Peoples* (22 September 2015)

1 HUMANITARIAN EMERGENCIES: ENSURING AN ADEQUATE RESPONSE

DEFEND HUMAN DIGNITY AND PROMOTE HUMANITARIAN LAW*

This 28th Conference takes place at a moment marked by rumbles of war and by an explosion of terrorism of such a magnitude unknown before today. Civilian victims of well-reported and of forgotten wars and of their destructive consequences run in the millions. In fact some States and non-State actors try to instrumentalize the desperation of endemic poverty and of extreme social inequality by promoting their private objectives through violent actions.

The world is confronted by a great challenge that raises dramatic questions right at this time when we are examining ways and means to strengthen our commitment to defend human dignity during armed conflicts and other emergency situations and to promote respect for humanitarian law.

In the effort to contain and overcome a wave of intolerable and unbearable violence, the temptation emerges to have recourse to methods of fighting not always respectful of the juridical rules adopted by the international community to ban war as a means to settle disputes and to protect the dignity of the person in every circumstance.

Unfortunately, humanitarian law appears at present as if hanging between its weak impact on armed conflicts and its limited relevance on the table of political negotiations. Some governments are reticent in accepting effective control mechanisms while public opinion seems to become accustomed to violations of humanitarian law as if the painful spectacle of so many victims were leading to resignation instead of prompting a reaction capable of influencing wrong political and military choices.

The Holy See looks at international humanitarian law as an important, invaluable, non-negotiable and still relevant instrument: 'Its observance or non-observance is a real test for the ethical foundation and for the very reason for existence of the international community' (Pope John Paul II, Address to the members of the International Institute of Humanitarian

* Statement delivered at the 28th Conference of the International Committee of the Red Cross and Red Crescent, 2–6 December 2003.

Law, 18 May, 1982). The Holy See will continue to promote appropriate initiatives of interreligious character to defend human dignity during armed conflicts and to increase respect for international humanitarian law especially through the vast network of Catholic educational institutions.

At this stage it is not so much a question of strengthening the normative framework, already significantly developed, but of finding the appropriate ways to make it effectively operational and of encouraging the political will for its global implementation.

A sadly eloquent sign among others of disregard toward humanitarian law is given by the attacks purposely directed against humanitarian personnel who generously serve in the midst of conflicts, in particular by the recent deadly attacks against the International Committee of the Red Cross.

In this troubling context, it becomes imperative to pursue an educational process directed not only at the dissemination of juridical instruments, but also at proposing the teaching of, and formation of conscience regarding the great principles inspiring humanitarian law: the dignity of every human being, the solidarity with victims, the primacy of law over force. In this regard, the Holy See carried out its pledge at the 27th Conference to enhance the formation of Catholic military chaplains in humanitarian law and it will continue to do so. And to prevent and contain the tendency to privatize the indiscriminate use of force a more determined effort can be undertaken to address the root causes of such a deep dissatisfaction exploding into violence, make them known in the mass communication media, and remedy them.

The dignity of the human person is at risk in other contemporary situations of forced displacement, catastrophes and infectious diseases, all generally affecting the poorest segments of the population and especially women and children. No stigma must be attached to human suffering. For this reason the Catholic Church has educational and assistance programs for persons affected by HIV/AIDS in 92 countries, the first partner of States in this social area and a sign of hope and a practical witness of their dignity for all these millions of patients.

The Movement of the Red Cross and the Red Crescent can count on the partnership and support of the Catholic Church. Collaboration with religious institutions and faith communities will make for a more effective humanitarian action. Religious motivation, we should not forget, gave a decisive push to the work of Henry Dunant, whose inspiration the present Conference carries on today.

A HOLISTIC CONCEPT OF HEALTH: THE HOLY SEE'S RESERVATIONS TO THE AGENDA FOR HUMANITARIAN ACTION*

The Holy See welcomes the adoption of the Declaration and the Agenda for Humanitarian Action by the 28th International Conference of the Red Cross and Red Crescent.

The Delegation of the Holy See has participated actively in the drafting work, but it intends to express a reservation on paragraphs 4.1.3 and 4.1.4 of the Agenda for Humanitarian Action under General Objective 4 regarding certain actions on reducing the risk and impact of diseases.

The Holy See, in conformity with its nature and particular mission, reaffirms all the reservations that it has previously expressed at the conclusion of the various United Nations Conferences and Summits, as well as the special sessions of the General Assembly for the review of those meetings.

Nothing that the Holy See has done during the discussions leading up to the adoption of the Agenda for Humanitarian Action should be understood or interpreted as an endorsement of concepts it cannot support for moral reasons.

Regarding the expression 'sexual and reproductive health care', the Holy See considers it as applying to a holistic concept of health, which embraces the person in the entirety of his or her personality, mind and body, and which fosters the achievement of personal maturity in sexuality and in the mutual love and decision-making that characterize the conjugal relationship in accordance with moral norms.

The Holy See wishes to emphasize that, with regard to the use of condoms as a means of preventing HIV infection, it has in no way changed its well-known moral position.

The Holy See asks that this reservation be included in the report of this 28th International Conference of the Red Cross and Red Crescent.

Thank you, Mr President.

* Statement delivered at the concluding session of the 28th Conference of the International Committee of the Red Cross and Red Crescent, 2–6 December 2003.

THE EMBLEM DEBATE: THE NEED TO RESPECT AND ACKNOWLEDGE THE NEUTRALITY, UNITY AND HUMANITY OF THE MOVEMENT*

Mr President,

On behalf of the Holy See Delegation I would like to express, first of all, our satisfaction to the Swiss Confederation for its excellent organization of this diplomatic Conference and especially for the important preparatory work. The Holy See will give her contribution in order to reach the desired outcomes.

Mr President,

For many years, the question of the emblem has been a serious problem to the Red Cross and Red Crescent Movement as a whole, and has complicated the implementation of international humanitarian law in certain regions of the world and has weakened the unity of the Movement. It is high time to find an effective and lasting solution.

The Holy See welcomes the agreements signed between Magen David Adom in Israel and the Palestinian Red Crescent Society, which pave the way for a global and comprehensive solution to the question of the Emblem. Even if this issue concerns the whole Movement, it remains nonetheless also closely linked to the Arab–Israeli conflict, which unfortunately has lasted too long. We want to see in the adoption of a third Protocol on the emblem another step on the road to a just and lasting peace in the Middle East.

First of all, the Holy See would like to see in it a strengthening of the recognition by all of the emblems of the Red Cross and Red Crescent Movement. These distinctive signs should give the necessary protection to all those who are committed to reduce the devastating impacts of armed conflict. Governments, non-State actors and individuals must comply, in all circumstances, with the principles that put some limits on the conduct of armed conflicts. The Emblem of the Red Cross and Red Crescent should remind us all of what is left of humanity when men succumb to the temptation to resolve their differences through violence. Certain limitations are essential.

* Statement delivered at the Diplomatic Conference on the Emblem of the Red Cross and Red Crescent Movement, 5–6 December 2005.

Mr President,

The proposed solution, which we hope will be adopted shortly, requires stronger efforts and commitments in order not to weaken the protective force of the new emblems, at least at the beginning. Training and awareness campaigns will be necessary, at the national and international levels, to make the new reality become an integral part of the collective consciousness and unconsciousness of humanity in situations of armed conflict or natural disasters. Anyhow, what has to be avoided in any case is that the proposed solution harms the perception of neutrality, humanity and unity of the Movement. Respect for the fundamental principles of the Movement and scrupulous implementation of the obligations stipulated in the draft of the proposed Third Protocol are prerequisites for the success of a lasting solution to the emblem debate.

Mr President,

The Holy See supports the solution suggested by the ICRC and the Federation of Red Cross and Red Crescent Societies, and will contribute to strengthen the unity of the Movement. Serenity and cooperation are the means to achieve the goals of humanity. Goals that we all share here in this room.

I thank you, Mr President.

TOGETHER FOR HUMANITY*

Madam President,

Beyond the tragedies and shortcomings of man-made conflicts, tensions and natural disasters, defacing the dignity of every person, a realistic and long-range solution to enhance humanitarian protection rests on the realization that the human family is really one. Solidarity within the human family finds concrete expression in collaborative action and in openness to dialogue and partnerships, a perspective summed up well in the theme of our Conference, 'Together for Humanity'. Among today's global concerns, this 30th International Conference of the Red Cross and Red Crescent has singled out for our discussion four particularly threatening developments: pandemics, international migration, urban violence and environmental degradation. The Mission of the Holy See recognizes in these challenges a reminder that coexistence among social and political communities, and the construction of a peaceful world order, are only possible on the basis of upholding the fundamental value of every person's human dignity.

The four areas that call for our immediate attention have serious humanitarian consequences for contemporary society as well as future generations. The will to work together to find adequate solutions for all cannot be shirked since upon it depends the material and ethical survival of humanity. Partial solutions that neglect a group of countries or a part of the national community are myopic, besides being unjust and unacceptable. A sound globalization will include the humanitarian imperative and thus avoid the uneven reality of the creation of regions of prosperity and peace and regions of poverty and conflict. When this happens, it is a political as well as an ethical failure.

Madam President,

It is only on the basis of such values that the Red Cross and Red Crescent Movement in all its components can muster the forces necessary to establish effective and lasting partnerships, respectful of differences and appreciative of the talents of each. In this context, the Holy See and the numerous Catholic aid agencies and organizations are ready to work

* Statement delivered at the 30th International Conference of the Red Cross and Red Crescent, 26–30 November 2007.

together with other countries and parties in order to offer the international community the wide experience acquired alongside the most vulnerable in every corner of the world.

It is also vital to realize that the solution to complex problems and emergencies concerning all of humanity are not only of a technical nature and cannot be reduced to mere assistance. In this instance, however, victims, both direct and indirect, deserve particular attention and care. In fact, it is the most vulnerable who suffer the worst from natural disasters, conflicts and violence, from the consequences of underdevelopment, poverty and pandemics. These persons, their families and communities, have rights and we need to do everything to respect them. Moreover, they deserve our human closeness, our psychological, moral and spiritual support, not as condescending pity, but as the expression of our solidarity. We constitute together one human family. Aid should be given as self-aid in order that local people may strengthen their own capacities and in this way fully exercise their freedom and responsibility.

My Delegation takes good note of the Resolutions before us and it hopes in particular that the implementation of the Memorandum of Understanding and the Agreement on Operational Arrangements between the Palestinian Red Crescent Society and Magen David Adom, signed in 2005, may soon be fully implemented. It supports any new effort directed at family reunion and at re-establishing lost contact and information about family members due to conflicts and disasters. It favours the adoption of a legally binding instrument for the prohibition and elimination of cluster munitions. It sees with satisfaction the return of the ICRC to the issue of protection of people caught up in population movements and in different degrees vulnerable to discrimination, marginalization and family separation. Humanitarian and human rights instruments have been developed, but the political will and the very complexity of the phenomenon of human mobility stand in the way of an adequate implementation especially when intergovernmental conferences and events keep prioritizing only economic and production dimensions of migrations leaving in the shadows the fact that they are persons, with inalienable dignity and rights, even when they are kept in detention camps and centers.

The different religions alongside other institutions can and must play a positive role. For its part, the Holy See has promoted initiatives of interreligious dialogue, which it considers a fundamental component in the construction of peace and the realization of the common good. As it had pledged in 2003, it has organized an interreligious scholarly event to promote the defence of human dignity and the respect of humanitarian law in case of armed conflict. It looks forward to further initiatives to promote the ethical foundation of humanitarian law and the defence of human dignity also in the case of armed conflict with non-State actors.

Madam President,

The exemplary approach of the Red Cross and Red Crescent rests on the ability to break down barriers and to build bridges across conflicting partners, aware of the common humanity binding us and that demands we move forward to the future together. The international community has the responsibility to prevent conflicts, provide protection and to build peace and a world in which a decent life is possible for the present and future generations.

THE HUMAN PERSON MUST ALWAYS BE AT THE CENTER OF HUMANITARIAN ASSISTANCE*

Madam President,

Natural and man-made disasters affect millions of persons each year and no region of the world is exempted. In particular, chronic armed conflicts have devastated societies in various corners of the globe, with innumerable civilian victims. The Holy See, therefore, welcomes the present humanitarian dialogue as an opportunity yet again to highlight the continued challenges and the need for an effective and coherent globalized response, guided by sound policy directives such as solidarity and the promotion of the inherent dignity of all. In this way, the right of persons, their families and communities to humanitarian assistance, and of care providers to unhindered access to these people in need of basic social, physical and spiritual attention, acquires a solid foundation and a motivation for action. While, for example, the year 2008 saw a decline in the number of refugees, still over 10 million men, women and children continue to live in refugee camps and 26 million remain internally displaced due to past and recent conflicts, insecurity and persecution. Asylum seekers, irregular migrants, uprooted people looking for survival and victims of natural disasters and climate change, are confined in hundreds of detention centers and makeshift camps. Although far from the media spotlight, these untenable situations wreak an immeasurable physical, mental, emotional and spiritual pain and lead to the breaking of the social fabric, destruction of families and communities, jeopardizing reconciliation and threaten the lives of thousands of innocent civilians.

The primary responsibility of protecting the lives of civilians lies first and foremost with the national authorities and parties engaged in an armed conflict. While the international community strives to prevent the eruption of conflicts, it is imperative that all parties recognize their responsibility for protecting the lives of civilians in areas under their jurisdiction or control and comply with and fully respect the rules and principles of international humanitarian law, among them, those related to the protection of humanitarian personnel and the unimpeded access to people in need. Further, in areas of natural disasters, States must work to promote, and allow access to, life-saving measures without using them

* Statement delivered at the Humanitarian Affairs Segment of the UN Economic and Social Council, 20 July 2009.

for political control or to condition a political guarantee of impunity for violation of human rights. The common good should be the guiding principle and the international humanitarian law should be implemented in all circumstances and without any condition.

At the same time, the international community remains a vital and indispensable actor in assisting the national authorities to respond to crises and, where these are unable to do so, it is called to provide access to emergency and life-saving regional and international actors. Naturally, in coordinating this internationalized response, the United Nations position places it in a unique role, with unique responsibilities to promote coordination and coherence for effective action and responsible management of available resources while preserving the basic humanitarian principles of neutrality, impartiality and humanity. Besides, by respecting subsidiarity and the ability of local groups and individuals, this coordination can better identify and implement a humanitarian strategy that would reach the people most in need. It is these local organizations, often faith-based, present on the ground before disaster strikes, that will be the ones present long after the international community has directed its focus of attention onto other crises. The Holy See Delegation, therefore, stresses the essential role of the civil society in situations of emergency and the need for policies to be adopted in a way which recognizes their long-term contribution and enables their capacity to respond to the needs of all.

New and old challenges have undermined the capacity and effectiveness of humanitarian actors to respond and provide assistance to millions of victims. The food crisis has led to a decrease in food distribution in famine areas, in camps and detention centers; the energy crises have added drastically to the cost of providing aid over long distances; and now the global economic crisis risks reducing funding to public and civil society, humanitarian agencies and organizations. The Holy See notes with appreciation that many States continue with generosity to shoulder the responsibility to assist, economic crisis notwithstanding. Failure to remain in solidarity with and provide for people in humanitarian crises during this difficult time will lead only to social and political instability which undermines society and its ability to come together and resolve the economic crisis.

Madam President,

My Delegation further calls on national authorities and groups in armed conflict to respect the rules of international humanitarian law, in particular the applicable Geneva Conventions and its optional protocols. The continued sexual violence perpetrated against women and girls within and around refugee camps violates all standards of international law and leads to the emotional, physical and mental devastation of these women which cannot be justified under any circumstances. Further, greater efforts must be made to provide for and ensure access to prisoners of war and others placed in various forms of detention. Deprivation of freedom, of the right to work, to family reunion, to education and personal development, among other human rights, cannot be simply discarded in emergencies. Camps and detention centers are meant to be temporary provisions and places where access is open and the dignity of persons remains a priority. With the cooperation of all actors, the international humanitarian community will retain the freedom to act in accordance with its mandates and principles, which should not be compromised by government interference.

The Holy See remains committed to addressing the needs of all individuals affected by humanitarian and man-made crises regardless of ethnicity and religious creed. Through its many institutions, it remains deeply involved in non-partisan humanitarian assistance and looks forward to sharing its best practices and ideas with other stakeholders. Guiding principles of assistance both in natural and human-made disasters need to be implemented, but, before all, we must put at the center of all our interventions the person and his/her material, psychological and spiritual needs.

THE NEED TO REAWAKEN PUBLIC CONSCIENCE*

Madam Chairperson,

Today's crises can arrive totally unexpectedly. Economic, political and humanitarian upheavals worry both the 'developing' and the 'developed' world. Centers of tension multiply. Violent conflicts are fought in urban conglomerates and it is difficult to distinguish between combatants and civilians who continue to be, by far, the first victims, dead, injured, disabled, of armed conflicts. Action for humanity becomes urgent and demands concrete answers. 'Public conscience' as referred to in the '*Martens' Clause*' needs to be reawakened.[1]

Areas of concern targeted for discussion are the worldwide impact of natural disasters and related displacement; the rapidly changing nature of human vulnerability; the evolving human and material cost of contemporary armed conflicts and other situations of violence, that make access to health more difficult; increasing global migration. These concerns indicate new developments that provoke human suffering. Life moves ahead of legislation and thus 'public conscience' serves well while the international community awaits legal measures to catch up with life. In the meantime the same effort must continue to develop rules that prevent suffering and save lives that marked the emergence of international humanitarian law from its beginning. The acquired patrimony of values and norms has to be preserved, applied and made more relevant and responsive to new situations. Yet the inhumanity of conflicts, particularly when the use of arms is chosen to resolve tensions and controversies that could be solved by means provided by dialogue and negotiation, and the inadequate response to some recent emergencies, are before our eyes. International humanitarian law, in the name of a common good, is always a warning to renounce violence on any person, civilian or combatant, prohibiting the indiscriminate and unrestrained use of violence and weapons. Increasingly it should become the basis for action inspired

* Statement delivered at the 31st International Conference of the Red Cross and Red Crescent, 28 November–2 December 2011.

[1] According to the *Martens' Clause*: 'populations and belligerents remain under the protection and empire of the principles of international law, as they result from the usages established between civilized nations, from the laws of humanity and from the requirements of the *public conscience*,' 1899 Hague Convention No. II, Preamble, 9.

by *solidarity* toward the direct or indirect victims of natural or man-made disasters.

There are moments when peoples and nations are compelled to claim the right to protect their existence, dignity and freedom. 'Public conscience', common to the human family, makes us aware that unfortunately this goal of protection often becomes an occasion to use degrading means both distant from the legal achievements of international law and ineffective in resolving conflicts and disputes. The adoption of dialogue and negotiation, including through the intervention of an impartial third party or of an international authority with sufficient powers, now is a choice no longer to be postponed.[2] Responsible dialogue will guarantee to opposing parties the respect of their legitimate aspirations and a durable peace.

The end of conflict always carries with it the problem of repatriation of prisoners of war, a humanitarian problem *par excellence*, that from the perspective of the Holy See includes the reunification of families and the resumption of normal affections, effective ways to ensure reconciliation and justice.

Following the indications of this Conference it will be necessary to consolidate proposals for effective *action plans*. The international community cannot ignore the persons kept away from their loved ones and their country without a justifiable reason; the victims of the devastating effects of violent conflicts and the civilians suffering from civil conflicts that by now have become endemic. Our thoughts turn to children, victims of war or uprooted from their families and recruited as child soldiers. Millions of refugees and displaced persons also are anxious to return to their land especially since, while forcibly relocated in other regions, they see threatened their ethnic, religious or linguistic identity, and even their very existence.

International humanitarian law should be able to respond to emergency situations determined by natural and man-made disasters. Effective action should be guided by solid ethical and moral principles. This task cannot be ignored by the various currents of thought, nor by faith communities, and the way forward is to retrace the same path that led to the great achievements of the protection of the human person. In such conflicts, humanitarian action, if inspired by solidarity, a spirit of brotherhood

[2] See Pope Benedict XVI, Encyclical Letter, *Caritas in Veritate*, § 67.

and loyal service,[3] will be integrated in a comprehensive and effective plan that includes, inter alia, reconstruction, medical care and a sense of justice.

The Holy See does not present technical solutions for the problems posed by today's emergencies. It considers it her duty, however, to point out at this Conference that no principle, no tradition, no claim – whatever its legitimacy – authorizes anyone to inflict on a people repressive actions or inhuman treatment – more so when it consists of innocent and defenceless civilians. It does so in the name of the supremacy of those 'principles of international law … and the requirements of public conscience' that remain the solid foundation of international humanitarian law. In this context, we are reminded that the simple application of the law is not sufficient. Pope John Paul II, reflecting on his experience under Nazi and Communist totalitarianism, wrote: 'True peace … is the fruit of justice, that moral virtue and legal guarantee which ensures full respect for rights and responsibilities, and the just distribution of benefits and burdens. But because human justice is always fragile and imperfect, subject as it is to the limitations and egoism of individuals and groups, it must include and, as it were, be completed by the *forgiveness which heals and rebuilds troubled human relations from their foundations*.'[4]

In the search for solutions, the Catholic Church offers a concrete contribution through education and action. It teaches that the source of human dignity and inalienable rights resides in the spiritual and physical unity of the person. Through the formation of conscience, citizens can be prepared to promote those values of humanity that international humanitarian law, more than juridical norms, has made operational exactly in situations where the dignity of the human person is violated and denied. When humanitarian action is reduced to a mere application of norms and procedures there is the risk of weakening the prohibition of inhuman or degrading treatment enshrined in the Geneva Conventions and their Additional Protocols, and perhaps of returning to the excesses that those instruments have solemnly and appropriately condemned. Catholic organizations all over the world carry out humanitarian assistance and promote humanitarian law in this spirit as the 2011 Report of the Holy See to the ICRC shows.

[3] See ibid., § 19.

[4] Pope John Paul II's Message for the 2002 World Day of Peace.

These, Madam Chairperson, are some thoughts that the Delegation of the Holy See wants to present to this Conference to encourage governments and international institutions to help break existing stalemates; to take specific and timely steps to overcome conflicts; to look in a new light at victims of cluster bombs, mines and other weapons; to renew concern for refugees and displaced persons; to enact generous forms of solidarity with all victims of disasters, catastrophes and conflicts and thus fulfill the aspiration for unity of the human family.

Thank you, Madam Chairperson.

PREVENTION OF NATURAL AND MAN-MADE DISASTER, A COLLECTIVE RESPONSIBILITY TO PRESERVE OUR COMMON HOME*

Mr President,

The current climate of violence, uprootedness and myopic politics makes the theme of this Humanitarian Segment timely and necessary. 'The future of humanitarian affairs: towards greater inclusiveness, coordination, interoperability and effectiveness' requires our commitment to integral human development and to cooperative solidarity. Natural and man-made disasters have produced millions of victims. To understand their plight we need to adopt their perspective, an approach that highlights the consequences, leads to identifying the causes of disasters, and to acting accordingly.

The priority of any humanitarian response are the needs of the victims. The capacities of the various responders, whether governments, local or national civil society actors, or partners in the Inter-Agency Standing Committee, should be leveraged towards that goal. To make the necessary cooperation work, the particular context with its specific needs, causes of emergencies, and available capacities to respond, should be taken into account.

While the more than US$ 11 billion provided for 2014 through interagency appeals was an all-time high, so too was the US$ 7.4 billion shortfall, highlighting the need to make the best use of available resources. Megatrends, such as climate change and environmental degradation, food and water scarcity and urbanization, are leading to greater vulnerability and exposure to hazards. Furthermore, crises are becoming more protracted, with 78 per cent of humanitarian spending by the members of the Development Assistance Committee of the Organisation for Economic Cooperation and Development going to protracted emergencies. Humanitarian appeals last for an average of seven years, and six countries have had appeals for ten consecutive years.

Climate change and natural disasters negatively affect the enjoyment of several human rights.[1] Under certain systems, such as the 1950

* Statement delivered to the 2015 Humanitarian Segment of the Economic and Social Council, 19 June 2015.

1 United Nations, Report of the Office of the United Nations High Commissioner for Human Rights on the relationship between climate change and human rights, UN Doc. A/HRC/10/61, New York, 2009, paras. 16–41.

European Convention on Human Rights, any human rights violation could, in theory, give rise to a *non-refoulement* obligation. Coherent with such a juridical tradition, the principle of *non-refoulement* could be applied by analogy to new categories of people whose life and human rights are threatened by the negative consequences of climate change and of a general situation of violence. Protection should focus primarily on avoiding the risk of present and future violations. Where this need is acknowledged, a clear protection status should also be granted. Existing human rights law, and the *non-refoulement* principle, do not provide a right to stay or specify the precise content of the protection. Nevertheless, it should include non-rejection at the border and provide a basis for some form of complementary, possibly temporary, but effective protection.

The reduction of disaster risks is an important part of the effort which aims at the eradication of poverty. There is growing evidence that the poorest people in the more vulnerable countries bear most of the burden of adapting to climate consequences they had almost no role in creating. The Report of the Secretary General illustrates the many devastating effects of natural and man-made disasters that people are confronting all over the world, year after year. Men and women working for international, national and local humanitarian organizations, many of which are faith-based, risk their lives and future to aid the victims of such catastrophes. It is for the safety of these humanitarian workers, and for the welfare of the suffering people they assist, that we must work for a truly effective, coordinated and humane disaster response system. Prevention starts with the recognition that 'creation' is not a possession: man is a steward and thus he should care for and respect nature. These catastrophes are a global phenomenon that exceeds the competence of any one community or country. An adequate response requires a mobilization comparable in size to the damage inflicted. At the same time, we must recognize that a moral requirement of solidarity arises since we are united together as one human family.

Over the last years, the high rate of natural disasters was tragically matched by many, and extremely costly, man-made ones. Armed conflicts have devastated societies in many places, taken lives, ruined economies, set back development and frustrated efforts to restore peace. The world has witnessed an indescribable suffering: women sold as chattel, Christians and other believers murdered simply because of their convictions, children killed or used as human shields, and millions of people forcibly uprooted. The international community appears to lack the political will to address these crises and there is a real risk of forgetting all of these victims.

In this context, providing tangible assistance is met with extraordinary difficulties because violence is ongoing and the territories that are controlled by extremist factions disregard the local population. As such, millions of people remain without adequate access to assistance. However, access to people in need is a prerequisite for needs assessment and effective humanitarian action. Some governments have devised cumbersome administrative procedures to restrict the movement of humanitarian convoys and the delivery of essential items. Parties in conflict have the primary responsibility for the protection and well-being of civilians under their control.[2]

Humanitarian personnel must be granted full and unimpeded access to people in need and they must be safeguarded and protected when doing so. In fact, all parties involved must comply fully with the rules and principles of international law and international humanitarian law. Likewise, the involved parties are obliged to guarantee civilians and victims of armed conflict safe and unhampered access to humanitarian aid.

Mr President,

The Holy See Delegation would like to reaffirm that the only way to a fair solution is through dialogue, the silencing of arms and a commitment to negotiate. Such a solution should give priority to the good of the countries involved and their people as well as to those who have taken refuge elsewhere, who maintain the right to return as soon as possible to their country.

Despite some progress to improve the coordination and effectiveness of the humanitarian response, important gaps remain. In particular, when the media attention is taken away from an emergency, often the local faith communities are left with the task of continuing the necessary assistance. For this reason, the establishment of a High-Level Panel on Humanitarian Financing may be useful in finding new ways for the humanitarian community to work with development actors and others. In this way, communities become more resilient to crises and less reliant on humanitarian aid. The international community should continue the process to enhance its operational effectiveness, building on the elements of the Inter-Agency Standing Committee Transformative Agenda.

[2] www.un.org/ga/search/view_doc.asp?symbol=E/2015/64.

Mr President,

In conclusion, the prevention of disasters is another chapter in the protection of creation; it calls for the cooperative action of all players to reinforce their common responsibility for the good of all. The sense of solidarity developed by the international community has to be preserved and applied and made more relevant and responsive to new situations. To solve disputes, the way forward is dialogue to prevent the scourge of war and the tragic consequences for the people affected. The current irrational explosion of violence shows the need for the urgent implementation of the objectives of this Humanitarian Segment. Indeed, International humanitarian law, as it promotes the common good, always prohibits the indiscriminate and unrestrained use of violence on any person, civilian or combatant. It should become, instead, the basis for a collaborative action inspired by solidarity toward the direct and indirect victims of disasters, whether natural or man-made.

Thank you, Mr President.

THE CONTINUED EROSION AND NON-COMPLIANCE WITH INTERNATIONAL HUMANITARIAN LAW*

Mr Chairman,

The Holy See Delegation is pleased to participate in this 32nd International Conference. It recognizes the outstanding contribution of the Red Cross and Red Crescent Movement in response to many human needs, especially in situations of humanitarian crisis and other emergencies. In particular, we wish to acknowledge the efforts of the RCRC in response to the Ebola epidemic that caused very great suffering in Guinea, Liberia and Sierra Leone. The Movement's engagement in providing Specialized Ebola Care, as well as safe and dignified burials, helped to prevent additional human anguish and loss of life, as a result of the outbreak. Many health care, social service and pastoral care institutions related to the Catholic Church, and other faith communities, worked side by side with the national and local members in the Ebola Response efforts. Thus, my Delegation concurs with the decision by this Conference to grant an Award to the volunteers, who selflessly responded to the families and local community members affected by this tragic outbreak.

The present Conference coincides with the 50th anniversary of the proclamation of the Fundamental Principles of the Movement: Humanity, Impartiality, Neutrality, Independence, Voluntary Service, Unity and Universality. These provide the overarching theme for this quadrennial gathering. Indeed, many humanitarian actors throughout the world, including religiously inspired organizations, share these same principles. So too, my Delegation supports the efforts of this Conference to strengthen International Humanitarian Law and to monitor carefully its implementation by States and by all other stakeholders.

Humanitarian needs are complex in nature and the response required by key stakeholders can run the risk of placing too much emphasis on those aspects with greater legal and technical implications, while downplaying or ignoring those aspects, which, in the judgment of the Holy See, are most essential – in other words, the principle of 'humanity', by which the Movement means '*protecting life and health and ensuring respect for the human being*', and through which it aims to '*promote mutual*

* Statement delivered at the 32nd International Conference of the Red Cross and Red Crescent, 8–10 December 2015.

understanding, friendship, cooperation and lasting peace amongst all peoples'.[1] During his recent address to the United Nations General Assembly, Pope Francis urged the international community to avoid the mistaken conclusion that 'the bureaucratic exercise of drawing up long lists of good proposals – goals, objectives and statistics ... will provide an answer to all the challenges' of today's world. He stressed that, 'we are dealing with real men and women who live, struggle and suffer, and are often forced to live in great poverty, deprived of all rights.'[2]

Mr Chairman,

The Holy See Delegation shares the concern expressed in the conceptual document for this Conference, that '[w]e are confronted today with a hugely complex humanitarian operating environment.' The current series of never-ending conflicts is bringing about increasingly difficult and tragic consequences. In a way, we face 'a true world war fought piecemeal', which affects numerous areas in our world in different forms and to varying degrees of intensity.[3]

Together with the international community, the Holy See, as well as Catholic Church-inspired organizations engaged in a humanitarian response in all parts of the world, is committed to preventing further deterioration of the situation. To this end, it participated in the World Conference on Disaster Risk Reduction, held in Sendai, Japan, during March 2015, and in the negotiations that led to the adoption of the post-2015 Framework for Disaster Risk Reduction. Increasing investment in disaster prevention and addressing the causes of disaster risk will eventually reduce the overwhelming costs, the tragic consequences, and the serial occurrences of natural disasters, due to environmental degradation and changes in climate. The means to achieve this objective are increased political will and economic input and a greater deployment of human resources, in conformity with internationally established standards and accords.

1 www.ifrc.org/en/who-we-are/vision-and-mission/the-seven-fundamental-principles/humanity/.

2 Pope Francis, Address to the Members of the United Nations General Assembly, 25 September 2015, http://w2.vatican.va/content/francesco/en/speeches/2015/september/documents/papa-francesco_20150925_onu-visita.html.

3 Address to the Members of the Diplomatic Corps accredited to the Holy See, 12 January 2015, http://w2.vatican.va/content/francesco/en/speeches/2015/january/documents/papa-francesco_20150112_corpo-diplomatico.html.

The best 'prevention', however, is through integral human development, which takes into account all aspects of human progress, including social, economic, educational, emotional and spiritual. Improvement of the quality of life, for both individuals and families, and the promotion of human rights and freedoms, most especially among poor and marginalized communities, can similarly prevent future occurrences of armed conflict, civil strife and failures in upholding the rule of law.

In the context of international humanitarian law, an alarming development seems to be gaining ground. The respect and promotion of international humanitarian law is increasingly ignored and violated. The Holy See is worried by these developments that can only lead to more violence, misery and suffering. It associates itself with the sober and urgent warning launched recently by the United Nations Secretary General and the President of the International Committee of the Red Cross. The description they give of the continued erosion of, and non-compliance with, the rules of international humanitarian law is alarming. These two senior leaders judge the current situation to be unacceptable. They see that the world is at a crossroads and that all State and non-State actors have the duty to engage to 'renew a contract for humanity' that should benefit millions of people affected by armed conflicts.

Mr Chairman,

Focusing on current and protracted conflicts, the international community should remain vigilant and tireless in calling attention to the needs of people who find themselves in the midst of humanitarian emergencies. The short attention span of the communications media, and of many others in the international community, should be challenged by regularly calling attention to the ongoing emergencies that seem to be multiplying in intensity and complexity. Let us emphasize the inter-connectedness of global phenomena and reject the 'throwaway culture' that plagues our world and feeds tendencies toward greed, corruption, violence, war, and environmental degradation. Let us insist that all citizens of this world have a responsibility to care for their neighbors. In this regard, the Holy See Delegation proposes a comprehensive definition for 'neighbor', since all persons are equal members of the one human family and should be in mutual solidarity. All of us are created with equal dignity and therefore are entitled to equal access to the goods of this world. Moreover, all persons should have an equal say in the formulation of policies and decisions that will affect their own lives and that of future generations.

Mr Chairman,

Preventive and remedial measures should go hand in hand. All players must address the root causes of the many problems our globalized world is facing. Based on a shared humanity and dignity, there is an urgent need to collectively confront the global issues affecting the whole human family. Disarmament, and nuclear disarmament in particular, migration, poverty, armed conflicts, respect for human rights and the rule of law, climate change and environmental problems, diseases, etc. are areas where States, the Red Cross and Red Crescent Movement, international organizations and the civil society should work together to secure a better future for coming generations.

2 RIGHT TO HEALTH AND ACCESS TO MEDICINES

WE MUST NOT FORGET AFRICA*

Madam President,

The Holy See Delegation wishes to convey its congratulations upon your election as President of this august assembly as well as its sincere gratitude to Dr Fernando Antezana Araníbar, who provided such excellent leadership for the World Health Organization Executive Board as it fulfilled its burdensome responsibility to discern succession to the post of Director General following the untimely death of Dr J. W. Lee.

My Delegation also expresses congratulations to Dr Margaret Chan upon her appointment as Director General of the World Health Organization. We welcome her designation of the health of women and of the people of Africa as major concerns during her tenure in office. The Catholic Church has traditionally been in the first line in the promotion of the authentic health of women, by helping them to harmonize their physical, psychological and social well-being with moral and spiritual values. In this line, the Catholic Church is also convinced of the God-given, equal, and complementary dignity of women and men. The Catholic Church also prioritizes the most fruitful expression of complementarity between woman and man – that is, the family which is founded upon lifelong and mutually faithful marriage and which continues to serve as the mainstay of human society. This vision of human dignity, strongly promoted by the Holy See, also is shared by citizens in many WHO Member States. In this same regard, it is the fervent hope of this Delegation that discussion on and implementation of Resolution EB 120.R6, 'Integrating Gender Analysis and Actions into the Work of WHO' will never be utilized to 'justify' doing harm to or destroying human life during one of its most vulnerable stages – when still within the mother's womb. Furthermore, the Holy See wishes to invite the WHO Member States once again to understand the term 'gender' as grounded in biological sexual identity, male or female.

Regarding Africa, the Popes have repeatedly expressed deep concern over its anguished history 'where many nations are still in the grip of famine, war, racial and tribal tensions, political instability and the

* Statement delivered at the 60th World Health Assembly, 14–23 May 2007.

violation of human rights',[1] and Pope Benedict XVI has exhorted the international community, 'we must not forget Africa ...'[2]

My Delegation wishes to commend, for particular attention by this Assembly, the resolutions and recommendations with regard to the pandemics of TB, malaria, and HIV, as well as those related to the projected exacerbation of avian and pandemic influenza. Much of the threat to health security caused by such diseases could adequately be addressed were the global human family to commit itself to affordable and action-oriented programs of research, vaccination, treatment and preventive education respectful of the natural moral law. On 23–25 November 2006, the Vatican's Pontifical Council for Health Pastoral Care convened more than 500 experts to reflect on 'Pastoral aspects of the treatment of infectious diseases'. In addressing those gathered, His Holiness Pope Benedict XVI emphasized the need to implement social justice in the sensitive area of treatment and nursing and therefore to ensure a fair distribution of resources for research and treatment.[3] In this same perspective, as the Chancellor of Germany prepared to assume the presidency of both the G8 countries and the European Union, the Holy Father, in a letter to her, expressed the hope that there would be 'a substantial investment of resources for research and for the development of medicines to treat AIDS, TB, malaria, and other tropical diseases ... There is also a need to make available medical and pharmaceutical technology and health care expertise without imposing legal or economic conditions.'[4]

The Holy See shares the concern expressed by the Secretariat of the World Health Organization in its Report on 'Better Medicines for Children', for the tragic loss of life each year among some 10.5 million children under five years of age; many of these children die of diseases that are treatable in adults but for which appropriate dosages and

[1] Apostolic Exhortation of Pope John Paul II, *Ecclesia in Africa*, § 51, www.vatican.va/holy_father/john_paul_ii/apost_exhortations/documents/hf_jp-ii_exh_14091995_ecclesia-in-africa_en.html.

[2] Address of Pope Benedict XVI to the Diplomatic Corps Accredited to the Holy See for the Traditional Exchange of New Year Greetings, 8 January 2007, www.vatican.va/holy_father/benedict_xvi/speeches/2007/january/documents/hf_ben-xvi_spe_20070108_diplomatic-corps_en.html.

[3] Address of Pope Benedict XVI to the Participants in the 21st International Congress Organized by the Pontifical Council for Health Pastoral Care, Clementine Hall, 24 November 2006, www.vatican.va/holy_father/benedict_xvi/speeches/2006/november/documents/hf_ben-xvi_spe_20061124_pc-health_en.html.

[4] Letter of Pope Benedict XVI to Her Excellency Dr Angela Merkel, Chancellor of the Federal Republic of Germany, 16 December 2006, www.evangelizatio.org/portale/adgentes/pontefici/pontefice.php?id=770.

formulations have not yet been developed for pediatric use.[5] Attention to this serious concern seems all the more compelling in light of the recently released report on 'Scaling up Priority HIV/AIDS Interventions in the Health Sector', which noted, with much regret, that only 15 per cent of HIV-positive children in need of antiretroviral treatment actually have access to these life-saving therapies. Such treatment coverage is approximately one-half that achieved for HIV-positive adults.[6] The international community can no longer turn a deaf ear to the life-threatening needs of children, many of whom can be counted among our most needy citizens but who represent, as well, the future of the human community. While steps are being taken to develop 'Better Medicines for Children' and to revise and regularly update the Model List of Essential Medicines in order to include those appropriate for pediatric use, research that is ethically based, transparent and carefully-monitored must be conducted on the safety of such medicines before they are approved for treatment of diseases affecting children.

As we approach the thirtieth anniversary of the historic Alma Ata Declaration on Primary Health Care, the Holy See Delegation is pleased to note the strategic attention being encouraged at this World Health Assembly on such crucial topics as Prevention and Control of Non-Communicable Diseases, Rational Use of Medicines, and, in particular, Health Promotion in a Globalized World with a special focus on primary health care. In all the deliberations during this Assembly and in the subsequent implementation of World Health Assembly Resolutions at national and local levels, my Delegation urges a perspective on health security that is grounded on an anthropology respectful of the human person in his or her integrity and looks far beyond the absence of disease to the full harmony and sound balance of the physical, emotional, spiritual and social forces within the human person.[7]

Thank you.

[5] 'Better Medicines for Children', Report by the Secretariat, World Health Organization, Sixtieth World Health Assembly, A60/25, 17 April 2007, www.who.int/gb/ebwha/pdf_files/WHA60/A60_25-en.pdf.

[6] Towards Universal Access: Scaling up Priority HIV/AIDS Interventions in the Health Sector, Progress Report by WHO, UNAIDS, UNICEF, April 2007, p. 6.

[7] Cf. Pope John Paul II, Message of the World Day of the Sick, 11 February 2000, § 3, www.vatican.va/holy_father/john_paul_ii/messages/sick/documents/hf_jp-ii_mes_19990806_world-day-of-the-sick-2000_en.html.

PROGRESS REPORT ON THE GLOBAL PLAN AND STOP TB STRATEGY*

Thank you, Mr Chairman. The Holy See Delegation wishes to thank the Secretariat for its excellent Progress Report on the Global Plan and Stop TB Strategy and for projecting, in a clear manner, the action necessary to overcome constraints encountered, at national and community levels, in attempts to implement this plan and strategy.

Our Delegation recognizes the urgency, especially in view of the patterns of co-infection of HIV and TB in many countries as well as the outbreaks of M-DR and X-DR TB, for this World Health Assembly to declare its full commitment to promote more effective TB programming in all countries affected by this pandemic and thus we encourage passage of the Resolution EB 120.R3.

On the basis of experience with community-based programs sponsored by the Catholic Church and other faith-based organizations in many highly affected, low-income countries, we note the importance of close collaboration among the WHO Secretariat, WHO Member States and civil society (including faith-based organizations) in order to address this pandemic in a more holistic, integrated and effective manner.

* Statement delivered at the 60th World Health Assembly: item 12.6 – Report on Progress with Global Plan and Stop TB Strategy as well as pending resolution for World Health Assembly Consideration, 17 May 2007.

THE RIGHT OF EVERYONE TO THE ENJOYMENT OF THE HIGHEST ATTAINABLE STANDARD OF PHYSICAL AND MENTAL HEALTH*

Mr President,

The Holy See Delegation welcomes the opportunity to offer its observations on the Report of the Special Rapporteur on the Right of Everyone to the Enjoyment of the Highest Attainable Standard of Physical and Mental Health.[1] First of all, we are pleased to note that the Report identifies this right as a 'fundamental building block of sustainable development, poverty reduction, and economic prosperity.'[2] In a similar manner, Pope Benedict XVI recently affirmed that '[t]he building of a more secure future for the human family means first and foremost working for the integral development of peoples, especially through the provision of adequate health care [and] the elimination of pandemics like AIDS … '[3]

The Report, Mr President, appropriately calls attention to the single policy framework for health that was embodied in the Declaration of Alma Ata on primary health care, promulgated, thirty years ago, by the world's Health Ministers. This framework outlined the underlying principles to assure equitable exercise of the right to health as well as the implementation of essential interventions to assure strong links between health and development.

We note, however, that, in accord with the Constitution of the World Health Organization, the definition of health extends beyond medical interventions and social determinants to include a 'state of complete physical, mental and social well-being and not merely the absence of disease or infirmity'.[4] The Holy See recognizes, as well, the need to assure

* Statement delivered at the 7th Session of the Human Rights Council – Item 3: *Promotion and Protection of All Human Rights, Civil, Political, Economic, Social and Cultural Rights, including the Right to Development*, 11 March 2008.

1 UN Doc. A/HRC/7/11, 31 January 2008. 2 Ibid., § 12.

3 Address of Pope Benedict XVI to H.E. Mrs Mary Ann Glendon, Ambassador of the United States of America to the Holy See, 29 February 2008, www.vatican.va/holy_father/benedict_xvi/speeches/2008/february/documents/hf_ben-xvi_spe_20080229_ambassador-usa_en.html.

4 Preamble to the Constitution of the World Health Organization as adopted by the International Health Conference, New York, 19 June–22 July 1946; signed on 22 July 1946 by the representatives of 61 States (Official Records of the World Health Organization, No. 2, p. 100) and entered into force on 7 April 1948.

access to spiritual assistance among those conditions which guarantee the full enjoyment of the right to health.[5]

The Report refers to the World Health Organization definition of 'health systems' that includes 'all organizations, people, and actions whose primary intent is to promote, restore, or maintain health'.[6] Moreover, while discussing the pre-conditions for a 'right-to-health' approach that strengthens health systems, he points out the entitlement of all individuals and communities to active and informed participation on issues relating to their health. In this regard, Mr President, my Delegation would like to focus on the key role that can and should be accorded to religious organizations as important stakeholders in the strengthening of health infrastructure.

Such organizations often assume significant responsibility for the burden of health care delivery, most especially to the poorest sectors of the population and to those living in rural areas. Too often, however, these faith-based service providers are not allowed a 'place at the table' during the formulation of health care plans on national or local levels. They also are deprived of an equitable share in the resources – both from the national/local budgets and from international donors. Such funding is essential to facilitate the maintenance of ongoing health systems; the training, recruitment, and retention of professional staff; as well as the scaling up necessary to address the ever-increasing burden of global pandemics such as HIV, TB, malaria and other infections and non-communicable diseases that disproportionately affect the poorest sectors of society.

Mr President, my Delegation was pleased to note, in this Report, the inclusion of 'non-discrimination' among the core obligations of health systems and the emphasis on the obligation of States to address the particular needs of disadvantaged individuals, communities and populations and to reach out to those living in poverty.[7]

With regard to those who require special protection, let us never ignore or deny the very right to life among those whose conditions are most vulnerable and may entirely depend on being safeguarded by others. Particular cases in point are children in the womb and those suffering from grave and life-threatening illnesses. My Delegation urgently hopes that references to 'emergency obstetric care' will never be misconstrued

[5] Charter for Health Care Workers, § 40, Pontifical Council for Health Pastoral Care, Vatican City, 1995. www.healthpastoral.org/pdffiles/Charter_06_Chapter2.pdf.

[6] UN Doc. A/HRC/7/11, 31 January 2008, § 34.

[7] Ibid., § 51.

to justify the forced ending of human life before birth and that the reference to a state's obligation to 'identify a minimum "basket" of health services'[8] and to 'striking balances'[9] will not be interpreted in a manner that denies essential services to the seriously ill. While the report claims that 'few human rights are absolute',[10] it is the firm belief of my Delegation, Mr President, that no compromise can be made with a person's right to life itself, from conception to natural death, nor with that person's ability to enjoy the dignity which flows from that right.

In conclusion, we note that the Report gave due recognition to 'health as a public good' which requires 'international cooperation' on 'trans-boundary health issues'. Urgent attention must be accorded to such issues since, in many countries, refugees, other migrants and internally displaced persons are deprived by host governments even of the most basic life-saving health services. In an attempt to fill such gaps, once again religious organizations often provide care, support and treatment to such populations without concern for their national or ethnic origins.

Thank you.

[8] Ibid., § 52. [9] Ibid., § 63. [10] Ibid.

RESPECT FOR THE DIGNITY OF THE HUMAN PERSON IN ALL HEALTH-RELATED CARE*

The Holy See Delegation congratulates you on your election as President of the 61st session of the World Health Assembly and makes his fervent wishes for the success of the work. I would also like to respectfully greet Dr Margaret Chan, Director General of the World Health Organization, and congratulate you on your authoritative guide of the Organization

While the World Health Organization marks the 60th anniversary of its establishment, I wish to express the gratitude of the Catholic Church for the important and decisive contribution that in recent decades has led the Organization to prevent, cure and eliminate diseases and pandemics that have caused countless deaths over the years. The emphasis placed on primary health care at the International Conference of Alma Ata, which celebrates its 30th anniversary this year, is placed in the same direction and remains very relevant.

Mr President,

My Delegation hopes that the issues on the agenda of this World Assembly find proper attention and greater cooperation, based on the respect for the dignity of the human person and his rights, which, as the common nature of all people, are inalienable. In recent years there have been positive signs of progress in eliminating polio through access to the package of essential vaccines for many children, even those living in areas of armed conflict.

According to data available in the Organization, this has led to the reduction in infections that are responsible for approximately 25 per cent of the 10 million deaths that occur each year among children less than five years old. However, they remain high and there are worrying rates of infant mortality, as well as HIV/AIDS, TB and other infectious diseases, especially in poor countries. If States do not seriously increase their commitment to the prevention and cure of these diseases by investing means and resources for the poor and by respecting the values enshrined

* Statement delivered by H.E. Cardinal Javier Lozano Barragán, Head of the Holy See Delegation to the 61st World Health Assembly, 22 May 2008.

in human nature, development will inevitably remain a good declaration of principle without proper monitoring.

The Delegation of the Holy See wishes to express its grave concern and rejection of all that is part of the strategy to promote reproductive health, harm the dignity of or even suppress prenatal life. In this perspective, such a strategy should also avoid equating conferences promoted with the substantial cooperation of NGOs with governmental meetings. The Delegation of the Holy See is still concerned about the impact of climate change on the health of the world's people, especially those with a low income who live in tropical and subtropical countries.

The gradual warming of the planet and the brutal increase in the frequency and severity of extreme weather events such as severe storms, heat waves, drought and floods has already begun to produce adverse health effects.

To this we must add the increasing environmental pollution caused by industrial and radioactive waste as well as water pollution of rivers in many developing countries. All this leads to negative effects on food production, the availability of drinking water, and air quality, creating unusual and disturbing social and health situations that require immediate and appropriate responses.

Mr President,

Faced with this serious and dangerous global picture, our response cannot do without the awareness of the human person's responsibility for the management of the earth, which is a gift of the Creator to humanity. Exploitation for selfish purposes, and profiteering from the environment, as has been seen in the last 50 years, endangers not only the health of the population but the very life of man and the world we live in.

This is what Pope Benedict XVI deemed necessary: 'to convert the model of global development' so as to respond to 'environmental and energy emergencies … by adopting a lifestyle and consumption compatible with the safeguarding of creation'.[1] In his recent speech at the United Nations, still talking about the ethical imperative to safeguard the environment, Pope Benedict XVI has stressed also that 'international action to preserve the environment and to protect various forms of life

[1] Pope Benedict XVI, Angelus, 12 November 2006, https://w2.vatican.va/content/benedict-xvi/en/angelus/2006/documents/hf_ben-xvi_ang_20061112.html.

on earth must not only guarantee a rational use of technology and science, but must also rediscover the authentic image of creation. This never requires a choice to be made between science and ethics: rather it is a question of adopting a scientific method that is truly respectful of ethical imperatives.'[2]

Thank you, Mr President.

[2] Pope Benedict XVI, Address to the 62nd Session of the United Nations General Assembly, 18 April 2008.

PRIMARY HEALTH CARE AND HEALTH SYSTEM STRENGTHENING*

Mr Chairperson,

The Holy See Delegation wishes to congratulate the WHO Secretariat for its report on this urgent topic and to encourage renewed commitment to promotion of primary health care services as it was envisioned thirty years ago by the Declaration of Alma Ata. This Delegation particularly was pleased to note, in the report, a reference to the values underlying such initiatives, including equity, solidarity and social justice, as well as the principles of multi-sectoral action and community participation. These same themes are echoed quite strongly in both the teaching and the practical service tradition of the Catholic Church's outreach to the most poor and vulnerable members of society.

The Report states that 'health authorities in many countries are aware that progress toward improved health outcomes ... is too slow and unequal, that performance does not meet expectations, and that they are ill-prepared to respond to challenges and demands'. In this regard, particular attention should be focused on the key role played by Church-related organizations both in the process that developed the Alma Ata Declaration and in its implementation during the past thirty years.

The Report further recommends that services 'have to be designed and organized around close-to-client networks of primary care teams'. My Delegation respectfully would like to point out that Church- and other faith-based organizations often reach communities in rural and otherwise isolated areas that do not benefit from services provided by national, provincial, district or even local government-sponsored services. These vital, faith-based links to 'health for all' actively contribute to health system strengthening, but, on the other hand, often are excluded from such policy-setting and are not allowed direct access to international or domestic funding.

Finally, the Holy See Delegation strongly affirms the recommendation of the World Health Report 2008 to enhance 'efforts to improve health by acting on wider social, economic, and environmental causes of ill health and health inequalities'. Striking a similar theme in his

* Statement delivered at the 124th Meeting of WHO Executive Board – Provisional agenda item 4.5: 'Primary Health Care, including Health System Strengthening', 19–27 January 2009.

Message for the 2009 World Day of Peace,[1] Pope Benedict XVI promoted a 'strong sense of *global solidarity* between rich and poor countries, as well as within individual countries, including affluent ones' and urged the global community, to develop 'gestures of creative solidarity', not only by 'giving from one's surplus', but above all by 'a change of life-styles, of models of production and consumption, and of the established structures of power which today govern societies'.[2]

Thank you, Mr Chairperson.

[1] www.vatican.va/holy_father/benedict_xvi/messages/peace/documents/hf_ben-xvi_mes_20081208_xlii-world-day-peace_en.html.

[2] Pope John Paul II, Encyclical Letter, *Centesimus Annus*, § 58.

HUMAN ORGAN AND TISSUE TRANSPLANTATION*

Mr Chairman,

The Holy See Delegation is well aware of the attention being dedicated by the WHO Secretariat and the membership of the Executive Board to this topic of such great urgency and relevance in modern health care. The World Health Organization itself estimates that, of the 66,000 kidney transplants that took place worldwide in 2007, nearly 10 per cent were illegal, as a result of the purchase and sale of kidneys, their trafficking across borders, and victimization of extremely poor persons, prisoners of war and conflict, and other vulnerable individuals to serve as involuntary, living donors of such organs.[1] His Holiness Pope Benedict XVI expressed grave concern about these abuses when he received the participants in an international conference on this topic on 7 November 2008 and appealed to those present and to all the 'scientific and medical community [to be] ready to unite in rejecting such unacceptable practices'.[2]

This Delegation greatly appreciates, therefore, the determination of the Director General to fulfill the mandate given by the 57th World Health Assembly to continue examining ethical issues related to Human Organ Transplantation in addition to the data related to clinical practices and epidemiological trends in this field.

The Holy See fully recognizes the urgent need to promote voluntary donation of organs, which the Catechism of the Catholic Church describes as 'a noble and meritorious act' and encourages as 'a manifestation of generous solidarity'.[3] We believe it necessary, however, to repeat a serious concern already asserted by this Delegation during the 123rd meeting of this body in May 2008, in relation to the reference to 'another source of organ donors', namely 'non-heartbeating donors' as contained in paragraph 11 of the Secretariat report. Particular care should be encouraged and taken in order to assure that, in all cases, the cessation of vital functions is truly irreversible and that it is certified by valid criteria.

* Statement delivered at the 124th Meeting of WHO Executive Board – Provisional agenda item 4.12: 'Human Organ and Tissue Transplantation', 19–27 January 2009.

1 'Trafficking of Human Organs, Fides Dossier, August 2008, Agency of the Congregation of the Evangelization of People, Vatican City.

2 www.vatican.va/holy_father/benedict_xvi/speeches/2008/november/documents/hf_ben-xvi_spe_20081107_acdlife_en.html.

3 *Catechism of the Catholic Church*, § 2296.

This Delegation is fully aware of the complex nature of the topic being discussed today and thus we would urge, as did Pope Benedict XVI, when he received in audience the participants in the previously mentioned international conference, to promote additional research and interdisciplinary reflection in order to present to the general public 'the most transparent truth on the anthropological, social, ethical and juridical implications of the practice of transplantation', while simultaneously assuring that 'the principal criteria of respect for the life of the donor must always prevail so that the extraction of organs be performed only in the case of his/her true death'.[4] Consultation with experts in this area suggests that such research is needed with children.

Mr Chairman, in the field of organ transplantation, clinical research has demonstrated the therapeutic benefits of interventions utilizing adult stem cells rather than embryonic cells. This direction of research guarantees respect for the dignity of each and every human being, even at the embryonic stage.

Thank you, Mr Chairman.

[4] www.vatican.va/holy_father/benedict_xvi/speeches/2008/november/documents/hf_ben-xvi_spe_20081107_acdlife_en.html. Cf. *Compendium of the Catechism of the Catholic Church*, London: Catholic Truth Society, 2006, § 476.

HEALTH CARE PERSONNEL IN THE CATHOLIC CHURCH*

Mr President,

Please allow me to convey the greetings and gratitude of Pope Benedict XVI for your efforts during this World Health Assembly and for the ongoing technical assistance offered by the World Health Organization. On this occasion, I would like to focus on the significant numbers of health care personnel engaged in Catholic Church-sponsored services throughout the world.

According to our most recent statistical data, the Catholic Church sponsors 114,053 health care institutions, of which there are 5,246 hospitals; 17,224 dispensaries; 684 leprosaria; 14,927 child care centres; 10,163 orphanages; 13,866 centres for marriage counselling; 30,531 centres for special education or social rehabilitation; and 10,516 performing various other services.[1] Moreover, we found that the Catholic Church is sponsoring 18 medical research centres.

In a study conducted by the Pontifical Council on Health Care, we found that 350,139 religious sisters work as nurses and are associated with 2,381 institutions and belong to 809 different religious orders.[2] Religious brothers and priests working in this same field come from 62 religious orders. In America, there are 647 religious orders working in the health sector; in Europe, 554 religious orders; in Africa, 694; in Asia, 307; and in Oceania, 52.[3]

We are especially grateful to those Church-related health care workers who remain faithful to their duties in extremely poor and war-torn countries when most other caregivers have left these areas out of concern for their own health and safety. In a similar way, we note that many such personnel live and work in extremely rural areas and which otherwise remain untouched by government-sponsored health care services and even by services sponsored by other civil society groups.

* Statement delivered by H.E. Archishop Zygmunt Zimowski, Head of the Holy See Delegation at the 62nd World Health Assembly, 18–27 May 2009.

1 Secretaria Status, *Statistical Year Book of the Church*, Libreria editrice Vaticana, 2004, p. 365.

2 Sister Teresa López Beorlegui, 'Las religiosas y su misión en el campo de la salud', in Pontificium Consilium pro valetudinis administris (pro pastorali valetudinis cura), *'Curate infirmos' y la vida consagrada/Pontificio Consejo para la Pastoral de los Agentes Sanitarios*, Vatican City: Vatican Press, 1994, pp. 97–8.

3 Secretaria Status, *Statistical Year Book of the Church*, pp. 355–66.

The Pontifical Council on Health Care launched a survey this year in order to prepare a more detailed analysis of the data reported earlier. Preliminary responses have been received from 121 national programs on five continents. At the present time, we have received 138 responses.[4] Data received so far indicate that a very broad range of professional disciplines are represented among the health care personnel engaged in such institutions.[5] All respondents have indicated the insufficient supply of professionally prepared personnel in the health care-related disciplines.[6]

The sheer numbers of those engaged in Catholic Church-sponsored health care services are most impressive; however, even more striking is the quality of care provided by them as well as their generosity and compassion toward those who are ill. Thus I will conclude with the words of gratitude addressed to such care-givers by Pope Benedict XVI: 'I would like to thank those who work in various ways and at various levels to ensure that the spirit of solidarity does not decline and that people persevere in looking after these brothers and sisters of ours, basing themselves on human and Gospel-based ideals and principles.'[7]

[4] Responses have been received to date from the following countries: Australia, Burundi, Chad, Colombia, South Korea, Ecuador, Spain, Ethiopia, France, Ghana, Guatemala, Iraq, Ireland, Mauritius, Italy, Mexico, New Zealand, Nigeria, Papua New Guinea, Portugal, Czech Republic, Dominican Republic, Thailand, Turkey, Uganda and Zimbabwe.

[5] Reported numbers include: 1,014 medical doctors, 125 psychologists, 49 sociologists, 399 physical therapists. 169 professional educators, 65 social workers, 2026 nurses, 678 technicians, 1,343 nursing assistants, 898 administrators, 1,394 volunteers, 69 chaplains, 317 religious priests, brothers, and sisters and 8 counsellors.

[6] Dr Fiorenza Deriù, Progress Report della indagine del Pontificio Consiglio per la Pastorale della Salute su 'Le risorse umane nelle strutture sanitarie cattoliche: quale sostenibilità per il futuro', Rome (May 2006), pp. 1–15.

[7] Pope Benedict XVI, Message on World Day of the Sick, 11 February 2006.

IMPACT ON HEALTH AND HEALTH CARE DURING THE GLOBAL ECONOMIC CRISIS*

Mr Chairman,

I wish to present the Holy See's sincere congratulations and good wishes on your appointment to this important office.

Recently appointed by His Holiness Pope Benedict XVI as the President of the Pontifical Council for Health Pastoral Care, I consider it a great honor to share with the delegates at this 62nd World Health Assembly some of the reflections and concerns of the Holy See. In relation to the impact on health and health care during this period of global economic crisis, the Holy See shares the preoccupation already expressed by other delegates.

The current crisis has raised the specter of the cancellation or drastic reduction of external assistance programs, especially for less developed countries. This will dramatically jeopardize the state of their health systems, which are already overburdened by endemic, epidemic and viral diseases. Pope Benedict XVI in his message to the G-20 observed that 'the way out of the current global crisis can only be reached together, avoiding solutions marked by any nationalistic selfishness or protectionism.' He therefore calls for 'a courageous and generous strengthening of international co-operation, capable of promoting a truly humane and integral development'.[1]

My Delegation also wishes to point out the high importance and the particular responsibility that is carried by faith-based organizations and thousands of Church-sponsored health care institutions in the provision of support and treatment to those living in poverty. The increasing financial burden placed on governments during this economic crisis is felt even more acutely by the Church-sponsored institutions that are often deprived of access to governmental or international funding and yet persevere in the struggle to serve those most in need. The values that motivate such service on the part of faith-based organizations, in addition to the overriding value of the sacredness and dignity of human life, include some of the same principles articulated in the Resolution

* Statement delivered by H.E. Archishop Zygmunt Zimowski, Head of the Holy See Delegation at the 62nd World Health Assembly, 18–27 May 2009.

1 Pope Benedict XVI, Letter to British Prime Minister Mr Gordon Brown ahead of the G20 Summit, 30 March 2009.

on Primary Health Care being considered by this Assembly. I refer to principles such as 'equity, solidarity, social justice and universal access to services'.[2]

Mr Chair,

In 1998, the Pontifical Council – prompted by the World Health Organization – conducted a research in local Churches on the challenges faced by the international community in the attainment of health for all. The results of this inquiry showed that one of the greatest challenges was the implementation of the principle of equity.[3] A decade later, I am afraid to note that this challenge still holds in most countries. My Delegation therefore notes with great attention the resolution concerning the Social Determinants of Health that is proposed for passage by this Assembly and is particularly interested in the urgent plea contained therein for governments 'to develop and implement goals and strategies to improve public health with a focus on health inequities'.[4]

Furthermore, there is a shared concern for the millions of children globally who do not reach their full potential due to the serious gaps in health equity. This same concern was addressed by Pope Benedict XVI to the participants at the 2008 International Conference of the Pontifical Council for Health Pastoral Care, when he called for 'a decisive action aimed at preventing illnesses as far as possible' among these children and when they are present, treating them 'by means of the most modern discoveries of medical science as well as by promoting better standards of hygiene and sanitation, especially in the less fortunate countries'.[5]

[2] www.who.int/gb/ebwha/pdf_files/EB124/B124_R8-en.pdf.

[3] Pontifical Council for the Pastoral Care of Health Care Workers, unpublished research, 'Projet de document de consultation pour l'actualisation de la stratégie mondiale de la santé pour tous', Rome, 1998.

[4] www.who.int/gb/ebwha/pdf_files/EB124/B124_R8-en.pdf.

[5] Pope Benedict XVI, Address to Participants in the 23rd International Congress on the Pastoral Care in the Treatment of Sick Children, 5 November 2008, Rome.

Mr Chair,

We cannot allow such defenseless children, their parents and other adults in low-income communities throughout this world to become even more vulnerable as a result of the global economic crisis, that is largely fueled by selfishness and greed. Thus the Holy Father insists that we 'need a strong sense of global solidarity between rich and poor countries, as well as within individual countries, including affluent ones. A common code of ethics is also needed, consisting of norms based not upon mere consensus, but rooted in the natural law inscribed by the Creator on the conscience of every human being (cf. Rom. 2:14–15).'[6] Because, 'justice cannot be created in the world solely through good economic models, necessary though they are. Justice is achieved only if there are upright people.'[7]

Thank you, Mr Chair.

[6] Pope Benedict XVI's Message for the 2009 World Day of Peace, § 8.

[7] Pope Benedict XVI, Address to the Parish Priests and Clergy of the Diocese of Rome, 26 February 2009.

CUTBACKS IN INTERNATIONAL AND PUBLIC HEALTH: A SHORT-TERM FINANCIAL BENEFIT VS. THE LONG-TERM HUMAN COST*

Madam President,

The international community is struggling to find solutions to the financial and economic crisis that greed and lack of ethical responsibility have brought about. While analysts debate the causes of the crisis, the social consequences of new poverty, loss of jobs, malnutrition and stifled development all impact on the most vulnerable groups of people and therefore call for effective and prompt answers. The Delegation of the Holy See appreciates the fact that the focus of attention is directed in this High-Level Segment, in a most timely manner, on 'Current global and national trends and their impact on social development, including public health'. The global economic crisis continues unabated. It is exacerbated by the emergence of a previously unknown influenza virus, A-H1N1 already recognized at pandemic proportion with a future impact that cannot be projected with much certainty, and by the global food security crisis that endangers the lives of millions of people, particularly the world's poorest, many of whom already suffer from acute and chronic malnutrition. These examples show once again the link between poverty and health and the disproportionate burden on developing countries and even on the poor in the developed ones. Faced with such urgent global challenges, the future is mortgaged in a way that young people risk inheriting a severely compromised economic system, a society without cohesion and a planet damaged in its sustainability as a home for the whole human family.

The Holy See Delegation notes with deep concern predictions by the World Bank that during 2009 an additional 53 million to 65 million people will be trapped in extreme poverty and that the number of people chronically hungry will exceed one billion, 800 million of whom live in rural areas where public health is weakest and where innovative health care initiatives are urgent. We can reasonably conclude that significant numbers of those extremely poor and hungry people will be more at risk of contracting both communicable and chronic, non-communicable diseases. Moreover, if they are faced with cutbacks in international aid

* Statement delivered at the 2009 High-Level Segment of the Economic and Social Council, 9 July 2009.

or if there is an increased number of people seeking care, the already fragile public health systems in developing countries will not be able to respond adequately to the health needs of their most vulnerable citizens. In addressing this problem, even more than an expression of solidarity, it is a matter of justice to overcome the temptation to reduce public services for a short-term benefit against the long-term human cost. In the same line, aid for development should be maintained and even increased as a critical factor in renewing the economy and leading us out of the crisis.

Madam President,

Another key obstacle to achieving the internationally articulated goals in public health is to address the inequalities that exist both between countries and within countries, and between racial and ethnic groups. Tragically, women continue in many regions to receive poorer-quality health care. This situation is well known to people and institutions working on the ground. The Catholic Church sponsors 5,378 hospitals, 18,088 health clinics, 15,448 homes for the elderly and disabled, and other health care programs throughout the world, but especially in the most isolated and marginalized areas and among people who rarely enjoy access to health care provided under national, provincial or district-level governmental health schemes. In this regard, special attention is given to Africa, where the Catholic Church has pledged to continue to stand alongside the poorest people in this continent in order to uphold the inherent dignity of all persons.

There is an increasing recognition that a plurality of actors, in the respect of the principle of subsidiarity, contribute to the implementation of the human right to primary health care. Among the civil society organizations assuring health care within various national systems, the programs sponsored by the Catholic Church and other faith-based organizations stand out as key stakeholders. WHO officials have acknowledged that such organizations 'provide a substantial portion of care in developing countries, often reaching vulnerable populations living under adverse conditions'.[1] However, despite their excellent and documented record in the field of HIV service delivery and primary health care, faith-based organizations do not receive an equitable share of the resources designated to support global, national and local health initiatives.

[1] De Cock, 'Faith-based organizations play a major role in HIV/AIDS care and treatment in sub-Saharan Africa'.

The mere quantitative tracking of aid flows and the multiplication of global health initiatives alone may not be sufficient to assure 'Health for All'. Access to primary health care and affordable life-saving drugs is vital to improving global health and fostering a shared globalized response to the basic needs of all. In an increasingly interdependent world, even sickness and viruses have no boundaries, and, therefore, greater global cooperation becomes not only a practical necessity, but, more importantly, an ethical imperative of solidarity. However, we must be guided by the best health care tradition that respects and promotes the right to life from conception until natural death for all regardless of race, disability, nationality, religion, sex and socio-economic status. Failure to place the promotion of life at the center of health care decisions results in a society in which an individual's absolute right to basic health care and life would be limited by the ability to pay, by the perceived quality of life and other subjective decisions which sacrifice life and health in exchange for short-term social, economic and political advantage.

In conclusion, Madam President, the Holy See Delegation wishes to call attention to the need for more than financial solutions to the challenges posed by the economic crisis to global efforts aimed at assuring universal access to health care. In his new Encyclical, Pope Benedict XVI states: 'Economic activity cannot solve all social problems through the simple application of *commercial logic*. This needs to be *directed towards the pursuit of the common good*, for which the political community in particular must also take responsibility.'[2]

An ethical approach to development is needed which implies a new model of global development centered on the human person rather than profit, and inclusive of the needs and aspirations of the entire human family.

[2] Pope Benedict XVI, Encyclical Letter, *Caritas in Veritate*, § 36.

MONITORING THE ACHIEVEMENTS OF THE HEALTH-RELATED MILLENNIUM DEVELOPMENT GOALS*

Mr Chairman,

The recent report on monitoring the achievements of the health-related Millennium Development Goals (A63/7) offers us an appraisal of the success and challenges. The Holy See Delegation would like to join other Delegations in acknowledging, among others, the growing success in reducing infant mortality, malaria control, widening of access to antiretroviral therapy for people living with HIV/AIDS, as well as treating and lowering the incidence rate of TB.

There have been positive efforts towards the achievement of some of the set goals. It is true, though, that the achievements vary from country to country and from goal to goal. On the other hand, my Delegation cannot agree with programs that promote abortion and contraceptives. We need to multiply initiatives that foster 'the achievement of personal maturity in sexuality and in the mutual love and decision-making that characterize the conjugal relationship in accordance with moral norms'.[1] The Holy See considers that abortion and contraceptive methods should not be promoted among targets for the new Millennium.

Furthermore, there are continuing inequities between health care systems in high-income countries and those of low-income countries, and, worse still, those in the so-called least developed countries. Moreover, even in high-income countries themselves, there are wide gaps in access to health care. Closely related to these problems is the lack of access among poor and marginalized people to medicines and other life-saving technology because of the lack of affordability or the poor health care infrastructure in their home countries. In 2008 more than 5 million people of the estimated 9.5 million in low- and middle-income countries living with HIV/AIDS were without access to treatment. It has also been established that access to treatment for other major diseases like malaria and TB is still inadequate, while more than a billion people are affected

* Statement delivered by H.E. Archbishop Zygmunt Zimowski, Head of the Holy See Delegation at the 63rd World Health Assembly, 17–21 May 2010.

1 Statement of the Holy See at the Concluding Session of the General Assembly for the Overall Review and Appraisal of the Implementation of the Programme of Action of the International Conference on Population and Development, New York, 2 July 1999.

by neglected tropical diseases.[2] Resources are badly needed by these poor countries to meet the funding shortfalls and strengthen their health systems.

Pope Benedict XVI in his recent Encyclical Letter, *Caritas in Veritate*, makes a strong appeal for the 'Co-operation of the Human Family'. The Holy Father stresses that 'the development of peoples depends, above all, on a recognition that the human race is a single family working together in true communion, not simply a group of subjects who happen to live side by side'.[3] And in order to avoid paternalistic social assistance, which is demeaning to those in need, the solidarity of the rich nations to the poor countries has to be closely linked with the principle of subsidiarity. In fact, '[e]conomic aid, in order to be true to its purpose, must not pursue secondary objectives. It must be distributed with the involvement not only of the governments of receiving countries, but also local economic agents and the bearers of culture within civil society, including local Churches. Aid programmes must increasingly acquire the characteristics of participation and completion from the grass roots.'[4]

Another complicating factor for the access to health care is the failure to find a balanced approach to intellectual property rights and the right to make a just profit from investments in research and development for pharmaceuticals and diagnostics vis-à-vis the emergency situation posed to the global community from such pandemics as HIV/AIDS and from major diseases that affect populations in low-income countries. I wish here to reiterate the appeal made by the Servant of God John Paul II, who in his address to the Conference on Economy and Health, promoted by the Pontifical Council for Health Care Workers, called upon pharmaceutical industries 'never to let financial gain prevail over the consideration of human values, but to be sensitive to the needs of those who do not enjoy social security, carrying out effective programmes to help the poorest and most marginalized'. He said, 'We must work to reduce and, if possible, eliminate the differences between the various continents, urging the more advanced countries to make available to the less developed their experience, technology and some of their economic wealth.'[5]

[2] Cf. World Health Organization, Report on Monitoring the Achievement of the Health-related Millennium Development Goals, A63/7.

[3] Pope Benedict XVI, Encyclical Letter, *Caritas in Veritate*, § 53. [4] Ibid., § 58.

[5] Pope John Paul II, Address to the 14th International Conference organized by the Pontifical Council for Health Care Workers, 19 November 1999, § 5.

My Delegation therefore hopes that the implementation of the resolution on a global strategy and plan of action on public health, innovation and intellectual property (WHA61.21) will be earnestly embraced by all stakeholders, so as to allow, among others, the transfer of pharmaceutical-related technology and production to developing countries.[6]

Mr Chairman,

I would like to draw attention to the problem of counterfeit medical products which presents a major public health risk and has grown in recent years to become a global challenge. In this regard, 'it should also be observed that in developing countries the level of counterfeiting is very high, principally because of insufficient human and financial resources and legislation that is weak as regards the production, distribution and importation of medical products.'[7] In such countries the phenomenon concerns in the main 'life-saving' drugs and medicines. Moreover, the counterfeiting and falsification of medical products afflicts first and foremost individuals of the pediatric age-group. There is need for a common ethical code in the production and distribution of medical products. It is our sincere hope that the campaign promoted by the World Health Organization, together with the necessary assistance to Member States will help make the combating of counterfeit medicines a high priority in all countries.

Regarding the draft resolution on 'Birth Defects' (A63/10) the Delegation of the Holy See would like to recall, that, since human life begins at the moment of conception, life must be defended even if the unborn child suffers from diseases or anomalies. Life as a precious gift should be always protected and never harmed or selected. This important aspect of health care programs that deal with birth defects, especially methods of prenatal diagnosis, should not be jeopardized by the wording of the resolution.

Lastly, today there are growing health concerns related to climate change and in the face of established evidence it would be irresponsible not to take the issue seriously. Thus Pope Benedict XVI, in his Message for the 2010 World Day of Peace called for urgent action to protect

[6] Cf. World Health Organization, Report on Public Health, Innovation and Intellectual Property: Global Strategy and Plan of Action A63/6.

[7] H.E. Archbishop Zygmunt Zimowski, Address to the World Congress of the International Federation of Catholic Pharmacists on 'The Safety of Medical Products: Ethics and the Conscience for Pharmacists', Poznan, Poland, 11–14 September 2009.

the environment and observed that climate change and environmental degradation have a profound impact on the exercise of human rights, such as the right to life, food, health and development.[8] He remarks that 'the ecological crisis offers an historic opportunity to develop a common plan of action aimed at orienting the model of global development towards greater respect for creation and for an integral human development inspired by the values proper to charity in truth.'[9] He therefore advocates 'the adoption of a model of development based on the centrality of the human person, on the promotion and sharing of the common good, on responsibility, on a realization of our need for a changed lifestyle, and on prudence, the virtue which tells us what needs to be done today in view of what might happen tomorrow.'[10]

Thank you, Mr Chairman, and God bless you all.

[8] Cf. Pope Benedict XVI's Message for the 2010 World Day of Peace.
[9] Ibid., § 9. [10] Ibid.

UNIVERSAL ACCESS TO MEDICINES AND DIAGNOSTIC TOOLS*

Mr President,

With regard to the right of everyone to the enjoyment of the highest attainable standard of physical and mental health, my Delegation wishes to raise additional concerns regarding the need for effective action in order to guarantee universal access to medicines and diagnostic tools for all persons. The Special Rapporteur focused on this issue during his Report to the Eleventh Session of this distinguished Council.[1] However, continued vigilance must be maintained in this regard.

As the members of this Council already are well aware, the right to health is universally recognized as a fundamental right. Article 25 of the Universal Declaration on Human Rights (UDHR) includes the right to health and medical care within the more general rubric of the right 'to enjoy an adequate standard of living'.[2] Article 12.1 of the International Covenant on Economic, Social, and Cultural Rights (ICESCR), however, directly recognizes the right to enjoy the best physical and mental condition.[3]

The Committee on Economic and Cultural Rights, in its General Comment No. 14,[4] moreover, identified the following minimum requirements for States to ensure: (1) the right of access to health care in a non-discriminatory way; (2) access to basic nutritional level; (3) access to housing, basic sanitation and a sufficient supply of drinking water; (4) the supply of essential drugs; (5) an equitable distribution of benefits and health services; and (6) adoption of national strategies to prevent and combat epidemics.

Mr President, the Catholic Church provides a major contribution to health care in all parts of the world – through local Churches, religious

* Statement delivered at the 14th Session of the Human Rights Council – Item 3: *General Debate*, 8 June 2010.

1 Report of the Special Rapporteur on the Right of Everyone to the Enjoyment of the Highest Attainable Standard of Physical and Mental Health to the Eleventh Session of the Human Rights Council, UN Doc. A/HRC/11/12, 31 March 2009.

2 www.ohchr.org/EN/UDHR/Documents/UDHR_Translations/eng.pdf.

3 www2.ohchr.org/english/law/cescr.htm.

4 Committee on Economic, Social and Cultural Rights, Twenty-second session, Geneva, 25 April–12 May 2000, E/C.12/2000/4, 11 August 2000, www.unhchr.ch/tbs/doc.nsf/(symbol)/E.C.12.2000.4.En.

institutions and private initiatives, which act on their own responsibility and in the respect of the law of each country – including the promotion of 5,378 hospitals, 18,088 dispensaries and clinics, 521 leprosaria, and 15,448 homes for the aged, the chronically ill, or disabled people. With information coming from these on-the-ground realities in some of the most poor, isolated, and marginalized communities, my Delegation is obliged to report that the rights detailed in the international instruments already mentioned are far from being realized.

One major impediment to the realization of these rights is the lack of access to affordable medicines and diagnostic tools that can be administered and utilized in low-income, low-technology settings. Among the disturbing trends and findings reported by the Special Rapporteur are the following: 'Diseases of poverty' still account for 50 per cent of the burden of disease in developing countries, nearly ten times higher than in developed countries;[5] more than 100 million people fall into poverty annually because they have to pay for health care;[6] in developing countries, patients themselves pay for 50 per cent to 90 per cent of essential medicines;[7] nearly 2 billion people lack access to essential medicines.[8]

One group particularly deprived of access to medicines is that of children. Many essential medicines have not been developed in appropriate formulations or dosages specific to pediatric use. Thus families and health care workers often are forced to engage in a 'guessing game' on how best to divide adult-size pills for use with children. This situation can result in the tragic loss of life or continued chronic illness among such needy children. For example, of the 2.1 million children estimated to be living with HIV infection,[9] only 38 per cent received life-saving antiretroviral medications at the end of 2008.[10] This treatment gap is partially due to the lack of 'child friendly' medications to treat the HIV infection.

Thus the Committee on the Rights of the Child has declared: 'The obligations of States Parties under the Convention extend to ensuring

[5] World Health Organization, *Public Health Innovation and Intellectual Property Rights, A Report of the Commission on Intellectual Property Rights, Innovation and Public Health*, Geneva, 2006, p. 3.

[6] World Health Organization, World Health Report, *Primary Health Care Now More than Ever*, Geneva, 2008.

[7] UN Doc. A/61/338, para. 75.

[8] World Health Organization, 'WHO Medicines Strategy: Countries at the Core, 2004–2007' (2004).

[9] UNAIDS, 2009, AIDS Epidemic Update, Geneva, November 2009.

[10] Children and AIDS: Fourth Stocktaking Report, UNICEF, 2009, p. 10.

that children have sustained and equal access to comprehensive treatment and care, including necessary HIV-related drugs … on a basis of non-discrimination.'[11]

My Delegation is well aware of the complexities inherent in the intellectual property aspects related to the issue of access to medicines. These considerations, including the flexibilities available to applying the Agreement on Trade-Related Aspects of Intellectual Property Rights, are well documented in the 2009 Report of the Special Rapporteur. We further recognize that serious efforts already have been undertaken to implement the Global Strategy and Plan of Action on Public Health, Innovation and Intellectual Property, established in 2008 by the 61st World Health Assembly. However, the intense debates recently pursued at the 63rd World Health Assembly demonstrate that the international community has not yet succeeded in its aim to provide equitable access to medicines and indicate the need for further creative reflection and action in this regard.

Mr President, my Delegation urges this Council to renew its commitment as a key stakeholder in efforts to assert and safeguard the right to health by guaranteeing equitable access to essential medicines. We do so with a firm conviction that 'treatment should be extended to every human being' and as an essential element of 'the search for the greatest possible human development' and with a strong belief that '[t]his ethical perspective [is] based on the dignity of the human person and on the fundamental rights and duties connected with it'.[12]

[11] Committee on the Rights of the Child, Thirty-Second Session, General Comment No. 3 (2003), HIV/AIDS and the Rights of the Child, CRC/GC/2003/3, www.unhchr.ch/tbs/doc.nsf/898586b1dc7b4043c1256a450044f331/309e8c3807aa8cb7c1256d2d0038caaa/$FILE/G0340816.pdf.

[12] Pope Benedict XVI, Address to the Plenary Assembly of The Pontifical Council for Health Pastoral Care, 22 March 2007, www.vatican.va/holy_father/benedict_xvi/speeches/2007/march/documents/hf_ben-xvi_spe_20070322_pc-salute_en.html.

SUSTAINABLE HEALTH FINANCING STRUCTURES AND UNIVERSAL COVERAGE*

Madam President,

My Delegation, in conjunction with other Delegations, wishes to reaffirm the Resolution on Sustainable Health Financing Structures and Universal Coverage (WHA64.9), which, among other things, urges Member States to aim for affordable universal coverage and access for all citizens on the basis of equity and solidarity. As Pope Benedict XVI emphasizes, 'in the health-care sector too, which is an integral part of everyone's life and of the common good, it is important to establish a real distributive justice which, on the basis of objective needs, guarantees adequate care to all. Consequently, if it is not to become inhuman, the world of health care cannot disregard the moral rules that must govern it.'[1]

The goal of the international community is to enable everyone to access health services without running the risk of financial hardship in doing so (WHA58.33). Despite the progress made in some countries, we are still a long way from this target. There is need therefore for greater commitment at all levels in order to ensure that the right to health care is rendered effective by furthering access to basic health care. In this regard, the Holy See Delegation supports the integration of universal coverage in high-level meetings related to health or social development, as well as its inclusion as a priority in the global development agenda.

At the recent Forum on Universal Health Coverage held in Mexico City, on 2 April, 2012, it was noted that more countries, especially those with emerging economies, are moving towards universal coverage, and this is very encouraging. The results obtained in these countries are not simply a fruit of financial resources; it has been observed that good policies that promote equity have guaranteed better health for a greater number of citizens in these countries. Therefore my Delegation strongly believes that in the endeavor to promote universal coverage, fundamental values such as equity, human rights and social justice need to become explicit policy objectives.

* Statement delivered by H.E. Archbishop Zygmunt Zimowski, Head of the Holy See Delegation, at the 65th World Health Assembly, 21–26 May 2012.

1 Pope Benedict XVI, Message to Participants in the 25th International Conference Organized by the Pontifical Council for Health Care Workers, 15 November 2010, Vatican City.

Secondly, Mme President, it has been shown by both low- and middle-income countries that progress towards universal coverage is not the prerogative of high-income countries. Nevertheless, most low-income countries need the support of the international community, especially of high-income countries and other development partners, in order to overcome the funding shortfalls in health. The Holy See Delegation therefore wishes to reiterate the call for greater global solidarity and commitment in development assistance for health. Evoking the words of the Holy Father, 'more economically developed nations should do all they can to allocate larger portions of their gross domestic product to development aid, thus respecting the obligations that the international community has undertaken in this regard.'[2]

Lastly, at the level of each single nation, the progress towards universal coverage cannot be the effort of the state machinery alone. It requires support from the civil society and communities, whose contribution to health service delivery is fundamental. In this regard States should, 'in accordance with the principle of subsidiarity, generously acknowledge and support initiatives arising from the different social forces and combine spontaneity with closeness to those in need'.[3] Faith-based organizations and Church-sponsored health care institutions, inspired by Charity, are part of those living forces in the health care field.

With over 120,000 social and health care institutions worldwide,[4] the Catholic Church is, in many developing countries, one of the key partners of the State in health care delivery, providing services in remote areas to rural low-income populations, enabling them to access services that would otherwise be out of their reach. The efforts and contribution of such organizations and institutions towards universal access merit the recognition and support of both the State and the international community, without obliging them to participate in activities they find morally abhorrent. Thus Pope Benedict XVI asks 'international agencies to acknowledge *them* and to offer *them* assistance, respecting their specific character and acting in a spirit of collaboration'.[5]

Thank you, Madam President, and God bless you all.

[2] Pope Benedict XVI, Encyclical Letter, *Caritas in Veritate*, § 60.

[3] Pope Benedict XVI, Encyclical Letter, *Deus Caritas Est*, § 28(b)

[4] Secretaria Status, *Statistical Year Book of the Church 2009*, Vatican City: Libreria Editrice Vaticana, 2009, pp. 355–65.

[5] Pope Benedict XVI, Post-Synodal Apostolic Exhortation, *Africae Munus*, § 73.

PRIORITIZING HEALTH IN THE NEXT GENERATION OF DEVELOPMENT GOALS*

Mr President, distinguished delegates,

I have the honor to convey to you the greetings and blessing of the Holy Father Pope Francis, who since the beginning of his Pontificate has shown great concern for the sick and suffering, and wishes this august assembly fruitful deliberations.

It has been duly emphasized that health contributes to the achievement of development and benefits from it. My Delegation welcomes the resolve to prioritize health in the next generation of global development goals. The task before us is that of describing health objectives in an appropriate and convincing way. In this regard, the Holy See strongly believes that setting universal coverage as an objective of health and development policy (A66/24) would be a surer way of accommodating the wide range of health concerns, which includes sustaining the gains made so far, as well as attending to the broadened health agenda.

Moreover, while acknowledging the close links between health and development, my Delegation wishes to underscore the need for integral development and not mere economic growth. Health and development ought to be integral if they are to respond fully to the needs of every human person. What we hold important is the human person – each person, each group of people, and humanity as a whole.[1] The essential quality of 'authentic' development is that it must be 'integral' in that it has to promote the good of every person and of the whole person, that is, in every single dimension.[2] Therefore both health care and development must attend to the spiritual state of the person as well as to the physical, emotional, economic and social factors that influence one's well-being.

Secondly, Mr President, within the framework of strengthening health through the life course, efforts are being made to save the lives of millions of women and children who continue to die every year from conditions that can easily be prevented with existing medical

* Statement of H.E. Archbishop Zygmunt Zimowski, Head of the Holy See Delegation, at the 66th World Health Assembly, 20–28 May 2013.

[1] Cf. Pope Paul VI, Encyclical Letter, *Populorum Progressio*, § 14.

[2] Cf. Pope Benedict XVI, Encyclical Letter, *Caritas in Veritate*, §§ 11, 18.

commodities. Thus Resolution EB132.R4, among others, urges Member States to improve the quality, supply and use of 13 'life-saving commodities'. The Holy See strongly agrees with the need to achieve further reductions in the loss of life and prevention of illness through increased access to inexpensive interventions that are respectful of the life and dignity of all mothers and children at all stages of life, from conception to natural death. In relation to this, the Holy See Delegation wishes to raise serious concerns about the Report of the Secretariat and the Resolution recommended by the Executive Board to promote the implementation of the recommendations of the Commission on Life-Saving Commodities for Women and Children. While indeed some of the recommendations are truly life-saving, that of 'emergency contraception' can hardly be labeled as such since it is well known that, when conception already has occurred, certain substances used in 'emergency contraception' produce an abortifacient effect. For my Delegation, it is totally unacceptable to refer to a medical product that constitutes a direct attack on the life of the child *in utero* as a 'life-saving commodity' and, much worse, to encourage 'increasing use of such substances in all parts of the world'.

Thirdly, Mr President, given the significant impact of non-communicable diseases on both morbidity and mortality in all parts of the world, the Holy See Delegation welcomes the proposed Global Action Plan for the control of non-communicable diseases 2013–2020 (A66/9). Moreover, we were especially pleased that the plan acknowledges the key role of civil society, including faith-based organizations, in mobilizing and engaging families and communities to prevent and treat such illnesses before they cause debilitating conditions or premature death. Our Delegation is aware that Catholic Church-inspired organizations and institutions throughout the world already have committed themselves to pursue such actions at global, regional, and local community levels.

In connection with Resolution WHA65.3 on strengthening non-communicable disease policies to promote active ageing, the Holy See wishes to participate in exploring the various aspects of prevention and control of non-communicable diseases in older age. Already thousands of faith-based institutions offer aged care services around the world, and they are growing rapidly as populations age. Our humble contribution to this venture will be an International Conference, to be held in the Vatican this coming November 21–23 on the topic: 'The Church at the Service of Sick Elderly People: Taking Care of People with Neurodegenerative Pathologies'.

Finally, Mr President, our Delegation wishes to register its support for the Draft action plan for the prevention of visual impairment 2014–2019 (A66/11) and the related resolution EB132.R1 calling for the endorsement of the 'universal eye health' plan of action.

Thank you, Mr President.

KEY ELEMENTS TO GUARANTEE ACCESS TO MEDICINES*

Mr President,

The Delegation of the Holy See has carefully reviewed the Report on Access to Medicines. While the Special Rapporteur maintains that 'Full realization of access to medicines requires the fulfillment of key elements of availability, accessibility, acceptability and quality,' my Delegation found that the Report gave insufficient attention to certain factors cited as 'key elements' by the Special Rapporteur.

With regard to accessibility, my Delegation believes that a comprehensive analysis of this crucial topic must reach beyond legal frameworks to include an examination of the social and political realities that deprive millions of people of enjoyment of the highest attainable standard of physical and mental health because of the obstacles that they place on access to medicines.

Article 25 of the Universal Declaration on Human Rights clearly adopted such a comprehensive perspective when it declared: 'Everyone has the right to a standard of living adequate for the health and well-being of himself and of his family, including food, clothing, housing and medical care and necessary social services, and the right to security in the event of unemployment, sickness, disability, widowhood, old age or other lack of livelihood in circumstances beyond his control.'

Thus the Holy See Delegation found that the Report paid insufficient attention to basic needs of individuals and families, at all stages of the life-cycle from conception to natural death. Such challenges often block access to medicines as much as, if not more than, the various legal factors that occupied the main focus of the Report.

Effective reversal of such obstacles requires an integral human development approach that promotes just legal frameworks as well as international solidarity, not only among States, but also among and between all peoples.

Thus the Holy See noted, with alarm, 'the difficulties millions of people face as they seek to obtain minimal subsistence and the medicines they need to cure themselves' and called for 'establishing true distributive

* Statement delivered at the 23rd Session of the UN Human Rights Council – Item 3: *Report of the Special Rapporteur on the Right to Health*, 28 May 2013.

justice which guarantees everyone adequate care on the basis of objective needs'.[1]

The Report made frequent references to the obligation of States to set the conditions for access to medicine. While governmental fulfillment of such responsibility is a clear prerequisite, the strong engagement of non-governmental and religious organizations in providing both medicines and a wide range of treatment and preventive measures to ensure the full enjoyment of the right to health also should have been acknowledged. From its contacts down to the grass-root level with 5,305 hospitals and 18,179 clinics,[2] inspired and organized under Catholic Church auspices throughout the world, the Holy See is well aware that these institutions serve the poorest sectors of society, many of whom live in rural and isolated areas or in conflict zones, where governmental health systems often do not reach. This fact has been confirmed by professional mapping exercises, with support and collaboration of the World Health Organization, which reported that 'between 30 and 70 per cent of the health infrastructure in Africa is currently owned by faith-based organizations.'[3]

Mr President, optimal facilitation of access to medicine is a complex endeavor and deserves comprehensive analysis and acknowledgement of all factors contributing to its promotion, rather than a more restricted analysis of legal, economic and political frameworks.

Thank you, Mr President.

[1] 'Health Care cannot divorce itself from moral rules', Message of Pope Benedict XVI to the participants in the 25th International Conference of the Pontifical Council for Health Pastoral Care, 18 November 2010, Vatican Information Service, VIS 20101118 (490).

[2] Catholic Church Statistics, Agenzia Fides, Vatican City, 21 October 2012.

[3] De Cock, 'Faith-based organizations play a major role in HIV/AIDS care and treatment in sub-Saharan Africa'.

EFFECTS OF CLIMATE CHANGE ON HEALTH*

Mr President,

The Holy See is cognizant of the devastating impact of climate change, as reported by the WHO Secretariat, in various reports and advisories. That impact often is estimated in terms of additional financial costs and burden of care to be assumed by both governmental and non-governmental health care structures. Climate change also deeply affects the social and environmental determinants of health, including clear air, safe drinking water, supply of sufficient and nutritious food, and adequate shelter. There is overwhelming evidence that human activities have greatly contributed to recent warming of the earth's surface, and that climate change as well as its consequences will continue into the future. It has also been observed that climate change will act mainly by aggravating health problems that already exist, and that most risks will apply in populations that are currently most affected by climate-related diseases.

Expressing his concern about the greedy exploitation of the environment, Pope Francis observed that 'Even if "nature is at our disposition", all too often we do not "respect it or consider it a gracious gift which we must care for and set at the service of our brothers and sisters, including future generations".'[1] He then called for responsibility on the part of all in pursuing policies that are respectful of the earth which is our common home.

In the face of signs of an 'ecological crisis',[2] my Delegation wishes to reiterate the call made by Benedict XVI, and the challenging questions he made. He said: 'Can we remain indifferent before the problems associated with such realities as climate change, desertification, the deterioration and loss of productivity in vast agricultural areas, the pollution of rivers and aquifers, the loss of biodiversity, the increase of natural catastrophes and the deforestation of equatorial and tropical regions? Can we disregard the growing phenomenon of "environmental refugees"?'[3] We must look beyond the purely scientific, medical, and economic issues related to climate change and come face to face with the persons whom it most affects.

* Statement delivered by H.E. Archbishop Zygmunt Zimowski, Head of the Holy See Delegation, at the 67th World Health Assembly, 19–24 May 2014.

1 Pope Francis, Address to the Diplomatic Corps Accredited to the Holy See, 13 January 2014.

2 Pope John Paul II's Message for the 1990 World Day of Peace, §§ 6–7.

3 Pope Benedict XVI's Message for the 2010 World Day of Peace, § 4.

As with most natural disasters, climate-related emergencies cause more suffering and personal loss to those who live in poverty, who cannot afford protective structures to shield them from extreme forces of nature and who have little or no resources to arrange for temporary shelter and other basic necessities once their homes have been severely damaged or totally destroyed. We therefore need to rethink the path we are traveling together.

Reflecting on these lamentable situations, Pope Benedict XVI appealed for greater solidarity to prevent or, at least, mitigate the impact of climate change on our more vulnerable brothers and sisters throughout the world. Such action will require more than economic allocations and policy-setting. He insisted that we must promote a different culture in all sectors of society and on the interpersonal level as well: 'it is necessary to rediscover those values engraved on the heart of every person that have always inspired their action: the sentiment of compassion and of humanity for others, the duty of solidarity and the commitment to justice must return to being the basis of all action, including what is done by the international community'.[4]

Mr President, the Holy See Delegation is happy to note that the reports before us and the WHO work-plan on climate change and health are part of this much-desired rethinking and solidarity.[5] This growing ecological awareness needs to be helped to develop and mature, and find fitting expression in concrete programmes and initiatives,[6] especially climate-resilient pathways for sustainable development, as well as appropriate transformations in economic, social, technological and political decisions and actions. '*The defense of life* and the consequent promotion of health, especially among very poor and developing peoples, will be simultaneously *the measure and the basic criterion of the ecological horizon* at both regional and world level.'[7]

Secondly, Mr President, my Delegation commends the secretariat for the report on efforts made for the management of autism spectrum disorders (A67/17), which among others shows progress made in creating

[4] Pope Benedict XVI, Message to the Director General of FAO on the Occasion of World Food Day 2011, www.vatican.va/holy_father/benedict_xvi/messages/food/documents/hf_ben-xvi_mes_20111017_world-food-day-2011_en.html.

[5] Cf. Pope John Paul II, Address to the Conference on Environment and Health, 24 March 1997; Pope Benedict XVI, Encyclical Letter, *Caritas in Veritate*, §§ 48–50.

[6] Cf. Pope John Paul II's Message for the 1990 World Day of Peace.

[7] Pope John Paul II, Address to the Conference on Environment and Health, 24 March 1997.

awareness, clearing some of the myths surrounding autism, forging partnerships with civil society organizations committed to improving services and setting priorities for national and sub-national actions. It is the sincere hope of my Delegation that the implementation of these guidelines at the national levels, with the continued policy guidance and support from WHO, will help to alleviate the plight of many families, who often have to shoulder alone the emotional and economic burden arising from the demanding responsibility of caring for the children with these disorders. The Holy See wishes to contribute to these efforts with an International Conference organized by the Pontifical Council for Health Care Workers to be held in the Vatican this coming November 20–22, on the topic: 'The Person with Autism Spectrum Disorders: Stir Hope'.

Finally, Mr President, with regard to maternal, infant and young child nutrition, the Holy See Delegation thanks the secretariat for the comprehensive report on this topic (A67/15), which reflects efforts to assure the health and well-being of children worldwide. It is our conviction that organizations with strong links in local communities should be integrated as key partners in the implementation of this global strategy.

My Delegation is also pleased to note that breastfeeding has been included as a Global Target in the Strategy and is proposed as a key indicator for monitoring progress towards achieving the targets. Breastfeeding is a major protection against early child malnutrition and should therefore be protected, promoted as part of primary health care. It should be guaranteed by laws governing workplace practice and there should be acceptance for breastfeeding even in public. Unlike many who openly disparage mothers who choose to breastfeed their children in public, Pope Francis, during a baptism function in the Sistine Chapel last January, encouraged mothers to overcome hesitation of breastfeeding their children when they are hungry.

My sincere wish is that the work of this Assembly will help to reaffirm the centrality of the human person in all our efforts for health promotion.

God bless you all!

Thank you, Mr President.

THE PRIMACY OF THE RIGHT TO HEALTH OVER THE FOCUS ON PROFIT*

Mr Chairman,

The Delegation of the Holy See acknowledges the responsibility of States to ensure that medicines are available, financially affordable, and physically accessible on a basis of non-discrimination to everyone and appreciates the decision of the Human Rights Council to dedicate this annual session of the Social Forum to this urgent issue. With regard to the availability of medicines, we take special note that 'scientific research has multiplied the possibilities of prevention and healing' and 'has allowed for the discovery of therapies that are indicated in caring for a variety of pathologies'. This represents 'a highly valuable commitment that aims to respond to the expectations and the hopes of many ill people across the world'.[1]

On the other hand, from the perspective of the Catholic Church's experience in caring for the sick in more than 5,000 hospitals and 18,000 dispensaries in every region of the world, my Delegation has called attention to the fact that States, in particular, and the international community, as a whole, have not fulfilled their responsibility to make medicines and diagnostic tools affordable and accessible to the poorest and most marginalized populations in low-income countries and even in certain areas and among certain groups of people in high- and middle-income countries. A major stumbling block in providing such access is found in restrictive applications and interpretations of intellectual property rights by many in the pharmaceutical industry.

* Statement delivered at the 2015 Social Forum of the Human Rights Council, 18 February 2015.

[1] Pope Francis, Address to the Participants to the Conference on Oncological Surgery, Vatican City, 12 April 2014, http://w2.vatican.va/content/francesco/en/speeches/2014/april/documents/papa-francesco_20140412_congresso-chirurgia-oncologica.html.

Mr Chairman,

Application of the intellectual property instruments, as it currently prevails in many parts of the world, interferes with the right to health in two ways. First of all, some pharmaceutical companies assert a claim to unrealistic profit and cost recovery margins even though most governments and individual buyers from developing countries do not have the financial capacity to purchase these products at such high cost. This system can lead to total disregard for those who cannot afford the price of certain medical products and allows an imbalanced free trade system, and thus constitutes a virtual monopoly.[2]

The second obstacle relates to research and development (R&D) in order to develop new and more effective medicines and other vital medical products, including diagnostic tools to facilitate early identification and treatment of certain life-threatening illnesses. The system, in fact, does not operate as an incentive to research on so-called 'no market' or 'low return on investment' treatments, such as those for neglected tropical diseases, rare diseases, or even for those illnesses that have higher prevalence among low-income people or in economically deprived regions, including HIV, TB, malaria, hepatitis and Ebola Virus Disease, which most recently has been ravaging coastal West Africa. It is most regrettable, therefore, that, due to an excessive focus on profit, we witness a preference within much of the pharmaceutical industry to orient research toward health issues that have greater market potential in wealthier industrialized countries.

One group particularly deprived of access to medicines is that of children. Many essential medicines have not been developed in appropriate formulations or dosages specific to pediatric use. Thus, families and health care workers often are forced to engage in a 'guessing game' on how best to divide adult-size pills for use with children. This situation can result in the tragic loss of life or continued chronic illness among needy children. While some progress to address this problem has been made in recent years, especially in relation to children living with HIV, many more challenges must be addressed in order to ensure access to medicines that are prepared in 'child-sized', fixed-dose combinations, of acceptable taste and form, and easy to administer to infants and very young children.

2 Cf. www.vatican.va/roman_curia/secretariat_state/documents/rc_seg-st_doc_20010620_wto_en.html.

Mr Chairman,

While fully respecting the right to private intellectual property, the Holy See urges a creative and innovative approach, with full use of the flexibilities allowed under the Trade Related Intellectual Property instruments, so that the right to health for all people without any form of discrimination can be fully guaranteed and implemented. We are convinced, therefore, that concern for the protection of intellectual property rights, while legitimate in itself, must be seen within the wider perspective of promoting the common good, building global solidarity and prioritizing the life and dignity of the world's most vulnerable people, many of whom bear an inequitable burden of both communicable and non-communicable diseases.

THE RURAL URBAN DIVIDE: RE-PRIORITIZE INVESTMENT IN HEALTH CARE*

Mr President,

The Holy See Delegation wishes to note the importance and the timeliness of the theme for the general discussion. The recent Ebola outbreak was a human and public health tragedy, which, among other things, showed that the need to build resilient health systems cannot be over-emphasized, as they are essential for the provision of universal health coverage and for a prompt response to outbreaks of disease.

There is an established awareness that the smooth and effective operation of health systems is critical to achieving both national and international health goals.[1] Unfortunately, most low-income countries, which are still afflicted by infectious disease and epidemics, have very poor health systems that need urgent intervention if they are to respond to the health needs of the whole population.

In fact, many health centers are unable to provide safely the services needed, as they lack staff, medicines, equipment and health information. This is aggravated by the chronic low public expenditure on health. We therefore need to re-prioritize investment in health care for the good of public health. This requires long-term commitment from national governments and international donors to support resilient health systems and to ensure universal coverage of health services, thus strengthening the capacity of national health systems to deliver equitable and quality health care services, and also stepping up their ability to respond to outbreaks and to improve community ownership and participation.

This means short- and long-term investment in a number of key elements of the health system; particularly, improved primary health care, an adequate number of trained health workers, availability of medicine, appropriate infrastructure, update statistical data, sufficient public financing, public–private partnership and scaling up the number of well-equipped health posts and district hospitals. It is also a challenge to donors to make a shift from short-term program funding to long-term comprehensive health service financing.

The recent report on Global evidence on inequities in rural health protection, by the International Labour Office, revealed that more than

* Statement delivered by H.E. Archbishop Zygmunt Zimowski, Head of the Holy See Delegation, at the 68th Assembly of the World Health Organization, 20 May 2015.

[1] Cf. A64/13 Health System Strengthening: Current Trends and Challenges.

half of the population in rural areas worldwide do not have access to basic health care, with many of them at risk of impoverishment or deepened poverty due to out of pocket payment for services.[2] This is clear evidence that, in 2015, we are still a long way from universal coverage. For various reasons, there are strong inequalities in access to health care between the rural and urban areas, with the latter often more advantaged than the former which are most deprived. Embracing the recommendation of the report, my Delegation wishes to note the urgent need to address this rural–urban divide in the post-2015 Development Agenda, bearing in mind that 'human life is always sacred and always has "quality"... There is no human life qualitatively more significant than another, only by virtue of resources, rights, greater social and economic opportunities.'[3] This means addressing the needs of the disadvantaged, marginalized and vulnerable rural populations. As Pope Francis reminds us, 'persons and peoples ask for justice to be put into practice: not only in a legal sense, but also in terms of contribution and distribution. Therefore, development plans and the work of international organizations must take into consideration the wish, so frequent among ordinary people, for respect for fundamental human rights and, in this case, the right *to social protection and health*.'[4]

In relation to this, the Holy See Delegation wishes to emphasize the role of public–private partnership in promoting universal coverage, especially in many low-income countries where primary health care services are accessed by a majority of the population in the rural and hard to reach areas, mainly from private not-for profit health centers and hospitals, managed by the Church and other faith-based institutions. In many countries, the Catholic Church is privileged to be one of the primary partners of the State in providing much needed health care services to populations in remote areas, through its over 110,000 health and social-welfare institutions around the world.[5] It is therefore important to offer

[2] Cf. International Labour Organization, *Global Evidence on Inequities in Rural Health Protection: New Data on Rural Deficits in Health Coverage for 174 Countries*, Geneva: 2015, pp. 6–12.

[3] Pope Francis, Address to participants in the commemorative Conference of the Italian Catholic Physicians' Association on the occasion of its 70th anniversary of foundation, 15 November 2014.

[4] Pope Francis, Address to FAO Nutrition Conference, 21 November 2014, § 2.

[5] The Catholic Church has a total of 116,185 health and social-welfare institutions world-wide, of which 5,034 hospitals, 16,627 dispensaries, 611 leprosaria, 15,518 homes for the aged, chronically ill, invalids and disabled, 9,770 orphanages, 3,896 special centres for social re-education and other social-welfare institutions. Cf.

them the necessary collaboration and support so as to enable them to bring the services close and to render them accessible to poor people in particular.[6] Indeed, in many low-income countries, the contribution of civil society and communities to health services delivery is fundamental.

Finally, Mr President, while remembering the many victims of the Ebola virus in Guinea, Liberia and Sierra Leone, as well as the many dedicated health care workers, from both public and private Church-owned health institutions, who lost their lives while assisting those affected, and aware of the impact of the outbreak on the already fragile health systems of the affected countries, whose capacity to provide essential health services has been greatly compromised, my Delegation welcomes the recommendations of the Resolution on Ebola (EBSS3.R1) and supports its review and approval by this august assembly (WHA68).

May I wish all the distinguished delegates a fruitful discussion and deliberation during this Assembly.

Thank you, Mr President.

Secretaria Status, *Statistical Yearbook of the Church 2013*, Vatican City: Libreria Editrice Vaticana, 2013, pp. 355–65.

[6] Cf. Pope Benedict XVI, Encyclical Letter, *Deus Caritas Est*, § 28(b).

SECURING THE REALIZATION OF THE RIGHT TO HEALTH THROUGH ACCESS TO MORE AFFORDABLE MEDICINES*

Mr President,

Let me start by thanking all the Members of the TRIPs Council for this decision and their constructive engagement. The classification of LDCs is contingent on a number of key human development indicators including levels of poverty, literacy, infant mortality and economic vulnerability. There are currently 48 countries that meet these criteria. Thirty-four of these countries are Members of the WTO and only four countries have graduated out of this category.[1]

LDCs are the world's most disadvantaged countries with the weakest technological capacity. With the recovery of the global economy remaining sluggish and uneven, the LDCs have continued to face a challenging external environment during the last biennium. Slow global economic growth, which translated into weaker international demand for commodities and a consequent decline in their prices, adversely affected the economic growth and export performance of several LDCs. Inflows of foreign direct investment (FDI) reached a record high and remittance inflows continued unabated, but official development assistance (ODA) started to show signs of stagnation. In 2013, the current account and merchandise trade balance of the LDCs as a group was weaker. The current account deficit in these countries continued to increase, reaching a historic peak of US$ 40 billion in 2013, and their merchandise trade deficit also widened, escalating by 29 per cent to US$ 21.1 billion. According to the 2014 market access study undertaken by the WTO, the share in world merchandise trade by LDCs, during 2013, was 1.24 per cent, with a staggering deficit of US$ 60.6 billion. LDCs now find themselves at a critical stage of development, and their socio-economic challenges are massive.

Access to affordable pharmaceutical products is a prerequisite for LDCs to deal with the numerous public health challenges that they face. LDCs are home to some of the world's most vulnerable people and bear considerable health burdens. They face growing burdens of neglected, infectious and chronic non-communicable diseases. UNAIDS reported

* Statement delivered to the World Trade Organization's Trade-Related Intellectual Property Rights Council, 6 November 2015.

[1] Botswana in 1994; Cape Verde in 2007; Maldives in 2011 and Samoa in 2014.

in its 2015 Gap Report that three out of five people living with HIV, and in need of antiretroviral therapy, still do not have access to such life-saving and life-prolonging medicines. Many of these people live in LDCs, and their numbers will increase dramatically if such countries are deprived of the price flexibilities from which they previously have benefited. Our engagement and our work should continue to be inspired by paragraph 7 of the Doha Declaration on the TRIPS Agreement and Public Health in recognition of the gravity of the public health problems afflicting LDCs and their acknowledged right to maximum flexibility to take steps to ensure access to medicines for all. They disproportionately suffer health risks associated with poverty such as malnutrition, unsafe water and poor sanitation.

In his recent address to the Congress of the USA, Pope Francis appealed, 'I know that you share my conviction that much more still needs to be done, and that in times of crisis and economic hardship a spirit of global solidarity must not be lost. At the same time I would encourage you to keep in mind all those people around us who are trapped in a cycle of poverty. They too need to be given hope. The fight against poverty and hunger must be fought constantly and on many fronts, especially in its causes.' The extension of the transition period, therefore, is critical to enable LDCs to be able to import affordable generic medicines as well as to strengthen local production capacity.

As already stated by my Delegation, a time-limited transition period creates an uncertain environment for the producers of affordable medicines, procurement agencies and donors, as well as for LDC governments, all of which rely on the specific pharmaceutical transition period to produce and import affordable medicines. This, in turn, jeopardizes the health situation of the people and communities within LDCs, and results in especially adverse consequences for the scaling up of HIV treatment. However, the decision that the obligations of LDC Members – under paragraphs 8 and 9 of Article 70 – shall be waived with respect to pharmaceutical products until 1 January 2033, represents a significant step forward.

In conclusion,

With deep interest in addressing these pressing public health needs, securing the ability to progressively realize the right to health, and ensuring continuous access to more affordable medicines of assured quality, the Delegation of the Holy See hopes that the consensus reached on the proposal of extension represents an important sign by the World Trade Organization, especially in anticipation of the next Ministerial Conference in Nairobi. The Holy See Delegation remains confident that a sense of common responsibility, as shown in the decision adopted, will bring us all to support such an extension as an accelerated step toward the human and economic progress of LDCs.

Thank you, Mr President.

3 THE RIGHTS OF ELDERLY PERSONS

THE RIGHT TO HEALTH OF OLDER PERSONS*

Madam President,

The Delegation of the Holy See wishes to express sincere interest and concern on this important topic for discussion. The expanding representation of older persons in the general population is well noted in the report, with estimates of persons 60 years of age and older being placed at 760 million at the end of 2010 and projections at one billion by the end of the current decade. This phenomenon is indeed cross-cutting and cross-cultural, with increasing numbers of older people to be found in the developing world. The report mentions the various social, economic, medical and psychological challenges to be confronted in the face of such demographic changes. Moreover, he makes the compelling point 'that the promotion and protection of human rights of older persons is not only in the interest of senior persons, but should also be of concern to everyone, because every person ages.'

The Special Rapporteur encourages a 'paradigm shift' in the current bio-medical view of ageing which too often is seen 'as an abnormal or pathological phenomenon' and thus 'equates advanced age with illness'. With similar reasoning, the World Health Organization promotes 'active ageing' that aims 'to optimize opportunities for health, participation and security amongst older persons in order to enhance their quality of life', through 'continuing participation in social, economic, cultural and civic affairs', rather than basing the criteria for such activity merely on physical stamina or participation in the labour force.

With regard to elderly persons who require special care, the Catholic Church, through its sponsorship of 15,448 homes for the aged, chronically ill and handicapped persons in all parts of the world, sees the growing number of ageing persons as a 'blessing' rather than as a burden on society. It further believes that 'every generation can learn from the experience and wisdom of the generation that preceded it. Indeed the provision of

* Statement delivered at the 18th Session of the Human Rights Council on the Thematic Study on the Realization of the Right to Health of Older Persons, 16 September 2011.

care for the elderly should be considered not so much an act of generosity as the repayment of a debt of gratitude'.[1]

Thus my Delegation would agree with the recommendation made by the Special Rapporteur that 'States should allocate more resources for the provision of geriatric health care in order to ensure that all health care workers, irrespective of specialty or profession, are adequately trained to deal with the particular health issues associated with ageing. They should also be trained on the right to health so that they interact with elderly patients in an appropriate, considerate and non-discriminatory manner.'

We further agree with the premise made in the Report that, in order to fully enjoy the right to health, older persons should be accorded the freedom 'to make independent decisions about one's health, which is to say freedom from State interference'. In addition, older persons are equally entitled to 'the provision of primary health care and social protection which recognizes and takes into account age-related elements', to home-based care and long-term care when and if such services become necessary, and access to 'the underlying determinants of health, such as access to water and sanitation, food and nutrition, education and housing'. We note, moreover, that the Report recognizes the deleterious impact on both the autonomy and dignity of frail elderly persons as well as the special need for protecting such persons against physical and emotional abuse by caregivers or even by family members.

Madam President, a significant number of palliative and hospice care programs are sponsored by the Catholic Church in order to assist elderly and other seriously ill persons to enter in the final stages of life with dignity and with minimal discomfort and pain. My Delegation wishes to take strong exception to a reference in the Report regarding 'issues of patient autonomy in respect of deciding to end life', even though the report writer notes that he 'is not treating such issues in the context of the present report'. We strongly believe that life is a gift that no person has the so-called 'right' to end, that death is the culmination of a natural process and no person, even the elderly or suffering person himself or

[1] Pope Benedict XVI, Address during visit to St Peter's Residence, Home for Older Persons, London Borough of Lambeth, 18 September 2010, www.vatican.va/holy_father/benedict_xvi/speeches/2010/september/documents/hf_ben-xvi_spe_20100918_st-peter-residence_en.html.

herself, is entitled to cause or hasten the natural process of dying through biomedical or any other means.

Thus, in conclusion, the Holy See 'exhorts scientists and doctors to undertake research to prevent and treat illnesses linked to old age without ever ceding to the temptation to have recourse to practices that shorten the life of the aged and sick, practices that would turn out to be, in fact, forms of euthanasia'.[2]

[2] Pope Benedict XVI, Address to the Participants in the 22nd International Congress of the Pontifical Council for Health Pastoral Care, Vatican City, 17 November 2007, www.vatican.va/holy_father/benedict_xvi/speeches/2007/november/documents/hf_ben-xvi_spe_20071117_xxii-operatori-sanitari_en.html.

THE SOCIAL ROLE OF OLDER PERSONS: GIVE SPACE TO THE ELDERLY TO GIVE SPACE TO LIFE*

Mr President,

My Delegation is grateful to the High Commissioner and to the Secretary General for their initiative to conduct a consultation with Member and Observer States, as well as civil society institutions, concerning the human rights situation and needs of older persons in today's society. The major challenges summarized by the High Commissioner, including the impact of the financial crisis on this population, high prevalence of poverty, food insecurity and homelessness among them, poor access to needed social protection and services, as well as health care, and the increasing isolation, institutionalization and discrimination toward our senior members of the community cause my Delegation grave concern. These problems are certainly well known to the Catholic Church, which sponsors 17,223 homes for the elderly, chronically ill and disabled persons, located in every region of the world,[1] and a range of community-based psycho-social and pastoral services that aim to maintain these persons in their own homes and actively engaged in family and social life.

The population of older persons is growing; the number of younger people to assist with family-centred care is decreasing. The demographic trends cited by the High Commissioner detailed this reality. As a response, there seems to be a tendency toward 'warehousing' older persons, thus depriving them of the place reserved for them in communal life. The wider population is thus deprived of the benefit that the lived experience and wisdom of these older members of the human community provide. The 2013 Report refers to the Public Consultation on this topic, and includes the claim that 'a decision had to be made about how long this longevity could be harnessed' and that '[t]he challenge was to "add life to years, not just years to life".' My Delegation certainly believes that ageing persons need to be assured the highest quality of life possible. We also strongly promote the right to life from conception to natural death and therefore unconditionally oppose any attempts to end the lives of older persons simply because they can no longer assume the role of

* Statement delivered at the 24nd Session of the Human Rights Council – Items 2 & 3: *Promotion and Protection of the Human Rights of Older Persons*, 13 September 2013.

1 'Catholic Church Statistics – 2012', Fides News Agency, 21 October 2012.

'contributing members of society' or because health care for this population entails rising costs. The dignity of persons remains always intact.

> [O]ften society, dominated by the logic of efficiency and profit, does not welcome … [longevity] as such; on the contrary, it often rejects it, considering the elderly as unproductive and useless … However, the elderly are a source of wisdom and a great resource. The quality of a society, of a civilization, may also be judged by how it treats its elderly and by the place reserved for them in communal life.[2]

Based on the data assembled and the expert testimonies gathered during the consultation process on this urgent issue, my Delegation would like to propose the following strategies in order to promote and to protect effectively the human rights of older persons:

1. *Affirm and preserve the social role of older persons.* This will necessitate a reflection on and development of more just and equitable policies aimed at redefining the concept of social utility for those who have retired from the system of paid employment but who are quite capable and needed to strengthen the fabric of society through volunteer service and social presence as respected and learned members of families and communities.
2. *Keep older people engaged in decision-making about their lives and their social integration.* Often these decisions are relegated to others even when older persons are competent to decide and discern their best interest. Respect for their human dignity and rights requires that they be engaged in such decisions and that others take over responsibility for determining their care only when there is verified evidence that they are incapable of doing so.
3. *Promote social solidarity in relation to the challenges faced by older persons.* Often limitations in funding are used as an excuse to deprive older persons of the highest quality of life. Provisions for social solidarity must be given priority by governments and by the entire human family.
4. *Guarantee access to health care and to community-based care.* The high cost of hospital and nursing home care can often be avoided by reinforcing primary care and community-based support and by providing financial support to families to maintain older persons in their own homes.

[2] Pope Benedict XVI, during visit to home for the elderly, Rome, 12 November 2012, www.news.va/en/news/to-give-space-to-the-elderly-is-to-give-space-to-1.

Mr President,

By giving due attention to the human rights of older persons and other related human rights the positive and constructive presence of older persons in society is valued. A binding instrument on the promotion and protection of all these rights would reinforce them and would make the international community accountable for their implementation. Contrary to the common stereotypes, older persons are an enrichment of society because of their experience and maturity, and they help us to see human affairs with greater wisdom.

ALLOW THE ELDERLY TO MAKE THEIR CONTRIBUTIONS TO SOCIETY*

Mr President,

The number of elderly persons within the general population is fast increasing, and is foreseen to double within the next decade, tripling by 2050, thus reaching the number of 2 billion older persons. Rightly, the Report of the Independent Expert highlights such information and the actions undertaken by her predecessor and, more recently, by her own efforts to promote and expand respect for the enjoyment of all human rights by older persons.

The significance of this demographic trend too often is calculated only on the basis of projected economic impact. Thus one global economic 'think tank' recently warned that '[t]he unprecedented pace of ageing will have a significant negative effect on economic growth over the next two decades across all regions,' and concluded that '[t]he demographic dividend that drove economic growth in the past will turn into a demographic tax.'[1] My Delegation is concerned, Mr President, that such limited vision could constitute a serious threat to the full enjoyment of rights by older people. Regrettably, today's efficient society tends to marginalize our vulnerable brothers and sisters, including older persons, as if they were only a 'weight' and a 'problem' for society.[2] To the contrary, the increasing number of older people, especially those who remain in good health, also means that they can make their contributions to society for longer periods of time. However, in order to assure that such positive developments will take place, we need to strategize and implement new approaches to structuring society in general, the world of work, health care infrastructure and delivery, the development of technology, intellectual property rights, social protection systems, and intergenerational social relationships.[3]

* Statement delivered at the 27th Session of the Human Rights Council – Item 3: *Report of the Independent Expert on the Promotion and Protection of Human Rights of Older Persons*, 15 September 2014.

1 'Population Aging Will Dampen Population Growth Over the Next Two Decades', Moody's Investor Service, 6 August 2014, p. 1.

2 Cf. Pope Benedict XVI, Address to the Participants in the 22nd International Conference of the Pontifical Council for Health Care Workers, on 'The Pastoral Care of the Elderly Sick People', Vatican City, 17 November 2007.

3 Cf. 'Recommendations on Good Practices for the Promotion of the Rights of the Elderly', Pontifical Council for Health Care Workers, Vatican City.

We noted with much interest, Mr President, the reference made by the Independent Expert to The Madrid International Plan of Action on Ageing that imposed on States the responsibility 'to take measures to address ageing in order to achieve a society for all ages' and to mainstream 'ageing into national and global development agendas'. Recall of this strategy is indeed timely during this period when the international community focuses its energy and attention on developing a Post-2015 Agenda. We feel compelled to raise the question, however, of how well this plan has been achieved to date, especially when we read of increasing numbers of ageing persons being constrained to leave their traditional and familiar homes in high-income countries to seek haven in developing regions of the world where the cost of long-term care is much less expensive. Surely, when we speak of preserving the enjoyment of all human rights, it is essential to respect and preserve as far as possible the bonds of older persons with loved ones and with a familiar environment. This is especially the case when long-term, facility-based care becomes necessary for those who are severely incapacitated or no longer are able to make safe and responsible decisions for themselves.

In her Report, the Independent Expert made explicit reference to the obligations of States, 'deriving from the rights to life and to a dignified death', while maintaining that imprisonment and/or application of the death penalty for older persons should be prohibited.[4] On various occasions, the Holy See has urged States in all parts of the world to abolish the death penalty within their respective jurisdictions. At the same time, the Holy See defends and upholds the right to life for all persons, from the moment of conception until natural death, and thus finds most alarming the increasing utilization of so-called 'assisted suicide', as well as the comments by some government officials that such extreme and harmful actions may warrant additional consideration since they could offer cost-saving benefits during a period of economic crisis.

Mr President, a purely economic and functional approach toward elderly persons risks creating a culture where the weakest and most fragile members of society – the unborn, the poorest, the sick and elderly, the

[4] Report of the Independent Expert on the enjoyment of all human rights by older persons, Rosa Kornfeld-Matte, United Nations General Assembly, UN Doc. A/HRC/27/46, 24 July 2014, para. 35.

seriously handicapped, etc. – are in danger of being 'thrown away' from a system that must be efficient at all costs[5] and thus impoverish society of their wisdom, experience, and enriching presence.

Thank you, Mr President.

[5] Pope Francis, Message to Catholics taking part in annual Day for Life in Britain and Ireland, 28 July 2013.

THE QUALITY OF OUR SOCIETIES IS MEASURED BY THE ATTENTION TO THE ELDERLY*

Mr President,

My Delegation would like to thank the Independent Expert for her Report on the enjoyment of all human rights by older persons.

Nowadays the world is ageing at a faster rate as is witnessed by the 900 million people over the age of 60. Forecasts predict that, at the increased rate of 3.26 per cent per year, the number of persons over 60 in the world will reach 1.4 billion by 2030 and 2.1 billion by 2050.[1] The so-called 'population ageing' phenomenon presents for the international community not only a challenge but an opportunity: to recognize the improvements made in health care access and quality of life and the contribution that older persons can make in our society.

In a rapidly changing social and technological environment, older persons are often set aside, discriminated against or even abandoned due to the current *throw-away culture* which considers them as 'persons who do not produce anymore'. These persons are becoming victimized through increased forms of violence and exploitation. We should bear in mind, as Pope Francis warns, that 'the elder is not an alien. We are that elder: in the near or far future, but inevitably, even if we don't think it. And if we don't learn how to treat the elder better, that is how we will be treated.'[2] There is a duty to care for the elderly: 'The quality of a society ... of a civilization, is also judged by how it treats elderly people and by the place it gives them in community life.'[3] 'Attention to the elderly makes the difference in a civilization ... This civilization will move forward if it knows how to respect wisdom, the wisdom of the elderly. In a civilization in which there is no room for the elderly or where they are thrown away because they create problems, this society carries with it the virus of death.'[4]

* Statement delivered at the 30th Session of the Human Rights Council – Item 3: *Independent Expert on the Rights of Older Persons*, 16 September 2015.

[1] Department of Economic and Social Affairs, Population Division, World Population Prospects: The 2015 Revision, https://esa.un.org/unpd/wpp/publications/files/key_findings_wpp_2015.pdf.

[2] Pope Francis, General Audience, Saint Peter's Square, 4 March 2015, Catechesis on the Family – Grandparents.

[3] Ibid. [4] Ibid.

It must be remembered that the caring for older persons is the primary responsibility of the family itself. This crucial role should not be undermined, discarded or taken for granted. Indeed, the State and its agencies cannot replace the family, but only have a subsidiary role. Sons and daughters, nephews and nieces and grandchildren are the first ones who must care for their older relatives.

Today, more than ever, the family is under stress to care for their elderly members. This is due, in large part, to the transformation of work relationships, the reduction of the size of families, the increased mobility and distance between relatives and the desire of older persons to live separately from their sons and daughters. For this reason, the family network must be seen as the main recipient of aid and public action so that it can be helped to fulfill its duties in caring for the elderly.

As often stated during the Madrid process,[5] a change of perspective is needed. Older persons should not be seen as passive actors, mere recipients of care, but active and full members of society. Their positive contributions to society are many: they are guardians of culture and knowledge, educators, volunteers. They also play a pivotal role in family life in caring for their children and grandchildren.

Our Delegation would like to recall the fact that the elderly are often mistreated, discarded with an attitude of abandonment as if their dignity and value were determined by their productivity or state of health. Such an attitude is the result of a utilitarian mentality which places economic interests before the dignity of the human person. Rather, the inherent value of the human person requires us to respect life in all its stages, even in its most vulnerable moments, until natural death.

Mr President,

The international community is called 'to patiently build a more diverse, more welcoming, more humane, more inclusive society that does not need to discard those who are weak in body and mind. On the contrary we need a society which measures its success on how the weak are cared for.'[6]

Thank you, Mr President.

5 UN, Open-ended Working Group on Ageing and the Independent Expert on Older Persons.

6 Meeting of the Pope with the elderly, Address of Pope Francis, Saint Peter's Square, 28 September 2014.

4 PROMOTING THE RIGHTS OF INDIGENOUS PEOPLES

THE NEED TO DIRECTLY INCLUDE INDIGENOUS PEOPLES IN THE DECISION-MAKING PROCESSES*

Mr President,

The social, personal and spiritual needs of the world's more than 370 million indigenous peoples in some 90 countries, in all regions of the world,[1] have been a long-standing concern of the Holy See.

Shortly, the World Conference on Indigenous Peoples will be held by the United Nations 'to share perspectives and best practices on the realization of the rights of indigenous peoples and to pursue the objectives of the United Nations Declaration on the Rights of Indigenous Peoples (UNDRIP)'.[2] This meeting represents another fundamental step to foster greater interest and respect for these communities and offers a unique opportunity to reaffirm the Declaration on the Rights of Indigenous Peoples, which sets the minimum standards for their survival, dignity and well-being and promotes their rights, inter alia, to self-determination; to land, territories and resources; and to economic, social and cultural development.

As we enter the Third International Decade of the World's Indigenous Peoples, the Holy See suggests that all eventual initiatives should be inspired and guided by the principle of respect for their identity and culture, including specific traditions, religious beliefs, and ability to decide their own development in cooperation with national governments.

As noted by the Special Rapporteur and in other United Nations documents, the human rights and fundamental freedoms of indigenous peoples regrettably continue to be violated, including through systemic discrimination and exclusion from political and economic power; lack of adequate access to justice; over-representation among the poorest,

* Statement delivered at the 27th Session of the Human Rights Council – Item 3: *General Debate*, 17 September 2014.

1 www.unric.org/en/indigenous-people/27307-the-sami-of-northern-europe–one-people-four-countries.

2 UN Doc. A/RES/65/198, Resolution adopted by the General Assembly on 21 December 2010 available at: http://daccess-dds-ny.un.org/doc/UNDOC/GEN/N10/524/42/PDF/N1052442.pdf?OpenElement.

the illiterate and the destitute; displacement by wars and environmental disasters;[3] and 'harassment, persecution, reprisals against, stigmatization and killings of indigenous human rights defenders'.[4] As a result, comprehensive development is delayed, if not denied.

A specific case regards the interaction between industrial and transnational companies and native populations. The Special Rapporteur refers, for example, to negative, even devastating, consequences for indigenous peoples that have been caused by the extractive industries. These corporations must overcome a specific focus on short-term economic advantage and adopt models of authentic development which do not violate the rights of indigenous peoples and encourage a responsible use of the environment.

Deserving attention, moreover, is the problem of defining and protecting folklore from becoming a commodity that can be used by anyone without consideration of the interests and rights of the communities within which they originated. Intellectual property and labour laws have created a body of legal and social requirements aimed at defending the rights of individual authors, composers and performers. Until now, however, the negotiations have not sufficiently provided safeguards to protect the rights deriving from folklore creations.

Mr President, it is expedient for this Council and other United Nations bodies to establish, as an indicator of respect for the rights of indigenous peoples, their direct inclusion in the decision-making processes related to the management of natural resources in their own territories. The Holy See Delegation urges the elimination of every attempt to marginalize indigenous peoples. This means, first of all, respecting their territories and the pacts made with them; likewise, efforts must be made to satisfy their legitimate social, health and cultural requirements. Finally, we cannot overlook the need for reconciliation between the indigenous peoples and the societies in which they are living.[5]

Thank you, Mr President.

[3] UN DESA, 'State of the World's Indigenous Peoples, 2009.

[4] UN Doc. A/HRC/23/32.

[5] Pope John Paul II, *Ecclesia in America*, § 64, www.vatican.va/holy_father/john_paul_ii/apost_exhortations/documents/hf_jp-ii_exh_22011999_ecclesia-in-america_en.html.

THE SYSTEMATIC VIOLATIONS OF INDIGENOUS PEOPLES' HUMAN RIGHTS AND THEIR TRADITIONAL KNOWLEDGE AND FOLKLORE'*

Mr President,

In recent years, the international community has advanced in its consideration and activity concerning issues and human rights of indigenous peoples, most especially in the landmark adoption of the UN Declaration on the Rights of Indigenous Peoples in 2007. A deep chasm, however, still divides the lived reality of many indigenous populations from the commitments, policies and legislative actions aiming to improve their lives. In many parts of the world, much still needs to be done to safeguard their human rights and fundamental freedoms. Greater efforts are still to be made – at the international, national and local levels – in setting development policies that truly involve indigenous peoples and respect their specific identity and cultures.

The World Conference on Indigenous Peoples Outcome Document presents the stepping stones that would bring the work of the international community on indigenous peoples' rights to the next level.[1] The commitments promote the full integration of indigenous peoples in today's society. Particularly beneficial is the initiative to consult and cooperate in good faith with indigenous peoples, through their own representatives, in order to obtain their free, prior and informed consent before adopting and implementing legislative or administrative measures that may affect them. The Outcome Document focuses on the human rights of indigenous women and addresses the problem of violence against women and youth. It highlights the grave challenges they face, from the difficulty in sustaining indigenous languages to preserving traditional knowledge and ensuring sustainable livelihood.

As noted by the Special Rapporteur, and other United Nations documents, the situation of indigenous peoples' human rights and their ongoing resistance against intrusions into their lands by extractive industries and land grabbers has improved. However, in some parts of the world, systematic violations of their human rights continue, ranging from

* Statement delivered at the 30th Session of the Human Rights Council: Annual Half-Day Panel Discussion on the Rights of Indigenous Peoples, 22 September 2015.

1 UN Doc. A/RES/65/198, Resolution adopted by the General Assembly on 21 December 2010, http://daccess-dds-ny.un.org/doc/UNDOC/GEN/N10/524/42/PDF/N1052442.pdf?OpenElement.

arbitrary arrests, torture and extrajudicial killings, to the labeling of indigenous organizations or naming leaders, activists and organizations as 'terrorists'. Their lack of access to basic social services and the violation of their cultural rights remain appalling. Violence against indigenous women is still pervasive in many countries. Many indigenous children are not able to finish primary school and indigenous women's access to health care services remains limited. All these issues will undercut the achievement of the Sustainable Development Goals which will soon be adopted.

The increasing arrival of foreign investments into many countries further exacerbates the loss of lands and resources of indigenous peoples and leads to significant environmental destruction of their territories. Exploitation by the mining industry and the increase of foreign investments which amount to more than 2,700 state-to-state bilateral investment treaties (BITs) continue to deteriorate the human rights of indigenous peoples. This only hinders their right and capacity to pursue their own economic, social and cultural development which is still very much challenged.[2]

Mr President,

At stake are the human rights of native populations that have developed the traditional knowledge and the expressions of folklore or who occupy the territories from which the genetic material comes, as well as the right of the countries to the resources associated with biological diversity; the right of the inventor or discoverer to remuneration for any intellectual value that they may have added, the possible rights and interests of companies and society's right to or interest in the stimulation of inventive activity and the development of science and the arts must be duly protected. Finally, the more general right of all mankind to be assured that the products of scientific progress will serve everyone equally and not only the sectors with the greatest acquisitive potential should also be guaranteed.[3] The ethical challenge to be met therefore is

[2] Statement of the UN Special Rapporteur on the Rights of Indigenous Peoples – see more at www.ohchr.org/EN/NewsEvents/Pages/DisplayNews.aspx?NewsID=16300&LangID=E#sthash.2e0djWqK.dpuf.

[3] The latter point is the central theme of the controversy surrounding access to drugs and their connection with intellectual property, a matter that is not directly related to the purpose of the Intergovernmental Committee on Genetic Resources, Traditional Knowledge and Folklore.

that of reconciling the various rights and interests in such a way that the legitimate economic interest does not compromise higher values such as the social function of inventions and knowledge and the human rights of the peoples from which the knowledge and resources originate.

The Holy See advocates a unitary approach of law that is structured on the basis of fundamental human rights. According to that vision, the value of justice in any set of enactments has to be measured by the possibility of perpetuating it and reconciling it with such human rights. In this way, the correct determination of the scope of ownership rights has to be made in relation to the principle of justice and the common good, which includes the universal destination and purpose of the goods of creation.

Thank you, Mr President.

EXPLANATORY NOTES

Agenda for Humanitarian Action Under General Objective 4 (2003)

Adopted at the 28th International Conference of the Red Cross and Red Crescent, the Agenda for Humanitarian Action focuses on the main theme and overall goal of the International Conference, namely Protecting Human Dignity, and sets out action-oriented goals and measures that States and the components of the International Red Cross and Red Crescent Movement can undertake to protect human dignity (https://www.icrc.org/eng/resources/documents/resolution/28-international-conference-resolution-1-2003.htm).

Alma Ata Declaration on Primary Health Care

The Alma Ata Declaration of 1978 emerged as a major milestone of the twentieth century in the field of public health, and it identified primary health care as the key to the attainment of the goal of Health for All. It raised urgent concerns about the existing gross inequality in the health status of the people, particularly between developed and developing countries. The people have a right and duty to participate individually and collectively in the planning and implementation of their health care (www.who.int/social_determinants/tools/multimedia/alma_ata/en/).

European Convention on Human Rights (1950)

On 4 November 1950, the Council of Europe agreed to the European Convention for the Protection of Human Rights and Fundamental Freedoms, the substantive provisions of which were based on a draft of what is now the International Covenant on Civil and Political Rights. Over the years, the enforcement mechanisms created by the convention have developed a considerable body of case law on questions regulated by the convention, which the States Parties typically have honoured and respected. In some European States, the provisions of the convention are deemed to be part of domestic constitutional or statutory law. Where that is not the case, the States Parties have taken other measures to make their domestic laws conform with their obligations under the convention (www.britannica.com/event/European-Convention-on-Human-Rights-Europe-1950).

Forum on Universal Health Coverage Held in Mexico City (2012)

This intergovernmental Forum played a key role in advancing global support for Universal Health coverage by issuing the Mexico City Political Declaration on Universal Health Coverage adopted in April 2012. Subsequently, on 12 December 2012, the United Nations General Assembly unanimously adopted a Resolution that emphasized health as an essential element of international development and urged governments to move towards providing all people with access to affordable, quality health care services (www.who.int/universal_health_coverage/un_resolution/en/index.html).

Geneva Conventions and their Additional Protocols

The Geneva Conventions and their Additional Protocols are at the core of international humanitarian law, the body of international law that regulates the conduct of armed conflict and seeks to limit its effects. They specifically protect people who are not taking part in the hostilities (civilians, health workers and aid workers) and those who are no longer participating in the hostilities, such as wounded, sick and shipwrecked soldiers and prisoners of war. The Conventions and their Protocols call for measures to be taken to prevent or put an end to all breaches. They contain stringent rules to deal with what are known as 'grave breaches'. Those responsible for grave breaches must be sought, tried or extradited, whatever nationality they may hold (https://www.icrc.org/eng/war-and-law/treaties-customary-law/geneva-conventions/overview-geneva-conventions.htm).

ICRC – International Committee of the Red Cross

The ICRC's exclusively humanitarian mission is to protect the lives and dignity of victims of armed conflict and other situations of violence and to provide them with assistance. It directs and coordinates the Red Cross and Red Crescent Movement's international relief activities during armed conflicts. Established in 1863, it is at the origin of the Movement (https://www.icrc.org/eng/who-we-are/movement/overview-the-movement.htm).

MDR TB

Multidrug-resistant TB (MDR TB) is TB that does not respond to at least isoniazid and rifampicin, the two most powerful anti-TB drugs. The reasons why multidrug resistance continues to emerge and spread are mismanagement of TB treatment and person-to-person transmission. Treatment options are limited and expensive, recommended medicines are not always available, and patients experience many adverse effects from the drugs (www.who.int/features/qa/79/en/).

MIPAA – Madrid International Plan of Action on Ageing

The Madrid International Plan of Action on Ageing was adopted in 2002 in Madrid, Spain. The Plan, commonly known as MIPAA, is a comprehensive list of commitments for United Nations Member States and focuses on three priority directions: older persons and development; advancing health and well-being into old age; and ensuring enabling and supportive environments (www.unece.org/population/mipaa.html).

Memorandum of Understanding and the Agreement on Operational Arrangements between the Palestinian Red Crescent Society and Magen David Adom

Magen David Adom in Israel (MDA) and the Palestine Red Crescent Society (PRCS), in an effort to facilitate the adoption of the 3rd Protocol Additional to the Geneva Conventions of 1949 and the entrance of both societies in the Red Cross and Red Crescent Movement, committed to operating in accordance with international humanitarian law and with the Statutes, Rules, and fundamental Principles of the International Red Cross and Red Crescent Movement, and signed this Memorandum of Understanding and Agreement in Geneva, on 28 November 2005 (https://www.icrc.org/eng/assets/files/red-cross-crescent-movement/31st-international-conference/31-int-conference-mou-mda-prcs-en.pdf).

Millennium Development Goals (MDGs)

The Millennium Development Goals were adopted at the UN Millennium Summit in New York in September 2000. The MDGs are eight time-bound international targets – that were committed to being achieved by 2015 – for addressing extreme poverty in its many dimensions such as income poverty, hunger, disease, lack of adequate shelter and exclusion, while promoting gender equality, education and environmental sustainability (www.unmillenniumproject.org/goals/).

Pontifical Council on Health Care

On 11 February 1985, John Paul II instituted the Pontifical Commission for the Pastoral Assistance to Health Care Workers, which, in 1988 became the Pontifical Council for the Pastoral Assistance to Health Care Workers. Its tasks are: to stimulate and promote the work of formation, study and action carried out by the diverse Catholic International Organizations (CIOs) in the health care field as well as other groups and associations which work in this sector, on different levels and in different ways and to coordinate the activities of different Vatican offices as they relate to the health care sector and its problems (www.vatican.va/roman_curia/pontifical_councils/hlthwork/documents/rc_pc_hlthwork_pro_20051996_en.html). As of 17 August 2016, this Pontifical Council was incorporated in the Dicastery for Promoting Integral Human Development.

RCRC – The Red Cross and Red Crescent Movement

The International Red Cross and Red Crescent Movement is the largest humanitarian network in the world. Its mission is to alleviate human suffering, protect life and health, and uphold human dignity especially during armed conflicts and other emergencies. It is present in every country and supported by millions of volunteers. The 'Movement' is made up of the following components: the International Committee of the Red Cross, the National Red Cross and Red Crescent Societies and the International Federation of Red Cross and Red Crescent Societies (https://www.icrc.org/en/who-we-are/movement).

Sendai's World Conference on Disaster Risk Reduction

The Third UN World Conference on Disaster Risk Reduction took place in Sendai, Japan on 14–18 March 2015. It adopted a post-2015 framework for disaster risk reduction, the so-called Sendai Framework, the first major agreement of the Post-2015 development agenda (www.wcdrr.org/conference).

Sustainable Development Goals (SDGs)

The Sustainable Development Goals are a universal set of goals, targets and indicators that UN Member States will be expected to use to frame their agendas and political policies over the next 15 years. They were adopted at the United Nations Sustainable Development Summit in September 2015 in New York, where world leaders adopted the 2030 Agenda for Sustainable Development: this Agenda includes a set of 17 SDGs to end poverty, fight inequality and injustice, and tackle climate change by 2030. The Sustainable Development Goals build on the Millennium Development Goals. While the MDGs, in theory, applied to all countries, in reality they were considered targets for poor countries to achieve, with finance from wealthy states. Conversely, every country will be expected to work towards achieving the SDGs (https://sustainabledevelopment.un.org/sdgs).

UNAIDS – Joint United Nations Programme on HIV/AIDS

Established in 1996 and based in Geneva, UNAIDS is the Joint United Nations Program on HIV/AIDS that leads and inspires the world in achieving universal access to HIV prevention, treatment, care and support. It is a joint venture of the United Nations family which brings together the efforts and resources of 11 UN system organizations to unite the world against AIDS: UNHCR (United Nations High Commissioner for Refugees), UNICEF (United Nations Children's Fund), World Bank, UNESCO (United Nations Educational, Scientific and Cultural Organization), UN Women (United Nations Entity for Gender Equality and the Empowerment of Women), UNDP (United Nations Development Programme), UNFPA (United Nations Populations Fund), WHO (World Health Organization), World Food Programme, UNODC (United Nations Office on Drugs and Crime), ILO (International Labour Organization) (www.unaids.org/en/).

UNDRIP – United Nations Declaration on the Rights of Indigenous Peoples

The United Nations Declaration on the Rights of Indigenous Peoples was adopted by the General Assembly on 13 September 2007. The Declaration establishes a universal framework of minimum standards for the survival, dignity, well-being and rights of the world's indigenous peoples.

The Declaration addresses both individual and collective rights; cultural rights and identity; rights to education, health, employment, language and others. It outlaws discrimination against indigenous peoples and promotes their full and effective participation in all matters that concern them. It also ensures their right to remain distinct and to pursue their own priorities in economic, social and cultural development (www.ohchr.org/EN/Issues/IPeoples/Pages/Declaration.aspx).

World Conference on Indigenous Peoples

The first World Conference on Indigenous Peoples, a high-level plenary meeting of the General Assembly, was held on 22–23 September 2014 in New York City (http://wcip2014.org/).

WHA – World Health Assembly

The World Health Assembly is the supreme decision-making body for the World Health Organization. It generally meets in Geneva in May each year, and is attended by Delegations from all 194 Member States. Its main function is to determine the policies of the Organization (www.who.int/governance/en/).

World Health Organization

Founded in 1948, WHO's primary role is to direct and coordinate international health within the United Nations system. WHO's main areas of work are health systems, promoting health through the life-course, non-communicable and communicable diseases, corporate services, and preparedness, surveillance and response (www.who.int/en/).

World Health Organization Executive Board

The Executive Board is composed of 34 individuals technically qualified in the field of health, each one designated by a Member State elected to do so by the World Health Assembly. Member States are elected for three-year terms. The Board meets at least twice a year and its main functions are to give effect to the decisions and policies of the Health Assembly, to advise it and generally to facilitate its work (www.who.int/governance/eb/en/).

World Health Organization Global Action Plan for the Control of Non-Communicable Diseases 2013–2020

Endorsed at the 66th Session of the World Health Assembly, the World Health Organization Global Action Plan for the Prevention and Control of NCDs 2013–2020 offers a paradigm shift by providing a road map and a menu of policy options for Member States, the World Health Organization, other UN organizations and intergovernmental organizations, NGOs and the private sector, which, when implemented collectively between 2013 and 2020, will attain nine voluntary global targets, including that of a 25 per cent relative reduction in premature mortality from NCDs by 2025 (www.who.int/nmh/events/ncd_action_plan/en/).

XDR TB

An abbreviation for extensively drug-resistant tuberculosis (TB), XDR TB is a form of TB which is resistant to at least four of the core anti-TB drugs. XDR TB patients can be cured, but with the current drugs available, the likelihood of success is much smaller than in patients with ordinary TB or even MDR TB. Cure depends on the extent of the drug resistance, the severity of the disease and whether the patient's immune system is compromised (www.who.int/tb/challenges/xdr/faqs/en/).

VI

People on the Move: The Challenge of the Twenty-first Century

Introduction

People on the move constitute an age-old experience and are important players in the unfolding of history.[1] Ours has been called the 'age of migration'.[2] With some 250 million people living and working in a country different from the one where they were born and with more than 700 million internal migrants, one in every seven persons in the world is a migrant.[3] Among these migrants are an unprecedented number of unaccompanied children and over 50 million forcibly displaced persons,[4] the highest number since the Second World War. There is little doubt that migration is one of the most powerful forces shaping the economic, social, political and cultural life in today's world.

Human mobility is indeed increasingly woven into the fabric of our society. However, we must never forget that, behind the statistics, we meet people with real stories of escape from persecution and systematic violation of their human rights, of search for a better quality of life, of hope of freedom from traffickers of human flesh, of resettlement made necessary by advancing desertification and climate changes forcing people to move elsewhere. New categories of forcibly displaced people are not yet protected by specific treaties and thus present a new challenge to the international community's sense of solidarity. Globalization is both a cause and a result of human mobility extending in many directions: South to North, South to South, and North to South. Projections for the future provide evidence that the phenomenon of human mobility will remain a critical social concern.

1 Michael H. Fisher, *Migration: A World History*, New York: Oxford University Press, 2014, p. 125: 'Migrations have deeply affected our identities, and museums, archives, and monuments throughout much of the world have attempted to reconstruct and commemorate them … These efforts counter-act anti-immigration sentiments and also preserve a sense of how our societies were constituted. Such efforts resonate with our widespread fascination with where we came from, because we are all migrants and migration history is the core of world history.'

2 Stephen Castles, Hein De Haas and Mark J. Miller, *The Age of Migration: International Population Movements in the Modern World*, New York: Palgrave Macmillan, 2014, p. 331: 'the inescapable central trends, the increasing ethnic and cultural diversity of most countries, the emergence of transnational networks which link emigration and immigration societies, and the growth of cultural interchange. The age of migration may yet be a period of greater unity in tackling the pressing problems that beset our small planet.'

3 http://siteresources.worldbank.org/INTPROSPECTS/Resources/334934-1288990760745/MigrationandDevelopmentBrief22.pdf.

4 www.unhcr.org/53a155bc6.html.

The present flow and diversity in the movements of people finds a parallel in the vast rearrangement of population distribution at the end of the Second World War that prompted the establishment of the main international structures and juridical provisions regarding population mobility. At that time, because of its international standing and network for social assistance, the Holy See was among 15 States invited by the UN Economic and Social Council, through Resolution 393B (XIII), to serve as members of an Advisory Committee on Refugees, a major human and political problem at the time. In 1951, when the UN General Assembly decided to convene a conference of plenipotentiaries with the task 'to consider the Draft Convention Relating to the Status of Refugees and the Draft Protocol Relating to the Status of Stateless Persons', an invitation to participate was extended to some States that were not members of the United Nations, including the Holy See, which, in fact, participated with full rights. The Conference produced one of the first conventions that the Holy See signed and subsequently ratified, the 1951 Convention Relating to the Status of Refugees and its subsequent 1967 Protocol.[5] This also marked the first occasion on which the United Nations called upon the Holy See to take a full part in one of its organizations.[6] From the post-war period, a gradual ascendancy of migrations as a policy issue for the international community has occurred. Migrations not only have taken greater visibility but also have undergone a change in perception: from mostly a function of the economy and a partial remedy of a demographic deficit to a social partnership for development with greater attention paid to the person of the migrant and to his/her inherent rights.[7]

The interventions delivered by the Mission of the Holy See in this regard aimed at supporting the process of a greater humanization of the global movement of people. They highlight the evidence that in

[5] www.unhcr.org/3b66c2aa10.html.

[6] Henry de Riedmatten, 'The Part Played by the Holy See in International Organizations', *Concilium* 8/6 (October 1970): 74–93.

[7] United Nations Development Programme, *Human Development Report, 2009. Overcoming Barriers: Human Mobility and Development*, New York: UNDP, 2009; Irena Omelaniuk, *Global Perspectives on Migration and Development: GFMD Puerto Vallarta and Beyond*, New York: Springer, 2012; Jospeh Chamie and Luca Dall'Oglio (eds), *International Migration and Development. Continuing the Dialogue: Legal and Policy Perspectives*, New York: Center for Migration Studies and International Organization for Migration, 2008; Stephen Castles and Raul Delgado Wise (eds), *Migration and Development: Perspectives from the South*, Geneva: International Organization for Migration, 2008.

the medium and long terms, migration benefits the countries of origin, arrival, and the migrants themselves.[8] The international community is reminded of the distinct causes that prompt people to leave their homes and of the consequent duty to respond accordingly. Distinctions are drawn concerning the moral obligations,[9] degrees of urgency and required policy responses to receive people seeking asylum because their lives are at serious risk and are targeted for destruction,[10] persons fleeing generalized violence, persons driven by climate changes from their native environments[11] and people seeking to improve their economic conditions.[12]

As a first step, recognition of the positive contribution of migration is proposed. In time, human talent and creativity prevail over emergency needs. Thus, the contradiction experienced by receiving countries where immigrants are welcome for their contribution to the economy but rejected because of their diversity will have to be confronted and resolved.[13] In this process, the social doctrine of the Church, presented on various occasions at the intergovernmental bodies dedicated to human mobility, is a valid contribution.[14] Debate on its implications is encouraged in order to add a particularly relevant dimension that always places the human person at the centre of concerns. Church teaching points out also that individual and national identity are not fossilized but in a continuous evolution on a 'two-way street'. This process results from the innovations and the new insights and cultural expressions that newcomers contribute and from the acceptance by the immigrants of the core

[8] Cf. the following interventions: 'Forcibly displaced persons and local integration' (2012); 'The protection of migrant workers and persons displaced by climate change and natural disasters' (2014).

[9] Cf. the following interventions: 'Make the responsibility to protect comprehensive' (2006); 'Enlarge the concept of protection of the sake of the common good' (2008); '50 million forcibly displaced persons have a right to recover their freedom and dignity' (2013).

[10] Cf. 'Why do we fail to take charge of refugees and displaced people?' (2009); 'Reducing the number of asylum-seekers' (2010); 'Migrants and refugees are not pawns on the chessboard of humanity: the admirable response of countries hosting Syrian refugees' (2013).

[11] Cf. 'Extend the protection to the people uprooted by desertification, famine, and climate change' (2008).

[12] Cf. 'The priority of persons over the economy' (2007).

[13] For a case of contradiction between acceptance and rejection of immigrants and the related debate, see Jeb Bush and Clint Bollick, *Immigration Wars: Forging an American Solution*, New York: Threshold Editions, 2013.

[14] Cf., for instance, 'Contribution to development and migrants' human rights' (2013).

values of their host society so that peaceful coexistence becomes possible. Relying on her millennial experience and the development of her social doctrine, the Holy See could raise international attention to a series of crucial problems directly linked to the first, often emergency, phases of the migration journey.[15] These include the detention of asylum seekers and unaccompanied minors,[16] the plight of refugees in protracted situations,[17] the right to return to one's home and property,[18] integration and participation in the life of society,[19] the particular situation of immigrants without proper documentation,[20] the frequently occurring phenomenon of discrimination against migrants.[21] Through the leverage of moral discourse, the diplomatic efforts of the Holy See have promoted the human rights both of host populations and of all people on the move, it created space for a more positive public opinion and prioritized greater acceptance of the presence of needy strangers.

On 5 December 2011, in order to strengthen its role as the voice of conscience and to facilitate more effective participation, the Holy See opted to become a Member State of the International Organization for Migrations (IOM) at the 100th Session of its Council.[22] The main reasons that prompted such a decision were, in fact, similar to those that motivate all Holy See engagement related to issues of human mobility: affirming the ethical dimension of population movements; offering its collaboration and partnership to the international services dedicated to

[15] On the social doctrine of the Catholic Church and migration, see: Silvano M. Tomasi, 'Human Rights as a Framework for Advocacy on Behalf of the Displaced: The Approach of the Catholic Church', in David Hollenbach, SJ (ed.), *Driven from Home: Protecting the Rights of Forced Migrants*, Washington, DC: Georgetown University Press, 2010. For an exhaustive treatment of the historical, pastoral, canonical and theological aspects of human mobility in the Catholic tradition, see: Graziano Battistella (ed.), *Migrazioni: Dizionario socio-pastorale*, Milan: Cisinello Balsamo, 2010.

[16] Cf. 'The scourge of trafficked children and their sexual exploitation' (2013); 'Children exodus: mechanism for family reunification' (2014).

[17] Cf. 'Solidarity for the suffering of refugees in Acholiland (Uganda)' (2006).

[18] Cf. 'Forcibly displaced persons – Iraq and neighboring countries: A call for coordinated help' (2007).

[19] Cf. 'Forcibly displaced persons and local integration' (2012).

[20] Cf. 'Prosecute the multi-billion-dollar industry of trafficking and rehabilitate the victims' (2004).

[21] Roger Zegers de Beijl (ed.), *Documenting Discrimination against Migrant Workers in the Labour Market: A Comparative Study of Four European Countries*, Geneva: International Labour Office, 2000; Leila Simona Talani (ed.), *Globalization, Migration, and the Future of Europe: Insiders and Outsiders*, London: Routledge, 2012.

[22] Cf. 'The Holy See becomes a member of the International Organization for Migration: The priority of human dignity and the right to life' (2011).

uprooted people; and providing comprehensive assistance on the basis of need, without distinction of race, colour or religious belief, or lack of it.

The statements by the Holy See, delivered at the UNHCR and the IOM, open wide horizons of reflection for action. Some principles serve as a foundation for these statements, including, for example, the conviction that we are one human family before the divisions of borders and hence have a moral responsibility to practise solidarity and to prevent the deaths of thousands attempting to escape conflicts and persecution.[23] Another contribution deals with the need for global governance of population movements, with a special attention to the most vulnerable groups.

The advocacy role of the Holy See extends to all human rights and duties specifically highlighted according to particular circumstances. Concerns and trends regarding uprooted people are identified and addressed within the framework of the social doctrine of the Church. A structural element of modernity, population movements impact societies in a deep way and become a catalyst of change. When migrants and asylum seekers arrive, they are not just potential workers, but persons with social, cultural and religious convictions. An enlightened management of the phenomenon of human mobility with its social, economic, political, cultural and religious implications calls for a far-sighted international policy of collaboration. In this regard, in the process through which States have finalized the goals of the Post-2015 Development Agenda, the Holy See has taken a clear position and supported an adequate inclusion of migration, the oldest action against poverty. This was done with the aim to reduce migration costs and to improve the human rights of migrants.[24] In fact, States and international organizations, together with civil society, have the responsibility to devise and implement migration policies, strategies, partnerships and agreements that would respect the

[23] *Fatal Journeys: Tracking Lives Lost during Migration*, Geneva: ILO, 2014. According to this report, it is estimated that since the year 2000 at least 40,000 migrants have died along migratory routes around the world while fleeing conflict, political instability and poverty. Many are dying on the journey to Europe, and from Central America to the United States of America through Mexico; drowning on their way from South Asia to Australia; drowning in the Red Sea and the Gulf of Aden trying to reach the Middle East from the Horn of Africa; and dying while attempting to cross the Sahara Desert to North Africa. Available at http://publications.iom.int/bookstore/free/FatalJourneys_CountingtheUncounted.pdf.

[24] Cf. the following statements: 'Forcibly displaced persons and local integration' (2012); 'Contribution to development and migrants' human rights' (2013); 'Persons left behind in the migration process' (2014); 'The protection of migrant workers and persons displaced by climate change and natural disasters' (2014).

personal dignity of the migrants. New norms may be required, but above all a new attitude of acceptance is needed that allows people on the move to become partners in building a common future in peaceful and constructive coexistence.[25] As Pope Francis urged in his message for the 101st World Day of Migrants and Refugees, 'it is necessary to respond to the globalization of migration with the globalization of charity and co-operation, in such a way as to make the conditions of migrants more humane.'[26] This is, in fact, the message voiced by the Holy See in the halls of the international organizations.

List of Statements

1 The Ethical Responsibility to Welcome Refugees

- PROVIDE SECURITY FOR THE CIVILIAN POPULATION, 55th Session of the Executive Committee of the Program of the United Nations High Commissioner for Refugees (4–8 October 2004)
- AVOID THE STIGMATIZATION AS CRIMINALS OF ASYLUM SEEKERS AND REFUGEES, 56th Session of the Executive Committee of UNHCR (5 October 2005)
- SOLIDARITY FOR THE SUFFERING OF REFUGEES IN ACHOLILAND (UGANDA), 35th Meeting of the Standing Committee of the UNHCR Standing Committee of the Executive Committee of the High Commissioner Program (8 March 2006)
- MAKE THE RESPONSIBILITY TO PROTECT COMPREHENSIVE, 57th Session of the Executive Committee of the High Commissioner's Program (4 October 2006)
- FORCIBLY DISPLACED PERSONS – IRAQ AND NEIGHBORING COUNTRIES: A CALL FOR COORDINATED HELP, International Conference on Addressing the Humanitarian Needs of the Refugees and Internally

[25] On the need for new norms and partnerships, see: Rahel Kunz, Sandra Lavenex and Marion Panizzon, *Multilayered Migration Governance: The Promise of Partnership*, London: Routledge, 2011; Sasha Baglay and Delphine Nakache, *Immigration Regulation in Federal States: Challenges and Responses in Comparative Perspectives*, New York: Springer, 2014; Susan F. Martin, *International Migration: Evolving Trends from the Early Twentieth Century to the Present*, New York: Cambridge University Press, 2014; Chris Skelcher, Helen Sullivan and Stephen Jeffares, *Hybrid Governance in European Cities: Neighbourhood, Migration and Democracy*, Basingstoke: Palgrave Macmillan, 2013.

[26] https://w2.vatican.va/content/francesco/en/messages/migration/documents/papa-francesco_20140903_world-migrants-day-2015.html.

Displaced Persons inside Iraq and in Neighboring Countries (17–18 April 2007)

- THE TERRIBLE LOSS OF LIVES IN THE ATTEMPT TO REACH A SAFE HAVEN: A NORMATIVE VACUUM?, 39th Meeting of the Standing Committee of the UNHCR Executive Committee of the High Commissioner's Programme (25 June 2007)
- HUMAN RIGHTS AND THE IMPLEMENTATION OF THE 1951 REFUGEES CONVENTION AND ITS RELATED 1967 PROTOCOL, 58th Session of the Executive Committee of the UNHCR (2 October 2007)
- ENLARGE THE CONCEPT OF PROTECTION FOR THE SAKE OF THE COMMON GOOD, 42nd Meeting of the Standing Committee of the UNHCR Executive Committee of the High Commissioner Programme (24 June 2008)
- EXTEND PROTECTION TO THE PEOPLE UPROOTED BY DESERTIFICATION, FAMINE, AND CLIMATE CHANGE, 59th Session of the Executive Committee of the UNHCR (7 October 2008)
- WHY DO WE FAIL TO TAKE CHARGE OF REFUGEES AND DISPLACED PEOPLE?, 44th Meeting of the Standing Committee of the UNHCR Executive Committee of the High Commissioner Program (3 March 2009)
- EFFECTIVE PREVENTION: UNDERSTAND AND ERADICATE THE ROOT CAUSES OF FORCED DISPLACEMENT, 60th Session of the Executive Committee of the UNHCR (29 September 2009).
- MIXED FLOWS, INTERNALLY DISPLACED AND URBAN REFUGEES: NEW CHALLENGES, 48th Meeting of the Standing Committee of the Executive Committee of the UNHCR (22 June 2010)
- REDUCING THE NUMBER OF ASYLUM SEEKERS, 61st Session of the Executive Committee of the UNHCR (5 October 2010)
- REFUGEES ARE NOT ANONYMOUS NUMBERS BUT PERSONS WITH DIGNITY, TALENTS AND ASPIRATIONS, 62nd Session of the Executive Committee of the UNHCR (4 October 2011)
- THE NEED TO MATCH POLITICAL WILL WITH THE UPDATE OF PROTECTION OBJECTIVES, Intergovernmental event at ministerial level on the occasion of the 60th anniversary of the 1951 Convention Relating to the Status of Refugees and the 50th anniversary of the 1961 Convention on the Reduction of Statelessness (7–8 December 2011)
- THE REFUGEES' DECISION TO FLEE THEIR COUNTRY IS AN ACT OF FAITH AND HOPE IN THE SOLIDARITY OF THE HUMAN FAMILY, 54th

Meeting of the Standing Committee of the Executive Committee of the UNHCR on International Protection (26 June 2012)

- INVEST IN EDUCATION TO HARVEST BENEFITS FOR THE FUTURE, 63rd Session of the Executive Committee of the UNHCR (2 October 2012)
- STRENGTHEN THE COOPERATION BETWEEN THE UNHCR AND FAITH COMMUNITIES, 57th Meeting of the Standing Committee of UNHCR (26 June 2013)
- MIGRANTS AND REFUGEES ARE NOT PAWNS ON THE CHESSBOARD OF HUMANITY: THE ADMIRABLE RESPONSE OF COUNTRIES HOSTING SYRIAN REFUGEES, 64th Session of the Executive Committee of UNHCR (2 October 2013)
- 50 MILLION FORCIBLY DISPLACED PERSONS HAVE A RIGHT TO RECOVER THEIR FREEDOM AND DIGNITY, 60th Session of the Standing Committee of UNHCR (1 July 2014)
- GLOBALIZATION OF SOLIDARITY FOR REFUGEES IN AFRICA, High-Level Segment of the 65th Session of the Executive Committee of UNHCR: *Enhancing International Cooperation, Solidarity, Local Capacities and Humanitarian Action for Refugees in Africa* (30 September 2014)
- PREVENTION AND LONG-TERM DEVELOPMENT STRATEGIES, 65th Session of the Executive Committee of UNHCR: *General Debate* (1 October 2014)
- TRANSLATE THE DUTY TO PROTECT INTO ACTION, 63rd Meeting of the Standing Committee of the UNHCR (24 June 2015)
- SAVE LIVES AND TAKE ACTION AGAINST THE ROOT CAUSES OF THE REFUGEE CRISIS, 66th Session of the Executive Committee of UNHCR (8 October 2015)

2 Migrants and their Contribution to Social Development

- MIGRANTS, BUILDERS OF BRIDGES AMONG SOCIETIES, 90th Session of the Council of the International Organization for Migration (29 November–2 December 2005)
- THE PRIORITY OF PERSONS OVER THE ECONOMY, 94th Session of the Council of the International Organization for Migration (27–30 November 2007)
- THE INADEQUACY OF THE CURRENT MIGRATION MANAGEMENT: THE INCREASING NUMBER OF IRREGULAR MIGRANTS, 98th Session of the Council of the International Organization for Migration (23–26 November 2009)

- THE DREADFUL TREATMENT OF STRANDED IMMIGRANTS, 99th Session of the Council of the International Organization for Migration (29 November–2 December 2010)
- THE HOLY SEE BECOMES A MEMBER OF THE INTERNATIONAL ORGANIZATION FOR MIGRATION: THE PRIORITY OF HUMAN DIGNITY AND THE RIGHT TO LIFE, 100th Session of the Council of the International Organization for Migration (5 December 2011)
- AN ADEQUATE AND POSITIVE GLOBAL MANAGEMENT OF MIGRATION FLOWS, 100th Session of the Council of the International Organization for Migration (6 December 2011)
- THE DETENTION OF IRREGULAR MIGRANTS AND THEIR DIGNITY, 20th Session of the Human Rights Council – Item 3: *Report of the Special Rapporteur on the Human Rights of Migrants* (22 June 2012)
- FORCIBLY DISPLACED PERSONS AND LOCAL INTEGRATION, 101st Session of the Council of the International Organization for Migration (27–30 November 2012)
- CONTRIBUTION TO DEVELOPMENT AND MIGRANTS' HUMAN RIGHTS, 103rd Session of the Council of the International Organization for Migration (26–29 November 2013)
- CHILDREN EXODUS: MECHANISMS FOR FAMILY REUNIFICATION, 26th Session of the Human Rights Council – Item 3: *Report of the Special Rapporteur on the Human Rights of Migrants* (13 June 2014)
- PERSONS LEFT BEHIND IN THE MIGRATION PROCESS, 2014 International Dialogue on Migration of the International Organization for Migration: *Migration and Families* (7–8 October 2014)
- THE PROTECTION OF MIGRANT WORKERS AND PERSONS DISPLACED BY CLIMATE CHANGE AND NATURAL DISASTERS, 105th Session of the Council of the International Organization for Migration (25–28 November 2014)
- THE FAILURE OF THE MULTILATERAL SYSTEM TO MANAGE MIGRATION: AN ABDICATION OF RESPONSIBILITY, 29th Session of the Human Rights Council, *Interactive Dialogue with the Special Rapporteur on Migrants* (15 June 2015)
- MIGRANTS AND CITIES: NEW PARTNERSHIPS TO MANAGE MOBILITY, International Dialogue on Migration – *Migrants and Cities: New Partnerships to Manage Mobility* (27 October 2015)
- VIABLE AND FORWARD-LOOKING SOLUTIONS FOR AN ENLIGHTENED MANAGEMENT OF HUMAN MOBILITY, 106th Session of the Council of the International Organization for Migration (24–27 November 2015)

3 The Scourge of Trafficking in Human Persons

- PROSECUTE THE MULTI-BILLION DOLLAR INDUSTRY OF TRAFFICKING AND REHABILITATE THE VICTIMS, 60th Session of the Commission on Human Rights – Item 14: *Specific groups and individuals* (8 April 2004)
- TRAFFICKING IN HUMAN BEINGS, A CONTEMPORARY FORM OF SLAVERY, 18th Session of the Human Rights Council – Item 3: *Contemporary Forms of Slavery* (14 September 2011)
- THE SCOURGE OF TRAFFICKED CHILDREN AND THEIR SEXUAL EXPLOITATION, 22nd Session of the Human Rights Council – Item 3: *Report of the Special Rapporteur on the Sale of Children, Child Prostitution and Child Pornography* (7 March 2013)

1 THE ETHICAL RESPONSIBILITY TO WELCOME REFUGEES

PROVIDE SECURITY FOR THE CIVILIAN POPULATION*

The Rights of Refugees and Protracted Situations

Mr Chairman,

On the occasion of this year's World Refugee Day, His Holiness Pope John Paul II stated: 'Every person needs a safe environment in which to live. Refugees aspire to this but, unfortunately, millions in various countries of the world are still living in refugee camps or prevented for long periods from fully exercising their rights.'[1] Indeed, Mr Chairman, the rights recognized to the refugees in international instruments too often remain mere words. In many countries, for example, refugees are not allowed to work, a basic right, and thus earn a livelihood.[2] Made dependent on food rations, they too often face real crises when these are reduced together with other necessities needed for existence with a minimum of dignity. Moreover, their movements are usually limited to the immediate surroundings of camps, often located in remote regions, where refugees and local people are forced to compete for scarce resources with a real risk of new conflicts unless the needs of both vulnerable populations are duly taken into account. The institutional capacity of the international community to realize the rights of refugees seems insufficient. The High Commissioner has renewed a concerted effort for refugee protection through initiatives like Convention Plus, so much needed in countries of first asylum in particular. But greater economic and financial investments, and especially political will, are required. Guaranteeing refugees their rights will assist them in becoming 'agents of development' even in their host country and not just recipients of aid or merely tolerated guests. The option of third country resettlement remains equally necessary and more efforts are called for it. In fact, if international cooperation is lacking, then we are left with a fourth *de facto*, albeit unofficial, solution: warehousing of millions of people in camps in subhuman

* Statement delivered at the 55th Session of the Executive Committee of the Program of the United Nations High Commissioner for Refugees, 4–8 October 2004.

[1] Angelus, Sunday, 20 June 2004.

[2] See Universal Declaration on Human Rights, Art. 23.

conditions, without a future and without the possibility of contributing their creativity. Camps must remain what they were intended to be: an emergency and therefore a temporary solution. Protracted refugee situations – 7 million of 12 million refugees worldwide have been refugees for ten years or more – seem a growing phenomenon with the consequence of masses of people without hope and generations of children becoming adults with a lost childhood.

Repatriation that is 'Voluntary'

Voluntary repatriation has today become the durable solution of choice. Fortunately, in some countries the situation has improved enough that refugees can return home on a large scale as the reasons why they fled gradually cease to exist, and people have the possibility to restart their lives. What makes all the difference between successful and unsuccessful voluntary repatriation is how people are returned home: if in, and to, conditions of safety and dignity; what kind of guaranteed benefits they receive and which follow-up activities are developed, whether it be de-mining, helping youngsters born in camps to adapt to rural areas, setting up micro-credit systems or similar programs. Provisions also need to be in place for settling property questions and land rights. These elements within a comprehensive structural development approach will show that the interest of refugees, as individuals or groups, is at the centre of any plan and it will prompt the refugees to return freely. Voluntary repatriation does not mean just going back. Otherwise there is the risk that people are moved from one difficult situation to a life of misery in their own country. Of course, these plans demand guaranteed possibilities of assistance with sufficient funding by international partners over a longer period to make implementation real. But that is the way of laying the foundation for a dignified return aimed at reintegration with reconstruction and reconciliation.

International Action

Continuing warfare still obliges numerous people to leave their homes because of fear of persecution, human rights violations, harassment and widespread violence, with a systematic use of rape as a war tactic. The cost of such forced movements is very high: the sufferings of people, the loss of lives, the process of eventually rebuilding society. We should not be shy in taking innovative steps, as was the case 20 years ago with the

Cartagena Declaration on Refugees that took into account generalized violence.

International human rights and humanitarian law oblige governments to provide for the security and well-being of all those under their jurisdiction. In particular, each citizen has a right to protection by his or her country. If, however, a State fails to, or cannot, take this responsibility and the human rights of a population continue to be trampled upon, then the international community can and should assert its concern, step in and take on this obligation. The responsibility of a 'humanitarian intervention' has to be considered. In this regard, I repeat the position of Pope John Paul II: 'Clearly, when a civilian population risks being overcome by the attacks of an unjust aggressor and political efforts and non-violent defence prove to be of no avail, it is legitimate and even obligatory to take concrete measures to disarm the aggressor. These measures, however, must be limited in time and precise in their aims. They must be carried out in full respect for international law, guaranteed by an authority that is internationally recognized and, in any event, never left to the outcome of armed intervention alone. The fullest and the best use must therefore be made of all the provisions of the United Nations Charter, further defining effective instruments and modes of intervention within the framework of international law. In this regard, the United Nations Organization itself must offer all its Member States an equal opportunity to be part of the decision-making process, eliminating privileges and discriminations which weaken its role and its credibility.'[3] The timeliness of this intervention is critical to save lives and a test of the international community's commitment to the cause of refugees.

In conclusion, Mr Chairman, it is measures like these that will help people separated from homes or their land to find a place to live that recognizes their human dignity and their right to security and peace.

[3] Message for the 2000 World Day of Peace.

AVOID THE STIGMATIZATION AS CRIMINALS OF ASYLUM SEEKERS AND REFUGEES*

Mr Chairman, allow me to congratulate you on your election as Chairman and to take this opportunity to welcome and to wish well to High Commissioner Antonio Guterres whose opening statement has been very much appreciated by the Delegation of the Holy See.

Mr Chairman,

The increase in the number of persons of concern to the UNHCR, while the number of refugees has been decreasing, raises some challenging questions about protection that remains at the heart of the UNHCR's mandate. While protection extends with appropriate modalities to conventional refugees, asylum seekers and internally displaced persons (IDP), its definition should reasonably evolve and become more inclusive in direct relation to a more adequate understanding of security. In recent debates dealing with the various elements that in combination afford a more comprehensive security to people, other requirements have been added to the absence of physical persecution, of threats to life, of violent conflicts. These include sufficient and safe food and minimal conditions of personal freedom and well-being that are necessary to safeguard the human dignity of every person. In this concerted and important development, however, grey areas exist that call for the creativity and the commitment of the international community to find better solutions. The Delegation of the Holy See would like to highlight a couple of these areas that directly affect people who are refugees and in refugee-like situations, namely the provision of food in camps and the policy of increasing detention of asylum seekers as a routine measure of deterrence.

The precarious condition of uprooted people living in camps often confines them away from agricultural pursuits to produce their own food and from income-generating activities through which they can support themselves. In such circumstances, they must depend on the international community. But budgetary resources have been inadequate for some years forcing food rationing that provokes dangerous coping mechanisms for survival. The solidarity of the international community provides food to the refugees and it recognizes access to food as a fundamental right.

* Statement delivered at the 56th Session of the Executive Committee of UNHCR, 5 October 2005.

When, however, there is a breakdown in the food pipeline, the ensuing crisis leads to well-documented unfortunate consequences: children stunted in their growth; the risk of trading sex for food; forced repatriation to a still unsafe environment. This Delegation joins in support for the option of local integration when possible, for the continued excellent collaboration between the World Food Program and the UNHCR, for an integrated development strategy inclusive of both local population and refugees settled in the same region. Such a comprehensive approach becomes a common responsibility of the international community and of non-governmental organizations. In this way, food security turns out to be the first step toward a return to a normal existence for people already traumatized by their forced exile and who should not be made more vulnerable by the uncertainty of their daily sustenance.

The widening sense of protection cannot overlook or underestimate the mushrooming of detention centres for asylum seekers. Hundreds of these centers dot the map of Europe and of other continents as well. The danger of stigmatizing asylum seekers and refugees as 'irregular migrants' and 'queue jumpers' and even 'criminals' (and there certainly are such members in these categories) can lead to a dehumanizing, emotional and not disinterested simplification of the asylum and migration nexus.

This policy of detention raises questions of a humanitarian, human rights and also juridical and legal nature. There are real concerns about its becoming a systematic policy to which many countries resort more as a rule than as an exception that is prompted by national order and security. In this complex question, weighing the consequences of deprivation of liberty and of inadequate standards and quality of treatment on the persons involved, especially on vulnerable groups like children and women, should be a must. Of course, States have a right to manage the movement of people across their borders. But confronted with the current pressure of people forced to move, as the UNHCR did in the past, taking into account the different conclusions on detention of this Committee and also the UNHCR Guidelines on detention, a renewed open and participatory reflection on the ethics of detention may be in order with greater focus on possible alternatives.

The consequences of a generalized policy of detention indicate the timeliness of a coordinated effort. In fact, the average conditions of detention show, in different degrees and places, staff inadequately trained, a mixing up of children and adults, elderly persons and women, and at times asylum seekers and common criminals. Lack of access to basic services and to education has equally a negative impact on the physical and mental health of the persons detained. There is as well a question of perception. In the public eye, the distinction is not easily made between detention, arbitrary detention, and administrative detention so that asylum seekers and irregular migrants are associated with criminals, an image that feeds racist and xenophobic behavior and is a deterrent to integration. Long detention in particular leaves scars on individuals who have already suffered hardship and abuse prior to arriving in countries where they are detained; scars that complicate their reintegration in society and in not a few cases lead them to take their own lives.

If national security demands that in exceptional cases asylum seekers should be detained, it should be under well-defined criteria and for the shortest possible time, with the possibility of having access to legal aid, doctors, members of their family, pastoral care and the outside world. While regional collaboration actively involving countries where asylum seekers come from and countries of transit and intended destination aims at preventing tragedies at sea and in desert crossing, care needs to be taken that protection is really provided and in conformity with international standards. Stated objectives and implementation are too often widely apart.

The search for alternatives and for constructive solutions cannot weaken the right to seek asylum. History shows that a policy of only control heightens the vulnerability of asylum seekers and their risk of exploitation. The present challenge consists in reducing the gap in the quality of life between developed and developing countries. A more comprehensive understanding of security can provide the will to address the root causes, both political and economic, that push large numbers of people criss-crossing the globe looking for protection, survival and a decent life.

SOLIDARITY FOR THE SUFFERING OF REFUGEES IN ACHOLILAND (UGANDA)*

Mr Chairman,

My Delegation is grateful for the regional Reports, especially those on Africa. The Delegation of the Holy See appreciates very much the UNHCR decision to extend its activities in the area of protection of refugees and of internally displaced persons in Africa.

Unfortunately the process of displacement continues even as we talk about refugees and IDPs. The cost in human suffering and stifled development is incalculable. In fact, there is the added and real risk that destabilization, as a result of cross-border violence and the flights of people looking for safety, may extend to new countries.

But among several similar situations, there is an old, protracted one of perhaps one million and a half IDPs about which the international media seems to be oblivious. I refer to the IDPs in Acholiland, Uganda, who survive in dozens of camps that are overcrowded, with limited security, with difficult access for some of them, with lack of clean water and a minimum of hygiene. There are indications that as many as 1,000 people a week die as a result of such constraints.

In the last months some positive steps have been taken with better coordination and more accurate information about security, a process that deserves support and further development.

As often is the case in these conditions of uprootedness and lack of security, women and children pay the highest price. Besides, access to food is difficult or even impossible for a significant percentage of IDPs and of refugees in that Ugandan region.

A massive effort is really needed to address these accumulated problems and perhaps a more detailed plan could be worked out by the UNHCR for this African region as part of an overall renewed commitment to all forcibly displaced people in the continent.

Mr Chairman, my Delegation hopes very much that the needed resources may be provided as a gesture of human solidarity, as an investment in peace, so that this long-uprooted population may not be forgotten.

Thank you.

* Statement delivered at the 35th Meeting of the UNHCR Standing Committee of the Executive Committee of the High Commissioner Program, 8 March 2006.

MAKE THE RESPONSIBILITY TO PROTECT COMPREHENSIVE*

Mr Chairman,

The Delegation of the Holy See adds its appreciation for your, and for the UNHCR High Commissioner's, able and committed leadership of the Executive Committee and in the cause of refugees and forcibly uprooted people.

The hundreds of victims whose lives have been lost in recent weeks and months in their desperate search for a more secure and decent existence is a red light of alarm that in our globalized world the international community is failing to uphold its goals of solidarity and protection. Around the world, through seas and deserts, people struggle to escape from war, from violation of their human rights, from famine. Motives and flows are mixed, a major challenge to the responsibility to protect, in our case responsibility to protect in general. While different mechanisms and institutional arrangements are in place to address different kinds of movement of people, clearly all of these people need protection. The valid distinction between migrants, asylum seekers and refugees has been blurred. A certain reluctance and fatigue to preserve such distinction in a fair way seem to prevail, thus weakening the protection role of the 1951 Convention on the Status of Refugees and the related 1967 Protocol as well as the 1969 Organization of African Unity Convention Governing the Specific Aspects of Refugee Problems in Africa, the OAU Convention. It seems reasonable, in both South–South and South–North population flows, that in the determination of admission the UNHCR should complement the often political approach of States and guarantee the quality of the process through its presence or the implementation of its specific guidelines about selection. In this way, asylum seekers, who are a small proportion in these movements, will not be exposed to *refoulement*.

The wider awareness of the responsibility to protect should encourage an added effort to alleviate the plight of asylum seekers who on subsistent living and in a virtual state of limbo are scattered in various regions like, for example, the recent flows of Iraqis throughout the Middle East. They are particularly vulnerable. Conflicts prevent them from returning and in the country of temporary residence their status is not well

* Statement delivered at the 57th Session of the Executive Committee of the High Commissioner's Program, 4 October 2006.

recognized; it is almost that of stateless persons. Political necessity conditions the interpretation of the refugee convention even though reality on the ground, often effectively witnessed to by civil society organizations, would demand recognition of these individuals and families as entitled to Convention protection and assistance. It has become obvious in the current discussions that more resources are called for to meet all protection requirements and to address not just populations in a state of limbo, but also the 5.7 million of the world's some 9 million refugees in protracted refugee situations, the more than 4 million Palestinian refugees, and the estimated 24 million internally displaced people (IDP). If international solidarity would add to its budget on aid to refugees a small proportion of the increase in arms expenses – from 1996 to 2005 military expenditure increased by 34 per cent to US$ 1.118 billion in current dollars – then a major step forward would be taken toward an adequate response to the pains of uprooted humanity.[1]

Funds are a necessary but not sufficient requirement. The political will is needed to make the responsibility to protect comprehensive enough to embrace the prevention of forced displacement tragedies. The way of dialogue and of respect of human rights should replace that of conflict. Refugee camps, official and unofficial, would no longer stain the map of the world. In the meantime the task on hand is the dissolution of these camps through the classical strategies of voluntary repatriation, local integration and resettlement. It seems to this Delegation that for some present complex situations the option of resettlement should be revisited. A larger number of countries can welcome a larger number of refugees anxious to start a new life in freedom and self-reliance. It is not only an ethical obligation but also a practical advantage since several developed receiving countries face scarcity of manpower for their economy and for a sustainable demography. In the preparation of refugees for resettlement, non-governmental as well as faith-based organizations can collaborate and provide competent help. In fact, as an expression of civil society NGOs can be good partners for their closeness to the reality on the ground, their experience and their capacity to create a favorable public opinion for newcomers. But an effective partnership has to take into account the security also of their personnel and, in the least developed countries especially, that their overheads cannot be supplied by local resources.

[1] Instituto de Investigación Internacional de la Paz de Estocolmo, *SIPRI Yearbook 2006: Armaments, Disarmaments, and International Security*, Oxford: Oxford University Press, 2006, pp. 259–386.

Mr Chairman,

The initiatives undertaken to make UNHCR more effective and flexible, the 'cluster approach', the reorganization of the budget, deserve support and they show its commitment and sensibility to the human face behind all statistics. Society at large should also renew its sense of responsibility to protect. First of all, education can transmit the values of solidarity and hospitality. Training of border officials will enable them to recognize asylum seekers. Labour unions, employers, schools and faith communities can prepare their constituencies to an increasingly frequent encounter with people in need and to welcome them to build a common future. With the human person and his/her dignity at the center of concern, the responsibility to protect will continue finding the creative capacity to respond in a humane and fair way to today's new developments.

Thank you, Mr Chairman.

FORCIBLY DISPLACED PERSONS – IRAQ AND NEIGHBORING COUNTRIES: A CALL FOR COORDINATED HELP*

Mr President,

In Iraq it seems 'easier to die than to live', as some media reported in the face of the increasing violence and daily atrocities that are destroying innumerable lives and the hope of an entire people. The initiative taken by the UNHCR to bring together representatives of governments and of humanitarian organizations is therefore an opportune and promising decision. The Delegation of the Holy See expresses its appreciation and looks forward, as a result of this conference, to heightened awareness on the part of the international community and to concrete forms of help for the uprooted populations of Iraq. Over the years, the UNHCR has rescued and given hope to millions of victims of persecution, conflicts and violation of basic human rights. We are all challenged to maintain this noble tradition.

The world is witnessing an unprecedented degree of hate and destructiveness in Iraq; this phenomenon concomitantly exerts a widening deadly impact in the entire Middle East region. Sectarian and tribal clashes, military actions, armed groups competing for power, kidnappings, rapes, international terrorism, threats to and murder of the innocent members of families simply because they uphold their ancestral faith – these are all elements that, in combination threaten human dignity and social well-being in the region. Targeting of unarmed civilians is a particularly tragic sign of total disregard of the sacredness of human life. While the consequences of this generalized violence affect the social and economic life of the country, they also are a stark reminder of the passionate appeals of the late Pope John Paul II to avoid 'the tremendous consequences that an international military operation would have for the population of Iraq and for the balance of the Middle East region already sorely tried, and for the extremisms that could stem from it'. He insistently called for negotiations even though he knew well that peace at any price might not be possible (Pope John Paul II, Angelus, 16 March 2003).

* Statement delivered at the International Conference on Addressing the Humanitarian Needs of the Refugees and Internally Displaced Persons inside Iraq and in Neighboring Countries, 17–18 April 2007.

Massive uprooting and displacement of the Iraqi population is now indeed a tremendous consequence. The figures are telling: some 2 million Iraqis currently displaced internally and 2 million others have already fled the country and between 40,000 and 50,000 are fleeing their homes each month. The very generous welcome provided by Jordan and Syria in particular and by the other countries is certainly highly commendable. Economic, social and security concerns, however, are putting to the test this willingness and capacity to welcome. It is urgent, therefore, for the international community to take up its responsibility and share in the task of protection and assistance, to answer the call for action now through the implementation on the ground and in practical decisions of the legal and moral commitments it patiently formulated and agreed upon. Where war and violence have destroyed the social tissue and the unity of Iraq, judicious political choices and a non-discriminatory humanitarian engagement would be the first step to re-establish a pluralistic unity.

There are special categories of victims that stand out in this largest Middle East exodus since the still unresolved Palestinian one of 1948. Displaced women, elderly and children bear the brunt of the tragedy. With the experience of daily violence and, even more tragically, with the killing of family members before their eyes, many children are traumatized and remain without professional care. Most uprooted Iraqi children wake up in their exile to a daily experience of uncertainty, deprivation, lack of schooling, and to hard labour just to attain the minimal essentials of human survival. One has to wonder how their psychological scars will condition the future. Christian and other religious minorities who have been a target of forced eviction and ethnic and religious cleansing by radical groups find themselves in limbo in their temporary place of refuge since they are unable to return to their homes and are without a possibility of local integration or resettlement. It is the suffering of all the victims that should prompt a coordinated, effective and generous response.

A comprehensive reconciliation and peace are the obvious responses that address the root of all forced displacement. As the international community pursues this complex goal, addressing immediately the needs of the millions of uprooted Iraqis and other refugees in the area will prevent further regional destabilization and will relieve their pain. This is not the time to look at technical definitions of a refugee, but to recall 'the exemplary value beyond its contractual scope' attributed by States from the very beginning, to the Convention Relating to the Status of Refugees (1951). Recently, the development of the concept of complementary protection has become a significant conclusion to support a humane response in massive displacement. Therefore, among the practical measures that must be upheld and implemented as means of due protection, are acceptance of all people fleeing generalized violence, respectful of their human rights and of the principle of *non-refoulement*, registration for an orderly assistance, provision of appropriate legal documentation.

In this humanitarian response, the countries hosting displaced Iraqis cannot be ignored by the international community and must receive tangible and prompt solidarity. A community-inclusive approach to assist vulnerable displaced people and hosts can be a winning strategy for an effective outreach even to needy persons who are the most isolated and vulnerable. In fact, without this solidarity, the victims escaping violence are at risk of new forms of exploitation and of being deprived of health and education services, housing and employment possibilities. Facing such vulnerability, some persons are tempted to place themselves in the hands of smugglers in order to escape but simply are confronted with additional difficulties in the countries they manage to reach.

While the first humanitarian need is peace, equally vital is a coordinated response that raises awareness of the immense crisis we face. Such a response must involve actors from States, civil society and United Nations. In order to ameliorate the plight of all displaced people inside and outside the country, this response must enjoy a responsible participation of all Iraqis.

All humanitarian workers who have been delivering active assistance, notwithstanding risk and sacrifice, deserve the appreciation from the global human family as well as adequate resources to carry out their mission. They serve as effective instruments, as shown, for example, by the tens of thousands of people of all backgrounds and convictions being helped daily by the Catholic charitable network in Iraq, Jordan, Syria, Lebanon, Turkey and Egypt. Local NGOs as well as faith-based organizations and others often have the best capacities to reach out to the neediest, build upon community solidarity and, in this moment of increased tensions between ethnic, tribal and religious groups, open up genuine dialogue. It makes good sense that they be empowered, financially supported and actively engaged in situation assessments and response programming.

In previous but similar crises of massive displacement, the mobilization of the international community proved effective in providing durable solutions. There is a need to match past effectiveness. While the right to return has to be kept alive for displaced Iraqis, other examples in recent history have demonstrated that the option of resettlement may need to be enhanced, and doors opened by more countries and for greater numbers, so that pressure within the region may be alleviated on a short-term basis. A renewed and concerted effort is called for, however, to make conditions in Iraq and in the whole region conducive to a decent and sustainable coexistence among all its citizens. The historical diversity of communities can contribute to a democratic experience and can link this society to the world. Such a contribution presupposes mutual acceptance, the rejection of homogenization and constructive pluralism. The implementation of all durable solutions to end displacement in this context can prevent the emergence of chronic, protracted situations that result in long-term and humiliating circumstances for large numbers of new refugees.

Mr President,

My Delegation is convinced that, at this juncture of the Middle East crisis, vigorous leadership is demanded of the international community. Surely, the greatest challenge is to find a way for reconciliation, to reconstruct the will to dialogue and to hope again so that peace may win. Generous, timely and coordinated humanitarian help for all the victims of such horrific violence will achieve justice for them and will begin the indispensable process of healing their tragic condition.

THE TERRIBLE LOSS OF LIVES IN THE ATTEMPT TO REACH A SAFE HAVEN: A NORMATIVE VACUUM?*

Mr Chairman,

First of all, the Delegation of the Holy See congratulates and welcomes the new Deputy High Commissioner and expresses its support for the continued attention given to protection.

The global refugee population has begun to increase again and the population of concern to the UNHCR Office is now well over 32 million. People forcibly displaced are a stark reminder of persisting conflicts and violations of human rights. The Delegation of the Holy See greatly appreciates the UNHCR's courageous service and openness to creative responses to the plight of all forcibly uprooted persons. In the present spiraling crisis of people obliged to move from their homes, while factual information is available, the complexity of the issues and perhaps some deficit of political will slow down the possibility of solutions.

Grey areas of concern seem to increase where existing protection instruments cannot apply or lack clarity of mandate. Reference is made to a phenomenon that now continues for some years – the terrible loss of life in the attempt to reach a safe haven on the part of thousands of people forced by desperate circumstances to look for survival outside their own country. The phenomenon is not just regional. It is present in the Mediterranean where people try to cross from Africa to Europe; in the Atlantic where they cross from West Africa to the Canary Islands. Other people lose their lives moving from East Africa to the Arabian Peninsula; from Caribbean islands to the American continent; from Mexico across the desert to the United States; in some areas of Asia. The questions arise of how the obligation to protect of the international community can be exercised in such a situation; if a normative vacuum exists for the protection of these victims who meet death in trying to escape some other forms of physical or psychological death. The UNHCR could raise the issue of a coordination of policies at the United Nations level that could focus on this trans-regional problem taking into account new developments, initiate a systematic study of how protection can be provided and even develop a specific protection cluster. Of course, in the long run a positive and preventive approach would require the transformation of

* Statement delivered at the 39th Meeting of the Standing Committee of the UNHCR Executive Committee of the High Commissioner's Programme, 25 June 2007.

conditions in the places of origin through greater security, respect of human rights, effective political participation, the creation of jobs and an environment of peace. But this local transformation cannot happen without the involvement of the international community for better-organized and wider legal channels for the movement of people and without fair agricultural, financial and trade policies that would not impact in a negative way on the poor countries thus triggering forced displacement.

A second point my Delegation wants to return to is that of the Middle East refugees and the worsening situation of ethnic and religious minorities cleansing. It seems that there is no way forward because of the inadequate acceptance of needy cases for resettlement and no way backward because of the impossibility of return due to persisting insecurity and refusal of coexistence among different religious communities. Christians in particular are confronted with a renewed era of martyrdom. Besides, the necessary funding for an adequate response to the suffering of Iraqi refugees is not yet sufficiently available. Adding his voice to the recent celebration of World Refugee Day the Holy Father Pope Benedict XVI stated: 'Welcoming refugees and giving them hospitality is a duty of human solidarity so that they may not feel isolated because of intolerance and lack of concern.' He appealed that asylum and the rights of refugees be guaranteed and that the leaders of Nations should offer protection to all in need of it. Burden sharing, both in terms of funds and provision of resettlement, remains a major challenge, as it is protection in the region.

Mr Chairman,

Critical refugee and internally displaced people situations around the world call for a renewed commitment and an active engagement on the part of the international community. It is an obvious form of solidarity within the human family. Today's developments in the vast world of forced displacements and tomorrow's consequences of climate change forcing people to move call for intellectual creativity and pragmatic programs of action that may give an answer to the new demands for protection.

Thank you, Mr Chairman.

HUMAN RIGHTS AND THE IMPLEMENTATION OF THE 1951 REFUGEES CONVENTION AND ITS RELATED 1967 PROTOCOL*

Mr Chairman,

Forcibly displaced people continue to be subjected to human rights violations. Regrettably, the number of refugees has increased again to some 10 million persons and internally displaced people to well over 24 million. The statistical trend shows that uprooting people from their homes is a major injustice caused by persisting conflicts that trigger this dehumanizing condition. Other forms of violence force people to leave their homes and native countries: these include extreme misery, environment degradation, religious intolerance and persecution, lack of freedom, lack of respect for advocacy activity on behalf of human rights. Millions of normal, ordinary human beings are thrust into situations of incredible humiliation and suffering. The frustration of the international community in trying to cope with the plight of refugees, internally displaced people (IDPs), stateless persons and asylum seekers, finds expression in the public anxiety and in the emotional political reactions about options for resettlement and for provisions of an adequate financial solidarity to meet emergencies and then enable the return of such uprooted people to a normal life back home with a minimum of dignity. Frustration, however, cannot be allowed to dictate the pace of the action required to protect the rights of the displaced.

An approach that opens to new commitments and that leads to practical measures of assistance and protection is based on rethinking the central place that human dignity and human rights should hold in refugee and asylum policies. On balance, among political considerations, institutional requirements, sudden crises and security mechanisms, priority should be given to uprooted people as persons with a claim on the international community. In fact the protection due to forcibly displaced people has been the motivation for the juridical instruments already developed by the international community. The respect of the rights of all displaced persons leads to a comprehensive response and protection so that a globalization of protection results from a globalization of rights.

* Statement delivered at the 58th Session of the Executive Committee of the UNHCR, 2 October 2007.

In this way, a more coordinated and effective implementation of existing protection instruments is possible while new instruments can be developed to remedy existing gaps, especially regarding vulnerable groups like women and girls, children, the elderly. The recent reflection in the preparation of new ExCom 'Conclusions' has been moving in this direction.

The perspective of human rights emanating from the dignity of every person offers a twofold advantage. First, a human rights approach means that the duty to protect reaches beyond the narrow national interest of single states and beyond the fear that it may be a disguised form of domination. A human rights-based approach to protection requires that the international community should respond actively to the needs of the displaced in ways that respect people displaced from their home nations and cultures as persons with equal dignity. Second, the human right to protection means that governments and other social groups have a duty not to drive people from their homes by denying them the possibility to survive there but to respond instead to the challenges of protection in a timely and effective way.

Some of the well-known challenges facing the forcibly displaced have been the subject of long debates, but they still remain of concern because no substantive solutions have been reached. Uprooted people have to flee because their rights are not recognized. In this exodus, their rights are again violated. Protection gaps and challenges still exist in the whole process, from the moment a person becomes a refugee to the moment of access to one of the durable solutions. State security is emphasized over the protection of persons; financial contributions are channeled elsewhere. The end result is human suffering. The evidence is given by the fact that access to asylum procedures has increasingly become difficult or even impossible to secure, sometimes leading to restricting access or leading to *refoulement*. The policy of detention is enforced beyond strictly necessary measures, while people are forced, more or less permanently, to stay in camps, without having their right to freedom of movement and access to work guaranteed, a situation that too often results in chronic malnutrition. Donor fatigue and insufficient funding lead to reduction in food rations in camps and in failure to provide the necessary minimum basic essentials to address needs. The combined effect of this situation impacts the individual and the family and leads to a breakdown of values. Reintegration programs should be in line with the national recovery program in post-conflict situations and should proceed smoothly from emergency assistance to development aid, and so guarantee a sustainable return of forcibly displaced people.

A comprehensive human rights perspective can indicate appropriate criteria and means that would apply from the moment a person is forced to leave home and to apply for asylum to the moment a durable solution is reached. In particular, renewed emphasis should be accorded to prevention and to peace-building, dialogue and reconciliation. The prevention of conflicts, which always are a source of human rights violations and of massive forced displacement, must become the main road in the efforts of the international community to eradicate the tragedy of forced displacement. Such a moral imperative is also pragmatically cost-effective. Moreover, the previously mentioned task of strengthening the institutional capacity to fulfill the protection mandate should encourage creative thinking, as has been the case in the cluster approach and in the ongoing restructuring within the UN system and some of its agencies. In this manner, the international community can succeed in developing a comprehensive instrument that embraces all forcibly uprooted persons. In this regard, the search for some monitoring mechanism or expert technical group could arrive at practical ways for a more effective implementation of the rights recognized to refugees in the 1951 Convention and its related Protocol as well as for a more convergent interpretation of these basic statutes.

Mr Chairman,

Around the world, crises leading to the movement of refugees and displaced people in the Middle East, in Africa and elsewhere are reported as a routine dimension of daily existence. Public opinion tends to accept almost as normal the fact that millions of fellow human beings are so uprooted and relegated to miserable and painful conditions. But welcoming refugees and giving them hospitality is, for everyone, a vital gesture of human solidarity in order to help them feel less isolated by intolerance and disinterest. The Delegation of the Holy See is happy to see that the UNHCR continues to witness such welcome and that it recognizes the welcome provided by representatives of the civil society, as is the case this year with the Nansen Refugee Award, given to a member of Jesuit Refugee Service (JRS). Pope Benedict XVI constantly appeals that these our brothers and sisters, so badly tested by suffering, should be guaranteed asylum and the recognition of their rights, and that public authorities should offer them protection in such delicate situations of need.

In conclusion, addressing the problem of uprooted people from their own perspective, and that of their dignity and rights, will lead the international community to search for more comprehensive and humane solutions and to find the motivation for undertaking bold steps for their implementation.

Thank you, Mr Chairman.

ENLARGE THE CONCEPT OF PROTECTION FOR THE SAKE OF THE COMMON GOOD*

Mr Chairman,

The Delegation of the Holy See joins previous speakers in expressing its appreciation for the presentations made, and the documents prepared by the UNHCR's Office. The perspective of human rights that has been adopted addressing refugees' protection is really timely.

The issue of protection comes back with greater urgency on the agenda of the UNHCR in dealing with violently uprooted people. People forcibly displaced by the ongoing conflicts in the Middle East have focused the attention of the international community both on the inadequate action being taken to protect a worldwide increasing number of refugees and of other persons entitled to protection as well as on the growing insensitivity to asylum seekers, whose number has also been increasing in industrialized and developing countries.

Unfortunately, on the global level, statistics show that close to 40 million people are currently uprooted by violence and persecution and are in need of different degrees of protection. A paradox emerges: as the wave of people seeking protection increases, political initiatives, proposed and implemented, move in the opposite direction of greater restriction and more control of access to safety. In the process, genuine victims from abuses of basic human rights and of specific hostility are confusedly catalogued with other people on the move.

Protection is a dynamic concept that has evolved since the Second World War exactly because the 1951 Convention on Refugees tied their protection to the Universal Declaration of Human Rights. Changing situations have required ever new solutions to offer a future to people who have been forced to flee. This possibility had already been foreseen in 1951. The Final Act of the United Nations Conference of Plenipotentiaries on the Status of Refugees and Stateless Persons says: 'The Conference expresses the hope that the Convention Relating to the Status of Refugees will have value as an example exceeding its contractual scope and that all nations will be guided by it in granting so far as possible to persons in their territory as refugees and who would not be covered by the terms of the Convention, the treatment for which it provides'

* Statement delivered at the 42nd Meeting of the Standing Committee of the UNHCR Executive Committee of the High Commissioner Program, 24 June 2008.

(A/CONF.2/108/Rev.1, 25 July 1951). In that spirit, as authorized by the UN General Assembly, the High Commissioner has exercised his protection mandate by using the concept of good offices to provide assistance to refugees outside the competence of the United Nations (United Nations General Assembly Resolution A/RES/1388, 20 November 1959).

Regional instruments have been developed, like the Convention of the Organization of African Unity (10 September 1969), which expand the definition of refugee to 'every person who, owing to external aggression, occupation, foreign domination or events seriously disturbing public order in either part or the whole of his country of origin or nationality, is compelled to leave his place of habitual residence in order to seek refuge in another place outside his country of origin or nationality'. The Cartagena Declaration on Refugees (22 November 1984), which addresses the situation in Central America, recommends to include as refugees persons 'threatened by generalized violence, foreign aggression, internal conflicts, massive violation of human rights or other circumstances which have seriously disturbed public order'.

With the passing of time, the General Assembly has extended UNHCR's protection capacities to groups who were not covered in the Convention like stateless people, returnees and certain groups of internally displaced people. The UNHCR Executive Committee's Conclusions, unanimously adopted, have indicated how to deal with specific situations. In addition, other human rights Conventions cover persons in need of protection, even when their requests for asylum are rejected. All these steps have been taken prompted by the conviction that international protection is not a static but an action-oriented commitment aimed at finding solutions so that uprooted people may restart their life with dignity.

A similar spirit should apply also to today's challenges and problems. A hopeful initiative is the proposed Convention for the Protection and Assistance of Internally Displaced Persons by the African Union, foreseen for adoption in November this year. Such a legally binding Convention could serve as a stimulus for the protection, prevention and assistance of IDPs in other continents.

Mr Chairman,

The experience of displacement in the world is further complicated by the fact that the precarious situation of all refugees is more acute in unstable regions where most of them are found; only 5 per cent are accepted in rich countries. For many, protracted exile turns into an added condition of suffering and some six million persons find themselves blocked in such a situation.

Today, therefore, protection remains a concept that can be further enlarged to include people with precise protection needs. There are some additional specific observations that can enter the protection discussion:

(a) the right to sufficient food within camps so that refugees may not feel forced to seek employment outside the camps and put themselves at the risk of arrest and deportation;
(b) the case of new countries becoming more accessible to asylum seekers as they are located at the outer boundaries of regional political groups to which technical assistance should be provided, in cooperation with the UNHCR, so that their decision-making process be correct;
(c) the need of adequate channels for legal entry and the critical evaluation of control-only policies so that asylum seekers may not be forced to take the same routes as irregular migrants, and thus become easily exposed to extortions and abuses within such groups and without distinction rejected with them;
(d) detention as such should be used as a last resort measure and avoided for minors for whom it is particularly traumatizing.

Finally, Mr Chairman, solidarity demands that the responsibility toward asylum seekers be not simply transferred to countries in the regions of origin of the refugees, but it should be shared according to the possibilities of each country or region for the sake of the common good.

Thank you, Mr Chairman.

EXTEND PROTECTION TO THE PEOPLE UPROOTED BY DESERTIFICATION, FAMINE, AND CLIMATE CHANGE*

Mr Chairman,

The spotlight of public opinion currently is placed on the crisis of financial markets, on the present form of economic organization, and on the irresponsibility and greed of some managers that led to it. The consequences of this enormously complicated crisis exert a grave impact on vulnerable groups in society and give concrete evidence of the interconnectedness and lack of equity in today's world. Additional challenges of great urgency confront the international community. Climate change leads to scarcity of food and lack of water, to the degradation of the environment and an increase of natural disasters. Together with related conflicts in some regions, all these factors result in an intensification of forced displacement of people and a greater uncertainty about our ability to provide them with the protection and assistance they need. This moment, on the other hand, can reawaken the awareness that it is really a common responsibility to determine whether the 'global village' thrives or suffers.

Natural and man-made disasters expose millions of persons and families to conditions of extreme poverty and to violations of their basic human rights. Such unbearable situations make it impossible for them to remain in their usual place of residence, much as they would like to do so. Looking at the future, the condition of uprooted people appears more bleak and ambiguous than ever. In view of the emergence and overlapping of these new complexities, our discussions about protection can be confronted with significant obstacles. Political responses, immediate assistance and technical know-how are necessary. However, a clear ethical dimension also must be acknowledged and should be placed at the center of debate as we formulate decisions on how to move forward with adequate protection.

The Delegation of the Holy See has participated with great interest in the discussions about protection. It has supported the priority accorded this urgent topic in recent UNHCR initiatives like the Conclusions on the Provision on International Protection Including Through Complementary Forms of Protection (2005), the Conclusion on Women

* Statement delivered at the 59th Session of the Executive Committee of the UNHCR, 7 October 2008.

and Girls at Risk (2006), the Conclusion on Children at Risk (2007), the Commissioner's Dialogue on Protection Challenges (2007), and the Agenda for Protection (2002). In fact, the UNHCR was mandated by the General Assembly to extend its protection capacities to new groups: stateless people, returnees and certain groups of internally displaced persons. Over the years, the concepts of 'group determination (*prima facie*)' and of 'temporary protection' were introduced when considering situations of mass influx movements. In addition, regional agreements and the cluster approach enlarged the field of protection and the capacity to respond.

The process of alerting States about new demands for protection shows both a pragmatic method and a dynamic understanding of the implications of the 1951 Refugee Convention and its related Protocol of 1967. In the same spirit, through regional instruments, States have examined their respective local reality and have agreed upon a more comprehensive and suitable approach by adapting juridical provisions to the evolution of forcible displacement and to geographical conditions. The latest General Conclusion on International Protection, now submitted for approval, rightly points out some current problems of intolerance and failure to meet the rights of asylum seekers while it simultaneously encourages maintenance of relevant international humanitarian and human rights law as a necessary point of reference. Indeed there seems to be an urgent need to expand reflection and statutory provisions to cover the whole range of the constantly changing situations of forcibly uprooted people.

The international community has managed to enact clear and courageous instruments to protect refugees from violence and persecution through the 1951 Refugee Convention and the 1967 Protocol, and through additional regional agreements. Existing refugee instruments constitute the start of a continuum, at the opposite end of which we could place the conventions and agreements enacted by the United Nations and by the International Labour Organization in order to protect labour migrants and their families. At present, between these two policy 'poles', are situated millions of other persons forcibly uprooted by desertification, famine, climate change, generalized oppression and abuse of their human rights. Many of these people remain within their own country without receiving the protection they need, and many cross the borders of neighbouring countries in search of relief. Some of these uprooted persons may come under the mandate of the UNHCR, as do those who become stateless. Many of them do not fit the typology of refugees or migrant workers, but the international community cannot ignore their plight nor can it deny the ethical obligation to extend protection to them, as difficult as this task can be.

In our interconnected world, we are linked with all displaced people by our common humanity and by the realization that the globalization of justice and solidarity is the best guarantee for peace and a common future. The question then to be addressed is of how to start a process to formalize ways and means for the protection of the millions of persons at the center of the continuum: the responsibility to protect them; providing assistance for immediate survival; criteria for their acceptance in other places; the structures of coordination. Existing best practices and human rights obligations can serve as a starting point to move toward a juridical instrument.

The experience of the international community with the implementation of legally binding conventions shows the value of the experts' committees that monitor and advise a converging interpretation of their content. Perhaps a similar group for the Refugee Convention can be a useful complement, possibly within the existing structures of the UNHCR, at this moment when courts, at times, diverge widely in their interpretative decisions.

In conclusion, Mr Chairman, the continued effort to safeguard the human rights of all forcibly displaced people is in line with a consistent ethic of life and with an ever more complete implementation of the Universal Declaration of Human Rights, whose 60th anniversary we mark this year. Displacement is not a phenomenon isolated from other social realities. It is the result of political decisions, of neglect and lack of preventive action, and also of unforeseen natural events. It falls within the responsibility of the State and the international community. An adequate response, therefore, is not possible without coherence in the action of agencies and actors involved and mandated to work for the best solutions. The creative alertness required for such solutions should move the international community to undertake new steps in protection. While juridical instruments are necessary, ultimately a culture of solidarity and the elimination of the root causes of displacement will sustain the protection system.

Thank you, Mr Chairman.

WHY DO WE FAIL TO TAKE CHARGE OF REFUGEES AND DISPLACED PEOPLE?*

Madam Chair,

The Delegation of the Holy See wishes to raise its grave concern with regard to a recurrent theme that was noted in the various regional updates prepared for this meeting of the UNHCR Standing Committee – that is, the difficulty experienced by asylum seekers to gain access to protection and to facilities through which they may present their request for asylum and subsequently expect an equitable consideration of their request in accord with established international standards and procedures.

The differences in receiving and processing asylum claims is quite significant among countries in Europe. The High Commissioner, during his address to the Ministerial Conference focused on 'Building a Europe of Asylum' in September 2008, noted that 'Protection rates for asylum-seekers [in Europe] … can range from zero to near 100%, depending on the country where the claim is examined.'[1] Madam Chair, my Delegation is in agreement with another remark of the High Commissioner: 'Each country is, of course, entitled to define its own migration policy, but international refugee protection norms must be respected.'[2] This appeal merits particular attention given the tragic situation that, during 2008, an estimated 1,502 persons, among whom presumably were a significant number fleeing persecution, met their death while attempting to enter European territory.[3] National and international policies and legal provisions need, therefore, to have a solid base on human rights, the right to life in the first place.

While these particular concerns are being raised with regard to Europe, we should not conclude that they are unique to this region of the world. Thus we note similar trends of constructing physical as well as bureaucratic, legislative and political barriers to asylum seekers in several developed and developing regions of the world.

* Statement delivered at the 44th Meeting of the Standing Committee of the UNHCR Executive Committee of the High Commissioner Program, 3 March 2009.

1 Ministerial Conference 'Building a Europe of Asylum', Paris, 8–9 September 2008, Remarks of United Nations High Commissioner for Refugees António Guterres,www.unhcr.org/admin/ADMIN/48c503f94.html.

2 Ibid.

3 Dossier Fides, 'Il Fenomeno delle Migrazioni in Europa', 31 January 2009.

Madam Chair, 60 years after the adoption of the Declaration on Human Rights and 57 years after the adoption of the Convention Relating to the Status of Refugees, the international community must not abandon its commitment to receive and protect those who seek to demonstrate their flight from a well-founded fear of persecution and are under threat to their very lives. The increasing phenomenon of unaccompanied minors seeking asylum calls for attention especially because it points toward the desperate situation of some families and because it is too often resolved by an ambiguous system of detention. Deeply preoccupied with the plight of refugees and asylum seekers worldwide, Pope Benedict XVI raised the following questions on the occasion of 95th World Day of Migrants and Refugees, observed on 18 January 2009: 'how can we fail to take charge of all those, particularly refugees and displaced people, who are in conditions of difficulty or hardship? How can we fail to meet the needs of those who are *de facto* the weakest and most defenseless, marked by precariousness and insecurity, marginalized and often excluded by society?'[4]

Thus my Delegation, Madam Chair, wishes to thank the High Commissioner for his appeal to keep asylum an effective option in all countries notwithstanding the hardships that the current financial and economic crisis brings about. At the same time, it is incumbent on everyone to address the root causes of forced displacement: a generous humanitarian response has to be matched by an equally committed political one. Finally, we urge that the foundations for a good asylum policy, not only in Europe, that is actively seeking to consolidate one, but throughout the world, fulfill the criteria of providing adequate and safe access to asylum seekers; provide clear, equitable, timely and professional processing of asylum claims; and be rooted in solidarity with all vulnerable and persecuted persons.

[4] Pope Benedict XVI, 'Message for 95th World Day of Migrants and Refugees, 18 January 2009, www.vatican.va/holy_father/benedict_xvi/messages/migration/documents/hf_ben-xvi_mes_20080824_world-migrants-day_en.html.

EFFECTIVE PREVENTION: UNDERSTAND AND ERADICATE THE ROOT CAUSES OF FORCED DISPLACEMENT*

Mr Chairman,

The Delegation of the Holy See extends its congratulations and thanks to you, to the High Commissioner and his staff for the leadership you are providing to assure protection and assistance to refugees and forcibly displaced populations, and for the excellent preparation of the reports and documents being examined.

The evidence provided shows that large numbers of people are still subjected to involuntary displacement and under threat of physical harm, emotional harassment and even death itself. Around the globe, we observe that the tragic plight of forcibly uprooted people continues to weigh on the conscience of the human family. To a great degree, the international community seems to lack the will or the ability to effectively address the suffering and vulnerability of such persons. But: 'how can we fail to take charge of… refugees and displaced people', asked Pope Benedict XVI on the occasion of the 95th World Day of Migrants and Refugees, 'who … are *de facto* the weakest and most defenseless, marked by precariousness and insecurity, marginalized and often excluded by society?'[1]

Mr Chairman, my Delegation believes that in order to achieve a correct analysis and, even more importantly, effective prevention of forced displacement, the global community must set the stage for a wider framework to understand the root causes of such migration. Among these causes are included violent political and cultural conflicts, random acts of violence and destruction in the absence of competent and responsible governmental authorities, systematic violation of universally recognized human rights and failure to respect the life and dignity of the human person. In addition to these long-standing causes, we now must add the deep human impact of climate-related emergencies and of the global economic crisis. These and other 'push' factors causing involuntary displacement demand a concerted and coherent response on the part of the entire international community. Indeed, a realistic framework to prevent

* Statement delivered at the 60th Session of the Executive Committee of the UNHCR, 29 September 2009.

1 www.vatican.va/holy_father/benedict_xvi/messages/migration/documents/hf_ben-xvi_mes_20080824_world-migrants-day_en.html.

the root causes of additional involuntary movements of people is urgently needed.

A more specific concern regards recent trends, in Europe and in other parts of the world, that point to a deterioration of adherence to the principle of *non-refoulement*. The global community must not allow xenophobia or self-interest to deprive victims of violence and persecution from an opportunity to establish a credible claim of asylum and to articulate a legitimate demand for protection. International collaboration and co-responsibility are to be fostered in order to deal with asylum requests with fairness. It is also necessary to ensure unhindered, attentive and law-abiding examination and processing of asylum claims by responsible authorities in countries that have committed themselves to internationally agreed-upon policies and practices in this regard.

My Delegation wishes to raise another urgent appeal – that is, for greater sensitivity to the needs of refugee families who deserve every opportunity, consistent with ethical legal provisions and practices, to remain united and to have unhindered enjoyment of family bonds and relationships. In anticipation of the twentieth Anniversary of the adoption of the Convention on the Rights of the Child, we cannot help but call attention to the increasing number of refugee and internally displaced children, accompanied as well as unaccompanied, caught up in such precarious situations as:

- being lost or otherwise separated from relatives as they start the search for asylum or along the way;
- enduring physical beatings, being maimed or even dying by suffocation when concealed in compartments or containers of trucks, trains or boats;
- falling into the hands of unscrupulous human traffickers;
- being placed into detention, without recourse to other reasonable and compassionate alternatives.

Mr Chairman, my Delegation commends the High Commissioner for his ongoing implementation of The 10-Point Plan of Action for Refugee Protection and Mixed Migration, and for the increasing engagement of States, of international organizations and of civil society in such measures as are specified in the Plan. This strategic document emphasizes a 'needs-first' approach to men, women and children arriving in mixed migration flows and outlines, a process by which the legal rights to various types of protection could be discerned, including that needed by refugees and asylum seekers, by their children, as well as by victims of human trafficking.

We further commend the High Commissioner for the recent formulation of the new 'Policy on Refugee Protection and Solutions in Urban Areas'. Since approximately one-half of the world's 10.5 million refugees now live in cities and towns, as compared to the one-third who live in camps, such attention truly is warranted. Too often, urban refugees and displaced persons remain anonymous and under-served in large conglomerates, forced to live in unspeakable conditions, without any access to legal assistance, with no opportunity to register the births of their children, and deprived of education, opportunities to gain livelihoods, health care, or other basic services. Moreover, such refugees face a wide range of protection risks that are difficult to contain or alleviate. The community-based approach promoted by UNHCR, as articulated in this new policy, is especially welcome, since it will help to mobilize and build capacity among the refugee populations and will promote their dignity, self-esteem and potential, and will help to preserve family unity within such groups.

My Delegation urges the Executive Committee to undertake a more comprehensive study of the relationship between forced migration and development. For the most part, such an analysis has been absent from other relevant international fora, including that of the Global Forum on Migration and Development, which, to date, has focused its attention mainly on the economic aspects of voluntary migration and on the prevention of irregular migration. Since a significant percentage of the world's uprooted people did not freely choose to leave their home territories, such refugees and internally displaced persons urgently need access to opportunities affording integral human development. Despite the gravity of their circumstances, forcibly displaced people possess valuable potential, in terms of skills, capacities and knowledge, that could be transformed into economic and other developmental benefits for their families, host communities, as well as for their countries and areas of origin. They, however, face obstacles in access to training and education and to decent work opportunities in their host communities. While they are placed on 'hold', often at significant expense to host and donor countries, opportunities for further development among such uprooted communities are seriously lacking. By investing in the development potential of internally displaced persons and refugees, host and donor countries can contribute toward the alleviation of the negative conditions that caused these and other populations to move in the first place. With such opportunities, forcibly displaced people could contribute not only to their host region but also could carry back their newly acquired knowledge, skills and work experience to their place of origin, once conditions there have improved to the point of allowing safe voluntary return.

Mr Chairman, the Holy See joins other Delegations in expressing sincere sympathy to the High Commissioner and his staff on the tragic deaths, during the past year, of their colleagues and of staff of implementing partners, as a result of deteriorating security conditions in countries in which they served, Our solidarity also is directed to their grieving families and loved ones. Unfortunately such tragedies confirm the shrinking of humanitarian space available to international and local agencies, including faith-based organizations, that are dedicated to emergency responses in the face of war, conflict and other humanitarian crises. In this regard, we might recall the address of His Holiness Pope Benedict XVI to the United Nations General Assembly, when he urged that every State fulfill its 'primary duty to protect its own population from grave and sustained violations of human rights, as well as from the consequences of humanitarian crises, whether natural or man-made', and pointed out that '[if] States are unable to guarantee such protection, the international community must intervene with the juridical means provided in the United Nations Charter and in other international instruments.'[2]

In conclusion, Mr Chairman, we all share in the heavy responsibility to assure adequate protection for forcibly displaced persons. States, regional and global political structures need to adhere to their international commitments to such vulnerable people, particularly by maintaining respect for and implementation of existing legal frameworks and international policies related to humanitarian emergencies, forced displacement flows, and asylum-seeking and by formulating new and equitable development and conflict-prevention frameworks that can effectively do away with involuntary uprooting of people in the future.

[2] Address of Pope Benedict XVI in Meeting with Members of the General Assembly of the United Nations Organization, New York, 18 April 2008, www.vatican.va/holy_father/benedict_xvi/speeches/2008/april/documents/hf_ben-xvi_spe_20080418_un-visit_en.html.

MIXED FLOWS, INTERNALLY DISPLACED AND URBAN REFUGEES: NEW CHALLENGES*

Mr Chairman,

The Holy See Delegation supports the intense effort made by the UNHCR to call attention to, to refine and to advance the priority of extending increased protection to refugees and persons of concern. Though it appears like a counter-trend to current political sensitivities, it is a timely response, since conflicts have been displacing more people and the forced return of potential asylum seekers gives evidence of a difficult political environment for uprooted people. The latest statistics indicate that involuntary movement of persons around the globe continues. The number of people of concern to the UNHCR has grown to 43.3 million worldwide in 2009, the highest number since the 1990s. A sign of current instability and change, for example, is the number of IDPs in Colombia that has reached 4.9 million at the end of 2009 – a record high – and the new huge wave of refugees from Kyrgyzstan. Confronted with such figures, and the suffering of persons hiding behind the statistics, the right course of action is continuing the enlargement process of categories of people to be protected as the international community has progressively included them in the mandate of the UNHCR. Among the new categories for which more targeted provisions can be developed, mixed flows, internally displaced and urban refugees have rightly been pointed out. The increasing attention given to internally displaced persons moves in this positive general direction. Now that over 50 per cent of the world population lives in urban areas, it is not surprising that refugees follow the same trend and move to cities in greater number, creating specific challenges for their protection from registration of their children at birth to avoid statelessness to employment possibilities, access to education and legal residence. Today's 'boat people' from Africa, Asia and elsewhere cannot simply be towed back to the port of origin of their journey as if distancing their presence would offer a real solution. Similarly, the automatic resort to detaining potential refugees and asylum seekers – often in appalling conditions – is inappropriate.

A combination of safety, respect of human dignity and human rights is necessary. To sustain such a combination, a renewed effort is required to

* Statement delivered at the 48th Meeting of the Standing Committee of the Executive Committee of the UNHCR, 22 June 2010.

prevent forced displacement before it starts and to anticipate events that could trigger protection issues. Equally important is maintaining a strong international consensus on the protection regime which is founded on international law at a time when non-State actors play outside its rules. In the end, protection is an ethical commitment that underlies and serves as a foundation for effective action. The responsibility we owe to vulnerable groups of our one human family prompts adequate answers to remedy the violation of rights and to assist the victims. The same sense of coherence needs to drive States in translating into appropriate protection services the commitments they have assumed. In the final analysis one cannot say that a state has met its responsibility when persons of concern are left in a state of destitution. It certainly is a commendable and encouraging sign that, notwithstanding the enormous difficulty that the current financial and economic crises have brought about, contributions provided for refugees have increased. A culture of friendly human interaction in our globalized world can nourish further solidarity.

The role of media in presenting a positive perception of forcibly displaced persons, a fair indication of the real causes of this displacement and a sound and realistic sense of solidarity can counteract disinformation and the political manipulation of fears of unknown cultures and people. It can show instead that refugees and forcibly displaced people have talents and capacities to offer and show as well the advantages of building together a common future.

Mr Chairman,

In conclusion, allow me to quote the words of Pope Benedict XVI on the occasion of World Refugee Day 2010: 'Refugees wish to find welcome and to be recognized in their dignity and their fundamental rights; at the same time, they intend to offer their contribution to the society that accepts them. We pray that, in a just reciprocity, an adequate response be given to such expectations and that the refugees show the respect they feel for the identity of the receiving community.'

Thank you, Mr Chairman.

REDUCING THE NUMBER OF ASYLUM SEEKERS*

Mr Chairman,

The Delegation of the Holy See extends its congratulations and thanks to you and in this 60th anniversary year of the Statute of the Office of the United Nations High Commissioner for Refugees and General Assembly Resolution 428, thanks the High Commissioner and his staff for the protection and assistance rendered to persons of concern throughout the world.

The first task imposed by the Statutes of the Office of the High Commissioner was to promote 'the conclusion and ratification of international conventions for the protection of refugees'. As we are all aware the year 2011 will mark the 60th anniversary of the Convention Relating to the Status of Refugees. A major response has been given.

Mr Chairman, the Statute imposes upon the High Commissioner the duty to 'improve the situation of refugees'. Of course, this is a responsibility shared with States, and over the years much has been accomplished. We were dismayed, however, to read in last year's report on *Global Strategic Priorities* (EC/60/SC/INF.2) that at the time of writing there had been 1,777 credible reports of *refoulement* occurring in at least 60 countries. These numbers did not reflect the tragic events occurring to some asylum seekers at the end of 2009. Were it possible also to consider *unreported* cases of *refoulement* and 'push-back' to unsafe countries, we would be face-to-face with a protection deficit of considerable proportion. All of us need to reflect seriously and remain engaged in how to give priority to people even though protection space is shrinking.

In the words of the Statute, refugees, persons needing and desiring international protection, are within 'the competence' of the High Commissioner, especially within the context of his particular competence by using his good offices to seek and frame solutions for refugees and other persons of concern. Recent initiatives on assuring protection in contexts of mixed migration, including regional and international processes to actualize the 10-Point Plan of Action, have wisely engaged the range of actors in States, international organizations and NGOs, and have been of increasing practical value. My Delegation would further welcome the adoption of an Executive Committee Conclusion about persons of

* Statement delivered at the 61st Session of the Executive Committee of the UNHCR, 5 October 2010.

concern with disabilities. At the same time, we wish to encourage the High Commissioner in his endeavors to address the problems of birth registration for people of concern.

Commitments to current solutions, however, are not sufficient, a fact painfully evident in today's 36 and a half million persons of concern to the UNHCR and, among them, in the distress of so many millions of refugees in protracted situations. Even with the welcome commitment to formal new resettlement programs by a number of countries, resettlement places worldwide have fallen to a level less than half of the resettlement need that UNHCR has identified for the coming year. The solution of resettlement merits greater support, as do voluntary repatriation and local integration, where numbers have also been low. With this in mind, my Delegation is supportive of the High Commissioner's exploration of channels of legal labour migration to provide additional refugee solutions. Indeed, refugees tell us how important legal livelihoods are to their own search for solutions and, as we all see, more than a few choose to go in this direction even outside of legal channels. The *sine qua non* of such a 'fourth durable solution', however, would have to be specific attention to the unique and enduring protection need of the refugees.

Mr Chairman, refugee protection is inextricably linked to recognition of status as a refugee. The Holy See continues to be alarmed by the trend among developed nations to externalize status determination procedures, especially to places with records of violation of human rights. A convergence of efforts seems called for to develop criteria of protection for vulnerable forcibly uprooted people still left in the gray areas of the law. My Delegation also deeply regrets the practice of detention of asylum seekers. This is particularly lamentable when it results in the separation of families and or the detention of children. We are pleased by UNHCR's participation and leadership in the round table on alternatives to detention which was held in Seoul, in April of this year. Before leaving the topic of status determination, my Delegation notes that in far too many States the responsibility for status determination is still left with UNHCR, even in States which are party to the Convention. While States need to undertake this duty, UNHCR has to ensure that all procedural and other safeguards it recommends to others in regard to status determination, particularly the assistance of counsel and right to a meaningful appeal process, be present in its status determination procedures.

The world and the High Commissioner's responsibilities have moved on since 1950. The General Assembly has encouraged the High Commissioner to extend his good offices on behalf of conflict-induced internally displaced persons. In 2009, for the first time, there were more internally displaced persons of concern to UNHCR than refugees. Like refugees, IDPs as presently defined are the product of violations of human rights which are part and parcel of any armed conflict. Any durable solution for IDPs must be based on recognition and protection of human rights.

Mr Chairman, in this year the two largest displacements of persons have been the result of natural disasters: the January 12th earthquake in Port-au-Prince and the enormous flooding in Pakistan. My Delegation compliments the role UNHCR played in coordinating protection and assistance in each of these calamities.

Lastly, Mr Chairman, we are reminded that the Statute instructs the High Commissioner 'to reduce the number requiring protection'. Such a reduction can only come about through the recognition, defense and fostering of human rights, be they political, social, cultural or economic. This way of avoiding destructive conflicts and of safeguarding the dignity of every person is the main road to promote the common good in any country and in the global community and the best prevention of forced displacement.

Thank you, Mr Chairman.

REFUGEES ARE NOT ANONYMOUS NUMBERS BUT PERSONS WITH DIGNITY, TALENTS AND ASPIRATIONS*

Mr Chairman,

In the past 60 years since the enactment of the 1951 Refugee Convention, the UNHCR, other relevant UN agencies, hosting States, faith-based and other organizations of civil society have undertaken tremendous efforts to ensure protection of refugees, to safeguard their human dignity and to provide for them a new start in life. In fact, the Convention has been receptive to new emergencies and has included in its protection new victims of persecution by non-State actors and of other forms of violence. The civilizing effect of a treaty giving rights to refugees, asylum seekers and other forcibly displaced persons, some 43 million of them, cannot be overestimated. However, there are still important gaps highlighted by recent dramatic events like the 'people's revolutions' in some parts of North Africa and the drought and conflict in the Horn of Africa that have sparked large refugee flows as well as by protracted refugee situations in the Middle East and elsewhere. Perhaps the most tragic evidence of an unfinished protection task comes from the more than 1,500 people who died while trying to cross the Mediterranean, others who drowned crossing the Gulf of Aden and the uncalculated numbers who have died walking out of Somalia in search for safety this year alone.

In its Preamble, the 1951 Refugee Convention sets as its purpose 'to assure refugees the widest possible exercise of their fundamental rights and freedoms'. But today in many regions of the world millions of refugees are yet unable to enjoy these rights. The noble goal set by the Convention at the end of the devastating experience of the Second World War has lately been eroded. My Delegation would like to point out just a few areas of concern.

Public opinion and political expediency have impacted the need for protection of asylum seekers in a negative way. Among these negative consequences, we note with deep regret that detention of asylum seekers and other people in need of protection is rising and it is no longer used as last resort for exceptional cases. These persons who are looking for protection or for ways of trying to survive are literally locked up and guarded as if they were criminal prisoners, and children too are

* Statement delivered at the 62nd Session of the Executive Committee of the UNHCR, 4 October 2011.

placed in the same conditions. Very often their living arrangements in detention lead to distinctively deteriorative effects upon the individual person. The prison-like environments existing in many detention centers, the isolation from the 'outside world', the unreliable flow of information and the disruption of a life plan, affect the physical and mental health of asylum seekers and bring about psychological stress, depression and self-uncertainty, decreased appetite and varying degrees of insomnia. The manner in how detainees see themselves is significantly impacted by detention. In this context, self-perception becomes an important indicator of the effects of detention because as an administrative measure it should not bring such detrimental personal consequences. It is, therefore, urgent that alternatives to detention be further developed and promoted as, for example, would be expanding community-based supervised programs, the introduction of monitoring and reporting mechanisms, the formation of support groups, of drop-in centers, adding to the capacity of open house projects so that at least families with children may reside in a safe living environment. In this way, administrative detention becomes the very last resort.

The policy of self-settlement outside camps has met with some success both with more educated and with poor refugees and these positive results seem to support trying it on a larger scale. Besides, the refugees warehoused in refugee camps are not necessarily more likely to repatriate than those who self-settle. Finally, although donors' solidarity is confronted with a more complex administrative task, it enhances the human development of refugees and gives them a better chance for their future.

Of concern to the Holy See and faith-based agencies are also the many refugees, asylum seekers and failed asylum seekers who find themselves trapped in situations of destitution. All over the world we can see people on the move who for good reasons cannot return to countries of origin and yet are completely excluded from social services in the countries where they are living. These persons are in limbo, in an impasse, without any perspective. It is not simply bad luck but policies of state authorities that completely exclude such groups of uprooted persons from any official assistance and leave them in distress and penury even though they need protection. Without access to housing, to health care, education, social assistance and work the situation of these people is especially worrisome. At present more than half of the refugee population is located outside camps and it is particularly vulnerable to destitution. National and local authorities should continue assuming responsibility for these refugees with the assured solidarity of international agencies.

Positive developments have already been initiated by UNHCR through innovative methods to reach 'urban' refugees including mailing SMS messages concerning the distribution of assistance, Internet access and videos on refugee rights, telephone hotlines to answer questions, and the distribution of bank cards to enable refugees to withdraw financial assistance at their convenience.

Hundreds of unauthorized, lone boys from the Middle East and other places are making their way across Europe challenging the protection system of the countries they cross. In fact, unaccompanied minors are in the thousands. In 2008 a total of 11,292 applications for asylum were lodged by unaccompanied minors in 22 Member States of the European Union. Some even die hidden in containers or in the undercarriage of trucks. The increased visibility acquired by unaccompanied minors claiming asylum in developed countries calls for a renewed attention to their need of protection and to the development of practical measures to help them adjust to the new environment.

Unaccompanied minors must be treated first and foremost as children and their best interest must be a primary consideration independently of the reason for their flight. For this reason, detention and closed accommodations prove to be inappropriate for minors in particular, as does the mixing of children with adults in these facilities. Research has shown that as a source of motivation and support religion is considered important by these minors who desire the availability of spiritual advisors. In this context, processing children's applications for asylum should be given a greater priority with the possibility for the unaccompanied minors who become adults to continue benefiting from the same determination procedure as those who are under 18 years of age. At times, unfortunately, unaccompanied minors arrive under false pretences as forerunners to trigger family reunion or as victims of smuggling and trafficking and therefore care should be taken to prevent their exploitation.

Mr Chairman,

The evolving political and humanitarian global situation raises continued challenges to the responsibility of the international community to protect the victims of forced displacement. New strategies and new policies are required that range from the understanding of root causes to border management and integration. Creative compassion becomes possible if there is a genuine sense of solidarity and responsibility toward the needier members of our human family. We should not forget these facts when discussing policies on refugee protection. Refugees are not anonymous numbers but persons, men, women and children with individual stories, with talents to offer and aspirations to be met.

Thank you, Mr Chairman.

THE NEED TO MATCH POLITICAL WILL WITH THE UPDATE OF PROTECTION OBJECTIVES*

Mr Chairman,

Refugees have always been part of history. Unfortunately today their number and their suffering still remain a wound in the social fabric of the international community. They continue to challenge our conscience, each one of the 33 million persons whom the UNHCR is currently mandated to protect and assist. 'A world where human rights are violated with impunity will never stop producing refugees of all kinds.'[1] Uprooted by wars, political upheavals, ethnic cleansing, religious persecution and other human rights violations, refugees are both the flashing red light of alarm pointing out deep social and political failures and an urgent call to remedy their suffering. The Holy See is pleased to take part in these commemorations of the 60th anniversary of the major instrument of refugee protection and of the 50th anniversary of the 1961 Convention on the Reduction of Statelessness. It is a special moment to express appreciation for the generous work carried out and to motivate renewed commitment and search for innovative responses. The Holy See was among the original 26 States that took part in the Conference of Plenipotentiaries in July of 1951 which gave rise to one of the conventions we commemorate today. Despite the tense geopolitical situation of the time, the parties held the hope that they could produce a convention that would make the world a better, safer, more humane place. They succeeded in the efforts and for 60 years people fleeing persecution have found protection. The Convention Relating to the Status of Refugees was a good document for the time and was left open for greater inclusiveness. Intervening events and international agreements suggest possibilities that now can update and make more realistic the protection objectives of the Convention, in line with developments in this first part of the twenty-first century.

* Statement delivered at the intergovernmental event at ministerial level on the occasion of the 60th anniversary of the 1951 Convention Relating to the Status of Refugees and the 50th anniversary of the 1961 Convention on the Reduction of Statelessness, 7–8 December 2011.

1 Cf. Pontifical Council 'Cor Unum' – Pontifical Council for the Pastoral Care of Migrants and Itinerant People; *Refugee: A Challenge to Solidarity*, Vatican City: Liberia Editrice Vaticana, 1992.

Mr Chairman,

At the close of last year's High Commissioner's Dialogue, he noted the lack of the right 'to run for one's life'. The refugee definition in Article 1 of the 1951 Convention provides for protection from persecution. Public culture and a greater awareness of human rights call for a new understanding of forced displacement to escape tragic situations that are equivalent to persecution, for example, natural disasters, or events that seriously disturb public order and mistaken economic policies which put a population in life-threatening conditions. A culture of protection entails a dynamic evolution of standards, which, in turn, will promote peaceful relations and the common good since they safeguard the dignity and the rights of every person at risk.

Moreover, the right to run for one's life entails the right to enter a foreign territory while at the same time consideration is given to both the good of the receiving society and the need of asylum seekers. Burden sharing in this regard is not limited to the provision of financial support by wealthier States to States hosting large numbers of refugees, but also implies their acceptance of persons fleeing conflict or disaster in similar proportion to poorer States. Recent examples have shown that the gap between poor and rich countries in welcoming refugees remains significantly wide.

Regional measures have advanced humanitarian law by adopting a more comprehensive understanding of protection for forcibly displaced persons. The universalization of such norms would be beneficial and would encourage a new mentality of welcome.

Mr Chairman,

Article 4 of the 1951 Convention recognizes the universal right to freedom of religion in the same manner as accorded to nationals of the receiving State. Subsequent human rights treaties, however, have recognized that States may not impose restrictions on this right. In this Delegation's view, Article 18 of the International Covenant on Civil and Political Rights (ICCPR) should be used to interpret and apply Article 4 and specifically recognize the right of a person to change his or her religion in accord with the dictates of his or her conscience.

In a similar fashion the rights to which refugees are entitled, for example, the right to freedom of movement and the human right to work to support one's family must be given more respect and further extended in the coming years. Encampment, in our view, is permissible, for a short period of time, in an influx situation. But use of encampment as a permanent policy, and making access to legal work almost impossible for most refugees, are both practices which should be progressively abandoned.

Mr Chairman,

Article 22 of the present convention ensures the right to primary education for refugees on an equal footing with nationals. Today this right should be extended to include secondary education and vocational training. In fact, no child anywhere can be prepared to contribute to society if his or her education ceases after primary school. In this regard we would note the special need to see that girls and young women receive education. In the first place, going to school is a form of protection. A well-supervised, well-run school is a deterrent to violence against women and girls. Moreover, providing education to girls and women affirms their equal dignity and prevents discrimination and confinement to secondary roles in society.

Mr Chairman,

As we commemorate the 60 years of the refugee convention and the 50 years of the convention on the reduction of Statelessness, these are some concerns the Delegation of the Holy See wishes to raise as an encouragement to pursue protection for forcibly uprooted people in line with contemporary circumstances. The practical implementation of adequate forms of protection demands a political will that only deep convictions of solidarity and mutual responsibility for the common good can provide. The dialectical tension between the ideal response and existential pragmatism will persist. The way into the future, however, requires both a renewed effort to eliminate the root causes of forced displacement and a more comprehensive protection when displacements occur. The task eludes the good will of any single country and calls for coherence and cooperation. Pope Benedict XVI expresses the hope that the concept of the family of nations can acquire real force. He writes: 'One senses the urgent need to find innovative ways of implementing the principle of the responsibility to protect and of giving poorer nations an effective voice in shared decision-making. This seems necessary in order to arrive at a political, juridical and economic order which can increase and give direction to international cooperation for the development of all peoples in solidarity. To manage the global economy … and to regulate migration: for all this, there is urgent need of a true world political authority … Without this, despite the great progress accomplished in various sectors, international law would risk being conditioned by the balance of power among the strongest nations. The integral development of peoples and international cooperation require the establishment of a greater degree of international ordering, marked by subsidiarity, for the management of globalization.'[2]

In the area of forcibly displaced people, this ethical approach can open a way to a future when all human rights are fully accorded to refugees and the right of any human being to run for his or her life is acknowledged and respected.

Thank you, Mr Chairman.

[2] Pope Benedict XVI, Encyclical Letter, *Caritas in Veritate*, § 67.

THE REFUGEES' DECISION TO FLEE THEIR COUNTRY IS AN ACT OF FAITH AND HOPE IN THE SOLIDARITY OF THE HUMAN FAMILY*

Mr Chairman,

Protection remains an urgent concern. With 42.5 million persons forced out from their homes or remaining in exile for fear of persecution and of violation of their fundamental human rights, and in many cases life-threatening hostility because of their religious convictions, the international community is challenged to devise creative responses adequate to today's circumstances. Unfortunately, the task is made more difficult by the fact that, in addition to the traditional armed conflicts, forced displacement is exacerbated by climate change, lack of food, natural disasters and by the complex situations created by war-lords and rebels and by breakaway regions. Moreover, the political will to help is weakened by economic and domestic crises that make public opinion less generous to offer asylum and restrict, rather than enlarge, the number of countries ready to provide it. The 1951 Convention on the status of refugees was an important step forward 61 years ago; it shows some limits now in addressing the needs of an increasingly connected, globalized and complex world. Under the current understanding of 'refugee' many individuals are excluded from receiving the proper protection that should be afforded to them based on their human rights and on human rights law as well as on our collective responsibility of solidarity.

Protection of these vulnerable groups – refugees, asylum seekers, internally displaced persons, stranded migrants and other people obliged to move for survival – is an international imperative that requires a positive, institutionalized approach to humanitarian assistance. Every person's innate dignity calls for a response especially in situations of suffering and uprootedness. As the Holy Father Benedict XVI said a few days ago on the occasion of the World Day of Refugees: 'I express the hope that their rights may always be respected.'[1]

The international community can move to a non-categorical approach to the forced displacement crises without regard to the status of the people involved. The primary concern of States and relevant

* Statement delivered at the 54th Meeting of the Standing Committee of the Executive Committee of the UNHCR on International Protection, 26 June 2012.

[1] Pope Benedict XVI, Angelus, Sunday, 17 June 2012.

stakeholders should be to protect and promote the fundamental human rights of those who are forcibly removed from their normal situations in their places of origins. Humanitarian assistance, freed from a consideration of the status of a person, should aim at supporting their immediate needs and to plan long-term solutions leading to a normal life.

A non-categorical approach to humanitarian assistance is important so that each individual person is recognized and attended to. In fact, the individual person has to be afforded protection and assistance as the implementation of his or her human rights, and more importantly because of his inalienable human dignity. A useful step to achieving the protection of all people seeking refuge is to universalize legal obligations on States in relation to protection and assistance of internally displaced persons.

An additional benefit of a non-categorical approach is a more comprehensive opportunity to sustainable resettlement with a shorter period to determine its implementation. At the same time, the unity of the family remains an important and even necessary resource in making any long-term solution really successful. Education also is a critical resource for protection. It should be provided to both boys and girls in order to give them tools to succeed and as a means against their falling victim of trafficking, abuse and other similar atrocities. These policies of international protection have to continue to be inclusive and non-discriminatory on matters of age, sex, religion or race.

In conclusion, as traditional distinctions among categories of people on the move are increasingly blurred, the existing normative framework can be interpreted with a serious concern for the human rights for all and reinforced by a sense of human solidarity. To remedy the protection gap at this moment when political and economic conditions do not seem favorable to new international norms, more generous interpretations should find wide agreement, national and regional policies should find greater support and more practical cooperation should develop among the existing institutions concerned with displaced people. Of course, the best solution resides in hearts disposed to peace and in a political determination to work at pre-empting conflicts in the first place.

The protection system needs greater policy attention. Affected countries should be helped in improving their capacity to protect and measures enacted to interdict and expedite removal and immigration-related security programs should not prevent bona fide asylum seekers and people looking for survival from reaching territorial protection.

Mr Chairman,

Persons fleeing their home leave because of fear and desperation. But, more importantly, their decision is an act of faith and hope that the solidarity of the human family and the actions of the international community will continue to witness and provide compassion and support that will enable them to enjoy again their human rights and a normal existence.

INVEST IN EDUCATION TO HARVEST BENEFITS FOR THE FUTURE*

Mr Chairman,

The surge in the number of recent conflicts has produced new waves of refugees and displaced persons. The futility of violence as a method for resolving disputes is evident in the price in suffering that hundreds of thousands of persons, mostly women and children, are paying as a consequence of political decisions that disregard their human impact. Forcibly uprooted people challenge the international community, that has failed to prevent it, to respond to their vulnerability. Family life has been disrupted, minors find themselves in a lonely life in refugee camps or in dangerous urban environments, and for all refugees the traumatic experience of death and destruction left behind marks their existence forever. These facts are all too familiar as they repeat themselves with every new crisis without, unfortunately, teaching us to avoid such tragedies.

The media spotlight focuses on the more politically interesting cases for them and leave in the shadows of public awareness other masses of displaced people forgotten and left to their tragic destiny. The Holy See Delegation takes note and is grateful for those countries which have kept their borders and their hearts open to receive refugees fleeing conflict in neighboring States and calls on all Member States to assist in sharing the burden these new refugee populations place on many of their hosts.

New complicating variables make the obligation to assist today's refugees more difficult. Not only the persisting economic crisis limits the options of response to the current emergencies, but also a devastating drought in some parts of the world has damaged crops and further weakened economic recovery. Food prices are volatile and foodstuff is excessively used for biofuels. Thus food for refugee camps costs more and risks being inadequate. It would be an additional tragedy if food speculation were to aggravate the delivery of humanitarian assistance to the increasing number of refugees and forcibly displaced persons.

Regarding burden sharing in the present circumstances, a country's wealth and level of development needs to be taken into account. Allow me to quote a pertinent remark by Pope Benedict XVI writing to the Chancellor of the Federal Republic of Germany: 'The Holy See has

* Statement delivered at the 63rd Session of the Executive Committee of the UNHCR, 2 October 2012.

repeatedly insisted that, while the governments of poorer countries have a responsibility with regard to good governance and the elimination of poverty, the active involvement of international partners is indispensable. This should not be seen as an "extra" or as a concession which could be postponed in the face of pressing national concerns. It is a grave and unconditional moral responsibility, founded on the unity of the human race, and on the common dignity and shared destiny of rich and poor alike, who are drawn ever closer by the process of globalization.'[1]

The limits now experienced with implementing the classical durable solutions of voluntary return, resettlement and local integration should encourage new efforts both to prevent refugee flows and to imagine some concrete mechanisms for a fairer distribution of responsibility in today's globalized world. The application of the concept of citizenship as an equalizing basic right instead of ethnic or religious affiliation for the population of a country could serve as a good example of a new understanding of social cohesion that helps to prevent conflicts. The commitment to formation of a reconciliation attitude instead of approving and teaching hatred and revenge to children, especially those affected by forced uprooting, will alleviate the risk of future revenge and violence and consequent refugee production. The vicious circle can be broken by forgiveness, dialogue and reconciliation.

Mr Chairman,

An inevitable consequence of protracted refugee situations is that children born into them get older. Like all children they need hope for their future and an opportunity to develop into productive adults. Education is a key factor in this development. My Delegation welcomes the UNHCR's expanded vision of education announced in its recent education policy. The preparation of teachers, the availability of education facilities no matter how simple, regular teaching programs, are invaluable resources, and good evidence of their value is provided by their implementation in the largest world refugee camp of Dadaab (Kenya). Very important is also the recognition in the UNHCR's policy that ending refugee education with primary education is to stunt development of the children in our care. The Holy See calls on States hosting refugee

[1] www.vatican.va/holy_father/benedict_xvi/letters/2006/documents/hf_ben-xvi_let_20061216_vertice-g8_en.html.

populations to remove all barriers to further education for these children, barriers such as study permits and lack of access to government-sponsored scholarships, so that their potential might be realized. For the countries unable to meet these objectives, international solidarity should help them. Even though resources are really stretched at the moment, investment in education assures benefits for the future.

Mr Chairman,

It is once again a fact this year that there are more persons internally displaced by conflict in the world than there are refugees. My Delegation is also aware that the topic of the extent of the UNHCR's involvement in providing assistance to IDPs is one on which States differ. In some instances there is a genuine fear of 'mission creep' and a concern that the core mission of the UNHCR, protection of refugees, will suffer. In other instances there is reason to suspect that the presence of neutral, international eyes during internal armed conflict or the provision of life-saving assistance to locally disfavored groups might not be welcome. The Holy See encourages the High Commissioner to continue to go the extra mile with regard to those displaced by armed conflict. This should be done in the first instance by seeking humanitarian access to affected populations to assess their protection needs, and in the second instance in coordination with other United Nations bodies by providing crucial assistance to these people. In connection with this the Holy See welcomes the humanitarian efforts being made by the UNHCR on behalf of the people of the Eastern area of the Democratic Republic of Congo. At the same, time my Delegation sincerely hopes that the pleas from the religious leaders of the region be heard and acted on by all parties to the conflict in that region that the killings, rapes and forced recruitment of child soldiers end.

Mr Chairman,

In conclusion, as armed clashes persist and new uprooted people are obliged to seek survival in exile and in precarious conditions of physical and psychological suffering it becomes our common responsibility to search and apply more creative and concrete forms of solidarity and protection.

Thank you, Mr Chairman.

STRENGTHEN THE COOPERATION BETWEEN THE UNHCR AND FAITH COMMUNITIES*

Madam Chair,

Violence once more is producing hundreds of thousands of forcibly displaced people. The Delegation of the Holy See notes with regret that the number of persons of concern to the UNHCR throughout the world has increased over the past twelve months. In almost all instances this increase is due to the continuation of armed conflicts while at the present time the States involved, the regional structures and the international community as a whole lack the political will to dialogue and to reach peaceful political solutions. Armaments will not help balancing fighting groups' influence and only will kill more civilians and uproot more families. This tragic evidence reconfirms that with war everything is lost and with peace everything is to be gained.

Madam Chair, my Delegation is pleased that in this moment of heightened displacement of people, the High Commissioner has initiated efforts to explore the role of faith communities in protection. The High Commissioner's dialogue on faith and protection last December was the successful expression of the convergence of people of faith in giving priority to compassion, solidarity and respectful dialogue as the appropriate method in responding to the plight of refugees. We note with approval the Affirmations of Faith Leaders which have been released recently as a follow up to the Dialogue. First-hand reports received from the areas of conflict show how faith communities are providers of protection. At the present time in Syria, one Catholic international organization is working through over 20 faith communities, Catholic, Orthodox, Protestant and Muslim, to provide food, medicines, shelter and psychosocial support to over 100,000 people in Damascus, Homs, Aleppo and surrounding rural areas. The recipients of these benefits are mostly Muslim, just as the population of Syria is in the majority Muslim. The benefits are not distributed according to creed, but according to need. It is a case of Syrians helping Syrians. These faith-based groups are not subject to the constraints of UNDSS security rules nor the tactics of politics which often impede the delivery of assistance. They are not part of the conflict, but are seeking to serve the needs of other non-combatants who are suffering. In my

* Statement delivered at the 57th Meeting of the Standing Committee of UNHCR, 26 June 2013.

Delegation's view it is vital that links between such groups and the UNHCR be strengthened so that the protection mandate may be better achieved.

Madam Chair,

This Delegation admires the generous efforts of Jordan, Lebanon, Turkey and Iraq in receiving over one and a half million refugees from Syria. This has been at great cost to these host countries as well as to the financial resources of UNHCR. The response of the international community to this emergency is indeed heartening. Much has been given, yet more is still needed. At the same time my Delegation is concerned that other emergencies, other people in need of protection, are being neglected as all the money moves to the Syrian emergency. We worry when we hear that needed protection services are being restricted in other parts of the world because there is no longer any money to pay for them. Madam President, a sick child requiring medicine in a refugee camp in Zambia is no different from a sick child requiring medicine in Damascus, or Amman. Each is in need and each deserves protection because the life of each is precious.

Madam Chair,

As a final point, my Delegation will address the question of access to protection space. The example of Jordan, Lebanon, Turkey and Iraq calls to mind their willingness to allow foreigners to enter their territory for protection. Indeed, these countries show the way to the rest of the international community. It is not enough to merely admire from afar the generous policies adopted and implemented by these countries and not emulate them. My Delegation, therefore, calls on the High Commissioner to continue his efforts to expand space for first asylum and space for resettlement and other durable solutions.

Thank you, Madam Chair.

MIGRANTS AND REFUGEES ARE NOT PAWNS ON THE CHESSBOARD OF HUMANITY: THE ADMIRABLE RESPONSE OF COUNTRIES HOSTING SYRIAN REFUGEES*

Madam President,

In recent years, crises have multiplied in different regions of the world, and they have produced growing numbers of forcibly displaced people. By some estimates, 100 million people have left their homes involuntarily in order to seek freedom, safety and survival outside their region or their country. These uprooted masses represent a protection concern that challenges States and the international community. Often going unnoticed among the available statistics are some particularly troubling trends: in 2012, there were 21,300 applications by unaccompanied or separated children among the overall number of 893,700 claims; 15.4 million refugees were counted in all parts of the world; mixed migration groups took to the sea, which caused increasingly complex normative and practical challenges for efforts to assist them; 26 million people were displaced by armed conflicts, violence and human rights violations and whose presence adds a serious strain on very weak national and local institutions. Syria is an emblematic case, as the special High-Level Segment has shown. Legal instruments have been developed for the protection of these people, but a significant gap persists between the implementation of agreed standards and reality on the ground. Thus it becomes clear that humanitarian solutions cannot be effective unless the underlying political factors are solved.

Emergencies, such as the conflicts in Syria and in the African and Asian continents, have motivated an admirable and generous response of host countries, that keep their borders open to even large numbers of persons in need of refuge, and the practical importance to further develop effective partnerships to meet the increasing demands. Faith-based communities are immediately open and responsive to the first impact of new arrivals and provide emergency relief. With limited resources, and putting to best use their identity and base in local communities, knowledge of the territory, and their influence, they strive to create a climate of acceptance and support. Their engagement continues on a long-term basis and, whenever possible, they accompany forcibly displaced people during their

* Statement delivered at the 64th Session of the Executive Committee of UNHCR, 2 October 2013.

life in camps, or in poor urban neighbourhoods, and provide counselling and education, job placement, food and shelter. By establishing friendly human relations with the refugees after their inhuman treatment, these organizations facilitate a healing process.

An important dimension of protection in the uncertainty, isolation and abandonment experienced by forcibly uprooted persons is offering them some hope about the future, a sense of meaning that may serve as a compass to their lives despite the disruptive and painful circumstances they face. In this way, refugees can muster the psychological strength to cope with their situation, plan for the future and maintain initiative no matter how depressing the environment. In this way they also become agents of development and creativity and enrich the communities that welcome them. Refugee children in particular – over one million of them have just crossed the Syrian borders – need access to education to serve as a guarantee for their future, so that immediate survival may turn into the beginning of a constructive journey toward a normal existence.

Madam President,

Solidarity and burden sharing on the part of countries receiving refugees should not diminish because of compassion fatigue. The long years of giving should be considered in relation to the protracted situations of some 7.5 million refugees trapped in exile and to the traumatic and multi-faceted suffering of newly produced forcibly displaced people. Today millions of uprooted persons send a new appeal to the international community: to share the means of survival; to recommit to prevention of new refugee flows; to ensure a good future for those who have fled. The links between extreme poverty, inequality and violations of human rights on one hand, and conflicts and wars on the other, is well established. The only reasonable and advantageous path ahead is dialogue to prevent new catastrophes, additional vulnerable groups, new victims, especially women and children, who, in many cases, are subjected to abuse, new suffering, expensive refugee response programs, and new instability for everyone. As already Pope John XXIII observed in 1962: 'Promoting, favouring, accepting conversations at all levels and in any time, is a rule of wisdom and prudence which attracts the blessings of heaven and earth.'

Madam President,

In conclusion, the Delegation of the Holy See shares in and supports the contribution to the cause of refugees, of host and donor countries, and of local communities. It constantly encourages concrete responses, especially on the part of religiously motivated communities and organizations, working in partnership with others. Pope Francis has recently said: 'Migrants and refugees are not pawns on the chessboard of humanity.'[1] Indeed, a new effort is required: to go at the root of refugee production and to address squarely the political responsibility to work together to prevent forcible uprooting of people and promote the respect of the God-given dignity of every person.

Thank you, Madam President.

[1] Pope Francis, Message for the World Day of Migrants and Refugees, 19 January 2014.

50 MILLION FORCIBLY DISPLACED PEOPLE HAVE A RIGHT TO RECOVER THEIR FREEDOM AND DIGNITY*

Mr Chairman,

Today's world is confronted with the highest number of people, over 50 million, fleeing their home, since the Second World War. The causes of such tragedy unfortunately have become too familiar: persecution, human rights violations, armed conflicts, life-threatening extreme poverty. Moreover, one needs to take into account those forced from their homes because of natural disasters and large-scale development schemes.

The first UN High Commissioner for refugees, Dr Gerrit Jan van Heuven Goedhart, summarized the solution as follows: 'The essence is to find a little place, which is not just a roof over one's head, not just a place to live in. It is the all-embracing term for a series of elements which together constitute a man's independence and therefore his freedom and his dignity' (Address, Oslo, 12 December 1955). We are all challenged to ensure that all uprooted persons may recover at least a minimum of freedom and dignity.

In fact, refugees and displaced persons are subjects of rights and duties as all human beings, and not merely the objects of assistance. They deserve protection, which should translate into concrete action the values and principles of respect for human rights and dignity. The evolution over the years of political and humanitarian circumstances have necessitated a wider interpretation of the concept of refugee. The UNHCR promoted this process by encouraging the international community to enlarge existing notions. The High Commissioner often has found it necessary to exercise his 'good offices'[1] in order to assure protection to refugees and other displaced persons. Such past actions need to be repeated, and even strengthened, at the present time. Protection of persons should take precedence over disproportionate concerns about State security. Nor should hospitality be limited to the private sphere. It needs to become part and parcel of the world of politics and thus make a difference at national and global levels. Burden sharing and solidarity extend

* Statement delivered at the 60th Session of the Standing Committee of UNHCR, 1 July 2014.

1 United Nations General Assembly Resolution, A/RES/1388, 20 November 1959, para. 2, authorizes the High Commissioner, in respect of refugees who do not come within the competence of the United Nations, to use his good offices in the transmission of contributions designed to provide assistance to these refugees.

to having more flexible borders policies and an easier access to asylum procedures. In addition, substantially increased resettlement possibilities could greatly advance the achievement of durable solutions.

In Europe, a common strategy is essential, so that the countries of first arrival may not be forced to bear the full burden alone. This requires a strategic accord that allocates refugees among all EU countries, taking into account criteria like the economic situation of the country, its size and population, and the talents and preferences of the people involved.

This further demands the education and sensitization of public opinion with regard to our common responsibility on the causes of conflict and on the search for peaceful solutions and co-existence. Faith communities, which are present everywhere, advocate a shared message of compassion and solidarity. They are particularly attentive to accompanying people on their journey to safety and can offer a unique contribution, that forced migration should be seen in a fuller perspective of individual, social and community consequences. This more inclusive, coherent and cohesive vision of forced migration facilitates a comprehensive analysis of causes and consequences motivated by full respect for human life and dignity.

In conclusion, the current situation shows the replay of a familiar tragedy with changed faces and new methods of escape. Arguments are restated on the ethical responsibility to eliminate the root causes of so much suffering. It remains urgent in the world of today to call for a renewed commitment and to implement the good conclusions reached. As Pope Francis has remarked: 'I ask leaders and legislators and the entire international community above all to confront the reality of those who have been displaced by force, with effective projects and new approaches in order to protect their dignity, to improve the quality of their life and to face the challenges that are emerging from modern forms of persecution, oppression and slavery.'[2]

Thank you, Mr Chairman.

[2] Speech Plenaria Pontifical Council for the Pastoral Care of Migrants and People on the Move, 24 May 2013.

GLOBALIZATION OF SOLIDARITY FOR REFUGEES IN AFRICA*

Mr President,

The Delegation of the Holy See supports the UNHCR Executive Committee Statement on Enhancing International Cooperation, Solidarity, Local Capacities and Humanitarian Action for Refugees in Africa. The Statement is a timely reminder of the persistent flow of forcibly uprooted peoples and a call to overcome the globalization of indifference to their suffering.

Within the African continent, as well as from Africa toward Europe and the world, the search of a safe haven and of a decent life pushes many people to abandon their homes and to cross borders to escape danger and oppressive conditions. Knowingly they even risk death on flimsy boats and often the cruelty of smugglers. Too many victims have turned the waters of the Mediterranean into a silent cemetery. Excessively restrictive border regulation policies, which lend themselves to the dangerous practice of smuggling of human persons as 'cargo', have pushed thousands of asylum seekers to undertake a fatal journey along which their dreams and their lives are shattered.

The hospitality of African countries proved to be a major life-saver in the many crises that have tormented the continent in recent decades. Refugees were received and given a chance to survive until repatriation became possible. In many cases, the opportunity to resettle locally was generously provided. International solidarity has often matched African generosity but neither is an inexhaustible resource. A renewed engagement in a policy of prevention is now urgent. The efforts of the international community to prevent conflicts, and bad governance which stifle development, are necessary in order to reduce the number of persons forcibly displaced. In essence, this requires a culture of peace, which is only possible when the human person is placed at the center of concerns, national plans and social goals, thus acknowledging his inherent dignity and the respect that his fundamental human rights deserve.

A change of mentality is required, one that rejects violence as a means of confronting personal and community differences and that

* Statement delivered at the High-Level Segment of the 65th Session of the Executive Committee of the UNHCR: Enhancing International Cooperation, Solidarity, Local Capacities and Humanitarian Action for Refugees in Africa, 30 September 2014.

transcends tribal, ethnic and national interests in the service of the common good.

African nations have invested political and economic capital in coordinating their continental action for a more efficient response to their need of development and peaceful resolution of differences. The juridical instruments produced for the protection of forcibly displaced populations offer useful tools to tackle the causes of forced displacement, so that today's asylum seekers and uprooted people may receive an adequate protection.

Additional practical steps are listed in the Executive Committee Statement. These measures can provide effective relief to the plight of asylum seekers and IDPs. Pope Francis pleads: 'Above all I ask leaders and legislators and the entire international community to confront the reality of those who have been displaced by force with effective projects and new approaches in order to protect their dignity, to improve the quality of their life and to face the challenges that are emerging from modern forms of persecution, oppression and slavery.'[1]

Mr President,

Unfortunately, forced displacement continues on the African continent as a result of violence used in the pursuit of selfish power and ideological imposition. Developing new strategies, by incorporating the best of experience-proven methods, is the only way to confront the current challenges. The political determination to prevent conflicts through dialogue and inclusiveness and an effective solidarity that bridges the gap between developing and developed regions of the world will open a path to a peaceful future.

Thank you, Mr President.

[1] Pope Francis, Address to Participants in the Plenary of the Pontifical Council for the Pastoral Care of Migrants and Itinerant People, 24 May 2013.

PREVENTION AND LONG-TERM DEVELOPMENT STRATEGIES*

Mr President,

Today, we have reached the highest number of forcibly displaced persons since the Second World War. It is not merely an increase in quantity but there is also a concomitant increase of complexity due to non-State actors in current conflicts and unpredictable massive displacement as a consequence.

The common goal of protection is an ever-growing challenge. This is due in large part to the unprecedented number of persons on the move; the lack of financial resources as a result of donor fatigue; ever more restrictive measures limiting access for asylum seekers; the reality of tensions which tend to arise between local populations and newly arrived; and, additionally, the phenomenon of unaccompanied minors, that is increasingly visible in the Americas, and also in Europe.

The practical preparedness of States to accommodate this increasing number of asylum seekers and refugees appears to be decreasing. But the generosity shown so far by the international community is a sign of hope, and it should continue by expressing solidarity to the victims of armed conflicts and situations of constant violation of fundamental human rights.

Such a state of affairs should help all of us who form the international community to reflect upon and urgently to devise preventive measures so that people are not forced to leave their homes in order to survive. This phenomenon creates a tremendous burden upon the host States, who must invest an exceptional amount of their resources, and thus places an obligation of solidarity by the wider community.

The necessary change of policy from focusing on assistance to prevention implies an important cultural shift, in which the human person, with his inviolable dignity and inalienable human rights, is the center of attention, rather than being a mere instrument for economic and political decisions. Such a perspective requires of the international community a reformulation of methods and structures of prevention, humanitarian assistance and long-term development.

* Statement delivered at the 65th Session of the Executive Committee of UNHCR: *General Debate*, 1 October 2014.

The Delegation of the Holy See encourages the continued extraordinary generosity of many donor countries and of those hosting societies that have welcomed, often at a great sacrifice, millions of forcibly displaced people. We also support the development of an increased global partnership, based more upon human solidarity and less upon selfish interests, to answer the plight of the current massive number of asylum seekers and refugees. Indeed, this solidarity is not simply an abstract idea, but a concrete moral imperative derived from the fact that together we form one human family. This is the first step to realizing reconciliation and restarting a productive life.

As Pope Francis emphasizes: 'It is necessary to respond to the globalization of migration with the globalization of charity and cooperation, in such a way as to make the conditions of migrants more humane. Solidarity with migrants and refugees must be accompanied by the courage and creativity necessary to develop, on a worldwide level, a more just and equitable financial and economic order, as well as an increasing commitment to peace, the indispensable condition for all authentic progress.'[1]

Mr President,

In conclusion, the continued, long-term stay of populations in camps and the increasing number of persons in overcrowded urban areas are in themselves a clear manifestation that violence can only destroy and fragment society. The present situation in the world is an appeal to the international community that the only positive way forward is to pursue the path of dialogue toward 'peaceful coexistence'.

[1] Pope Francis, 'Message for World Day of Migrants and Refugees', 23 September 2014.

TRANSLATE THE DUTY TO PROTECT INTO ACTION*

Mr Chairman,

Protection of forcibly uprooted people remains a priority for the international community. The UNHCR High Commissioner reminded the world that in 2014 a daily average of 42,500 people became refugees, asylum seekers or internally displaced persons. More than 60 million people for a variety of reasons are displaced from their homes, the highest number since the end of the Second World War.

The plight of so many exiles moves one to have both compassion and indignation because of the unjust suffering inflicted on them. It also generates an irrational hostility in some groups as if the victims of violence and abuse of their human rights were the culprits for their own condition. The international community has to go beyond emotions, however, and translate its duty to protect into action. This is the real test of solidarity. The first step is an attitude of acceptance that should start at the borders, as indicated in the guidelines produced by the UN Office of the High Commissioner for Human Rights in *Recommended Principles and Guidelines on Human Rights at International Borders* (A/69/CRP.1, 23 July 2014). In these present disconcerting circumstances, extraordinary solidarity is called for, specifically a more generous resettlement policy and a stronger commitment to responsibility sharing.

The present situation is also producing asylum seekers who are not protected by existing juridical instruments. For example, Pope Francis writes in his new Encyclical on the care of our common home (*Laudato Si'*): 'There has been a tragic rise in the number of migrants seeking to flee from the growing poverty caused by environmental degradation. They are not recognized by international conventions as refugees; they bear the loss of the lives they have left behind, without enjoying any legal protection whatsoever' (§ 25). A similar concern is addressed by the timely Nansen Initiative, that aims at meeting the needs of people displaced across borders in the context of disasters and climate change.

Thus, the current emergency can become an opportunity to be more innovative and to explore new legal forms of protection like: the use of humanitarian visas in a wider way, the encouragement of community-based sponsorships of individuals and families, the opening of legal

* Statement delivered at the 63rd Meeting of the Standing Committee of the UNHCR, 24 June 2015.

channels of passage so asylum seekers may not have to risk their lives on rickety boats or deadly land-crossing or have to pay exorbitant sums to reach a safe haven where to apply for protection. An exclusively security-oriented approach overlooks two important facts: that asylum seekers are not a problem but human persons who are themselves the living victims of tragedies that forced them into exile; and that the common good extends beyond the national borders of a single State.

The dramatic increase in the number of persons requiring international protection is related to the growing phenomenon of failed States, the recourse to violence to solve disputes and the ravages of climate change. These crises, in turn, speak of failed global governance and of global powers becoming passive observers or a distant manipulative influence in the conflicts driving so many innocent civilians from their homes. The critical variable to end the bloodshed and the forced exodus of the population seems to be missing, the political will to reach a concrete solution as also underlined in the UNHCR's document *Solution Strategies*. While funding is necessary, prevention is to be pursued more urgently: it will spare much suffering and it will be much less burdensome financially. Again, a variety of national and regional interests impede both the necessary political dialogue and the contextualization of displacement as a consequence of confrontational international relations.

Neighboring countries to failed States, and to States at war, carry the heaviest burden of caring for the refugees they have welcomed into their territory. The international community, however, has to shoulder collectively the responsibility of assisting the victims of the many ongoing conflicts. Thus, in the distribution of financial resources for development on the part of international institutions, special consideration should be given to refugee-hosting countries. It is a practical measure that strengthens these countries and prevents the risk of their destabilization and the eventual production of more internally displaced persons and refugees.

Looking ahead, the refugee and displaced persons situation will unfortunately continue for some time. A changed outlook is needed. Forcibly uprooted people can be a resource for their own country's reconstruction and stabilization in any political effort of reconciliation and peaceful coexistence. In countries of new residence, they contribute their intelligence and their skills in building a common future that benefits all. They are human persons first and the protection of their rights and dignity is an investment that guarantees the respect and protection of the dignity of all.

SAVE LIVES AND TAKE ACTION AGAINST THE ROOT CAUSES OF THE REFUGEE CRISIS*

Madam President,

Today, as already pointed out, more than 60 million people have been forced to leave their home. It is an exceptional moment of crisis that sees people being persecuted, as victims of war, or obliged to leave their host countries because of lack of hope. The Syrian case presents this situation in a very dramatic way.

The 1951 Convention clearly states that refugees are a common responsibility of the international community. Gradually, however, this responsibility has shifted to the host countries in the developing world notwithstanding their own limited means. They continue to bear the burden with financial assistance from donors. Many times the combined assistance is inadequate and refugees find themselves in very difficult predicaments. Nevertheless, geographical proximity does not define responsibility. Many powers destabilize the countries of origin of asylum seekers and they should, therefore, take responsibility for the consequences of their actions.

Syrian refugees and other asylum seekers now are reaching Europe through desperate paths that leave many casualties at sea and on land. So far this year some 3,000 asylum seekers and migrants drowned in the Mediterranean where they lay buried together with their dreams of a more dignified life. They arrive directly from conflict areas, or they leave situations with no hope and no prospect for the future. They escape extreme poverty and a systemic violation of their human rights. The host communities are under strain. Humanitarian programs remain underfunded. These asylum seekers cannot use normal transport since carriers want to see the documentation required by countries of destination and they do not have such documentation and, in fact, do not need to have it. Access to the European territory to apply for asylum has thus become almost impossible. Huge amounts are paid to smugglers as a result. Humanitarian visas would be a remedy. One might even consider the lifting of carrier sanctions. Asylum seekers could then arrive safely in Europe without risking their lives.

* Statement delivered at the 66th Session of the Executive Committee of UNHCR, 8 October 2015.

The increased number of asylum seekers and refugees challenges the European Union. Measures have been taken to relocate asylum seekers and to provide additional donor money. However admirable, these measures remain only a first step. A parallel agenda is also in place: reinforcing borders and trying to prevent people from arriving. The question remains whether EU obligations to refugees will be put in the first place or that securing borders gets the upper hand.

There is fear that too many people are knocking at the door of the EU and its 28 countries. Arguments are presented that too much strain would be placed on EU structures and societies and that it would be better to settle refugees in their region of origin. However, a sense of perspective is called for. Most refugees are in fact in their region of origin, in the neighbouring countries of Lebanon, Jordan and Turkey. More accurate information and balanced reporting in the media would dispel unfounded fears and support the needed political will to show concrete solidarity in solving the current difficulties.

The political priority remains the need to save lives. Then the legal obligation deriving from the treaties should be honored. The current emergency calls also for a more effectively coordinated global governance of population movements. This emergency is not new. Unfortunately, at regular intervals the world has to witness refugee emergencies. In 1956, 220,000 Hungarians crossed into Austria in three weeks. In 1975 the end of the Vietnam War caused more than a million refugees, boat people and others, to look for a refuge. Millions of refugees were produced by the independence and civil wars in Mozambique, Congo, Angola. In the 1990s, when the peace agreement was signed to end the Balkan wars, more than 3 million people from the region were displaced, an estimated 1.3 million were internally displaced, approximately 500,000 refugees had fled to neighboring countries, and some 700,000 refugees were in Western Europe. Elsewhere, there are new 'boat people' looking for a welcome. Yesterday and today the causes of so much suffering are the same: wars, persecution, policies of oppression, discrimination, tyranny and extreme poverty.

The international community cannot afford to continue along this path. Innovative reflection needs to be undertaken, keeping in mind the situations of the past, through initiatives like the International Conference on Assistance to Refugees in Africa (ICARA I and II) or the Global Consultations on International Protection. Above all, the root causes of forced displacement have to be addressed by ensuring peace and sustainable development, the two tracks on which run a future without asylum seekers.

At this turning point when practical decisions are urgently required, Pope Francis' words to the American and to the European political representatives are timely in pointing the way forward: 'Our world is facing a refugee crisis of a magnitude not seen since the Second World War. This presents us with great challenges and many hard decisions ... We must not be taken aback by their numbers, but rather view them as persons, seeing their faces and listening to their stories, trying to respond as best we can to their situation ... in a way which is always humane, just and fraternal. We need to avoid a common temptation nowadays: to discard whatever proves troublesome.

Europe will be able to confront the problems associated with immigration only if it is capable of clearly asserting its own cultural identity ... Only if it is capable of adopting fair, courageous and realistic policies which can assist the countries of origin in their own social and political development and in their efforts to resolve internal conflicts – the principal cause of this phenomenon – rather than adopting policies motivated by self-interest, which increase and feed such conflicts. We need to take action against the causes and not only the effects.'

Madam President, allow me to add a word of thanks to the High Commissioner António Guterres, his leadership, *humanitas*, determination, compassion, have marked his service, inspired us and provided effective protection and assistance to millions of uprooted persons. My Delegation wishes him God's speed and a happy future.

Thank you, Madam President.

2 MIGRANTS AND THEIR CONTRIBUTION TO SOCIAL DEVELOPMENT

MIGRANTS, BUILDERS OF BRIDGES AMONG SOCIETIES*

Mr President,

In his first message for this year's World Day of Migrants and Refugees, Pope Benedict XVI wrote that 'one of the recognizable signs of the times today is undoubtedly migration', a phenomenon which has taken on structural characteristics, becoming an important factor of the labor market worldwide, a consequence among other variables of the enormous impact of globalization.[1] In fact, the visibility of migration on the international agenda has never been so high; it is debated regularly in national parliaments, in regional conferences and at the global level. This unprecedented interest is not without ambiguity. The popular perception of immigrants reflects anxiety over economic competition, national security and cultural identity. Policy-makers tend to emphasize the economic and demographic function played by foreign professionals and labourers. On the other hand, the extraordinary positive contribution of migrants to the economy of their families and of their countries of origin through the flow of remittances and newly acquired skills, and to the realization of economic objectives in their host countries, and the contribution of their creativity and spiritual gifts, are seldom in the limelight. There is a need to overcome this ambiguity and the occasional political manipulation of the immigrants for electoral purposes, and to educate public opinion to a more objective appreciation of our new neighbors.

A way forward for a positive change of attitude are the current efforts to develop an effective policy coherence in migration. This policy certainly deserves support, as it represents a concerted will of sending, transit and receiving countries to respond in a comprehensive and inclusive way to contemporary migrations by taking into account both countries' labour needs and migrants' human rights and responsibilities. The added value of this approach is its timeliness. Migration pressures will continue as will continue the request for manpower in many developed countries.

* Statement delivered at the 90th Session of the Council of the International Organization for Migration, 29 November–2 December 2005.

[1] Pope Benedict XVI, Message for the 92nd World Day of Migrants and Refugees. Vatican, 18 October 2005.

Experience has shown that control alone is not the answer. In fact, an exclusive focus on control brings about lack of appreciation for the root causes of migration and a real risk of reducing the migrant to his or her service function forgetting the human fundamental dimension. It also relegates into the shadows the many victims of today's increased movements of people: the migrants who die trying to reach their destinations, the women and children trafficked, the thousands of migrants and asylum seekers in detention centers, the millions of undocumented migrants. A patient and determined multilateral dialogue, among States and with immigrant communities, gives reasonable hope for realistic agreements and laws: it is the road ahead.

In the complexity of relationships and implications that the international movement of people entails, in no way comparable to the movement of capital and goods, the dignity and the human rights of the migrant person have to take precedence. For this reason it seems urgent to revisit the question of integration if the end result of the migration process should lead to an enriching and peaceful coexistence of different cultural expressions in society. If only the worker or only the technician is taken into account, and not the human persons they are, with aspirations, family ties, religious convictions and traditions, formed identities, then lack of adjustment can easily be predicted. Integration takes place from a position of strength of the newcomer and from this position can take place the transition to a new identity as cultures evolve and adapt to each other. In the long run the interest of the receiving society is served by its acceptance of newcomers in their difference and in its openness to progressively incorporate them in view of a common future. In this perspective, policies based on rights turn out to be more useful in the formation of a cohesive society and in the management of migration since they provide a common ground to negotiate competing interests. Two recent projects among those undertaken by the IOM have addressed important aspects of migration that have a critical bearing on immigrants' integration and hopefully will continue to be discussed and further elaborated. The first is the initiative to support the development and the teaching of the international right of migrations, that is the rights and duties of migrants and of States. It breaks new ground in bringing together partners in the migration process and in indicating a base on which to develop a fair integration of immigrants. The second initiative is the decision to address the role that religion plays in the process of integration; it involves the relation of immigrants with the receiving country and with other religions at a moment when most societies are confronted with religious pluralism. It is interesting to see how the religious variable touches the personal and group ethnic identity, inspires social services that assist immigrants to integrate, and can help to transcend nationalisms.

Finally, a word of caution seems in order as a renewed interest emerges in favor of temporary migrations. The failure of past migrant workers programs should make us aware that a rights-based migration policy cannot overlook the problematic aspects of guest worker and circular migration models like compulsory employment with a specific employer as a condition, and the consequent vulnerability to abuse and isolation from the host society rather than integration.

Mr President,

In conclusion, migrations are not just a sign of the times; they are a great resource for economic and human development, but the migrants must remain protagonists as builders of bridges among societies with the support of coherent and humane policies on the part of the international community.

THE PRIORITY OF PERSONS OVER THE ECONOMY*

Mr President,

The diversity of population movements around the world has increasingly caught the attention of international organizations and States: temporary and permanent migrant workers, refugees, asylum seekers, internally displaced persons, trafficked women and men, multinational corporations, transferred personnel. New categories emerge like internal and cross-border displaced people forced to move by the degradation of the environment, certain types of development projects and climate change. The Delegation of the Holy See appreciates the strategic choice made by the IOM to address the migratory phenomenon from 'an integral and holistic perspective' while focusing on its specific mandate. While targeted responses render effective the protection and assistance due to all uprooted persons, a comprehensive perspective is needed. In fact, today's economic and political interdependence has shown that international migrations have become a structural component of modern societies. In particular, the global labour market attracts workers from an ever wider range of countries, making the migration for work the largest segment of all population movements. People vote with their feet, searching to meet their aspirations for security and a decent life for themselves and their families.

Estimates now give more than 200 million persons in the world living and working in countries different than the one in which they were born or were citizens and the 90 million workers among them are almost 3 per cent of the three-billion-strong labour force. The numbers, in a way, are the tip of the iceberg revealing the complexity of a phenomenon that affects countries of origin, transit and destination, laws and administrative regulations, cultural, religious and social modalities of coexistence. A cooperative approach to migrations becomes unavoidable and it should be inclusive of States, intergovernmental bodies, civil society. Non-governmental organizations and faith-communities in particular, with their ear to the ground and a geographically diversified experience, can provide insights and collaboration both in policy formation and in operational assistance. This Delegation appreciates as a positive development the formalized process for exchange of views and information

* Statement delivered at the 94th Session of the Council of the International Organization for Migration, 27–30 November 2007.

on the part of the Heads of United Nations agencies with responsibility for one or the other aspect of human mobility. But coherence among the various players seems still at an initial stage and it would be beneficial if some participation of representatives of migrants' organizations and interests would be included at all levels of policy development.

Migrant workers, skilled and unskilled, have taken central place in many current debates. This type of migration is looked at as a positive force for development of countries of origin, especially through the billions of dollars in remittances sent home by the migrants – US$ 167 billion sent to developing countries in 2005 – as well as for the economy of receiving countries. In fact, for a growing number of countries, immigrants have become a necessity to compensate for the dwindling workforce and for their demographic deficit. But the pragmatic advantages accepted through the admission of migrants are on several occasions overshadowed by an ambivalent attitude that is manifest in media and public opinion that allows for stereotyping and negative generalizations of newcomers. Fairness in recognizing the contribution immigrants make can serve as a good base for their integration.

Two important dimensions of contemporary migrations are not adequately discussed and paid attention to in the formulation of policies: the victims of migration flows and the priority that persons have over the economy. The whole system of protection and of human rights is relegated to a secondary supporting role instead of serving, as it was intended, as an assurance that the dignity of all human persons must take precedence. Just a few days ago, 64 migrants drowned before the shores of Yemen, where the previous month another 66 desperate asylum seekers had died or were missing after being thrown overboard by traffickers. Some media report that about 500 persons have met their death this year in the dangerous enterprise of crossing illegally from Mexico into the United States. As many as 6,000 people have died or disappeared in 2006 alone just trying to cross the waters from the West coast of Africa to the Canary Islands. Unaccompanied children are found in these traumatic flows across seas and borders. New creative forms of prevention, of humanitarian assistance and protection mechanisms are called for.

An inclusive approach that takes into account all components of the migrants' journey: the decisions to emigrate and how many immigrants to admit; the modalities of participation of various types of migrants in the host society; the role played by migrants in the economic development and in society; the migrants' entitlement to protection and the exercise of their rights, seems the appropriate way to proceed. Present political trends appear clear and slanted in the direction of responding to the more emotional and vocal demands of public opinion for control and integration. In the long run, however, a fair and effective solution will come from a comprehensive approach that embraces all policy components: the rights of the State and of the receiving community, of the migrants, and of the international common good. A growing consensus supports the convenience of such an inclusive approach and the necessity to pay more attention to migrants themselves and not only to their economic role as temporary workforce or permanent settlers. International treaties and conventions that directly, or in a general way, include references to the rights of migrants have adopted the centrality of the human person as their supporting base. In a parallel way, the social teaching of the Catholic Church, and in fact that of all religious traditions, looks at migrants as human beings in the first place and then as citizens or guests, or as economic and cultural agents. The ethical dimension in the discussion of migration results from a larger anthropological framework in which secular and religious people can find a common ground in order to address the inevitable tension between different principles. In the case of migrants, this tension appears in the moral obligations of governments to ensure the safety and well-being of their own populations and a more universal ethic that values the well-being of all mankind and of each person. In this sense, the High-Level Dialogue on Migration and Development could state: 'Respect for the fundamental rights and freedoms of all migrants was considered essential for reaping the full benefits of international migration.'

Mr President,

As the concerted effort to refine ways and means to manage the different aspects of human mobility moves forward, the Delegation of the Holy See considers it more urgent to muster the political will to ratify and implement the human rights instruments already developed and to make them the foundation of a truly humane and comprehensive policy. Education can play a major role. Migrants, aware of their rights, can be more secure in offering their services and talents and the receiving community, well informed and respectful of these rights, will feel freer in extending its solidarity in order to build together a common future.

THE INADEQUACY OF THE CURRENT MIGRATION MANAGEMENT: THE INCREASING NUMBER OF IRREGULAR MIGRANTS*

Mr Chairman,

The Delegation of the Holy See expresses its appreciation for the effective leadership of the Director General, welcomes the new Deputy Director General and congratulates you on your election.

Mr Chairman,

The increasing number of people on the move across the globe, especially the vast majority of those forcibly displaced by lack of survival opportunities, by violence and climate change, has raised new and complex demands for solidarity, humanitarian assistance and protection. The challenge to international organizations, governments and the civil society comes from the fact that while necessity is the common factor that pushes these people out of their country, the legal norms that define their status apply differently and in some cases are blurred or even disregarded. Migrant workers, convention refugees, asylum seekers, temporary migrants, mixed flows, boat people, climate refugees, victims of smuggling and of trafficking, are all categories of persons included in current policy discussions. The International Organization for Migration, sensitive to the evolving situation, commendably has begun to deepen its own approach, in collaboration with other partners, to a major concern in the management of migration and a sign of its present inadequacy: irregular migrants.

Data from the UN and governments about people who enter another country without authorization or who overstay their visa or engage in activities different from the authorization they had received are only estimates, given that the nature of such movement escapes registration. But numbers are impressive. Migrants in irregular administrative status are approximately 30 million to 40 million, a number that amounts to 15 per cent to 20 per cent of all international migrants. This phenomenon is global. Europe is home to an estimated 5 million to 8 million irregular migrants; the United States to over 10 million; South Africa to

* Statement delivered at the 98th Session of the Council of the International Organization for Migration, 23–26 November 2009.

some 500,000. In Asia, around 30 per cent to 40 per cent of all migration flows are estimated to take place through irregular channels. A reflection of both the challenges and the most sensible response, various regularizations in quite a number of countries of Europe and Latin America have settled hundreds of thousands of irregular migrants: my Delegation welcomes signals that the United States is also advancing a similar strategy.

Many countries on all continents, as these examples indicate, experience the presence of irregular migrants, a reality that will remain with us as long as insecurity due to environment degradation, violations of human rights, wars and lack of opportunity persist. In fact irregular migration needs to be looked at and analyzed as linked to regular migration: often the same root causes and mechanisms are at work in both cases; many times migrants are diverted to irregular channels because no legal channels are effectively available to them.

It is also rather well documented that irregular migration often matches the labour market demand in countries of destination. The International Labour Organization (ILO) and other international and regional bodies as well as our own Church organizations and partners working with migrants and refugees of all kinds around the world report that nearly all of the irregular migrants who are adults, and a growing number of the children, are working, predominantly either in the informal economy or in informal employment arrangements. For the most part, they fill huge gaps in providing essential labour and services, often of the most demanding kind, in both highly and lesser skilled occupations. The impressive proportion of migrant workers busy growing food and constructing houses, buildings and cities speaks to how important they are to their new societies as a whole. Their growing role in the home, health and child-care sectors of so many countries of the North and the South illustrates their role in one-to-one, day-to-day *solidarity*, a building block of families and communities worldwide.

And yet, a consequence of their status is that irregular migrants become vulnerable to widespread exploitation and abuse, can be used for unfair competition, and experience serious, but avoidable personal and public health concerns. Moreover, irregular migrants are commonly pictured for political and media purposes – and at times perceived by public opinion – as simply losers, job stealers or worse, and a burden to social services when in fact they are active contributors to the economy. Indeed, most are young and responsible providers for their families. They are often marginalized, and scared by public policies that are expressed or implied, enforcement that is ad hoc as well as targeted, and discrimination. The majority finds invisibility in shadows that carry risk for any democracy and social cohesion.

Experience has shown that irregular migrations have been growing notwithstanding increased control of borders and of work places. Bound up in all these considerations, the dignity and inalienable human rights of irregular migrants call for a new management strategy. States, while exercising their sovereign right to regulate immigration, should work for concerted policy answers directed to positive outcomes. In this complex effort, some significant elements should be taken into account.

First, as so many states and others are increasingly emphasizing at international and regional fora like this meeting, migrants are human beings, with human aspirations and human vulnerabilities that at times evoke a specific form of human solidarity. This is particularly evident during the often long and life-threatening experience of many migrants in irregular flows on desperate migratory routes. The very human responses of rescue, of assistance especially in emergencies, and of protection, especially for refugees, children, women and victims of torture, trafficking, trauma or violence in transit, these are all responses that deserve greater attention and organization in addressing the dangers and suffering in irregular migration today. My Delegation welcomes the thinking that the IOM has been doing in this area, and particularly in the approach of collaboration not competition with the expertise and presence of UNHCR, the Red Cross system and local non-government organizations on the ground, including the many Church entities directly engaged in this work.

My Delegation calls for new attention to the horrific phenomenon of 'gauntlet migration', that is, what it means to be and properly respond to, a man, woman or child who has been serially brutalized, multiple times and repetitively, along the many roads and crossings of a migration journey across land, desert and water borders in Africa, in South and Southeast Asia, and in the Americas and Caribbean, for example. What may be needed is not so much new rights or policies but, as the background paper for this session suggests in its reference to the IOM's work with UNHCR under the 10-Point Plan of Action, the elaboration of common standards and practical mechanisms for better *operationalizing* assistance and protection in such situations.

My Delegation also wishes to encourage the IOM, in the course of and beyond this reflection on irregular migration, to return, together with its members and with partners in UNHCR, other international organizations and civil society, to the important but unfinished business of distinguishing between forced or survival migration and migration that is genuinely voluntary. This opportunity for reflection, and new, more human and practical responses to those who truly have no choice other than to migrate, seems especially promising in light of the clear convergence that recent processes, including the Global Forum on Migration and Development, have demonstrated on recognizing and building appropriate policy frameworks to address the difference between migration that is a choice and migration that is a necessity.

Secondly, given the unprecedented rise in mobility as our economies, labor markets and even families become ever more globalized, it is important to fully consider that, however grave their circumstances, these millions of migrants possess valuable development potential in terms of skills, capacity and knowledge. Under the right conditions, i.e., the enjoyment of basic rights, they can use their potential to rebuild their communities and their livelihoods and contribute to the economy and society that hosts them. But those considered to be in irregular status – including, most regrettably, large numbers of refugees stuck in protracted situations – lack the ability to find legal work, sufficient freedom of movement and access to training and education. While they are kept in the shadows, development opportunities are lost. Hence the need to provide the necessary legal framework to prevent such a loss.

Thirdly, to arrive at such a framework, popular stereotypes, that often block fair legislation, should be overcome through education and a more realistic portraying of irregular migrants in the media. It is a misconception that irregular migrants take away jobs or reside only in developed countries. A concerted negotiation between governments, employers and labor unions appears necessary. If one takes into account that small and medium-sized enterprises are often drawn to employ irregular migrants to avoid costs, an effective solution would provide a way to accommodate the mutual need of the employers for workers and those workers for jobs by offering legal employment together with some tax benefits and scaled payment for social benefits without prejudice to fundamental work rights and without creating unfair competition with national workers. Devising such forms of regularization is not without economic benefits since it is better for the state to have businesses and regular migrants that may contribute slightly less to the social security and tax regimes than irregular ones that do not contribute at all.

A fourth observation regards the need of balance for an eventual comprehensive framework where control, interests of the economy and human rights are considered together. The social consequences of migration cannot be left out of the equation. Migrants add a human face to the ongoing process of globalization and can be instrument and promoters of peaceful relations among countries making visible the reality that we are one human family. In this connection, policies of detention should be revisited not only because of the human rights questions they raise, but also because they hold hostage and inactive a productive population at very high financial costs. Much less practical and respectful, as the UN Human Rights Council has underlined, is the recourse to criminalization of irregular migrants simply because of their status.

Finally, confronted with such a complex and almost intractable issue, the IOM could intensify the promotion of serious research into contemporary irregular migration to advance an understanding of the mechanisms involved, especially of the organized underground industry that plays an intermediary role with its international ramifications in fostering irregular migration. For a successful task, cooperation among countries of departure, transit and destination becomes even more necessary in this type of migration. The various attempts undertaken to stimulate a global coordination of migrations remain still at an embryonic stage, but they show the felt need of some global entity that can effectively support the management of today's population movements. It is a challenge that demands creative and courageous imagination.

Mr Chairman,

The inclusion of migrations in the fight against poverty and in the process of development would fall short of its goals if the large percentage of irregular migrants is left out. If a new framework of wider channels for legal immigration and other provisions to regularize their presence and to uphold their fundamental human rights is achieved, everyone will gain: migrants, national economies and peaceful coexistence. The way forward rests on the acceptance of every person as a protagonist in development and on the responsibility of States and the international community to create the conditions that allow everyone's talent to be fruitful in a transparent and legal situation. As Pope Benedict XVI reminds us in his recent social Encyclical, authentic development is inclusive and solicitous of the most vulnerable members of society. He says: 'The more we strive to secure a common good corresponding to the real needs of our neighbors, the more effectively we love them ... In an increasingly globalized society, the common good and the effort to obtain it cannot fail to assume the dimensions of the whole human family.'[1] Irregular migrants are part of this family.

[1] Pope Benedict XVI, Encyclical Letter, *Caritas in Veritate*, § 7.

THE DREADFUL TREATMENT OF STRANDED IMMIGRANTS*

Mr President,

The persisting economic crisis has caused a negative impact on many sectors of society. Immigrants also have paid a price. The limits imposed on legal immigration, the reinforcement of border controls, the non-renewal of work permits, for example, are measures that often responded to widespread and legitimate security concerns but also to the pressure of public opinion and sometimes have created a perception of rejection and of fear that immigrants may exacerbate competition for jobs as well as become a threat to national cohesion. Voting patterns across continents give evidence of how a distorted image of immigrants can affect political behaviour. A contradiction emerges that, on one hand, sees the market of developed and emerging economies demand and absorb immigrants, while, on the other hand, the receiving societies begrudge and reject these same persons. Public policies to address the phenomenon of immigration from a human rights perspective often meet with great resistance on the ground. There is a need, therefore, to renew practical efforts at counteracting the negative trend and stereotypes, which are accentuated by the present economic situation, a trend that prevents sound legislative reforms and ignores the great contribution of migrants. It is necessary, as well, to avoid taking hasty legal and administrative measures that impose a disproportionate burden on the immigrants. A fair and coordinated re-examination by all States involved in certain practices regarding detention, especially of children, borders and high sea 'push backs', policies toward irregular migrants, and the conditions to which returnees are subjected, would signal respect for the basic requirements of human rights and give a message of hope that will facilitate the future process of integration.

Stranded immigrants are a clear example of the ambiguity we witness in the current treatment of immigrants. The Church and its agencies, as well as other faith-based organizations, closely accompany migrants and have collected numerous testimonies of migrants who are stranded, persons who are unable to return to a country of nationality or former residence due to legal, or intractable humanitarian or logistical,

* Statement delivered at the 99th Session of the Council of the International Organization for Migration, 29 November–2 December 2010.

reasons.[1] They cannot move forward nor back. Many of these stranded migrants share the same dreadful situation: they are denied access to basic social rights and services and live in constant fear of being detained and deported. Even if they already have stayed for several years in the same country they completely lack future prospects and chances to build up their lives. These persons may not fall under the technical definition of refugee, and cannot escape the situation in the countries of transit because they are denied access to a country of destination. Their condition when they are in detention places is even worse. The international community hopefully will not turn a blind eye on the dreadful treatment of these trapped migrants in need of protection on the other side of the borders of the more developed countries. New protection mechanisms have been devised; now they need adequate support to become truly effective.

Cooperation among countries, on the other hand, can be the practical road to achieve effective results in the governance of today's massive migrations. Suspicions and objections toward an international management of migrations are not lacking as emphasis is placed on national responses and defence of sovereignty. But grave transnational phenomena, such as trafficking and smuggling and irregular migration flows, or the important attraction of labour from less to more developed and secure countries by the global market, all require better and comprehensive planning and action. The establishment of an international framework for some cross-border issues like trade, labour, human rights, intellectual property and climate has proven doable and useful. Individual States, citizens and migrants alike would find it advantageous to adopt and implement an international approach that would enhance collaboration and governance in the area of human mobility. The growing number of migrants around the world who are vulnerable and exploited and not adequately reached and protected by States and international institutions, as are stranded migrants, would certainly benefit from a global system that could close this and other protection gaps. Concrete steps can be taken starting with a greater coherence at the national level to exchanges of information and agreements among regional migration entities and to a greater collaboration engagement on the part of international organizations with a mandate to deal with migration. As indicated in its strategy,

1 Stefanie Grant, 'The Legal Protection of Stranded Migrants', in Ryszard Cholewinski, Richard Perruchoud and Euan MacDonald (eds), *International Migration Law: Developing Paradigms and Key Challenges*, The Hague: T.M.C. Asser Press, 2007, pp. 29–47, at p. 30.

and as part of its priorities, the IOM can provide leadership to enhance, in accord with international law, the humane and orderly management of migrations and the respect of the human rights of migrants.

In conclusion, Mr President, as international migration is expected to continue to grow in scale, global reach and variety, cooperation becomes urgent to achieve the fundamental goal of allowing migrants to be partners in economic development and as potential citizens by recognizing their human rights and the fact that they are already equal members of our one human family. As the Holy Father Benedict XVI has written in his Message for the next World Day for Migrants and Refugees: 'In this regard, the Church does not cease to recall that the deep sense of this epochal process and its fundamental ethical criterion are given by the unity of the human family and its development towards what is good (cf. Benedict XVI, Encyclical Letter, *Caritas in Veritate*, § 42). All, therefore, belong to one family, migrants and the local populations that welcome them, and all have the same right to enjoy the goods of the earth whose destination is universal.'[2]

Thank you, Mr President.

[2] Pope Benedict XVI, Message of Benedict XVI for the 97th World Day of Migrants and Refugees (2011): 'One human family'.

THE HOLY SEE BECOMES A MEMBER OF THE INTERNATIONAL ORGANIZATION FOR MIGRATION: THE PRIORITY OF HUMAN DIGNITY AND THE RIGHT TO LIFE*

Mr President,

Allow me to express a word of appreciation for the decision, just taken, to admit the Holy See as a Member of the IOM. Around the globe, the movement of people who are looking for work or survival from famine, conflicts and the violation of their basic human rights continues to increase. Thus, the responsibility of the international community to respond in an effective and humane way becomes more evident and more urgent. As it marks its 60th Anniversary, the International Organization for Migration can celebrate a record of great service to displaced people and of collaboration with States and with civil society organizations in finding realistic solutions without compromising on basic principles of protection and respect for human rights. Through its membership in the Organization the Holy See intends to support this tradition in accord with its specific nature, principles and norms. In particular, I would like to highlight three points.

Rather than decreasing their numbers the present economic crisis further complicates the life of uprooted people, and it raises a challenging question of how to provide security, not just to States, but also to migrants. From the perspective of this Delegation, the ethical implications of the current situation seem to require a renewed discussion on how to prevent the deaths and respond to the staggering trauma of people attempting to escape from their countries across the Mediterranean, the Red Sea, the desert of Arizona or transit countries like Egypt and the Sinai peninsula or Indonesia toward Australia, and the list goes on. Today the ethical dimension of population movements should take its place among other major concerns such as their effect on development, on national identity, on the evolution of democracy. When the dignity of the human person and the right to life are at stake, these values should take priority. In this difficult area of reflection and of balancing of rights, this Delegation will try to contribute its part.

The experience of Catholic agencies and associations in Geneva and on the ground worldwide, for example, of the International Catholic

* Statement delivered at the 100th Session of the Council of the International Organization for Migration, 5 December 2011.

Migration Commission and the many national Caritas organizations, is well established and extensive. By providing assistance to displaced people in camps and urban settings, by coordinating resettlement operations, and by devising integration programs, these agencies and associations have gained invaluable experience and delivered effective service that has enabled thousands of families and individuals to start a new life and to become constructive partners in the host societies. For this reason, operational collaboration appears an important and even necessary way to facilitate the convergence of all available energies in order to help uprooted people of all kinds through joint or delegated programs and through regular sharing of information.

A third observation regards the distinct features of the services provided by Catholic agencies and associations around the world. This response is dictated by the needs of the person without distinction of race, colour, religious belief or lack of it, and it embraces everyone in a truly comprehensive manner. In fact, the deep conviction that prompts involvement and action in helping all uprooted people is based in the belief of the unique dignity and common belonging to the same human family of every human person, that is antecedent to any cultural, religious, social, political or other consideration. This disinterested service values the accompaniment of uprooted persons and combines professional care with generous love and results in greater efficiency and long-term benefits. Thus it seems only right that public authorities acknowledge this contribution and, in a genuine sense of democracy, make room for conscience-based service that, in turn, becomes a guarantee of freedom for everyone.

In conclusion, Mr President, the participation of the Holy See as a Member of the IOM is a commitment to collaboration and support in the common search of solutions and assistance to people caught up in this major phenomenon of our globalized world and in need of a friendly hand to make them protagonists of their future and active partners in their adoptive societies and in the world.

AN ADEQUATE AND POSITIVE GLOBAL MANAGEMENT OF MIGRATION FLOWS*

Mr President,

At this 100th session of the IOM Council, migration remains as urgent a global concern – if not more so – as when the IOM started its services 60 years ago. The current economic crisis, in fact, has more complicated the lives of migrants rather than significantly reduced their number. Reliable projections indicate a probable growth in the international movement of people from the present 214 plus millions making migration a megatrend of the twenty-first century. This truly international and very complex phenomenon, however, is not statistical play, but directly involves and affects millions of human beings, their families, and the people of the countries of origin, transit and destination. It is above all the human dimension that should place migration at the forefront of the responsibility of States, public institutions and civil society. The experience of migration changes entire societies as well as individual lives and yet there is limited reflection on its long-term consequences, and limited coordinated planning. Unfortunately, attitudes of self-protection prevail, aggravated by the economic crisis and the rise in pressure on the borders of developed countries. Migration becomes a test for the respect and implementation of human rights especially when policies are centered on control and national security, forgetting the equally important security of the persons on the move across the planet. The search for an efficient and comprehensive answer assumes greater urgency as new motives for emigration are given by natural and human-made catastrophes, climate change and violence, whether among States or by non-State groups.

Mr President, my Delegation would like to congratulate the IOM for its 60 years of service and at the same time to call for further reflection and research on some topics that can shape a positive answer to the future of population movements.

The international answer provided to date remains fragmentary and lacks coordination. IOM has been at the forefront of the answer to the needs of people on the move while maintaining a specific vision and a pragmatic organization. For example, in a number of emergencies it has effectively embraced partnership with the UNHCR, indicating both the

* Statement delivered at the 100th Session of the Council of the International Organization for Migration, 6 December 2011.

usefulness and move toward a wider collaboration. But a dozen or so international agencies have a stake in migration, often with a particular interest in certain aspects for which they could assume respective responsibilities. With regard to migration management, sixty years on the issue of governance appears as an inevitable next step to consider. Attempts to address this issue meet with reluctance and misgivings since public opinion often is reported to be hostile and anti-immigration parties are gaining ground in the rich countries. But increased cooperation within the multilateral system and a specific contribution by the IOM to the debate on coherence of migration policies can make a significant and strategic contribution to attaining more assistance and protection for all migrants. In fact, globalization intensifies the interdependence of countries in need of manpower with those that have younger populations; a sensible and rights-oriented approach to these dynamics can create a synergy that is beneficial for both. The achievement of such synergy should also be the goal of multilateral institutions so that the action of one will not contradict or create confusion for activities undertaken by another. The development of an appropriate global architecture for the management of migration is certainly a huge challenge, but, if based on common values, mutual acknowledgement of and work for the complementarity of policies and decisions, and the will to resolve common difficulties, it may result in the positive beginning of a real partnership and a clear line of leadership.

A second observation deals with the need to promote and strengthen a positive perception of migrants. There is clear and accumulating evidence about the positive economic contribution made by migrants to their new countries through the taxes they pay, the new businesses they start and the variety of services they provide that range from jobs that are considered socially less attractive, although necessary, to the care of family members who are disabled, elderly or very young. Migrants make visible the link that binds the whole human family together, the richness of cultures and the resource for development exchanges and trade networks constituted by diaspora communities. For their part, the positive contribution of the presence of migrants becomes effective when they too open themselves to receive and appreciate the basic values of the new society so that a common and richer future may be built together. The role played by the media and by education is crucial in this regard. Migrants should not be used as a distraction for lack of jobs and unresolved economic crises nor be seen as threats to security. The effort to overcome an overly biased and emotional approach will result in a more balanced and factual presentation and will better serve the formation of public opinion. Overly technical rules on border management, on visas and infrastructures, on strictly economic services, necessary as they are, do not reflect the importance of migration as a social and political phenomenon with a transformative capacity for entire societies. Multicultural societies create a new reality that confronts elected officials and legislators with new questions.

Modern communications raise expectations and aspirations of potential migrants by projecting images – often exaggerated – of other types of societies and life-styles. Clearly, however, the push factors to emigrate are no longer merely economic in nature, but also include the search for security and freedom, the possibility of personal and professional development and of a better quality of life. All these elements play a part in the decision to leave. In this process, a major consideration is given to the families left behind, not just in terms of sending them money, but, more importantly, of finding a way to be reunited. In the development of immigration policies, therefore, these central sensibilities should be taken into account. Financial aid and technology transfer do not seem to offer the promise of development sufficiently capable to convince potential migrants that they have a choice to remain at home. Cooperation on the part of the international community will need to sustain a social environment where fundamental human rights and freedoms are guaranteed.

Mr President, the achievement of an adequate global management of migration flows, a positive understanding of them, and the approach to *human* development may seem long-range goals. But the speed of the journey is less important than proceeding in the right direction. In the meantime there are also some immediate situations that demand a response. Among these, for example, are included the growing migration of unaccompanied children; the endemic violence and trauma suffered by migrants in transit, especially women and children; attention owed to migrants being deported back to their countries and then left in particularly destitute conditions; and the sole reliance on control and deportation methods in dealing with irregular migrants, which, instead of halting irregular migration, reconfigures mobility flows via more dangerous migration routes and encourages trafficking in human persons. The solution to these and related problems begins with the awareness, as Pope Benedict XVI writes in his Message for the 97th World Day of Migrants and Refugees (2011), of the 'profound link between all human beings ... who form one family of brothers and sisters in societies that are becoming ever more multi-ethnic and intercultural, where also people of various religions are urged to take part in dialogue, so that a serene and fruitful coexistence with respect for legitimate differences may be found.' As the IOM celebrates its 60th anniversary, the complexity of the challenges posed by population movements multiply. This milestone in the Organization's history offers the occasion for a renewed vision and commitment at the service of all persons uprooted and searching for a better and productive life.

THE DETENTION OF IRREGULAR MIGRANTS AND THEIR DIGNITY*

Madam President,

Migration is a natural response to internal disorder, fear of persecution or violence, and poor economic opportunity. These reasons result inter alia in the migration of millions of people every year. The displacement of individuals from their homes, whether within their native country or in a foreign country, poses a significant challenge to the international community for the preservation of human rights. Migration has developed into a structural reality intertwined with the global labour market resulting from, in part, the drive of globalizing influences. State responses to high levels of migration must uphold basic human rights.

Madam President,

The Delegation of the Holy See takes note of the Special Rapporteur's submission on the human rights of migrants, and his particular focus on detention practices. It is apparent that detention of migrants is an unfortunate aspect of the migrant experience, and the development of international norms that respect the individuality of the person are necessary to safeguard migrants from abuse. Unfortunately, in many places irregular migrants are treated as criminals and the resulting punishment is punitive and many times arbitrary.

The first concern with detention is that irregular migration should not be treated as a criminal act. The migrant must be empowered to act appropriately within the necessary legal framework to secure his or her safety and future. Second, detention does not act as a deterrent to migration. The inescapable reality is that migrants will continue to cross borders and seek refuge in neighbouring States even though the condition in the host State may result in serious difficulties. Often, migrants risk these consequences because the cost of remaining in their native country is much greater than punishment in a receiving country. Furthermore, detention of migrants in any form, and especially indefinite detention, is a violation of a migrant's basic human right to freedom and has no

* Statement delivered at the 20th Session of the Human Rights Council – Item 3: *Report of the Special Rapporteur on the Human Rights of Migrants*, 22 June 2012.

support in international law and should not be upheld by international norms.

Detention is certainly a pressing component of the larger story of the rights and freedoms of migrants. Most world religions encourage a practice of hospitality and compassion and of care for the least among us. Migrants, because of socioeconomic conditions and the adversities of their presence in a foreign environment, often fall into the category of the least among us. Rejection and dislike of the stranger in need, especially when this attitude is motivated by racial stereotypes, is clearly contrary to core universalist ideas of Christian belief. This unique charge for welcome and solidarity requires the careful consideration for and protection of migrants.

Madam President,

The Holy See supports a person-centric approach to migration policies. In order to respond fully to the needs of migrants and ensure their human rights are protected, the individual must be the focus of policy and praxis. Discriminatory laws and practices, based on race, ethnicity, sex and religion are a test in a State's treatment of migrants. Discrimination reinforces a culture of fear of detention and fear of discovery of irregular situations which in turn produces a limitation of personal freedoms and rights of migrants, such as health services, education, housing, movement and sometimes even the right to publicly and communally partake in religious expression.

Furthermore, practices of detention have negative effects on families, which are the vital cells of society. The family is the foundation upon which stable social, cultural and economic situations can arise and is central to establishing societies that serve the good of man and practice social responsibility.[1]

As a policy alternative, subsidiarity in the form of the family provides a structure for migrants to integrate into the host country, while also diversifying it, and establish themselves as contributing and positive members of the society. The State, though well equipped for many projects, eliminates the possibility of true participation in society through policies that force migrants to leave families in their native countries or to separate from their spouses or children upon arrival. Ethical migration

[1] 'The Family, the Vital Cell of Society', *Compendium of the Social Doctrine of the Church*, 2004.

policies must preserve the family not only to ensure the human rights of migrants but also for the benefit of the State.

Madam President,

All people, including and especially migrants, must exist in environments that are non-discriminatory and value the cultural, social and economic contributions of all people. Furthermore, it is essential that migrants, due to their inherent human dignity as persons, receive fully the complete range of their human rights and freedoms. States must not degrade the dignity of the person through policy, practice or attitude whether through the criminalization of migration, the detention of irregular migrants or any other practice that divides families or victimizes migrants who are very often much needed by these same States.

Madam President,

In closing, the Holy See Delegation recalls the important role of religions in promoting the rights of migrants as a fundamental feature of their sense of compassion and solidarity that make migration a beneficial experience for the migrants themselves and for the societies of origin and destination. Pope John Paul II wisely observed that the moral and social attitude of interdependence is solidarity. It 'is not a feeling of vague compassion or shallow distress at the misfortunes of so many people, both near and far. On the contrary, it is a firm and persevering determination to commit oneself to the common good; that is to say to the good of all and of each individual, because we are all really responsible for all.'[2]

[2] John Paull II, Encyclical Letter, *Sollicitudo Rei Socialis* (1987).

FORCIBLY DISPLACED PERSONS AND LOCAL INTEGRATION*

Mr Chairman,

My Delegation congratulates you on your election and extends a cordial welcome to the new IOM Members and its sincere appreciation to the Director General Ambassador Swing for his leadership.

Mr Chairman,

The 72 million forcibly displaced people, refugees, IDPs, stateless persons, victims of violent conflicts, other persons uprooted by natural disasters and development projects, are all witnesses of today's crises, that the political will of the international community either has failed or has been unable to prevent.[1] Thus, the percentage of forcibly displaced people as part of the overall migration phenomenon is increasing, a situation that calls for a humanitarian response that is coordinated, generous and effective.

These crises are precipitated by non-State actors, by persecution and by State repression, generalized violence and conflicts that are particularly destructive in urban areas. The difficult challenge is providing a humanitarian response that is determined by the degree of vulnerability and need rather than legal categories. The theme of the 2012 International Dialogue on Migration selected by the IOM Member States was dedicated to migration crises and how international actors manage them. A human rights approach seems helpful in developing an adequate response. Further reflection on the forcible displacement of people by increasingly unpredictable disasters and explosions of violence can be another tangible contribution of the IOM.

In these circumstances, the expression of international solidarity becomes quite urgent and necessary, but it remains critical to look at forcibly displaced people as protagonists themselves, within the limits of their situation, in finding appropriate solutions to their plight and to their need of protection.

* Statement delivered at the 101st Session of the Council of the International Organization for Migration, 27–30 November 2012.

[1] Roger Zetter (ed.), *World Disasters Report: Focus on Forced Migration and Displacement*, Geneva: International Federation of Red Cross and Red Crescent Societies, 2012, p. 304.

A related concern comes from the protracted situation in which many forcibly displaced people find themselves: more than 7 million refugees and more than 13 million IDPs have been languishing for years in a condition of marginalization and inactivity. These human resources could progressively be integrated in the host societies and contribute their talents to development and the building of a common future. Overcoming political resistance to local integration is a daunting challenge that only a joint effort of donors, local communities and national governments could address in new ways in the search for some solution.

As migrations grow in number and complexity, and with the persistence of displacement producing crises, leadership in developing a comprehensive framework to guide international actors in responding to crises appears as another timely undertaking. The various attempts made so far remain at an embryonic stage, but they show the felt need of some global entity that can effectively support the management of today's population movements.

Likewise, the establishment of the Migration Emergency Funding Mechanism[2] represents a substantial step towards ensuring a more effective response to migrants stranded in crisis situations. Recent major emergencies have highlighted the need for a funding mechanism to facilitate the IOM's rapid response and intervention. As guests in a foreign country, these persons are vulnerable in times of crisis, often unable to access support networks or resources either from the host country or their country of origin. The IOM is increasingly called upon to step into the breach and provide assistance to migrants who have nowhere else to turn. This funding mechanism should be able to reinforce the IOM's operational and emergency response capacity by providing the Organization with funds to bridge the gap between the period when an emergency occurs and when donor funding is received.

Mr Chairman,

Problems for migrants do not end once these persons are evacuated or repatriated to their home countries; to the contrary, return to their communities means additional difficulties related to poverty, psychosocial trauma and lack of employment. Home countries are very often already burdened by poverty, and, in fact, they are very much dependent on

[2] www.iom.int/jahia/webdav/shared/shared/mainsite/about_iom/en/council/100/MC_2335.pdf (last consulted 16 January 2017).

remittances sent back by migrants. Thus, for migrants the crisis in host countries risks becoming a protracted crisis in their home. Moreover, many young migrants, faced with lack of resources and job opportunities at home choose to emigrate again even to crisis-affected areas or give in to the pressure of recruitment and joining rebel groups in their regions.

Therefore, to alleviate both the burden of migrants and of their home communities, international actors need to combine short-term humanitarian assistance with long-term development initiatives that address reconstruction, stabilization and rehabilitation of migrants and sending countries. Migrants could be forgotten too easily once a crisis is over. Many continue risking their lives to ensure their families a decent life, others may become victims of human trafficking and smuggling and even may die while trying to reach better destinations through deserts and seas.

All these issues should become part of any post-2015 global framework since better-managed migration is a critical enabler for inclusive social and economic development. Economic and other contributions of migrants to their sending and host countries need to be more fully utilized.[3]

International migration is bringing benefits to both countries of origin and countries of destination, including remittances and reduced labour shortages. The transfer of resources, skills, knowledge, ideas and networks through migration is difficult to quantify, yet significant. Many millions of migrants also have benefited from their experience that helps building a better future for themselves and their families. However, too many migrants continue to work and live in insecure, precarious and dangerous conditions, often marginalized and subject to discrimination and without access to social and health care services. Moreover, disruptions to their family life can have significant social consequences, particularly in the country of origin. However, the link between migration and development is complex. Adequate policies need to be in place to mitigate some of the well-known risks, such as brain drain and health issues.

[3] www.oxfamblogs.org/fp2p/?p=10831 (last consulted 16 November 2012).

Mr Chairman,

In conclusion, the Delegation of the Holy See would like to recall that beyond being considered an additional strain to host communities, migrants are a resource for our societies. Besides the new and rich values and perspectives they are contributing, migrants sustain the economy through their work. In the planning by the international community migrations need to find their place, not only as functional to development and demography, but as a major human rights commitment and comprehensive humanitarian responsibility. Only in this way, will the interdependence, of which migrations are a result and a cause, make our common future a positive force for all.

CONTRIBUTION TO DEVELOPMENT AND MIGRANTS' HUMAN RIGHTS*

Chairperson, my Delegation welcomes the new member States and congratulates you and the Bureau on your election.

This Council convenes at a propitious moment in the evolution of migration governance, policy formulation and practice. As the international community develops its strategies for the post-2015 Development Agenda, the priority-setting that is required to address the needs and rights of the 232 million migrants worldwide, who constitute 3.2 per cent of the global population, cannot be ignored.[1] By comparing the number of international migrants with those reported in past years, 175 million in 2000 and 154 million in 1990, we can better understand the growing significance and impact of this reality. While people on the move are motivated by different needs and aspirations, we must recognize the unique human dignity of such persons and acknowledge the gifts, talents, skills, experience and cultural patrimony offered by all migrants who serve as bridges between their respective countries of origin and the countries that receive them. We must also recognize the difficult conditions that lead or compel persons to seek a better, more secure life in a foreign land. Many flee intense privation, violence or natural disaster. Most decide to migrate as part of a family survival strategy. All make extraordinary sacrifices to further their own and their family members' prospects and potential. As Pope Francis has put it, migrants and refugees 'share a legitimate desire for knowing and having, but above all for *being* more' (italics added).[2]

Migrants also substantially contribute to the well-being and development of their countries of origin and adoption. Wage increases from migration exceed all of the world's formal development and anti-poverty interventions in developing nations combined. Globally, the world's international migrants are expected to remit earnings worth US$ 550 billion this year, including US$ 414 billion to developing countries. Diaspora savings, which can be mobilized to help finance development goals, are

* Statement delivered at the 103rd Session of the Council of the International Organization for Migration, 26–29 November 2013.

1 http://esa.un.org/unmigration/wallchart2013.htm.

2 Message of Pope Francis for the World Day of Migrants and Refugees, Vatican City, 24 September 2013, www.news.va/en/news/popes-message-for-word-day-of-migrants-and-refugee.

estimated to exceed US$ 400 billion. Thus migration provides a fast path to poverty reduction in countries of origin. Countries of destination, in turn, benefit from necessary workers, tax revenue and other contributions from immigrants.

In these circumstances, it is worth considering the gains from movement for labour. The intermediate and long-term positive effects of migration should weigh more than the emotional and often prejudicial political manipulation of migration debates. For this reason, nations should adopt a person-centered approach to migration that takes into account the concrete contributions that result from what is often an expression of human creativity and entrepreneurship. The positive effects and potential of migration calls for serious analysis and for recommendations for global action on urgent concerns: access to a territory and asylum when needed, respect of fundamental human rights and recognition of innate and acquired rights for all migrants.

These reflections arise from consideration of persons that leave their countries of birth and persons displaced within their own countries due to conditions of conflict, persecution or oppression that put their very lives and futures at risk,[3] as well as categories of migrants demanding renewed attention, especially domestic workers and workers in general.

Access to territory for Asylum Seekers.In early July 2013, Pope Francis chose Lampedusa as the destination for his first trip outside Rome since assuming office as Pope. This island between Southern Italy and the African continent, in the Mediterranean Sea, where more than 20,000 African immigrants have lost their lives in recent years while trying to escape abject poverty, cruel wars and ethnic violence in unseaworthy boats. There he launched a challenge, which seems most appropriate for the work of this Council: 'In this globalized world, we have fallen into globalized indifference. We have become used to the suffering of others: it doesn't affect me; it doesn't concern me; it's none of my business!'[4]

Three months later, the same venue marked the tragic deaths of more than 300 migrants seeking freedom and a dignified life who perished in a fire that broke out on their unseaworthy vessel. In expressing his personal grief at this disaster, Pope Francis reminded the international

[3] In fact, the 2012 World Disasters Report estimated some 72 million forced migrants in the world, who 'face serious humanitarian and human rights challenges. With their support systems removed, they are often unable to access basic health, welfare and education services. They may lose links with families and communities, and experience severe socio-economic loss and impoverishment.'

[4] www.vatican.va/holy_father/francesco/homilies/2013/documents/papa-francesco_20130708_omelia-lampedusa_en.html.

community of the 'shame' that we all must bear for denying, ignoring or merely tolerating such conditions inflicted upon our sisters and brothers in the human family.

The Director General of this Organization has made his own visit to Lampedusa, and recalled that these tragedies are not just being witnessed in the Mediterranean but also in Asia, the South China Sea, the Atlantic, and the Gulf of Aden and in the sands of deserts. He pointed out that 'these deaths are taking place on a frightening scale', and urged that 'the top priority now has to be saving life.'[5] Good planning, data collection on labor market needs and a renewed commitment to everyone's right to work, to family unity, to equity, to human security and to solidarity, can help the opening of legal migration channels and prevent useless loss of lives. The IOM can continue to remind Member States of their responsibilities to provide access to fair status determination procedures.

Chairperson,

Respect for Human Rights. The inalienable rights of all migrants must be recognized and respected, as the Declaration of the High-Level Dialogue on International Migration and Development affirms. My Delegation makes a strong 'appeal for the protection of the dignity and centrality of every person, respecting his fundamental rights'.[6] 'All [persons], in fact, enjoy rights and duties that are not arbitrary, because they stem from human nature itself'[7] and 'thus are … universal, inviolable, [and] inalienable.'[8]

With much regret, the Holy See notes increasing trends toward infringement of the rights of migrants, many of whom become victims of extortion and trafficking and are held against their will and in inhuman conditions, whose identity documents are confiscated, and who are subjected to physical and psychological violence. An increasing number of governments, in fact, make it extraordinarily difficult, if not impossible,

[5] Interview with Ambassador William Lacy Swing, Director General of the International Organization for Migration, Vatican Radio, 14 October 2013.

[6] Address of Pope Francis to the Plenary Meeting of the Pontifical Council for the Pastoral Care of Migrants and Travelers, Vatican City, 24 May 2013, www.vatican.va/holy_father/francesco/speeches/2013/may/documents/papa-francesco_20130524_migranti-itineranti_en.html.

[7] Address of Pope Benedict XVI to the Plenary Meeting of the Pontifical Council for the Pastoral Care of Migrants and Travelers, Vatican City, 28 May 2012, www.vatican.va/holy_father/benedict_xvi/speeches/2010/may/documents/hf_ben-xvi_spe_20100528_migranti_en.html.

[8] Pope John XXIII, Encyclical Letter, *Pacem in Terris* (1963), § 5.

for those fleeing for their lives to reach territory where they might make a claim for protection. Migrants who manage to enter another country are frequently held in detention centers for protracted periods, sometimes without the opportunity to present a request for asylum in a timely way or to pursue other legitimate claims for legal residency. Summary expulsions have also become commonplace.

The relationship between rights and development is at the heart of the migration and development dialogue. Respect for rights enhances the ability of migrants to contribute to their countries of origin and countries of destination. Irregular or unauthorized status makes it harder for migrants to earn as much and thus to contribute as much to their new communities and to invest as substantially in their countries of origin as those with more secure status. Respect for rights contributes to the stability, reputation, human capital and growth of migrant-sending nations, and thus encourages investment by expatriates, diaspora groups and others. At the same time, respect for migrant rights in receiving countries increases the socioeconomic well-being of immigrants and thus their potential to contribute to the development of sending and receiving communities.

My Delegation particularly supports the IOM's approach to the scourge of human trafficking which links the victims of trafficking to other migrants in situations of vulnerability and seeks to promote migration control systems which are respectful of human rights.

Finally, Chairperson, due recognition is called for the rights of migrants acquired in the destination country. These rights, based often on the development of strong equitable ties, facilitate integration and are a requirement of justice and a contribution to the common good and to peaceful coexistence.

My Delegation feels a deep obligation as well to plead for proper care and attention to child migrants, consistent with their best interests. Increasing numbers of unaccompanied minor migrants have been reported in North America and elsewhere. For example, statistics from Mexico's National Migration Institute indicate that in 2012, between January and July, 3,391 Guatemalan, Honduran and Salvadoran children were deported, 50 per cent more than in the same period in 2011. Of these, 2,801 were unaccompanied, many of whom became victims of 'coyotes' or people smugglers.[9] The United States has reported a tripling

[9] 'Mexico: The End of the Dream for Child Migrants', InterPress Service News Agency, 5 November 2012, www.ipsnews.net/2012/10/mexico-the-end-of-the-american-dream-for-child-migrants/.

of unaccompanied minors crossing its border with Mexico over a four-year period.[10]

Chairperson, I will conclude by citing the Declaration of the High-Level Dialogue on International Migration and Development, in which key policy-makers and expert practitioners associated with both governments and civil society organizations reaffirmed 'the need to promote and protect effectively the human rights and fundamental freedoms of all migrants', and resolved 'to address international migration through international, regional or bilateral cooperation and dialogue, through a comprehensive and balanced approach' and to avoid approaches that might aggravate 'the vulnerability of migrants'.[11] In this way, the debate on the post-2015 priorities can become the occasion to look in a new, positive way at migration as an enabler of development and a constructive shaper of history.

Thank you, Chairperson.

10 Pamela Prah, 'Number of Undocumented Children Who Cross U.S. Border Alone Has Tripled', 9 May 2013, www.pewstates.org/projects/stateline/headlines/number-of-undocumented-children-who-cross-us-border-alone-has-tripled-85899474787; Center for Migration Studies of New York, 'The Rise in Unaccompanied Minors: A Global Humanitarian Crisis', 15 October 2012, http://cmsny.org/2012/10/15/the-rise-in-unaccompanied-minors-a-global-humanitarian-crisis/.

11 www.un.org/ga/search/view_doc.asp?symbol=A/68/L.5&referer=www.un.org/en/ga/68/meetings/migration/&Lang=E.

CHILDREN EXODUS: MECHANISMS FOR FAMILY REUNIFICATION*

Mr President,

The Special Rapporteur on the human rights of migrants clearly points out several critical issues concerning exploitation of migrants and underlines the emergence of new vulnerable groups among people on the move. He also has rightly emphasizes that the role of the recruitment agencies should be analyzed in a specific way. Migration is certainly beneficial for all involved, for countries of origin, of arrival and for migrants themselves. After the anxiety and adjustment difficulties of the first impact between newcomers and host population, ample documentation supports the conclusion of the overall beneficial contribution of migrants, a fact that should be highlighted for an appropriate public perception of this phenomenon. As recalled by Pope Francis, 'A change of attitude towards migrants and refugees is needed on the part of everyone, moving away from attitudes of defensiveness and fear, indifference and marginalization – all typical of a throwaway culture – towards attitudes based on a culture of encounter, the only culture capable of building a better, more just and fraternal world.'[1] There remains, however, a tragic and suffering side of this experience: trafficking of persons, abuse of migrant domestic workers and slave labor. Among the relatively new categories of people on the move who call for a new form of protection and urgently demand the attention of the international community are unaccompanied minors, whose numbers and abuses are fast growing

Forced displacement of people caused by current wars and the multiplication of violent conflicts in several regions of the globe is pushing hundreds of thousands of people to risk their lives in the search for survival. A poignant reminder of the futility of violence is the thousands of children who leave their homes and become asylum seekers. In 2011, 12,225 unaccompanied minors applied for asylum in Europe. They represented all the trouble spots of the Middle East and Africa. Symptomatic is also the explosion of child migrants travelling alone in the hope of crossing the border into the United States. The child migrants surge has resulted in a steady increase from 2008 to today; so much so that in 2013,

* Statement delivered at the 26th Session of the Human Rights Council – Item 3: *Report of the Special Rapporteur on the Human Rights of Migrants*, 13 June 2014.

[1] Pope Francis, Message for the World Day for Migrants and Refugees, 2014.

38,883 unaccompanied minors were apprehended at the United States–Mexican border and authorities anticipate that the numbers will double to well over 70,000 for 2014. On make-shift boats that cross the Mediterranean or on the railroads that connect from Central America to the North, these children are exposed to sexual violations, to starvation, to mutilations when they fall and even to the loss of life when their boats sink or they get lost in the desert. This child exodus is primarily caused by the destabilization and endemic violence in the home countries. Some children want to exercise their natural right to be with their families since these may be for years residing in another country without proper documentation. Others are faced with the necessity to escape an environment where more than 90 per cent of the victims of homicide are young male adults and where, as well, 90 per cent of those who commit homicide are young male adults: both are prompted to escape for survival. Others still prefer to die on the way to a dreamed destination of survival rather than dying of hunger or being killed by gangs and organized crime at home. Finally, the allure of a different life-style presented by television pre-socializes other children to move.

In this complex situation it would be useful if the Special Rapporteur would add his contribution in helping governments to devise some urgently needed solutions. Children on the move constitute a humanitarian emergency that calls for immediate remedies. Detention of minors is not an option and the best interest of the child should prevail even in these challenging circumstances. In an effort to prevent the continual flow of minors, international solidarity can be effective by helping to address urban violence at the source of the children's exodus. Legal channels for family reunification will also avoid children resorting to unsafe routes where their exploitation becomes almost unavoidable. Humanitarian values suggest as well the creation of some mechanisms of regularization that would allow children to live with their parents. This natural human right certainly takes priority over administrative infringement of border regulations. Finally, joint projects could open up some educational and employment opportunities for young people that would give them a sense of hope for the future and the reason to stay at home.

Thank you, Mr President.

PERSONS LEFT BEHIND IN THE MIGRATION PROCESS*

Mr Chairman,

The migrant family is a critical component of the growing phenomenon of migration in our globalized world. Thus the Delegation of the Holy See finds it most opportune to have chosen this topic for reflection at the 2014 International Dialogue on Migration (IDM).

Migrants very often move out of concern for the needs of their families; at times, they even risk their lives on flimsy boats or in dangerous deserts in the hope of ensuring their families a decent life as the IOM Report documents. Through their work, the taxes they pay, the new businesses they start and a variety of services they provide, most migrants offer a positive economic and social contribution to the receiving societies. Women domestic workers, for example, leave their children behind in the home country in order to become caregivers for children, disabled and elderly persons abroad. While migrants are a positive presence in their host societies, they face the risk that their own children and relatives remain in the shadow and deprived of their affection at home. The remittances sent home focus the debate on the financial benefits generated by migrants. While this money is important to improve health and education for the family members left behind, it does not quite compensate for other needs: human affection, a necessary presence to educate in values and integrity, a reference model for responsible behaviour, especially for young people. The human emptiness felt when a father or mother emigrates becomes a reminder of the ambivalence of emigration and of the fundamental right to be able to stay at home in dignity. Especially when mothers emigrate, other negative consequences emerge: children's school attendance declines, early marriages of adolescent girls increase, and there is a heightened risk of drug abuse. As Pope Francis recently stated, 'it is necessary to respond to the globalization of migration with the globalization of charity and cooperation, in such a way as to make the conditions of migrants more humane. At the same time, greater efforts are needed to guarantee the easing of conditions, often brought about by war or famine, which compel whole peoples to leave their native countries'.[1]

* Statement delivered at the 2014 International Dialogue on Migration of the International Organization for Migration: *Migration and Families*, 7–8 October 2014.

1 Message of Pope Francis for the 2015 World Day of Migrants and Refugees, http://w2.vatican.va/content/francesco/en/messages/migration/documents/papa-francesco_20140903_world-migrants-day-2015.html.

Children, therefore, as well as elderly persons and spouses left behind, must become a high priority in any migration policy and debate: they are particularly vulnerable, and hence should receive special protection. Policy and program development should aim at maximizing the benefits of remittances, limiting the negative effects of migration and emphasizing family ties as a primary concern in the management of immigration by States. Policy formulation often treats family and labor migration as two distinct realms, 'social' and 'economic'. In reality, the two concepts are closely intertwined.[2] In the planning by the international community and in discussions focused on the post-2015 Development Agenda, migration must have a proper place, not only as functional to development and demography, but as a major human rights commitment aimed at safeguarding the dignity of every human person and the centrality of the family.

Indeed an urgently needed immigration reform involves the formulation of a legal framework that helps keep families together. The life and dignity of every human person is lived within the family. All children need their parents. Parents have the responsibility to protect and nurture their children, and yet deported parents are prevented from living out this fundamental vocation. Too many families are now torn apart. By allowing children to emigrate unaccompanied further problems arise as they are exposed to lawlessness and despair. The family structure, however, should be the place where hope, compassion, justice and mercy are taught most effectively. Family is the basic unit of coexistence, its foundation and the ultimate remedy against social fragmentation.[3]

Finally, achievable measures could be implemented in a realistic and sensitive manner. Migrants, who are restricted or prevented from traveling home in order to provide personal care for elderly parents or affection to their kin, should be entitled to occasional leaves and should benefit from special prices for their trip home. Interest fees for the transfer of remittances must be lowered. The process to obtain a visa for a spouse or close family member (which in certain countries takes several years) needs to be speeded up. Ad hoc 'family counselors' to serve in regions with a very high rate of migrants should be engaged in order to provide assistance and advice to members of the family 'left behind' and to facilitate timely

[2] Brenda S. A. Yeoh and Cheng Yi'En, 'Family Migration', in *The Encyclopedia of Global Human Migration*, Hoboken, NJ: Wiley-Blackwell, 2013, p. 2.

[3] 'Family Beyond Borders', an open letter from the Bishops of the Border region of Mexico, Texas and New Mexico.

reunification of the family. In fact, when return migrants revert to day-to-day interaction with their societies of origin, they experience a 'reverse culture shock'.[4] The changes in family dynamics that result from migration do not end when the migrant returns to the society of origin; in fact, migrants generally return to a family situation that is very different from that before departure. Family members can become 'strangers' since they have been absent from each other's lives and since relations between them are largely based on the sending of money and goods or sporadically maintained by new forms of Internet communications.

In conclusion, it is mandatory to avoid treating the 'left behind' population merely as passive recipients of the effects of migration. In this context, family migration needs to be reconceived using frameworks of trans-nationalism that grant more flexibility to the movement of people, especially in countries where the presence of the family of the migrant workers is legally impeded. Healthy interaction and personal relations among family members are obstructed by borders. States and civil society are prompted by their own future to give priority to the family and thus make migration a more positive experience for all.

[4] www.scielo.org.mx/scielo.php?pid=S1665–89062013000100001&script=sci_arttext.

THE PROTECTION OF MIGRANT WORKERS AND PERSONS DISPLACED BY CLIMATE CHANGE AND NATURAL DISASTERS*

Mr Chairperson,

My Delegation extends congratulations to you, Ambassador Eddico and to the Council Bureau, on your election and thanks Ambassador Enrique Chávez Basagoitia of Peru, for his work as Chair of the Council over the course of the last year. It also welcomes the Independent State of Samoa as a new IOM Member.

At present, one in every seven persons worldwide lives in some sort of migration status. The world witnesses, as migrants, an unprecedented and appalling number of unaccompanied children; complex health and humanitarian emergencies, and over 50 million forcibly displaced persons, the highest number since the Second World War. There is little doubt that migration is one of the most powerful forces shaping the economic, social, political and cultural life in today's world. While often accompanied by challenges, this phenomenon results in benefits for countries of origin, destination, and for the migrants themselves. In fact, it is a well-established fact that migrants can make an even richer contribution when their dignity is respected, integration in their country of residence is favored, their human rights secured, and the development of their talents and energy encouraged.

The time has come for States and the international community to respond to the globalization of migration with the globalization of solidarity and cooperation, in such a way as to make the conditions of migrants more humane.[1] From a path of confrontation, we need to move to one of dialogue and encounter. From migration control and the use of the rising number of migrants dying in transit toward a dreamed destination as deterrence,[2] we must strive to regulate openness and devise legal ways to facilitate mobility.

* Statement delivered at the 105th Session of the Council of the International Organization for Migration, 25–28 November 2014.

1 http://w2.vatican.va/content/francesco/en/messages/migration/documents/papa-francesco_20140903_world-migrants-day-2015.html (Message of Pope Francis for the 2015 World Day of Migrants and Refugees).

2 www.ohchr.org/EN/NewsEvents/Pages/DisplayNews.aspx?NewsID=15239&LangID=E.

Mr Chairperson,

Among the various aspects of migration, I wish to focus briefly on two concerns: on migrant workers and on those persons displaced by climate change and natural disasters.

The persistent inequalities and the increasing levels of poverty prompt many workers in developing countries to seek work abroad.[3] This type of migration, however, 'is still too frequently associated with unacceptable labor abuses and exploitation in the face of which inaction is an abdication of responsibility'.[4] In particular, migrant domestic workers, the majority of whom are women, find themselves especially vulnerable and are often victims of human trafficking. The recruitment process for migrants, therefore, needs to be further formalized and facilitated in order to prevent exploitation. Legislation must be enforced to ensure that migrant workers' rights are respected. Within such a framework, a closer cooperation between the private sector and governments is needed to enhance global knowledge about national and international recruitment practices, to promote fair business standards as well as to strengthen laws, policies and enforcement mechanisms.

The international instruments on labor and migration[5] adopted over the years are crucial for safeguarding the dignity and rights of migrant workers; however, existing regulations in many countries are often inconsistent with, or fail to uphold, them.

Mr Chairperson,

My Delegation would also like to underscore the role that climate change and other environmental factors are increasingly playing in the movement of persons. Perhaps more than ever, concerns of accelerating climate change call for a renewed consideration of its effects upon migration. At the moment, there is little consensus on a definition of migrants forced to move by environmental degradation or climate change, but

3 http://ilo.org/global/standards/subjects-covered-by-international-labour-standards/migrant-workers/lang–en/index.htm.

4 ILO's Director General remarks during the 103rd International Labour Conference, May 28, 2014 www.ilo.org/ilc/ILCSessions/103/reports/reports-to-the-conference/WCMS_242879/lang–en/index.htm.

5 For example, the UN Guiding Principles on Business and Human Rights, the International Convention on the Protection of all Migrant Workers and their families, and several ILO Conventions.

there must be a term that corresponds to this reality which could provide sufficient rationale to create the necessary framework to protect them.[6] The number of environmental-degradation- and climate-change-induced migrants has reached an annual average of 27 million people.[7] The humanitarian and human rights impact on people should be the priority. Neither the 1992 United Nations Framework Convention on Climate Change ('UNFCCC') nor its Kyoto Protocol of 1997 includes any provisions concerning specific assistance or protection for those directly affected by the effects of climate change. Likewise, the most recent G-20 communiqué[8] does not make any single reference to the humanitarian consequences of climate change on the populations affected. In this context, the Delegation of the Holy See finds it most opportune that the IOM decided to convene a Conference on the topic of 'Migrants and Cities' in October 2015. In fact, while most policies are formulated at the State level, the large majority of internal and international migrants actually move to large metropolitan areas, in many cases residing in precarious informal settlements and slums, a degraded and problematic environment.

The upcoming World Conference on Disaster-Risk Reduction in Sendai, the 8th Global Forum on Migration and Development in 2015, and the World Humanitarian Summit in 2016, offer opportunities to highlight the essential humanitarian aspects of migration. The Delegation of the Holy See hopes that the good sense of the international community will prevail. Dignity has no nationality: it is equal for every person. No country can singlehandedly face the difficulties associated with this phenomenon.[9] Respect for the human rights of migrants – it is not just a responsibility we all share; it is an ethical duty.

[6] Rabab Fatima, Anita Jawadurovna Wadud and Sabira Coelho, 'Human Rights, Climate Change, Environmental Degradation and Migration: A New Paradigm', Washington, DC: Migration Policy Institute, March 2014.

[7] www.internal-displacement.org/global-figures#natural.

[8] https://www.g20.org/sites/default/files/g20_resources/library/brisbane_g20_leaders_summit_communique.pdf.

[9] Message of Pope Francis for the 2014 World Day of Migrants and Refugees, http://w2.vatican.va/content/francesco/en/messages/migration/documents/papa-francesco_20130805_world-migrants-day.html.

Mr Chairperson,

No man or woman, having the possibility to live in his/her homeland with dignity, would feel compelled to flee his/her country. We must, then, strive to create the proper environment 'at home'. In light of current demographic trends and projections that anticipate continued migration flows, it is necessary to tackle the root causes of migration: extreme poverty, unstable political situations, health crises, persecutions, climate change. The goal ahead is to make migration a choice and not a compulsive necessity. In the meantime, the 'presence of migrants is a reminder of the need to eradicate inequality, injustice and abuses'.[10]

In conclusion, it makes sense to integrate migration, the 'oldest action against poverty', into the Post-2015 Development Agenda. States and international organizations, together with civil society, have the responsibility to devise and implement migration policies, strategies and agreements to make more humane the experience of migration in its old and new forms and thus ensure its benefits for all.

10 Pope Francis, Message to Participants on 7th World Congress for the Pastoral Care of Migrants, 21 November 2014.

THE FAILURE OF THE MULTILATERAL SYSTEM TO MANAGE MIGRATION: AN ABDICATION OF RESPONSIBILITY*

Mr President,

The multilateral system, and immigration countries in particular, have not yet succeeded in effectively managing migration. While much generosity in receiving asylum seekers and migrants has been evident, a long-range immigration strategy is still lacking. The consequence, in Pope Francis' words, is abdication of responsibility, because 'leaving our brothers on boats to die ... is an attack against life.'[1] In fact, since January 2015, well over 1,800 migrants have already lost their lives while attempting to cross the Mediterranean.[2] An estimated 25,000 Rohingyas and Bangladeshi have boarded smugglers' boats destined for Thailand and Malaysia[3] in the first three months of 2015. A shocking total of 68,000 unaccompanied children were apprehended by the US Border Patrol from October 2013 to September 2014.[4]

Mr President,

The push factors for such gigantic migration and refugee flows are well-known to the international community: the organized business of human trafficking that exploits people in desperate situations; no end to poverty; lack of jobs; unstable political situations, discrimination, health crises, persecutions, bloody wars and famines. The multilateral system needs to work better together: migration and climate change are major challenges of the twenty-first century. In the long term, it is necessary to address the root causes of such a global phenomenon. The clock is ticking, and the longer we wait, the higher the costs will be. All these persons on the move for different reasons have rights that the national and international communities must protect and respect in practice. The Delegation of the Holy See would like to suggest some concrete steps.

* Statement delivered to the 29th Session of the Human Rights Council, Interactive Dialogue with the Special Rapporteur on Migrants, 15 June 2015.

1 Pope Francis, Address to participants in the meeting sponsored by the Science and Life Association, 30 May 2015.

2 http://missingmigrants.iom.int/sites/default/files/pictures/IOM-Mediterranean-Update-26May2015.jpg.

3 www.unhcr.org/554c8adf9.html.

4 www.wola.org/commentary/latest_border_stats_point_to_heavy_child_family_migration_in_2015.

First, search and rescue operations should continue and be further strengthened, as the need to protect the right to life of all, regardless of their status, must remain the priority; second, resettlement in Europe, as well as in other parts of the world, should be effectively carried out and more fairly distributed, with due attention for security and social needs, but without acquiescing in irrational populist pressures; third, competent authorities should provide safer legal channels of emigration and practical acceptance so as to reconcile migrants' rights and the legitimate interests of the receiving societies.

Mr President,

The perception of migrants as a burden runs against the evidence of their contribution to the national economy of the host countries, to the social security system and to the demographic deficit.[5] Accumulating evidence shows that, besides enriching the national culture with new values and perspectives, migrants contribute through the taxes they pay, the new businesses they start, as well as the array of services they provide. For instance, some stunning 497,000 new enterprises were run by foreign citizens in Italy in 2013,[6] and, according to the Organisation for Economic Co-operation and Development (OECD), migrants accounted for 47 per cent of the increase in the workforce in the United States and 70 per cent in Europe over the past ten years.[7] Far from being an obstacle, newcomers therefore prove to be a crucial positive factor for the economy and a creative presence in society.

Mr President,

At the same time, other long-range strategies are required. The issue of migration is not an isolated variable, but an important component in the context of political, economic and trade relations between sending and receiving countries. No person with the possibility of living with dignity in his or her home country would feel compelled to flee it. International solidarity should then strive to create the proper environment 'at home', thus making migration a choice and not a compulsive necessity.

[5] Report of the ILO Director General to the International Labour Conference, 'Fair Migration: Setting an ILO Agenda', 2014, p. 4.

[6] 2015 ISTAT Annual Report, available at www.istat.it/it/files/2015/05/Rapporto-Annuale-2015.pdf.

[7] www.oecd.org/migration/mig/OECD%20Migration%20Policy%20Debates%20Numero%202.pdf, p. 2

This may be accomplished by creating quality and decent jobs, promoting a more just and equitable financial and economic order, improving access to markets, trade and competition, by exchanging innovative technology, raising participation and political stability.

An increasing number of people are moving to urban centers, a development that calls for fresh reflection on integration to ensure peaceful coexistence in society. Aside from mere economic reasons, the interest of the receiving society is served in the long run by the acceptance of newcomers in their difference and by their openness to progressive integration in the new environment by accepting the fundamental values, rights and obligations that make possible a common future.

Fairness demands that a positive image of newcomers be adopted with a common, friendly and appropriate terminology for media at the national level, so as to avoid ambiguity, demagoguery and the stirring up of racism, discrimination, exploitation by unscrupulous politicians. Above all, respect for the dignity of the human person remains the touchstone. At the same time, receiving countries should put in place proper mechanisms for social acceptance of migrants, for example, by drafting Charters on rights and responsibilities of migrants, which are readily comprehensible, so as better to integrate migrants and provide them with a secure legal status, with clear and specific rights and responsibilities.

In conclusion, we thank the Special Rapporteur for the best practices outlined in his report and for playing an important role in maintaining a high level of public awareness and we welcome resolution 26/19 of the Human Rights Council which further extended his mandate.

Mr President,

The proper implementation of human rights becomes truly beneficial for migrants, as well as for the sending and receiving countries. The measures suggested are not a mere concession to migrants. They are in the interest of migrants, host societies and the international community at large. Promoting and respecting the human rights of migrants and their dignity ensures that everyone's rights and dignity in society are fully respected.

MIGRANTS AND CITIES: NEW PARTNERSHIPS TO MANAGE MOBILITY*

Madam Chairperson,

The Delegation of the Holy See is pleased to participate in this High-Level Conference on Migrants and Cities, a theme which is filled with challenges and opportunities. As is well known, urbanization is a global reality that has witnessed exponential increases in the last decades. Over 54 per cent of people across the globe were living in urban areas in 2014. It is estimated that the number of people living in cities will nearly double to some 6.4 billion by 2050, turning much of the world into a global city.[1] For the first time in human history, we are witnessing the density of population in urban areas surpassing the population in rural areas. In general, urban settings constitute a pull factor, offering the promise of economic progress, of upward social mobility, of greater access to jobs, as well as improved education opportunities and better health care. Such a changing demographic provides challenges and opportunities for the migrants themselves and the host cities, on both the cultural and social and economic levels.

Many cities have tried to approach these challenges by forming urban areas for migrants. In countries with a significant gap between the haves and have-nots, public spaces are often made exclusive, the so-called *gated communities*. These areas function as a type of exclusive social 'barrier', a sort of enclave for the wealthy classes, who shelter themselves up within walls as protection against the insecurity that derives from social inequalities. Within such areas, the standard of living, including the amenities and civil infrastructure, is not comparable to those conditions experienced by those who are outside those walls. This situation poses the need to rethink the relationship between the city and migrants from the urban space to which they are destined, as well as their interactions with other social groups. Therefore, it is necessary to think on how to break a pattern of development that unravels the social fabric of urban life and design a new public policy of the city, directed to increase sustainable relationships between inhabitants.

* Statement delivered at the International Dialogue on Migration – Migrants and Cities: New Partnerships to Manage Mobility, 27 October 2015.

1 Cf. International Organization for Migration (IOM), World Migration Report 2015, https://www.iom.int/sites/default/files/country/docs/syria/IOM-World-Migration-Report-2015-Overview.pdf.

Urban centers constitute the largest hubs of the world's economy. They are the places where the most industry, investment, innovation are found, with the potential of job opportunities at all levels. In fact, it is well known that most wealthy nations are predominantly urban in their demographic. Hence, there exists a strong association between scale of economic growth and increase in level of urbanization which is inherently linked to the reality of migration. As a result, the reality of today's urban aggregations can be described through the concept of 'super-diversity', due to the heterogeneous migratory backgrounds and to their intersection with other types of diversity, often described as fostering economic competitiveness and common well-being. Migration flows not only provide a cheap labor force to sustain the everyday functioning of the urban economies, they also bring about new entrepreneurs, new contributors to an ever-evolving social setting.

When considering the role of migrants' contribution to the economic and social development of hosting societies, a specific focus must be put on their civic engagement and desirable involvement in voluntary work within both ethnic and mainstream organizations. Besides producing a positive impact on the migrants' empowerment and well-being, supporting their process of integration, their involvement in the social and civil life of the urban community, permits them to give back to the host country what they have received, according to the logic of reciprocity, and to feel more appreciated and welcomed. Moreover, migrants' involvement in the civic and associative spheres has a positive impact on social cohesion. The presence of migrants among the staff of mainstream organizations makes it possible to mediate cultural values, to promote the dialogue between cultures, to improve the linguistic and cultural skills of other volunteers.

Migrants' social involvement increases the associations' expertise and expands their offer; enriches the problem-solving process; promotes international contacts and cooperation with the sending countries. Moreover, it allows local communities and newcomers to meet and to become involved together in issues of common interest thus boosting interethnic, interreligious and intercultural interactions, enabling them to deal with social change and to recognize the opportunities arising from a society that embraces cultural diversity. This promotes an attitude of openness to other cultures both in the receiving society's population and in the ethnic communities, and leads to the development of a feeling of mutual trust and confidence that contributes to the dynamic two-way integration process required for the creation of a shared citizenship.

Migrants themselves share an essential element of the design of a new public policy of the city, from their own contributions to social cohesion; in other words, through their perception of public problems and their social commitment. Within their civic and popular organizations, we can highlight those that contribute to the reduction of social inequality and the acquisition of social capital because these strengthen relationships within and among groups.

In spite of the asymmetry with regard to society, migrants establish groups for mutual aid also linked with members of other collectives. Through these organizations, religious organizations in particular, migrants increase the level of social cohesion, receive and offer ethical and civic guidance and create other spaces for sharing, for dialogue and mutual acceptance. Recent studies have evidenced the contributions towards social cohesion on two levels. The first such contribution is through the insertion to their own organizations, of groups of volunteers or religious affiliation groups from the native population; second, at the level of cooperation with NGOs and groups from various religious denominations, in projects that can range from courses to learn the local language, or food banks, to theater workshops, intercultural festivals or information regarding election processes. Migrant organizations offer an open field for the formation of leaders and the recovery of self-esteem among the people whose education or working experience is not recognized by government agencies or private enterprise.

Madam Chairperson,

'The multicultural character of society today … call[s] us to deepen and strengthen the values needed to guarantee peaceful coexistence between persons and cultures. Achieving mere tolerance that respects diversity and ways of sharing between different backgrounds and cultures is not sufficient … a more decisive and constructive action is required, one which relies on a universal network of cooperation, based on safeguarding the dignity and centrality of every human person. This will lead to greater effectiveness in the fight against the shameful and criminal trafficking of human beings, the violation of fundamental rights, and all forms of violence, oppression and enslavement.'[2]

Thank you, Madam Chairperson.

2 Pope Francis, Message on the World Day of Migrants, 2014.

VIABLE AND FORWARD-LOOKING SOLUTIONS FOR AN ENLIGHTENED MANAGEMENT OF HUMAN MOBILITY*

Mr Chairperson,

My Delegation wishes to thank the Director General for his comprehensive report and extend congratulations to you, Ambassador Bertrand de Crombrugghe, and to the Council Bureau, on your election, while recognizing Ambassador Eddico of Ghana for his work as Chair of the Council over the course of the last year. In addition, we welcome the Democratic Republic of São Tomé and Príncipe, the Federation of Saint Kitts and Nevis, Eritrea, Saint Lucia and the Republic of Kiribati as new IOM Members.

Mr Chairperson,

Violent conflicts and deep inequalities persist in many regions of the globe and precipitate a large displacement of people. As a result, we are witnessing around 240 million international migrants, of whom more than 60 million have been forcefully displaced. Human mobility is a megatrend of our times. It is not limited to the Mediterranean; it is a global challenge to which the international community needs to respond with a concerted political strategy and common humanitarian values, rather than with populist rhetoric. This 'year of the migrant' is a defining moment for the evolution of our societies. The recently adopted 2030 Agenda for Sustainable Development gives a clear sign that the international community has made a remarkable effort to act as a real family of nations. Recent terrorist attacks, however, have shifted public and political attention from development to security. The response to migration risks being jeopardized, becoming inadequate and disordered.

Mr Chairperson,

As we gather today, thousands of men, women and children are trying to find their way to safe havens. Globalization has allowed for a free flow of money and of trade in goods and services; but as for human mobility – and especially that of migrants and refugees in need – enormous obstacles remain. The remedy begins with a realistic evaluation of

* Statement delivered at the 106th Session of the Council of the International Organization for Migration, 24–27 November 2015.

the positive aspects of this phenomenon. Migrants provide a solid contribution to receiving societies through the taxes they pay, the skilled and unskilled labor they provide and the balance they represent for the demographic circumstances of ageing host populations. More than a crisis of numbers, we face a crisis of trust and solidarity. An enlightened management of migration requires a mobilization of political will and the vision to adopt viable and forward-looking solutions.

First and foremost, the priority must be to save lives, no matter what their migratory status. Simply closing borders and building barriers heightens the vulnerability of migrants in transit, giving opportunities to human traffickers to carry on their criminal business. Instead, training law enforcement officials to treat migrants in transit with dignity, and investing in cross-border partnerships for a speedy and just assessment of their status, is a more effective approach.

If we wish to address the root causes that trigger displacement, we must first address the destabilizing elements in the countries of origin of today's flows of displaced people. This may necessitate, among other things, supporting incremental peace processes to end ongoing conflicts and address humanitarian suffering, establishing and enforcing safe zones where civilians are protected from indiscriminate acts of violence, or undertaking the responsibility to protect wherever terrorists are acting with impunity. Without such steps, mass exoduses cannot be prevented.

Reception centres and well-functioning asylum systems, together with safe and legal channels of emigration created without being preselective with respect to background or origin, while ensuring that the truly needy are helped and effectively protected from new pressures and abuses, will make current flows more orderly and beneficial.

As reported by the Director General, 'the migration debate today is largely one-sided, with emphasis on the short term and a strong security focus, driven by fears and destructive stereotypes'.[1] In this regard, it would be useful if the forthcoming environment Conference, COP 21, were to look at the population consequences of environmental degradation. 'There has been a tragic rise in the number of migrants seeking to flee from the growing poverty caused by environmental degradation', observes Pope Francis. 'They are not recognized by international conventions as refugees; they bear the loss of the lives they have left behind, without enjoying any legal protection whatsoever. Sadly, there is widespread indifference to such suffering, which is even now taking place throughout

[1] DG Report to the 106th Session of the IOM Council.

our world. Our lack of response to these tragedies involving our brothers and sisters points to the loss of that sense of responsibility for our fellow men and women upon which all civil society is founded.'[2]

International migration is a very sensitive issue as it touches on national sovereignty and identity. It is therefore important to rebuild trust in migration policies and institutions. Sustainable Development Goal 16 of the 2030 Development Agenda seeks to 'promote peaceful and inclusive societies for sustainable development, provide access to justice for all and build effective, accountable and inclusive institutions at all levels'.[3] This objective cannot be achieved without an effective channeling of multiculturalism and diversity.

Finally, a failure of political will to address current population movements, in an objective and constructive way at the international and national levels, would contradict the overarching need to manage migration in view of the common good. As Pope Francis recalls in his message for the 2016 World Day of Migrants and Refugees: 'at this moment in human history, marked by great movements of migration, identity is not a secondary issue. Those who migrate are forced to change some of their most distinctive characteristics and, whether they like it or not, even those who welcome them are also forced to change.'[4] Newcomers and local populations can develop together a richer identity. Integration, however, requires the acceptance of some basic values that allow for a peaceful and constructive coexistence: mutual respect, freedom of conscience, separation of religion and politics, acceptance of democracy and all fundamental human rights. Cities and local governments are the front line in the management of integration as they are the first to meet arriving migrants who move more and more into the urban context.

[2] Pope Francis, *Laudato Si'*, § 25.

[3] https://sustainabledevelopment.un.org/topics.

[4] Message of Pope Francis for the World Day of Migrants and Refugees, 17 January 2016, http://w2.vatican.va/content/francesco/en/messages/migration/documents/papa-francesco_20150912_world-migrants-day-2016.html (4 October 2015).

Mr Chairperson,

In conclusion, migrants constitute an invitation to look anew at international relations and at our solidarity as a single family of nations, so that unjust inequalities and violence may not disrupt peaceful coexistence. Migrants can be builders of bridges among cultures, bringing their contribution in hard work, energy and new ideas. But their acceptance of fundamental human rights is indispensable for the development of a successful integration, for a successful story of mutual enrichment and renewed confidence in the future.

Thank you, Mr Chairperson.

3 THE SCOURGE OF TRAFFICKING IN HUMAN PERSONS

PROSECUTE THE MULTI-BILLION DOLLAR INDUSTRY OF TRAFFICKING AND REHABILITATE THE VICTIMS*

Mr Chairman,

The vast and growing phenomenon of human mobility reaches into the tens of millions today: every country – of origin, transit and arrival – is directly affected by it. These masses on the move are actors of globalization and development through the contribution of their culture, their work and the remittances they send home, higher than those given by rich countries as aid to development. While basically a positive factor of modern societies, people on the move become a source of political and social concern, and of untold suffering to themselves, when their presence in a new environment is the result of forced expulsions and violent conflicts, as in the case of refugees and internally displaced persons, or of deception and exploitation, as in the case of trafficked and smuggled persons. The international community has developed structures and initiatives to address the needs and rights of the different categories of people on the move. It studies ways and means to manage in a more rational and productive manner a phenomenon with major national and global implications. The Commission on Human Rights has focused its attention on the more vulnerable groups, rightly beginning with women and children. There are, in fact, subgroups of people among those moving across the globe that call for a specific and continued concern because their human rights are more blatantly trampled upon. The Delegation of the Holy See adds its appreciation for the valuable reports of the Secretary General and of the Special Rapporteur addressing these situations and looks forward to their continued contribution to better the plight of all vulnerable migrants.

Among the violations of migrants' rights, traffic in humans is the worst. It involves up to 1 million persons transported annually across national borders. It is carried out for various types of exploitation of children, women and men, subjecting them to slave-like conditions in work, sexual abuse and begging, thus stripping people of their God-given

* Statement delivered at the 60th Session of the Commission on Human Rights – Item 14: *Specific Groups and Individuals*, 8 April 2004.

dignity and fueling instead corruption and organized crime. Trafficking has turned into a multi-billion-dollar industry. The recent entry into force of the Protocol to Prevent, Suppress and Punish Trafficking in Persons, especially Women and Children, is an important step in protection. But regional mechanisms and national legislation are equally important to eradicate this scourge. Besides, it would be opportune for national legislators to take into consideration the High Commissioner for Human Rights' Recommended Principles and Guidelines on Human Rights and Human Trafficking. In the multilateral approach required to combat trafficking, the collection and sharing of data, including of the strategies and routes used by traffickers, becomes a significant tool to step up both investigations and prosecutions. In the effort to dismantle criminal networks the information that the victims of trafficking can provide is invaluable. But clear legal protection for victims must be assured. However, the victim's readiness to testify in court should not be the condition for affording protection. The best practice seems that of granting at least a temporary residence permit to the victim as an encouragement to cooperate with the judicial system but also as a possible opening for social integration in the host society. This becomes a moral necessity if the return home would expose the victim to retaliation. In any case, providing assistance and protection in both countries of destination and origin and during the repatriation and reintegration process is a generally recognized obligation.

If most of the trafficked persons are migrants who by different strategies have been pressed into servitude, there are other vulnerable migrants who have started their journey on their own and by any means of fortune and find themselves in an irregular position in the receiving society. In the shadowy world of their irregular status, fear and inability to stand up for their rights leave these migrants at risk of unfair treatment and of being co-opted in illegal activity. Immigration policies that realistically reflect the labor and demographic needs of the receiving societies would favor their own and the immigrants' interest by opening regular channels of immigration adequately wide to at least prevent the worst tragedies of lost young lives of migrants crossing deserts or seas looking for a decent living. The application of labor laws can also go a long way in the protection of irregular-status migrants and to discourage this type of movement. Now that the International Convention on the Protection of the Rights of Migrant Workers and Members of Their Families has entered into force and its monitoring Committee been established, all migrants have an important instrument at their disposal.

At the root of the migration push we often find extreme poverty and the alluring appeal of possible jobs, and a freer and more humane life, in the countries of destination, as powerfully projected by the global media.

In conclusion, Mr Chairman, a multi-pronged approach appears necessary to make human mobility a motor for progress even for its most vulnerable segments: international cooperation in the prevention and prosecution of trafficking and the rehabilitation of victims; less restrictive and more realistic immigration policies; concerted promotion of sustainable economic and social development in poor countries; a continued formation to a culture of human rights and respect of the dignity of every person.

TRAFFICKING IN HUMAN BEINGS, A CONTEMPORARY FORM OF SLAVERY*

Madam Chairperson,

The trade in human beings, especially of women and minors, has become a powerful global business involving many countries of origin, transit and destination. The victims of trafficking in persons are estimated at almost three million a year, a lucrative trade that generates an annual income of over US$ 30 billion. After a risky journey, these women and minors become bonded to their masters as slaves, with passports and personal documents seized, and a sense of identity destroyed. What is new is the globalization of this trade, the development of a global market which exploits the extreme poverty and vulnerability of many women and minors who try to escape intolerable conditions of misery and violence. The consequences of this enslavement are a loss of psycho-physical identity, of personal dignity and freedom. In this systemic violation of human rights, in particular, a woman comes to consider herself as an object, a thing, a piece of merchandise and is forced to live as an illegal, a social and cultural outcast, emptied by sexual abuse of her deepest values, her femininity, self-esteem and her concept of love and life. Such degradation stifles any dream of a bright future

The international community and national legislations have enacted several good measures directed at preventing the exploitation of people and at providing remedy for the victims of trafficking. The trade in human beings, however, does not tend to diminish and only takes on new forms. Endemic poverty and armed conflicts affect women and children in greater part. Corruption is another cause that favors the exploitation of more vulnerable persons. Then, the ignorance and lack of experience of the victims themselves allow for their deception and subjugation as tools for easy gains. Laws and conventions need to be adequately applied if trafficking is to be stopped and its victims protected. Indeed legal provisions point in some constructive directions.

First, prevention has to be prioritized. Programs of information and formation in the countries of origin, often generously provided by faith-based communities, intend to prevent the exodus toward richer countries. But a more effective prevention can and must be exercised by

* Statement delivered at the 18th Session of the Human Rights Council – Item 3: *Contemporary Forms of Slavery*, 14 September 2011.

eliminating the demand for sexual services and the creation of a new culture where interpersonal relations between a man and a woman are based on reciprocal respect and not on merchandizing the body.

Second, concrete initiatives are indicated for the protection and social re-integration of the victims of trafficking, in particular for those that ask for help to exit their context of exploitation and enslavement. Thousands of young women, for example, have been welcomed into family-like homes established to host them as they escaped from their exploiters. The young women find in these homes protection, guidance and a friendly environment that sustains their return to a more human, normal and even spiritual and legal situation. They are helped to heal the wounds caused by their exploitation and to become again protagonists of their future. Existing good practices, for example, carried out by women religious, who network among countries for an effective action, could become a standard answer to this huge problem of trafficking.

Third, the prosecution of traffickers has to be strengthened through a fair and effective application of legislation. Traffickers have earned much money that they use to evade the law and even the sentences received and their quick exit from prison places their victims once more at risk together with their families in the countries of origin.

Madam Chairperson,

To counteract the scourge of trafficking of women and children with greater determination and more concrete results, a convergence of efforts is necessary: a mentality that is centred on the unique dignity of every person, a sure punishment of traffickers, fight against corruption, a correct teaching in schools of the mutual relations between man and woman, the fairness of mass media in reporting the damages created by trafficking. Finally, collaboration among the various organisms concerned with this problem is critical. In fact, while legislation should be continuously adjusted and adapted to the evolution of the phenomenon of trafficking, the working together of public and private institutions and the contribution of volunteers will guarantee that no person may be bought or sold in violation of his/her dignity and fundamental human rights because he/she is created free and in God's image and not to be treated as a slave.

Thank you, Madam Chairperson.

THE SCOURGE OF TRAFFICKED CHILDREN AND THEIR SEXUAL EXPLOITATION*

Mr President,

Far from abating, the scourge of human trafficking is growing and it becomes more diversified with the increase of human mobility and with the globalization of communication and trade. The focus on the sale, prostitution of children and child pornography by the latest Report of the Special Rapporteur underlines a *global* trend of human trafficking. The latest Report by the UN Office of Drugs and Crime on Human Trafficking (2012) paints a grim picture of the millions of people trafficked for sexual exploitation and forced labor: they come from at least 136 different nationalities and have been found in 118 countries. Although the majority of such persons are women (55 per cent to 60 per cent), the flow of children is growing alarmingly quickly from 20 per cent between 2003 and 2006 to 27 per cent between 2007 and 2010. Among the total of trafficking cases identified globally, trafficking for sexual exploitation accounts for 58 per cent.

The Report of the Special Rapporteur shows with accuracy how children can become victims of the sexual fantasies of adults. The phenomenon is certainly not new, but recently it has been unleashed by the liberalization of sexual behaviour. Past and current studies have made it clear that the goal of traffickers is mainly economic. They seek to maximise their profit-making activities by using human beings as 'commodities'. The international community is confronted with a criminal market that generates billions of dollars for the traffickers. When the risks of engaging in such activity are low, high profits become tempting. The Special Rapporteur's Report shows that, in the case of trafficking children, risks are low in many ways and in many parts of the world. There is a clear need to update legislation, increase international and regional cooperation, share information and good practices, combat impunity and corruption, enhance judicial practices, care for the victims and provide ways to reintegrate them into a normal and dignified life in society.

* Statement delivered at the 22nd Session of the Human Rights Council – Item 3: *Report of the Special Rapporteur on the Sale of Children, Child Prostitution and Child Pornography*, 7 March 2013.

Mr President,

As in every market, the offer serves a demand. Child trafficking exists because there is a demand. To disrupt the market, we need to confront and fight the 'consumers' who are willing to pay for the 'services' of children. Such activities could be effectively prevented by enacting and implementing legislation that criminalizes the consumption of child pornography or the sexual abuse of a child.

Legal measures, however, are not enough. As the Report of the Special Rapporteur points out, prevention also should address the consumerist culture that stimulates and promotes the unhealthy and immature sexual desires that drive 'consumers' to this market. Legitimate questions should be posed about why many tourists seek such 'services' that cause such irreversible harm to children. Prevention should dare to ask what has happened to the tourist seeking that kind of 'service'. How is the consumer market for sexual exploitation created in the first place? If the understanding of individual freedom rejects the ethical boundaries imposed by nature itself, the trafficking of persons and the violation of their innate dignity will continue to occur, and the action of the State will be ineffective.

The persistent economic crisis, current wars and civil conflicts, the high prices of food, famine, abject poverty and migration, political upheavals, failed States, these are as many opportunities for human traffickers to prey upon vulnerable victims. The predator practice of traffickers feeds on the weakest, people already in need and therefore easy to kidnap, enslave and reduce to 'commodities'. A concrete example of human trafficking is the ring operating in the Horn of Africa and the Sinai region: it offers a 'real-life' sample of the cycle of abuse that is unleashed by trafficking of human persons. To prevent this scourge we must reinforce human security and address the root causes that make people vulnerable. To combat this trade is to discourage criminal groups from seeking out and exploiting innocent victims.

Mr President,

Among the shocking practices of human trafficking, the case of children requires special and urgent attention and action on both humanitarian and moral grounds. Identifying survivors, providing them support, preparing them for a productive life free of traumas, and developing an effective prosecution of traffickers are the joint tasks of the private and public sectors of society. Victims, however, will find real protection if the prevention task is taken seriously by changing a culture that justifies their exploitation and tolerates with impunity the violation of human security, a breeding ground of human vulnerability.

Pope John Paul II, in a Letter on the occasion of the International Conference, '21st Century Slavery – The Human Rights Dimension to Trafficking in Human Beings,' stated that human trafficking 'constitutes a shocking offense against human dignity and a grave violation of fundamental human rights. In particular, the sexual exploitation of women and children is an especially repugnant aspect of this trade, and must be recognized as an intrinsic violation of human dignity and human rights.'[1]

[1] Pope John Paul II, Letter to Archbishop Jean-Louis Tauran on the Occasion of the International Conference on 21st Century Slavery – The Human Rights Dimension to Trafficking in Human Beings, 15 May 2002.

EXPLANATORY NOTES

Affirmations of Faith Leaders

In December 2012, the High Commissioner's Dialogue on Protection Challenges focused on the theme of Faith and Protection. The Dialogue brought together faith leaders, faith-based organizations (FBOs), academics and government representatives to explore how asylum and the protection of refugees, stateless persons and the internally displaced are reflected in religious values and traditions, and how to improve cooperation between UNHCR and faith actors (www.unhcr.org/524ac7fd9.pdf).

Asylum Seekers

The terms asylum seeker and refugee are often confused: an asylum seeker is someone who says he or she is a refugee, but whose claim has not yet been definitively evaluated. On average, about 1 million people seek asylum on an individual basis every year (www.unhcr.org/pages/49c3646c137.html).

Cartagena Declaration on Refugees

The Cartagena Declaration on Refugees is a non-binding agreement adopted by the Colloquium on the International Protection of Refugees in Latin America, Mexico and Panama, held at Cartagena, Colombia from 19 to 22 November 1984. It is the landmark regional refugee instrument, which broadened the refugee definition for Latin America and proposed new approaches to the humanitarian needs of refugees and displaced persons with a spirit of solidarity and cooperation (www.unhcr.org/45dc19084.html).

CMW – International Convention on the Protection of the Rights of All Migrant Workers and Members of Their Families

The Convention was adopted by Resolution 45/158 of 18 December 1990 by the General Assembly of the United Nations (www2.ohchr.org/english/bodies/cmw/cmw.htm).

Convention Relating to the Status of Refugees (1951) and the Related 1967 Protocol

The 1951 Convention Relating to the Status of Refugees is the key legal document in defining who is a refugee, their rights and the legal obligations of states. The 1967 Protocol removed geographical and temporal restrictions from the Convention (www.unhcr.org/pages/49da0e466.html).

COP 21 – Conference of the Parties 21

The 2015 United Nations Climate Change Conference in Paris, also referred to as COP 21, was held in Paris, France, from 30 November to 12 December 2015. It was the 21st yearly session of the Conference of the Parties to the United Nations Framework Convention on Climate Change (UNFCCC) adopted in Rio in 1992 and the 11th Session of the Meeting of the Parties to the 1997 Kyoto Protocol (www.cop21paris.org/).

CRC – Convention on the Rights of the Child

The Convention on the Rights of the Child was adopted by the General Assembly Resolution 44/25 of 20 November 1989 and entered into force on 2 September 1990. Two Optional Protocols to the Convention, on involvement of children in armed conflict and on sale of children, child prostitution and child pornography were adopted in 2000 by the United Nations General Assembly, while a third Optional Protocol on a communications procedure, which allows individual children to submit complaints regarding specific violations of their rights under the Convention and its first two Optional Protocols, was adopted in 2011 (www.ohchr.org/EN/ProfessionalInterest/Pages/CRC.aspx).

Declaration of the High-Level Dialogue on International Migration and Development

This Declaration was unanimously adopted by the General Assembly on 3–4 October 2013. It calls for the respect of human rights and international labor standards, reiterates the commitment to fight human trafficking and strongly condemns manifestations of racism and intolerance (www.un.org/ga/search/view_doc.asp?symbol=A/68/L.5).

ExCom – Executive Committee (UNHCR)

The ExCom meets in Geneva annually to review and approve UNHCR's programs and budget, advise on international protection and discuss a wide range of other issues with UNHCR and its intergovernmental and non-governmental partners (www.unhcr.org/pages/49c3646c83.html).

GFMD – Global Forum on Migration and Development

The Global Forum on Migration and Development (GFMD) was created during the United Nations General Assembly 14–15 September 2006 High-Level Dialogue on International Migration and Development to address the linkages between migration and development in practical and action-oriented ways. It is an informal, non-binding, voluntary and government-led process that marks the culmination of more than a decade of international dialogue on the growing importance of the linkages between migration and development (www.gfmd.org/).

High Commissioner's Dialogue on Protection Challenges

In 2007, then UN High Commissioner for Refugees António Guterres launched the first in a series of Dialogues on Protection Challenges. This annual event in Geneva facilitates a lively and informal discussion on new or emerging global protection issues. Over the years, the Dialogue has become an important forum to discuss protection challenges related to UNHCR's mandate and work, and identify ways to strengthen the protection of people of concern to the refugee agency (www.unhcr.org/pages/501a39166.html).

ICCPR – International Covenant on Civil and Political Rights

The ICCPR was adopted in 1966 by General Assembly Resolution 2200A. Together with the ICESCR, it is a reinforcement concerning the Universal Declaration of Human Rights (www.ohchr.org/en/professionalinterest/pages/ccpr.aspx).

IDM – International Dialogue on Migration

The IDM is the IOM's principal forum for migration policy dialogue. The IDM provides a space to analyze current and emerging issues in migration governance and to exchange experiences, policy approaches and effective practices. Every year, the IDM is guided by an overarching theme selected by the IOM Member States (https://www.iom.int/idm).

IDPs – Internally Displaced Persons

Unlike refugees, IDPs have not crossed an international border to find sanctuary but have remained inside their home countries. Even if they have fled for similar reasons as refugees (armed conflict, generalized violence, human rights violations), IDPs legally remain under the protection of their own government – even though that government might be the cause of their flight. As citizens, they retain all of their rights and protection under both human rights and international humanitarian law. UNHCR´s original mandate does not specifically cover IDPs, but because of the agency´s expertise on displacement it has for many years been protecting and assisting millions of them (www.unhcr.org/pages/49c3646c146.html).

IOM – International Organization for Migration

Established in 1951, the IOM is the leading intergovernmental organization in the field of migration and works closely with governmental, intergovernmental and non-governmental partners. The IOM is dedicated to promoting humane and orderly migration for the benefit of all. It does so by providing services and advice to governments and migrants (www.iom.int/about-iom).

IOM's High-Level Conference on Migrants and Cities

This High-Level Conference, part of the IOM's International Dialogue on Migration, was held in Geneva on 26–27 October 2015. It brought together ministers, mayors and high-level officials to debate the complex dynamics of human mobility in cities and how challenges can be managed and development opportunities maximized (https://www.iom.int/idmcmc).

Nansen Refugee Award

Established in 1954, the Nansen Refugee Award is named after Fridtjof Nansen, the first High Commissioner for Refugees. The award is bestowed to a person or group for outstanding work on behalf of the forcibly displaced (www.unhcr.org/nansen/503743f86.html).

Non-Refoulement

The principle of *non-refoulement* is often referred to as the cornerstone of international protection. This principle, first introduced in the 1951 Convention Relating to the Status of Refugees, has acquired the status of customary international law, meaning that it has become binding on all States, regardless of whether or not they are signatories to the 1951 Convention. *Non-refoulement* prohibits States from returning a refugee or asylum seeker to territories where there is a risk that his or her life or freedom would be threatened on account of race, religion, nationality, membership of a particular social group or political opinion (www.unhcr.org/4d9486929.pdf).

OAU Convention – Organization of African Unity Convention Governing the Specific Aspects of Refugee Problems in Africa

Adopted in 1969, the OAU Convention entered into force in 1974 (www.unhcr.org/45dc1a682.html).

Protocol to Prevent, Suppress and Punish Trafficking in Persons, especially Women and Children

The Protocol to Prevent, Suppress and Punish Trafficking in Persons, especially Women and Children is one of the three Protocols to the Convention against Transnational Organised Crime, adopted by the General Assembly in 2000. This Convention is further supplemented by two other protocols: the Protocol against the Smuggling of Migrants by Land, Sea and Air; and the Protocol against the Illicit Manufacturing of and Trafficking in Firearms, their Parts and Components and Ammunition (https://www.unodc.org/unodc/treaties/CTOC/).

Standing Committee (UNHCHR)

ExCom's subsidiary body, the Standing Committee, meets several times each year to carry on the UNHCR's work between plenary sessions (www.unhcr.org/pages/49c3646c8f.html).

Sustainable Development Goals (SDGs)

The Sustainable Development Goals are a universal set of goals, targets and indicators that UN Member States will be expected to use to frame their agendas and political policies over the next 15 years. They were adopted at the United Nations Sustainable Development Summit in September 2015 in New York, where world leaders also adopted the 2030 Agenda for Sustainable Development: this Agenda includes a set of 17 SDGs to end poverty, fight inequality and injustice, and tackle climate change by 2030. The Sustainable Development Goals build on the Millennium Development Goals. While the MDGs, in theory, applied to all countries, in reality they were considered targets for poor countries to achieve, with finance from wealthy states. Conversely, every country will be expected to work towards achieving the SDGs (https://sustainabledevelopment.un.org/sdgs).

The 10-Point Plan of Action for Refugee Protection and Mixed Migration

The 10-Point Plan of Action was issued by UNHCR in June 2006. The Plan of Action offers a framework to assist States in ensuring that persons in need of international protection who are travelling within broader mixed migratory movements can be identified and provided with an appropriate response. The Plan is especially relevant to situations where refugees are at risk of *refoulement* or irregular onward movement (www.unhcr.org/4688b4af2.html).

UNHCR – United Nations High Commissioner for Refugees

The Office of the United Nations High Commissioner for Refugees was established on 14 December 1950 by the United Nations General Assembly. The agency is mandated to lead and co-ordinate international action to protect refugees and resolve refugee problems worldwide. Its primary purpose is to safeguard the rights and well-being of refugees (www.unhcr.org/pages/49c3646c2.html).

CONCLUSION

A Beacon of Inspiration for the Family of Nations

ANTÓNIO MANUEL DE OLIVEIRA GUTERRES*

The quest for peace, the respect of human rights and the dignity of the human person, the promotion of justice and social progress: these are the founding principles that the leaders of the world agreed to abide by in 1945 in the wake of that abyss of blood and darkness that civilization had plunged into.[1] These four pillars are the expression of the just aspirations of man, and should guide the relations among States.

Seventy years after this solemn declaration, its realization remains unfulfilled. Transgressions of human rights are still massive in extent and scope in various part of the globe. Millions of people are still suffering persecution, exile, enslavement and unemployment, while society stands by in silence. Inequalities are on the rise. The gap between the poor and the rich grows and bodes ill for the future. In 2016, the best-off 1 per cent owned more wealth than the remaining 99 per cent. We have stretched our natural resource systems to their limits. With the intensifying struggle to develop a coherent response to the spiralling migrant crisis whose victims turn our seas into cemeteries, what emerges is a dismal picture, indicating a loss of faith in human capabilities and moral values.

Confronted with today's inequalities, violence and destruction, Pope Francis warned about a 'piecemeal World War III'. In this context, the Holy See prompts the international community and its institutions to take the 'risk of solidarity'. We must never forget the root values on which the United Nations were established. These are values that seek to bring

* António Manuel de Oliveira Guterres is the Secretary General of the United Nations. He served as United Nations High Commissioner for Refugees from June 2005 to December 2015. Prior to that, from 1995 to 2002, he also served as Portuguese Prime Minster.

1 UN Charter, Preamble. Available at: www.un.org/en/documents/charter/preamble .shtml.'We the people of the United Nations determined:

- to save succeeding generations from the scourge of war, which twice in our lifetime has brought untold sorrow to mankind, and
- to reaffirm faith in fundamental human rights, in the dignity and worth of the human person, in the equal rights of men and women and of nations large and small, and
- to establish conditions under which justice and respect for the obligations arising from treaties and other sources of international law can be maintained, and
- to promote social progress and better standards of life in larger freedom.'

the human family to a future of mutual trust, peace and development, to a future that is truly inclusive for everyone, without any marginalization. 'Now is the time for *new hope*, which calls us to expel the paralyzing burden of cynicism from the future of politics and of human life.'[2]

The Holy See at the United Nations and at other international organizations in Geneva is engaged in renewing the moral dimension in international relations, thus allowing the human family to live peacefully and develop including everyone. This means overcoming the present absence of strong convictions and long-term programmes that have resulted in a profound, paralyzing crisis of those values on which the foundation of social cohesion has always rested. Unfortunately, the Machiavellian national interests of certain countries so powerful as to influence international decisions are often hindering this process. A case in point, in the Middle East, the United Nations has been powerless in many aspects. It has not been able to find a way – or a united, political will – to stop bloodshed and persecutions, especially against Christians and minorities, thus failing to fulfil its responsibility to protect.

The name 'United Nations' itself suggests the idea of a 'family of nations'. The statements of the Holy See call for international relations inspired and governed by the principle of subsidiarity and solidarity. This approach is all the more necessary at this time when we experience that multilateral consensus is continuously in crisis because still subordinated to the decisions of a few. The world's problems, however, call for interventions in the form of collective action by the international community. Now is the time to renew trust in the 'family of nations'.

Why is it so hard for the human family to imagine a different, better future based on the dignity of the human person? This question finds an answer in the statements of Archbishop Silvano M. Tomasi, Permanent Observer of the Holy See to the United Nations in Geneva, which present a clear ethical perspective. The diplomatic contribution of the Holy See is not limited to the mere observation of unfolding events or to the proclamation of solemn principles. It intends to affect – and often succeeds in affecting – the decision-making process, often proposing solutions to situations of impasse, for example, through her good offices, as we have recently witnessed in the significant role it played in the normalization of USA–Cuba relations. And she does so in order to facilitate

2 https://w2.vatican.va/content/john-paul-ii/en/speeches/1995/october/documents/hf_jp-ii_spe_05101995_address-to-uno.html.

coexistence and cohabitation among the various nations and to promote a genuine fraternity among peoples.

The active presence of the Holy See in Geneva, the international hub where the operational dimension of the UN is coordinated, reminds the world of the meaning of the brotherhood of nations. It is indeed a beacon of inspiration for all nations. Former UN Secretary General Dag Hammarskjöld observed that the UN 'was not created to lead mankind to heaven, but to save humanity from hell'. The Holy See, however, serves a double mission: to help humanity from plunging into the dark abysses of destruction and war and to promote a culture of dialogue and respect. The various sections of this volume point out the way to achieve this goal.

1 HUMAN RIGHTS – THE INDIVISIBILITY AND UNIVERSALITY OF HUMAN RIGHTS

The great progress achieved in articulating human rights and in improving their application was due in large part to the wisdom of the framers of the Universal Declaration of Human Rights. In this foundational document, the universal value of the inherent dignity and worth of the human person was deliberately agreed upon as the cornerstone of all rights.

In 1993, the Vienna Declaration and Programme of Action, adopted by the World Conference on Human Rights, proclaimed the indivisibility and universality of all human rights. However, as different perceptions and convictions build barriers, the effort to give substance to the stated equal importance and interdependence of civil and political rights and of economic, social and cultural rights, is still hindered.

Much work remains to be done to make the universality and indivisibility of human rights a reality. The Holy See appeals to the international community for a greater commitment in closing the gap between ideals and lived reality, to ensure that the UN Charter and its principles are not given mere lip service, but also implemented. In defending and promoting the universality of human rights, we must never lose sight of the human person who is at the centre of those rights. In this sense, the Holy See calls particular attention to the suffering of the most vulnerable and upholds the most fundamental and non-negotiable human right, the right to life.

The activity of the Holy See in the United Nations in Geneva is rather vast, with interventions defending the right to access to safe drinking water and basic sanitation ('the availability of fresh water has now become correlated more obviously to human rights like the right to life and health'),[3] the right to adequate housing, the right to education and the right to food. In particular, the fight against poverty and hunger requires more and more targeted interventions and solidarity in order to guarantee universal access to water for personal survival, health and for the development of agriculture and the production of food. The Holy See repeatedly calls for the urgent need for governments and the global society to respect, protect, facilitate and fulfil the human right to food, appealing to solidarity among the human family. 'Solidarity at the international level is equally important in efforts to guarantee the right to food ... ensure that the right to food is not reduced to a right not to starve and will truly be acknowledged as an inclusive right to an adequate diet and all the nutritional elements needed to live a healthy and active life, and the means to access them.'[4]

The rights of the child, the most vulnerable members of society, are addressed in several statements. With thousands of children involved in armed conflicts around the world, the scourge of recruiting child soldiers today continues to be a harsh reality in several countries, including among national security forces. 'Children in many countries are used as combatants, messengers, porters, cooks, suicide-bombers and are even forced to have sexual relations.' Sometimes, a village may be forced to provide a certain number of children as soldiers in exchange for protection against other gangs or militias; some children are volunteered by their parents due to extreme poverty and hunger at home, 'lured by false promises of an escape from extreme poverty'.[5] Not only is it a matter of governance and sound economics, but an ethical responsibility to protect children from violence. 'Society should not allow the talents and energies of children and young people to be dispersed in pursuit of destructive goals but rather assist that they be focused on the common good and on constructing a culture of peace, dialogue and solidarity. Indispensable to achieve the elimination of the social wound of child soldiers is the work and achievement of peace'[6]

[3] 'THE RIGHT TO SAFE DRINKING WATER AND BASIC SANITATION', 15th Session of the Human Rights Council: *Interactive Dialogue on Human Rights*, 16 September 2010.

[4] 'THE RIGHT TO FOOD REQUIRES SOCIAL SOLIDARITY AMONG ALL PEOPLES', 25th Session of the Human Rights Council – Item 3: *Report of the Special Rapporteur on the Right to Food*, 10 March 2014.

[5] 'THE SOCIAL WOUND OF FORCED CONSCRIPTION OF CHILDREN', 24th Session of the Human Rights Council – Item 3: *Children and Armed Conflict*, 10 September 2013.

[6] Ibid.

Another key position that the Holy See has developed relates to the family as the fundamental cell of human society. Such understanding of the family has been embraced throughout history by all cultures. The family 'continually exhibits a vigor much greater than that of the many forces that have tried to eliminate it as a relic of the past, or an obstacle to the emancipation of the individual, or to the creation of a freer, egalitarian and happy society'.[7]

Finally, culminating in Pope Francis' prophetic Encyclical on climate change, the Holy See has long been drawing attention to the global, common responsibility towards the environment. '[D]egradation can and does adversely affect the enjoyment of a broad range of human rights. This is an issue of justice, respect and equity.'[8] Climate change and inequality are inextricably linked, and an impediment to solving a looming planetary and human rights crisis. 'In the present condition of global society, where injustices abound and growing numbers of people are deprived of basic human rights and considered expendable, the principle of the common good immediately becomes, logically and inevitably, a summons to solidarity and a preferential option for the poorest of our brothers and sisters.'[9]

For the Holy See, to deny the universality and indivisibility of human rights is to deny that there is a human nature shared by everyone. The quest for freedom in our time has its basis in those universal, inviolable and inherent rights, which human beings enjoy by the very fact of their humanity. Hence, the Holy See seeks to build bridges between people, helping the human family to promote a culture of peace. *Historia magistra vitae*, and those who ignore history are bound to repeat its mistakes. The poor not only suffer injustice, they also struggle against it. That the human person should remain at the centre of our quest for development becomes even more urgent. 'If everyone's political, religious and economic rights and freedoms are respected, we will shift the paradigm from merely trying to manage poverty, to creating wealth; from viewing the poor as a burden, to welcoming them as part of the solution.'[10]

[7] 'The family must remain the fundamental cell of society', 26th Session of the Human Rights Council, Item 8: General Debate, Geneva, 24 June 2014.

[8] 'Our common responsibility towards Creation', 28th Session of the Human Rights Council – Item 3: *Human Rights Obligations Relating to the Enjoyment of a Safe, Clean, Healthy and Sustainable Environment*, 9 March 2015.

[9] Pope Francis' Encyclical Letter, *Laudato Si'*, § 168.

[10] http://en.radiovaticana.va/news/2015/09/01/cardinal_turkson_peace_is_a_fruit_of_justice/1168878.

2 FREEDOM OF RELIGION – IT SHOULD NEVER BE NECESSARY TO DENY GOD TO ENJOY ONE'S FREEDOM

Human rights, of course, must include the right to religious freedom which includes both an individual and a communitarian dimension distinguishing between the dimension of the citizen and that of the believer.[11]

The commitment to religious freedom and to the elimination of all forms of religious intolerance remains an important priority for the Holy See, as proved by the copious statements delivered at the United Nations. Violations of freedom of religion are not lessening, but have in fact increased, and religious minority groups suffer the most. Article 1 of the 'Declaration of the Rights of Man and of the Citizen' of 1789, which together with the American Declaration of Independence contributed to inspire the UDHR for a large part, states that 'Men are born and remain free and equal in rights' and consequently implies the freedom of thought and religion and the equality of each person before the law. Article 18 of UDHR indeed states that 'Everyone has the right to freedom of thought, conscience and religion; this right includes freedom to change his religion or belief, and freedom, either alone or in community with others and in public or private, to manifest his religion or belief in teaching, practice, worship and observance.' Unfortunately, religious freedom remains one of the most frequently and widely denied and restricted rights in the world.

What appears clear from the statements of the Holy See is that freedom of religion is a fundamental human right, which 'must remain among the issues of concern to the world community since its violation continues and even deteriorates in some cases with regard to both Christians and other religious groups, especially if their situation is that of a minority'.[12] In fact, 'together with religious freedom, all other freedoms develop and thrive.' Freedom of thought, conscience and religion is a right upheld by international human rights norms for individuals, communities and their institutional structures, three inseparable dimensions. Hence, the full implementation of this right is the persistent challenge ahead of us today.

[11] http://w2.vatican.va/content/benedict-xvi/en/speeches/2008/april/documents/hf_ben-xvi_spe_20080418_un-visit.html.

[12] 'Religious freedom: a touchstone for the observance of the other fundamental rights', 61st Session of the Human Rights Commission – Item 11: *Civil and Political Rights*, 1 April 2005.

Freedom is a challenge that must be constantly won over for the cause of good.

Unfortunately, in a large number of countries freedom of religion is not yet fully guaranteed. In certain regions followers of minority religions, that are not recognized by law, confess their faith in hiding and illegally, with fear of prison terms and persecution. 'Several other international human rights texts, General Assembly and Human Rights Council resolutions unambiguously state that everyone has the right to freedom of thought, conscience and religion or belief. The freedom to manifest one's religion or belief in teaching, practice, worship and observance is also guaranteed. It is inconceivable that believers should have to suppress a part of themselves – their faith – in order to be active citizens. It should never be necessary to deny God in order to enjoy one's rights.'[13]

The Holy See calls upon States to respect and promote the right to freedom of religion in all its aspects, through national legislation, including appropriate sanctions against violators to eradicate impunity. 'Victims of discrimination and violent attacks have a right to obtain redress and compensation for the harm done to them by public or private agents. The State has the responsibility of protecting the fundamental human rights of all people in its territory.'[14] In order to obtain such just redress, standard and objective methods should be included in national legislation without distinction on the ground of race, colour, sex or religion. Only through a peaceful coexistence built on mutual respect, solidarity and cooperation, will 'a healthy social pluralism and a prosperous life for all members of our one human family'[15] be achieved. This is why the Holy See supports a continued engagement in highlighting the often invisible or underplayed abuses that receive only a faint echo in the international arena.

The Holy See also warned of the risk of a double standard in the protection of human rights with regard to the delicate and complex issue of freedom of expression vis-à-vis freedom of religion. 'Some limits to freedom of expression are selectively imposed by law and accepted; meanwhile, systematic, provocative and verbally violent attacks on religion which hurt the personal identity of believers are endorsed.'[16]

[13] 'It should never be necessary to deny God to enjoy one's rights', 20th Session of the Human Rights Council – Item 8: *Freedom of Religion*, 3 July 2012.

[14] 'An urgent need to delineate a positive and open secularity', 13th Session of the Human Rights Council – Item 3: *General Debate*, 12 March 2010.

[15] Ibid.

[16] 'Freedom of expression vs. freedom of religion', 28th Session of the Human Rights Council – Item 3: *Report of the Special Rapporteur on Freedom of Religion or Belief*, 11 March 2015.

The Holy See denounces the intolerance that leads to violence, persecution and death of many innocent people simply because of their religious convictions. There is a 'need to protect and defend the right to religious freedom, which is clearly under attack in some parts of the world today. This is a fundamental human right based on the right of freedom of conscience. Experience shows that when this right is respected all other rights are as well.'[17] 'The positions of extreme individualism and collectivism offer a partial view of the human person: the first leads her to isolation; the second cancels and absorbs her into the abstract idea of a social or ideological collectivity. These two perspectives do not allow for dialogue, rather make it impossible, because both counter the reality of human nature.'[18]

3 ECONOMY – NO TO AN ECONOMY OF INEQUALITY AND EXCLUSION

For those who ignore the deep involvement of the Holy See in the field of economy, or merely believe that it is an idealistic, unattainable Utopia isolated from the real world, the numerous statements contained in Part III will really surprise the reader. They not only provide a critical explanation of the global financial and economic crisis that broke out in 2008, which left millions of people without work and in situations of acute hardship, swelling the ranks of those already in poverty and insecurity. When despair was becoming pervasive, the Holy See proposed a solution for the dismal state of affairs based on the centrality of the human person in development.

Indeed, the revulsion towards an economy predicated upon the notion of individualism, motivated by private greed, and a cogent critique of reckless globalization, has been a coherent response of the Holy See. 'Human beings are themselves considered consumer goods to be used and then discarded. We have created a "throw away" culture which is now spreading.' At the root of this situation is an individualistic ideology, one described by Pope Francis as 'an economy of exclusion and inequality' (*Evangelii Gaudium*, § 53). It rests on the 'presumption' that human

17 'The need to protect and defend the right to religious freedom worldwide' (Statement delivered at the 27th Session of the Human Rights Council – Item 2: *On the Opening Remarks of the High Commissioner for Human Rights*, 8 September 2014.

18 'Religion must not be a criterion for discrimination' (Statement delivered at the 15th Session of the Human Rights Council – Item 9, 28 September 2010.

beings are naturally selfish and on the automatic ability of a free market, unhindered by regulations, to generate increased efficiency and aggregate growth. 'This ideology describes the future not in terms of uncertainty but in terms of risk based on probability. The consequences of any action may be rationally assessed and the bottom line is determined by profit maximization.'[19]

As a result, the very foundations of a democratic, egalitarian and just economy are shaking. The fruits of the toil of millions are boldly stolen to build up colossal fortunes for a few, while the vast majority is gripped by fear and desperation, even in the developed countries. The closed doors of nations must be opened not for another round of ruthless exploitation, transgressing against the sovereignty of unwilling nations, but for the true enjoyment of the benefits of progress. 'Debt and the accumulation of interest also make it difficult for countries to realize the potential of their own economies and keep citizens from enjoying their real purchasing power. In this system, which tends to devour everything which stands in the way of increased profits, whatever is fragile, like the environment, is defenseless before the interests of a deified market, which become the only rule.'[20]

Moreover, the volatility of food prices in recent years has caused great harm to farmers, in both the global North and South, which has led to more lives lost to hunger. In recent years the Holy See consistently has expressed concern about food security, issuing 'an invitation to rethink and renew our food systems from a perspective of solidarity, overcoming the logic of unbridled exploitation of creation and orienting better our commitment to cultivate and look after the environment and its resources, to guarantee food security and progress towards sufficient and healthy food for all.'[21]

The effects of globalization have the potential to compound and magnify existing vulnerabilities. Every person has a shared responsibility to respond to the 'cries' of needy nations that are seeking a larger share in the benefits of civilization and striving for fuller growth. If we all agree

19 'The vocation of business: contribute to the common good and respect human rights', 3rd Forum on Business and Human Rights: *High-Level Discussion on Strengthening the Links between the Global Economic Architecture and the Business and Human Rights Agenda*, 3 December 2014.

20 'The last call for the credibility of the multilateral trade system', 9th Session of the Ministerial Conference of the World Trade Organization, Bali, Indonesia, 4 December 2013.

21 Ibid.

on the global goal to fight the 'war on poverty', then we cannot proceed to increase the wealth and power of the rich while the needy remain entrenched in greater poverty. We need to seek constantly for a just economic system, a fairly shared tax burden based on wealth, a diffusion of decent labour practices and safety-net instruments for the poor, a promotion of equal economic policies for men and women alike. Only then will we be able to tackle inequality, promote the common good and help nations discover the road to cultural and social progress, while remaining faithful to the native genius of their land.

Pope Francis' address to the 2014 International Labour Conference, delivered by Archbishop Tomasi, touched upon some critical issues: jobs, equity, sustainability of human security, labour mobility, social dialogue, youth unemployment, which is tragically expanding the frontiers of poverty, and the mass migration of people forced to seek work away from their homelands. The latter, despite their hopes for a better future, frequently encounter mistrust, false promises and unethical recruitment, to say nothing of experiencing tragedies and disasters. Having made such sacrifices, these men and women often fail to find dignified work and fall victim to a certain "globalization of indifference". Their situation exposes them to further dangers such as the horror of human trafficking, forced labour and enslavement. The Pope also called for a re-evaluation of the responsibilities of international corporations in the countries where they operate, including the areas of profit and investment management.[22]

Finally, a key objective for the Holy See has been advocating affordable access to medicines for less developed countries. 'Intellectual property deserves protection since it creates incentives for innovation. Such protection, however, must be tempered to allow the spreading of the benefits of innovation as widely as possible.'[23] The benefits of innovation, with the connected IP rights, however, 'should aim primarily at serving the common good of the human community'. For this reason, the 'poor should be helped to acquire expertise, to enter the circle of exchange, and to develop their skills in order to make the best use of their capacities and resources.'[24]

22 'Message of Pope Francis on the occasion of the 103rd session of the Conference of the International Labour Organization (ILO): "Better work to enhance human dignity"', 103rd Session of the International Labour Conference, 9 June 2014.

23 'The ultimate goal of intellectual property is to serve the common good', 49th Series of Meetings of the WIPO General Assemblies, 27 September 2011.

24 Ibid.

The litmus test of our progress is not whether we keep adding more to the abundance of those who have much, it is whether we provide enough for those many who only have little. We have a collective responsibility to uphold the principles of human dignity, equality and equity at the global level, especially for the most vulnerable and, in particular, for the children of the world, to whom the future belongs. The measure of restoration lies in the extent to which we apply social values more noble than mere monetary profit. Indeed, this inequality is 'the root of social evil'.

4 DISARMAMENT – PEACE AS A CONDITION FOR HUMAN RIGHTS

No long-lasting peace can ever be achieved without a true recognition of the dignity of every human person. And since peace is inconceivable without justice, a culture of peace requires a culture of justice. This is the touchstone of the engagement of the Holy See in the field of disarmament. In order to lead the process and to lend her moral voice to the debate, the Holy See has acceded to and ratified practically all the instruments relating to arms control and disarmament.

Since the UN's founding, we have avoided the catastrophe of a third all-out global war, but we have also witnessed several international and civil conflicts of varying duration and intensity. Papal diplomacy has made it a priority to respond to the expectations of people suffering and struggling because of armed conflicts and widespread violence, and aims at security through disarmament. The Holy See has taken a clear and strong position on the elimination of nuclear weapons. Ever since the emergence of the nuclear era, Papal diplomacy advocated the abolition of nuclear weapons 'which are seemingly without any military logic. Since the Encyclical *Pacem in Terris* of Pope John XXIII (1963), the Holy See continues to question the ethical basis to the so-called doctrine of nuclear deterrence. Ethical and humanitarian consequences of the possession and use of nuclear weapons are catastrophic and beyond the rational and reasonable.'[25] Confronted with the recent crisis and spiralling security dilemma posed by the arms race, the Holy See underscored once again that 'Nuclear weapons are a global problem. They impact future

[25] 'The ethical and humanitarian consequences of nuclear weapons', Conference on the Humanitarian Impact of Nuclear Weapons, 9 December 2014.

generations and the entire planet that is our home. The reduction of the nuclear threat and disarmament require a global ethic.'[26] Indeed, only an ethic rooted in solidarity and peaceful coexistence can lead to a peaceful future for humanity. Moreover, the world is confronted with several enormous challenges (environmental problems, migration flows, military conflicts, extreme poverty, regular economic crises, etc.), and yet, paradoxically, money continues to be squandered on expensive weapon systems. Lofty rhetoric and the justification of war as a noble crusade for democracy have always been pushed by international racketeers, bent upon gaining profit through a game of arming the world to fight itself. War means unconscionable and unjust profits for a few, but destruction for the majority of the human family.

The Holy See never fails to raise her moral voice and condemn the large-scale occurrence of serious violations of human rights and of humanitarian law. For example, concerning the dismal picture of the long-lasting conflict in Syria, the Holy See all along has insisted that only peaceful negotiations will 'lead to an acceptable solution of the crisis and that participation in an eventual government and in positions of responsibility by representatives of all citizens can ensure a constructive and lasting peaceful coexistence of all component communities of Syrian society.' To combat violence and its detrimental consequences we must avoid becoming accustomed to killing. Mindful that violence only begets violence, the Holy See repeatedly calls for negotiations and for putting an end to violence, and encourages all to pursue negotiations in a constructive dialogue for the peaceful future of the Syrian people: 'people should take precedence over power and revenge. Their unspeakable suffering must not be ignored by any of the parties involved as they are all called to act now for peace, reconstruction and a new beginning of human relations based on human rights and the common interest of the one human family.'[27]

Maintaining the priority of the dignity of the human person, the position of the Holy See is unyielding on the responsibility to protect. Yet, this has to be assumed in good faith, within the framework of international law and humanitarian law. Civil society in general, and religious

[26] Ibid.

[27] 'A DURABLE AND ACCEPTABLE SOLUTION IN SYRIA THROUGH PEACEFUL NEGOTIATIONS', 23rd Session of the Human Rights Council: *Urgent Debate on the Deteriorating Situation of Human Rights in the Syrian Arab Republic and the Recent Killings in Al Qusayr*, 29 May 2013.

and ethnic communities in particular, should not become an instrument of regional and international geopolitical games. 'Crimes in the name of religion are never justified. Massacring innocent people in the name of God is not religion but the manipulation of religion for ulterior motives.' In fact, 'believers, both Christians and Muslim, have experienced a common tragic outcome, at the hands of people who claim to be religious, but who instead abuse religion, to make of it an ideology for their own distorted interests of exploitation and murder.'[28]

In situation of conflicts, there is always a blurred line between military interests and humanitarian urgency. While in many fields autonomous technology may indeed prove beneficial to humanity, the application of autonomy to weapons technology is entirely distinct: it seeks to place a machine in the position of deciding over life and death. The Holy See supports the view that 'autonomous weapon systems, like drones, have a huge deficit which cannot be addressed only by respecting the rules of international humanitarian law. To comply, these systems would require human qualities that they inherently lack. The ethical consequences of such systems if deployed and used cannot be overlooked and underestimated'.[29]

Finally, it is worth recalling that Papal diplomacy, although far from trumpeting her own success, achieved great results in the field of disarmament. The Conference on Cluster Munitions is one such example. Adopted on 30 May 2008 in Dublin, Ireland and signed on 3–4 December 2008 in Oslo, Norway, the Convention on Cluster Munitions (CCM) entered into force on 1 August 2010. As of 11 September 2015, a total of 117 states have joined the Convention, as 96 States Parties and 21 Signatories.[30] This international treaty addresses the humanitarian consequences and unacceptable harm to civilians caused by cluster munitions through a categorical prohibition of them. Insisting on the priority of human dignity and fighting the abject indifference towards thousands of victims, the Holy See has greatly contributed to the CCM. 'International humanitarian law is not a cold body of rules written for the past.

[28] Pope Francis, Letter to the Bishops of Nigeria, 17 March 2015.

[29] 'MACHINES CAN NEVER TRULY REPLACE HUMANS IN MORAL DECISIONS OVER LIFE AND DEATH: THE ACCOUNTABILITY VACUUM', Meeting of Experts on Lethal Autonomous Weapons Systems of the High Contracting Parties to the Convention on Prohibitions or Restrictions on the Use of Certain Conventional Weapons Which May Be Deemed to Be Excessively Injurious or to Have Indiscriminate Effects, 13 May 2014.

[30] www.clusterconvention.org/.

International humanitarian law has to evolve and to become more protective of the civilian populations.'[31]

5 SOLIDARITY WITH ALL HUMANITY – 'NO MAN IS AN ISLAND IN HIMSELF'

The principle of solidarity inspires the action of the Holy See. It is centred on the plight of the poorest and most vulnerable members of society, upon those who often are marginalized from access to social protection, care and enjoyment of rights and dignity. For the Holy See, the solidarity with the vulnerable, with the marginalized is not mere lip service. The sheer numbers of those engaged in Catholic Church-sponsored health care services are most impressive; however, even more striking is the quality of care provided by them as well as their generosity and compassion toward the most vulnerable in every corner of the world

The fundamental principle for the Holy See remains the uncompromising, non-negotiable belief in the sanctity of human life, from conception to natural death, fully respecting the dignity of the human person. A similar defence and emphasis are also placed upon the right of everyone to the highest attainable standards of physical and mental health through the promotion of just public health policies, without distinction of race, religion, political belief, economic or social condition. Such objectives are also expressed in the Constitution of the World Health Organization, 'basic to the happiness, harmonious relations and security of all peoples'.[32]

The vision of human dignity promoted by the Holy See has been reinforced during the hardship brought by the global financial and economic crisis, which has raised the spectre of the cancellation or drastic reduction of external assistance programmes, especially for less developed countries. Cutbacks in financial aid would dramatically jeopardize the state of their health systems, which are already overburdened by endemic, epidemic and viral diseases.

One group particularly deprived of access to medicines, especially during hard times, are children. This is why the Holy See always voices her concerns for the most vulnerable, reaffirming 'the responsibility of States to ensure that medicines are available, financially affordable and

31 'Dublin Diplomatic Conference on Cluster Munitions: human dignity, prevention, and assistance to victims'. Statement delivered at the Dublin Diplomatic Conference on Cluster Munitions, 19 May 2008 (Dublin, Ireland).

32 www.who.int/governance/eb/who_constitution_en.pdf.

physically accessible on a basis of non-discrimination to everyone'.[33] A major stumbling block in providing such access is found in restrictive applications and interpretations of intellectual property rights by the pharmaceutical industry. While fully respecting the right to private intellectual property, the Holy See urges a creative and innovative approach, 'with full use of the flexibilities allowed under the Trade Related Intellectual Property instruments, so that the right to health for all people without any form of discrimination can be fully guaranteed and implemented',[34] prioritizing the life and dignity of the world's most vulnerable people.

As part of this 'solidarity with all humanity', the Holy See encourages governments and international institutions to help break existing stalemates and 'to take specific and timely steps to overcome conflicts; to look in a new light at victims of cluster bombs, mines and other weapons; to renew concern for refugees and displaced persons; to enact generous forms of solidarity with all victims of disasters, catastrophes and conflicts and thus fulfill the aspiration for unity of the human family'.[35] Such actions for humanity become urgent and demand concrete answers. '"Public conscience" as referred to in the "*Martens' Clause*" needs to be reawakened.'[36]

Finally, the Holy See strongly denounced the negative, even devastating, consequences for indigenous peoples caused by extractive industries. 'These corporations must overcome a specific focus on short-term economic advantage and adopt models of authentic development which do not violate the rights of indigenous peoples and encourage a responsible use of the environment.'[37] In any case, 'all eventual initiatives should be inspired and guided by the principle of respect for their identity and culture, including specific traditions, religious beliefs and ability

[33] 'Impact on health and health care during the period of global economic crisis', 62nd World Health Assembly, 18–27 May 2009.

[34] 'The primacy of the right to health over the focus on profit', 2015 Social Forum of the Human Rights Council, 18 February 2015.

[35] 'The need to reawaken public conscience', 31st International Conference of the Red Cross and Red Crescent, 28 November–2 December 2011.

[36] Ibid. According to the *Martens' Clause*: 'populations and belligerents remain under the protection and empire of the principles of international law, as they result from the usages established between civilized nations, from the laws of humanity and from the requirements of the *public conscience*'; 1899 Hague Convention No. II, Preamble, 9.

[37] 'The need to directly include Indigenous Peoples in the decisionmaking processes', 27th Session of the Human Rights Council – Item 3: *General Debate*, 17 September 2014.

to decide their own development in cooperation with their national governments.'[38]

6 PEOPLE ON THE MOVE – THE GREAT CHALLENGE OF OUR CENTURY

With the massive influx of refugees in certain parts of the world, we are confronted with a geopolitical challenge. This is a moment of change in rules and structures for the international community. If, on the one hand, the inclusion of migration in the Post-2015 Development Agenda was a success, on the other hand, the stark reality of current migrations makes it hard to celebrate. Unfortunately, today the number of migrants and their suffering still remain a wound in the social fabric of the international community. They continue to challenge our consciences. Never before have John Donne's words rung more true: 'Any man's death diminishes me, because I am involved in mankind.' The international community has not yet devised a proper global governance to manage human mobility and thus there is a lack of policy in the response to migratory flows. We have seen mixed approaches by different countries and a lack of a global strategy. When considering the current crisis we should not forget the foundational principles and rules which guided the international community thus far. The Holy See ratified the Convention Relating to the Status of Refugees in 1951, a Convention which emerged in the aftermath of the devastating experience of the Second World War whose purpose was 'to assure refugees the widest possible exercise of their fundamental rights and freedoms'. When confronted with the current situation, it appears that the noble goal set out by the Convention has dwindled in its meaning.

The interventions delivered by the Holy See aim at supporting the process of a greater humanization of the global movement of people. They draw attention to issues emerging in the migration journey, such as the illegal detention of asylum seekers, unaccompanied minors, the plight of refugees in protracted situations and the right to return to one's home. Evidence shows that in the medium and long term, migration benefits the countries of origin, arrival and the migrants themselves. But rather than to focus on migration, these statements focus on the human person, on the migrants. Raising her moral voice, the Holy See has promoted the human rights of all people on the move, creating a more

[38] Ibid.

positive public opinion, and prioritizing greater acceptance of their presence. After all, migration is the oldest action against poverty: when migrants and asylum seekers arrive, not just potential workers arrive, but persons who contribute with their social, cultural and religious convictions. An enlightened management of human mobility with its social, economic, political, cultural and religious implications calls for far-sighted domestic and international policies of collaboration that will respect the dignity of the migrants.

The statements also invite the developed world not to forget their responsibility. 'Neighboring countries to failed States, and to States at war, carry the heaviest burden of caring for the refugees they have welcomed into their territory. The international community, however, has to shoulder collectively the responsibility of assisting the victims of the many on-going conflicts.'[39] The Holy See reminds us that human mobility requires a common, global, shared responsibility and that proximity does not mean necessarily increased responsibility. Again, 'no man is an island by himself.'

As traditional distinctions among categories of people on the move are increasingly blurred, the existing normative framework leaves a serious concern in regard to human rights and should be reinforced by a sense of human solidarity. Of particular concern for the Holy See are also the many refugees, asylum seekers and rejected asylum seekers who find themselves trapped in a frustrating limbo. These persons, who are not protected by existing juridical instruments, are increasing as they seek to flee from the growing poverty caused by environmental degradation. 'Persons fleeing their home leave because of fear and desperation. But, more importantly, their decision is an act of faith and hope that the solidarity of the human family and the actions of the international community will continue to witness and provide compassion and support that will enable them to enjoy again their human rights and a normal existence.'[40]

Migration is a great resource for economic and human development, but 'the migrants must remain protagonists as builders of bridges among societies with the support of coherent and humane policies on the part

39 'Translate the duty to protect into action', 63rd Meeting of the Standing Committee of the UNHCR, 24 June 2015.

40 'The refugees' decision to flee their country is an act of faith and hope in the solidarity of the human family', 54th Meeting of the Standing Committee of the Executive Committee of the UNHCR on International Protection, 26 June 2012.

of the international community'. The 'pragmatic advantages accepted by the admission of migrants are on several occasions overshadowed by an ambivalent attitude that is manifest in media and public opinion that allows for stereotyping and negative generalizations of newcomers.'[41] This positive image of migrants and their contribution to development is therefore the key point of the Holy See statements: 'While people on the move are motivated by different needs and aspirations, we must recognize the unique human dignity of such persons and acknowledge the gifts, talents, skills, experience and cultural patrimony offered by all migrants who serve as bridges between their respective countries of origin and the countries that receive them. We must also recognize the difficult conditions that lead or compel persons to seek a better, more secure life in a foreign land. Many flee intense privation, violence or natural disasters. Most decide to migrate as part of a family survival strategy. All make extraordinary sacrifices to further their own and their family members' prospects and potential.' Migrants and refugees 'share a legitimate desire for knowing and having, but above all for *being* more'.[42] Indeed, the perception of migrants as a burden runs against the evidence of their contribution to the national economy of the host countries, to the social security system and to the demographic deficit,[43] through the taxes they pay, the new businesses they start as well as the array of services they provide. Therefore 'Fairness demands that a positive image of newcomers be adopted with a common, friendly and appropriate terminology for media at the national level, so as to avoid ambiguity, demagoguery and the stirring up of racism, discrimination, exploitation by unscrupulous politicians. Above all, respect for the dignity of the human person remains the touchstone.'[44]

At the same time, the Holy See never ceases to remind the international community that no person with the possibility of living with dignity in his or her home country would feel compelled to flee it. 'International solidarity should then strive to create the proper environment "at home", thus making migration a choice and not a compulsive necessity. This

41 'The priority of persons over the economy', 94th Session of the Council of the International Organization for Migration, 27–30 November 2007.

42 'Contribution to development and migrants' human rights', 103rd Session of the Council of the International Organization for Migration, 26–29 November 2013.

43 Report of the ILO Director General to the International Labour Conference, 'Fair Migration: Setting an ILO Agenda', 2014, p. 4.

44 'The failure of the multilateral system to manage migration: an abdication of responsibility', 29th Session of the Human Rights Council, *Interactive Dialogue with the Special Rapporteur on Migrants*, 15 June 2015.

may be accomplished by creating quality and decent jobs, promoting a more just and equitable financial and economic order, improving access to markets, trade and competition, by exchanging innovative technology, raising participation and political stability.'[45]

Finally, in the statements delivered in the Human Rights Council, the Holy See openly cautioned against the exploitation of the human persons by criminal transnational organizations. The millions of young people trafficked for sexual exploitation and forced labour are cause for great alarm and demand a renewed sense of moral responsibility. 'As in every market, the offer serves a demand. Child trafficking exists because there is a demand. To disrupt the market, we need to confront and fight the "consumers" who are willing to pay for the services of children.'[46]

In conclusion, migrants are not statistics but persons, men, women and children with individual stories, with talents to offer and aspirations to be met. The plight of so many exiles should rightly move us to have both compassion and indignation because of the unjust suffering inflicted upon them. Yet, as rightfully pointed out by the Holy See, the international community has to go beyond emotions and translate its duty to protect into action, the litmus test of solidarity among the family of nations.

Agenda 2030 – A New Vision for a Culture of Solidarity and Social Justice: From Existence with Others to Existence for Others

The United Nations represent for many people a hope for a better, sustainable future. The presence and active engagement of the Holy See strives to turn this hope into a reality, into a more just and inclusive future. The year 2015 is a favourable time of commemoration and recognition of the important changes that have taken place in the realization of human rights. Nevertheless, it is also a strategic opportunity to reflect on the persisting challenges that compromise the sustainable and lasting development of peoples and the growth of nations. The new Agenda seeks to address the biggest challenges before us, such as extreme poverty, the growing economic inequality among people, the exclusion of the weak and the most vulnerable, and the progressive degradation of 'our

[45] Ibid.

[46] 'THE SCOURGE OF TRAFFICKED CHILDREN AND THEIR SEXUAL EXPLOITATION', 22nd Session of the Human Rights Council – Item 3: *Report of the Special Rapporteur on the Sale of Children, Child Prostitution and Child Pornography*, 7 March 2013.

common home', the environment. The United Nations has the duty to carry out this historic, momentous task of promoting this *paradigm shift* in the life of the international community. This goal will only be reached if the human person is placed at the centre of development. While the human person is the primary beneficiary of sustainable development, it is also its agent and its steward, responding to the persistent question of 'what are you doing for others?'.

In his address to the United Nations General Assembly, Pope Francis said: 'the simplest and best measure and indicator of the implementation of the new Agenda for development will be effective, practical and immediate access, on the part of all, to essential material and spiritual goods: housing, dignified and properly remunerated employment, adequate food and drinking water; religious freedom and, more generally, spiritual freedom and education. These pillars of integral human development have a common foundation, which is the right to life and, more generally, what we could call the right to existence of human nature itself.'

In a similar way, in 2008, Pope Benedict XVI expressed the hope that the family of nations become a greater reality. 'One senses the urgent need to find innovative ways of implementing the principle of the responsibility to protect and of giving poorer nations an effective voice in shared decision-making. This seems necessary in order to arrive at a political, juridical and economic order which can increase and give direction to international cooperation for the development of all peoples in solidarity. To manage the global economy … and to regulate migration: for all this, there is urgent need of a true world political authority … Without this, despite the great progress accomplished in various sectors, international law would risk being conditioned by the balance of power among the strongest nations. The integral development of peoples and international cooperation require the establishment of a greater degree of international ordering, marked by subsidiarity, for the management of globalization.'[47]

The statements delivered by the Holy See offer great motivation and some fundamental concepts, many already articulated in the UDHR itself. These can serve as a major source of inspiration in the development of a new vision designed to encourage and not to frustrate. This vision rests on the unity of origin and the shared destiny of the human family; the equal dignity of every person; that the human person is the protagonist of integral development, and at the centre of every

[47] Pope Benedict XVI, Encyclical Letter, *Caritas in Veritate*, § 67.

social activity following solidarity and subsidiarity. Indeed, true prosperity is the result of well-placed confidence in fellow human beings and ourselves.

Confronted with the persisting challenges of inequality and injustice, the United Nations is called to move beyond promises toward real and verifiable results through the newly adopted development agenda. The UN 'needs to rise more and more above the cold status of an administrative institution and to become a moral centre where all the nations of the world feel at home and develop a shared awareness of being a family of nations'.[48] The presence of the Holy See at the United Nations is indeed a constant reminder and proponent of this goal.

[48] https://w2.vatican.va/content/john-paul-ii/en/speeches/1995/october/documents/hf_jp-ii_spe_05101995_address-to-uno.html.

APPENDIX

Intergovernmental Organizations and Bodies, and International Programmes in which the Holy See Participates

AALCO	Asian-African Legal Consultative Organization, New Delhi, Guest
AU	African Union, Addis Ababa, Non-Member Accredited State
CE	Council of Europe, Strasbourg, Observer
CIEC	International Commission on Civil Status, Strasbourg, Observer
CTBTO	Preparatory Commission for the Comprehensive Nuclear-Test Ban Treaty Organization, Vienna, Member
FAO	United Nations Food and Agriculture Organization, Rome, Observer
IAEA	International Atomic Energy Agency, Vienna, Member
ICMM	International Committee of Military Medicine, Brussels, Member
IFAD	International Fund for Agricultural Development, Rome, Observer
ILO	International Labour Organization, Geneva, Observer
INTOSAI	International Organization of Supreme Audit Institutions, Vienna, Member
IOM	International Organization for Migration, Geneva, Member
LAS	League of Arab States, Cairo, Member of a bilateral agreement of cooperation
OAS	Organization of American States, Washington, Observer
OPCW	Organization for the Prohibition of Chemical Weapons, The Hague, Member
OSCE	Organization for Security and Cooperation in Europe, Vienna, Member
UL	Latin Union, Paris, Permanent Guest
UN	United Nations Organization, New York, Observer
UN-HABITAT	United Nations Centre for Human Settlements, Nairobi, Observer

UNCTAD	United Nations Conference on Trade and Development, Geneva, Member
UNDP	United Nations Development Programme
UNEP	United Nations Environment Programme, Nairobi, Observer
UNESCO	United Nations Educational, Scientific and Cultural Organization, Paris, Observer
UNHCR	United Nations High Commissioner for Refugees, Geneva, Member
UNIDO	United Nations Industrial Development Organization, Vienna, Observer
UNIDROIT	International Institute for the Unification of Private Law, Rome, Member
UNOG	United Nations Office in Geneva, Geneva, Observer
UNON	United Nations Office in Nairobi, Nairobi, Observer
UNOV	United Nations Office in Vienna, Vienna, Observer
UNWTO	United Nations World Tourist Organization, Madrid, Observer
WFP	World Food Programme, Rome, Observer
WHO	World Health Organization, Geneva, Observer
WIPO	World Intellectual Property Organization, Geneva, Member
WMO	World Meteorological Organization, Geneva, Observer
WTO	World Trade Organization, Geneva, Observer

International and Intergovernmental Organizations the Vatican City State participates in:

CEPT	European Conference of Postal and Telecommunications, Copenhagen, Member
EUTELSATIGO	European Telecommunication Satellite Organization, Paris, Member
IGC	International Grains Council, London, Member
IISA	International Institute of Administrative Sciences, Brussels, Member
ITSO	International Telecommunications Satellite Organization, Washington DC, Member
ITU	International Telecommunication Union, Geneva, Member
UPU	Universal Postal Union, Berne, Member

INDEX